ARGONAUTS OF THE WESTERN PACIFIC

BRONISLAW MALINOWSKI (1884-1942), Anglo-Polish anthropologist, was born in what was then Austrian Poland of a long line of Polish nobility and landed gentry. He was educated at the Polish University of Cracow, from which he received his doctorate in 1908 with the highest honors of the Austro-Hungarian Empire. He also studied at the University of Leipzig and later went on to London, where from 1910 he was associated with the London School of Economics. From 1914 to 1918 Dr. Malinowski was a member of the Robert Mond Expedition to New Guinea and North Melanesia, and it was the research done on this expedition that was later published as *Argonauts of the Western Pacific*. In later years Dr. Malinowski taught at the University of London, at Cornell University, and at Yale. His books include the following: *Myth in Primitive Society* (1926), *Crime and Custom in Savage Society* (1926), *Sex and Repression in Savage Society* (1927), *The Sexual Life of Savages* (1929).

ARGONAUTS OF THE WESTERN PACIFIC was first published in 1922.

A CEREMONIAL ACT OF THE KULA (See p. 472)

ARGONAUTS

OF THE

WESTERN PACIFIC

AN ACCOUNT OF NATIVE ENTERPRISE
AND ADVENTURE IN THE ARCHIPELAGOES
OF MELANESIAN NEW GUINEA

by

BRONISLAW MALINOWSKI

Preface by

SIR JAMES G. FRASER

A Dutton  *Paperback*

With 66 Illustrations and 5 Maps

NEW YORK

E. P. DUTTON

This paperback edition of
"Argonauts of the Western Pacific"
Published 1961 by E. P. Dutton & Co., Inc.
All rights reserved. Printed in the U.S.A.

SBN 0-525-47074-3

TO

MY FRIEND AND TEACHER

PROFESSOR C. G. SELIGMAN, F.R.S.

PREFACE

By Sir James G. Frazer

My esteemed friend, Dr. B. Malinowski has asked me to write a preface to his book, and I willingly comply with his request, though I can hardly think that any words of mine will add to the value of the remarkable record of anthropological research which he has given us in this volume. My observations, such as they are, will deal partly with the writer's method and partly with the matter of his book.

In regard to method, Dr. Malinowski has done his work, as it appears to me, under the best conditions and in the manner calculated to secure the best possible results. Both by theoretical training and by practical experience he was well equipped for the task which he undertook. Of his theoretical training he had given proof in his learned and thoughtful treatise on the family among the aborigines of Australia*; of his practical experience he had produced no less satisfactory evidence in his account of the natives of Mailu in New Guinea, based on a residence of six months among them.† In the Trobriand Islands, to the east of New Guinea, to which he next turned his attention, Dr. Malinowski lived as a native among the natives for many months together, watching them daily at work and at play, conversing with them in their own tongue, and deriving all his information from the surest sources—personal observation and statements made to him directly by the

---

* The Family among the Australian Aborigines : A Sociological Study. London: University of London Press, 1913.

† " The Natives of Mailu : Preliminary Results of the Robert Mond Research Work in British New Guinea." Transactions of the Royal Society of South Australia, vol. xxxix., 1915.

natives in their own language without the intervention
of an interpreter.   In this way he has accumulated a large
mass of materials, of high scientific value, bearing on the
social, religious, and economic or industrial life of the
Trobriand Islanders.   These he hopes and intends to
publish hereafter in full ; meantime he has given us in
the present volume a preliminary study of an interesting
and peculiar feature in Trobriand society, the remarkable system of exchange, only in part economic or
commercial, which the islanders maintain among themselves and with the inhabitants of neighbouring islands.

Little reflection is needed to convince us of the fundamental importance of economic forces at all stages of
man's career from the humblest to the highest.   After
all, the human species is part of the animal creation, and
as such, like the rest of the animals, it reposes on a
material foundation ; on which a higher life, intellectual,
moral, social, may be built, but without which no such
superstructure is possible.   That material foundation,
consisting in the necessity of food and of a certain degree
of warmth and shelter from the elements, forms the
economic or industrial basis and prime condition of human
life.   If anthropologists have hitherto unduly neglected
it, we may suppose that it was rather because they were
attracted to the higher side of man's nature than because
they deliberately ignored and undervalued the importance
and indeed necessity of the lower.   In excuse for their
neglect we may also remember that anthropology is still
a young science, and that the multitude of problems
which await the student cannot all be attacked at once,
but must be grappled with one by one.   Be that as it
may, Dr. Malinowski has done well to emphasise the great
significance of primitive economics by singling out the
notable exchange system of the Trobriand Islanders for
special consideration.

Further, he has wisely refused to limit himself to a
mere description of the processes of the exchange, and
has set himself to penetrate the motives which underlie
it and the feelings which it excites in the minds of the

natives. It appears to be sometimes held that pure sociology should confine itself to the description of acts and should leave the problems of motives and feelings to psychology. Doubtless it is true that the analysis of motives and feelings is logically distinguishable from the description of acts, and that it falls, strictly speaking, within the sphere of psychology ; but in practice an act has no meaning for an observer unless he knows or infers the thoughts and emotions of the agent ; hence to describe a series of acts, without any reference to the state of mind of the agent, would not answer the purpose of sociology, the aim of which is not merely to register but to understand the actions of men in society. Thus sociology cannot fulfil its task without calling in at every turn the aid of psychology.

It is characteristic of Dr. Malinowski's method that he takes full account of the complexity of human nature. He sees man, so to say, in the round and not in the flat. He remembers that man is a creature of emotion at least as much as of reason, and he is constantly at pains to discover the emotional as well as the rational basis of human action. The man of science, like the man of letters, is too apt to view mankind only in the abstract, selecting for his consideration a single side of our complex and many-sided being. Of this one-sided treatment Molière is a conspicuous example among great writers. All his characters are seen only in the flat : one of them is a miser, another a hypocrite, another a coxcomb, and so on ; but not one of them is a man. All are dummies dressed up to look very like human beings ; but the likeness is only on the surface, all within is hollow and empty, because truth to nature has been sacrificed to literary effect. Very different is the presentation of human nature in the greater artists, such as Cervantes and Shakespeare : their characters are solid, being drawn not from one side only but from many. No doubt in science a certain abstractness of treatment is not merely legitimate, but necessary, since science is nothing but knowledge raised to the highest power, and all knowledge implies a process of abstraction and general-isation : even the recognition of an individual whom we see every day is only possible as the result of an abstract idea of him formed by generalisation from his appear-ances in the past. Thus the science of man is forced to abstract certain aspects of human nature and to con-sider them apart from the concrete reality ; or rather it falls into a number of sciences, each of which considers a single part of man's complex organism, it may be the physical, the intellectual, the moral, or the social side of his being ; and the general conclusions which it draws will present a more or less incomplete picture of man as a whole, because the lines which compose it are necessarily but a few picked out of a multitude.

In the present treatise Dr. Malinowski is mainly concerned with what at first sight might seem a purely economic activity of the Trobriand Islanders ; but, with his usual width of outlook and fineness of perception, he is careful to point out that the curious circulation of valuables, which takes place between the inhabitants of the Trobriand and other islands, while it is accompanied by ordinary trade, is by no means itself a purely com-mercial transaction ; he shows that it is not based on a simple calculation of utility, of profit and loss, but that it satisfies emotional and æsthetic needs of a higher order than the mere gratification of animal wants. This leads Dr. Malinowski to pass some severe strictures on the conception of the Primitive Economic Man as a kind of bogey who, it appears, still haunts economic text-books and even extends his blighting influence to the minds of certain anthropologists. Rigged out in cast-off garments of Mr. Jeremy Bentham and Mr. Gradgrind, this horrible phantom is apparently actuated by no other motive than that of filthy lucre, which he pursues relentlessly, on Spencerian principles, along the line of least resistance. If such a dismal fiction is really regarded by serious inquirers as having any counterpart in savage society, and not simply as a useful abstraction, Dr. Malinowski's account of the *Kula* in this book should help to lay the phantom by the heels ; for he proves that the trade in useful objects, which forms part of the *Kula* system, is in the minds of the natives entirely subordinate in importance to the exchange of other objects, which serve no utilitarian purpose whatever. In its combination of commercial enterprise, social organisation, mythical background, and magical ritual, to say nothing of the wide geographical range of its operations, this singular institution appears to have no exact parallel in the existing anthropological record ; but its discoverer, Dr. Malinowski, may very well be right in surmising that it is probably a type of institution of which analogous, if not precisely similar, instances will hereafter be brought to light by further research among savage and barbarous peoples.

Not the least interesting and instructive feature of the *Kula*, as it is described for us by Dr. Malinowski, is the extremely important part which magic is seen to play in the institution. From his description it appears that in the minds of the natives the performance of magical rites and the utterance of magical words are indispensable for the success of the enterprise in all its phases, from the felling of the trees out of which the canoes are to be hollowed, down to the moment when, the expedition successfully accomplished, the argosy with its precious cargo is about to start on its homeward voyage. And incidentally we learn that magical ceremonies and spells are deemed no less necessary for the cultivation of gardens and for success in fishing, the two forms of industrial enterprise which furnish the islanders with their principal means of support ; hence the garden magician, whose business it is to promote the growth of the garden produce by his hocus-pocus, is one of the most important men in the village, ranking next after the chief and the sorcerer. In short, magic is believed to be an absolutely essential adjunct of every industrial undertaking, being just as requisite for its success as the mechanical operations involved in it, such as the caulking, painting and launching of a canoe, the planting of a garden, and the setting of a fish-trap. " A belief in magic," says Dr. Malinowski, " is one of the main psychological forces which allow for organisation and systematisation of economic effort in the Trobriands."

This valuable account of magic as a factor of fundamental economic importance for the welfare and indeed for the very existence of the community should suffice to dispel the erroneous view that magic, as opposed to religion, is in its nature essentially maleficent and anti-social, being always used by an individual for the promotion of his own selfish ends and the injury of his enemies, quite regardless of its effect on the common weal. No doubt magic may be so employed, and has in fact probably been so employed, in every part of the world ; in the Trobriand Islands themselves it is believed to be similarly practised for nefarious purposes by sorcerers, who inspire the natives with the deepest dread and the most constant concern. But in itself magic is neither beneficent nor maleficent ; it is simply an imaginary power of controlling the forces of nature, and this control may be exercised by the magician for good or evil, for the benefit or injury of individuals and of the community. In this respect, magic is exactly on the same footing with the sciences, of which it is the bastard sister. They, too, in themselves, are neither good nor evil, though they become the source of one or other according to their application. It would be absurd, for example, to stigmatise pharmacy as anti-social, because a knowledge of the properties of drugs is often employed to destroy men as well as to heal them. It is equally absurd to neglect the beneficent application of magic and to single out its maleficent use as the characteristic property by which to define it. The processes of nature, over which science exercises a real and magic an imaginary control, are not affected by the moral disposition, the good or bad intention, of the individual who uses his knowledge to set them in motion. The action of drugs on the human body is precisely the same whether they are administered by a physician or by a poisoner.

Nature and her handmaid Science are neither friendly nor hostile to morality ; they are simply indifferent to it and equally ready to do the bidding of the saint and of the sinner, provided only that he gives them the proper word of command. If the guns are well loaded and well aimed, the fire of the battery will be equally destructive, whether the gunners are patriots fighting in defence of their country or invaders waging a war of unjust aggression. The fallacy of differentiating a science or an art according to its application and the moral intention of the agent is obvious enough with regard to pharmacy and artillery ; it is equally real, though to many people apparently it is less obvious, with regard to magic.

The immense influence wielded by magic over the whole life and thought of the Trobriand Islanders is perhaps the feature of Dr. Malinowski's book which makes the most abiding impression on the mind of the reader. He tells us that " magic, the attempt of man to govern the forces of nature directly by means of a special lore, is all-pervading and all-important in the Trobriands " ; it is " interwoven into all the many industrial and communal activities " ; " all the data which have been so far mustered disclose the extreme importance of magic in the Kula. But if it were a questions of treating of any other aspect of the tribal life of these natives, it would also be found that, whenever they approach any concern of vital importance, they summon magic to their aid. It can be said without exaggeration that magic, according to their ideas, governs human destinies ; that it supplies man with the power of mastering the forces of nature ; and that it is his weapon and armour against the many dangers which crowd in upon him on every side."

Thus in the view of the Trobriand Islanders, magic is a power of supreme importance either for good or evil ; it can make or mar the life of man ; it can sustain and protect the individual and the community, or it can injure and destroy them. Compared to this universal and deep-rooted conviction, the belief in the existence of the spirits of the dead would seem to exercise but little influence on the life of these people. Contrary to the general attitude of savages towards the souls of the departed, they are reported to be almost completely devoid of any fear of ghosts. They believe, indeed, that the ghosts return to their villages once a year to partake of the great annual feast ; but " in general the spirits do not influence human beings very much, for better or worse "; " there is nothing of the mutual inter-action, of the intimate collaboration between man and spirit which are the essence of religious cult." This conspicuous predominance of magic over religion, at least over the worship of the dead, is a very notable feature in the culture of a people so comparatively high in the scale of savagery as the Trobriand Islanders. It furnishes a fresh proof of the extraordinary strength and tenacity of the hold which this world-wide delusion has had, and still has, upon the human mind.

We shall doubtless learn much as to the relation of magic and religion among the Trobrianders from the full report of Dr. Malinowski's researches in the islands. From the patient observation which he has devoted to a single institution, and from the wealth of details with which he has illustrated it, we may judge of the extent and value of the larger work which he has in preparation. It promises to be one of the completest and most scientific accounts ever given of a savage people.

J. G. FRAZER.

The Temple, London.
  7th March, 1922.

FOREWORD

By the Author

ETHNOLOGY is in the sadly ludicrous, not to say tragic, position, that at the very moment when it begins to put its workshop in order, to forge its proper tools, to start ready for work on its appointed task, the material of its study melts away with hopeless rapidity. Just now, when the methods and aims of scientific field ethnology have taken shape, when men fully trained for the work have begun to travel into savage countries and study their inhabitants—these die away under our very eyes.

The research which has been done on native races by men of academic training has proved beyond doubt and cavil that scientific, methodic inquiry can give us results far more abundant and of better quality than those of even the best amateur's work. Most, though not all, of the modern scientific accounts have opened up quite new and unexpected aspects of tribal life. They have given us, in clear outline, the picture of social institutions often surprisingly vast and complex ; they have brought before us the vision of the native as he is, in his religious and magical beliefs and practices. They have allowed us to penetrate into his mind far more deeply than we have ever done before. From this new material, scientifically hall-marked, students of comparative Ethnology have already drawn some very important conclusions on the origin of human customs, beliefs and institutions ; on the history of cultures, and their spread and contact ; on the laws of human behaviour in society, and of the human mind.

The hope of gaining a new vision of savage humanity through the labours of scientific specialists opens out like a mirage, vanishing almost as soon as perceived.

For though at present, there is still a large number of
native communities available for scientific study, within
a generation or two, they or their cultures will have practically disappeared. The need for energetic work is urgent,
and the time is short. Nor, alas, up to the present, has
any adequate interest been taken by the public in these
studies. The number of workers is small, the encouragement they receive scanty. I feel therefore no need to
justify an ethnological contribution which is the result
of specialised research in the field.

In this volume I give an account of one phase of savage
life only, in describing certain forms of inter-tribal, trading
relations among the natives of New Guinea. This
account has been culled, as a preliminary monograph,
from Ethnographic material, covering the whole extent
of the tribal culture of one district. One of the first
conditions of acceptable Ethnographic work certainly is
that it should deal with the totality of all social, cultural
and psychological aspects of the community, for they are
so interwoven that not one can be understood without
taking into consideration all the others. The reader of
this monograph will clearly see that, though its main
theme is economic—for it deals with commercial enterprise, exchange and trade—constant reference has to be
made to social organisation, the power of magic, to
mythology and folklore, and indeed to all other aspects
as well as the main one.

The geographical area of which the book treats is
limited to the Archipelagoes lying off the eastern end of
New Guinea. Even within this, the main field of research
was in one district, that of the Trobriand Islands. This,
however, has been studied minutely. I have lived in that
one archipelago for about two years, in the course of three
expeditions to New Guinea, during which time I naturally
acquired a thorough knowledge of the language. I did
my work entirely alone, living for the greater part of the
time right in the villages. I therefore had constantly the
daily life of the natives before my eyes, while accidental,
dramatic occurrences, deaths, quarrels, village brawls,

public and ceremonial events, could not escape my notice.

In the present state of Ethnography, when so much has still to be done in paving the way for forthcoming research and in fixing its scope, each new contribution ought to justify its appearance in several points. It ought to show some advance in method ; it ought to push research beyond its previous limits in depth, in width, or in both ; finally, it ought to endeavour to present its results in a manner exact, but not dry. The specialist interested in method, in reading this work, will find set out in the Introduction, Divisions II-IX and in Chapter XVIII, the exposition of my points of view and efforts in this direction. The reader who is concerned with results, rather than with the way of obtaining them, will find in Chapters IV to XXI a consecutive narrative of the Kula expeditions, and the various associated customs and beliefs. The student who is interested, not only in the narrative, but in the ethnographic background for it, and a clear definition of the institution, will find the first in Chapters I and II, and the latter in Chapter III.

To Mr. Robert Mond I tender my sincerest thanks. It is to his generous endowment that I owe the possibility of carrying on for several years the research of which the present volume is a partial result. To Mr. Atlee Hunt, C.M.G., Secretary of the Home and Territories Department of the Commonwealth of Australia, I am indebted for the financial assistance of the Department, and also for much help given on the spot. In the Trobriands, I was immensely helped in my work by Mr. B. Hancock, pearl trader, to whom I am grateful not only for assistance and services, but for many acts of friendship.

Much of the argument in this book has been greatly improved by the criticism given me by my friend, Mr. Paul Khuner, of Vienna, an expert in the practical affairs of modern industry and a highly competent thinker on economic matters. Professor L. T. Hobhouse has kindly read the proofs and given me valuable advice on several points.

Sir James Frazer, by writing his Preface, has enhanced the value of this volume beyond its merit and it is not only a great honour and advantage for me to be introduced by him, but also a special pleasure, for my first love for ethnology is associated with the reading of the " Golden Bough," then in its second edition.

Last, not least, I wish to mention Professor C. G. Seligman, to whom this book is dedicated. The initiative of my expedition was given by him and I owe him more than I can express for the encouragement and scientific counsel which he has so generously given me during the progress of my work in New Guinea.

B.M.

El Boquin,
    Icod de los Vinos,
        Tenerife.
April, 1921.

ACKNOWLEDGEMENTS

It is in the nature of the research, that an Ethnographer has to rely upon the assistance of others to an extent much greater than is the case with other scientific workers. I have therefore to express in this special place my obligations to the many who have helped me. As said in the Preface, financially I owe most to Mr. Robert Mond, who made my work possible by bestowing on me the Robert Mond Travelling Scholarship (University of London) of £250 per annum for five years (for 1914 and for 1917 –1920). I was substantially helped by a grant of £250 from the Home and Territories Department of Australia, obtained by the good offices of Mr. Atlee Hunt, C.M.G. The London School of Economics awarded me the Constance Hutchinson Scholarship of £100 yearly for two years, 1915-1916. Professor Seligman, to whom in this, as in other matters I owe so much, besides helping me in obtaining all the other grants, gave himself £100 towards the cost of the expedition and equipped me with a camera, a phonograph, anthropometric instruments and other paraphernalia of ethnographic work. I went out to Australia with the British Association for the Advancement of Science in 1914, as a guest, and at the expense, of the Commonwealth Government of Australia.

It may be interesting for intending field-workers to observe that I carried out my ethnographic research for six years— 1914 to 1920—making three expeditions to the field of my work, and devoting the intervals between expeditions to the working out of my material and to the study of special literature, on little more than £250 a year. I defrayed out of this, not only all the expenses of travel and research, such as fares, wages to native servants, payments of interpreters, but I was also able to collect a fair amount of ethnographic specimens, of which part has been presented to the Melbourne Museum as the Robert Mond Collection. This would not have been possible for me, had I not received much help from residents in New Guinea. My friend, Mr. B. Hancock, of Gusaweta, Trobriand Islands, allowed me to use his house and store as base for my gear and provisions ; he lent me his cutter on various occasions and provided me with a home, where I could always repair in need or sickness. He helped me in my photographic work, and gave me a good number of his own photographic plates, of which several are reproduced in this book (Plates XI, XXXVII, and L-LII).

Other pearl traders and buyers of the Trobriands were also very kind to me, especially M. and Mme. Raphael Brudo, of

Paris, Messrs. C. and G. Auerbach, and the late Mr. Mick George, all of whom helped me in various ways and extended to me their kind hospitality.

In my interim studies in Melbourne, I received much help from the staff of the excellent Public Library of Victoria, for which I have to thank the Librarian, Mr. E. La Touche Armstrong, my friend Mr. E. Pitt, Mr. Cooke and others.

Two maps and two plates are reproduced by kind permission of Professor Seligman from his " Melanesians of British New Guinea." I have to thank the Editor of *Man* (Captain T. A. Joyce) for his permission to use here again the plates which were previously published in that paper.

Mr. William Swan Stallybrass, Senior Managing Director of Messrs. Geo. Routledge & Sons, Ltd., has spared no trouble in meeting all my wishes as to scientific details in the publication of this book, for which I wish to express my sincere thanks.

PHONETIC NOTE.

The native names and words in this book are written according to the simple rules, recommended by the Royal Geographical Society and the Royal Anthropological Institute. That is, the vowels are to be pronounced as in Italian and the consonants as in English. This spelling suits the sounds of the Melanesian languages of New Guinea sufficiently well. The apostrophe placed between two vowels indicates that they should be pronounced separately and not merged into a diphthong. The accent is almost always on the penultimate, rarely on the anti-penultimate. All the syllables must be pronounced clearly and distinctly.

TABLE OF CONTENTS

LIST OF ILLUSTRATIONS

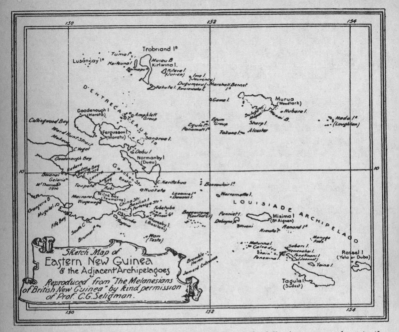

MAP I—The native names and their spelling on this and the following map conform to the traditional nomenclature to be found on charts and old maps. Maps III-V show the native names as ascertained by myself and phonetically spelled.

INTRODUCTION

THE SUBJECT, METHOD AND SCOPE OF THIS INQUIRY

I

THE coastal populations of the South Sea Islands, with very few exceptions, are, or were before their extinction, expert navigators and traders. Several of them had evolved excellent types of large sea-going canoes, and used to embark in them on distant trade expeditions or raids of war and conquest. The Papuo-Melanesians, who inhabit the coast and the outlying islands of New Guinea, are no exception to this rule. In general they are daring sailors, industrious manufacturers, and keen traders. The manufacturing centres of important articles, such as pottery, stone implements, canoes, fine baskets, valued ornaments, are localised in several places, according to the skill of the inhabitants, their inherited tribal tradition, and special facilities offered by the district ; thence they are traded over wide areas, sometimes travelling more than hundreds of miles.

Definite forms of exchange along definite trade routes are to be found established between the various tribes. A most remarkable form of intertribal trade is that obtaining between the Motu of Port Moresby and the tribes of the Papuan Gulf. The Motu sail for hundreds of miles in heavy, unwieldy canoes, called *lakatoi*, which are provided with the characteristic crab-claw sails. They bring pottery and shell ornaments, in olden days, stone blades, to Gulf Papuans, from whom they obtain in exchange sago and the heavy dug-outs, which are used afterwards by the Motu for the construction of their *lakatoi* canoes.*

---

* The *hiri*, as these expeditions are called in Motuan, have been described with a great wealth of detail and clearness of outline by Captain F. Barton, in C. G. Seligman's " The Melanesians of British New Guinea," Cambridge, 1910, Chapter viii.

Further East, on the South coast, there lives the industrious, sea-faring population of the Mailu, who link the East End of New Guinea with the central coast tribes by means of annual trading expeditions.* Finally, the natives of the islands and archipelagoes, scattered around the East End, are in constant trading relations with one another. We possess in Professor Seligman's book an excellent description of the subject, especially of the nearer trades routes between the various islands inhabited by the Southern Massim.† There exists, however, another, a very extensive and highly complex trading system, embracing with its ramifications, not only the islands near the East End, but also the Louisiades, Woodlark Island, the Trobriand Archipelago, and the d'Entrecasteaux group ; it penetrates into the mainland of New Guinea, and exerts an indirect influence over several outlying districts, such as Rossel Island, and some parts of the Northern and Southern coast of New Guinea. This trading system, the Kula, is the subject I am setting out to describe in this volume, and it will be seen that it is an economic phenomenon of considera-able theoretical importance. It looms paramount in the tribal life of those natives who live within its circuit, and its impor-tance is fully realised by the tribesmen themselves, whose ideas, ambitions, desires and vanities are very much bound up with the Kula

II

Before proceeding to the account of the Kula, it will be well to give a description of the methods used in the collecting of the ethnographic material. The results of scientific research in any branch of learning ought to be presented in a manner absolutely candid and above board. No one would dream of making an experimental contribution to physical or chemical science, without giving a detailed account of all the arrange-ments of the experiments ; an exact description of the apparatus used ; of the manner in which the observations were conducted ; of their number ; of the length of time devoted to them, and of the degree of approximation with which each measurement was made. In less exact sciences, as in biology or geology,

* Cf. "The Mailu," by B. Malinowski, in Transactions of the R. Society of S. Australia, 1915 ; Chapter iv. 4, pp. 612 to 629.

† Op. cit. Chapter xl.

this cannot be done as rigorously, but every student will do his best to bring home to the reader all the conditions in which the experiment or the observations were made. In Ethnography, where a candid account of such data is perhaps even more necessary, it has unfortunately in the past not always been supplied with sufficient generosity, and many writers do not ply the full searchlight of methodic sincerity, as they move among their facts but produce them before us out of complete obscurity.

It would be easy to quote works of high repute, and with a scientific hall-mark on them, in which wholesale generalisations are laid down before us, and we are not informed at all by what actual experiences the writers have reached their conclusion. No special chapter or paragraph is devoted to describing to us the conditions under which observations were made and information collected. I consider that only such ethnographic sources are of unquestionable scientific value, in which we can clearly draw the line between, on the one hand, the results of direct observation and of native statements and interpretations, and on the other, the inferences of the author, based on his common sense and psycholgical insight.* Indeed, some such survey, as that contained in the table, given below (Div. VI of this chapter) ought to be forthcoming, so that at a glance the reader could estimate with precision the degree of the writer's personal acquaintance with the facts which he describes, and form an idea under what conditions information had been obtained from the natives.

Again, in historical science, no one could expect to be seriously treated if he made any mystery of his sources and spoke of the past as if he knew it by divination. In Ethnography, the writer is his own chronicler and the historian at the same time, while his sources are no doubt easily accessible, but also supremely elusive and complex ; they are not embodied in fixed, material documents, but in the behaviour and in the memory of living men. In Ethnography, the distance is often enormous between the brute material of

* On this point of method again, we are indebted to the Cambridge School of Anthropology for having introduced the really scientific way of dealing with the question. More especially in the writings of Haddon, Rivers and Seligman, the distinction between inference and observation is always clearly drawn, and we can visualise with perfect precision the conditions under which the work was done.

information—as it is presented to the student in his own observations, in native statement, in the kaleidoscope of tribal life— and the final authoritative presentation of the results. The Ethnographer has to traverse this distance in the laborious years between the moment when he sets foot upon a native beach, and makes his first attempts to get into touch with the natives, and the time when he writes down the final version of his results. A brief outline of an Ethnographer's tribulations, as lived through by myself, may throw more light on the question, than any long abstract discussion could do.

III

Imagine yourself suddenly set down surrounded by all your gear, alone on a tropical beach close to a native village, while the launch or dinghy which has brought you sails away out of sight. Since you take up your abode in the compound of some neighbouring white man, trader or missionary, you have nothing to do, but to start at once on your ethnographic work. Imagine further that you are a beginner, without previous experience, with nothing to guide you and no one to help you. For the white man is temporarily absent, or else unable or unwilling to waste any of his time on you. This exactly describes my first initiation into field work on the south coast of New Guinea. I well remember the long visits I paid to the villages during the first weeks ; the feeling of hopelessness and despair after many obstinate but futile attempts had entirely failed to bring me into real touch with the natives, or supply me with any material. I had periods of despondency, when I buried myself in the reading of novels, as a man might take to drink in a fit of tropical depression and boredom.

Imagine yourself then, making your first entry into the village, alone or in company with your white cicerone. Some natives flock round you, especially if they smell tobacco. Others, the more dignified and elderly, remain seated where they are. Your white companion has his routine way of treating the natives, and he neither understands, nor is very much concerned with the manner in which you, as an ethnographer, will have to approach them. The first visit leaves you with a hopeful feeling that when you return alone, things will be easier. Such was my hope at least.

I came back duly, and soon gathered an audience around me. A few compliments in pidgin-English on both sides, some tobacco changing hands, induced an atmosphere of mutual amiability. I tried then to proceed to business. First, to begin with subjects which might arouse no suspicion, I started to " do " technology. A few natives were engaged in manufacturing some object or other. It was easy to look at it and obtain the names of the tools, and even some technical expressions about the proceedings, but there the matter ended. It must be borne in mind that pidgin-English is a very imperfect instrument for expressing one's ideas, and that before one gets a good training in framing questions and understanding answers one has the uncomfortable feeling that free communication in it with the natives will never be attained ; and I was quite unable to enter into any more detailed or explicit conversation with them at first. I knew well that the best remedy for this was to collect concrete data, and accordingly I took a village census, wrote down genealogies, drew up plans and collected the terms of kinship. But all this remained dead material, which led no further into the understanding of real native mentality or behaviour, since I could neither procure a good native interpretation of any of these items, nor get what could be called the hang of tribal life. As to obtaining their ideas about religion, and magic, their beliefs in sorcery and spirits, nothing was forthcoming except a few superficial items of folk-lore, mangled by being forced into pidgin English.

Information which I received from some white residents in the district, valuable as it was in itself, was more discouraging than anything else with regard to my own work. Here were men who had lived for years in the place with constant opportunities of observing the natives and communicating with them, and who yet hardly knew one thing about them really well. How could I therefore in a few months or a year, hope to overtake and go beyond them ? Moreover, the manner in which my white informants spoke about the natives and put their views was, naturally, that of untrained minds, unaccustomed to formulate their thoughts with any degree of consistency and precision. And they were for the most part, naturally enough, full of the biassed and pre-judged opinions inevitable in the average practical man, whether administrator, missionary, or trader , yet so strongly repulsive to a mind striving after the

objective, scientific view of things.   The habit of treating with
a self-satisfied frivolity what is really serious to the ethnographer ; the cheap rating of what to him is a scientific treasure,
that is to say, the native's cultural and mental peculiarities and
independence—these features, so well known in the inferior
amateur's writing, I found in the tone of the majority of white
residents.*

Indeed, in my first piece of Ethnographic research on the
South coast, it was not until I was alone in the district that I
began to make some headway ; and, at any rate, I found out
where lay the secret of effective field-work.   What is then this
ethnographer's magic, by which he is able to evoke the real
spirit of the natives, the true picture of tribal life ?   As usual,
success can only be obtained by a patient and systematic
application of a number of rules of common sense and well-
known scientific principles, and not by the discovery of any
marvellous short-cut leading to the desired results without
effort or trouble.   The principles of method can be grouped
under three main headings ; first of all, naturally, the student
must possess real scientific aims, and know the values and
criteria of modern ethnography.   Secondly, he ought to put
himself in good conditions of work. that is, in the main, to live
without other white men, right among the natives.   Finally,
he has to apply a number of special methods of collecting,
manipulating and fixing his evidence.   A few words must be
said about these three foundation stones of field work, beginning
with the second as the most elementary.

IV

Proper conditions for ethnographic work.   These, as said,
consist mainly in cutting oneself off from the company of other
white men, and remaining in as close contact with the natives
as possible, which really can only be achieved by camping right
in their villages (see Plates I and II).   It is very nice to have
a base in a white man's compound for the stores, and to know
there is a refuge there in times of sickness and surfeit of native.
But it must be far enough away not to become a permanent
milieu in which you live and from which you emerge at fixed

---

* I may note at once that there were a few delightful exceptions to that,
to mention only my friends Billy Hancock in the Trobriands ; M. Raffael
Brudo, another pearl trader ; and the missionary, Mr. M. K. Gilmour.

hours only to " do the village." It should not even be near enough to fly to at any moment for recreation. For the native is not the natural companion for a white man, and after you have been working with him for several hours, seeing how he does his gardens, or letting him tell you items of folk-lore, or discussing his customs, you will naturally hanker after the company of your own kind. But if you are alone in a village beyond reach of this, you go for a solitary walk for an hour or so, return again and then quite naturally seek out the natives' society, this time as a relief from loneliness, just as you would any other companionship. And by means of this natural intercourse, you learn to know him, and you become familiar with his customs and beliefs far better than when he is a paid, and often bored, informant.

There is all the difference between a sporadic plunging into the company of natives, and being really in contact with them. What does this latter mean ? On the Ethnographer's side, it means that his life in the village, which at first is a strange, sometimes unpleasant, sometimes intensely interesting adventure, soon adopts quite a natural course very much in harmony with his surroundings.

Soon after I had established myself in Omarakana (Tro-briand Islands), I began to take part, in a way, in the village life, to look forward to the important or festive events, to take personal interest in the gossip and the developments of the small village occurrences ; to wake up every morning to a day, presenting itself to me more or less as it does to the native. I would get out from under my mosquito net, to find around me the village life beginning to stir, or the people well advanced in their working day according to the hour and also to the season, for they get up and begin their labours early or late, as work presses. As I went on my morning walk through the village, I could see intimate details of family life, of toilet, cooking, taking of meals ; I could see the arrangements for the day's work, people starting on their errands, or groups of men and women busy at some manufacturing tasks (see Plate III). Quarrels, jokes, family scenes, events usually trivial, some-times dramatic but always significant, formed the atmosphere of my daily life, as well as of theirs. It must be remembered that as the natives saw me constantly every day, they ceased to be interested or alarmed, or made self-conscious by my presence, and I ceased to be a disturbing element in the tribal life which I was to study, altering it by my very approach, as always happens with a new-comer to every savage community. In fact, as they knew that I would thrust my nose into everything, even where a well-mannered native would not dream of intruding, they finished by regarding me as part and parcel of their life, a necessary evil or nuisance, mitigated by donations of tobacco.

Later on in the day, whatever happened was within easy reach, and there was no possibility of its escaping my notice. Alarms about the sorcerer's approach in the evening, one or two big, really important quarrels and rifts within the community, cases of illness, attempted cures and deaths, magical rites which had to be performed, all these I had not to pursue, fearful of missing them, but they took place under my very eyes, at my own doorstep, so to speak (see Plate IV). And it must be emphasised whenever anything dramatic or important occurs it is essential to investigate it at the very moment of happening, because the natives cannot but talk about it, are too excited to be reticent, and too interested to be mentally lazy in supplying details. Also, over and over again, I committed breaches of etiquette, which the natives, familiar enough with me, were not slow in pointing out. I had to learn how to behave, and to a certain extent, I acquired " the feeling " for native good and bad manners. With this, and with the capacity of enjoying their company and sharing some of their games and amusements, I began to feel that I was indeed in touch with the natives, and this is certainly the preliminary condition of being able to carry on successful field work.

V

But the Ethnographer has not only to spread his nets in the right place, and wait for what will fall into them. He must be an active huntsman, and drive his quarry into them and follow it up to its most inaccessible lairs. And that leads us to the more active methods of pursuing ethnographic evidence. It has been mentioned at the end of Division III that the Ethnographer has to be inspired by the knowledge of the most modern results of scientific study, by its principles and aims. I shall not enlarge upon this subject, except by way of one remark, to avoid the possibility of misunderstanding. Good training in theory, and acquaintance with its latest results, is not identical with being burdened with " preconceived ideas." If a man sets out on an expedition, determined to prove certain hypotheses, if he is incapable of changing his views constantly and casting them off ungrudgingly under the pressure of evidence, needless to say his work will be worthless. But the more problems he brings with him into the field, the more he is in the habit of moulding his theories according to facts, and of seeing facts in their bearing upon theory, the better he is equipped for the work. Preconceived ideas are pernicious in any scientific work, but foreshadowed problems are the main endowment of a scientific thinker, and these problems are first revealed to the observer by his theoretical studies.

In Ethnology the early efforts of Bastian, Tylor, Morgan, the German Völkerpsychologen have remoulded the older crude information of travellers, missionaries, etc., and have shown us the importance of applying deeper conceptions and discarding crude and misleading ones.*

The concept of animism superseded that of " fetichism " or " devil-worship," both meaningless terms. The understanding of the classificatory systems of relationship paved the way for the brilliant, modern researches on native sociology in the field-work of the Cambridge school. The psychological analysis of the German thinkers has brought forth an abundant crop of most valuable information in the results obtained by the recent German expeditions to Africa, South America and the Pacific, while the theoretical works of Frazer, Durkheim and others have already, and will no doubt still for a long time inspire field workers and lead them to new results. The field worker relies entirely upon inspiration from theory. Of course he may be also a theoretical thinker and worker, and there he can draw on himself for stimulus. But the two functions are separate, and in actual research they have to be separated both in time and conditions of work.

As always happens when scientific interest turns towards and begins to labour on a field so far only prospected by the curiosity of amateurs, Ethnology has introduced law and order into what seemed chaotic and freakish. It has transformed for us the sensational, wild and unaccountable world of

* According to a useful habit of the terminology of science, I use the word Ethnography for the empirical and descriptive results of the science of Man, and the word Ethnology for speculative and comparative theories.

" savages " into a number of well ordered communities,
governed by law, behaving and thinking according to consistent
principles. The word " savage," whatever association it might
have had originally, connotes ideas of boundless liberty, of
irregularity, of something extremely and extraordinarily quaint.
In popular thinking, we imagine that the natives live on the
bosom of Nature, more or less as they can and like, the prey of
irregular, phantasmagoric beliefs and apprehensions. Modern
science, on the contrary, shows that their social institutions have
a very definite organisation, that they are governed by authority, law and order in their public and personal relations, while
the latter are, besides, under the control of extremely complex
ties of kinship and clanship. Indeed, we see them entangled
in a mesh of duties, functions and privileges which correspond
to an elaborate tribal, communal and kinship organisation
(see Plate IV). Their beliefs and practices do not by any
means lack consistency of a certain type, and their knowledge
of the outer world is sufficient to guide them in many of their
strenuous enterprises and activities. Their artistic productions again lack neither meaning nor beauty.

It is a very far cry from the famous answer given long ago
by a representative authority who, asked, what are the manners
and customs of the natives, answered, " Customs none, manners
beastly," to the position of the modern Ethnographer ! This
latter, with his tables of kinship terms, genealogies, maps,
plans and diagrams, proves the existence of an extensive and big
organisation, shows the constitution of the tribe, of the clan, of the
family ; and he gives us a picture of the natives subjected to a
strict code of behaviour and good manners, to which in comparison
the life at the Court of Versailles or Escurial was free and easy.*

Thus the first and basic ideal of ethnographic field-work is
to give a clear and firm outline of the social constitution, and
disentangle the laws and regularities of all cultural phenomena

---

* The legendary " early authority " who found the natives only beastly
and without customs is left behind by a modern writer, who, speaking about
the Southern Massim with whom he lived and worked " in close contact " for
many years, says :—" . . . We teach lawless men to become obedient,
inhuman men to love, and savage men to change." And again :—" Guided
in his conduct by nothing but his instincts and propensities, and governed by
his unchecked passions. . . ." " Lawless, inhuman and savage ! " A
grosser misstatement of the real state of things could not be invented by anyone
wishing to parody the Missionary point of view. Quoted from the Rev. C. W.
Abel, of the London Missionary Society, " Savage Life in New Guinea," no
date.

from the irrelevances. The firm skeleton of the tribal life has to be first ascertained. This ideal imposes in the first place the fundamental obligation of giving a complete survey of the phenomena, and not of picking out the sensational, the singular, still less the funny and quaint. The time when we could tolerate accounts presenting us the native as a distorted, childish caricature of a human being are gone. This picture is false, and like many other falsehoods, it has been killed by Science. The field Ethnographer has seriously and soberly to cover the full extent of the phenomena in each aspect of tribal culture studied, making no difference between what is commonplace, or drab, or ordinary, and what strikes him as astonishing and out-of-the-way. At the same time, the whole area of tribal culture *in all its aspects* has to be gone over in research. The consistency, the law and order which obtain within each aspect make also for joining them into one coherent whole.

An Ethnographer who sets out to study only religion, or only technology, or only social organisation cuts out an artificial field for inquiry, and he will be seriously handicapped in his work.

<h2 style="text-align:center">VI</h2>

Having settled this very general rule, let us descend to more detailed consideration of method. The Ethnographer has in the field, according to what has just been said, the duty before him of drawing up all the rules and regularities of tribal life ; all that is permanent and fixed ; of giving an anatomy of their culture, of depicting the constitution of their society. But these things, though crystallised and set, are nowhere *formulated*. There is no written or explicitly expressed code of laws, and their whole tribal tradition, the whole structure of their society, are embodied in the most elusive of all materials; the human being. But not even in human mind or memory are these laws to be found definitely formulated. The natives obey the forces and commands of the tribal code, but they do not comprehend them ; exactly as they obey their instincts and their impulses, but could not lay down a single law of psychology. The regularities in native institutions are an automatic result of the interaction of the mental forces of tradition, and of the material conditions of environment. Exactly as a humble member of any modern institution, whether it be the state, or the church, or the army, is *of* it and *in* it, but has no vision of the resulting integral action of the whole, still less could furnish any account of its organisation, so it would be futile to attempt questioning a native in abstract, sociological terms. The difference is that, in our society, every institution has its intelligent members, its historians, and its archives and documents, whereas in a native society there are none of these. After this is realised an expedient has to be found to overcome this difficulty. This expedient for an Ethnographer consists in collecting concrete data of evidence. and drawing the general inferences for himself. This seems obvious on the face of it, but was not found out or at least practised in Ethnography till field work was taken up by men of science. Moreover, in giving it practical effect, it is neither easy to devise the concrete applications of this method, nor to carry them out systematically and consistently.

Though we cannot ask a native about abstract, general rules, we can always enquire how a given case would be treated. Thus for instance, in asking how they would treat crime, or punish it, it would be vain to put to a native a sweeping question such as, " How do you treat and punish a criminal ? " for even words could not be found to express it in native, or in pidgin. But an imaginary case, or still better, a real occurrence, will stimulate a native to express his opinion and to supply plentiful information. A real case indeed will start the natives on a wave of discussion, evoke expressions of indignation, show them taking sides—all of which talk will probably contain a wealth of definite views, of moral censures, as well as reveal the social mechanism set in motion by the crime committed. From there, it will be easy to lead them on to speak of other similar cases, to remember other actual occurrences or to discuss them in all their implications and aspects. From this material, which ought to cover the widest possible range of facts, the inference is obtained by simple induction. The *scientific* treatment differs from that of good common sense, first in that a student will extend the completeness and minuteness of survey much further and in a pedantically systematic and methodical manner ; and secondly, in that the scientifically trained mind, will push the inquiry along really relevant lines, and towards aims possessing real importance. Indeed, the object of scientific training is to provide the empirical investigator with a *mental chart*, in accordance with which he can take his bearings and lay his course.

To return to our example, a number of definite cases discussed will reveal to the Ethnographer the social machinery for punishment. This is one part, one aspect of tribal authority. Imagine further that by a similar method of inference from definite data, he arrives at understanding leadership in war, in economic enterprise, in tribal festivities—there he has at once all the data necessary to answer the questions about tribal government and social authority. In actual field work, the comparison of such data, the attempt to piece them together, will often reveal rifts and gaps in the information which lead on to further investigations.

From my own experience, I can say that, very often, a problem seemed settled, everything fixed and clear, till I began to write down a short preliminary sketch of my results. And only then, did I see the enormous deficiencies, which would show me where lay new problems, and lead me on to new work. In fact, I spent a few months between my first and second expeditions, and over a year between that and the subsequent one, in going over all my material, and making parts of it almost ready for publication each time, though each time I knew I would have to re-write it. Such cross-fertilisation of constructive work and observation, I found most valuable, and I do not think I could have made real headway without it. I give this bit of my own history merely to show that what has been said so far is not only an empty programme, but the result of personal experience. In this volume, the description is given of a big institution connected with ever so many associated activities, and presenting many aspects. To anyone who reflects on the subject, it will be clear that the information about a phenomenon of such high complexity and of so many ramifications, could not be obtained with any degree of exactitude and completeness, without a constant interplay of constructive attempts and empirical checking. In fact, I have written up an outline of the Kula institution at least half a dozen times while in the field and in the intervals between my expeditions. Each time, new problems and difficulties presented themselves.

The collecting of concrete data over a wide range of facts is thus one of the main points of field method. The obligation is not to enumerate a few examples only, but to exhaust as far as possible all the cases within reach ; and, on this search for cases, the investigator will score most whose mental chart is clearest. But, whenever the material of the search allows it, this mental chart ought to be transformed into a real one ; it ought to materialise into a diagram, a plan, an exhaustive, synoptic table of cases. Long since, in all tolerably good modern books on natives, we expect to find a full list or table of kinship terms, which includes all the data relative to it, and does not just pick out a few strange and anomalous relation-ships or expressions. In the investigation of kinship, the following up of one relation after another in concrete cases leads naturally to the construction of genealogical tables. Practised already by the best early writers, such as Munzinger, and, if I remember rightly, Kubary, this method has been developed to its fullest extent in the works of Dr. Rivers. Again, studying the concrete data of economic transactions, in order to trace the history of a valuable object, and to gauge the nature of its circulation, the principle of completeness and thoroughness would lead to construct tables of transactions, such as we find in the work of Professor Seligman.* It is in following Professor Seligman's example in this matter that I was able to settle certain of the more difficult and detailed rules of the Kula. The method of reducing information, if possible, into charts or synoptic tables ought to be extended to the study of practically all aspects of native life. All types of economic transactions may be studied by following up con-nected, actual cases, and putting them into a synoptic chart ; again, a table ought to be drawn up of all the gifts and presents customary in a given society , a table including the sociological, ceremonial, and economic definition of every item. Also, systems of magic, connected series of ceremonies, types of legal acts, all could be charted, allowing each entry to be synoptically defined under a number of headings. Besides this, of course, the genealogical census of every community, studied more in detail, extensive maps, plans and diagrams, illustrating ownership in garden land, hunting and fishing privileges, etc., serve as the more fundamental documents of ethnographic research.

A genealogy is nothing else but a synoptic chart of a number

* For instance, the tables of circulation of the valuable axe blades, op. cit., pp. 531, 532.

of connected relations of kinship. Its value as an instrument of research consists in that it allows the investigator to put questions which he formulates to himself *in abstracto*, but can put concretely to the native informant. As a document, its value consists in that it gives a number of authenticated data, presented in their natural grouping. A synoptic chart of magic fulfils the same function. As an instrument of research, I have used it in order to ascertain, for instance, the ideas about the nature of magical power. With a chart before me, I could easily and conveniently go over one item after the other, and note down the relevant practices and beliefs contained in each of them. The answer to my abstract problem could then be obtained by drawing a general inference from all the cases, and the procedure is illustrated in Chapters XVII and XVIII.* I cannot enter further into the discussion of this question, which would need further distinctions, such as between a chart of concrete, actual data, such as is a genealogy, and a chart summarising the outlines of a custom or belief, as a chart of a magical system would be.

Returning once more to the question of methodological candour, discussed previously in Division II, I wish to point out here, that the procedure of concrete and tabularised presentation of data ought to be applied first to the Ethnographer's own credentials. That is, an Ethnographer, who wishes to be trusted, must show clearly and concisely, in a tabularised form, which are his own direct observations, and which the indirect information that form the bases of his account. The Table on the next page will serve as an example of this procedure and help the reader of this book to form an idea of the trustworthiness of any statement he is specially anxious to check. With the help of this Table and the many references scattered throughout the text, as to how, under what circumstances, and with what degree of accuracy I arrived at a given item of knowledge, there will, I hope remain no obscurity whatever as to the sources of the book.

---

* In this book, besides the adjoining Table, which does not strictly belong to the class of document of which I speak here, the reader will find only a few samples of synoptic tables, such as the list of Kula partners mentioned and analysed in Chapter XIII, Division II, the list of gifts and presents in Chapter VI, Division VI, not tabularised, only described ; the synoptic data of a Kula expedition in Chapter XVI, and the table of Kula magic given in Chapter XVII. Here, I have not wanted to overload the account with charts, etc., preferring to reserve them till the full publication of my material.

CHRONOLOGICAL LIST OF KULA EVENTS WITNESSED
BY THE WRITER

FIRST EXPEDITION, August, 1914—March, 1915.

> *March*, 1915. In the village of Dikoyas (Woodlark Island) a few ceremonial offerings seen. Preliminary information obtained.

SECOND EXPEDITION, May, 1915—May, 1916.

> *June*, 1915. A Kabigidoya visit arrives from Vakuta to Kiriwina. Its anchoring at Kavataria witnessed and the men seen at Omarakana, where information collected.
>
> *July*, 1915. Several parties from Kitava land on the beach of Kaulukuba. The men examined in Omarakana. Much information collected in that period.
>
> *September*, 1915. Unsuccessful attempt to sail to Kitava with To'uluwa, the chief of Omarakana.
>
> *October-November*, 1915. Departure noticed of three expeditions from Kiriwina to Kitava. Each time To'uluwa brings home a haul of *mwali* (armshells).
>
> *November*, 1915—*March*, 1916. Preparations for a big overseas expedition from Kiriwina to the Marshall Bennett Islands. Construction of a canoe ; renovating of another ; sail making in Omarakana ; launching ; *tasasoria* on the beach of Kaulukuba. At the same time, information is being obtained about these and the associated subjects. Some magical texts of canoe building and Kula magic obtained.

THIRD EXPEDITION, October, 1917—October, 1918.

> *November*, 1917—*December*, 1917. Inland Kula ; some data obtained in Tukwaukwa.
>
> *December*—*February*, 1918. Parties from Kitava arrive in Wawela. Collection of information about the *yoyova*. Magic and spells of Kaygau obtained.
>
> *March*, 1918. Preparations in Sanaroa ; preparations in the Amphletts ; the Dobuan fleet arrives in the Amphletts. The *uvalaku* expedition from Dobu followed to Boyowa.
>
> *April*, 1918. Their arrival ; their reception in Sinaketa ; the Kula transactions ; the big intertribal gathering. Some magical formulæ obtained.
>
> *May*, 1918. Party from Kitava seen in Vakuta.
>
> *June*, *July*, 1918. Information about Kula magic and customs checked and amplified in Omarakana, especially with regard to its Eastern branches.
>
> *August*, *September*, 1918. Magical texts obtained in Sinaketa.
>
> *October*, 1918. Information obtained from a number of natives in Dobu and Southern Massim district (examined in Samarai).

PLATE I

THE ETHNOGRAPHER'S TENT ON THE BEACH OF NU'AGASI

This illustrates the manner of life among the natives, described on p. 6. Note (with reference to Chs. IV and V) the dug-out log of a large canoe beside the tent, and the *masawa* canoe, beached under palm leaves to the left

PLATE II

THE CHIEF'S LISIGA (PERSONAL HUT) IN OMARAKANA

To'uluwa, the present chief, is standing in front (cf. Ch. II, Div. V) ; to the left, among the palms, is the Ethnographer's tent (see p. 6), with a group of natives squatting in front of it

PLATE III

STREET OF KASANA'I (INKIRIWINA, TROBRIAND ISLANDS)

An everyday scene, showing groups of people at their ordinary occupations. (See p. 7.)

PLATE IV

SCENE IN YOURAWOTU (TROBRIANDS)

A complex, but well-defined, act of a *sagali* (ceremonial distribution) is going on. There is a definite system of sociological, economic and ceremonial principles at the bottom of the apparently confused proceedings. (See p. 8.)

To summarise the first, cardinal point of method, I may say each phenomenon ought to be studied through the broadest range possible of its concrete manifestations ; each studied by an exhaustive survey of detailed examples. If possible, the results ought to be tabulated into some sort of synoptic chart, both to be used as an instrument of study, and to be presented as an ethnological document. With the help of such documents and such study of actualities the clear outline of the framework of the natives' culture in the widest sense of the word, and the constitution of their society, can be presented. This method could be called *the method of statistic documentation by concrete evidence.*

VII

Needless to add, in this respect, the scientific field-work is far above even the best amateur productions. There is, however, one point in which the latter often excel. This is, in the presentation of intimate touches of native life, in bringing home to us these aspects of it with which one is made familiar only through being in close contact with the natives, one way or the other, for a long period of time. In certain results of scientific work—especially that which has been called " survey work "—we are given an excellent skeleton, so to speak, of the tribal constitution, but it lacks flesh and blood. We learn much about the framework of their society, but within it, we cannot perceive or imagine the realities of human life, the even flow of everyday events, the occasional ripples of excitement over a feast, or ceremony, or some singular occurrence. In working out the rules and regularities of native custom, and in obtaining a precise formula for them from the collection of data and native statements, we find that this very precision is foreign to real life, which never adheres rigidly to any rules. It must be supplemented by the observation of the manner in which a given custom is carried out, of the behaviour of the natives in obeying the rules so exactly formulated by the ethnographer, of the very exceptions which in sociological phenomena almost always occur.

If all the conclusions are solely based on the statements of informants, or deduced from objective documents, it is of course impossible to supplement them in actually observed data of real behaviour. And that is the reason why certain works of amateur residents of long standing, such as educated traders and planters, medical men and officials, and last, but not least, the few intelligent and unbiassed missionaries to whom Ethnography owes so much, surpass in plasticity and in vividness most of the purely scientific accounts. But if the specialised field-worker can adopt the conditions of living described above, he is in a far better position to be really in touch with the natives than any other white resident. For none of them lives right in a native village, except for very short periods, and everyone has his own business, which takes up a considerable part of his time. Moreover, if, like a trader or a missionary or an official he enters into active relations with the native, if he has to transform or influence or make use of him, this makes a real, unbiassed, impartial observation impossible, and precludes all-round sincerity, at least in the case of the missionaries and officials.

Living in the village with no other business but to follow native life, one sees the customs, ceremonies and transactions over and over again, one has examples of their beliefs as they are actually lived through, and the full body and blood of actual native life fills out soon the skeleton of abstract constructions. That is the reason why, working under such conditions as previously described, the Ethnographer is enabled to add something essential to the bare outline of tribal constitution, and to supplement it by all the details of behaviour, setting and small incident. He is able in each case to state whether an act is public or private ; how a public assembly behaves, and what it looks like ; he can judge whether an event is ordinary or an exciting and singular one ; whether natives bring to it a great deal of sincere and earnest spirit, or perform it in fun ; whether they do it in a perfunctory manner, or with zeal and deliberation.

In other words, there is a series of phenomena of great importance which cannot possibly be recorded by questioning or computing documents, but have to be observed in their full actuality. Let us call them *the inponderabilia of actual life*. Here belong such things as the routine of a man's working day, the details of his care of the body, of the manner of taking food and preparing it ; the tone of conversational and social life around the village fires, the existence of strong friendships or hostilities, and of passing sympathies and dislikes between people ; the subtle yet unmistakable manner in which personal vanities and ambitions are reflected in the behaviour of the individual and in the emotional reactions of those who surround him. All these facts can and ought to be scientifically formulated and recorded, but it is necessary that this be done, not by a superficial registration of details, as is usually done by untrained observers, but with an effort at penetrating the mental attitude expressed in them. And that is the reason why the work of scientifically trained observers, once seriously applied to the study of this aspect, will, I believe, yield results of surpassing value. So far, it has been done only by amateurs, and therefore done, on the whole, indifferently.

Indeed, if we remember that these imponderable yet all important facts of actual life are part of the real substance of the social fabric, that in them are spun the innumerable threads which keep together the family, the clan, the village community, the tribe—their significance becomes clear. The more crystallised bonds of social grouping, such as the definite ritual, the economic and legal duties, the obligations, the ceremonial gifts and formal marks of regard, though equally important for the student, are certainly felt less strongly by the individual who has to fulfil them. Applying this to ourselves, we all know that " family life " means for us, first and foremost, the atmosphere of home, all the innumerable small acts and attentions in which are expressed the affection, the mutual interest, the little preferences, and the little antipathies which constitute intimacy. That we may inherit from this person, that we shall have to walk after the hearse of the other, though sociologically these facts belong to the definition of " family " and " family life," in personal perspective of what family truly is to us, they normally stand very much in the background.

Exactly the same applies to a native community, and if the Ethnographer wants to bring their real life home to his readers, he must on no account neglect this. Neither aspect, the intimate, as little as the legal, ought to be glossed over. Yet as a rule in ethnographic accounts we have not both but either the one or the other—and, so far, the intimate one has hardly ever been properly treated. In all social relations besides the family ties, even those between mere tribesmen and, beyond that, between hostile or friendly members of different tribes, meeting on any sort of social business, there is this intimate side, expressed by the typical details of intercourse, the tone of their behaviour in the presence of one another. This side is different from the definite, crystalised legal frame of the relationship, and it has to be studied and stated in its own right.

In the same way, in studying the conspicuous acts of tribal life, such as ceremonies, rites, festivities, etc., the details and tone of behaviour ought to be given, besides the bare out-line of events. The importance of this may be exemplified by one instance. Much has been said and written about survival. Yet the survival character of an act is expressed in nothing so well as in the concomitant behaviour, in the way in which it is carried out. Take any example from our own culture, whether it be the pomp and pageantry of a state ceremony, or a picturesque custom kept up by street urchins, its " outline " will not tell you whether the rite flourishes still with full vigour in the hearts of those who perform it or assist at the performance or whether they regard it as almost a dead thing, kept alive for tradition's sake. But observe and fix the data of their behaviour, and at once the degree of vitality of the act will become clear. There is no doubt, from all points of socio-logical, or psychological analysis, and in any question of theory, the manner and type of behaviour observed in the performance of an act is of the highest importance. Indeed behaviour is a fact, a relevant fact, and one that can be recorded. And foolish indeed and short-sighted would be the man of science who would pass by a whole class of phenomena, ready to be garnered, and leave them to waste, even though he did not see at the moment to what theoretical use they might be put !

As to the actual method of observing and recording in field-work these *imponderabilia of actual life and of typical behaviour*, there is no doubt that the personal equation of the observer comes in here more prominently, than in the collection of crystalised, ethnographic data. But here also the main endeavour must be to let facts speak for themselves. If in making a daily round of the village, certain small incidents, characteristic forms of taking food, of conversing, of doing work (see for instance Plate III) are found occuring over and over again, they should be noted down at once. It is also important that this work of collecting and fixing impressions should begin early in the course of working out a district.

Because certain subtle peculiarities, which make an impression as long as they are novel, cease to be noticed as soon as they become familiar. Others again can only be perceived with a better knowledge of the local conditions. An ethnographic diary, carried on systematically throughout the course of one's work in a district would be the ideal instrument for this sort of study. And if, side by side with the normal and typical, the ethnographer carefully notes the slight, or the more pronounced deviations from it, he will be able to indicate the two extremes within which the normal moves.

In observing ceremonies or other tribal events, such, for instance as the scene depicted in Plate IV, it is necessary, not only to note down those occurrences and details which are prescribed by tradition and custom to be the essential course of the act, but also the Ethnographer ought to record carefully and precisely, one after the other, the actions of the actors and of the spectators. Forgetting for a moment that he knows and understands the structure of this ceremony, the main dogmatic ideas underlying it, he might try to find himself only in the midst of an assembly of human-beings, who behave seriously or jocularly, with earnest concentration or with bored frivolity, who are either in the same mood as he finds them every day, or else are screwed up to a high pitch of excitement, and so on and so on. With his attention constantly directed to this aspect of tribal life, with the constant endeavour to fix it, to express it in terms of actual fact, a good deal of reliable and expressive material finds its way into his notes. He will be able to " set " the act into its proper place in tribal life, that is to show whether it is exceptional or commonplace, one in which the natives behave ordinarily, or one in which their whole behaviour is transformed. And he will also be able to bring all this home to his readers in a clear, convincing manner.

Again, in this type of work, it is good for the Ethnographer sometimes to put aside camera, note book and pencil, and to join in himself in what is going on. He can take part in the natives' games, he can follow them on their visits and walks, sit down and listen and share in their conversations. I am not certain if this is equally easy for everyone—perhaps the Slavonic nature is more plastic and more naturally savage than that of Western Europeans—but though the degree of success varies, the attempt is possible for everyone. Out of such

plunges into the life of the natives—and I made them frequently
not only for study's sake but because everyone needs human
company—I have carried away a distinct feeling that their
behaviour, their manner of being, in all sorts of tribal transactions, became more transparent and easily understandable
than it had been before. All these methodological remarks,
the reader will find again illustrated in the following
chapters.

VIII

Finally, let us pass to the third and last aim of scientific
field-work, to the last type of phenomenon which ought to be
recorded in order to give a full and adequate picture of native
culture. Besides the firm outline of tribal constitution and
crystallised cultural items which form the skeleton, besides the
data of daily life and ordinary behaviour, which are, so to
speak, its flesh and blood, there is still to be recorded the
spirit—the natives' views and opinions and utterances. For,
in every act of tribal life, there is, first, the routine prescribed
by custom and tradition, then there is the manner in which it
is carried out, and lastly there is the commentary to it, contained in the natives' mind. A man who submits to various
customary obligations, who follows a traditional course of
action, does it impelled by certain motives, to the accompaniment of certain feelings, guided by certain ideas. These ideas,
feelings, and impulses are moulded and conditioned by the
culture in which we find them, and are therefore an ethnic
peculiarity of the given society. An attempt must be made
therefore, to study and record them.

But is this possible ? Are these subjective states not too
elusive and shapeless ? And, even granted that people
usually do feel or think or experience certain psychological
states in association with the performance of customary acts,
the majority of them surely are not able to formulate these
states, to put them into words. This latter point must certainly
be granted, and it is perhaps the real Gordian knot in the study
of the facts of social psychology. Without trying to cut or
untie this knot, that is to solve the problem theoretically, or to
enter further into the field of general methodology, I shall
make directly for the question of practical means to overcome
some of the difficulties involved.

First of all, it has to be laid down that we have to study here stereotyped manners of thinking and feeling. As sociologists, we are not interested in what A or B may feel *qua* individuals, in the accidental course of their own personal experiences—we are interested only in what they feel and think *qua* members of a given community. Now in this capacity, their mental states receive a certain stamp, become stereotyped by the institutions in which they live, by the influence of tradition and folk-lore, by the very vehicle of thought, that is by language. The social and cultural environment in which they move forces them to think and feel in a definite manner. Thus, a man who lives in a polyandrous community cannot experience the same feelings of jealousy, as a strict monogynist, though he might have the elements of them. A man who lives within the sphere of the Kula cannot become permanently and senti-mentally attached to certain of his possessions, in spite of the fact that he values them most of all. These examples are crude, but better ones will be found in the text of this book.

So, the third commandment of field-work runs : Find out the typical ways of thinking and feeling, corresponding to the institutions and culture of a given community, and formulate the results in the most convincing manner. What will be the method of procedure ? The best ethnographical writers—here again the Cambridge school with Haddon, Rivers, and Seligman rank first among English Ethnographers—have always tried to quote *verbatim* statements of crucial importance. They also adduce terms of native classification ; sociological, psychological and industrial *termini technici*, and have rendered the verbal contour of native thought as precisely as possible. One step further in this line can be made by the Ethnographer, who acquires a knowledge of the native language and can use it as an instrument of inquiry. In working in the Kiriwinian language, I found still some difficulty in writing down the statement directly in translation which at first I used to do in the act of taking notes. The translation often robbed the text of all its significant characteristics—rubbed off all its points—so that gradually I was led to note down certain important phrases just as they were spoken, in the native tongue. As my knowledge of the language progressed, I put down more and more in Kiriwinian, till at last I found myself writing exclusively in that language, rapidly taking notes, word for word, of each statement. No sooner had I arrived at this point, than I recognised that I was thus acquiring at the same time an abundant linguistic material, and a series of ethnographic documents which ought to be reproduced as I had fixed them, besides being utilised in the writing up of my account.* This *corpus inscriptionum Kiriwiniensium* can be utilised, not only by myself, but by all those who, through their better penetration and ability of interpreting them, may find points which escape my attention, very much as the other *corpora* form the basis for the various interpretations of ancient and prehistoric cultures ; only, these ethnographic inscriptions are all decipherable and clear, have been almost all translated fully and unambiguously, and have been provided with native cross-commentaries or *scholia* obtained from living sources.

No more need be said on this subject here, as later on a whole chapter (Chapter XVIII) is devoted to it, and to its exemplification by several native texts. The *Corpus* will of course be published separately at a later date.

IX

Our considerations thus indicate that the goal of ethnographic field-work must be approached through three avenues :

1. *The organisation of the tribe, and the anatomy of its culture* must be recorded in firm, clear outline. The method of *concrete, statistical documentation* is the means through which such an outline has to be given.

2. Within this frame, the *imponderabilia of actual life*, and the *type of behaviour* have to be filled in. They have to be collected through minute, detailed observations, in the form of some sort of ethnographic diary, made possible by close contact with native life.

3. A collection of ethnographic statements, characteristic narratives, typical utterances, items of folk-lore and magical formulæ has to be given as a *corpus inscriptionum*, as documents of native mentality.

* It was soon after I had adopted this course that I received a letter from Dr. A. H. Gardiner, the well-known Egyptologist, urging me to do this very thing. From his point of view as archæologist, he naturally saw the enormous possibilities for an Ethnographer of obtaining a similar body of written sources as have been preserved to us from ancient cultures, plus the possibility of illuminating them by personal knowledge of the full life of that culture.

These three lines of approach lead to the final goal, of which an Ethnographer should never lose sight. This goal is, briefly, to grasp the native's point of view, his relation to life, to realise *his* vision of *his* world. We have to study man, and we must study what concerns him most intimately, that is, the hold which life has on him. In each culture, the values are slightly different ; people aspire after different aims, follow different impulses, yearn after a different form of happiness. In each culture, we find different institutions in which man pursues his life-interest, different customs by which he satisfies his aspirations, different codes of law and morality which reward his virtues or punish his defections. To study the institutions, customs, and codes or to study the behaviour and mentality without the subjective desire of feeling by what these people live, of realising the substance of their happiness—is, in my opinion, to miss the greatest reward which we can hope to obtain from the study of man.

These generalities the reader will find illustrated in the following chapters. We shall see there the savage striving to satisfy certain aspirations, to attain his type of value, to follow his line of social ambition. We shall see him led on to perilous and difficult enterprises by a tradition of magical and heroical exploits, shall see him following the lure of his own romance. Perhaps as we read the account of these remote customs there may emerge a feeling of solidarity with the endeavours and ambitions of these natives. Perhaps man's mentality will be revealed to us, and brought near, along some lines which we never have followed before. Perhaps through realising human nature in a shape very distant and foreign to us, we shall have some light shed on our own. In this, and in this case only, we shall be justified in feeling that it has been worth our while to understand these natives, their institutions and customs, and that we have gathered some profit from the Kula.

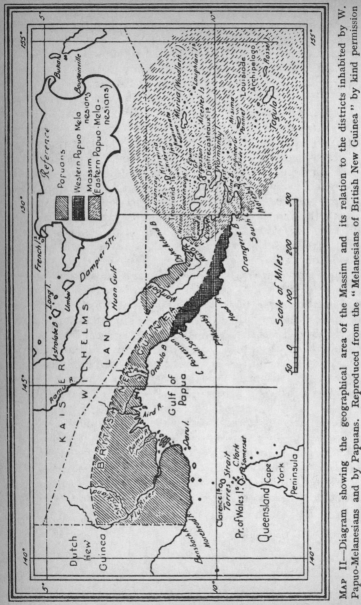

MAP II—Diagram showing the geographical area of the Massim and its relation to the districts inhabited by W. Papuo-Melanesians and by Papuans. Reproduced from the "Melanesians of British New Guinea" by kind permission of Professor C. G. Seligman.

Chapter I

THE COUNTRY AND INHABITANTS OF THE KULA DISTRICT

I

THE tribes who live within the sphere of the Kula system of trading belong, one and all—with the exception perhaps, of the Rossel Island natives, of whom we know next to nothing—to the same racial group. These tribes inhabit the easternmost end of the mainland of New Guinea and those islands, scattered in the form of the long-drawn archipelago, which continue in the same south-easterly trend as the mainland, as if to bridge over the gap between New Guinea and the Solomons.

New Guinea is a mountainous island-continent, very difficult of access in its interior, and also at certain portions of the coast, where barrier reefs, swamps and rocks practically prevent landing or even approach for native craft. Such a country would obviously not offer the same opportunities in all its parts to the drifting migrations which in all probability are responsible for the composition of the present population of the South Seas. The easily accessible portions of the coast and the outlying islands would certainly offer a hospitable reception to immigrants of a higher stock ; but, on the other hand, the high hills, the impregnable fastnesses in swampy flats and shores where landing was difficult and dangerous, would give easy protection to the aborigines, and discourage the influx of migrators.

The actual distribution of races in New Guinea completely justifies these hypotheses. Map II shows the Eastern part of the main island and archipelagoes of New Guinea and the racial distribution of the natives. The interior of the continent, the low sago swamps and deltas of the Gulf of Papua—probably the greater part of the North Coast and of the South-West Coast of New Guinea, are inhabited by a "relatively tall, dark-skinned, frizzly-haired " race, called by Dr. Seligman *Papuan*, and in the hills more especially by pygmy tribes. We know little about these people, swamp tribes and hill tribes alike, who probably are the autochtons in this part of the world.* As we shall also not meet them in the following account, it will be better to pass to the tribes who inhabit the accessible parts of New Guinea. " The Eastern Papuasians, that is, the generally smaller, lighter coloured, frizzly-haired races of the eastern peninsula of New Guinea and its archipelagoes now require a name, and since the true Melanesian element is dominant in them, they may be called Papuo-Melanesians. With regard to these Eastern Papuasians, Dr. A. C. Haddon first recognised that they came into the country as the result of a ' Melanesian migration into New Guinea,' and further, ' That a single wandering would not account for certain puzzling facts.' "† The Papuo-Melanesians again can be divided into two groups, a Western and an Eastern one, which, following Dr. Seligman's terminology, we shall call the Western Papuo-Melanesians and the Massim respectively. It is with these latter we shall become acquainted in the following pages.

If we glance at a map and follow the orographical features of Eastern New Guinea and its coast line, we see at once that the high main range of mountains drops off between the 149th and 150th meridians, and again that the fringing reef disappears at the same point, that is, at the west end of Orangerie Bay. This means that the extreme East End of New Guinea, with its archipelagoes, in other words, the Massim country, is the most easily accessible area, and might be expected to be inhabited by a homogeneous stock of people, consisting of

---

* The best accounts we possess of the inland tribes are those of W. H. Williamson, " The Mafulu," 1912, and of C. Keysser, " Aus dem Leben der Kaileute," in R. Neuhauss, " Deutsch Neu Guinea," Vol. III. Berlin, 1911. The preliminary publications of G. Landtmann on the Kiwai, " Papuan magic in the Building of Houses," " Acta Arboenses, Humanora." I. Abo, 1920, and " The Folk-Tales of the Kiwai Papuans," Helsingfors, 1917, promise that the full account will dispel some of the mysteries surrounding the Gulf of Papua. Meanwhile a good semi-popular account of these natives is to be found in W. N. Beaver's " Unexplored New Guinea," 1920. Personally I doubt very much whether the hill tribes and the swamp tribes belong to the same stock or have the same culture. Compare also the most recent contribution to this problem : " Migrations of Cultures in British New Guinea," by A. C. Haddon, Huxley Memorial Lecture for 1921, published by the R. Anthrop Institute.

† See C. G. Seligman, " The Melanesians of British New Guinea," Cambridge, 1910.

immigrants almost unmixed with the autochtons (Cf. Map II). " Indeed, while the condition actually existing in the Massim area suggests that there was no slow mingling of the invaders with a previous stock, the geographical features of the territory of the Western Papuo-Melanesians with its hills, mountains and swamps, are such that invaders could not have speedily overrun the country, nor failed to have been influenced by the original inhabitants. . . ."*

I shall assume that the reader is acquainted with the quoted work of Dr. Seligman, where a thorough account is given of all the main types of Papuo-Melahesian sociology and culture one after the other. But the tribes of the Eastern Papuo-Melanesian or Massim area, must be described here somewhat more in detail, as it is within this fairly homogeneous area that the Kula takes place. Indeed, the Kula sphere of influence and the ethnographic area of the Massim tribes almost completely overlap, and we can speak about the Kula type of culture and the Massim culture almost synonymously.

II

The adjacent Map III shows the Kula district, that is, the easternmost end of the main island and the archipelagoes lying to its East and North-East. As Professor C. G. Seligman says : " This area can be divided into two parts, a small northern portion comprising the Trobriands, the Marshall Bennets, the Woodlarks (Murua), as well as a number of smaller islands such as the Laughlans (Nada), and a far larger southern portion comprising the remainder of the Massim domain " (op. cit., p. 7).

This division is represented on Map III by the thick line isolating to the North the Amphletts, the Trobriands, the small Marshall Bennet Group, Woodlark Island and the Laughlan Group. The Southern portion, I found convenient to divide further into two divisions by a vertical line, leaving to the East Misima, Sud-Est Island and Rossel Island. As our information about this district is extremely scanty, I have preferred to exclude it from the area of the Southern Massim. In this excluded area, only the natives of Misima enter into the Kula, but their participation will play a very small part only in the following account. The western segment, and this is

* Cf. C. G. Seligman, op. cit., p. 5.

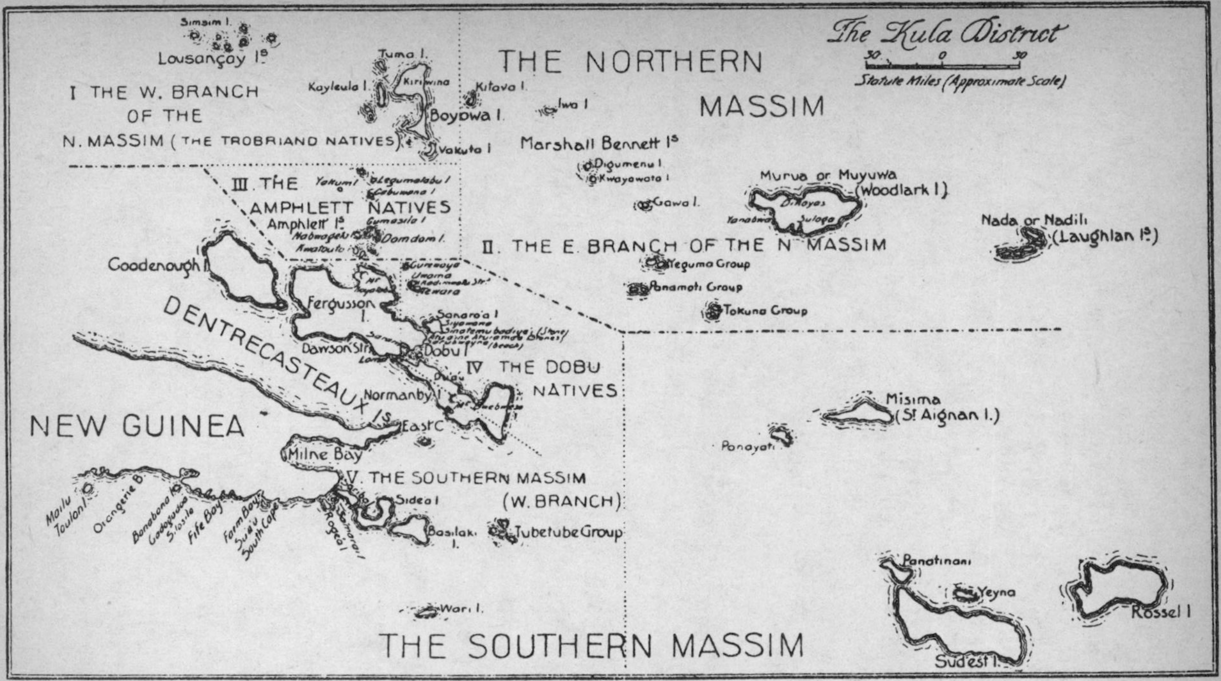

Map III—The Kula district. Sketch map, showing the sub-divisions of the Massim and the principal places of importance in the Kula.

the part of which we shall speak as the district of the Southern
Massim, comprises first the East End of the mainland, the few
adjacent islands, Sariba, Roge'a, Side'a, and Basilaki; to the
South, the island of Wari, to the East the important, though
small archipelago of Tubetube (Engineer Group) ; and to the
North, the big archipelago of the d'Entrecasteaux Islands.
From this latter, only one district, that of Dobu, interests us
more specially. The culturally homogeneous tribes of the
Southern Massim have been marked off on our map as district
V, the Doubans as district IV.

Returning to the two main divisions into the Southern
and Northern portion, this latter is occupied by a very homogeneous population, homogeneous both in language and
culture, and in the clear recognition of their own ethnic unity.
To quote further Professor Seligman, it " is characterised by
the absence of cannibalism, which, until put down by the
Government, existed throughout the remaining portion of the
district ; another peculiarity of the Northern Massim is their
recognition " in certain districts, though not in all, of chieftans
who wield extensive powers (op. cit. p. 7). The natives of that
northern area used to practise—I say used because wars are
a thing of the past—a type of warfare open and chivalrous,
very different from the raids of the Southern Massim. Their
villages are built in big compact blocks, and they have storehouses on piles for storing food, distinct from their rather
miserable dwellings, which stand directly on the ground and
are not raised on piles. As can be seen on the map, it has been
necessary to sub-divide this Northern Massim further into
three groups, first, that of the Trobriand Islanders, or the
Boyowans (the Western Branch) ; secondly that of the natives
of Woodlark Island and the Marshall Bennets (the Eastern
Branch); and, thirdly, the small group of the Amphlett natives.

The other big sub-division of the Kula tribes is composed
of the Southern Massim, of which, as just said, the western
branch mainly concerns us. These last natives are smaller
in stature, and with, broadly speaking, a much less attractive
appearance than those of the North.* They live in widely

---

* A number of good portraits of the S. Massim type are to be found in
the valuable book of the Rev. H. Newton, " In Far New Guinea," 1914 and in
the amusingly written though superficial and often unreliable booklet of the
Rev. C. W. Abel (London Missionary Society), " Savage Life in New Guinea "
(No date).

scattered communities, each house or group of houses standing in its own little grove of palm and fruit trees, apart from the others. Formerly they were cannibals and head-hunters, and used to make unexpected raids on their adversaries. There is no chieftainship, authority being exercised by the elders in each community. They build very elaborately constructed and beautifully decorated houses on piles.

I have found it necessary for the purpose of this study to cut out of the western branch of the southern portion of the Massim the two areas (marked IV and V on the Map III), as they are of special importance to the Kula. It must, however, be borne in mind that our present knowledge does not allow of any final classification of the Southern Massim.

Such are the general characteristics of the Northern and Southern Massim respectively, given in a few words. But before proceeding with our subject, it will be good to give a short but more detailed sketch of each of these tribes. I shall begin with the southernmost section, following the order in which a visitor, travelling from Port Moresby with the Mail boat, would come in contact with these districts, the way indeed in which I received my first impressions of them. My personal knowledge of the various tribes is, however, very uneven, based on a long residence among the Trobriand Islanders (District I), on a month's study of the Amphletts (District III) ; on a few weeks spent in Woodlark Island or Murua (District II), the neighbourhood of Samarai (District V), and the South Coast of New Guinea (also V) ; and on three short visits to Dobu (District IV). My knowledge of some of the remaining localities which enter into the Kula is derived only from a few conversations I had with natives of this district, and on second-hand information derived from white residents. The work of Professor C. G. Seligman, however, supplements my personal acquaintance in so far as the districts of Tubetube, Woodlark Island, the Marshall Bennets, and several others are concerned.

The whole account of the Kula will therefore naturally be given from the perspective, so to speak, of the Trobriand district. This district is often called in this book by its native name, Boyowa, and the language is spoken of as Kiriwinian, Kiriwina being the main province of the district, and its language considered by the natives as a standard speech. But

PLATE V

SCENES ON THE BEACH OF SILOSILO (SOUTHERN MASSIM
DISTRICT)

These represent phases of a big annual feast, the *so'i*. (See p. 37 and
compare also Ch. XXI.) Note the prominent part taken by women in the
proceedings ; the use of the " ceremonial " axe handles ; the manner
of carrying pigs, and the canoes beached on the shore

Plate VI

VILLAGE SCENES DURING A SO'I FEAST

These show types of Southern Massim and their decorations ; again note the prominent part taken by women in the ceremonial actions. (See p. 37.)

I may add at once that in studying the Kula in that part, I *ipso facto* studied its adjacent branches between the Trobriands and the Amphletts, between the Trobriands and Kitava, and between the Trobriands and Dobu ; seeing not only the preparations and departures in Boyowa, but also the arrival of the natives from other districts, in fact, following one or two of such expeditions in person.* Moreover, the Kula being an international affair, the natives of one tribe know more about Kula customs abroad than they would about any other subject. And in all its essentials, the customs and tribal rules of the exchange are identical throughout the whole Kula area.

III

Let us imagine that we are sailing along the South coast of New Guinea towards its Eastern end. At about the middle of Orangerie Bay we arrive at the boundary of the Massim, which runs from this point north-westwards till it strikes the northern coast near Cape Nelson (see Map II). As mentioned before, the boundary of the district inhabited by this tribe corresponds to definite geographical conditions, that is, to the absence of natural, inland fastnesses, or of any obstacles to landing. Indeed, it is here that the Great Barrier Reef becomes finally submerged, while again the Main Range of mountains, which follows up to this point, always separated from the foreshore by minor ranges, comes to an end.

Orangerie Bay is closed, on its Eastern side, by a headland, the first of a series of hills, rising directly out of the sea. As we approach the land, we can see distinctly the steep, folded slopes, covered with dense, rank jungle, brightened here and there by bold patches of lalang grass. The coast is broken first by a series of small, land-locked bays or lagoons ; then, after Fife Bay, come one or two larger bays, with a flat, alluvial foreshore, and then from South Cape the coast stretches in an almost unbroken line, for several miles, to the end of the mainland.

The East End of New Guinea is a tropical region, where the distinction between the dry and wet season is not felt very sharply. In fact, there is no pronounced dry season there, and so the land is always clad in intense, shining green, which forms a crude contrast with the blue sea. The summits of the

* See Table in the Introduction (p. 16), and also Chapters XVI and XX.

hills are often shrouded in trailing mist, whilst white clouds brood or race over the sea, breaking up the monotony of saturated, stiff blue and green. To someone not acquainted with the South Sea landscape it is difficult to convey the permanent impression of smiling festiveness, the alluring clearness of the beach, fringed by jungle trees and palms, skirted by white foam and blue sea, above it the slopes ascending in rich, stiff folds of dark and light green, piebald and shaded over towards the summit by steamy, tropical mists.

When I first sailed along this coast, it was after a few months' residence and field work in the neighbouring district of the Mailu. From Toulon Island, the main centre and most important settlement of the Mailu, I used to look towards the East end of Orangerie Bay, and on clear days I could see the pyramidal hills of Bonabona, of Gadogado'a, as blue silhouettes in the distance. Under the influence of my work, I came to regard this country within the somewhat narrow native horizon, as the distant land to which perilous, seasonal voyages are made, from whence come certain objects—baskets, decorated carvings, weapons, ornaments—particularly well formed, and superior to the local ones ; the land to which the natives point with awe and distrust, when speaking of specially evil and virulent forms of sorcery ; the home of a folk mentioned with horror as cannibals. Any really fine touch of artistic taste, in Mailu carvings, would always be directly imported or imitated from the East, and I also found that the softest and most melodious songs and the finest dances came from the Massim. Many of their customs and institutions would be quoted to me as quaint and unusual, and thus, I, the ethno-grapher working on the borderland of two cultures, naturally had my interest and curiosity aroused. It seemed as if the Eastern people must be much more complex, in one direction towards the cruel, man-eating savage, in the other towards the finely-gifted, poetical lord of primitive forest and seas, when I compared them with the relatively coarse and dull native of Mailu. No wonder, therefore, that on approaching their coast—travelling on that occasion in a small launch—I scanned the landscape with keen interest, anxious to catch my first glimpse of natives, or of their traces.

The first distinctly visible signs of human existence in this neighbourhood are the patches of garden land. These big clearings, triangular in shape, with the apex pointing uphill, look as if they were plastered on to the steep slopes. From August to November, the season when the natives cut and burn the bush, they can be seen, at night, alight with slowly-blazing logs, and in daytime, their smoke clings over the clearings, and slowly drifts along the hill side. Later on in the year, when the plantation sprouts, they form a bright spot, with the light green of their fresh leaves.

The villages in this district are to be found only on the foreshore, at the foot of the hills, hidden in groves of trees, with here and there a golden or purplish bit of thatch showing through the dark green of the leaves. In calm weather a few canoes are probably not far off, fishing. If the visitor is lucky enough to pass at the time of feasts, trading expeditions, or any other big tribal gathering, many a fine sea-going canoe may be seen approaching the village, the sound of conch shells blowing melodiously.

In order to visit one of the typical, large settlements of these natives, let us say near Fife Bay, on the South coast, or on the island of Sariba, or Roge'a, it would be best to go ashore in some big, sheltered bay, or on one of the extensive beaches at the foot of a hilly island. We enter a clear, lofty grove, composed of palms, bread fruit, mangoes, and other fruit trees, often with a sandy subsoil, well weeded-out and clean, where grow clumps of ornamental bushes, such as the red-flowering hybiscus, croton or aromatic shrub. Here we find the village. Fascinating as may be the Motuan habitations standing on high piles in the middle of a lagoon, or the neat streets of an Aroma or Mailu settlement, or the irregular warren of small huts on the Trobriand coast, all these cannot compete in picturesqueness or charm with the villages of the Southern Massim. When, on a hot day, we enter the deep shadow of fruit trees and palms, and find ourselves in the midst of the wonderfully designed and ornamented houses hiding here and there in irregular groups among the green, surrounded by little decorative gardens of shells and flowers, with pebble-bordered paths and stone-paved sitting circles, it seems as if the visions of a primeval, happy, savage life were suddenly realised, even if only in a fleeting impression. Big bodies of canoes are drawn high up the beach and covered with palm leaves ; here and there nets are drying, spread out on special stands, and on the platforms in front of the houses sit groups of men and women, busy at some domestic work, smoking and chatting.

Walking along the paths which lead on for miles, we come every few hundred yards on another hamlet of a few houses. Some of these are evidently new and freshly decorated, while others are abandoned, and a heap of broken household objects is lying on the ground, showing that the death of one of the village elders has caused it to be deserted. As the evening approaches, the life becomes more active, fires are kindled, and the natives busy themselves cooking and eating food. In the dancing season, towards dusk, groups of men and women foregather, singing, dancing, and beating drums.

When we approach the natives closer and scan their personal appearance, we are struck—if we compare them with their Western neighbours—by the extreme lightness of their skin, their sturdy, even lumpy stature, and a sort of soft, almost effete general impression which their physique produces. Their fat, broad faces, their squashed noses, and frequently oblique eyes, make them appear quaint and grotesque rather than impressively savage. Their hair, not so woolly as that of the pure Papuans, nor growing into the enormous halo of the Motuans, is worn in big mops, which they often cut at the sides so as to give the head an oblong, almost cylindrical shape. Their manner is shy and diffident, but not unfriendly—rather smiling and almost servile, in very great contrast to the morose Papuan, or the unfriendly, reserved South Coast Mailu or Aroma. On the whole, they give at first approach not so much the impression of wild savages as of smug and self-satisfied bourgeois.

Their ornaments are much less elaborate and more toned down than those of their Western neighbours. Belts and armlets plaited of a dark brown fern vine, small red shell disks and turtle shell rings as ear ornaments are the only permanent, every-day decorations worn. Like all Melanesians of Eastern New Guinea, they are quite cleanly in their persons, and a personal approach to them does not offend any of our senses. They are very fond of red hibiscus flowers stuck in their hair, of scented flower wreaths on their head, of aromatic leaves thrust into their belts and armlets. Their grand, festive head-dress is extremely modest compared with the enormous erections of feathers used by the Western tribes, and consists mainly of a round halo of white cockatoo feathers stuck into their hair (see Plate V and VI).

In olden days, before the advent of white men, these pleasant, apparently effete people were inveterate cannibals and head-hunters, and in their large war-canoes they carried on treacherous, cruel raids, falling upon sleeping villages, killing man, woman and child, and feasting on their bodies. The attractive stone circles in their villages were associated with their cannibal feasts.*

The traveller, who could settle down in one of their villages and remain there sufficiently long to study their habits and enter into their tribal life, would soon be struck by the absence of a well recognised general authority. In this, however, the natives resemble not only the other Western Melanesians of New Guinea, but also the natives of the Melanesian Archipelago. The authority in the Southern Massim tribe, as in many others, is vested in the village elders. In each hamlet the eldest man has a position of personal influence and power, and these collectively would in all cases represent the tribe and carry out and enforce their decisions—always arrived at in strict accord with tribal tradition.

Deeper sociological study would reveal the characteristic totemism of these natives, and also the matrilineal construction of their society. Descent, inheritance, and social position follow the female line—a man always belongs to his mother's totemic division and local group, and inherits from his mother's brother. Women also enjoy a very independent position, and are exceedingly well treated, and in tribal and festive affairs they play a prominent part (see Plates V and VI). Some women, even, owing to their magical powers, wield a considerable influence.†

The sexual life of these natives is extremely lax. Even when we remember the very free standard of sex morals in the Melanesian tribes of New Guinea, such as the Motu or the Mailu, we still find these natives exceedingly loose in such matters. Certain reserves and appearances which are usually kept up in other tribes, are here completely abandoned. As is probably the case in many communities where sex morals are

* Cf. Professor C. G. Seligman, op. cit., Chapters XL and XLII.
† Professor C. G. Seligman, op. cit., Chapters XXXV, XXXVI, XXXVII.

lax, there is a complete absence of unnatural practices and sex perversions. Marriage is concluded as the natural end of a long and lasting liaison.*

These natives are efficient and industrious manufacturers, and great traders. They own large sea-going canoes, which, however, they do not manufacture themselves, but which they import from the Northern Massim district, or from Panayati. Another feature of their culture, which we shall meet again, consists of their big feasts, called *So'i* (see Plates V and VI), associated with mortuary celebrations and with a special mortuary taboo called *gwara*. In the big inter-tribal trading of the Kula, these feasts play a considerable rôle.

This general, and necessarily somewhat superficial description, is meant to give the reader a definite impression of these tribes, provide them, so to speak, with a physiognomy, rather than to give a full account of their tribal constitution. For this the reader is referred to Professor C. G. Seligman's treatise, our main source of knowledge on the Melanesians of New Guinea. The above sketch refers to what Professor Seligman calls the Southern Massim, or more exactly to the portion marked off in the Ethnographic sketch Map No. III as " V, the Southern Massim "—the inhabitants of the Easternmost mainland and the adjacent archipelago.

IV

Let us now move North, towards the district marked " IV, the Dobu," in our map, which forms one of the most important links in the chain of Kula and a very influential centre of cultural influence. As we sail North, passing East Cape, the Easternmost point of the main island—a long, flat promontory covered with palms and fruit belts, and harbouring a very dense population—a new world, new both geographically and ethnographically, opens up before us. At first it is only a faint, bluish silhouette, like a shadow of a distant mountain range, hovering far north over the horizon. As we approach, the hills of Normanby, the nearest of three big islands of the d'Entrecasteaux Archipelago, become clearer and take more definite shape and substance. A few high summits stand out more distinctly through the usual tropical haze, among them the characteristic double-peaked top of Bwebweso, the mountain

* Cf. Professor C. G. Seligman, Chapters XXXVII and XXXVIII.

where, according to native legend, the spirits of the dead in these parts lead their latter existence. The South Coast of Normanby, and the interior are inhabited by a tribe or tribes of which we know nothing ethnographically, except that they differ culturally from the rest of their neighbours. These tribes also take no direct part in the Kula.

The Northern end of Normanby, both sides of the Dawson Straits which separate the two islands of Normanby and Fergusson, and the South-eastern tip of Fergusson, are inhabited by a very important tribe, the Dobu. The heart of their district is the small extinct volcano forming an island at the Eastern entrance to Dawson Straits—Dobu, after which island they are named. To reach it, we have to sail through this extremely picturesque channel. On either side of the winding, narrow strait, green hills descend, and close it in, till it is more like a mountain lake. Here and there they recede, and a lagoon opens out. Or again they rise in fairly steep slopes, on which there can be plainly seen triangular gardens, native houses on piles, large tracts of unbroken jungle and patches of grass land. As we proceed, the narrow straits broaden, and we see on our right a wide flank of Mt. Sulomona'i on Normanby Island. On our left, there is a shallow bay, and behind it a large, flat plain, stretching far into the interior of Fergusson Island, and over it, we look into wide valleys, and on to several distant mountain ranges. After another turn, we enter a big bay, on both sides bordered by a flat foreshore, and in the middle of it rises out of a girdle of tropical vegetation, the creased cone of an extinct volcano, the island of Dobu.

We are now in the centre of a densely populated and ethnographically important district. From this island, in olden days, fierce and daring cannibal and head-hunting expeditions were periodically launched, to the dread of the neighbouring tribes. The natives of the immediately surrounding districts, of the flat foreshore on both sides of the straits, and of the big neighbouring islands were allies. But the more distant districts, often over a hundred miles away by sail, never felt safe from the Dobuans. Again, this was, and still is, one of the main links in the Kula, a centre of trade, industries and general cultural influence. It is characteristic of the international position of the Dobuans that their language is spoken as a lingua franca all over the d'Entrecasteaux

Archipelago, in the Amphletts, and as far north as the Trobriands. In the southern part of these latter islands, almost
everyone speaks Dobuan, although in Dobu the language of
the Trobriands or Kiriwinian is hardly spoken by anyone.
This is a remarkable fact, which cannot be easily explained
in terms of the present conditions, as the Trobrianders, if
anything, are on a higher level of cultural development than
Dobuans, are more numerous, and enjoy the same general
prestige.*

Another remarkable fact about Dobu and its district is
that it is studded with spots of special, mythological interest.
Its charming scenery, of volcanic cones, of wide, calm bays,
and lagoons overhung by lofty, green mountains, with the
reef-riddled, island-strewn ocean on the North, has deep,
legendary meaning for the native. Here is the land and sea
where the magically inspired sailors and heroes of the dim past
performed feats of daring and power. As we sail from the
entrance into Dawson Straits, through Dobu and the Amphletts
to Boyowa, almost every new configuration of the land which
we pass is the scene of some legendary exploit. Here the
narrow gorge has been broken through by a magic canoe flying
in the air. There the two rocks standing in the sea are the
petrified bodies of two mythological heroes who were stranded
at this spot after a quarrel. Here again, a land-locked lagoon
has been a port of refuge to a mythical crew. Apart from its
legends, the scenery before us, fine as it is, derives still more
charm from the knowledge that it is, and has been a distant
Eldorado, a land of promise and hope to generation after
generation of really daring native sailors from the Northern
islands. And in the past these lands and seas must have been
the scene of migrations and fights, of tribal invasions, and of
gradual infiltrations of peoples and cultures.

In personal appearance, the Dobuans have a very distinct
physique, which differentiates them sharply from the Southern
Massim and from the Trobrianders ; very dark-skinned, small
of stature, with big heads and rounded shoulders, they give a

---

* My knowledge of the Dobuans is fragmentary, derived from three short
visits in their district, from conversation with several Dobu natives whom I
had in my service, and from frequent parallels and allusions about Dobuan
customs, which are met when doing field-work among the Southern Trobrianders.
There is a short, sketchy account of certain of their customs and beliefs by the
Rev. W. E. Bromilow, first missionary in Dobu, which I have also consulted,
in the records of the Australasian Association for the Advancement of Science.

strange, almost gnome-like impression on a first encounter. In their manner, and their tribal character, there is something definitely pleasant, honest and open—an impression which long acquaintance with them confirms and strengthens. They are the general favourites of the whites, form the best and most reliable servants, and traders who have resided long among them compare them favourably with other natives.

Their villages, like those of the previously described Massim, are scattered over wide areas. The fertile and flat foreshores which they inhabit are studded with small, compact hamlets of a dozen or so houses, hidden in the midst of one continuous plantation of fruit trees, palms, bananas and yams. The houses are built on piles, but are cruder architecturally than those of the S. Massim, and almost without any decorations, though in the olden days of head-hunting some of them were ornamented with skulls.

In their social constitution, the people are totemic, being divided into a number of exogamous clans with linked totems. There is no institution of regular chieftainship, nor have they any system of rank or caste such as we shall meet in the Trobriands. Authority is vested in the elders of the tribe. In each hamlet there is a man who wields the greatest influence locally, and acts as its representative on such tribal councils as may arise in connection with ceremonies and expeditions.

Their system of kinship is matrilineal, and women hold a very good position, and wield great influence. They also seem to take a much more permanent and prominent part in tribal life than is the case among the neighbouring populations. There is notably one of the features of Dobuan society, which seems to strike the Trobrianders as peculiar, and to which they will direct attention while giving information, even although in the Trobriands also women have a good enough social position. In Dobu, women take an important part in gardening, and have a share in performing garden magic, and this in itself gives them a high status. Again, the main instrument for wielding power and inflicting penalties in these lands, sorcery, is to a great extent in the hands of women. The flying witches, so characteristic of the Eastern New Guinea type of culture, here have one of their strongholds. We shall have to go into this subject more in detail when speaking about shipwreck and the dangers of sailing. Besides this, women practice ordinary sorcery, which in other tribes is only man's prerogative.

As a rule, amongst natives, a high position of women is associated with sex laxity. In this, Dobu is an exception. Not only are married women expected to remain faithful, and adultery considered a great crime, but, in sharp contrast to all surrounding tribes, the unmarried girls of Dobu remain strictly chaste. There are no ceremonial or customary forms of licence, and an intrigue would be certainly regarded as an offence.

A few more words must be said here about sorcery, as this is a matter of great importance in all inter-tribal relations. The dread of sorcery is enormous, and when the natives visit distant parts, this dread is enhanced by the additional awe of the unknown and foreign. Besides the flying witches, there are, in Dobu, men and women who, by their knowledge of magical spells and rites, can inflict disease and cause death. The methods of these sorcerers, and all the beliefs clustering round this subject are very much the same as those in the Trobriands which we shall meet later on. These methods are characterised by being very rational and direct, and implying hardly any supernatural element. The sorcerer has to utter a spell over some substance, and this must be administered by mouth, or else burnt over the fire in the victim's hut. The pointing stick is also used by the sorcerers in certain rites.

If his methods are compared with those used by flying witches, who eat the heart and lungs, drink the blood, snap the bones of their enemies, and moreover possess the powers of invisibility and of flying, the Dobuan sorcerer seems to have but simple and clumsy means at his disposal. He is also very much behind his Mailu or Motu namesakes—I say namesakes, because sorcerers throughout the Massim are called *Bara'u*, and the same word is used in Mailu, while the Motu use the reduplicated *Babara'u*. The magicians in these parts use such powerful methods as those of killing the victim first, opening up the body, removing, lacerating or charming the inside, then bringing the victim to life again, only that he may soon sicken and eventually die.*

* Professor C. G. Seligman, op. cit., pp. 170 and 171 ; 187 and 188 about the Koita and Motu ; and B. Malinowski, *The Mailu*, pp. 647-652.

According to Dobuan belief, the spirits of the dead go to the top of Mt. Bwebweso on Normanby Island. This confined space harbours the shades of practically all the natives of the d'Entrecasteaux Archipelago, except those of Northern Goodenough Island, who, as I was told by some local informants, go after death to the spirit land of the Trobrianders.* The Dobuans have also the belief in a double soul—one, shadowy and impersonal, surviving the bodily death for a few days only, and remaining in the vicinity of the grave, the other the real spirit, who goes to Bwebweso.

It is interesting to note how natives, living on the boundary between two cultures and between two types of belief, regard the ensuing differences. A native of, say, Southern Boyowa, confronted with the question :—how it is that the Dobuans place spirit-land on Bwebweso, whereas they, the Trobrianders, place it in Tuma ?—does not see any difficulty in solving the problem. He does not regard the difference as due to a dogmatic conflict in doctrine. Quite simply he answers :— " Their dead go to Bwebweso and ours to Tuma." The metaphysical laws of existence are not yet considered subject to one invariable truth. As human destinies in life change, according to varieties in tribal custom, so also the doings of the spirit ! An interesting theory is evolved to harmonise the two beliefs in a mixed case. There is a belief that if a Trobriander were to die in Dobu, when on a Kula expedition, he would go for a time to Bwebweso. In due season, the spirits of the Trobrianders would sail from Tuma, the spirit land, to Bwebweso, on a spirit Kula, and the newly departed one would join their party and sail with them back to Tuma.

On leaving Dobu, we sail the open sea, a sea studded with coral patches and sand-banks, and seamed with long barrier reefs, where treacherous tides, running sometimes as much as five knots, make sailing really dangerous, especially for helpless native craft. This is the Kula sea, the scene of the inter-tribal expeditions and adventures which will be the theme of our future descriptions.

The Eastern shore of Ferguson Island, near Dobu, along which we are sailing, consists first of a series of volcanic cones and capes, giving the landscape the aspect of something

* Comp. D. Jenness and A. Ballantyne, " The Northern d'Entrecasteaux," Oxford, 1920, Chapter XII.

unfinished and crudely put together. At the foot of the hills there stretches for several miles beyond Dobu a broad alluvial flat covered with villages—Deide'i, Tu'utauna, Bwayowa, all important centres of trade, and the homes of the direct Kula partners of the Trobrianders. Heavy fumes can be seen floating above the jungle, coming from the hot geysers of Deide'i, which spurt up in high jets every few minutes.

Soon we come abreast of two characteristically shaped, dark rocks, one half hidden in the vegetation of the shore, the other standing in the sea at the end of a narrow sand-spit dividing the two. These are Atu'a'ine and Aturamo'a, two men turned into stone, as mythical tradition has it. Here the big sailing expeditions, those starting northwards from Dobu, as well as those arriving from the North, still make a halt—just as they have done for centuries, and, under observation of many taboos, give sacrificial offerings to the stones, with ritual invocations for propitious trade.

In the lee of these two rocks, runs a small bay with a clean, sandy beach, called Sarubwoyna. Here a visitor, lucky enough to pass at the right moment of the right season would see a picturesque and interesting scene. There before him would lie a huge fleet of some fifty to a hundred canoes, anchored in the shallow water, with swarms of natives upon them, all engaged in some strange and mysterious task. Some of these, bent over heaps of herbs, would be mumbling incantations ; others would be painting and adorning their bodies. An onlooker of two generations ago coming upon the same scene would no doubt have been led to suspect that he was watching the preparations for some dramatic tribal contest, for one of those big onslaughts in which the existence of whole villages and tribes were wiped out. It would even have been difficult for him to discern from the behaviour of the natives whether they were moved more by fear or by the spirit of aggression, as both these passions might have been read—and correctly so—into their attitudes and movements. That the scene contained no element of warfare ; that this fleet had come here from about a hundred miles sailing distance on a well regulated tribal visit ; that it had drawn up here for the final and most important preparations—this would not have been an easy guess to make. Nowadays—for this is carried out to this day with undiminished pomp—it would be an equally picturesque, but of course, tamer affair, since the romance of danger has gone from native life. As we learn in the course of this study to know more about these natives, their general ways and customs, and more especially about their Kula cycle of beliefs, ideas and sentiments, we shall be able to look with understanding eyes upon this scene, and comprehend this mixture of awe with intense, almost aggressive eagerness and this behaviour, which appears cowed and fierce at the same time.

V

Immediately after leaving Sarubwoyna and rounding the promontory of the two rocks, we come in sight of the island of Sanaroa, a big, sprawling, coral flat, with a range of volcanic hills on its western side. On the wide lagoon to the East of this island are the fishing grounds, where year after year the Trobrianders, returning from Dobu, look for the valuable spondylus shell, which, after their arrival home, is worked into the red discs, which form one of the main objects of native wealth. In the North of Sanaroa there is a stone in one of the tidal creeks called Sinatemubadiye'i, once a woman, the sister of Atu'a'ine and Aturamo'a, who, with her brothers came in here and was petrified before the last stage of the journey. She also receives offerings from canoes, coming either way on Kula expeditions.

Sailing further, some fine scenery unfolds itself on our left, where the high mountain range comes nearer to the sea shore, and where small bays, deep valleys and wooded slopes succeed one another. By carefully scanning the slopes, we can see small batches of some three to six miserable huts. These are the dwellings of the inhabitants, who are of a distinctly lower culture than the Dobuans, take no part in the Kula, and in olden days were the cowed and unhappy victims of their neighbours.

On our right there emerge behind Sanaroa the islands of Uwama and Tewara, the latter inhabited by Dobuan natives. Tewara is of interest to us, because one of the myths which we shall get to know later on makes it the cradle of the Kula. As we sail on, rounding one after the other the Eastern promontories of Fergusson Island, a group of strongly marked monumental profiles appears far on the horizon from behind the receding headlands. These are the Amphlett Islands, the link, both geographically and culturally, between the coastal tribes of the volcanic region of Dobu and the inhabitants of the flat coral archipelago of the Trobriands. This portion of the sea is very picturesque, and has a charm of its own even in this land of fine and varied scenery. On the main island of Fergusson, overlooking the Amphletts from the South, and ascending straight out of the sea in a slim and graceful pyramid, lies the tall mountain of Koyatabu, the highest peak on the island. Its big, green surface is cut in half by the white ribbon of a watercourse, starting almost half-way up and running down to the sea. Scattered under the lea of Koyatabu are the numerous smaller and bigger islands of the Amphlett Archipelago—steep, rocky hills, shaped into pyramids, sphynxes and cupolas, the whole a strange and picturesque assemblage of characteristic forms.

With a strong South-Easterly wind, which blows here for three quarters of the year, we approach the islands very fast, and the two most important ones, Gumawana and Ome'a, almost seem to leap out of the mist. As we anchor in front of Gumawana village at the S.E. end of the island, we cannot but feel impressed. Built on a narrow strip of foreshore, open to the breakers, and squeezed down to the water's edge by an almost precipitously rising jungle at its back, the village has been made sea-proof by walls of stone surrounding the houses with several bulwarks, and by stone dykes forming small artificial harbours along the sea front. The shabby and unornamented huts, built on piles, look very picturesque in these surroundings (see Plates VII and XLIII).

The inhabitants of this village, and of the four remaining ones in the archipelago, are a queer people. They are a numerically weak tribe, easily assailable from the sea, getting hardly enough to eat from their rocky islands ; and yet, through their unique skill in pottery, their great daring and efficiency as sailors, and their central position half way between Dobu and the Trobriands, they have succeeded in becoming in several respects the monopolists of this part of the world. They have also the main characteristics of monopolists : grasping and mean, inhospitable and greedy, keen on keeping the trade and exchange in their own hands, yet unprepared to make any sacrifice towards improving it ; shy, yet arrogant to anyone who has any dealings with them ; they contrast unfavourably with their southern and northern neighbours. And this is not only the white man's impression.* The Trobrianders, as well as the Dobuans, give the Amphlett natives a very bad name, as being stingy and unfair in all Kula transactions, and as having no real sense of generosity and hospitality.

When our boat anchors there, the natives approach it in their canoes, offering clay pots for sale. But if we want to go ashore and have a look at their village, there is a great commotion, and all the women disappear from the open places. The younger ones run and hide in the jungle behind the village, and even the old hags conceal themselves in the houses. So that if we want to see the making of pottery, which is almost exclusively women's work, we must first lure some old woman out of her retreat with generous promises of tobacco and assurances of honourable intentions.

This has been mentioned here, because it is of ethnographic interest, as it is not only white men who inspire this shyness ; if native strangers, coming from a distance for trade, put in for a short time in the Amphletts, the women also disappear in this fashion. This very ostentatious coyness is, however, not a sham, because in the Amphletts, even more than in Dobu, married and unmarried life is characterised by strict chastity and fidelity. Women here have also a good deal of influence, and take a great part in gardening and the performance of garden magic. In social institutions and customs, the natives present a mixture of Northern and Southern Massim elements. There are no chiefs, but influential elders wield authority, and in each village there is a head man who takes the lead in ceremonies and other big tribal affairs. Their totemic clans are identical with those of Murua (District II). Their somewhat precarious food supply comes partly from the poor gardens, partly from fishing with kite and fish trap, which, however, can only seldom be carried out, and does not yield very much. They are not self-supporting, and receive, in form of presents and by trade, a good deal of vegetable food as well as pigs from the mainland, from Dobu and the

* I spent about a month in these islands, and found the natives surprisingly intractable and difficult to work with ethnographically. The Amphlett " boys " are renowned as good boat-hands, but in general they are not such capable and willing workers as the Dobuans.

Trobriands. In personal appearance they are very much like the Trobrianders, that is, taller than the Dobuans, lighter skinned, and with finer features.

We must now leave the Amphletts and proceed to the Trobriand Islands, the scene of most of the occurrences described in this book, and the country concerning which I possess by far the largest amount of ethnographic information.

PLATE VII

IN THE AMPHLETTS
The sea-front of the main village (or Gumawana).   (See p. 46.)

[face p. 48

PLATE VIII

GROUP OF NATIVES IN THE VILLAGE OF TUKWA'UKWA
This shows the type of coastal village, with the natives squatting round.
(See p. 5.)

PLATE IX

MEN OF RANK FROM KIRIWINA

Tokulubakiki, a chief's son ; Towese'i and Yobukwa'u, of the highest and somewhat
inferior rank respectively.   All three show fine features and intelligent expressions ; they were
among my best informants.   (See p. 52.)

PLATE X

FISHERMEN FROM TEYAVA

Types of commoners from a Lagoon village.   (See p. 52.)

PLATE XI

A TYPICAL NAKUBUKWABUYA
(UNMARRIED WOMAN)

This shows the coarse, though fine-looking, type of a commoner woman.
(See p. 52.)

Chapter II

THE NATIVES OF THE TROBRIAND ISLANDS

I

LEAVING the bronzed rocks and the dark jungle of the Amphletts for the present—for we shall have to revisit them in the course of our study, and then shall learn more about their inhabitants—we sail North into an entirely different world of flat coral islands ; into an ethnographic district, which stands out by ever so many peculiar manners and customs from the rest of Papuo-Melanesia. So far, we have sailed over intensely blue, clear seas, where in shallow places the coral bottom, with its variety of colour and form, with its wonderful plant and fish life, is a fascinating spectacle in itself—a sea framed in all the splendours of tropical jungle, of volcanic and mountainous scenery, with lively watercourses and falls, with steamy clouds trailing in the high valleys. From all this we take a final farewell as we sail North. The outlines of the Amphletts soon fade away in tropical haze, till only Koyatabu's slender pyramid, lifted over them, remains on the horizon, the graceful form, which follows us even as far as the Lagoon of Kiriwina.

We now enter an opaque, greenish sea, whose monotony is broken only by a few sandbanks, some bare and awash, others with a few pandanus trees squatting on their air roots, high in the sand. To these banks, the Amphlett natives come and there they spend weeks on end, fishing for turtle and dugong. Here is also laid the scene of several of the mythical incidents of primeval Kula. Further ahead, through the misty spray, the line of horizon thickens here and there, as if faint pencil marks had been drawn upon it. These become more substantial, one of them lengthens and broadens, the others spring into the distinct shapes of small islands, and we find ourselves in the big Lagoon of the Trobriands, with Boyowa, the largest island, on our right, and with many others, inhabited and uninhabited, to the North and North-West.

MAP IV—The Trobriand Archipelago, also called Boyowa or Kiriwina.

As we sail in the Lagoon, following the intricate passages between the shallows, and as we approach the main island, the thick, tangled matting of the low jungle breaks here and there over a beach, and we can see into a palm grove, like an interior, supported by pillars. This indicates the site of a village. We step ashore on to the sea front, as a rule covered with mud and refuse, with canoes drawn up high and dry, and passing through the grove, we enter the village itself (see Plate VIII).

Soon we are seated on one of the platforms built in front of a yam-house, shaded by its overhanging roof. The round, grey logs, worn smooth by contact with naked feet and bodies ; the trodden ground of the village-street ; the brown skins of the natives, who immediately surround the visitor in large groups—all these form a colour scheme of bronze and grey, unforgetable to anyone, who, like myself, has lived among these people.

It is difficult to convey the feelings of intense interest and suspense with which an Ethnographer enters for the first time the district that is to be the future scene of his field-work. Certain salient features, characteristic of the place, at once rivet his attention, and fill him with hopes or apprehensions. The appearance of the natives, their manners, their types of behaviour, may augur well or ill for the possibilities of rapid and easy research. One is on the lookout for symptoms of deeper, sociological facts, one suspects many hidden and mysterious ethnographic phenomena behind the commonplace aspect of things. Perhaps that queer-looking, intelligent native is a renowned sorcerer ; perhaps between those two groups of men there exists some important rivalry or vendetta which may throw much light on the customs and character of the people if one can only lay hands upon it ? Such at least were my thoughts and feelings as on the day of my arrival in Boyowa I sat scanning a chatting group of Trobriand natives.

The great variety in their physical appearance is what strikes one first in Boyowa.* There are men and women of tall stature, fine bearing, and delicate features, with clear-cut aquiline profile and high foreheads, well formed nose and chin,

---

* Already Dr. C. G. Seligman has noticed that there are people of an outstanding fine physical type among the Northern Massim, of whom the Trobrianders form the Western section, people who are " generally taller (often very notably so) than the individuals of the short-faced, broad-nosed type, in whom the bridge of the nose is very low." Op. cit., p. 8.

and an open, intelligent expression (see Plates IX, XV, XVII). And besides these, there are others with prognatic, negroid faces, broad, thick-lipped mouths, narrow foreheads, and a coarse expression (see Plates X, XI, XII). The better featured have also a markedly lighter skin. Even their hair differs, varying from quite straight locks to the frizzly mop of the typical Melanesian. They wear the same classes of ornaments as the other Massim, consisting mainly of fibre armlets and belts, earrings cf turtle shell and spondylus discs, and they are very fond of using, for personal decoration, flowers and aromatic herbs. In manner they are much freer, more familiar and confident, than any of the natives we have so far met. As soon as an interesting stranger arrives, half the village assembles around him, talking loudly and making remarks about him, frequently uncomplimentary, and alto-gether assuming a tone of jocular familiarity.

One of the main sociological features at once strikes an observant newcomer—the existence of rank and social differ-entiation. Some of the natives—very frequently those of the finer looking type—are treated with most marked deference by others, and in return, these chiefs and persons of rank behave in quite a different way towards the strangers. In fact, they show excellent manners in the full meaning of this word.

When a chief is present, no commoner dares to remain in a physically higher position ; he has to bend his body or squat. Similarly, when the chief sits down, no one would dare to stand. The institution of definite chieftainship, to which are shown such extreme marks of deference, with a sort of rudi-mentary Court ceremonial, with insignia of rank and authority, is so entirely foreign to the whole spirit of Melanesian tribal life, that at first sight it transports the Ethnographer into a different world. In the course of our inquiry, we shall con-stantly meet with manifestation of the Kiriwinian chief's authority, we shall notice the difference in this respect between the Trobrianders and the other tribes, and the resulting adjustments of tribal usage.

II

Another sociological feature, which forcibly obtrudes itself on the visitor's notice is the social position of the women. Their behaviour, after the cool aloofness of the Dobuan women, and the very uninviting treatment which strangers receive from those of the Amphletts, comes almost as a shock in its friendly familiarity. Naturally, here also, the manners of women of rank are quite different from those of low class commoners. But, on the whole, high and low alike, though by no means reserved, have a genial, pleasant approach, and many of them are very fine-looking (see Plates XI, XII). Their dress is also different from any so far observed. All the Melanesian women in New Guinea wear a petticoat made of fibre. Among the Southern Massim, this fibre skirt is long, reaching to the knees or below, whereas in the Trobriands it is much shorter and fuller, consisting of several layers standing out round the body like a ruff (compare the S. Massim women on Plates V and VI with the Trobrianders on Plate IV). The highly ornamental effect of that dress is enhanced by the elaborate decorations made in three colours on the several layers forming the top skirt. On the whole, it is very becoming to fine young women, and gives to small slender girls a graceful, elfish appearance.

Chastity is an unknown virtue among these natives. At an incredibly early age they become initiated into sexual life, and many of the innocent looking plays of childhood are not as innocuous as they appear. As they grow up, they live in promiscuous free-love, which gradually develops into more permanent attachments, one of which ends in marriage. But before this is reached, unmarried girls are openly supposed to be quite free to do what they like, and there are even cere-monial arrangements by which the girls of a village repair in a body to another place ; there they publicly range themselves for inspection, and each is chosen by a local boy, with whom she spends a night. This is called *katuyausi* (see Plate XII). Again, when a visiting party arrives from another district, food is brought to them by the unmarried girls, who are also expected to satisfy their sexual wants. At the big mortuary vigils round the corpse of a newly deceased person, people from neighbouring villages come in large bodies to take part in the wailing and singing. The girls of the visiting party are expected by usage to comfort the boys of the bereaved village, in a manner which gives much anguish to their official lovers. There is another remarkable form of ceremonial licence, in which indeed women are openly the initiators. During the gardening season, at the time of weeding, the women do communal work, and any strange man who ventures to pass through the district runs a considerable risk, for the women will run after him, seize him, tear off his pubic leaf, and ill-treat him orgiastically in the most ignominous manner. Side by side with these ceremonial forms of licence, there go, in the normal course of events, constant private intrigues, more intense during the festive seasons, becoming less prominent as garden work, trading expeditions, or harvesting take up the energies and attention of the tribe.

Marriage is associated with hardly any public or private rite or ceremony. The woman simply joins her husband in his house, and later on, there is a series of exchanges of gifts, which in no way can be interpreted as purchase money for the wife. As a matter of fact, the most important feature of the Trobriand marriage is the fact that the wife's family have to contribute, and that in a very substantial manner, to the economics of her household, and also they have to perform all sorts of services for the husband. In her married life, the woman is supposed to remain faithful to her husband, but this rule is neither very strictly kept nor enforced. In all other ways, she retains a great measure of independence, and her husband has to treat her well and with consideration. If he does not, the woman simply leaves him and returns to her family, and as the husband is as a rule economically the loser by her action, he has to exert himself to get her back—which he does by means of presents and persuasions. If she chooses, she can leave him for good, and she can always find someone else to marry.

In tribal life, the position of women is also very high. They do not as a rule join the councils of men, but in many matters they have their own way, and control several aspects of tribal life. Thus, some of the garden work is their business ; and this is considered a privilege as well as a duty. They also look after certain stages in the big, ceremonial divisions of food, associated with the very complete and elaborate mortuary ritual of the Boyowans (see Plate IV). Certain forms of magic—that performed over a first-born baby, beauty-magic made at tribal ceremonies, some classes of sorcery—are also the monopoly of women. Women of rank share the privileges incidental to it, and men of low caste will bend before them and observe all the necessary formalities and taboos due to a chief. A woman of chief's rank, married to commoner, retains her status, even with regard to her husband, and has to be treated accordingly.

The Trobrianders are matrilineal, that is, in tracing descent and settling inheritance, they follow the maternal line. A child belongs to the clan and village community of its mother, and wealth, as well as social position, are inherited, not from father to son, but from maternal uncle to nephew. This rule admits of certain important and interesting exceptions, which we shall come across in the course of this study.

III

Returning to our imaginary first visit ashore, the next interesting thing to do, after we have sufficiently taken in the appearance and manners of the natives, is to walk round the village. In doing this, again we would come across much, which to a trained eye, would reveal at once deeper sociological facts. In the Trobriands however, it would be better to make our first observations in one of the large, inland villages, situated on even, flat ground with plenty of space, so that it has been possible to build it in the typical pattern. In the coastal villages, placed on marshy ground and coral outcrop, the irregularity of the soil and cramped space have obliterated the design, and they present quite a chaotic appearance. The big villages of the central districts, on the other hands, are built one and all with an almost geometrical regularity.

In the middle, a big circular space is surrounded by a ring of yam houses. These latter are built on piles, and present a fine, decorative front, with walls of big, round logs, laid crosswise on one another, so as to leave wide interstices through which the stored yams can be seen (see Plates XV, XXXII, XXXIII). Some of the store-houses strike us at once as being better built, larger, and higher than the rest, and these have also big, ornamented boards, running round the gable and across it. These are the yam houses of the chief or of persons of rank. Each yam house also has, as a rule, a small platform in front of it, on which groups of men will sit and chat in the evening, and where visitors can rest.

Concentrically with the circular row of yam houses, there runs a ring of dwelling huts, and thus a street going all round the village is formed between the two rows (see Plates III, IV,

VIII). The dwellings are lower than the yam houses, and instead of being on piles, are built directly on the ground. The interior is dark and very stuffy, and the only opening into it is through the door, and that is usually closed. Each hut is occupied by one family (see Plate XV), that is, husband, wife and small children, while adolescent and grown-up boys and girls live in separate small bachelor's houses, harbouring some two to six inmates. Chiefs and people of rank have their special, personal houses, besides those of their wives. The Chief's house often stands in the central ring of the store-houses facing the main place.

The broad inspection of the village would therefore reveal to us the rôle of decoration as insignia of rank, the existence of bachelors' and spinsters' houses, the great importance attached to the yam-harvest—all these small symptoms which, followed up, would lead us deep into the problems of native sociology. Moreover, such an inspection would have led us to inquire as to the part played by the different divisions of the village in tribal life. We should then learn that the *baku*, the central circular space, is the scene of public ceremonies and festivities, such as dancing (see Plates XIII, XIV), division of food, tribal feasts, mortuary vigils, in short, of all doings that represent the village as a whole. In the circular street between the stores and living houses, everyday life goes on, that is, the preparation of food, the eating of meals, and the usual exchange of gossip and ordinary social amenities. The interior of the houses is only used at night, or on wet days, and is more a sleeping than a living room. The backs of the houses and the contiguous groves are the scene of the children's play and the women's occupations. Further away, remote parts of the grove are reserved for sanitary purposes, each sex having its own retreat.

The *baku* (central place) is the most picturesque part, and there the somewhat monotonous colour scheme of the brown and grey is broken by the overhanging foliage of the grove, seen above the neat fronts and gaudy ornamentation of the yam-houses and by the decorations worn by the crowd when a dance or ceremony is taking place (see Plates XIII, XXXIII). Dancing is done only at one time in the year, in connection with the harvest festivities, called *milamala*, at which season also the spirits of the dead return from Tuma, the nether-world, to the villages from which they hail. Sometimes the dancing season lasts only for a few weeks or even days, sometimes it is extended into a special dancing period called *usigola*. During such a time of festivities, the inhabitants of a village will dance day after day, for a month or longer, the period being inaugurated by a feast, punctuated by several more, and ending in a big culminating performance. At this many villages assist as spectators, and distributions of food take place. During an *usigola*, dancing is done in full dress, that is, with facial painting, floral decorations, valuable ornaments, and a head-dress of white cockatoo feathers (see Plates XIII, XIV). A performmance consists always of a dance executed in a ring to the accompaniment of singing and drum-beating, both of which are done by a group of people standing in the middle. Some dances are done with the carved dancing shield.

Sociologically, the village is an important unit in the Trobriands. Even the mightiest chief in the Trobriands wields his authority primarily over his own village and only secondarily over the district. The village community exploit jointly their garden lands, perform ceremonies, wage warfare, undertake trading expeditions, and sail in the same canoe or fleet of canoes as one group.

After the first inspection of the village, we would be naturally interested to know more of the surrounding country, and would take a walk through the bush. Here, however, if we hoped for a picturesque and varied landscape, we should receive a great disappointment. The extensive, flat island consists only of one fertile plain, with a low coral ridge running along portions of the coast. It is almost entirely under intermittent cultivation, and the bush, regularly cleared away every few years, has no time to grow high. A low, dense jungle grows in a matted tangle, and practically wherever we move on the island we walk along between two green walls, presenting no variety, allowing of no broader view. The monotony is broken only by an occasional clump of old trees left standing—usually a tabooed place—or by one of the numerous villages which we meet with every mile or two in this densely populated country. The main element, both of picturesqueness and ethnographic interest, is afforded by the native gardens. Each year about one quarter or one fifth of the total area is under actual cultivation as gardens, and these

are well tended, and present a pleasant change from the
monotony of the scrub. In its early stages, the garden site
is simply a bare, cleared space, allowing of a wider outlook
upon the distant coral ridge in the East, and upon the tall
groves, scattered over the horizon, which indicate villages or
tabooed tree clumps. Later on, when the yam-vines, taro,
and sugar cane begin to grow and bud, the bare brown soil
is covered with the fresh green of the tender plants. After
some more time still, tall, stout poles are planted over each
yam-plant ; the vine climbs round them, grows into a full,
shady garland of foliage, and the whole gives the impression
of a large, exuberant hop-yard.

IV

Half of the natives' working life is spent in the garden,
and around it centres perhaps more than half of his interests
and ambitions. And here we must pause and make an attempt
to understand his attitude in this matter, as it is typical of the
way in which he goes about all his work. If we remain under
the delusion that the native is a happy-go-lucky, lazy child of
nature, who shuns as far as possible all labour and effort, waiting
till the ripe fruits, so bountifully supplied by generous tropical
Nature, fall into his mouth, we shall not be able to understand
in the least his aims and motives in carrying out the Kula or
any other enterprise. On the contrary, the truth is that the
native can and, under circumstances, does work hard, and
work systematically, with endurance and purpose, nor does he
wait till he is pressed to work by his immediate needs.

In gardening, for instance, the natives produce much more
than they actually require, and in any average year they
harvest perhaps twice as much as they can eat. Nowadays,
this surplus is exported by Europeans to feed plantation hands
in other parts of New Guinea ; in olden days it was simply
allowed to rot. Again, they produce this surplus in a manner
which entails much more work than is strictly necessary for
obtaining the crops. Much time and labour is given up to
æsthetic purposes, to making the gardens tidy, clean, cleared of
all debris ; to building fine, solid, fences, to providing specially
strong and big yam-poles. All these things are to some
extent required for the growth of the plant ; but there can be
no doubt that the natives push their conscientiousness far

beyond the limit of the purely necessary. The non-utilitarian element in their garden work is still more clearly perceptible in the various tasks which they carry out entirely for the sake of ornamentation, in connection with magical ceremonies, and in obedience to tribal usage. Thus, after the ground has been scrupulously cleared and is ready for planting, the natives divide each garden plot into small squares, each a few yards in length and width, and this is done only in obedience to usage, in order to make the gardens look neat. No self-respecting man would dream of omitting to do this. Again, in especially well trimmed gardens, long horizontal poles are tied to the yam supports in order to embellish them. Another, and perhaps the most interesting example of non-utilitarian work is afforded by the big, prismatic erections called *kamkokola*, which serve ornamental and magical purposes, but have nothing to do with the growth of plants (comp. Plate LIX).

Among the forces and beliefs which bear upon and regulate garden work, perhaps magic is the most important. It is a department of its own, and the garden magician, next to the chief and the sorcerer, is the most important personage of the village. The position is hereditary, and, in each village, a special system of magic is handed on in the female line from one generation to another. I have called it a *system*, because the magician has to perform a series of rites and spells over the garden, which run parallel with the labour, and which, in fact, initiate each stage of the work and each new development of the plant life. Even before any gardening is begun at all, the magician has to consecrate the site with a big ceremonial performance in which all the men of the village take part. This ceremony officially opens the season's gardening, and only after it is performed do the villagers begin to cut the scrub on their plots. Then, in a series of rites, the magician inaugurates successively all the various stages which follow one another—the burning of the scrub, the clearing, the planting, the weeding and the harvesting. Also, in another series of rites and spells, he magically assists the plant in sprouting, in budding, in bursting into leaf, in climbing, in forming the rich garlands of foliage, and in producing the edible tubers.

The garden magician, according to native ideas, thus controls both the work of man and the forces of Nature. He also acts directly as supervisor of gardening, sees to it that people do not skimp their work, or lag behind with it.   Thus magic is a systematising, regulating, and controlling influence in garden work.   The magician, in carrying out the rites, sets the pace, compels people to apply themselves to certain tasks, and to accomplish them properly and in time.   Incidentally, magic also imposes on the tribe a good deal of extra work, of apparently unnecessary, hampering taboos and regulations. In the long run, however, there is no doubt that by its influence in ordering, systematising and regulating work, magic is economically invaluable for the natives.*

Another notion which must be exploded, once and for ever, is that of the Primitive Economic Man of some current economic text books.   This fanciful, dummy creature, who has been very tenacious of existence in popular and semi-popular economic literature, and whose shadow haunts even the minds of competent anthropologists, blighting their outlook with a preconceived idea, is an imaginary, primitive man, or savage, prompted in all his actions by a rationalistic conception of self-interest, and achieving his aims directly and with the minimum of effort.   Even *one* well established instance should show how preposterous is this assumption that man, and especially man on a low level of culture, should be actuated by pure economic motives of enlightened self-interest.   The primitive Trobriander furnishes us with such an instance, contradicting this fallacious theory.   He works prompted by motives of a highly complex, social and traditional nature, and towards aims which are certainly not directed towards the satisfaction of present wants, or to the direct achievement of utilitarian purposes.   Thus, in the first place, as we have seen, work is not carried out on the principle of the least effort.   On the contrary, much time and energy is spent on wholly unnecessary effort, that is, from a utilitarian point of view.   Again, work and effort, instead of being merely a means to an end, are, in a way an end in themselves.   A good garden worker in the Trobriands derives a direct prestige from the amount of labour he can do, and the size of garden he can till. The title *tokwaybagula*, which means " good " or " efficient gardener," is bestowed with discrimination, and borne with pride.   Several of my friends, renowned as *tokwaybagula*,

* I have dealt with the subject of garden work in the Trobriands and with its economic importance more fully in an article entitled " The Primitive Economics of the Trobriand Islanders " in *The Economic Journal*, March, 1921.

would boast to me how long they worked, how much ground they tilled, and would compare their efforts with those of less efficient men. When the labour, some of which is done communally, is being actually carried out, a good deal of competition goes on. Men vie with one another in their speed, in their thoroughness, and in the weights they can lift, when bringing big poles to the garden, or in carrying away the harvested yams.

The most important point about this is, however, that all, or almost all the fruits of his work, and certainly any surplus which he can achieve by extra effort, goes not to the man himself, but to his relatives-in-law. Without entering into details of the system of the apportionment of the harvest, of which the sociology is rather complex and would require a preliminary account of the Trobriand kinship system and kinship ideas, it may be said that about three quarters of a man's crops go partly as tribute to the chief, partly as his due to his sister's (or mother's) husband and family.

But although he thus derives practically no personal benefit in the utilitarian sense from his harvest, the gardener receives much praise and renown from its size and quality, and that in a direct and circumstantial manner. For all the crops, after being harvested, are displayed for some time afterwards in the gardens, piled up in neat, conical heaps under small shelters made of yam vine. Each man's harvest is thus exhibited for criticism in his own plot, and parties of natives walk about from garden to garden, admiring, comparing and praising the best results. The importance of the food display can be gauged by the fact that, in olden days, when the chief's power was much more considerable than now, it was dangerous for a man who was not either of high rank himself, or working for such a one, to show crops which might compare too favourably with those of the chief.

In years when the harvest promises to be plentiful, the chief will proclaim a *kayasa* harvest, that is to say, ceremonial, competitive display of food, and then the straining for good results and the interest taken in them are still higher. We shall meet later on with ceremonial enterprises of the *kayasa* type, and find that they play a considerable part in the Kula. All this shows how entirely the real native of flesh and bone differs from the shadowy Primitive Economic Man, on whose imaginary behaviour many of the scholastic deductions of abstract economics are based.* The Trobriander works in a roundabout way, to a large extent for the sake of the work itself, and puts a great deal of æsthetic polish on the arrangement and general appearance of his garden. He is not guided primarily by the desire to satisfy his wants, but by a very complex set of traditional forces, duties and obligations, beliefs in magic, social ambitions and vanities. He wants, if he is a *man*, to achieve social distinction as a *good gardener* and a good worker in general.

I have dwelt at this length upon these points concerning the motives and aims of the Trobrianders in their garden work, because, in the chapters that follow, we shall be studying economic activities, and the reader will grasp the attitude of the natives best if he has it illustrated to him by various examples. All that has been said in this matter about the Trobrianders applies also to the neighbouring tribes.

V

With the help of this new insight gained into the mind of the native, and into their social scheme of harvest distribution, it will be easier to describe the nature of the chief's authority. Chieftainship in the Trobriands is the combination of two institutions : first, that of headmanship, or village authority ; secondly, that of totemic clanship, that is the division of the community into classes or castes, each with a certain more or less definite rank.

In every community in the Trobriands, there is one man who wields the greatest authority, though often this does not amount to very much. He is, in many cases, nothing more than the *primus inter pares* in a group of village elders, who deliberate on all important matters together, and arrive at a decision by common consent. It must not be forgotten that there is hardly ever much room for doubt or deliberation, as natives communally, as well as individually, never act except on traditional and conventional lines. This village headman is, as a rule,

* This does not mean that the general economic conclusions are wrong. The economic nature of Man is as a rule illustrated on imaginary savages for didactic purposes only, and the conclusions of the authors are in reality based on their study of the facts of developed economics. But, nevertheless, quite apart from the fact that pedagogically it is a wrong principle to make matters look more simple by introducing a falsehood, it is the Ethnographer's duty and right to protest against the introduction from outside of false facts into his own field of study.

therefore, not much more than a master of tribal ceremonies, and the main speaker within and without the tribe, whenever one is needed.

But the position of headman becomes much more than this, when he is a person of high rank, which is by no means always the case. In the Trobriands there exist four totemic clans, and each of these is divided into a number of smaller sub-clans, —which could also be called families or castes, for the members of each claim common descent from one ancestress, and each of them holds a certain, specified rank. These sub-clans have also a local character, because the original ancestress emerged from a hole in the ground, as a rule somewhere in the neighbourhood of their village community. There is not one sub-clan in the Trobriands whose members cannot indicate its original locality, where their group, in the form of the ancestress, first saw the light of the sun. Coral outcrops, water-holes, small caves or grottoes, are generally pointed out as the original " holes " or " houses," as they are called. Often such a hole is surrounded by one of the tabooed clumps of trees alluded to before. Many of them are situated in the groves surrounding a village, and a few near the sea shore. Not one is on the cultivable land.

The highest sub-clan is that of the Tabalu, belonging to the Malasi totem clan. To this sub-clan belongs the main chief of Kiriwina, To'uluwa, who resides in the village of Omarakana (see Plate II and Frontispiece). He is in the first place the headman of his own village, and in contrast to the headmen of low rank, he has quite a considerable amount of power. His high rank inspires everyone about him with the greatest and most genuine respect and awe, and the remnants of his power are still surprisingly large, even now, when white authorities, very foolishly and with fatal results, do their utmost to undermine his prestige and influence.

Not only does the chief—by which word I shall designate a headman of rank—possess a high degree of authority within his own village, but his sphere of influence extends far beyond it. A number of villages are tributary to him, and in several respects subject to his authority. In case of war, they are his allies, and have to foregather in his village. When he needs men to perform some task, he can send to his subject villages, and they will supply him with workers. In all big festivities the villages of his district will join, and the chief will act as master of ceremonies. Nevertheless, for all these services rendered to him he has to pay. He even has to pay for any tributes received out of his stores of wealth. Wealth, in the Trobriands, is the outward sign and the substance of power, and the means also of exercising it. But how does he acquire his wealth ? And here we come to the main duty of the vassal villages to the chief. From each subject village, he takes a wife, whose family, according to the Trobriand law, has to supply him with large amounts of crops. This wife is always the sister or some relation of the headman of the subject village, and thus practically the whole community has to work for him. In olden days, the chief of Omarakana had up to as many as forty consorts, and received perhaps as much as thirty to fifty per cent. of all the garden produce of Kiriwina. Even now, when his wives number only sixteen, he has enormous storehouses, and they are full to the roof with yams every harvest time.

With this supply, he is able to pay for the many services he requires, to furnish with food the participants in big feasts, in tribal gatherings or distant expeditions. Part of the food he uses to acquire objects of native wealth, or to pay for the making of them. In brief, through his privilege of practising polygamy, the chief is kept supplied with an abundance of wealth in food stuffs and in valuables, which he uses to maintain his high position ; to organise tribal festivities and enterprises, and to pay, according to custom, for the many personal services to which he is entitled.

One point in connection with the chief's authority deserves special mention. Power implies not only the possibility of rewarding, but also the means of punishing. This in the Trobriands is as a rule done indirectly, by means of sorcery. The chief has the best sorcerers of the district always at his beck and call. Of course he also has to reward them when they do him a service. If anyone offends him, or trespasses upon his authority, the chief summons the sorcerer, and orders that the culprit shall die by black magic. And here the chief is powerfully helped in achieving his end by the fact that he can do this openly, so that everybody, and the victim himself knows that a sorcerer is after him. As the natives are very deeply and genuinely afraid of sorcery, the feeling of being

PLATE XII

BOYOWAN GIRLS

Such facial painting and decorations are used when they go on a *katuyausi* expedition. (See p. 52.)

PLATE XIII

KAYDEBU DANCE

The circular dance with the carved shield on the *baku* of Omarakana. (See p. 57.) Note the plain, though picturesque, headdress of cockatoo feathers

PLATE XIV

DANCERS IN FULL DECORATION

A segment of the dancing circle, in a *kayleku* dance, village of Yalaka. (See p. 57.)

Plate XV

A FAMILY GROUP

Tokulubakiki of Omarakana, with his mother, wife and children. (See p. 57.) Note the storehouse, with yams showing through the interstices

hunted, of imagining themselves doomed, is in itself enough to doom them in reality. Only in extreme cases, does a chief inflict direct punishment on a culprit. He has one or two hereditary henchmen, whose duty it is to kill the man who has so deeply offended him, that actual death is the only sufficient punishment. As a matter of fact, very few cases of this are on record, and it is now, of course, entirely in abeyance.

Thus the chief's position can be grasped only through the realisation of the high importance of wealth, of the necessity of paying for everything, even for services which are due to him, and which could not be withheld. Again, this wealth comes to the chief from his relations-in-law, and it is through his right to practise polygamy that he actually achieves his position, and exercises his power.

Side by side with this rather complex mechanism of authority, the prestige of rank, the direct recognition of his personal superiority, give the chief an immense power, even outside his district. Except for the few of his own rank, no native in the Trobriands will remain erect when the great chief of Omarakana approaches, even in these days of tribal dis-integration. Wherever he goes, he is considered as the most important person, is seated on a high platform, and treated with consideration. Of course the fact that he is accorded marks of great deference, and approached in the manner as if he were a supreme despot, does not mean that perfect good fellowship and sociability do not reign in his personal relations with his companions and vassals. There is no difference in interests or outlook between him and his subjects. They sit together and chat, they exchange village gossip, the only difference being that the chief is always on his guard, and much more reticent and diplomatic than his companion, though he is no less interested. The chief, unless he is too old, joins in dances and even in games, and indeed he takes precedence as a matter of course.

In trying to realise the social conditions among the Trobrianders and their neighbours, it must not be forgotten that their social organisation is in certain respects complex and ill-defined. Besides very definite laws which are strictly obeyed, there exist a number of quaint usages, of vague graduations in rules, of others where the exceptions are so many, that they rather obliterate the rule than confirm it. The narrow social outlook of the native who does not see beyond his own district, the prevalence of singularities and exceptional cases is one of the leading characteristics of native sociology, one which for many reasons has not been sufficiently recognised. But the main outlines of chieftainship here presented, will be enough to give a clear idea of it and of some of the flavour of their institutions, as much, in fact, as is necessary, in order to understand the chief's rôle in the Kula. But it must to a certain extent be supplemented by the concrete data, bearing upon the political divisions of the Trobriands.

The most important chief is, as said, the one who resides in Omarakana and rules Kiriwina, agriculturally the richest and most important district. His family, or sub-clan, the Tabalu, are acknowledged to have by far the highest rank in all the Archipelago. Their fame is spread over the whole Kula district ; the entire province of Kiriwina derives prestige from its chief, and its inhabitants also keep all his personal taboos, which is a duty but also a distinction. Next to the high chief, there resides in a village some two miles distant, a personage who, though in several respects his vassal, is also his main foe and rival, the headman of Kabwaku, and ruler of the province of Tilataula. The present holder of this title is an old rogue named Moliasi. From time to time, in the old days, war used to break out between the two provinces, each of which could muster some twelve villages for the fight. These wars were never very bloody or of long duration, and they were in many ways fought in a competitive, sporting manner, since, unlike with the Dobuans and Southern Massim, there were neither head-hunting nor cannibalistic practices among the Boyowans. Nevertheless, defeat was a serious matter. It meant a temporary destruction of the loser's villages, and exile for a year or two. After that, a ceremony of reconciliation took place, and friend and foe would help to rebuild the villages.* The ruler of Tilataula has an intermediate rank, and outside his district he does not enjoy much prestige ; but within it, he has a considerable amount of power, and a good

---

* Compare Professor C. G. Seligman, op. cit., pp. 663-668 ; also the Author, article on " War and Weapons among the Trobriand Islanders," in *Man*, January, 1918.

deal of wealth, in the shape of stored food and ceremonial articles. All the villages under his rule, have, of course, their own independent headman, who, being of low rank, have only a small degree of local authority.

In the west of the big, northern half of Boyowa (that is of the main island of the Trobriand Group) are again two districts, in past times often at war with one another. One of them, Kuboma, subject to the chief of Gumilababa, of high rank, though inferior to the chief of Kiriwina, consists of some ten inland villages, and is very important as a centre of industry. Among these villages are included those of Yalaka, Buduwaylaka, Kudukwaykela, where the quicklime is prepared for betel chewing, and also the lime pots made. The highly artistic designs, burnt in on the lime pots, are the speciality of these villagers, but unfortunately the industry is fast decaying. The inhabitabts of Luya are renowned for their basket work, of which the finest specimens are their production. But the most remarkable of all is the village of Bwoytalu, whose inhabitants are at the same time the most despised pariahs, the most dreaded sorcerers, and the most skilful and industrious craftsmen in the island. They belong to several sub-clans, all originating in the neighbourhood of the village, near which also, according to tradition, the original sorcerer came out of the soil in the form of a crab. They eat the flesh of bush-pigs, and they catch and eat the stingaree, both objects of strict taboos and of genuine loathing to the other inhabitants of Northern Boyowa. For this reason they are despised and regarded as unclean by the others. In olden days they would have to crouch lower and more abjectly than anyone else. No man or woman would mate with anyone from Bwoytalu, whether in marriage or in an intrigue. Yet in wood carving, and especially in the working out of the wonderful, round dishes, in the manufacture of plaited fibre work, and in the production of combs, they are far more skilful than anyone else, and acknowledged to be such ; they are the wholesale manufacturers of these objects for export, and they can produce work not to be rivalled by any other village.

The five villages lying on the western coast of the northern half, on the shores of the Lagoon, form the district of Kulumata. They are all fishing villages, but differ in their methods, and each has its own fishing grounds and its own methods of exploiting them.* The district is much less homogeneous than any of those before mentioned. It posesses no paramount chief, and even in war the villagers used not to fight on the same side. But it is impossible to enter here into all these shades and singularities of political organisation.

In the southern part of Boyowa, there is first the province of Luba, occupying the waist of the island, the part where it narrows down to a long isthmus. This part is ruled by a chief of high rank, who resides in Olivilevi. He belongs to the same family as the chief of Omarakana, and this southern dominion is the result of a younger line's having branched off some three generations ago. This happened after an unsuccessful war. when the whole tribe of Kiriwina fled south to Luba, and lived there for two years in a temporary village. The main body returned afterwards, but a number remained behind with the chief's brother, and thus the village of Olivilevi was founded. Wawela, which was formerly a very big village, now consists of hardly more than twenty huts. The only one on the Eastern shore which lies right on the sea, it is very picturesquely situated, overlooking a wide bay with a clean beach. It is of importance as the traditional centre of astronomical knowledge. From here, for generation after generation up to the present day, the calendar of the natives has been regulated. This means that some of the most important dates are fixed, especially that of the great annual festival, the *Milamala*, always held at full moon. Again, Wawela is one of the villages where the second form of sorcery, that of the flying witches, has its main Trobriand home. In fact, according to native belief, this form of sorcery has its seat only in the Southern half, and is unknown to the women in the North, though the Southern witches extend their field of operations all over Boyowa. Wawela, which lies facing the east, and which is always in close touch with the villages of Kitava and the rest of the Marshall Bennetts, shares with these islands the reputation of harbouring many women who can fly, kill by magic, who also feed on corpses, and are especially dangerous to seamen in peril.

Further down to the south, on the western shore of the Lagoon, we come to the big settlement of Sinaketa, consisting of some six villages lying within a few hundred yards from one

* Compare the Author's article on " Fishing and Fishing Magic in the Trobriands," *Man*, June, 1918.

another, but each having its own headman and a certain amount of local characteristics. These villages form, however, one community for purposes of war and of the Kula. Some of the local headmen of Sinaketa claim the highest rank, some are commoners ; but on the whole, both the principle of rank and the power of the chief break down more and more as we move south. Beyond Sinaketa, we meet a few more villages, who practice a local Kula, and with whom we shall have to deal later on. Sinaketa itself will loom very largely in the descriptions that follow. The southern part of the island is sometimes called Kaybwagina, but it does not constitute a definite political unit, like the northern districts.

Finally, south of the main island, divided from it by a narrow channel, lies the half-moon-shaped island of Vakuta, to which belong four small villages and one big one. Within recent times, perhaps four to six generations ago, there came down and settled in this last mentioned one a branch of the real Tabalu, the chiefly family of highest rank. But their power here never assumed the proportions even of the small chiefs of Sinaketa. In Vakuta, the typical Papuo-Melanesian system of government by tribal elders—with one more prominent than the others, but not paramount—is in full vigour.

The two big settlements of Sinaketa and Vakuta play a great part in the Kula, and they also are the only two communities in the whole Trobriands where the red shell discs are made. This industry, as we shall see, is closely associated with the Kula. Politically, Sinaketa and Vakuta are rivals, and in olden days were periodically at war with one another.

Another district which forms a definite political and cultural unit is the large island of Kayleula, in the West. The inhabitants are fishermen, canoe-builders, and traders, and undertake big expeditions to the western d'Entrecasteaux islands, trading for betel nut, sago, pottery and turtle shell in exchange for their own industrial produce.

It has been necessary to give a somewhat detailed description of chieftainship and political divisions, as a firm grasp of the main, political institutions is essential to the understanding of the Kula. All departments of tribal life, religion, magic, economics are interwoven, but the *social organisation* of the tribe lies at the foundation of everything else. Thus it is essential to bear in mind that the Trobriands form one cultural unit, speaking the same language, having the same institutions, obeying the same laws and regulations, swayed by the same beliefs and conventions. The districts just enumerated, into which the Trobriands are subdivided, are distinct politically and not culturally ; that is, each of them comprises the same kind of natives, only obeying or at least acknowledging their own chief, having their own interests and pursuits, and in case of war each fighting their own fight.

Again, within each district, the several village communities have each a great deal of independence. A village community is represented by a headman, its members make their gardens in one block and under the guidance of their own garden magician ; they carry on their own feasts and ceremonial arrangements, mourn their dead in common, and perform, in remembrance of their departed ones, an endless series of food distributions. In all big affairs, whether of the district or of the tribe, members of a village community keep together, and act in one group.

VI

Right across the political and local divisions cut the totemic clans, each having a series of linked totems, with a bird as principal one.* The members of these four clans are scattered over the whole tribe of Boyowa, and in each village community, members of all four are to be found, and even in every house, there are at least two classes represented, since a husband must be of a different clan from his wife and children. There is a certain amount of solidarity within the clan, based on the very vague feeling of communal affinity to the totem birds and animals, but much more on the many social duties, such as the performance of certain ceremonies, especially the mortuary ones, which band the members of a clan together. But real solidarity obtains only between members of a sub-clan. A sub-clan is a local division of a clan, whose members claim common ancestry, and hence real identity of bodily substance, and also are attached to the locality where their ancestors emerged. It is to these sub-clans that the idea of a definite

* The discovery of the existence of " linked " totems, and the introduction of this term and conception are due to Professor C. G. Seligman. Op. cit., pp. 9, 11 ; see also Index.

rank attaches. One of the totemic clans, the Malasi, includes the most aristocratic sub-clan, the Tabalu, as well as the lowest one, the local division of the Malasi in Bwoytalu. A chief of the Tabalu feels very insulted if it is ever hinted that he is akin to one of the stingaree-eaters of the unclean village, although they are Malasi like himself. The principle of rank attached to totemic divisions is to be met only in Trobriand sociology ; it is entirely foreign to all the other Papuo-Melanesian tribes.

As regards kinship, the main thing to be remembered is that the natives are matrilineal, and that the succession of rank, membership in all the social groups, and the inheritance of possessions descend in the maternal line. The mother's brother is considered the real guardian of a boy, and there is a series of mutual duties and obligations, which establish a very close and important relation between the two. The real kinship, the real identity of substance is considered to exist only between a man and his mother's relations. In the first rank of these, his brothers and sisters are specially near to him. For his sister or sisters he has to work as soon as they are grown up and married. But, in spite of that, a most rigorous taboo exists between them, beginning quite early in life. No man would joke and talk freely in the presence of his sister, or even look at her. The slightest allusion to the sexual affairs, whether illicit or matrimonial, of a brother or sister in the presence of the other, is the deadliest insult and mortification. When a man approaches a group of people where his sister is talking, either she withdraws or he turns away.

The father's relation to his children is remarkable Physiological fatherhood* is unknown, and no tie of kinship or relationship is supposed to exist between father and child, except that between a mother's husband and the wife's child. Nevertheless, the father is by far the nearest and most affec-tionate friend of his children. In ever so many cases, I could observe that when a child, a young boy or girl, was in trouble or sick; when there was a question of some one exposing himself to difficulties or danger for the child's sake, it was

---

* See the Author's article, " Baloma, Spirits of the Dead," Part VII, J.R.A.I., 1917, where this statement has been substantiated with abundant evidence. Further information obtained during another expedition to the Trobriands, established by an additional wealth of detail the complete ignorance of physiological fatherhood.

always the father who worried, who would undergo all the hardships needed, and never the maternal uncle. This state of things is quite clearly recognised, and explicitly put into words by the natives. In matters of inheritance and handing over of possessions, a man always shows the tendency to do as much for his children as he is able, considering his obligations to his sister's family.

It is difficult, in one phrase or two, to epitomise the distinction between the two relations, that between a boy and his maternal uncle, and that between a son and a father. The best way to put it shortly might be by saying that the maternal uncle's position of close relation is regarded as right by law and usage, whereas the father's interest and affection for his children are due to sentiment, and to the intimate personal relations existing between them. He has watched the children grow up, he has assisted the mother in many of the small and tender cares given to an infant, he has carried the child about, and given it such education as it gets from watching the elder ones at work, and gradually joining in. In matters of inheritance, the father gives the children all that he can, and gives it freely and with pleasure ; the maternal uncle gives under the compulsion of custom what he cannot withhold and keep for his own children.

VII

A few more words must be said about some of the magico-religious ideas of the Trobrianders. The main thing that struck me in connection with their belief in the spirits of the dead, was that they are almost completely devoid of any fear of ghosts, of any of these uncanny feelings with which we face the idea of a possible return of the dead. All the fears and dreads of the natives are reserved for black magic, flying witches, malevolent disease-bringing beings, but above all for sorcerers and witches. The spirits migrate immediately after death to the island of Tuma, lying in the North-West of Boyowa, and there they exist for another span of time, underground, say some, on the surface of the earth, though invisible, say others. They return to visit their own villages once a year, and take part in the big annual feast, *milamala*, where they receive offerings. Sometimes, at this season, they show themselves to the living, who are, however, not alarmed by it, and in general the spirits do not influence human beings very much, for better or worse.* In a number of magical formulæ, there is an invocation of ancestral spirits, and they receive offerings in several rites. But there is nothing of the mutual interaction, of the intimate collaboration between man and spirit which are the essence of religious cult.

On the other hand, magic, the attempt of man to govern the forces of nature directly, by means of a special lore, is all-pervading, and all-important in the Trobriands.† Sorcery and garden magic have already been mentioned. Here it must suffice to add, that everything that vitally affects the native is accompanied by magic. All economic activities have their magic ; love, welfare of babies, talents and crafts, beauty and agility—all can be fostered or frustrated by magic. In dealing with the Kula—a pursuit of immense importance to the natives, and playing on almost all their social passions and ambitions—we shall meet with another system of magic, and we shall have then to go more into detail about the subject in general.

Disease, health, or death are also the result of magic or counter-magic. The Trobrianders have a very complex and very definite set of theoretical views on these matters. Good health is primarily of course the natural, normal state. Minor ills may be contracted by exposure, over-eating, over-strain, bad food, or other ordinary causes. Such ailments never last, and have never any really bad effects, nor are they of immediate danger. But, if a man sickens for any length of time, and his strength seems to be really sapped, then the evil forces are at work. By far the most prevalent form of black magic, is that of the *bwaga'u*, that is the black sorcerer, of whom there are a number in each district. Usually even in each village there are one or two men more or less dreaded as *bwaga'u*. To be one does not require any special initiation except the knowledge of the spells. To learn these—that is, to learn them in such a manner as to become an acknowledged

* See the Author's article " Baloma, Spirits of the Dead," quoted above.

† I am using the words *religion* and *magic* according to Sir James Frazer's distinction (see " Golden Bough," vol. I). Frazer's definition suits the Kiriwinian facts much better than any other one. In fact, although I started my field work convinced that the theories of religion and magic expounded in the " Golden Bough " are inadequate, I was forced by all my observations in New Guinea to come over to Frazer's position.

bwaga'u—can only be done by means of high payment, or in exceptional circumstances. Thus, a father will often " give " his sorcery to his son, always, however, without payment ; or a commoner will teach it to a man of rank, or a man to his sister's son. In these two latter cases a very high payment would have to be given. It is important as a characteristic of the kinship conditions of this people, that a man receives sorcery gratis from his father, who according to the traditional kinship system is no blood-relation, whereas he has to pay for it to his maternal uncle, whose natural heir he is.

When a man has acquired the black art, he applies it to a first victim, and this has always to be some one of his own family. It is a firm and definite belief among all the natives that if a man's sorcery has to be any good, it must first be practised on his mother or sister, or any of his maternal kindred. Such a matricidal act makes him a genuine *bwaga'u*. His art then can be practised on others, and becomes an established source of income.

The beliefs about sorcery are complex ; they differ according as to whether taken from a real sorcerer, or from an outsider ; and there are also evidently strata of belief, due perhaps to local variation, perhaps to superimposed versions. Here a short summary must suffice.

When a sorcerer wants to attack someone, the first step is to cast a light spell over his habitual haunts, a spell which will affect him with a slight illness and compel him to keep to his bed in his house, where he will try to cure himself by lying over a small fire and warming his body. His first ailment, called *kaynagola*, comprises pains in the body, such as (speaking from our point of view) would be brought about by rheumatism, general cold, influenza, or any incipient disease. When the victim is in bed, with a fire burning under him, and also, as a rule, one in the middle of the hut, the *bwaga'u* stealthily approaches the house. He is accompanied by a few night-birds, owls and night-jars, which keep guard over him, and he is surrounded by a halo of legendary terrors which make all natives shiver at the idea of meeting a sorcerer on such a nocturnal visit. He then tries to insert through the thatch wall a bunch of herbs impregnated with some deadly charm and tied to a long stick, and these he attempts to thrust into the fire over which the sick man is lying. If he succeeds, the fumes of the burnt leaves will be inhaled by the victim, whose name has been uttered in the charm, and he will be seized by one or other of the deadly diseases of which the natives have a long list, with a definite symptomatology, as well as a magical etiology. Thus the preliminary sorcery was necessary, in order to keep the victim to his house, in which spot only can the mortal magic be performed.

Of course, the sick man is on the defensive as well. First of all, his friends and relatives—this is one of the main duties of the wife's brothers—will keep a close watch over him, sitting with spears round the hut, and at all approaches to it. Often have I come across such vigils, when walking late at night through some village. Then, the services of some rival *bwaga'u* are invoked (for the art of killing and curing is always in the same hand), and he utters counter-spells, so that at times the efforts of the first sorcerer, even should he succeed in burning the herbs according to the dreaded *toginivayu* rite, are fruitless.

Should this be so, he resorts to the final and most fatal rite, that of the pointing-bone. Uttering powerful spells, the *bwaga'u* and one or two accomplices, boil some coco-nut oil in a small pot, far away in a dense patch of jungle. Leaves of herbs are soaked in the oil, and then wrapped round a sharp stingaree spine, or some similar pointed object, and the final incantation, most deadly of all, is chanted over it. Then the *bwaga'u* steals towards the village, catches sight of his victim, and hiding himself behind a shrub or house, points the magical dagger at him. In fact, he violently and viciously turns it round in the air, as if to stab the victim, and to twist and wrench the point in the wound. This, if carried out properly, and not counteracted by a still more powerful magician, will never fail to kill a man.

I have here summarised the bare outlines of the successive application of black magic as it is believed by sorcerer and outsider alike to be done, and to act in producing disease and death. There can be no doubt that the acts of sorcery are really carried out by those who believe themselves to possess the black powers. It is equally certain that the nervous strain of knowing one's life to be threatened by a *bwaga'u* is very great, and probably it is much worse when a man knows that behind the sorcerer stands the might of the chief, and this apprehension certainly contributes powerfully towards the success of black magic. On the other hand, a chief, if attacked, would have a good guard to protect him, and the most powerful wizards to back him up, and also the authority to deal directly with anyone suspected of plotting against him. Thus sorcery, which is one of the means of carrying on the established order, is in its turn strengthened by it.

If we remember that, as in all belief in the miraculous and supernatural, so also here, there is the loophole of counter-forces, and of the sorcery being incorrectly or inefficiently applied, spoilt by broken taboos, mispronounced spells, or what not ; again, that suggestion strongly influences the victim, and undermines his natural resistance ; further that all disease is invariably traced back to some sorcerer or other, who, whether it is true or not, often frankly admits his responsi-bility in order to enhance his reputation, there is then no difficulty in understanding why the belief in black magic flourishes, why no empirical evidence can ever dispel it, and why the sorcerer no less than the victim, has confidence in his own powers. At least, the difficulty is the same as in explaining many contemporary examples of results achieved by miracles and faith healing, such as Christian Science or Lourdes, or in any cure by prayers and devotion.

Although by far the most important of them all, the *bwaga'u* is only one among the beings who can cause disease and death. The often-mentioned flying-witches, who come always from the Southern half of the island, or from the East, from the islands of Kitava, Iwa, Gava, or Murua, are even more deadly. All very rapid and violent diseases, more especially such as show no direct, perceptible symptoms, are attributed to the *mulukwausi*, as they are called. Invisible, they fly through the air, and perch on trees, house-tops, and other high places. From there, they pounce upon a man or woman and remove and hide " the inside," that is, the lungs, heart and guts, or the brains and tongue. Such a victim will die within a day or two, unless another witch, called for the purpose and well paid, goes in search and restores the missing "inside." Of course, sometimes it is too late to do it, as the meal has been eaten in the meantime ! Then the victim must die.

Another powerful agency of death consists of the *tauva'u*, non-human though anthropomorphic beings, who cause all epidemic disease. When, at the end of the rainy season the new and unripe yams have come in, and dysentery rages, decimating the villages ; or, when in hot and damp years an infectious disease passes over the district, taking heavy toll, this means that the *tauva'u* have come from the South, and that, invisible, they march through the villages, rattling their lime gourds, and with their sword-clubs or sticks hitting their victims, who immediately sicken and die. The *tauva'u* can, at will, assume the shape of man or reptile. He appears then as a snake, or crab, or lizard, and you recognise him at once, for he will not run away from you, and he has as a rule a patch of some gaudy colour on his skin. It 'would be a fatal thing to kill such a reptile. On the contrary, it has to be taken up cautiously and treated as a chief ; that is to say, it is placed on a high platform, and some of the valuable tokens of wealth —a polished green stone blade, or a pair of arm-shells, or a necklace of spondylus shell beads must be put before it as an offering.

It is very interesting to note that the *tauva'u* are believed to come from the Northern coast of Normanby Island, from the district of Du'a'u, and more especially from a place called Sewatupa. This is the very place where, according to Dobuan belief and myth, their sorcery originated. Thus, what to the local tribes of the originating place is ordinary sorcery, practised by men, becomes, when looked at from a great distance, and from an alien tribe, a non-human agency, endowed with such super-normal powers as changing of shape, invisibility, and a direct, infallible method of inflicting death.

The *tauva'u* have sometimes sexual intercourse with women ; several present cases are on record, and such women who have a familar *tauva'u* become dangerous witches, though how they practise their witchcraft is not quite clear to the natives.

A much less dangerous being is the *tokway*, a wood sprite, living in trees and rocks, stealing crops from the field and from the yam-houses, and inflicting slight ailments. Some men in the past have acquired the knowledge of how to do this from the *tokway*, and have handed it on to their descendants.

So we see that, except for the very light ailments which pass quickly and easily, all disease is attributed to sorcery.

Even accidents are not believed to happen without cause. That this is the case also with drowning, we shall learn more in detail, when we have to follow the Trobrianders in their dangerous sea-trips. Natural death, caused by old age, is admittedly possible, but when I asked in several concrete cases, in which age was obviously the cause, why such and such a man died, I was always told that a *bwaga'u* was at the back of it. Only suicide and death in battle have a different place in the mind of the natives, and this is also confirmed by the belief that people killed in war, those that commit suicide, and those who are bewitched to death have, each class, their own way to the other world.

This sketch of Trobriand tribal life, belief and customs must suffice, and we shall still have opportunities of enlarging upon these subjects that most matter to us for the present study.

VIII

Two more districts remain to be mentioned, through which the Kula trade passes on its circuit, before it returns to the place from where we started. One of them is the Eastern portion of the Northern Massim, comprising the Marshall Bennett Islands (Kitava, Iwa, Gawa, Kwayawata), and Woodlark Island (Murua), with the small group of Nada Islands The other district is that of St. Aignan Island, called by the natives Masima, or Misima, with the smaller island Panayati.

Looking from the rocky shores of Boyowa, at its narrowest point, we can see over the white breakers on the fringing reef and over the sea, here always blue and limpid, the silhouette of a flat-topped, low rock, almost due East. This is Kitava. To the Trobrianders of the eastern districts, this island and those behind it are the promised land of the Kula, just as Dobu is to the natives of Southern Boyowa. But here, not as in the south, they have to deal with tribesmen who speak their own language, with dialectic differences only, and who have very much the same institutions and customs. In fact, the nearest island, Kitava, differs only very little from the Trobriands. Although the more distant islands, especially Murua, have a slightly different form of totemism, with hardly any idea of rank attached to the sub-clans, and consequently no chieftainship in the Trobriand sense, yet their social

organisation is also much the same as in the western province.*
I know the natives only from having seen them very frequently
and in great numbers in the Trobriands, where they come on
Kula expeditions. In Murua, however, I spent a short time
doing field work in the village of Dikoyas. In appearance,
dress, ornaments and manners, the natives are indistinguishable
from the Trobrianders. Their ideas and customs in matters of
sex, marriage, and kinship are, with variations in detail only,
the same as in Boyowa. In beliefs and mythology, they also
belong to the same culture.

To the Trobrianders, the Eastern islands are also the chief
home and stronghold of the dreaded *mulukwausi* (flying
witches) ; the land whence love magic came, originating in the
island of Iwa ; the distant shores towards which the mythical
hero Tudava sailed, performing many feats, till he finally
disappeared, no one knows where. The most recent version is
that he most likely finished his career in the white man's
country. To the eastern islands, says native belief, the
spirits of the dead, killed by sorcery, go round on a short visit
not stopping there, only floating through the air like clouds,
before they turn round to the north- west to Tuma.

From these islands, many important products come to
Boyowa (the Trobriands), but none half as important as the
tough, homogeneous green-stone, from which all their implements were made in the past, and of which the ceremonial axes
are made up till now. Some of these places are renowned for
their yam gardens, especially Kitava, and it is recognised that
the best carving in black ebony comes from there. The most
important point of difference between the natives of this
district and the Trobrianders, lies in the method of mortuary
distributions, to which subject we shall have to return in a
later part of the book, as it is closely connected with Kula.

From Murua (Woodlark Island) the Kula track curves over
to the South in two different branches, one direct to Tubetube,
and the other to Misima, and thence to Tubetube and Wari.
The district of Misima is almost entirely unknown to me—I
have only spoken once or twice with natives of this island,
and there is not, to my knowledge, any reliable published

* Compare Professor C. G. Seligman, op. cit., the parallel description of
the social institutions in the Trobriands, Marshall Bennetts, Woodlark Island
and the Loughlands, Chapters XLIX—LV.

information about that district, so we shall have to pass it
over with a very few words. This is, however, not so serious,
because it is certain, even from the little I know about them,
that the natives do not essentially differ from the other Massim.
They are totemic and matrilineal ; there is no chieftainship,
and the form of authority is the same as in the Southern
Massim.   Their sorcerers and witches resemble those of the
Southern Massim and Dobuans.   In industries, they specialise
in canoe-building, and in the small island of Panayati produce
the same type of craft as the natives of Gawa and Woodlark
Island, slightly different only from the Trobriand canoe.   In
the island of Misima, a very big supply of areca (betel) nut is
produced, as there is a custom of planting a number of these
nuts after a man's death.

The small islands of Tubetube and Wari, which form the
final link of the Kula, lie already within the district of the
Southern Massim.   In fact, the island of Tubetube is one of
the places studied in detail by Professor Seligman, and its
ethnographical description is one of three parallel monographs
which form the division of the Southern Massim in the treatise
so often quoted.

Finally, I want to point out again that the descriptions
of the various Kula districts given in this and in the
previous chapter, though accurate in every detail, are
not meant to be an exhaustive ethnographic sketch
of the tribes.   They have been given with a few light
touches in order to produce a vivid and so-to-speak personal
impression of the various type of natives, and countries and
of cultures.   If I have succeeded in giving a physiognomy to
each of the various tribes, to the Trobrianders, to the
Amphlettans, the Dobuans, and the Southern Massim, and in
arousing some interest in them, the main purpose has been
achieved, and the necessary ethnographic background for the
Kula has been supplied.

PLATE XVII

TWO MEN WEARING ARMSHELLS

This illustrates the manner in which the armshells are usually adorned with beads, pendants and ribbons of dried pandanus. I do not remember having seen more than once or twice men wearing armshells, and then they were in full dancing array. (See p. 81.)

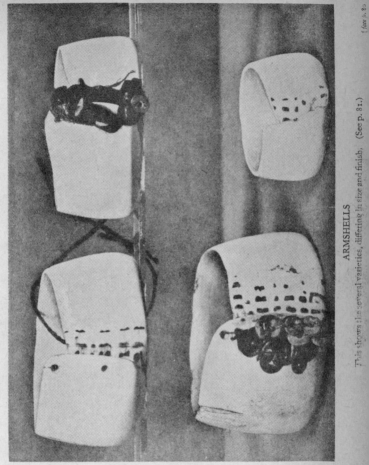

Plate XVI

ARMSHELLS

This shows the several varieties, differing in size and finish. (See p. 81.)

(See p. 81.)

PLATE XVIII

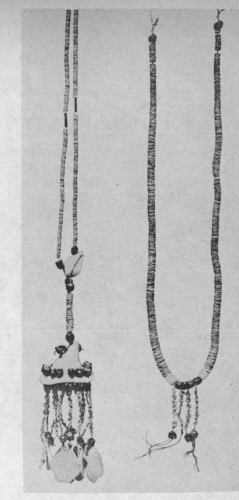

TWO NECKLACES, MADE OF RED SPONDYLUS
DISCS

On the left, the *soulava*, or *bagi*, the real Kula article. On
the right, the *katudababile* (or *samakupa*, as it is called
among the Southern Massim), made of bigger discs,
manufactured in the villages of Sinaketa and Vakuta
(Trobriand Islands). This latter article does not play any
important part in the Kula. (See p. 81. Ch. XIV,
Div. II : Ch. XV, Divs. II and III.)

TWO WOMEN ADORNED WITH NECKLACES

This shows the manner in which a *soulava* is worn, when used as a decoration.   (See p. 82.)

" once in the Kula, always in the Kula," and a partnership between two men is a permanent and lifelong affair. Again, any given *mwali* or *soulava* may always be found travelling and changing hands, and there is no question of its ever settling down, so that the principle " once in the Kula, always in the Kula " applies also to the valuables themselves.

The ceremonial exchange of the two articles is the main, the fundamental aspect of the Kula. But associated with it, and done under its cover, we find a great number of secondary activities and features. Thus, side by side with the ritual exchange of arm-shells and necklaces, the natives carry on ordinary trade, bartering from one island to another a great number of utilities, often unprocurable in the district to which they are imported, and indispensable there. Further, there are other activities, preliminary to the Kula, or associated with it, such as the building of sea-going canoes for the expeditions, certain big forms of mortuary ceremonies, and preparatory taboos.

The Kula is thus an extremely big and complex institution, both in its geographical extent, and in the manifoldness of its component pursuits. It welds together a considerable number of tribes, and it embraces a vast complex of activities, interconnected, and playing into one another, so as to form one organic whole.

Yet it must be remembered that what appears to us an extensive, complicated, and yet well ordered institution is the outcome of ever so many doings and pursuits, carried on by savages, who have no laws or aims or charters definitely laid down. They have no knowledge of the *total outline* of any of their social structure. They know their own motives, know the purpose of individual actions and the rules which apply to them, but how, out of these, the whole collective institution shapes, this is beyond their mental range. Not even the most intelligent native has any clear idea of the Kula as a big, organised social construction, still less of its sociological function and implications. If you were to ask him what the Kula is, he would answer by giving a few details, most likely by giving his personal experiences and subjective views on the Kula, but nothing approaching the definition just given here. Not even a partial coherent account could be obtained. For the integral picture does not exist in his mind ; he is in it, and cannot see the whole from the outside.

The integration of all the details observed, the achievement of a sociological synthesis of all the various, relevant symptoms, is the task of the Ethnographer. First of all, he has to find out that certain activities, which at first sight might appear incoherent and not correlated, have a meaning. He then has to find out what is constant and relevant in these activities, and what accidental and inessential, that is, to find out the laws and rules of all the transactions. Again, the Ethnographer has to *construct* the picture of the big institution, very much as the physicist constructs his theory from the experimental data, which always have been within reach of everybody, but which needed a consistent interpretation. I have touched on this point of method in the Introduction (Divisions V and VI), but I have repeated it here, as it is necessary to grasp it clearly in order not to lose the right perspective of conditions as they really exist among the natives.

II

In giving the above abstract and concise definition, I had to reverse the order of research, as this is done in ethnographic field-work, where the most generalised inferences are obtained as the result of long inquiries and laborious inductions. The general definition of the Kula will serve as a sort of plan or diagram in our further concrete and detailed descriptions. And this is the more necessary as the Kula is concerned with the exchange of wealth and utilities, and therefore it is an economic institution, and there is no other aspect of primitive life where our knowledge is more scanty and our understanding more superficial than in Economics. Hence misconception is rampant, and it is necessary to clear the ground when approaching any economic subject.

Thus in the Introduction we called the Kula a " form of trade," and we ranged it alongside other systems of barter. This is quite correct, if we give the word " *trade* " a sufficiently wide interpretation, and mean by it any exchange of goods. But the word " trade " is used in current Ethnography and economic literature with so many different implications that a whole lot of misleading, preconceived ideas have to be brushed aside in order to grasp the facts correctly. Thus the *a priori* current notion of primitive trade would be that of an exchange of indispensable or useful articles, done without much ceremony

or regulation, under stress of dearth or need, in spasmodic, irregular intervals—and this done either by direct barter, everyone looking out sharply not to be done out of his due, or, if the savages were too timid and distrustful to face one another, by some customary arrangement, securing by means of heavy penalties compliance in the obligations incurred or imposed *
Waiving for the present the question how far this conception is valid or not in general—in my opinion it is quite misleading —we have to realise clearly that the Kula contradicts in almost every point the above definition of " savage trade." It shows us primitive exchange in an entirely different light.

The Kula is not a surreptitious and precarious form of exchange. It is, quite on the contrary, rooted in myth, backed by traditional law, and surrounded with magical rites. All its main transactions are public and ceremonial, and carried out according to definite rules. It is not done on the spur of the moment, but happens periodically, at dates settled in advance, and it is carried on along definite trade routes, which must lead to fixed trysting places. Sociologically, though transacted between tribes differing in language, culture, and probably even in race, it is based on a fixed and permanent status, on a partnership which binds into couples some thousands of individuals. This partnership is a lifelong relationship, it implies various mutual duties and privileges, and constitutes a type of inter-tribal relationship on an enormous scale. As to the economic mechanism of the transactions, this is based on a specific form of credit, which implies a high degree of mutual

* By " current view," I mean such as is to be found in text-books and in passing remarks, scattered through economic and ethnological literature. As a matter of fact, Economics is a subject very seldom touched upon either in theoretical works on Ethnology, or in accounts of field-work. I have enlarged on this deficiency in the article on " Primitive Economics," published in the *Economic Journal*, March, 1921.

The best analysis of the problem of savage economy is to be found, in spite of its many shortcomings, in K. Bücher's " Industrial Evolution," English Translation, 1901. On primitive trade, however, his views are inadequate. In accordance with his general view that savages have no national economy, he maintains that any spread of goods among natives is achieved by non-economic means, such as robbery, tributes and gifts. The information contained in the present volume is incompatible with Bücher's views, nor could he have maintained them had he been acquainted with Barton's description of the Hiri (contained in Seligman's " Melanesians.")

A summary of the research done on Primitive Economics, showing incidentally, how little real, sound work has been accomplished, will be found in Pater W. Kopper's " Die Ethnologische Wirtschaftsforschung " in *Anthropos*, X—XI, 1915-16, pp. 611-651, and 971-1079. The article is very useful, where the author summarises the views of others.

trust and commercial honour—and this refers also to the subsidiary, minor trade, which accompanies the Kula proper. Finally, the Kula is not done under stress of any need, since its main aim is to exchange articles which are of no practical use.

From the concise definition of Kula given at the beginning of this chapter, we see that in its final essence, divested of all trappings and accessories, it is a very simple affair, which at first sight might even appear tame and unromantic. After all, it only consists of an exchange, interminably repeated, of two articles intended for ornamentation, but not even used for that to any extent. Yet this simple action—this passing from hand to hand of two meaningless and quite useless objects— has somehow succeeded in becoming the foundation of a big inter-tribal institution, in being associated with ever so many other activities, Myth, magic and tradition have built up around it definite ritual and ceremonial forms, have given it a halo of romance and value in the minds of the natives, have indeed created a passion in their hearts for this simple exchange.

The definition of the Kula must now be amplified, and we must describe one after the other its fundamental character- istics and main rules, so that it may be clearly grasped by what mechanism the mere exchange of two articles results in an institution so vast, complex, and deeply rooted.

III

First of all, a few words must be said about the two principal objects of exchange, the arm-shells (*mwali*) and the necklaces (*soulava*). The arm-shells are obtained by breaking off the top and the narrow end of a big, cone-shaped shell (*Conus millepunctatus*), and then polishing up the remaining ring. These bracelets are highly coveted by all the Papuo- Melanesians of New Guinea, and they spread even into the pure Papuan district of the Gulf.* The manner of wearing the arm-shells is illustrated by Plate XVII, where the men have put them on on purpose to be photographed.

The use of the small discs of red spondylus shell, out of which the *soulava* are made, is also of a very wide diffusion.

---

* Professor C. G. Seligman, op. cit., p. 93, states that arm-shells, *toea*, as they are called by the Motu, are traded from the Port Moresby district westward to the Gulf of Papua. Among the Motu and Koita, near Port Moresby, they are highly valued, and nowadays attain very high prices, up to £30, much more than is paid for the same article among the Massim.

There is a manufacturing centre of them in one of the villages in Port Moresby, and also in several places in Eastern New Guinea, notably in Rossell Island, and in the Trobriands. I have said " *use* " on purpose here, because these small beads, each of them a flat, round disc with a hole in the centre, coloured anything from muddy brown to carmine red, are employed in various ways for ornamentation. They are most generally used as part of earrings, made of rings of turtle shell, which are attached to the ear lobe, and from which hang a cluster of the shell discs. These earrings are very much worn, and, especially among the Massim, you see them on the ears of every second man or woman, while others are satisfied with turtle shell alone, unornamented with the shell discs. Another everyday ornament, frequently met with and worn, especially by young girls and boys, consists of a short necklace, just encircling the neck, made of the red spondylus discs, with one or more cowrie shell pendants. These shell discs can be, and often are, used in the make-up of the various classes of the more elaborate ornaments, worn on festive occasions only. Here, however, we are more especially concerned with the very long necklaces, measuring from two to five metres, made of spondylus discs, of which there are two main varieties, one, much the finer, with a big shell pendant, the other made of bigger discs, and with a few cowrie shells or black banana seeds in the centre (see Plate XVIII).

The arm-shells on the one hand, and the long spondylus shell strings on the other, the two main Kula articles, are primarily ornaments. As such, they are used with the most elaborate dancing dress only, and on very festive occasions such as big ceremonial dances, great feasts, and big gatherings, where several villages are represented, as can be seen in Plate VI. Never could they be used as everyday ornaments, nor on occasions of minor importance, such as a small dance in the village, a harvest gathering, a love-making expedition, when facial painting, floral decoration and smaller though not quite everyday ornaments are worn (see Plates XII and XIII). But even though usable and sometimes used, this is not the main function of these articles. Thus, a chief may have several shell strings in his possession, and a few arm-shells. Supposing that a big dance is held in his or in a neighbouring village, he will not put on his ornaments himself if he goes to assist at it, unless he intends to dance and decorate himself, but any of his relatives, his children or his friends and even vassals, can have the use of them for the asking. If you go to a feast or a dance where there are a number of men wearing such ornaments, and ask anyone of them at random to whom it belongs, the chances are that more than half of them will answer that they themselves are not the owners, but that they had the articles lent to them. These objects are not owned in order to be used ; the privilege of decorating oneself with them is not the real aim of possession.

Indeed—and this is more significant—by far the greater number of the arm-shells, easily ninety per cent., are of too small a size to be worn even by young boys and girls. A few are so big and valuable that they would not be worn at all, except once in a decade by a very important man on a very festive day. Though all the shell-strings can be worn, some of them are again considered too valuable, and are cumbersome for frequent use, and would be worn on very exceptional occasions only.

This negative description leaves us with the questions : why, then, are these objects valued, what purpose do they serve ? The full answer to this question will emerge out of the whole story contained in the following chapters, but an approximate idea must be given at once. As it is always better to approach the unknown through the known, let us consider for a moment whether among ourselves we have not some type of objects which play a similar rôle and which are used and possessed in the same manner. When, after a six years' absence in the South Seas and Australia, I returned to Europe and did my first bit of sight-seeing in Edinburgh Castle, I was shown the Crown jewels. The keeper told many stories of how they were worn by this or that king or queen on such and such occasion, of how some of them had been taken over to London, to the great and just indignation of the whole Scottish nation, how they were restored, and how now everyone can be pleased, since they are safe under lock and key, and no one can touch them. As I was looking at them and thinking how ugly, useless, ungainly, even tawdry they were, I had the feeling that something similar had been told to me of late, and that I had seen many other objects of this sort, which made a similar impression on me.

And then arose before me the vision of a native village on coral soil, and a small, rickety platform temporarily erected under a pandanus thatch, surrounded by a number of brown, naked men, and one of them showing me long, thin red strings, and big, white, worn-out objects, clumsy to sight and greasy to touch. With reverence he also would name them, and tell their history, and by whom and when they were worn, and how they changed hands, and how their temporary possession was a great sign of the importance and glory of the village. The analogy between the European and the Trobriand *vaygu'a* (valuables) must be delimited with more precision. The Crown Jewels, in fact, any heirlooms too valuable and too cumbersome to be worn, represent the same type as *vaygu'a* in that they are merely possessed for the sake of possession itself, and the ownership of them with the ensuing renown is the main source of their value. Also both heirlooms and *vaygu'a* are cherished because of the historical sentiment which surrounds them. However ugly, useless, and—according to current standards—valueless an object may be, if it has figured in historical scenes and passed through the hands of historic persons, and is therefore an unfailing vehicle of important sentimental associations, it cannot but be precious to us. This historic sentimentalism, which indeed has a large share in our general interest in studies of past events, exists also in the South Seas. Every really good Kula article has its individual name, round each there is a sort of history and romance in the traditions of the natives. Crown jewels or heirlooms are insignia of rank and symbols of wealth respectively, and in olden days with us, and in New Guinea up till a few years ago, both rank and wealth went together. The main point of difference is that the Kula goods are only in possession for a time, whereas the European treasure must be permanently owned in order to have full value.

Taking a broader, ethnological view of the question, we may class the Kula valuables among the many " ceremonial " objects of wealth ; enormous, carved and decorated weapons, stone implements, articles of domestic and industrial nature, too well decorated and too clumsy for use. Such things are usually called " ceremonial," but this word seems to cover a great number of meanings and much that has no meaning at all. In fact, very often, especially on museum labels, an article is called " ceremonial " simply because nothing is known about its uses and general nature. Speaking only about museum exhibits from New Guinea, I can say that many so-called ceremonial objects are nothing but simply overgrown objects of use, which preciousness of material and amount of labour expended have transformed into reservoirs of condensed economic value. Again, others are used on festive occasions, but play no part whatever in rites and ceremonies, and serve for decoration only, and these might be called *objects of parade* (comp. Chap VI, Div. I). Finally, a number of these articles function actually as instruments of a magical or religious rite, and belong to the intrinsic apparatus of a ceremony. Such and such only could be correctly called *ceremonial*. During the *So'i* feasts among the Southern Massim, women carrying polished axe blades in fine carved handles, accompany with a rythmic step to the beat of drums, the entry of the pigs and mango saplings into the village (see Plates V and VI). As this is part of the ceremony and the axes are an indispensable accessory, their use in this case can be legitimately called " ceremonial." Again, in certain magical ceremonies in the Trobriands, the *towosi* (garden magician) has to carry a mounted axe blade on his shoulders, and with it he delivers a ritual blow at a *kamkokola* structure (see Plate LIX; compare Chapter II, Division IV).

The *vaygu'a*—the Kula valuables—in one of their aspects are overgrown objects of use. They are also, however, *ceremonial* objects in the narrow and correct sense of the word. This will become clear after perusal of the following pages, and to this point we shall return in the last chapter.

It must be kept in mind that here we are trying to obtain a clear and vivid idea of what the Kula valuables are to the natives, and not to give a detailed and circumstantial description of them, nor to define them with precision. The comparison with the European heirlooms or Crown jewels was given in order to show that this type of ownership is not entirely a fantastic South Sea custom, untranslatable into our ideas. For—and this is a point I want to stress—the comparison I have made is not based on purely external, superficial similarity. The psychological and sociological forces at work are the same, it is really the same mental attitude which makes us value our heirlooms, and makes the natives in New Guinea value their *vaygu'a*.

IV

The exchange of these two classes of *vaygu'a*, of the arm-shells and the necklaces, constitutes the main act of the Kula. This exchange is not done freely, right and left, as opportunity offers, and where the whim leads. It is subject indeed to strict limitations and regulations. One of these refers to the sociology of the exchange, and entails that Kula transactions can be done only between partners. A man who is in the Kula —for not everyone within its district is entitled to carry it on —has only a limited number of people with whom he deals This partnership is entered upon in a definite manner, under fulfilment of certain formalities, and it constitutes a life-long relationship. The number of partners a man has varies with his rank and importance. A commoner in the Trobriands would have a few partners only, whereas a chief would number hundreds of them. There is no special social mechanism to limit the partnership of some people and extend that of the others, but a man would naturally know to what number of partners he was entitled by his rank and position. And there would be always the example of his immediate ancestors to guide him. In other tribes, where the distinction of rank is not so pronounced, an old man of standing, or a headman of a hamlet or village would also have hundreds of Kula associates, whereas a man of minor importance would have but few.

Two Kula partners have to *kula* with one another, and exchange other gifts incidentally ; they behave as friends, and have a number of mutual duties and obligations, which vary with the distance between their villages and with their reciprocal status. An average man has a few partners near by, as a rule his relations-in-law or his friends, and with these partners, he is generally on very friendly terms. The Kula partnership is one of the special bonds which unite two men into one of the standing relations of mutual exchange of gifts and services so characteristic of these natives. Again, the average man will have one or two chiefs in his or in the neighbouring districts with whom he *kulas*. In such a case, he would be bound to assist and serve them in various ways, and to offer them the pick of his *vaygu'a* when he gets a fresh supply. On the other hand he would expect them to be specially liberal to him.

The overseas partner is, on the other hand, a host, patron and ally in a land of danger and insecurity. Nowadays, though the feeling of danger still persists, and natives never feel safe and comfortable in a strange district, this danger is rather felt as a magical one, and it is more the fear of foreign sorcery that besets them. In olden days, more tangible dangers were apprehended, and the partner was the main guarantee of safety. He also provides with food, gives presents, and his house, though never used to sleep in, is the place in which to foregather while in the village. Thus the Kula partnership provides every man within its ring with a few friends near at hand, and with some friendly allies in the far-away, dangerous, foreign districts. These are the only people with whom he can *kula*, but, of course, amongst all his partners, he is free to choose to which one he will offer which object.

Let us now try to cast a broad glance at the cumulative effects of the rules of partnership. We see that all around the ring of Kula there is a network of relationships, and that naturally the whole forms one interwoven fabric. Men living at hundreds of miles' sailing distance from one another are bound together by direct or intermediate partnership, exchange with each other, know of each other, and on certain occasions meet in a large intertribal gathering (Plate XX). Objects given by one, in time reach some very distant indirect partner or other, and not only Kula objects, but various articles of domestic use and minor gifts. It is easy to see that in the long run, not only objects of material culture, but also customs, songs, art motives and general cultural influences travel along the Kula route. It is a vast, inter-tribal net of relationships, a big institution, consisting of thousands of men, all bound together by one common passion for Kula exchange, and secondarily, by many minor ties and interests.

Returning again to the personal aspect of the Kula, let us take a concrete example, that of *an average man* who lives, let us assume, in the village of Sinaketa, an important Kula centre in the Southern Trobriands. He has a few partners, near and far, but they again fall into categories, those who give him arm-shells, and those who give him necklaces. For it is

naturally an invariable rule of the Kula that arm-shells and
necklaces are never received from the same man, since they must
travel in different directions. If one partner gives the armshells, and I return to him a necklace, all future operations
have to be of the same type. More than that, the nature of
the operation between me, the man of Sinaketa, and my
partner, is determined by our relative positions with regard to
the points of the compass. Thus I, in Sinaketa, would receive
from the North and East only arm-shells ; from the South and
West, necklaces are given to me. If I have a near partner
next door to me, if his abode is North or East of mine, he will
always be giving me arm-shells and receiving necklaces from
me. If, at a later time he were to shift his residence within the
village, the old relationship would obtain, but if he became a
member of another village community on the other side of me
the relationship would be reversed. The partners in villages
to the North of Sinaketa, in the district of Luba, Kulumata, or
Kiriwina all supply me with arm-shells. These I hand over to
my partners in the South, and receive from them necklaces.
The South in this case means the southern districts of Boyowa,
as well as the Amphletts and Dobu.

Thus every man has to obey definite rules as to the geographical direction of his transactions. At any point in the
Kula ring, if we imagine him turned towards the centre of the
circle, he receives the arm-shells with his left hand, and the
necklaces with his right, and then hands them both on. In
other words, he constantly passes the arm-shells from left to
right, and the necklaces from right to left.

Applying this rule of personal conduct to the whole Kula
ring, we can see at once what the aggregate result is. The sum
total of exchanges will not result in an aimless shifting of the
two classes of article, in a fortuitous come and go of the armshells and necklaces. Two continuous streams will constantly
flow on, the one of necklaces following the hands of a clock,
and the other, composed of the arm-shells, in the opposite
direction. We see thus that it is quite correct to speak of the
circular exchange of the Kula, of a ring or circuit of moving
articles (comp. Map V). On this ring, all the villages are
placed in a definitely fixed position with regard to one another,
so that one is always on either the arm-shell or on the necklace
side of the other.

Now we pass to another rule of the Kula, of the greatest importance. As just explained " the armshells and shell-strings always travel in their own respective directions on the ring, and they are never, under any circumstances, traded back in the wrong direction. Also, they never stop. It seems almost incredible at first, but it is the fact, nevertheless, that no one ever keeps any of the Kula valuables for any length of time. Indeed, in the whole of the Trobriands there are perhaps only one or two specially fine armshells and shell-necklaces permanently owned as heirlooms, and these are set apart as a special class, and are once and for all out of the Kula. ' Ownership,' therefore, in Kula, is quite a special economic relation. A man who is in the Kula never keeps any article for longer than, say, a year or two. Even this exposes him to the reproach of being niggardly, and certain districts have the bad reputation of being ' slow ' and ' hard ' in the Kula. On the other hand, each man has an enormous number of articles passing through his hands during his life time, of which he enjoys a temporary possession, and which he keeps in trust for a time. This possession hardly ever makes him use the articles, and he remains under the obligation soon again to hand them on to one of his partners. But the temporary ownership allows him to draw a great deal of renown, to exhibit his article, to tell how he obtained it, and to plan to whom he is going to give it. And all this forms one of the favourite subjects of tribal conversation and gossip, in which the feats and the glory in Kula of chiefs or commoners are constantly discussed and re-discussed."* Thus every article moves in one direction only, never comes back, never permanently stops, and takes as a rule some two to ten years to make the round.

This feature of the Kula is perhaps its most remarkable one, since it creates a new type of ownership, and places the two Kula articles in a class of their own. Here we can return to the comparison drawn between the *vaygu'a* (Kiriwinian valuables) and the European heirlooms. This comparison broke down on one point : in the European objects of this class, permanent ownership, lasting association with the hereditary dignity or rank or with a family, is one of its main features.

* This and the following quotations are from the Author's preliminary article on the Kula in *Man*, July, 1920. Article number 51, p. 100.

In this the Kula articles differ from heirlooms, but resemble another type of valued object, that is, trophies, gauges of superiority, sporting cups, objects which are kept for a time only by the winning party, whether a group or an individual. Though held only in trust, only for a period, though never used in any utilitarian way, yet the holders get from them a special type of pleasure by the mere fact of owning them, of being entitled to them. Here again, it is not only a superficial, external resemblance, but very much the same mental attitude, favoured by similar social arrangements. The resemblance goes so far that in the Kula there exists also the element of pride in merit, an element which forms the main ingredient in the pleasure felt by a man or group holding a trophy. Success in Kula is ascribed to special, personal power, due mainly to magic, and men are very proud of it. Again, the whole community glories in a specially fine Kula trophy, obtained by one of its members.

All the rules so far enumerated—looking at them from the individual point of view—limit the social range and the direction of the transactions as well as the duration of ownership of the articles. Looking at them from the point of view of their integral effect, they shape the general outline of the Kula, give it the character of the double-closed circuit. Now a few words must be said about the nature of each individual transaction, in so far as its *commercial technicalities* are concerned. Here very definite rules also obtain.

V

The main principle underlying the regulations of actual exchange is that the Kula consists in the bestowing of a ceremonial gift, which has to be repaid by an equivalent counter-gift after a lapse of time, be it a few hours or even minutes, though sometimes as much as a year or more may elapse between payments.* But it can never be exchanged from hand to hand, with the equivalence between the two objects discussed, bargained about and computed. The decorum of the Kula transaction is strictly kept, and highly

---

* In order not to be guilty of inconsistency in using loosely the word " ceremonial " I shall define it briefly. I shall call an action ceremonial, if it is (1) public ; (2) carried on under observance of definite formalities ; (3) if it has sociological, religious, or magical import, and carries with it obligations.

valued.   The natives sharply distinguish it from barter, which they practise extensively, of which they have a clear idea, and for which they have a settled term—in Kiriwinian : *gimwali*. Often, when criticising an incorrect, too hasty, or indecorous procedure of Kula, they will say : " He conducts his Kula as if it were *gimwali*."

The second very important principle is that the equivalence of the counter-gift is left to the giver, and it cannot be enforced by any kind of coercion.   A partner who has received a Kula gift is expected to give back fair and full value, that is, to give as good an arm-shell as the necklace he receives, or vice versa.   Again, a very fine article must be replaced by one of equivalent value, and not by several minor ones, though intermediate gifts may be given to mark time before the real repayment takes place.

If the article given as counter-gift is not equivalent, the recipient will be disappointed and angry, but he has no direct means of redress, no means of coercing his partner, or of putting an end to the whole transaction.   What then are the forces at work which keep the partners to the terms of the bargain ?   Here we come up against a very important feature of the native's mental attitude towards wealth and value. The great misconception of attributing to the savage a pure economic nature, might lead us to reason incorrectly thus : " The passion of acquiring, the loathing to lose or give away, is the fundamental and most primitive element in man's attitude to wealth.   In primitive man, this primitive characteristic will appear in its simplest and purest form. *Grab and never let go* will be the guiding principle of his life."* The fundamental error in this reasoning is that it assumes that " primitive man," as represented by the present-day savage, lives, at least in economic matters, untrammelled by conventions and social restrictions.   Quite the reverse is the case   Although, like every human being, the Kula native loves to possess and therefore desires to acquire and dreads to lose, the social code of rules, with regard to give and take by far overrides his natural acquisitive tendency.

* This is not a fanciful construction of what an erroneous opinion might be, for I could give actual examples proving that such opinions have been set forth, but as I am not giving here a criticism of existing theories of Primitive Economics, I do not want to overload this chapter with quotations.

PLATE XX

A KULU GATHERING ON THE BEACH OF SINAKETA

Along about half a mile's length of shore, over eighty canoes are beached or moored, and in the village, on the beach, and in the surrounding country there are assembled some two thousand natives from several districts, ranging from Kitava to Dobu. This illustrates the manner in which the Kula brings together large numbers of people belonging to different cultures ; in this case, that of Kitava, Boyowa, the Amphletts and Dobu. (See p. 92, and Ch. XVI, Div. II.)

PLATE XXI

A MASAWA CANOE

Nigada Bu'a, the sea-going canoe of Omarakana, showing general form, ornamentation of prowboards, the leaf-shaped paddles and the form of the out-rigger log. (See p. 106, also next Chapter.)

PLATE XXII

PUTTING A CANOE INTO ITS HANGAR

The canoes on the East shores of Boyowa are seldom used, and when idle are housed in shelters, built very much like ordinary huts, only much larger. (See p. 106.)

PLATE XXIII

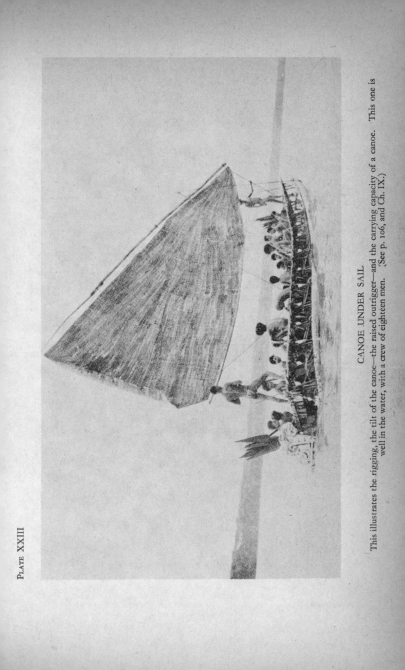

CANOE UNDER SAIL.

This illustrates the rigging, the tilt of the canoe—the raised outrigger—and the carrying capacity of a canoe.   This one is
well in the water, with a crew of eighteen men.   (See p. 106, and Ch. IX.)

PLATE XXIV

FISHING CANOE (KALIPOULO)

Above the profile of a canoe, shows the outline of the dug-out, the relative width of the gunwale planks and the hull, and the general shape of the canoe. The bottom picture shows the attachment of the outrigger to the hull, the prow, the prow-boards and the platform. (See p. 106.)

This social code, such as we find it among the natives of the Kula is, however, far from weakening the natural desirability of possession ; on the contrary, it lays down that to possess is to be great, and that wealth is the indispensable appanage of social rank and attribute of personal virtue. But the important point is that with them to possess is to give —and here the natives differ from us notably. A man who owns a thing is naturally expected to share it, to distribute it, to be its trustee and dispenser. And the higher the rank the greater the obligation. A chief will naturally be expected to give food to any stranger, visitor, even loiterer from another end of the village. He will be expected to share any of the betel-nut or tobacco he has about him. So that a man of rank will have to hide away any surplus of these articles which he wants to preserve for his further use. In the Eastern end of New Guinea a type of large basket, with three layers, manufactured in the Trobriands, was specially popular among people of consequence, because one could hide away one's small treasures in the lower compartments. Thus the main symptom of being powerful is to be wealthy, and of wealth is to be generous. Meanness, indeed, is the most despised vice, and the only thing about which the natives have strong moral views, while generosity is the essence of goodness.

This moral injunction and ensuing habit of generosity, superficially observed and misinterpreted, is responsible for another wide-spread misconception, that of the *primitive communism of savages*. This, quite as much as the diametrically opposed figment of the acquisitive and ruthlessly tenacious native, is definitely erroneous, and this will be seen with sufficient clearness in the following chapters.

Thus the fundamental principle of the natives' moral code in this matter makes a man do his fair share in Kula transaction and the more important he is, the more will he desire to shine by his generosity. *Noblesse oblige* is in reality the social norm regulating their conduct This does not mean that people are always satisfied, and that there are no squabbles about the transactions, no resentments and even feuds. It is obvious that, however much a man may want to give a good equivalent for the object received, he may not be able to do so. And then, as there is always a keen competition to be the most generous giver, a man who has received less than he gave will not keep his grievance to himself, but will brag about his own generosity and compare it to his partner's meanness ; the other resents it, and the quarrel is ready to break out. But it is very important to realise that there is no actual haggling, no tendency to do a man out of his share. The giver is quite as keen as the receiver that the gift should be generous, though for different reasons. Then, of course, there is the important consideration that a man who is fair and generous in the Kula will attract a larger stream to himself than a mean one.

The two main principles, namely, first that the Kula is a gift repaid after an interval of time by a counter-gift, and not a bartering ; and second, that the equivalent rests with the giver, and cannot be enforced, nor can there be any haggling or going back on the exchange—these underlie all the transactions. A concrete outline of how they are carried on, will give a sufficient preliminary idea.

" Let us suppose that I, a Sinaketa man, am in possession of a pair of big armshells. An overseas expedition from Dobu in the d'Entrecasteaux Archipelago, arrives at my village. Blowing a conch shell, I take my armshell pair and I offer it to my overseas partner, with some such words as ' This is a *vaga* (opening gift)—in due time, thou returnest to me a big *soulava* (necklace) for it ! ' Next year, when I visit my partner's village, he either is in possession of an equivalent necklace, and this he gives to me as *yotile* (return gift), or he has not a necklace good enough to repay my last gift. In this case he will give me a small necklace—avowedly not equivalent to my gift—and he will give it to me as *basi* (intermediary gift). This means that the main gift has to be repaid on a future occasion, and the *basi* is given in token of good faith—but it, in turn, must be repaid by me in the meantime by a gift of small arm-shells. The final gift, which will be given to me to clinch the whole transaction, would then be called *kudu* (clinching gift) in contrast to *basi* " (loc. cit., p. 99).

Although haggling and bargaining are completely ruled out of the Kula, there are customary and regulated ways of bidding for a piece of *vaygu'a* known to be in the possession of one's partner. This is done by the offer of what we shall call solicitary gifts, of which there are several types. " If I, an inhabitant of Sinaketa, happen to be in possession of a pair of arm-shells more than usually good, the fame of it spreads, for it must be remembered that each one of the first-class arm-shells and necklaces has a personal name and a history of its own, and as they circulate around the big ring of the Kula, they are all well known, and their appearance in a given district always creates a sensation. Now, all my partners—whether from overseas or from within the district—compete for the favour of receiving this particular article of mine, and those who are specially keen try to obtain it by giving me *pokala* (offerings) and *kaributu* (solicitary gifts). The former (*pokala*) consist as a rule of pigs, especially fine bananas, and yams or taro ; the latter (*kaributu*) are of greater value : the valuable, large axe-blades (called *beku*), or lime spoons of whale bone are given " (*loc. cit*, p. 100). The further complication in the repayment of these solicitary gifts and a few more technicalities and technical expressions connected herewith will be given later on in Chapter IV.

VI

I have enumerated the main rules of the Kula in a manner sufficient for a preliminary definition, and now a few words must be said about the associated activities and secondary aspects of the Kula. If we realise that at times the exchange has to take place between districts divided by dangerous seas, over which a great number of people have to travel by sail, and do so keeping to appointed dates, it becomes clear at once that considerable preparations are necessary to carry out the expedition. Many preliminary activities are intimately associated with the Kula. Such are, particularly, the building of canoes, preparation of the outfit, the provisioning of the expedition, the fixing of dates and social organisation of the enterprise. All these are subsidiary to the Kula, and as they are carried on in pursuit of it, and form one connected series, a description of the Kula must embrace an account of these preliminary activities. The detailed account of canoe building, of the ceremonial attached to it, of the incidental magical rites, of the launching and trial run, of the associated customs which aim at preparing the outfit—all this will be described in detail in the next few chapters.

Another important pursuit inextricably bound up with the Kula, is that of the *secondary trade*. Voyaging to far-off countries, endowed with natural resources unknown in their own homes, the Kula sailors return each time richly laden with these, the spoils of their enterprise. Again, in order to be able to offer presents to his partner, every outward bound canoe carries a cargo of such things as are known to be most desirable in the overseas district. Some of this is given away in presents to the partners, but a good deal is carried in order to pay for the objects desired at home. In certain cases, the visiting natives exploit on their own account during the journey some of the natural resources overseas. For example, the Sinaketans dive for the spondylus in Sanaroa Lagoon, and the Dobuans fish in the Trobriands on a beach on the southern end of the island. The secondary trade is complicated still more by the fact that such big Kula centres as, for instance, Sinaketa, are not efficient in any of the industries of special value to the Dobuans. Thus, Sinaketans have to procure the necessary store of goods from the inland villages of Kuboma, and this they do on minor trading expeditions preliminary to the Kula. Like the canoe-building, the secondary trading will be described in detail later on, and has only to be mentioned here.

Here, however, these subsidiary and associated activities must be put in proper relation with regard to one another and to the main transaction. Both the canoe-building and the ordinary trade have been spoken of as secondary or subsidiary to the Kula proper. This requires a comment. I do not, by thus subordinating the two things in importance to the Kula, mean to express a philosophical reflection or a personal opinion as to the relative value of these pursuits from the point of view of some social teleology. Indeed, it is clear that if we look at the acts from the outside, as comparative sociologists, and gauge their real utility, trade and canoe-building will appear to us as the really important achievements, whereas we shall regard the Kula only as an indirect stimulus, impelling the natives to sail and to trade. Here, however, I am not dealing in sociological, but in pure ethnographical description, and any sociological analysis I have given is only what has been absolutely indispensable to clear away misconceptions and to define terms.*

* It is hardly necessary perhaps to make it quite clear that all questions of origins, of development or history of the institutions have been rigorously ruled out of this work. The mixing up of speculative or hypothetical views with an account of facts is, in my opinion an unpardonable sin against ethnographic method.

By ranging the Kula as the primary and chief activity, and the rest as secondary ones, I mean that this precedence is implied in the institutions themselves. By studying the behaviour of the natives and all the customs in question, we see that the Kula is in all respects the main aim : the dates are fixed, the preliminaries settled, the expeditions arranged, the social organisation determined, not with regard to trade, but with regard to Kula. On an expedition, the big ceremonial feast, held at the start, refers to the Kula ; the final ceremony of reckoning and counting the spoil refers to Kula, not to the objects of trade obtained. Finally, the magic, which is one of the main factors of all the procedure, refers only to the Kula, and this applies even to a part of the magic carried out over the canoe. Some rites in the whole cycle are done for the sake of the canoe itself, and others for the sake of Kula. The construction of the canoes is always carried on directly in connection with a Kula expedition. All this, of course, will become really clear and convincing only after the detailed account is given. But it was necessary at this point to set the right perspective in the relation between the main Kula and the trade.

Of course not only many of the surrounding tribes who know nothing of the Kula do build canoes and sail far and daringly on trading expeditions, but even within the Kula ring, in the Trobriands for instance, there are several villages who do not kula, yet have canoes and carry on energetic overseas trade. But where the Kula is practised, it governs all the other allied activities, and canoe building and trade are made subsidiary to it. And this is expressed both by the nature of the institutions and the working of all the arrangements on the one hand, and by the behaviour and explicit statements of the natives on the other.

The Kula—it becomes, I hope, more and more clear—is a big, complicated institution, insignificant though its nucleus might appear. To the natives, it represents one of the most vital interests in life, and as such it has a ceremonial character and is surrounded by magic. We can well imagine that articles of wealth might pass from hand to hand without ceremony or ritual, but in the Kula they never do. Even when at times only small parties in one or two canoes sail overseas and bring back *vaygu'a*, certain taboos are observed, and a customary course is taken in departing, in sailing, and in arriving ; even the smallest expedition in one canoe is a tribal event of some importance, known and spoken of over the whole district. But the characteristic expedition is one in which a considerable number of canoes take part, organised in a certain manner, and forming one body. Feasts, distributions of food, and other public ceremonies are held, there is one leader and master of the expedition, and various rules are adhered to, in addition to the ordinary Kula taboos and observances.

The ceremonial nature of the Kula is strictly bound up with another of its aspects—magic. " The belief in the efficiency of magic dominates the Kula, as it does ever so many other tribal activities of the natives. Magical rites must be performed over the sea-going canoe when it is built, in order to make it swift, steady and safe ; also magic is done over a canoe to make it lucky in the Kula. Another system of magical rites is done in order to avert the dangers of sailing. The third system of magic connected with overseas expeditions is the *mwasila* or the Kula magic proper. This system consists in numerous rites and spells, all of which act directly on the mind (*nanola*) of one's partner, and make him soft, unsteady in mind, and eager to give Kula gifts " (loc. cit., p. 100).

It is clear than an institution so closely associated with magical and ceremonial elements, as is the Kula, not only rests on a firm, traditional foundation, but also has its large store of legends. " There is a rich mythology of the Kula, in which stories are told about far-off times when mythical ancestors sailed on distant and daring expeditions. Owing to their magical knowledge they were able to escape dangers, to conquer their enemies, to surmount obstacles, and by their feats they established many a precedent which is now closely followed by tribal custom. But their importance for their descendants lies mainly in the fact that they handed on their magic, and this made the Kula possible for the following generations " (loc. cit., p. 100).

The Kula is also associated in certain districts, to which the Trobriands do not belong, with the mortuary feasts, called *so'i*. The association is interesting and important, and in Chapter XX an account of it will be given.

The big Kula expeditions are carried on by a great number of natives, a whole district together. But the geographical limits, from which the members of an expedition are recruited, are well defined. Glancing at Map V, " we see a number of circles, each of which represents a certain sociological unit which we shall call a Kula community. A Kula community consists of a village or a number of villages, who go out together on big overseas expeditions, and who act as a body in the Kula transactions, perform their magic in common, have common leaders, and have the same outer and inner social sphere, within which they exchange their valuables. The Kula consists, therefore, first of the small, internal transactions within a Kula community or contiguous communities, and secondly, of the big over-seas expeditions in which the exchange of articles takes place between two communities divided by sea. In the first, there is a chronic, permanent trickling of articles from one village to another, and even within the village. In the second, a whole lot of valuables, amounting to over a thousand articles at a time, are exchanged in one enormous transaction, or, more correctly, in ever so many transactions taking place simultaneously " (loc. cit., p. 101). " The Kula trade consists of a series of such periodical overseas expeditions, which link together the various island groups, and annually bring over big quantities of *vaygu'a* and of subsidiary trade from one district to another. The trade is used and used up, but the *vaygu'a*—the arm-shells and necklets—go round and round the ring" (loc. cit., p. 105).

In this chapter, a short, summary definition of the Kula has been given. I enumerated one after the other its most salient features, the most remarkable rules as they are laid down in native custom, belief and behaviour. This was necessary in order to give a general idea of the institution before describing its working in detail. But no abridged definition can give to the reader the full understanding of a human social institution. It is necessary for this, to explain its working concretely, to bring the reader into contact with the people, show how they proceed at each successive stage, and to describe all the actual manifestations of the general rules laid down in abstract.

As has been said above, the Kula exchange is carried on by enterprises of two sorts ; first there are the big overseas expeditions, in which a more or less considerable amount of valuables are carried at one time. Then there is the inland trade in which the articles are passed from hand to hand, often changing several owners before they move a few miles.

The big overseas expeditions are by far the more spectacular part of the Kula. They also contain much more public ceremonial, magical ritual, and customary usage. They require also, of course, more of preparation and preliminary activity. I shall therefore have a good deal more to say about the overseas Kula expeditions than about the internal exchange.

As the Kula customs and beliefs have been mainly studied in Boyowa, that is, the Trobriand Islands, and from the Boyowan point of view, I shall describe, in the first place, the typical course of an overseas expedition, as it is prepared, organised, and carried out from the Trobriands. Beginning with the construction of the canoes, proceeding to the ceremonial launching and the visits of formal presentation of canoes, we shall choose then the community of Sinaketa, and follow the natives on one of their overseas trips, describing it in all details. This will serve us as a type of a Kula expedition to distant lands. It will then be indicated in what particulars such expeditions may differ in other branches of the Kula, and for this purpose I shall describe an expedition from Dobu, and one between Kiriwina and Kitava. An account of inland Kula in the Trobriands, of some associated forms of trading and of Kula in the remaining branches will complete the account.

In the next chapter I pass, therefore, to the preliminary stages of the Kula, in the Trobriands, beginning with a description of the canoes.

CHAPTER IV

CANOES AND SAILING

I

A CANOE is an item of material culture, and as such it can be described, photographed and even bodily transported into a museum. But—and this is a truth too often overlooked— the ethnographic reality of the canoe would not be brought much nearer to a student at home, even by placing a perfect specimen right before him

The canoe is made for a certain use, and with a definite purpose ; it is a means to an end, and we, who study native life, must not reverse this relation, and make a fetish of the object itself. In the study of the economic purposes for which a canoe is made, of the various uses to which it is submitted, we find the first approach to a deeper ethnographic treatment. Further sociological data, referring to its ownership, accounts of who sails in it, and how it is done ; information regarding the ceremonies and customs of its construction, a sort of typical life history of a native craft— all that brings us nearer still to the understanding of what his canoe truly means to the native.

Even this, however, does not touch the most vital reality of a native canoe. For a craft, whether of bark or wood, iron or steel, lives in the life of its sailors, and it is more to a sailor than a mere bit of shaped matter. To the native, not less than to the white seaman, a craft is surrounded by an atmosphere of romance, built up of tradition and of personal experience. It is an object of cult and admiration, a living thing, possessing its own individuality.

We Europeans—whether we know native craft by experience or through descriptions—accustomed to our extraordinarily developed means of water transport, are apt to look down on a native canoe and see it in a false perspective —regarding it almost as a child's plaything, an abortive, imperfect attempt to tackle the problem of sailing, which we ourselves have satisfactorily solved.* But to the native his cumbersome, sprawling canoe is a marvellous, almost miraculous achievement, and a thing of beauty (see Plates XXI, XXIII, XL, XLVII, LV). He has spun a tradition around it, and he adorns it with his best carvings, he colours and decorates it. It is to him a powerful contrivance for the mastery of Nature, which allows him to cross perilous seas to distant places. It is associated with journeys by sail, full of threatening dangers, of living hopes and desires to which he gives expression in song and story. In short, in the tradition of the natives, in their customs, in their behaviour, and in their direct statements, there can be found the deep love, the admiration, the specific attachment as to something alive and personal, so characteristic of the sailors' attitude towards his craft.

And it is in this emotional attitude of the natives towards their canoes that I see the deepest ethnographic reality, which must guide us right through the study of other aspects—the customs and technicalities of construction and of use ; the economic conditions and the associated beliefs and traditions. Ethnology or Anthropology, the science of Man, must not shun him in his innermost self, in his instinctive and emotional life.

A look at the pictures (for instance Plates XXI, XXIV, XXXIX, or XLVII) will give us some idea of the general structure of the native canoes : the body is a long, deep well, connected with an outrigger float, which stretches parallel with the body for almost all its length (see Plates XXI and XXIII), and with a platform going across from one side to the other. The lightness of the material permits it to be much more deeply immersed than any sea-going European craft, and gives it greater buoyancy. It skims the surface, gliding up and down the waves, now hidden by the crests, now riding on top

* Comparing the frail yet clumsy native canoe with a fine European yacht, we feel inclined to regard the former almost in the light of a joke. This is the pervading note in many amateur ethnographic accounts of sailing, where cheap fun is made by speaking of roughly hewn dug-outs in terms of "dreadnoughts " or "Royal Yachts," just as simple, savage chiefs are referred to as " Kings " in a jocular vein. Such humour is doubtless natural and refreshing, but when we approach these matters scientifically, on the one hand we must refrain from any distortion of facts, and on the other, enter into the finer shades of the natives' thought and feeling with regard to his own creations.

of them. It is a precarious but delightful sensation to sit in the slender body, while the canoe darts on with the float raised, the platform steeply slanting, and water constantly breaking over ; or else, still better, to perch on the platform or on the float—the latter only feasible in the bigger canoes—and be carried across on the sea on a sort of suspended raft, gliding over the waves in a manner almost uncanny. Occasionally a wave leaps up and above the platform, and the canoe—unwieldy, square raft as it seems at first—heaves lengthways and crossways, mounting the furrows with graceful agility. When the sail is hoisted, its heavy, stiff folds of golden matting unroll with a characteristic swishing and crackling noise, and the canoe begins to make way ; when the water rushes away below with a hiss, and the yellow sail glows against the intense blue of sea and sky—then indeed the romance of sailing seems to open through a new vista.

The natural reflection on this description is that it presents the feelings of the Ethnographer, not those of the native. Indeed there is a great difficulty in disentangling our own sensations from a correct reading of the innermost native mind. But if an investigator, speaking the native's language and living among them for some time, were to try to share and understand their feelings, he will find that he can gauge them correctly. Soon he will learn to distinguish when the native's behaviour is in harmony with his own, and when, as it sometimes happens, the two are at variance.

Thus, in this case, there is no mistaking the natives' great admiration of a good canoe ; of their quickness in appreciating differences in speed, buoyancy and stability, and of their emotional reaction to such difference. When, on a calm day, suddenly a fresh breeze rises, the sail is set, and fills, and the canoe lifts its *lamina* (outrigger float) out of the water, and races along, flinging the spray to right and left—there is no mistaking the keen enjoyment of the natives. All rush to their posts and keenly watch the movements of the boat ; some break out into song, and the younger men lean over and play with the water. They are never tired of discussing the good points of their canoes, and analysing the various craft. In the coastal villages of the Lagoon, boys and young men will often sail out in small canoes on mere pleasure cruises, when they race each other, explore less familiar nooks of the

Lagoon, and in general undoubtedly enjoy the outing, in just the same manner as we would do.

Seen from outside, after you have grasped its construction and appreciated through personal experience its fitness for its purpose, the canoe is no less attractive and full of character than from within. When, on a trading expedition or as a visiting party, a fleet of native canoes appears in the offing, with their triangular sails like butterfly wings scattered over the water (see Plates XLVIII), with the harmonious calls of conch shells blown in unison, the effect is unforgettable.* When the canoes then approach, and you see them rocking in the blue water in all the splendour of their fresh white, red, and black paint, with their finely designed prowboards, and clanking array of large, white cowrie shells (see Plates XLIX, LV)—you understand well the admiring love which results in all this care bestowed by the native on the decoration of his canoe.

Even when not in actual use, when lying idle beached on the sea front of a village, the canoe is a characteristic element in the scenery, not without its share in the village life. The very big canoes are in some cases housed in large sheds (see Plate XXII), which are by far the largest buildings erected by the Trobrianders. In other villages, where sailing is always being done, a canoe is simply covered with palm leaves (see Plates I, LIII), as protection from the sun, and the natives often sit on its platform, chatting, and chewing betel-nut, and gazing at the sea. The smaller canoes, beached near the sea-front in long parallel rows, are ready to be launched at any moment. With their curved outline and intricate framework of poles and sticks, they form one of the most characteristic settings of a native coastal village

II

A few words must be said now about the technological essentials of the canoe. Here again, a simple enumeration of the various parts of the canoe, and a description of them,

* The crab-claw sails, used on the South Coast, from Mailu where I used to see them, to westwards where they are used with the double-masted *lakatoi* of Port Moresby, are still more picturesque. In fact, I can hardly imagine anything more strangely impressive than a fleet of crab-claw sailed canoes. They have been depicted in the British New Guinea stamp, as issued by Captain Francis Barton, the late Governor of the Colony. See also Plate XII of Seligman's " Melanesians."

a pulling to pieces of a lifeless object will not satisfy us. I shall instead try to show how, given its purpose on the one hand, and the limitations in technical means and in material on the other, the native ship-builders have coped with the difficulties before them.

A sailing craft requires a water-tight, immersible vessel of some considerable volume. This is supplied to our natives by a hollowed-out log. Such a log might carry fairly heavy loads, for wood is light, and the hollowed space adds to its buoyancy. Yet it possesses no lateral stability, as can easily be seen. A look at the diagrammatic section of a canoe Fig. I (1), shows that a weight with its centre of gravity in

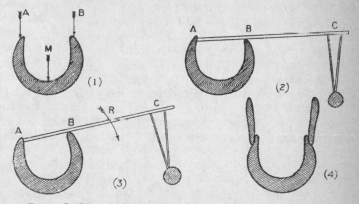

FIGURE I—Diagram showing in transversal section some principles of canoe stability and construction.

the middle, that is, distributed symmetrically, will not upset the equilibrium, but any load placed so as to produce a momentum of rotation (that is, a turning force) at the sides (as indicated by arrows at A or B) will cause the canoe to turn round and capsize.

If, however, as shown in Fig. I (2), another smaller, solid log (C) be attached to the dug-out, a greater stability is achieved, though not a symmetrical one. If we press down the one side of the canoe (A) this will cause the canoe to turn round a longitudinal axis, so that its other side (B) is raised, Fig. I (3). The log (C) will be lifted out of the water, and its weight will produce a momentum (turning force) proportional to the displacement, and the rest of the canoe will come to equilibrium. This momentum is represented in the diagram by the arrow R. Thus a great stability relative to any stress exercised upon A, will be achieved. A stress on B causes the log to be immersed, to which its buoyancy opposes a slight resistance. But it can easily be seen that the stability on this side is much smaller than on the other. This assymetrical* stability plays a great part in the technique of sailing. Thus, as we shall see, the canoe is always so sailed that its outrigger float (C) remains in the wind side. The pressure of the sail then lifts the canoe, so that A is pressed into the water, and B and C are lifted, a position in which they are extremely stable, and can stand great force of wind. Whereas the slightest breeze would cause the canoe to turn turtle, if it fell on the other side, and thus pressed B—C into the water.

Another look at Fig. I (2) and (3) will help us to realise that the stability of the canoe will depend upon (i) the volume, and especially the depth of the dug-out ; (ii) the distance B—C between the dug-out and the log ; (iii) the size of the log C. The greater all these three magnitudes are, the greater the stability of the canoes. A shallow canoe, without much freeboard, will be easily forced into the water ; moreover, if sailed in rough weather, waves will break over it, and fill it with water.

(i) *The volume of the dug-out log* naturally depends upon the length, and thickness of the log. Fairly stable canoes are made of simply scooped-out logs. There are limits, however, to the capacity of these, which are very soon reached. But by building out the side, by adding one or several planks to them, as shown in Figure I (4) the volume and the depth can be greatly increased without much increase in weight. So that such a canoe has a good deal of freeboard to prevent water from breaking in. The longitudinal boards in Kiriwinian canoes are closed in at each end by transversal prow-boards, which are also carved with more or less perfection (see Plates XXIV c, XLVII).

(ii) *The greater the distance B—C between dug-out and outrigger float*, the greater the stability of the canoe. Since

* A constructive expedient to achieve a symmetrical stability is exemplified by the Mailu system of canoe-building, where a platform bridges two parallel, hollowed-out logs. Cf. Author's article in the Transactions of the Royal Society of S. Australia, Vol. XXXIX, 1915, pp. 494-706. Chapter IV, 612-599. Plates XXXV-XXXVII.

the momentum of rotation is the product of B—C (Fig. I), and the weight of the log C, it is clear, therefore, that the greater the distance, the greater will be the momentum. Too great a distance, however, would interfere with the wieldiness of the canoe. Any force acting on the log would easily tip the canoe, and as the natives, in order to manage the craft, have to walk upon the outrigger, the distance B—C must not be too great. In the Trobriands the distance B—C is about one-quarter, or less, of the total length of the canoe. In the big, sea-going canoes, it is always covered with a platform. In certain other districts, the distance is much bigger, and the canoes have another type of rigging.

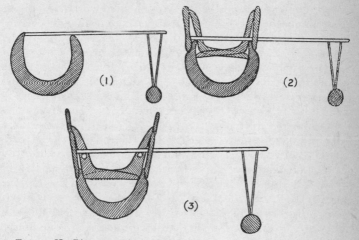

FIGURE II—Diagrammatic sections of the three types of Trobriand Canoe

(1) *Kewo'u*　　(2) *Kalipoulo*　　(3) *Masawa*

(iii) *The size of the log (C) of which the float is formed.* This, in sea-going canoes, is usually of considerable dimensions. But, as a solid piece of wood becomes heavy if soaked by water, too thick a log would not be good.

These are all the essentials of construction in their functional aspect, which will make clear further descriptions of sailing, of building, and of using. For, indeed, though I have said that technicalities are of secondary importance, still without grasping them, we cannot understand references to the managing and rigging of the canoes.

The Trobrianders use their craft for three main purposes, and these correspond to the three types of canoe. Coastal transport, especially in the Lagoon, requires small, light, handy canoes called *kewo'u* (see Fig. II (1), and Plates XXIV, top foreground, and XXXVI, to the right) ; for fishing, bigger and more seaworthy canoes called *kalipoulo* (see Fig. II (2), and Plates XXIV, and XXXVI, to the left, also XXXVII) are used ; finally, for deep sea sailing, the biggest type is needed, with a considerable carrying capacity, greater displacement, and stronger construction. These are called *masawa* (see Fig. II (3) and Plates XXI, XXIII, etc.). The word *waga* is a general designation for all kinds of sailing craft.

Only a few words need to be said about the first two types, so as to make, by means of comparison, the third type clearer. The construction of the smallest canoes is sufficiently illustrated by the diagram (1) in Fig. II. From this it is clear that it is a simple dug-out log, connected with a float. It never has any built-up planking, and no carved boards, nor as a rule any platform. In its economic aspect, it is always owned by one individual, and serves his personal needs. No mythology or magic is attached to it.

Type (2), as can be seen in Fig. II (2), differs in construction from (1), in so far that it has its well enclosed by built-out planking and carved prow-boards. A framework of six ribs helps to keep the planks firmly attached to the dug-out and to hold them together. It is used in fishing villages. These villages are organised into several fishing detachments, each with a headman. He is the owner of the canoe, he performs the fish magic, and among other privileges, obtains the main yield of fish. But all his crew *de facto* have the right to use the canoe and share in the yield. Here we come across the fact that native ownership is not a simple institution, since it implies definite rights of a number of men, combined with the paramount right and title of one. There is a good deal of fishing magic, taboos and customs connected with the construction of these canoes, and also with their use, and they form the subject of a number of minor myths.

By far the most elaborate technically, the most seaworthy and carefully built, are the sea-going canoes of the third type (see Fig. II (3)). These are undoubtedly the greatest achievement of craftsmanship of these natives. Technically, they differ from the previously described kinds, in the amount of time spent over their construction and the care given to details, rather than in essentials. The well is formed by a planking built over a hollowed log and closed up at both ends by carved, transversal prow-boards, kept in position by others, longitudinal and of oval form. The whole planking remains in place by means of ribs, as in the second type of canoes, the *kalipoulo*, the fishing canoes, but all the parts are finished and fitted much more perfectly, lashed with a better creeper, and more thoroughly caulked. The carving, which in the fishing canoes is often quite indifferent, here is perfect. Ownership of these canoes is even more complex, and its construction is permeated with tribal customs, ceremonial, and magic, the last based on mythology. The magic is always performed in direct association with Kula expeditions.

III

After having thus spoken about, first, the general impression made by a canoe and its psychological import, and then about the fundamental features of its technology, we have to turn to the social implications of a *masawa* (sea-going canoe).

The canoe is constructed by a group of people, it is owned, used and enjoyed communally, and this is done according to definite rules. There is therefore a social organisation underlying the building, the owning, and the sailing of a canoe. Under these three headings, we shall give an outline of the canoe's sociology, always bearing in mind that these outlines have to be filled in in the subsequent account.

(A) *Social organisation of labour in constructing a Canoe.*

In studying the construction of a canoe, we see the natives engaged in an economic enterprise on a big scale. Technical difficulties face them, which require knowledge, and can only be overcome by a continuous, systematic effort, and at certain stages must be met by means of communal labour. All this obviously implies some social organisation. All the stages of work, at which various people have to co-operate, must be co-ordinated, there must be someone in authority who takes the initiative and gives decisions ; and there must be also someone with a technical capacity, who directs the construction. Finally, in Kiriwina, communal labour, and the services of experts have to be paid for, and there must be someone who has the means and is prepared to do it.* This economic organisation rests on two fundamental facts—(1) the socio-logical differentiation of functions, and (2) the magical regulation of work.

(1) *The sociological differentiation of functions.*—First of all there is the owner of the canoe, that is, the chief, or the headman of a village or of a smaller sub-division, who takes the responsibility for the undertaking. He pays for the work, engages the expert, gives orders, and commands communal labour.

Besides the owner, there is next another office of great sociological importance, namely, that of the expert. He is the man who knows how to construct the canoe, how to do the carvings, and, last, not least, how to perform the magic. All these functions of the expert may be, but not necessarily are, united in one person. The owner is always one individual, but there may be two or even three experts.

Finally, the third sociological factor in canoe-building, consists of the workers. And here there is a further division. First there is a smaller group, consisting of the relations and close friends of the owner or of the expert, who help throughout the whole process of construction ; and, secondly, there is, besides them, the main body of villagers, who take part in the work at those stages where communal labour is necessary.

(2) *The magical regulation of work.*—The belief in the efficiency of magic is supreme among the natives of Boyowa, and they associate it with all their vital concerns. In fact, we shall find magic interwoven into all the many industrial and communal activities to be described later on, as well as associated with every pursuit where either danger or chance conspicuously enter. We shall have to describe, besides the magic of canoe-making, that of propitious sailing, of ship-wreck and salvage, of Kula and of trade, of fishing, of obtaining *spondylus* and *Conus* shell, and of protection against attack in foreign parts. It is imperative that we should thoroughly grasp what magic means to the natives and the rôle it plays in all their vital pursuits, and a special chapter will be devoted

---

* The whole tribal life is based on a continuous material give and take ; cf. the above mentioned article in the *Economic Journal*, March, 1921, and the disgression on this subject in Chapter VI, Division IV-VII.

to magical ideas and magical practices in Kiriwina. Here, however, it is necessary to sketch the main outlines, at least as far as canoe magic is concerned.

First of all, it must be realised that the natives firmly believe in the value of magic, and that this conviction, when put to the test of their actions, is quite unwavering, even nowadays when so much of native belief and custom has been undermined. We may speak of the sociological weight of tradition, that is of the degree to which the behaviour of a community is affected by the traditional commands of tribal law and customs. In the Trobriands, the general injunction for always building canoes under the guidance of magic is obeyed without the slightest deviation, for the tradition here weighs very heavily. Up to the present, not one single *masawa* canoe has been constructed without magic, indeed without the full observance of all the rites and ceremonial. The forces that keep the natives to their traditional course of behaviour are, in the first place, the specific social inertia which obtains in all human societies and is the basis of all conservative tendencies, and then the strong conviction that if the traditional course were not taken, evil results would ensue. In the case of canoes, the Trobrianders would be so firmly persuaded that a canoe built without magic would be unseaworthy, slow in sailing, and unlucky in the Kula, that no one would dream of omitting the magic rites.

In the myths related elsewhere (Chap. XII) we shall see plainly the power ascribed to magic in imparting speed and other qualities to a canoe. According to native mythology, which is literally accepted, and strongly believed, canoes could be even made to fly, had not the necessary magic fallen into oblivion.

It is also important to understand rightly the natives' ideas about the relation between magical efficiency and the results of craftsmanship. Both are considered indispensable, but both are understood to act independently. That is, the natives will understand that magic, however efficient, will not make up for bad workmanship. Each of these two has its own province : the builder by his skill and knowledge makes the canoe stable and swift, and magic gives it an additional stability and swiftness. If a canoe is obviously badly built, the natives will know why it sails slowly and is unwieldy.

But if one of two canoes, both apparently equally well constructed surpasses the other in some respect, this will be attributed to magic.

Finally, speaking from a sociological point of view, what is the economic function of magic in the process of canoe making ? Is it simply an extraneous action, having nothing to do with the real work or its organisation ? Is magic, from the economic point of view, a mere waste of time ? By no means. In reading the account which follows, it will be seen clearly that magic puts order and sequence into the various activities, and that it and its associated ceremonial are instrumental in securing the co-operation of the community, and the organisation of communal labour. As has been said before, it inspires the builders with great confidence in the efficiency of their work, a mental state essential in any enterprise of complicated and difficult character. The belief that the magician is a man endowed with special powers, controling the canoe, makes him a natural leader whose command is obeyed, who can fix dates, apportion work, and keep the worker up to the mark.

Magic, far from being a useless appendage, or even a burden on the work, supplies the psychological influence, which keeps people confident about the success of their labour, and provides them with a sort of natural leader.* Thus the organisation of labour in canoe-building rests on the one hand on the division of functions, those of the owner, the expert and the helpers, and on the other on the co-operation between labour and magic.

IV

(B) *Sociology of Canoe Ownership.*

Ownership, giving this word its broadest sense, is the relation, often very complex, between an object and the social community in which it is found. In ethnology it is extremely important not to use this word in any narrower sense than that just defined, because the types of ownership found in various parts of the world differ widely. It is especially a grave

---

* This view has been more fully elaborated in the article on " Primitive Economics " in the *Economic Journal*, March, 1921 ; compare also the remarks on systematic magic in Chapter XVII, Division VII.

error to use the word ownership with the very definite connotation given to it in our own society. For it is obvious that this connotation presupposes the existence of very highly developed economic and legal conditions, such as they are amongst ourselves, and therefore the term " own " as we use it is meaningless, when applied to a native society. Or indeed, what is worse, such an application smuggles a number of preconceived ideas into our description, and before we have begun to give an account of the native conditions, we have distorted the reader's outlook.

Ownership has naturally in every type of native society, a different specific meaning, as in each type, custom and tradition attach a different set of functions, rites and privileges to the word. Moreover, the social range of those who enjoy these privileges varies. Between pure individual ownership and collectivism, there is a whole scale of intermediate blendings and combinations.

In the Trobriands, there is a word which may be said approximately to denote ownership, the prefix *toli*—followed by the name of the object owned. Thus the compound word (pronounced without hiatus) *toli waga*, means " owner " or " master " of a canoe (*waga*) ; *toli-bagula*, the master of the garden (*bagula*—garden) ; *toli-bunukwa*, owner of the pig; *toli-megwa* (owner, expert in magic, etc.) This word has to be used as a clue to the understanding of native ideas, but here again such a clue must be used with caution. For, in the first place, like all abstract native words, it covers a wide range, and has different meanings in different contexts. And even with regard to one object, a number of people may lay claim to ownership, claim to be *toli*—with regard to it. In the second place, people having the full *de facto* right of using an object, might not be allowed to call themselves *toli*—of this object. This will be made clear in the concrete example of the canoe.

The word *toli*—in this example is restricted to one man only, who calls himself *toli-waga*. Sometimes his nearest maternal relatives, such as his brothers and maternal nephews, might call themselves collectively *toli-waga*, but this would be an abuse of the term. Now even the mere privilege of using exclusively this title is very highly valued by the natives. With this feature of the Trobriand social psychology, that is with their characteristic ambition, vanity and desire to be renowned and well spoken of, the reader of the following pages will become very familiar. The natives, to whom the Kula and the sailing expeditions are so important, will associate the name of the canoe with that of its *toli ;* they will identify his magical powers and its good luck in sailing and in the Kula ; they will often speak of So-and-so's sailing here and there, of his being very fast in sailing, etc., using in this the man's name for that of the canoe.

Turning now to the detailed determination of this relationship, the most important point about it is that it always rests in the person of the chief or headman.   As we have seen in our short account of the Trobrianders' sociology, the village community is always subject to the authority of one chief or headman.   Each one of these, whether his authority extends over a small sectional village, or over a whole district, has the means of accumulating a certain amount of garden produce, considerable in the case of a chief, relatively small in that of a headman, but always sufficient to defray the extra expenses incidental to all communal enterprise.   He also owns native wealth condensed into the form of the objects of value called *vaygu'a*.   Again, a headman will have little, a big chief a large amount.   But everyone who is not a mere nobody, must possess at least a few stone blades, a few *kaloma* belts, and some *kuwa* (small necklets).   Thus in all types of tribal enterprises, the chief or headman is able to bear the burden of expense, and he also derives the main benefit from the affair.   In the case of the canoe, the chief, as we saw, acts as main organiser in the construction, and he also enjoys the title of *toli*.

This strong economic position runs side by side with his direct power, due to high rank, or traditional authority.   In the case of a small headman, it is due to the fact that he is at the head of a big kinship group (the totemic sub-clan).   Both combined, allow him to command labour and to reward for it.

This title of *toliwaga*, besides the general social distinction which it confers, implies further a definite series of social functions with regard to its individual bearer.

(1) There are first the formal and ceremonial privileges. Thus, the *toliwaga* has the privilege of acting as spokesman of

his community in all matters of sailing or construction. He assembles the council, informal or formal as the case may be, and opens the question of when the sailing will take place. This right of initiative is a purely a nominal one, because both in construction and sailing, the date of enterprise is determined by outward causes, such as reciprocity to overseas tribes, seasons, customs, etc. Nevertheless, the formal privilege is strictly confined to the *toliwaga*, and highly valued. The position of master and leader of ceremonies, of general spokesman, lasts right through the successive stages of the building of the canoe, and its subsequent use, and we shall meet with it in all the ceremonial phases of the Kula.

(2) The economic uses and advantages derived from a canoe are not limited to the *toliwaga*. He, however, gets the lion's share. He has, of course, in all circumstances, the privilege of absolute priority in being included in the party. He also receives always by far the greatest proportion of Kula valuables, and other articles on every occasion. This, however, is in virtue of his general position as chief or headman, and should perhaps not be included under this heading. But a very definite and strictly individual advantage is that of being able to dispose of the canoe for hire, and of receiving the payment for it. The canoe can be, and often is, hired out from a headman, who at a given season has no intention of sailing, by another one, as a rule from a different district, who embarks on an expedition. The reason of this is, that the chief or headman who borrows, may at that time not be able to have his own canoe repaired, or construct another new one. The payment for hire is called *toguna*, and it consists of a *vaygu'a*. Besides this, the best *vaygu'a* obtained on the expedition would be kula'd to the man from whom the canoe was hired.*

(3) The *toliwaga* has definite social privileges, and exercises definite functions, in the running of a canoe. Thus, he selects his companions, who will sail in his canoe, and has the nominal right to choose or reject those who may go on the expedition with him. Here again the privilege is much shorn of its

* The way of hiring a *masawa* (sea-going) canoe is different from the usual transaction, when hiring a fishing canoe. In the latter case, the payment consists of giving part of the yield of fish, and this is called *uwaga*. The same term applies to all payments for objects hired. Thus, if fishing nets or hunting implements, or a small canoe for trading along the coast are hired out, part of the proceeds are given as *uwaga*.

value by many restrictions imposed on the chief by the nature
of things. Thus, on the one hand, his *veyola* (maternal
kinsmen) have, according to all native ideas of right and law,
a strong claim on the canoe. Again, a man of rank in a
community could be excluded from an expedition only with
difficulty, if he wished to go and there were no special grievance
against him. But if there were such a cause, if the man had
offended the chief, and were on bad terms with him, he himself
would not even try to embark. There are actual examples
of this on record. Another class of people having a *de facto*
right to sail are the sailing experts. In the coastal villages
like Sinaketa there are many of these ; in inland ones, like
Omarakana, there are few. So in one of these inland places,
there are men who always go in a canoe, whenever it is used ;
who have even a good deal to say in all matters connected
with sailing, yet who would never dare to use the title of *toliwaga*, and would even definitely disclaim it if it were given to
them. To sum up : the chief's privilege of choice is limited
by two conditions, the rank and the seamanship of those he
may select. As we have seen, he fulfils definite functions in
the construction of the canoe. We shall see later on that he
has also definite functions in sailing.

(4) A special feature, implied in the title of *toliwaga*, is
the performance of magical duties. It will be made clear that
magic during the process of construction is done by the expert,
but magic done in connection with sailing and Kula is done by
the *toliwaga*. The latter must, by definition, know canoe
magic. The rôle of magic in this, and the taboos, ceremonial activities, and special customs associated with it,
will come out clearly in the consecutive account of a Kula
expedition.

V

(3) *The Social Division of Functions in the Manning and Sailing
of the Canoe.*

Very little is to be said under this heading here, since to
understand this we must know more about the technicalities
of sailing. We shall deal with this subject later on (Chap. IX,
Div. II), and there the social organisation within the canoe—
such as it is—will be indicated. Here it may be said that a

number of men have definite tasks assigned to them, and they keep to these. As a rule a man will specialise, let us say, as steersman, and will always have the rudder given to his care. Captainship, carrying with it definite duties, powers and responsibilities, as a position distinct from that of the *toliwaga*. does not exist. The owner of the canoe will always take the lead and give orders, provided that he is a good sailor. Otherwise the best sailor from the crew will say what is to be done when difficulties or dangers arise. As a rule, however, everyone knows his task, and everyone performs it in the normal course of events.

A short outline of the concrete details referring to the distribution of canoes in the Trobriands must be given here. A glance at the map of Boyowa shows that various districts have not the same opportunities for sailing, and not all of them direct access to the sea. Moreover, the fishing villages on the Lagoon, where fishing and sailing have constantly to be done, will naturally have more opportunities for cultivating the arts of sailing and ship-building. And indeed we find that the villages of the two inland districts, Tilataula and Kuboma, know nothing about shipbuilding and sailing, and possess no canoes ; the villages in Kiriwina and Luba, on the east coast, with indirect access to the sea, have only one canoe each, and few building experts ; while some villagers on the Lagoon are good sailors and excellent builders. The best centres for canoe-building are found in the islands of Vakuta and Kayleula and to a lesser degree this craft flourishes in the village of Sinaketa. The island of Kitava is the traditional building centre, and at present the finest canoes as well as the best canoe carvings come from there. In this description of canoes, this island, which really belongs to the Eastern rather than to the Western branch of the N. Massim, must be included in the account, since all Boyowan canoe mythology and canoe industry is associated with Kitava.

There are at present some sixty-four Masawa canoes in the Trobriands and Kitava. Out of these, some four belong to the Northern district, where Kula is not practised ; all the rest are built and used for the Kula. In the foregoing chapters I have spoken about " Kula communities," that is, such groups of villages as carry on the Kula as a whole, sail together on overseas expeditions, and do their internal Kula with one another. We shall group the canoes according to the Kula community to which they belong.

Kiriwina ..	..	..	8	canoes.
Luba ..	..	..	3	,,
Sinaketa ..	..	..	8	,,
Vakuta ..	..	..	22	,,
Kayleula ..	..	about	20	,,
Kitava ..	..	about	12	,,

Total for all Kula communities   60 canoes.

To this number, the canoes of the Northern district must be added, but they are never used in the Kula. In olden days, this figure was, on a rough estimate, more than double of what it is now, because, first of all, there are some villages which had canoes in the old days and now have none, and then the number of villages which became extinct a few generations ago is considerable. About half a century ago, there were in Vakuta alone about sixty canoes, in Sinaketa at least twenty, in Kitava thirty, in Kiriwina twenty, and in Luba ten. When all the canoes from Sinaketa and Vakuta sailed south, and some twenty to thirty more joined them from the Amphletts and Tewara, quite a stately fleet would approach Dobu.

Turning now to the list of ownership in Kiriwina, the most important canoe is, of course, that owned by the chief of Omarakana. This canoe always leads the fleet ; that is to say, on big ceremonial Kula sailings, called *uvalaku*, it has the privileged position. It lives in a big shed on the beach of Kaulukuba (see Plates XXII, XXX), distant about one mile from the village, the beach on which also each new canoe is made. The present canoe (see Plates XXI and XLI) is called Nigada Bu'a—" begging for an areca-nut." Every canoe has a personal name of its own, sometimes just an appropriate expression, like the one quoted, sometimes derived from some special incident. When a new canoe is built, it often inherits the name of its predecessor, but sometimes it gets a new name. The present Omarakana canoe was constructed by a master-builder from Kitava, who also carved the ornamental prow-board. There is no one now in Omarakana who can build or carve properly. The magic over the latter stages ought to have been recited by the present chief, To'uluwa, but as he has very little capacity for remembering spells, the magic was performed by one of his kinsmen.

All the other canoes of Kiriwina are also housed in hangars, each on a beach of clean, white sand on the Eastern coast. The chief or headman of each village is the *toliwaga*. In Kasana'i, the sub-village of Omarakana, the canoe, called in feigned modesty *tokwabu* (something like "landlubber"), was built by Ibena, a chief of equal rank, but smaller power than To'uluwa, and he is also the *toliwaga*. Some other characteristic names of the canoes are :—Kuyamataym'—"Take care of yourself," that is, " because I shall get ahead of you "; the canoe of Liluta, called Siya'i, which is the name of a Government station, where some people from Liluta were once imprisoned ; Topusa—a flying fish ; Yagwa'u—a scarecrow ; Akamta'u—" I shall eat men," because the canoe was a gift from the cannibals of Dobu.

In the district of Luba there are at present only three canoes; one belongs to the chief of highest rank in the village of Olivilevi.   This is the biggest canoe in all the Trobriands. Two are in the village of Wawela, and belong to two headmen, each ruling over a section of the village ; one of them is seen being relashed on Plate XXVII.

The big settlement of Sinaketa, consisting of sectional villages, has also canoes.   There are about four expert builders and carvers, and almost every man there knows a good deal about construction.   In Vakuta the experts are even more numerous, and this is also the case in Kayleula and Kitava.

CHAPTER V

THE CEREMONIAL BUILDING OF A WAGA

I

THE building of the sea-going canoe (*masawa*) is inextricably bound up with the general proceedings of the Kula. As we have said before, in all villages where Kula is practised the *masawa* canoes are built and repaired only in direct connection with it. That is, as soon as a Kula expedition is decided upon, and its date fixed, all the canoes of the village must be overhauled, and those too old for repair must be replaced by new ones. As the overhauling differs only slightly from building in the later, ceremonial stages of the procedure, the account in this chapter covers both.

To the native, the construction of the canoe is the first link in the chain of the Kula performances. From the moment that the tree is felled till the return of the oversea party, there is one continuous flow of events, following in regular succession. Not only that : as we shall see, the technicalities of construction are interrupted and punctuated by magical rites. Some of these refer to the canoe, others belong to the Kula. Thus, canoe-building and the first stage of Kula dovetail into one another. Again, the launching of the canoe, and especially the *kabigidoya* (the formal presentation visit) are in one respect the final acts of canoe-building, and in another they belong to the Kula. In giving the account of canoe-building, therefore, we start on the long sequence of events which form a Kula expedition. No account of the Kula could be considered complete in which canoe-building had been omitted.

In this chapter, the incidents will be related one after the other as they happen in the normal routine of tribal life, obeying the commands of custom, and the indications of belief, the latter acting more rigidly and strongly even than the former. It will be necessary, in following this consecutive account, to keep in mind the definite, sociological mechanism underlying the activities, and the system of ideas at work in regulating labour and magic. The social organisation has been described in the previous chapter. We shall remember that the owner, the expert or experts, a small group of helpers, and the whole community are the social factors, each of which fulfils a different function in the organisation and performance of work. As to the magical ideas which govern the various rites, they will be analysed later on in the course of this and some of the following chapters, and also in Chapter XVII. Here it must suffice to say that they belong to several different systems of ideas. The one based on the myth of the flying canoe refers directly to the canoe; it aims at imparting a general excellence, and more especially the quality of speed to the canoe. The rites of the other type are really exorcisms directed against evil bewitchment (*bulubwalata*) of which the natives are much afraid. The third system of magic (performed during canoe construction) is the Kula magic, based on its own mythological cycle, and although performed on the canoe, yet aiming at the imparting of success to the *toliwaga* in his Kula transactions. Finally, at the beginnings of the proceedings there is some magic addressed to the *tokway*, the malignant wood sprite.

The construction of the canoe is done in two main stages, differing from one another in the character of the work, in the accompanying magic, and in the general sociological setting. In the first stage, the component parts of the canoe are prepared. A big tree is cut, trimmed into a log, then hollowed out and made into the basic dug-out ; the planks, boards, poles, and sticks are prepared. This is achieved by slow, leisurely work, and it is done by the canoe-builder with the assistance of a few helpers, usually his relatives or friends or else those of the *toliwaga*. This stage generally takes a long time, some two to six months, and is done in fits and starts, as other occupations allow, or the mood comes. The spells and rites which accompany it belong to the *tokway* magic, and to that of the flying canoe cycle. To this first stage also belongs the carving of the decorative prow-boards. This is done sometimes by the builder, sometimes by another expert, if the builder cannot carve.

The second stage is done by means of intense communal labour. As a rule this stage is spread over a short time, only perhaps a week or two—including the pauses between work.

The actual labour, in which the whole community is energetically engaged, takes up only some three to five days. The work consists of the piecing together of the planks and prowboards, and, in case these do not fit well, of trimming them appropriately, and then of the lashing them together. Next comes the piecing and lashing of the outrigger, caulking and painting of the canoe. Sail-making is also done at this time, and belongs to this stage. As a rule, the main body of the canoe is constructed at one sitting, lasting about a day ; that is, the prow-boards are put in, the ribs and planks fitted together, trimmed and lashed. Another day is devoted to the attaching of the float and binding of the outrigger frame and the platform. Caulking and painting are done at another sitting, or perhaps at two more, while the sail is made on yet another day. These times are only approximate, since the size of the canoe, as well as the number of people participating in communal labour, greatly varies. The second stage of canoe-building is accompanied by Kula magic, and by a series of exorcisms on the canoe, and the magic is performed by the owner of the canoe, and not by the builder or expert. This latter, however, directs the technicalities of the proceedings, in which he is assisted and advised by builders from other villages ; by sailing experts, and by the *toliwaga* and other notables. The lashing of the canoe with a specially strong creeper, called *wayugo*, is accompanied by perhaps the most important of the rites and spells belonging to the flying canoe magic.

II

After the decision to build a *waga* has been taken, a tree suitable for the main log has to be chosen. This, in the Trobriands, is not a very easy task. As the whole plain is taken up by garden land, only the small patches of fertile soil in the coral ridge which runs all round the island, remain covered with jungle. There the tree must be found, there felled, and thence transported to the village.

Once the tree is chosen, the *toliwaga*, the builder and a few helpers repair to the spot, and a preliminary rite must be performed, before they begin to cut it down. A small incision is made into the trunk, so that a particle of food, or a bit of areca-nut can be put into it. Giving this as an offering to the *tokway* (wood sprite), the magician utters an incantation :—

Vabusi Tokway Spell.

" Come down, O wood sprites, O *Tokway*, dwellers in branches, come down ! Come down, dwellers in branch forks, in branch shoots ! Come down, come, eat ! Go to your coral outcrop over there ; crowd there, swarm there, be noisy there, scream there !

" Step down from our tree, old men ! This is a canoe ill spoken of ; this is a canoe out of which you have been shamed ; this is a canoe out of which you have been expelled ! At sunrise and morning, you help us in felling the canoe ; this our tree, old men, let it go and fall down ! "

This spell, given in free translation, which, however, follows the original very closely, word for word, is far clearer than the average sample of Trobriand magic. In the first part, the *tokway* is invoked under various names, and invited to leave his abode, and to move to some other place, and there to be at his ease In the second part, the canoe is mentioned with several epithets, all of which denote an act of discourtesy or ill-omen. This is obviously done to compel the *tokway* to leave the tree. In Boyowa, the *yoba*, the chasing away, is under circumstances a great insult, and at times it commands immediate compliance. This is always the case when the chaser belongs to the local sub-clan of a village, and the person expelled does not. But the *yoba* is always an act of considerable consequence, never used lightly, and in this spell, it carries these sociological associations with it. In the usual anticipatory way, characteristic of native speech, the tree is called in the spell " canoe " (*waga*).

The object of this spell is written very plainly in every word of it, and the natives also confirm it by saying that it is absolutely necessary to get rid of the *tokway*. What would happen, however, if the *tokway* were not expelled, is not so unequivocally laid down by tradition, and it cannot be read out of the spell or the rite. Some informants say that the canoe would be heavy ; others that the wood would be full of knots, and that there would be holes in the canoe, or that it would quickly rot.

But though the rationale of the expulsion is not so well defined, the belief in the *tokway's* evil influence, and in the dangers associated with his presence is positive. And this is in keeping with the general nature of the *tokway*, as we find him delineated by native belief. The *tokway* is on the whole a harmful being, though the harm he does is seldom more than an unpleasant trick, perhaps a sudden fright, an attack of shooting pains, or a theft. The *tokway* live in trees or in coral rocks and boulders, usually in the *raybwag*, the primeval jungle, growing on the coastal ridge, full of outcrops and rocks. Some people have seen a *tokway*, although he is invisible at will. His skin is brown, like that of any Boyowan, but he has long, sleek hair, and a long beard. He comes often at night, and frightens people. But, though seldom seen, the *tokway's* wailing is often heard from the branches of a big tree, and some trees evidently harbour more *tokways* than others, since you can hear them very easily there. Sometimes, over such trees, where people often hear the *tokway* and get a fright, the above quoted incantation and rite are performed.

In their contact with men, the *tokway* show their unpleasant side ; often they come at night and steal food. Many cases can be quoted when a man, as it seemed, was surprised in the act of stealing yams out of a storehouse, but lo ! when approached he disappeared—it was a *tokway*. Then, sickness in some of its lighter forms is caused by the *tokway*. Shooting pains, pricking and stabbing in one's inside, are often due to him, for he is in possession of magic by which he can insert small, sharp-edged and sharp-pointed objects into the body. Fortunately some men know magic by which to extract such objects. These men, of course, according to the general rule of sorcery, can also inflict the same ailments. In olden days, the *tokway* gave both the harmful and beneficent magic to some men, and ever since, this form of sorcery and of concomitant healing have been handed on from one generation to another.

Let us return to our canoe, however. After the rite has been performed, the tree is felled. In olden days, when stone implements were used, this must have been a laborious process, in which a number of men were engaged in wielding the axe, and others in re-sharpening the blunted or broken blades. The old technique was more like nibbling away the wood in small chips, and it must have taken a long time to cut out a sufficiently deep incision to fell the tree. After the tree is on the ground, the preliminary trimming is done on the spot. The branches are lopped off, and the log of appropriate length is made out of the tree. This log is cut into the rough shape of a canoe, so as to make it as light as possible, for now it has to be pulled to the village or to the beach.

The transporting of the log is not an easy task, as it has to be taken out of the uneven, rocky *raybwag*, and then pulled along very bad roads. Pieces of wood are put on the ground every few metres, to serve as slips on which the log can more easily glide than on the rocks and uneven soil. In spite of that, and in spite of the fact that many men are summoned to assist, the work of pulling the log is very heavy. The men receive food in payment for it. Pig flesh is cooked and distributed with baked yams ; at intervals during the work they refresh themselves with green coco-nut drinks and with sucking sugar cane. Gifts of such food, given during work in payment of communal labour, are called *puwaya*. To describe how heavy the work sometimes is, the native will say, in a characteristically figurative manner :

> " The pig, the coco drinks, the yams are finished, and yet we pull—very heavy ! "

In such cases the natives resort to a magical rite which makes the canoe lighter. A piece of dry banana leaf is put on top of the log. The owner or builder beats the log with a bunch of dry lalang grass and utters the following spell :

KAYMOMWA'U SPELL.

" Come down, come down, defilement by contact with excrement ! Come down, defilement by contact with refuse ! Come down, heaviness ! Come down, rot ! Come down fungus ! . . ." and so on, invoking a number of deteriorations to leave the log, and then a number of defilements and broken taboos. In other words, the heaviness and slowness, due to all these magical causes, are thrown out of the log.

This bunch of grass is then ritually thrown away. It is called *momwa'u*, or the " heavy bunch." Another handful of the long lalang grass, seared and dry, is taken, and this is the *gagabile*, the " light bunch," and with this the canoe is again beaten. The meaning of the rite is quite plain : the first bunch takes into it the heaviness of the log, and the second imparts lightness to it. Both spells also express this meaning in plain terms. The second spell, recited with the *gagabile* bunch, runs thus :

Kaygagabile Spell

" He fails to outrun me " (repeated many times). " The canoe trembles with speed " (many times). A few untranslatable words are uttered ; then a long chain of ancestral names is invoked. " I lash you, O tree ; the tree flies ; the tree becomes like a breath of wind ; the tree becomes like a butterfly ; the tree becomes like a cotton seed fluff. One sun " (i.e., time) " for my companions, midday sun, setting sun ; another sun for me——" (here the reciter's name is uttered)—" the rising sun, the rays of the (rising) sun, (the time of) opening the huts, (the time of the) rising of the morning star ! " The last part means : " My companions arrive at sunset, while I arrive with the rising sun "—(indicating how far my canoe exceeds them in speed.)*

These formulæ are used both to make the log lighter for the present purpose of pulling it into the village, and in order to give it greater speed in general, when it is made up into a *waga*.

After the log has been finally brought into the village, and left on the *baku*, the main central place, the creeper by means of which it has been pulled and which is called in this connection *duku*, is not cut away at once. This is done ceremonially on the morning of the following day, sometimes after even two or three days have passed. The men of the community assemble, and the one who will scoop out the canoe, the builder (*tota'ila waga*, " the cutter of the canoe ") performs a magical rite. He takes his adze (*ligogu*) and wraps some very light and thin herbs round the blade with a piece of dried banana leaf, itself associated with the idea of lightness. This he wraps only half round, so that a broad opening is left, and the breath and voice have free access to the herbs and blade of the adze. Into this opening, the magician chants the following long spell :

Kapitunena Duku Spell.

" I shall wave them back, (i.e., prevent all other canoes from overtaking me) ! " repeated many times. " On the top of Si'a Hill ; women of Tokuna ; my mother a sorceress, myself a sorcerer. It dashes forward, it flies ahead. The canoe body is light ; the pandanus streamers are

---

* The words within brackets in this and in some of the following spells are free additions, necessary to make the meaning clear in the English version. They are implied by the context in the native original, though not explicitly contained.

aflutter; the prow skims the waves; the ornamental boards leap, like dolphins; the *tabuyo* (small prow-board) breaks the waves; the *lagim'* (transversal prow-board) breaks the waves. Thou sleepest in the mountain, thou sleepest in Kuyawa Island. We shall kindle a small fire of lalang grass, we shall burn aromatic herbs (i.e., at our destination in the mountains)! Whether new or old, thou goest ahead."

This is the exordium of the formula. Then comes a very long middle part, in a form very characteristic of Trobriand magic. This form resembles a litany, in so far as a key word or expression is repeated many times with a series of complementary words and expressions. Then the first key word is replaced by another, which in its turn, is repeated with the same series of expressions; then comes another key word, and so on. We have thus two series of words; each term of the first is repeated over and over again, with all terms of the second, and in this manner, with a limited number of words, a spell is very much lengthened out, since its length is the product of the length of both series. In shorter spells, there may be only one key word, and in fact, this is the more usual type. In this spell, the first series consists of nouns denoting different parts of the canoe; the second are verbs, such as: to cut, to fly, to speed, to cleave a fleet of other canoes, to disappear, to skim over the waves. Thus the litany runs in such a fashion: "The tip of my canoe starts, the tip of my canoe flies, the tip of my canoe speeds, etc., etc." After the long litany has been chanted, the magician repeats the exordium, and finishes it off with the conventional onomatopoetic word *saydididi*— which is meant to imitate the flying of the witches.

After the recital of this long spell over the herbs and blade of his adze, the magician wraps up the dry banana leaf, thus imprisoning the magical virtue of the spell round the blade, and with this, he strikes and cuts through the *duku* (the creeper used for the pulling of the canoes.)

With this, the magic is not over yet, for on the same evening, when the canoe is put on transversal logs (*nigakulu*), another rite has to be carried out. Some herbs are placed on the transversals between them and the body of the big canoe log. Over these herbs, again, another spell has to be uttered. In order not to overload this account with magical texts, I shall not adduce this spell in detail. Its wording also plainly indicates that it is speed magic, and it is a short formula running on directly, without cross-repetitions.

After that, for some days, the outside of the canoe body is worked. Its two ends must be cut into tapering shape, and the bottom evened and smoothed. After that is done, the canoe has to be turned over, this time into its natural position, bottom down, and what is to be the opening, upwards. Before the scooping out begins, another formula has to be recited over the *kavilali*, a special *ligogu* (adze), used for scooping out, which is inserted into a handle with a moveable part, which then allows the cutting to be done at varying angles to the plane of striking.

The rite stands in close connection to the myth of the flying canoe, localised in Kudayuri, a place in the Island of Kitava, and many allusions are made to this myth.* After a short exordium, containing untranslatable magical words, and geographical references, the spell runs :

LIGOGU SPELL.

" I shall take hold of an adze, I shall strike ! I shall enter my canoe, I shall make thee fly, O canoe, I shall make thee jump ! We shall fly like butterflies, like wind ; we shall disappear in mist, we shall vanish. You will pierce the straits of Kadimwatu (between the islands of Tewara and Uwama) you will break the promontory of Saramwa (near Dobu), pierce the passage of Loma (in Dawson Straits), die away in the distance, die away with the wind, fade away with the mist, vanish away. Break through your seaweeds (i.e., on coming against the shore). Put on your wreath (probably an allusion to the sea-weeds), make your bed in the sand. I turn round, I see the Vakuta men, the Kitava men behind me ; my sea, the sea of Pilolu (i.e., the sea between the Trobriands and the Amphletts) ; to-day the Kudayuri men will burn their fires (i.e., on the shores of Dobu). Bind your grass skirt together, O canoe " (here the personal name of the canoe is mentioned), " fly ! " The last phrase contains an implicit hint that the canoe partakes of the nature of a flying witch, as it should, according to the Kudayuri myth.

After this, the canoe-builder proceeds to scoop out the log. This is a long task, and a heavy one, and one which requires a good deal of skill, especially towards the end, when the walls of the dug-out have to be made sufficiently thin, and when

* Compare therefore Chapter XII, Division IV.

the wood has to be taken off evenly over the whole surface. Thus, although at the beginning the canoe carpenter is usually helped by a few men—his sons or brothers or nephews who in assisting him also learn the trade—towards the end he has to do the work single-handed. It, therefore, always happens that this stage takes a very long time. Often the canoe will lie for weeks, untouched, covered with palm leaves against the sun, and filled with some water to prevent drying and cracking (see Plate XXV). Then the carpenter will set to work for a few days, and pause again. In almost all villages, the canoe is put up in the central place, or before the builder's hut. In some of the Eastern villages, the scooping out is done on the sea beach, to avoid pulling the heavy log to and from the village.

Parallel with the process of hollowing out, the other parts of the canoe are made ready to be pieced together. Four broad and long planks form the gunwale ; L-shaped pieces of wood are cut into ribs ; long poles are prepared for longitudinal support of the ribs, and for platform rafters ; short poles are made ready as transversals of the platform and main supports of the outrigging ; small sticks to connect the float with the transversals ; finally, the float itself, a long, bulky log. These are the main, constituent parts of a canoe, to be made by the builder. The four carved boards are also made by him if he knows how to carve, otherwise another expert has to do this part of the work (see Plate XXVI).

When all the parts are ready, another magical rite has to be performed. It is called " *kapitunela nanola waga* " : " the cutting off of the canoe's mind," an expression which denotes *a change of mind*, a *final determination*. In this case, the canoe makes up its mind to run quickly. The formula is short, contains at the beginning a few obscure words, and then a few geographical references to some places in the d'Entrecasteaux Archipelago. It is recited over a few drops of coco-nut oil, which is then wrapped up in a small bundle. The same spell is then again spoken over the *ligogu* blade, round which a piece of dry banana has been wrapped in the manner described above. The canoe is turned bottom up, the bundle with coco-nut oil placed on it and struck with the adze. With this the canoe is ready to be pieced together, and the first stage of its construction is over.

III

As has been said above, the two stages differ from one another in the nature of work done and in their sociological and ceremonial setting.　So far, we have seen only a few men engaged in cutting the tree and scooping it out and then preparing the various parts of the canoe.　Industriously, but slowly and deliberately, with many pauses, they toil over their work, sitting on the brown, trodden soil of the village in front of the huts, or scooping the canoe in the central place.　The first part of the task, the felling of the tree, took us to the tall jungle and intricate undergrowth, climbing and festooned around the fantastic shapes of coral rocks.

Now, with the second stage, the scene shifts to the clean, snow-white sand of a coral beach, where hundreds of natives in festive array crowd around the freshly scraped body of the canoe.　The carved boards, painted in black, white and red, the green fringe of palms and jungle trees, the blue of the sea —all lend colour to the vivid and lively scene.　Thus I saw the building of a canoe done on the East shore of the Trobriands, and in this setting I remember it.　In Sinaketa, instead of the blue, open sea, breaking in a belt of white foam outside on the fringing reef and coming in limpid waves to the beach, there are the dull, muddy browns and greens of the Lagoon, playing into pure emerald tints where the clean sandy bottom begins.

Into one of these two scenes, we must now imagine the dug-out transported from the village, after all is ready, and after the summons of the chief or headman has gone round the neighbouring villages.　In the case of a big chief, several hundreds of natives will assemble to help, or to gaze on the performance.　When a small community with a second-rate headman construct their canoe, only a few dozen people will come, the relatives-in-law of the headman and of other notables, and their close friends.

After the body of the canoe and all the accessories have been placed in readiness, the proceedings are opened by a magical rite, called *Katuliliva tabuyo*.　This rite belongs to the Kula magic, for which the natives have a special expression ; they call it *mwasila*.　It is connected with the inserting of the ornamental prow-boards into their grooves at both ends of the canoe.　These ornamental parts of the canoe are put in first of all, and this is done ceremonially.　A few sprigs of the mint plant are inserted under the boards, as they are put in, and the *toliwaga* (owner of the canoe) hammers the boards in by means of a special stone imported from Dobu, and ritually repeats a formula of the *mwasila* magic. The mint plant (*sulumwoya*) plays an important part in the *mwasila* (Kula magic) as well as in love spells, and in the magic of beauty. Whenever a substance is to be medicated for the purpose of charming, seducing, or persuading, as a rule *sulumwoya* is used. This plant figures also in several myths, where it plays a similar part, the mythical hero always conquering the foe or winning a woman by the use of the *sulumwoya*.

I shall not adduce the magical formulæ in this account, with the exception of the most important one. Even a short summary of each of them would obstruct the narrative, and it would blur completely the outline of the consecutive account of the various activities. The various complexities of the magical ritual and of the formulæ will be set forth in Chapter XVII. It may be mentioned here, however, that not only are there several types of magic performed during canoe building, such as the *mwasila* (Kula magic), the canoe speed magic, exorcisms against evil magic, and exorcism of the *tokway*, but within each of these types, there are different systems of magic, each with its own mythological basis, each localised in a different district, and each having of course different formulæ and slightly different rites.*

After the prow-boards are put in, and before the next bit of technical work is done, another magical rite has to be performed. The body of the canoe, now bright with the three-coloured boards, is pushed into the water. A handful of leaves, of a shrub called *bobi'u*, is charmed by the owner or by the builder, and the body of the canoe is washed in sea water with the leaves. All the men participate in the washing, and this rite is intended to make the canoe fast, by removing the traces of any evil influence, which might still have remained, in spite of the previous magic, performed on the *waga*. After the *waga* has been rubbed and washed, it is pulled ashore again and placed on the skid logs.

Now the natives proceed to the main and most important constructive part of their work; this consists of the erection of the gunwale planks at the sides of the dug-out log, so as to

* All this is discussed at length in Chapter XVII, Division IV.

form the deep and wide well of the built-up canoe. They are kept in position by an internal framework of some twelve to twenty pairs of ribs, and all of this is lashed together with a special creeper called *wayugo*, and the holes and interstices are caulked with a resinous substance.

I cannot enter here into details of building, though from the technological point of view, this is the most interesting phase, showing us the native at grips with real problems of construction. He has a whole array of component parts, and he must make them fit together with a considerable degree of precision, and that without having any exact means of measurement. By a rough appreciation based on long experience and great skill, he estimates the relative shapes and sizes of the planks, the angles and dimensions of the ribs, and the lengths of the various poles. Then, in shaping them out, the builder tests and fits them in a preliminary manner as work goes on, and as a rule the result is good. But now, when all these component parts have to be pieced finally together, it nearly always happens that some bit or other fails to fit properly with the rest. These details have to be adjusted, a bit taken off the body of the canoe, a plank or pole shortened, or even a piece added. The natives have a very efficient way of lashing on a whole bit of a plank, if this proves too short, or if, by some accident, it breaks at the end. After all has been finally fitted, and made to tally, the framework of ribs is put into the canoe (see Plate XXVII), and the natives proceed to lash them to the body of the dug-out, and to the two longitudinal poles to which the ribs are threaded.

And now a few words must be said about the *wayugo*, the lashing creeper. Only one species of creeper is used for the lashing of boats, and it is of the utmost importance that this creeper should be sound and strong. It is this alone that maintains the cohesion of the various parts, and in rough weather, very much depends on how the lashings will stand the strain. The other parts of the canoe—the outrigger poles—can be more easily tested, and as they are made of strong elastic wood, they usually stand any weather quite well. Thus the element of danger and uncertainty in a canoe is due mainly to the creeper. No wonder, therefore, that the magic of the creeper is considered as one of the most important ritual items in canoe-building.

In fact, *wayugo*, the name of that creeper species, is also used as a general term for canoe magic. When a man has the reputation of building or owning a good and fast canoe, the usual way of explaining it is to say that he has, or knows " a good *wayugo*." For, as in all other magic, there are several types of *wayugo* spells. The ritual is always practically the same : five coils of the creeper are, on the previous day, placed on a large wooden dish and chanted over in the owner's hut by himself. Only exceptionally can this magic be done by the builder. Next day they are brought to the beach ceremonially on the wooden plate. In one of the *wayugo* systems, there is an additional rite, in which the *toliwaga* (canoe owner) takes a piece of the creeper, inserts it into one of the holes pierced in the rim of the dug-out for the lashing, and pulling it to and fro, recites once more the spell.

In consideration of the importance of this magic, the formula will be here adduced in full. It consists of an exordium (*u'ula*), a double main part (*tapwana*), and a concluding period (*dogina*).*

Wayugo Spell.

In the *u'ula* he first repeats " Sacred (or ritual) eating of fish, sacred inside," thus alluding to a belief that the *toliwaga* has in connection with this magic to partake ritually of baked fish. Then come the words—" Flutter, betel plant, leaving behind," all associated with leading ideas of canoe magic—the flutter of pandanus streamers ; the betel nut, which the ancestral spirits in other rites are invited to partake of ; the speed by which all comrades will be left behind !

A list of ancestral names follows. Two of them, probably mythical personages, have significative names ; " Stormy sea " and " Foaming." Then the *baloma* (spirits) of these ancestors are asked to sit on the canoe slips and to chew betel, and they are invoked to take the pandanus streamer of the Kudayuri—a place in Kitava, where the flying canoe magic originated—and plant it on top of Teula or Tewara, the small island off the East coast of Fergusson.

The magician after that chants : " I shall turn, I shall turn towards you, O men of Kitava, you remain behind

* It is necessary to be acquainted with the mythology of canoe-building and of the Kula (Chapter XII) in order to understand thoroughly the meaning of this spell.

on the To'uru beach (in the Lagoon of Vakuta). Before
you lies the sea arm of Pilolu. To-day, they kindle the
festive fire of the Kudayuri, thou, O my boat " (here the
personal name of the boat is uttered), " bind thy skirts
together and fly ! " In this passage—which is almost
identical with one in the previously quoted *Ligogu* spell—
there is a direct allusion to the Kudayuri myth, and to
the custom of festive fires. Again the canoe is addressed
as a woman who has to bind her grass petticoat together
during her flight, a reference to the belief that a flying
witch binds her skirts when starting into the air and to
the tradition that this myth originates from Na'ukuwakula,
one of the flying Kudayuri sisters. The following main
part continues with this mythical allusion : Na'ukuwakula
flew from Kitava through Sinaketa and Kayleula to
Simsim, where she settled down and transmitted the
magic to her progeny. In this spell the three places :
Kuyawa (a creek and hillock near Sinaketa), Dikutuwa (a
rock near Kayleula), and La'u (a cleft rock in the sea
near Simsim, in the Lousançay Islands) are the leading
words of the *tapwana*.

The last sentence of the first part, forming a transition
into the *tapwana*, runs as follows : " I shall grasp the
handle of the adze, I shall grip all the component parts
of the canoe "—perhaps another allusion to the mythical
construction of the Kudayuri canoe (comp. Chap. XII,
Div. IV)—" I shall fly on the top of Kuyawa, I shall
disappear ; dissolve in mist, in smoke ; become like a
wind eddy, become alone—on top of Kuyawa." The same
words are then repeated, substituting for Kuyawa the
two other above-mentioned spots, one after the other,
and thus retracing the flight of Na'ukuwakula.

Then the magician returns to the beginning and recites
the spell over again up to the phrase : " bind thy skirt
together and fly," which is followed this time by a second
tapwana : " I shall outdistance all my comrades with the
bottom of my canoe ; I shall out-distance all my comrades
with the prow-board of my canoe, etc., etc.," repeating
the prophetic boast with all the parts of the canoe, as is
usual in the middle part of magical spells.

In the *dogina*, the last part, the magician addresses
the *waga* in mythological terms, with allusions to the
Kudayuri myth, and adds : " Canoe thou art a ghost,
thou art like a wind eddy ; vanish, O my canoe, fly ;
break through your sea-passage of Kadimwatu, cleave
through the promontory of Saramwa, pass through Loma ;

die away, disappear, vanish with an eddy, vanish with
the mist ; make your imprint in the sand, cut through
the seaweed, go, put on your wreath of aromatic herbs."*

After the *wayugo* has been ritually brought in, the lashing
of the canoe begins. First of all the ribs are lashed into position
then the planks, and with this the body of the canoe is ready.
This takes a varying time, according to the number of
people at work, and to the amount of tallying and adjusting
to be done at the final fitting. Sometimes one whole day's
work is spent on this stage, and the next piece of work, the
construction of the outrigger, has to be postponed to another
day. This is the next stage, and there is no magic to punctuate
the course of technical activities. The big, solid log is put
alongside the canoe, and a number of short, pointed sticks are
driven into it. The sticks are put in crossways on the top of
the float (*lamina*). Then the tops of these sticks are again
attached to a number of horizontal poles, which have to be
thrust through one side of the canoe-body, and attached to
the other. All this naturally requires again adjusting and
fitting. When these sticks and poles are bound together,
there results a strong yet elastic frame, in which the canoe and
the float are held together in parallel positions, and across them
transversely there run the several horizontal poles which keep
them together. Next, these poles are bridged over by many
longitudinal sticks lashed together, and thus a platform is
made between the edge of the canoe and the tops of the float
sticks.

When that is done, the whole frame of the canoe is ready,
and there remains only to caulk the holes and interstices.
The caulking substance is prepared in the hut of the *toliwaga*,
and a spell is recited over it on the evening before the work is
begun. Then again, the whole community turn out and do
the work in one day's sitting.

The canoe is now ready for the sea, except for the painting,
which is only for ornamentation. Three more magical rites
have to be performed, however, before it is painted and then
launched. All three refer directly to the canoe, and aim at
giving it speed. At the same time all three are exorcisms
against evil influences, resulting from various defilements or
broken taboos, which possibly might have desecrated the *waga*.

* Compare the linguistic analysis of this spell in Chapter XVIII.

The first is called *Vakasulu*, which means something like " ritual cooking " of the canoe. The *toliwaga* has to prepare a real witches' cauldron of all sorts of things, which afterwards are burnt under the bottom of the canoe, and the smoke is supposed to exercise a speed-giving and cleansing influence. The ingredients are : the wings of a bat, the nest of a very small bird called *posisiku*, some dried bracken leaves, a bit of cotton fluff, and some lalang grass. All the substances are associated with flying and lightness. The wood used for kindling the fire is that of the light-timbered mimosa tree (*liga*). The twigs have to be obtained by throwing at the tree a piece of wood (never a stone), and when the broken-off twig falls, it must be caught in the hand, and not allowed to touch the ground.

The second rite, called *Vaguri*, is an exorcism only, and it consists of charming a stick, and then knocking the body of the canoe all over with it. This expells the evil witchery (*bulub-walata*), which it is only wise to suspect has been cast by some envious rivals, or persons jealous of the *toliwaga*.

Finally, the third of these rites, the *Kaytapena waga*, consists in medicating a torch of coco-leaf with the appropriate spell, and fumigating with it the inside of the canoe. This gives speed and once more cleanses the canoe.

After another sitting of a few days, the whole outside of the canoe is painted in three colours. Over each of them a special spell is chanted again, the most important one over the black colour. This is never omitted, while the red and white spells are optional. In the rite of the black colour, again, a whole mixture of sunstances is used—a dry bracken leaf, grass, and a *posisiku* nest—all this is charred with some coco-nut husk, and the first strokes of the black paint are made with the mixture. The rest is painted with a watery mixture of charred coco-nut. For red colour, a sort of ochre, imported from the d'Entrecasteaux Islands, is used ; the white one is made of a chalky earth, found in certain parts of the sea shore.

Sail-making is done on another day, usually in the village, by communal labour, and, with a number of people helping, the tedious and complicated work is performed in a relatively short time. The triangular outline of the sail is first pegged out on the ground, as a rule the old sail being used as a pattern. After this is done, tapes of dried pandanus leaf (see Plates XXVIII, XXIX) are stretched on the ground and first fixed along the borders of the sail. Then, starting at the apex of the triangle, the sail-makers put tapes radiating towards the base, sewing them together with awls of flying fox bone, and using as thread narrow strips of specially toughened pandanus leaf. Two layers of tapes are sewn one on top of the other to make a solid fabric.

IV

The canoe is now quite ready to be launched. But before we go on to an account of the ceremonial launching and the associated festivities, one or two general remarks must be made retrospectively about the proceedings just described.

The whole of the first stage of canoe-building, that is, the cutting of the tree, the scooping out of the log, and the preparation of the other component parts, with all their associated magic, is done only when a new canoe is built.

But the second stage has to be performed over all the canoes before every great overseas Kula expedition. On such an occasion, all the canoes have to be re-lashed, re-caulked, and re-painted. This obviously requires that they should all be taken to pieces and then lashed, caulked and painted exactly as is done with a new canoe. All the magic incidental to these three processes is then performed, in its due order, over the renovated canoe. So that we can say about the second stage of canoe-building that not only is it always performed in association with the Kula, but that no big expedition ever takes place without it.

We have had a description of the magical rites, and the ideas which are implied in every one of them have been specified. But there are one or two more general characteristics which must be mentioned here. First, there is what could be called the " ceremonial dimension " of magical rites. That is, how far is the performance of the rite attended by the members of the community, if at all ; and if so, do they actively take part in it, or do they simply pay keen attention and behave as an interested audience ; or, though being present, do they pay little heed and show only small interest ?

In the first stage of canoe-building, the rites are performed by the magician himself, with only a few helpers in attendance. The general village public do not feel sufficiently interested and attracted to assist, nor are they bound by custom to do so.

The general character of these rites is more like the perform-ance of a technicality of work than of a ceremony. The preparing of herbs for the *ligogu* magic, for instance, and the charming it over, is carried out in a matter-of-fact, business-like manner, and nothing in the behaviour of the magician and those casually grouped around him would indicate that anything specially interesting in the routine work is happening.

The rites of the second stage are *ipso facto* attended by all those who help in piecing together and lashing, but on the whole those present have no special task assigned to them in the per-formance of these rites. As to the attention and behaviour during the performance of the magic, much depends of course on whether the magician officiating is a chief of great importance or someone of low rank. A certain decorum and even silence would be observed in any case. But many of those present would turn aside and go away, if they wanted to do so. The magician does not produce the impression of an officiating high priest performing a solemn ceremony, but rather of a specialised workman doing a particularly important piece of work. It must be remembered that all the rites are simple, and the chanting of the spells in public is done in a low voice, and quickly, without any specially effective vocal production. Again, the caulking and the *wayugo* rites are, in some types of magic at least, performed in the magician's hut, without any attendance whatever, and so is that of the black paint.

Another point of general importance is what could be called the stringency of magic rites. In canoe magic, for instance, the expulsion of the *tokway*, the ritual cutting of the pulling rope, the magic of the adze (*ligogu*), that of the lashing creeper (*wayugo*), of the caulking, and of the black paint can never be omitted. Whereas the other rites are optional, though as a rule some of them are performed. But even those which are considered indispensable do not all occupy the same place of importance in native mythology and in native ideas, which is clearly expressed in the behaviour of the natives and their manner of speaking of them. Thus, the general term for canoe magic is either *wayugo* or *ligogu*, from which we can see that these two spells are considered the most important. A man will speak about his *wayugo* being better than that of the other, or of having learnt his *ligogu* from his father. Again, as we shall see in the canoe myth, both these rites are explicitly mentioned there. Although the expulsion of the *tokway* is always done, it is definitely recognised by the natives as being of lesser importance. So are also the magic of caulking and of the black paint.

A less general point, of great interest, however, is that of evil magic (*bulubwalata*) and of broken taboos. I had to mention several exorcisms against those influences, and something must be said about them here. The term *bulubwalata* covers all forms of evil magic or witchery. There is that which, directed against pigs, makes them run away from their owners into the bush ; there is *bulubwalata* for alienating the affections of a wife or sweetheart ; there is evil magic against gardens, and—perhaps the most dreaded one—evil magic against rain, producing drought and famine. The evil magic against canoes, making them slow, heavy, and unseaworthy, is also much feared. Many men profess to know it, but it is very difficult for the Ethnographer to obtain a formula, and I succeeded only in taking down one. It is always supposed to be practised by canoe-owners upon the craft which they regard as dangerous rivals of their own.

There are many taboos referring to an already constructed canoe, and we shall meet with them later when speaking about sailing and handling the canoe. But before that stage is reached, any defilement with any unclean substance of the log out of which the canoe is scooped, would make it slow and bad; or if anybody were to walk over a canoe log or stand on it there would be the same evil result.

One more point must be mentioned here. As we have seen, the first magical rite, of the second stage of construction, is performed over the prow-boards. The question obtrudes itself as to whether the designs on these boards have any magical meaning. It must be clearly understood that any guesswork or speculations about origins must be rigidly excluded from ethnographic field work like this. For a sociologically empirical answer, the Ethnographer must look to two classes of facts. First of all, he may directly question the natives as to whether the prow-boards themselves or any of the motives upon them are done for magical purposes. Whether he questions the average man, or even the specialist in canoe magic and carving, to this he will always receive in Kiriwina a negative answer. He can then enquire whether in the magical

ritual for formulæ there are no references to the prow-boards,
or to any of the decorative motives on them.   Here also, the
evidence on the whole is negative.   In one spell perhaps, and
that belonging not to canoe but to the Kula magic (comp
below, Chap. XIII, Div. II, the Kayikuna Tabuyo spell),
there can be found an allusion to the prow-boards, but only
to the term describing them in general, and not to any special
decorative motive.   Thus the only association between canoe
decoration and canoe magic consists in the fact that two magical
rites are performed over them, one mentioned already, and the
other to be mentioned at the beginning of the next chapter.

The description of canoe-building, in fact, all the data
given in this chapter, refer only to one of the two types of
sea-going canoe to be found in the Kula district.   For the
natives of the Eastern half of the ring use craft bigger, and in
certain respects better, than the *masawa*.   The main difference
between the Eastern and Western type consists in the fact
that the bigger canoes have a higher gunwale or side, and
consequently a greater carrying capacity, and they can be
immersed deeper.   The larger water board offers more
resistance against making leeway, and this allows the canoes
to be sailed closer to the wind.   Consequently, the Eastern
canoes can beat, and these natives are therefore much more
independent of the direction of the wind in their sailings.
With this is connected the position of the mast, which in this
type is stepped in the middle, and it is also permanently fixed,
and is not taken down every time after sailing.   It obviously,
therefore, need not be changed in its position every time the
canoe goes on another tack.

I have not seen the construction of a *nagega*, as these
canoes are called, but I think that it is technically a much
more difficult task than the building of a *masawa*.   I was told
that both magic and ceremonial of construction are very much
the same in the building of both canoes.

The *nagega*, that is the larger and more seaworthy type,
is used on the section of the Kula ring beginning in Gawa and
ending in Tubetube.   It is also used in certain parts of the
Massim district, which lie outside the Kula ring, such as the
Island of Sud-Est, and surrounding smaller islands, and it is
used among the Southern Massim of the mainland.   But
though its use is very widely spread, its manufacture is confined

PLATE XXV

THE DUG-OUT IN THE VILLAGE

A canoe hull in the process of being hollowed out, in the *baku* of one of the villages of Sinaketa. The parts
not being worked are covered with cocoanut leaves. (See p. 112.)

CARVING A TABUYO

Molilakwa, a *tokabitam* (master carver), giving the final touches to an oval prowboard (*tabuyo*), made for a new canoe in Olivilevi. The carving is done with a long iron nail (formerly a wallaby bone was used), which is driven by means of a wooden hammer. (See p. 112.)

CONSTRUCTION OF A WAGA

This canoe has been partly dismembered, in the process of being relashed. It shows the construction of the ribs and the fixtures on the outrigger log. The men were just in the act of fitting in a new gunwale plank (to be seen in the background) which has to fit into the carved prowboards and into the groove at the top of the hull. (See p. 123.) The owner and magician can be seen to the left of the picture

Plate XXVIII

SAIL MAKING

Within a couple of hours a number of men perform this enormous task of sewing together
small bands of pandanus leaf (see p. 140 and Chapter VI, Div. II) till they form a sail. Among
the workers there is an albino

Plate XXIX

ROLLS OF DRIED PANDANUS LEAF

This is the material of which the sail is made. The *bisila* (pandanus streamer) is made of a
softer variety of pandanus leaf, bleached at a fire. (See p. 146.)

to only a few places. The most important centres of *nagega* building are Gawa, a few villages on Woodlark Islands, the Island of Panayati, and perhaps one or two places on Misima. From there, the canoes are traded all over the district, and indeed this is one of the most important forms of trade in this part of the world. The *masawa* canoes are used and manufactured in the district of Dobu, in the Amphletts, in the Trobriands, in Kitava and Iwa.

One point of great importance in the relation of these two forms of canoe is that one of them has, within the last two generations, been expanding at the expense of the other. According to reliable information, gathered at several points in the Trobriands and the Amphletts, the *nagega* type, that is the heavier, more seaworthy and better-sailing canoe, was driven out some time ago from the Amphletts and Trobriands. The *masawa*, in many respects inferior, but less difficult to build, and swifter, has supplanted the bigger type. In olden days, that is, about two or three generations ago, the *nagega* was used exclusively in Iwa, Kitava, Kiriwina, Vakuta, and Sinaketa, while the Amphlettans and the natives of Kayleula would usually use the *nagega*, though sometimes they would sail in *masawa* canoes. Dobu was the real home and head-quarters of the *masawa*. When the shifting began, and when it was completed, I could not ascertain. But the fact is that nowadays even the villages of Kitava and Iwa manufacture the smaller *masawa* canoe. Thus, one of the most important cultural items is spreading from South to North. There is, however, one point on which I could not obtain definite information : that is, whether in the Trobriands the *nagega* in olden days was imported from Kitava, or whether it was manufactured locally by imported craftsmen (as is done even nowadays in Kiriwina at times), or whether the Trobrianders themselves knew how to make the big canoes. There is no doubt, however, that in olden days, the natives of Kitava and Iwa used themselves to make the *nagega* canoes. The Kudayuri myth (see Chapter XII), and the connected magic, refer to this type of canoe. Thus in this district at any rate, and probably in the Trobriands and Amphletts as well, not only the use, but also the manufacture of the bigger canoe has been superseded by that of the smaller one, the *masawa*, now found in all these parts.

Chapter VI

LAUNCHING OF A CANOE AND CEREMONIAL VISITING—TRIBAL ECONOMICS IN THE TROBRIANDS

I

The canoe, painted and decorated, stands now ready to be launched, a source of pride to the owners and to the makers, and an object of admiration to the other beholders. A new sailing craft is not only another utility created ; it is more : if is a new entity sprung into being, something with which the future destinies of the sailors will be bound up, and on which they will depend. There can be no doubt that this sentiment is also felt by the natives and expressed in their customs and behaviour. The canoe receives a personal name, it becomes an object of intense interest to the whole district. Its qualities, points of beauty, and of probable perfection or faultiness are canvassed round the fires at night. The owner and his kinsmen and fellow villagers will speak of it with the usual boasting and exaggerations, and the others will all be very keen to see it, and to watch its performances. Thus the institution of ceremonial launching is not a mere formality prescribed by custom ; it corresponds to the psychological needs of the community, it rouses a great interest, and is very well attended even when the canoe belongs to a small community. When a big chief's canoe is launched, whether that of Kasanai or Omarakana, Olivilevi or Sinaketa, up to a thousand natives will assemble on the beach.

This festive and public display of a finished canoe, with its full paint and ornament, is not only in harmony with the natives' sentiments towards a new sailing craft ; it also agrees with the way they treat in general the results of their economic activities. Whether in gardening or in fishing, in the building of houses or in industrial achievements, there is a tendency to display the products, to arrange them, and even adorn at least certain classes of them, so as to produce a big, æsthetic effect. In fishing, there are only traces of this tendency, but in gardening, it assumes very great proportions, and the handling, arranging and display of garden produce is one of the most characteristic features of their tribal life, and it takes up much time and work.*

Soon after the painting and adorning of the canoe, a date is fixed for the ceremonial launching and trial run, the *tasasoria* festivities, as they are called. Word is passed to the chiefs and headmen of the neighbouring villages. Those of them who own canoes and who belong to the same Kula community have always to come with their canoes and take part in a sort of regatta held on the occasion. As the new canoe is always constructed in connection with a Kula expedition, and as the other canoes of the same Kula community have to be either done up or replaced, it is the rule that on the *tasasoria* day a whole fleet of brand new or renovated canoes assemble on the beach, all resplendent in fresh colours and decoration of cowrie shells and bleached pandanus streamers.

The launching itself is inaugurated with a rite of the *mwasila* (Kula magic), called *Kaytalula wadola waga* ("staining red of the mouth of the canoe"). After the natives have taken off the plaited coco-nut leaves with which the canoe is protected against the sun, the *toliwaga* chants a spell over some red ochre, and stains both bow and stern of the canoe. A special cowrie shell, attached to the prow-board (*tabuyo*) is stained at each end. After that the canoe is launched, the villagers pushing it into the water over pieces of wood transversely placed which act as slips (see Plate XXX). This is done amidst shouts and ululations, such as are made on all occasions when some piece of work has to be done in a festive and ceremonial manner, when, for instance, the harvest is brought in and given ceremonially by a man to his brother-in-law, or when a gift of yams or taro is laid down before a fisherman's house by an inland gardener, or the return gift of fish is made.

Thus the canoe is finally launched after the long series of mingled work and ceremony, technical effort and magical rite.

After the launching is done, there takes place a feast, or, more correctly, a distribution of food (*sagali*) under observation of all sorts of formalities and ritual. Such a distribution

* Cf. Chapter II, Divisions III and IV, and some of the following Divisions of this Chapter.

is always made when the *toliwaga* has not built the canoe himself, and when he therefore has to repay the cutter of the
canoe and his helpers. It also takes place whenever the canoe
of a big chief is launched, in order to celebrate the occasion,
to show off his wealth and generosity, and to give food to the
many people who have been summoned to assist in the
construction.

After the *sagali* (ceremonial distribution of food) is over,
as a rule, in the afternoon, the new canoe is rigged, the mast
is put up, the sail attached, and this and all the other boats
make a trial run. It is not a competitive race in the strict
sense of the word. The chief's canoe, which indeed would as
a rule be best and fastest, in any case always wins the race.
If it did not sail fastest, the others would probably keep back.
The trial run is rather a display of the new canoe, side by side
with the others.

In order to give one concrete illustration of the ceremonial
connected with canoe building and launching, it may be well
to relate an actual event. I shall therefore describe the
tasasoria, seen on the beach of Kaulukuba, in February, 1916,
when the new canoe of Kasana'i was launched. Eight canoes
took part in the trial run, that is, all the canoes of Kiriwina,
which forms what I have called the " Kula community," the
social group who make their Kula expeditions in a body, and
who have the same limits within which they carry on their
exchange of valuables.

The great event which was the cause of the building and
renovating of the canoes, was a Kula expedition planned by
To'ulawa and his Kula community. They were to go to the
East, to Kitava, to Iwa or Gawa, perhaps even to Muruwa
(Woodlark Island), though with this island the natives do not
carry on the Kula directly. As is usual in such cases, months
before the approximate date of sailing, plans and forecasts were
made, stories of previous voyages were recounted, old men dwelt
on their own reminiscences and reported what they had been
told by their elders of the days when iron was unknown and
everyone had to sail to the East in order to get the green
stone quarried in Suloga on Woodlark Island. And so, as it
always happens when future events are talked over round
village fires, imagination outran all bounds of probability ;
and the hopes and anticipations grew bigger and bigger. In

the end, everyone really believed his party would go at least to the Easternmost Marshall Bennetts (Gawa), whereas, as events turned out, they did not sail beyond Kitava.

For this occasion a new canoe had to be constructed in Kasana'i, and this was done by Ibena himself, the chief of that village, a man of rank equal to the highest chief (his kinsman, in fact) but of smaller power. Ibena is a skilled builder as well as a fair carver, and there is no class of magic in which he does not profess to be versed. The canoe was built, under his guidance ; he carved the boards himself, he also performed the magic, and he was, of course, the *toliwaga*.

In Omarakana, the canoe had to be slightly altered in construction ; it had to be re-lashed and re-painted. To do this To'uluwa, the chief, had summoned a master builder and carver from the island of Kitava, the same one who a couple of years before, had built this canoe. Also a new sail had to be made for the Omarakana boat, as the old one was too small. The ceremony of *tasasoria* (launching and regatta) ought by rights to have been held on the beach of Kasana'i, but as its sister village, Omarakana, is so much more important, it took place on Kaulukuba, the sea shore of the latter.

As the date approached, the whole district was alive with preparations, since the coastal villages had to put their canoes in order, while in the inland communities, new festive dresses and food had to be made ready. The food was not to be eaten, but to be offered to the chief for his *sagali* (ceremonial distribution). Only in Omarakana, the women had to cook for a big festive repast to be eaten on return from the *tasasoria*. In the Trobriands it is always a sign that a festive event is pending when all the women go in the evening to the bush to collect plenty of firewood. Next morning, this will be used for the *kumkumuli*, the baking of food in the ground, which is one of the forms of cooking used on festive occasions. On the evening of the *tasasoria* ceremony, people in Omarakana and Kasana'i were also busy with the numerous other preparations, running to the shore and back, filling baskets with yams for the *sagali*, getting ready their festive dress and decorations for the morrow. Festive dress means, for a woman, a new grass skirt, resplendent in fresh red, white and purple, and for the man a newly bleached, snow-white pubic leaf, made of the stalk of areca palm leaf.

Early in the morning of the appointed day, the food was packed into baskets of plaited leaf, the personal apparel on top of it, all covered as usual with folded mats and conveyed to the beach. The women carried on their heads the large baskets, shaped like big inverted bells, the men shouldered a stick with two bag-shaped baskets at each end. Other men had to carry the oars, paddles, rigging and sail, as these paraphenalia are always kept in the village. From one of the villages, one of the large, prismatic receptacles for food made of sticks was carried by several men right over the *raybwag* (coral ridge) to be offered to the chief of Omarakana as a share in the *sagali*. The whole village was astir, and on its outskirts, through the surrounding groves, parties from inland could be seen making their way rapidly to the shore. I left the village with a party of notables at about eight o'clock in the morning. After leaving the grove of fruit and palm trees which grows especially densely around the village of Omarakana, we entered between the two walls of green, the usual monotonous Trobriand road, which passes through the low scrub. Soon, emerging on a garden space, we could see, beyond a gentle declivity, the rising slope of the *raybwag*, a mixture of rank vegetation with monumental boulders of grey coral standing out here and there. Through this, the path led on, following in an intricate course between small precipices and towering outcrops, passing huge, ancient ficus trees, spreading around them their many trunks and aerial roots. At the top of the ridge, all of a sudden the blue sea shone through the foliage, and the roar of waves breaking on the reef struck our ears. Soon we found ourselves among the crowd assembled on the beach, near to the big boat-shed of Omarakana.

By about nine o'clock, everybody was ready on the beach. It was fully exposed to the Eastern sun, but this was not yet sufficiently high to drop its light right from above, and thus to produce that deadly effect of tropical mid-day, where the shadows instead of modelling out the details, blur every vertical surface and make everything dull and formless. The beach appeared bright and gaudy, and the lively brown bodies looked well against the background of green foliage and white sand. The natives were anointed with coco-nut oil, and decorated with flowers and facial paint. Large red hibiscus blossoms were stuck into their hair, and wreaths of the white, wonderfully scented *butia* flowers crowned the dense black mops. There was a good display of ebony carvings, sticks and lime spoons. There were decorated lime pots, and such objects of personal adornment as belts of red shell discs or of small cowrie shells, nose sticks (very rarely used nowadays), and other articles so well known to everybody from ethnological collections in museums, and usually called "ceremonial," though, as said above (Chapter III, Div. III) the description "objects of parade" would be much more in agreement with the correct meaning of the words.

Such popular festivities as the one just being described are the occasions on which these objects of parade, some of which astonish us by their artistic perfection, appear in native life. Before I had opportunities to see savage art in actual display, in its proper, "living" setting, there seemed to me always to exist some incongruity between the artistic finish of such objects and the general crudity of savage life, a crudity marked precisely on the æsthetic side. One imagines greasy, dirty, naked bodies, moppy hair full of vermin, and other realistic features which make up one's idea of the "savage," and in some respects reality bears out imagination. As a matter of fact though, the incongruity does not exist when once one has seen native art actually displayed in its own setting. A festive mob of natives, with the wonderful golden-brown colour of their skins brought out by washing and anointing and set off by the gaudy white, red and black of facial paint, feathers and ornaments, with their exquisitely carved and polished ebony objects, with their finely worked lime pots, has a distinct elegance of its own, without striking one as grotesque or incongruous in any æsthetic detail. There is an evident harmony between their festive mood, the display of colours and forms, and the manner in which they put on and bear their ornaments.

Those who have come from a distance, and who would spoil their decorations by the long march, wash with water and anoint themselves with coco-nut grease immediately before arriving at the scene of festivities. As a rule the best paint is put on later on, when the climax of the proceedings approaches. On this occasion, after the preliminaries (distribution of food, arrival of other canoes) were over, and when the races were just going to be started, the aristocracy of Omarakana—the wives and children of To'uluwa, his relatives and himself—withdrew behind the shelters, near the boat shed, and proceeded to put on the red, white and black of full facial paint. They crushed young betel-nut, mixed it with lime, and put it on with the pestles of betel mortars ; then some of the aromatic black resin (*sayaku*) and white lime were applied. As the habit of mirrors is not quite well established yet in the Trobriands, the painting was done by one person on the face of another, and great care and patience were displayed on both sides.

The numerous crowd spent the day without taking much refreshment—a feature strongly differentiating Kiriwinian festivities from our ideal of an entertainment or picnic. No cooking was done, and only a few bananas were eaten here and there, and green coco-nuts were drunk and eaten. But even these refreshments were consumed with great frugality.

As always on such occasions, the people collected together in sets, the visitors from each village forming a group apart. The local natives kept to their own boat houses, those of Omarakana and Kurokaiwa having their natural centres on the beach of Kaulukuba. The other visitors similarly kept together in their position on the beach, according to their local distribution ; thus, men from the Northern villages would keep to the Northern section of the beach, those from the South would stick to that point of the compass, so that villages which were neighbours in reality would also be side by side on the shore. There was no mingling in the crowd, and individuals would not walk about from one group to another. The aristocrats, out of personal dignity, humble folk because of a modesty imposed by custom, would keep in their places. To'uluwa sat practically during the whole performance, on the platform erected for this purpose, except when he went over to his boat, to trim it for the race.

The boat shed of Omarakana, round which the chief, his family and the other villagers were grouped, was the centre of all the proceedings. Under one of the palms, a fairly high platform was put up to accommodate To'uluwa. In a row in front of the sheds and shelters, there stood the prismatic food receptacles (*pwata'i*). They had been erected by the inhabitants of Omarakana and Kasana'i, on the previous day, and partially filled with yams. The rest had to be supplied by people from the other villages, on the day of the boat races. As the natives came to the beach on that day, village after village, they brought their contribution, and before settling down on their particular spot on the shore, they paid a visit to the chief and offered him their tributes. These would be put into one of the *pwata'i*. All the villages did not contribute their share, but the majority did, though some of them brought only a few baskets. One of the villages brought one complete *pwata'i*, filled with yams, and offered the whole to the chief.

In the meantime, the eight canoes arrived, including that of Kasana'i, which had been ceremonially launched that morning with the accompanying magical rite, on its own beach about half a mile away. The canoe of Omarakana had also been launched on this morning (Plate XXX), and the same rite performed over it. It ought to have been done by To'uluwa, the chief. As he, however, is quite incapable of remembering magical spells—in fact, he never does any of the magic which his rank and office impose on him—the rite was performed on this occasion by one of his kinsmen. This is a typical case of a rule very stringently formulated by all informants when you ask about it, yet in reality often observed with laxity. If you inquire directly, everyone will tell you that this rite, as all others of the *mwasila* (Kula magic) has to be done by the *toliwaga*. But every time when he ought to perform it, To'uluwa will find some excuse, and delegate it to another.

When all the canoes were present, as well as all the important villages, at about eleven o'clock a.m., there took place the *sagali* (ceremonial distribution). The food was given to people from various villages, especially such as took part in the races, or had assisted in the building of the new canoe. So we see that food contributed by all the villages before the *sagali* was simply redistributed among them, a considerable quantity having been added first by the chief; and this indeed is the usual procedure at a *sagali*. In this case, of course, the lion's share was taken by the Kitavans who helped at the building.

After the *sagali* was over, the canoes were all brought up to one spot, and the natives began to prepare them for the race. The masts were stepped, the fastenings trimmed, the sails made ready (see Plate XXXI). After that the canoes all put off and gathered about half a mile off the shore, beyond the fringing reef ; and at a sign given by some one on one of them, they all started. As said before, such a run is not a race properly speaking, in which the canoes would start scrupulously at the same minute, have the same distance to cover, and which would clearly show which is the fastest. In this case, it was merely, as always, a review of the boats sailing along as well as they were able, a review in which they all began to move, more or less at the same time, went in the same direction, and covered practically the same distance.

As to the time table of the events, the *sagali* was over before mid-day. There was a pause ; and then, at about one p.m., the natives began rigging the canoes. Then all hands had a spell, and not before three p.m. were the races started. The whole affair was over by about four o'clock, and half an hour later, the boats from the other villages started to sail home, the people on the shore dispersed, so that by sunset, that is, about six o'clock, the beach was almost deserted.

Such was the *tasasoria* ceremony which I saw in February, 1916. It was a fine sight from the spectacular point of view. A superficial onlooker could have hardly perceived any sign of white man's influence or interference. I was the only white man present, and besides myself only some two or three native missionary teachers were dressed in white cotton. Amongst the rest of us there could be seen sparsely a coloured rag, tied round as a neckerchief or head-dress. But otherwise there was only a swarm of naked brown bodies, shining with coco-nut oil, adorned in new festive dress, with here and there the three-coloured grass skirt of a woman (see Plates XXX and XXXI).

But alas, for one who could look below the surface and read the various symptoms of decay, deep changes would be discernible from what must have been the original conditions of such a native gathering. In fact, some three generations ago, even its appearances would have been different. The natives then would have been armed with shields and spears ; some would have borne decorative weapons, such as the big sword-clubs of hard wood, or massive ebony cudgels, or small throwing-sticks. A closer inspection would have shown many more decorations and ornaments, such as nose-sticks, finely carved lime spatulæ, gourds with burnt-in designs, some of which are now out of use, or those used of inferior workmanship or without decoration.

But other and much deeper changes have taken place in the social conditions. Three generations ago both the canoes in the water and the people on the shore would have been more numerous. As mentioned above, in the olden days there would have been some twenty canoes in Kiriwina, as against eight at the present time. Again, the far stronger influence of the chief, and the much greater relative importance of the event would have attracted a larger proportion out of the then more numerous population. Nowadays, other interests, such as diving for pearls, working on white man's plantations, divert the native attention, while many events connected with Missions, Government and trading, eclipse the importance of old customs.

Again, the people on the shore would have had to adhere in olden days even more closely to the local distribution, men of the same village community keeping together still more strictly, and looking with mistrust and perhaps even hostility, at other groups, especially those with whom they had hereditary feuds. The general tension would often be broken by squabbles or even miniature fights, especially at the moment of dispersing, and on the way home.

One of the important features of the performance, and the one of which the natives think perhaps most—the display of food—would also have been quite different. The chief whom I saw sitting on a platform surrounded by a few wives only, and with small attendance would, under the old conditions, have been the owner of thrice as many wives and consequently relatives-in-law, and as it is these from whom he derives most of his income, he would have provided a much bigger *sagali* than he is able to do nowadays.

Three generations ago the whole event would have been much more solemn and dramatic to the natives. The very distance to the neighbouring island of Kitava is nowadays dwarfed. In the past, it would not, as now, be quickly obliterated by a white man's steam-launch. Then, the canoes on the beach were the only means of arriving there, and their value in the eyes of the natives must have, therefore, been even higher, although they think so much of them now. The outlines of the distant island and the small fleet of canoes on the beach formed for the natives the first act of a big over seas expedition, an event of far deeper significance to them then than now. A rich haul of arm-shells, the arrival of many much-coveted utilities, the bringing back of news from the far-off land, all this meant much more in older days than it can mean at present. War, dancing, and the Kula supplied tribal life with its romantic and heroic elements. Nowadays, with war prohibited by the Government, with dancing discredited by missionary influence, the Kula alone remains, and even that is stripped of some of its glamour.

II

Before we proceed to the next stage, we must pause in following the events of a Kula expedition, and consider one or two points of more general importance. I have touched in the narrative, but not dwelt upon, certain problems of the sociology of work. At the outset of the preceding chapter it was mentioned that canoe-building requires a definite organisation of work, and in fact we saw that in the course of construction, various kinds of labour were employed, and more especially towards the end, much use was made of communal labour. Again, we saw that during the launching ceremony payment was given by the owner to the expert and his helpers. These two points therefore, the organisation of labour and communal labour in particular, and the system of payment for experts' work must be here developed.

Organisation of Labour.—First of all, it is important to realise that a Kiriwinian is capable of working well, efficiently and in a continuous manner. But he must work under an effective incentive : he must be prompted by some duty imposed by tribal standards, or he must be lured by ambitions and values also dictated by custom and tradition. Gain, such as is often the stimulus for work in more civilised communities, never acts as an impulse to work under the original native conditions. It succeeds very badly, therefore, when a white man tries to use this incentive to make a native work.

This is the reason why the traditional view of the lazy and indolent native is not only a constant refrain of the average white settler, but finds its way into good books of travel, and even serious ethnographic records. With us, labour is, or was till fairly recently, a commodity sold as any other, in the open market. A man accustomed to think in terms of current economic theory will naturally apply the conceptions of supply and demand to labour, and he applies them therefore to native labour. The untrained person does the same, though in less sophisticated terms, and as they see that the native will not work well for the white man, even if tempted by considerable payment and treated fairly well, they conclude that his capacity for labour is very small. This error is due to the same cause which lies at the bottom of all our misconceptions about people of different cultures. If you remove a man from his social milieu, you *eo ipso* deprive him of almost all his stimuli to moral steadfastness and economic efficiency and even of interest in life. If then you measure him by moral, legal or economic standards, also essentially foreign to him, you cannot but obtain a caricature in your estimate.

But the natives are not only capable of energetic, continuous and skilful work ; their social conditions also make it possible for them to employ organised labour. At the beginning of Chapter IV, the sociology of canoe-building was given in outline, and now, after the details of its successive stages have been filled in, it is possible to confirm what has been said there, and draw some conclusions as to this organisation of labour. And first, as we are using this expression so often, I must insist again on the fact that the natives are capable of it, and that this contention is not a truism, as the following considerations should show. The just mentioned view of the lazy, individualistic and selfish savage, who lives on the bounties of nature as they fall ripe and ready for him, implicitly precludes the possibility of his doing effective work, *integrated into an organised effort by social forces*. Again, the view, almost universally accepted by specialists, is that the lowest savages are in the pre-economic stage of individualistic search for food, whereas the more developed ones, such as the Trobrianders, for instance, live at the stage of isolated household economy. This view also ignores, when it does not deny explicitly, the possibility of socially organised labour.

The view generally held is that, in native communities each individual works for himself, or members of a household work so as to provide each family with the necessities of life. Of course, a canoe, even a *masawa*, could obviously be made by the members of a household, though with less efficiency and in a longer time. So that there is *a priori* nothing to foretell whether organised labour, or the unaided efforts of an individual or a small group of people should be used in the work. As a matter of fact, we have seen in canoe-building a number of men engaged in performing each a definite and difficult task, though united to one purpose. The tasks were differentiated in their sociological setting ; some of the workers were actually to own the canoe ; others belonged to a different community, and did it only as an act of service to the chief. Some worked in order to derive direct benefit from the use of the canoe, others were to be paid. We saw also that the work of felling, of scooping, of decorating, would in some cases be performed by various men, or it might be performed by one only. Certainly the minute tasks of lashing, caulking and painting, as well as sail-making, were done by communal labour as opposed to individual. And all these different tasks were directed towards one aim : the providing the chief or headman with the title of ownership of a canoe, and his whole community with its use.

It is clear that this differentiation of tasks, co-ordinated to a general purpose, requires a well developed social apparatus to back it up, and that on the other hand, this social mechanism must be associated and permeated with economic elements. There must be a chief, regarded as representative of a group ; he must have certain formal rights and privileges, and a certain amount of authority, and also he must dispose of part of the wealth of the community. There must also be a man or men with knowledge sufficient to direct and co-ordinate the technical operations. All this is obvious. But it must be clearly set forth that the real force which binds all the people and ties them down in their tasks is obedience to custom, to tradition.

Every man knows what is expected from him, in virtue of his position, and he does it, whether it means the obtaining of a privilege, the performance of a task, or the acquiescence in a *status quo*. He knows that it always has been thus, and thus it is all around him, and thus it always must remain. The chief's authority, his privileges, the customary give and take which exist between him and the community, all that is merely, so to speak, the mechanism through which the force of tradition acts. For there is no organised physical means by which those in authority could enforce their will in a case like this. Order is kept by direct force of everybody's adhesion to custom, rules and laws, by the same psychological influences which in our society prevent a man of the world doing something which is not "the right thing." The expression "might is right" would certainly not apply to Trobriand society. "Tradition is right, and what is right *has* might"—this rather is the rule governing the social forces in Boyowa, and I dare say in almost all native communities at this stage of culture.

All the details of custom, all the magical formulæ, the whole fringe of ceremonial and rite which accompany canoe-building, all these things add weight to the social scheme of duties. The importance of magical ideas and rites as integrating forces has been indicated at the outset of this description. It is easy to see how all the appurtenances of ceremony, that is, magic, decoration, and public attendance welded together into one whole with labour, serve to put order and organisation into it.

Another point must be enlarged upon somewhat more. I have spoken of *organised labour*, and of *communal labour*. These two conceptions are not synonymous, and it is well to keep them apart. As already defined, organised labour implies the co-operation of several socially and economically different elements. It is quite another thing, however, when a number of people are engaged side by side, performing the same work, without any technical division of labour, or social differentiation of function. Thus, the whole enterprise of canoe-building is, in Kiriwina, the result of *organised labour*. But the work of some twenty to thirty men, who side by side do the lashing or caulking of the canoe, is *communal labour*. This latter form of work has a great psychological advantage. It is much more stimulating and more interesting, and it allows of emulation, and therefore of a better quality of work. For one or two men, it would require about a month to do the work which twenty to thirty men can do in a day. In certain cases, as in the pulling of the heavy log from the jungle to the village, the joining of forces is almost indispensable. True, the canoe could be scooped out in the *raybwag*, and then a few men might be able to pull it along, applying some skill. But it would entail great hardships. Thus, in some cases, communal labour is of extreme importance, and in all cases it furthers the course of work considerably. Sociologically, it is important, because it implies mutual help, exchange of services, and solidarity in work within a wide range .

Communal labour is an important factor in the tribal economy of the Trobriand natives. They resort to it in the building of living-huts and storehouses, in certain forms of industrial work, and in the transport of things, especially at harvest time, when great quantities of produce have to be shifted from one village to another, often over a great distance. In fishing, when several canoes go out together and fish each for itself, then we cannot speak of communal labour. When on the other hand, they fish in one band, each canoe having an appointed task, as is sometimes done, then we have to do with organised labour. Communal labour is also based upon the duties of *urigubu*, or relatives-in-law. That is, a man's relatives-in-law have to assist him, whenever he needs their co-operation. In the case of a chief, there is an assistance on a grand scale, and whole villages will turn out. In the case of a commoner, only a few people will help. There is always a distribution of food after the work has been done, but this can hardly be considered as payment, for is is not proportional to the work each individual does.

By far the most important part communal labour has to play, is in gardening. There are as many as five different forms of communal labour in the gardens, each called by a different name, and each distinct in its sociological nature. When a chief or headman summons the members of a village community, and they agree to do their gardens communally, it is called *tamgogula*. When this is decided upon, and the time grows near for cutting the scrub for new gardens, a festive eating is held on the central place, and there all men go, and *takayva* (cut down) the scrub on the chief's plot. After that, they cut in turn the garden plots of everyone, all men working on the one plot during a day, and getting on that day food from the owner. This procedure is reproduced at each successive stage of gardening ; at the fencing, planting of yams, bringing in supports, and finally, at the weeding, which is done by women. At certain stages, the gardening is often done by each one working for himself, namely at the clearing of the gardens after they are burnt, at the cleaning of the roots

PLATE XXX

LAUNCHING OF A CANOE

Nigada Bu'a after its renovation, being pushed into the water. (See p. 147.)

PLATE XXXI

THE TASASORIA ON THE BEACH OF KAULUKUBA

Stepping the masts and getting the sails ready for the run. In the foreground, To'uluwa, the chief of Kiriwina, standing at the mast, supervises the rigging of Nigada Bu'a. (See p. 154.)

A CHIEF'S YAM HOUSE IN KASANA'I

This illustrates the display of yams in the interstices between the logs of the wall, and the decorations of cocoanuts, running round the gable, along the supports and the walls. This yam house was quite recently put up and its barge boards had not yet been erected. (See p. 168.)

Plate XXXIII

FILLING A YAM HOUSE IN YALUMUGWA

The yams are taken from the conical heaps and put into the *bwayma* (store houses) by the brother-in-law (wife's brother) of the owner. Note the decorations on the gable—the owner being a *gumguya'u* (chief of lower rank). (See p. 170.)

DISPLAY OF PIGS AND YAMS AT A DISTRIBUTION (SAGALI)

All food to be given away is several times displayed before, during, and after the ceremony. Exhibiting the food in large, prismatic receptacles (*pwata'i*) is one of the typical features of Trobriand custom. (See p. 170.)

PLATE XXXV

COMMUNAL COOKING OF MONA (TARO DUMPLINGS)

Large claypots, imported from the Amphletts, are used for the purpose ; in these, coconut oil is brought to a boil, pieces of pounded taro being thrown in afterwards, while a man stirs the contents with a long, decorated, wooden ladle. (See p. 171.)

PLATE XXXVI

SCENE IN THE WASI (CEREMONIAL EXCHANGE OF VEGETABLES FOR FISH)

The inland party have brought their yams by boat to the village of Oburaku, which is practically inaccessible by land. They are putting up the vegetables into square, wooden crates in order to carry them ceremonially and to place each before the partner's house. (See p. 18.)

PLATE XXXVII

VAVA, DIRECT BARTER OF VEGETABLES FOR FISH

In the picture, the inland natives exchange bundles of taro directly for fish, without observing the rites and ceremonies obligatory in a *wasi*. (See p. 190.)

of yams when they begin to produce tubers, and at harvesting.

There are, as a rule, several communal feasts during the progress, and one at the end of a *tamgogula* period. Gardens are generally worked in this fashion, in years when big ceremonial dancing or some other tribal festivity is held. This usually makes the work very late, and it has then to be done quickly and energetically, and communal labour has evidently been found suitable for this purpose.

When several villages agree to work their gardens by communal labour, this is called *lubalabisa*. The two forms do not differ very much except by name, and also by the fact that, in the latter form, more than one chief or headman has to direct the process. The *lubalabisa* would only be held when there are several small villages, clustered together, as is the case in the village compounds of Sinaketa, Kavataria, Kabwaku or Yalaka.

When a chief or headman, or man of wealth and influence summons his dependents or his relatives-in-law to work for him, the name *kabutu* is given to the proceedings. The owner has to give food to all those co-operating. A *kabutu* may be instituted for one bit of gardening, for example, a headman may invite his villagers to do his cutting for him, or his planting or his fencing. It is clear that whenever communal labour is required by one man in the construction of his house or yam store, the labour is of the *kabutu* type, and it is thus called by the natives.

The fourth form of communal labour is called *ta'ula*, and takes place whenever a number of villagers agree to do one stage of gardening in common, on the basis of reciprocity. No great or special payments take place. The same sort of communal labour extending over all stages of gardening, is called *kari'ula*, and it may be counted as the fifth form of communal labour in the gardens. Finally, a special word, *tavile'i*, is used when they wish to say that the gardens are done by individual labour, and that everyone works on his own plot. It is a rule, however, that the chief's plots, especially those of an influential chief of high rank, are always gardened by communal labour, and this latter is also used with regard to certain privileged plots, on which, in a given year, the garden magic is performed first, and with the greatest display.

Thus there is a number of distinct forms of communal labour, and they show many more interesting features which cannot be mentioned in this short outline. The communal labour used in canoe-building is obviously of the *kabutu* type. In having a canoe made, the chief is able to summon big numbers of the inhabitants of a whole district, the headman of an important village receives the assistance of his whole community, whereas a man of small importance, such as one of the smaller headmen of Sinaketa or Vakuta, would have to rely on his fellow villagers and relations-in-law. In all these cases, it would be the call of duty, laid down by custom, which would make them work. The payment would be of secondary importance, though in certain circumstances, it would be a considerable one. The distribution of food during launching forms such a payment, as we have seen in Division I of this chapter. In olden days, a meal of pigs, an abundance of betel-nut and coco-nut and sugar cane would have made a veritable feast for the natives.

Another point of importance from the economic aspect is the payment given by the chief to the builder of the canoe. The canoe of Omarakana was made, as we saw, for To'uluwa by a specialist from Kitava, who was well paid with a quantity of food, pigs and *vaygua* (native valuables). Nowadays, when the power of the chiefs is broken, when they have much less wealth than formerly to back up their position, and cannot use even the little force they ever did and when the general breaking up of custom has undermined the traditional deference and loyalty of their subjects, the production of canoes and other forms of wealth by the specialist for the chief is only a vestige of what it once was. In olden days it was, economically, one of the most important features of the Trobriand tribal life. In the construction of the canoe, which a chief in olden days would never build himself, we meet with an example of this.

Here it will be enough to say that whenever a canoe is built for a chief or headman by a builder, this has to be paid for by an initial gift of food. Then, as long as the man is at work, provisional gifts of food are given him. If he lives away from home, like the Kitavan builder on the beach of Omarakana, he is fed by the *toliwaga* and supplied with dainties such as coco-nut, betel-nut, pigs' flesh, fish and fruits. When he works

in his own home, the *toliwaga* will bring him choice food at
frequent intervals, inspecting, as he does so, the progress of
the work.   This feeding of the worker or bringing him extra
choice food is called *vakapula*.   After the canoe is finished, a
substantial gift is given to the master-builder during the
ceremonial distribution of food.   The proper amount would be
a few hundred basketfuls of yams, a pig or two, bunches of
betel-nut, and a great number of coco-nuts ; also, a large stone
blade or a pig, or a belt of red shell discs, and some smaller
vaygua of the non-Kula type.

In Vakuta, where chieftainship is not very distinct, and the
difference in wealth less great, a *toliwaga* also has to feed the
workers during the time of hollowing out, preparing, and
building a canoe.   Then, after the caulking, some fifty baskets-
ful are given to the builder.   After the launching and trial
run, this builder gives a rope, symbol of the canoe, to his wife,
who, blowing the conch shell, presents the rope to the *toliwaga*.
He, on the spot, gives her a bunch of betel or bananas.   Next
day, a considerable present of food, known as *yomelu*, is given
by the chief, and then at the next harvest, another fifty or
sixty basketfuls of yams as *kuribudaboda* or closing up gift.

I have chosen the data from two concrete cases, one noted
in Kiriwina, the other in Vakuta— that is, in the district where
the chief's power is greatest, and in that where there never
has been more than a rudimentary distance in rank and wealth
between chief and commoner.   In both cases there is a payment, but in Kiriwina the payment is greater.   In Vakuta,
it is obviously rather an exchange of services, whereas in
Kiriwina the chief maintains, as well as rewards his builder.
In both cases we have the exchange of skilled services against
maintenance by supply of food.

III

We shall pass now to the next ceremonial and customary
performance in the succession of Kula events, to the display
of a new canoe to the friends and relatives of the *toliwaga*.
This custom is called *kabigidoya*.   The *tasasoria* (launching
and trial run) is obviously at the same time the last act of ship-
building, and by its associated magical rite, by the foretaste of
sailing, it is also one of the beginning stages of the Kula.
The *kabigidoya* being a presentation of the new canoe, belongs

to the series of building ceremonials ; but in so far as it is a provisioning trip, it belongs to the Kula.

The canoe is manned with the usual crew, it is rigged and fitted out with all its paraphernalia, such as paddles, baler, and conch shell, and it sets out on a short trip to the beaches of the neighbouring villages. When the canoe belongs to a compound settlement like Sinaketa, then it will stop at every beach of the sister villages. The conch shell is blown, and people in the village will know " The *kabigidoya* men have arrived." The crew remains in the canoe, the *toliwaga* goes ashore, taking one paddle with him. He goes to the house of his fellow-headman, and thrusts the paddle into the frame of the house, with the words : " I offer thee thy *bisila* (pandanus streamer) ; take a *vaygua* (valuable), catch a pig and break the head of my new canoe." To which the local headman will answer—giving a present : " This is the *katuvisala dabala* (the breaking of the head) of thy new canoe ! " This is an example of the quaint, customary wording used in the exchange of gifts, and in other ceremonial transactions. The *bisila* (pandanus streamer) is often used as a symbol for the canoe, in magical spells, in customary expressions, and in idiomatic terms of speech. Bleached pandanus streamers are tied to the mast, rigging and sail ; a specially medicated strip is often attached to the prow of the canoe to give it speed, and there is also other *bisila* magic to make a district partner inclined for Kula.

The gifts given are not always up to the standard of those mentioned in the above customary phrase. The *kabigidoya*, especially from the neighbouring villages, often brings only a few mats, a few dozen coco-nuts, some betel-nut, a couple of paddles, and such articles of minor value. And even in these trifles there is not much gain from the short *kabigidoya*. For as we know, at the beginning of the Kula all the canoes of, say, Sinaketa or Kiriwina are either rebuilt or renewed. What therefore one canoe receives on its *kabigidoya* round, from all the others, will have to be more or less returned to them, when they in their turn *kabigidoya* one after the other. Soon afterwards, however, on an appointed day, all the canoes sail together on a visit to the other districts, and on this *kabigidoya*, they receive as a rule much more substantial presents, and these they will only have to return much later, after a year or two, when the visited district will come back to them on their own *kabigidoya*. Thus, when the canoes of Kirwina are built and renovated for a big Kula expedition, they will sail South along the coast, and stop first in Olivilevi, receiving presents from the chief there, and walking on a round of the inland villages of Luba. Then they will proceed to the next sea village, that of Wawela, leaving their canoes there, and going from there across to Sinaketa. Thence they proceed still further South, to Vakuta. The villages on the Lagoon, such as Sinaketa and Vakuta, will return these visits, sailing North along the Western shore on the Lagoon side. Then they stop at Tukwaukwa or Kavataria, and from there walk inland to Kiriwina, where they receive presents (see Map IV, p. 50).

The *kabigidoya* trips of the Vakutans and Sinaketans are more important than those of the Northern or Eastern districts, because they are combined with a preliminary trade, in which the visitors replenish their stock of goods, which they will need presently on their trip South to Dobu. The reader will remember that Kuboma is the industrial district of the Trobriands, where are manufactured most of the useful articles, for which these islands are renowned in the whole of Eastern New Guinea. It lies in the Northern half of the island, and from Kiriwina it is only a few miles walk, but to reach it from Sinaketa or Vakuta it is necessary to sail North. The Southern villages therefore go to Kavataria, and from there walk inland to Bwoytalu, Luya, Yalaka and Kadukwaykela, where they make their purchases. The inhabitants of these villages also when they hear that the Sinaketans are anchored in Kavataria, bring their wares to the canoes.

A brisk trade is carried on during the day or two that the Sinaketans remain in Kavataria. The natives of Kuboma are always eager to buy yams, as they live in an unfertile district, and devote themselves more to industrial productions than to gardening. And they are still more eager to acquire coco-nuts and betel-nut, of which they have a great scarcity. They desire besides to receive in exchange for their produce the red shell discs manufactured in Sinaketa and Vakuta, and the turtle-shell rings. For objects of great value, the Sinaketans would give the big clay pots which they receive directly from the Amphletts. For that they obtain different articles according to the villages with which they are exchanging. From Bwoytalu, they get the wonderfully fashioned and decorated wooden dishes of various sizes, depths and finish, made out of either hard or soft wood ; from Bwaytelu, Wabutuma and Buduwaylaka, armlets of plaited fern fibre, and wooden combs ; from Buduwaylaka, Yalaka, and Kaduk-waykela, lime pots of different qualities and sizes.   From the villages of Tilatauia, the district North-east of Kuboma, the polished axe blades used to be acquired in olden days.

I shall not enter into the technicalities of this exchange, nor shall I give here the approximate list of prices which obtain. We shall have to follow the traded goods further on to Dobu, and there we shall see how they change hands again, and under what conditions.   This will allow us to compare the prices and thus to gauge the nature of the transaction as a whole. It will be better therefore to defer all details till then.

IV

Here, however, its seems necessary to make another digression from the straight narrative of the Kula, and give an outline of the various forms of trade and exchange as we find them in the Trobriands.   Indeed, the main theme of this volume is the Kula, a form of exchange, and I would be untrue to my chief principle of method, were I to give the description of one form of exchange torn out of its most intimate context ; that is, were I to give an account of the Kula without giving at least a general outline of the forms of Kiriwinian payments and gifts and barter.

In Chapter II, speaking of some features of Trobriand tribal life, I was led to criticise the current views of primitive economic man.   They depict him as a being indolent, inde-pendent, happy-go-lucky, yet at the same time governed exclusively by strictly rational and utilitarian motives, and logical and consistent in his behaviour.   In this chapter again, in Division II, I pointed out another fallacy implied in this conception, a fallacy which declares that a savage is capable only of very simple, unorganised and unsystematic forms of labour.   Another error more or less explicitly expressed in all writings on primitive economics, is that the natives possess only rudimentary forms of trade and exchange ; that these forms play no essential part in the tribal life, are carried on only spasmodically and at rare intervals, and as necessity dictates.

Whether we have to deal with the wide-spread fallacy of the primitive Golden Age, characterised mainly by the absence of any distinction between *mine* and *thine* ; or whether we take the more sophisticated view, which postulates stages of individual search for food, and of isolated household catering ; or if we consider for the moment the numerous theories which see nothing in primitive economics but simple pursuits for the maintenance of existence—in none of these can we find reflected even a hint of the real state of affairs as found in the Trobriands ; namely, that *the whole tribal life is permeated by a constant give and take ;* that every ceremony, every legal and customary act is done to the accompaniment of material gift and counter gift ; that wealth, given and taken, is one of the main instruments of social organisation, of the power of the chief, of the bonds of kinship, and of relationship in law.*

These views on primitive trade, prevalent though erroneous, appear no doubt quite consistent, that is, if we grant certain premises. Now these premises seem plausible, and yet they are false, and it will be good to have a careful look at them so that we can discard them once and for all. They are based on some sort of reasoning, such as the following one : If, in tropical conditions, there is a plenty of all utilities, why trouble about exchanging them ? Then, why attach any value to them ? Is there any reason for striving after wealth, where everyone can have as much as he wants without much effort ? Is there indeed any room for value, if this latter is the result of

* I am adducing these views not for any controversial purposes, but to justify and make clear why I stress certain general features of Trobriand Economic Sociology. My contentions might run the danger of appearing as gratuitous truisms if not thus justified. The opinion that primitive humanity and savages have no individual property is an old prejudice shared by many modern writers, especially in support of communistic theories, and the so-called materialistic view of history. The " communism of savages " is a phrase very often read, and needs no special quotation. The views of individual search for food and household economy are those of Karl Bücher, and they have directly influenced all the best modern writings on Primitive Economics. Finally, the view that we have done with Primitive Economics if we have described the way in which the natives procure their food, is obviously a fundamental premise of all the naïve, evolutionary theories which construct the successive stages of economic development. This view is summarised in the following sentence : " . . . . In many simple communities, the actual food quest, and operations immediately arising from it, occupy by far the greater part of the people's time and energy, leaving little opportunity for the satisfaction of any lesser needs." This sentence, quoted out of " Notes and Queries on Anthropology," p. 160, article on the " Economics of the Social Group," represents what may be called the official view of contemporary Ethnology on the subject, and in perusing the rest of the article, it can be easily seen that all the manifold economic problems, with which we are dealing in this book, have been so far more or less neglected.

scarcity as well as utility, in a community, in which all the useful things are plentiful ?   On the other hand, in those savage communities where the necessities of life are scarce, there is obviously no possibility of accumulating them, and thus creating wealth.

Again, since, in savage communities, whether bountifully or badly provided for by nature, everyone has the same free access to all the necessities, is there any need to exchange them ? Why give a basketful of fruit or vegetables, if everybody has practically the same quantity and the same means of procuring it ?   Why make a present of it, if it cannot be returned except in the same form ?*

There are two main sources of error at the bottom of this faulty reasoning.   The first is that the relation of the savage to material goods is a purely rational one, and that consequently, in his conditions, there is no room for wealth or value. The second erroneous assumption is that there can be no need for exchange if anyone and everyone can, by industry and skill, produce all that represents value through its quantity or its quality.

As regards the first proposition, it is not true either with regard to what may be called primary wealth, that is, food stuffs, nor with regard to articles of luxury, which are by no means absent in Trobriand society.   First as to food-stuffs, they are not merely regarded by the natives as nourishment, not merely valued because of their utility.   They accumulate them not so much because they know that yams can be stored and used for a future date, but also because they like to display their possessions in food.   Their yam houses are built so that the quantity of the food can be gauged, and its quality ascertained through the wide interstices between the beams (see Plates XXXII and XXXIII).   The yams are so arranged that the best specimens come to the outside and are well visible.   Special

---

* These views had to be adduced at length, although touched upon already in Chapter II, Division IV, because they imply a serious error with regard to human nature in one of its most fundamental aspects.   We can show up their fallacy on one example only, that of the Trobriand Society, but even this is enough to shatter their universal validity and show that the problem must be re-stated.   The criticised views contain very general propositions, which, however, can be answered only empirically.   And it is the duty of the field Ethnographer to answer and correct them.   Because a statement is very general, it can none the less be a statement of empirical fact.   General views must not be mixed up with hypothetical ones.   The latter must be banished from field work ;   the former cannot receive too much attention.

varieties of yams, which grow up to two metres length, and weigh as much as several kilograms each, are framed in wood and decorated with paint, and hung on the outside of the yam houses. That the right to display food is highly valued can be seen from the fact that in villages where a chief of high rank resides, the commoners' storehouses have to be closed up with coco-nut leaves, so as not to compete with his.

All this shows that the accumulation of food is not only the result of economic foresight, but also prompted by the desire of display and enhancement of social prestige through possession of wealth.

When I speak about ideas underlying accumulation of food stuffs in the Trobriands, I refer to the present, actual psychology of the natives, and I must emphatically declare that I am not offering here any conjectures about the " origins " or about the " history " of the customs and their psychology, leaving this to theoretical and comparative research.

Another institution which illuminates the native ideas about food storage is the magic called *vilamalya*, performed over the crops after harvest, and at one or two other stages. This magic is intended to make the food last long. Before the store-house is filled with yams, the magician places a special kind of heavy stone on the floor, and recites a long magical spell. On the evening of the same day, after the food houses have been filled, he spits over them with medicated ginger root, and he also performs a rite over all the roads entering into the village, and over the central place. All this will make food plentiful in that village, and will make the supplies last long. But, and this is the important point for us, this magic is conceived to act, not on the food, but on the inhabitants of the village. It makes their appetites poor, it makes them, as the natives put it, inclined to eat wild fruit of the bush, the mango and bread fruit of the village grove, and refuse to eat yams, or at least be satisfied with very little. They will boast that when this magic is performed well, half of the yams will rot away in the storehouses, and be thrown on the *wawa*, the rubbish heap at the back of the houses, to make room for the new harvest. Here again we meet the typical idea that the main aim of accumulating food is to keep it exhibited in the yam houses till it rots, and then can be replaced by a new étalage.

The filling of the storehouses involves a double display of food, and a good deal of ceremonial handling. When the tubers are taken out of the ground they are first displayed in the gardens. A shed of poles is erected, and covered with *taitu* vine, which is thrown thickly over it. In such arbours, a circle is pegged out on the ground, and within this the *taitu* (the ordinary small yams of the Trobriands which form the staple harvest) are carefully piled up into a conical heap. A great deal of care is lavished on this task, the biggest are selected, scrupulously cleaned, and put on the outside of the heap. After a fortnight or more of keeping the yams in the garden, where they are much admired by visiting parties, the owner of the garden plot summons a party of friends or relatives-in-law, and these transport them into a village. As we know already, from Chapter II, such yams will be offered to the owner's sister's husband. It is to his village that they are brought, where again they are displayed in conical heaps, placed before his yam house. Only after they have thus remained for several days—sometimes up to a fortnight—are they put into the storehouse (see Plate XXXIII).

Indeed, it would be enough for anyone to see how the natives handle the yams, how they admire big tubers, how they pick out freaks and sports and exhibit them, to realise that there is a deep, socially standardised sentiment centring round this staple product of their gardens. In many phases of their ceremonial life, big displays of food form the central feature. Extensive mortuary distributions called *sagali*, are, in one of their aspects, enormous exhibitions of food, connected with their re-apportionment (see Plate XXXIV). At harvest of the early yams (*kuvi*) there is an offering of first fruits to the memory of the recently dead. At the later, main harvest of *taitu* (small yams), the first tubers are dug out ceremonially brought into the village and admired by the whole community. Food contests between two villages at harvest, in olden days often followed by actual fighting, are also one of the characteristic features which throw light on the natives' attitude towards edible wealth. In fact, one could almost speak of a " cult of food " among these natives, in so far as food is the central object of most of their public ceremonies.

In the preparation of food, it must be noted that many taboos are associated with cooking, and especially with the cooking pots. The wooden dishes on which the natives serve their food are called *kaboma*, which means " tabooed wood." The act of eating is as a rule strictly individual. People eat within their family circles, and even when there is public ceremonial cooking of the taro pudding (*mona*) in the big clay pots, especially tabooed for this purpose (see Plate XXXV), they do not eat in one body, but in small groups. A clay pot is carried into the different parts of the village, and men from that part squat round it and eat, followed afterwards by the women. Sometimes again the pudding is taken out, placed on wooden dishes, and eaten within the family.

I cannot enter here into the many details of what could be called the social psychology of eating, but it is important to note that the centre of gravity of the feast lies, not in the eating, but in the display and ceremonial preparation of the food (see Plate XXXV). When a pig is to be killed, which is a great culinary and festive event, it will be first carried about, and shown perhaps in one or two villages ; then roasted alive, the whole village and neighbours enjoying the spectacle and the squeals of the animal. It is then ceremonially, and with a definite ritual, cut into pieces and distributed. But the eating of it is a casual affair ; it will take place either within a hut, or else people will just cook a piece of flesh and eat it on the road, or walking about in the village. The relics of a feast such as pigs' jaws and fish tails, however, are often collected and displayed in houses or yam stores.*

The quantity of food eaten, whether in prospect or retrospect, is what matters most. " We shall eat, and eat till we vomit," is a stock phrase, often heard at feasts, intended to express enjoyment of the occasion, a close parallel to the pleasure felt at the idea of stores rotting away in the yam house. All this shows that the social act of eating and the associated conviviality are not present in the minds or customs of the Trobrianders, and what is socially enjoyed is the common admiration of fine and plentiful food, and the knowledge of its abundance. Naturally, like all animals, human or otherwise, civilised or savage, the Trobrianders enjoy their eating as one of the chief pleasures of life, but this remains an individual

* As a matter of fact, this custom is not so prominent in the Trobriands as in other Massim districts and all over the Papuo-Melanesian world, cf. for instance Seligman, *op. cit.*, p. 56 and Plate VI, Fig. 6.

act, and neither its performance nor the sentiments attached to it have been socialised.

It is this indirect sentiment, rooted of course in reality in the pleasures of eating, which makes for the value of food in the eyes of the natives. This value again makes accumulated food a symbol, and a vehicle of power. Hence the need for storing and displaying it. Value is not the result of utility and rarity, intellectually compounded, but is the result of a sentiment grown round things, which, through satisfying human needs, are capable of evoking emotions.

The value of manufactured objects of use must also be explained through man's emotional nature, and not by reference to his logical construction of utilitarian views. Here, however, I think that the explanation must take into account, not so much the user of these objects, as the workman who produces them. These natives are industrious, and keen workers. They do not work under the spur of necessity, or to gain their living, but on the impulse of talent and fancy, with a high sense and enjoyment of their art, which they often conceive as the result of magical inspiration. This refers especially to those who produce objects of high value, and who are always good craftsmen and are fond of their workmanship. Now these native artists have a keen appreciation of good material, and of perfection in craft. When they find a specially good piece of material it lures them on to lavish on it an excess of labour, and to produce things too good to be used, but only so much the more desirable for possession.

The careful manner of working, the perfection of craftmanship, the discrimination in material, the inexhaustible patience in giving the final touches, have been often noted by those who have seen natives at work. These observations have also come under the notice of some theoretical economists, but it is necessary to see these facts in their bearing upon the theory of value. That is, namely, that this loving attitude towards material and work must produce a sentiment of attachment to rare materials and well-worked objects, and that this must result in their being valued. Value will be attached to rare forms of such materials as the craftsman generally uses : classes of shell which are scarce, lending themselves especially to fashioning and polishing ; kinds of wood which are also rare, like ebony ; and more particularly, special varieties of that stone out of which implements are made.*

We can now compare our results with the fallacious views on Primitive Economic Man, sketched out at the beginning of this Division. We see that value and wealth exist, in spite of abundance of things, that indeed this abundance is valued for its own sake. Great quantities are produced beyond any possible utility they could possess, out of mere love of accumulation for its own sake ; food is allowed to rot, and though they have all they could desire in necessities, yet the natives want always more, to serve in its character of wealth. Again, in manufactured objects, and more especially in objects of the *vaygu'a* type (comp. Chapter III, Div. III), it is not rarity within utility which creates value, but a rarity sought out by human skill within the workable materials. In other words, not those things are valued, which being useful or even indispensable are hard to get, since all the necessities of life are within easy reach of the Trobriand Islander. But such an article is valued where the workman, having found specially fine or sportive material, has been induced to spend a disproportionate amount of labour on it. By doing so, he creates an object which is a kind of economic monstrosity, too good, too big, too frail, or too overcharged with ornament to be used, yet just because of that, highly valued.

V

Thus the first assumption is exploded, " that there is no room for wealth or value in native societies." What about the other assumption, namely, " That there is no need to exchange if anyone can by industry and skill, produce all that represents value through its quantity or its quality ? " This assumption is confuted by realising a fundamental fact of native usage and psychology : the love of give and take for its own sake ; the active enjoyment in possession of wealth, through handing it over.

In studying any sociological questions in the Trobriands, in describing the ceremonial side of tribal life, or religion and magic, we constantly meet with this give and take, with

* Again, in explaining value, I do not wish to trace its possible origins, but I try simply to show what are the actual and observable elements into which the natives' attitude towards the object valued can be analysed.

exchange of gifts and payments. I had occasion several times to mention this general feature, and in the short outline of the Trobriand sociology in Chapter II, I gave some examples of it. Even a walk across the island, such as we imagined in that chapter, would reveal to an open-eyed Ethnographer this economic truth. He would see visiting parties—women carrying big food baskets on their head, men with loads on their shoulders—and on inquiring he would learn that these were gifts to be presented under one of the many names they bear, in fulfilment of some social obligation. Offerings of first fruits are given to the chief or to relatives-in-law, when the mango or bread fruit or sugar cane are ripe. Big quantities of sugar cane being borne to a chief, carried by some twenty to thirty men running along the road, produce the impressions of a tropical Birnam Wood moving through the jungle. At harvest time all the roads are full of big parties of men carrying food, or returning with empty baskets. From the far North of Kiriwina a party will have to run for some twelve miles to the creek of Tukwa'ukwa, get into canoes, punt for miles along the shallow Lagoon, and have another good walk inland from Sinaketa ; and all this is in order to fill the yam house of a man who could do it quite well for himself, if it were not that he is under obligation to give all the harvest to his sister's husband ! Displays of gifts associated with marriage, with *sagali* (food distributions), with payments for magic, all these are some of the most picturesque characteristics of the Trobriand garden, road and village, and must impress themselves upon even a superficial observer.

The second fallacy, that man keeps all he needs and never spontaneously gives it away, must therefore be completely discarded. Not that the natives do not possess a strongly retentive tendency. To imagine that they differ from other human beings in this, would be to fall out of one fallacy into the opposite one also already mentioned, namely that there is a sort of primitive communism among the natives. On the contrary, just because they think so much of giving, the distinction between mine and thine is not obliterated but enhanced ; for the presents are by no means given haphazardly, but practically always in fulfilment of definite obligations, and with a great deal of formal punctilio. The very fundamental motive of giving, the vanity of a display of possession and power, *a limine* rules out any assumption of communistic tendencies or institutions. Not in all cases, but in many of them, the handing over of wealth is the expression of the superiority of the giver over the recipient. In others, it represents subordination to a chief, or a kinship relation or relationship-in-law. And it is important to realise that in almost all forms of exchange in the Trobriands, there is not even a trace of gain, nor is there any reason for looking at it from the purely utilitarian and economic standpoint, since there is no enhancement of mutual utility through the exchange.

Thus, it is quite a usual thing in the Trobriands for a type of transaction to take place in which A gives twenty baskets of yams to B, receiving for it a small polished blade, only to have the whole transaction reversed in a few weeks' time. Again, at a certain stage of mortuary ritual, a present of valuables is given, and on the same day later on, the identical articles are returned to the giver. Cases like that described in the *kabigidoya* custom (Div. III of this chapter), where each owner of a new canoe made a round of all the others, each thus giving away again what he receives, are typical. In the *wasi*— exchange of fish for yams, to be described presently—through a practically useless gift, a burdensome obligation is imposed, and one might speak of an increase of burdens rather than an increase of utilities.

The view that the native can live in a state of individual search for food, or catering for his own household only, in isolation from any interchange of goods, implies a calculating, cold egotism, the possibility of enjoyment by man of utilities for their sake. This view, and all the previously criticised assumptions, ignore the fundamental human impulse to display, to share, to bestow. They ignore the deep tendency to create social ties through exchange of gifts. Apart from any consideration as to whether the gifts are necessary or even useful, giving for the sake of giving is one of the most important features of Trobriand sociology, and, from its very general and fundamental nature, I submit that it is a universal feature of all primitive societies.

I have dwelt at length on economic facts which on the surface are not directly connected with the Kula. But if we realise that in these facts we may be able to read the native's attitude towards wealth and value, their importance for the main theme becomes obvious. The Kula is the highest and the most dramatic expression of the native's conception of value, and if we want to understand all the customs and actions of the Kula in their real bearings we must, first and foremost, grasp the psychology that lies at its basis.

VI

I have on purpose spoken of forms of exchange, of gifts and counter-gifts, rather than of barter or trade, because, although there exist forms of barter pure and simple, there are so many transitions and gradations between that and simple gift, that it is impossible to draw any fixed line between trade on the one hand, and exchange of gifts on the other. Indeed, the drawing of any lines to suit our own terminology and our own distinctions is contrary to sound method. In order to deal with these facts correctly it is necessary to give a complete survey of all forms of payment or present. In this survey there will be at one end the extreme case of pure gift, that is an offering for which nothing is given in return. Then, through many customary forms of gift or payment, partially or conditionally returned, which shade into each other, there come forms of exchange, where more or less strict equivalence is observed, arriving finally at real barter. In the following survey I shall roughly classify each transaction according to the principle of its equivalence.

Such tabularised accounts cannot give the same clear vision of facts as a concrete description might do, and they even produce the impression of artificiality, but, and this must be emphatically stated, I shall not introduce here artificial categories, foreign to the native mind. Nothing is so misleading in ethnographic accounts as the description of facts of native civilisations in terms of our own. This, however, shall not be done here. The principles of arrangement, although quite beyond the comprehension of the natives, are nevertheless contained in their social organisation, customs, and even in their linguistic terminology. This latter always affords the simplest and surest means of approach towards the understanding of native distinctions and classifications. But it also must be remembered that, though important as a clue to native ideas, the knowledge of terminology is not a miraculous short-cut into the native's mind. As a matter of fact, there

exist many salient and extremely important features of
Trobriand sociology and social psychology, which are not
covered by any term, whereas their language distinguishes
sub-divisions and subtleties which are quite irrelevant with
regard to actual conditions. Thus, a survey of terminology
must always be supplemented by a direct analysis of ethnographic fact and inquiry into the native's ideas, that is, by
collecting a body of opinions, typical expressions, and
customary phrases by direct cross-questioning. The most
conclusive and deepest insight, however, must always be
obtained by a study of behaviour, by analysis of ethnographic
custom and concrete cases of traditional rules.

LIST OF GIFTS, PAYMENTS, AND COMMERCIAL TRANSACTIONS.

1. *Pure Gifts.*—By this, as just mentioned, we understand
an act, in which an individual gives an object or renders a
service without expecting or getting any return. This is not
a type of transaction very frequently met in Trobriand tribal
life. It must be remembered that accidental or spontaneous
gifts, such as alms or charities, do not exist, since everybody
in need would be maintained by his or her family. Again,
there are so many well-defined economic obligations, connected with kinship and relationship-in-law, that anyone
wanting a thing or a service would know where to go and ask
for it. And then, of course, it would not be a free gift, but one
imposed by some social obligation. Moreover, since gifts in the
Trobriands are conceived as definite acts with a social meaning,
rather than transmissions of objects, it results that where
social duties do not directly impose them, gifts are very rare.

The most important type of free gift are the presents
characteristic of relations between husband and wife, and
parents and children. Among the Trobrianders, husband and
wife own their things separately. There are man's and
woman's possessions, and each of the two partners has a special
part of the household goods under control. When one of them
dies, his or her relations inherit the things. But though the
possessions are not joint, they very often give presents to one
another, more especially a husband to his wife.

As to the parents' gifts to the children, it is clear that in a
matrilineal society, where the mother is the nearest of kin to

her children in a sense quite different to that in our society, they share in and inherit from her all her possessions. It is more remarkable that the father, who, according to native belief and law, is only the mother's husband, and not the kinsman of the children, is the only relation from whom free gifts are expected.* The father will give freely of his valuables to a son, and he will transmit to him his relationships in the Kula, according to the definite rules by which it is done (see Chapter XI, Division II). Also, one of the most valuable and valued possessions, the knowledge of magic, is handed over willingly, and free of any counter-gift, from father to son. The ownership of trees in the village grove and ownership in garden plots is ceded by the father to his son during the lifetime of the former. At his death, it often has to be returned to the man's rightful heirs, that is, his sister's children. All the objects of use embraced by the term *gugua* will be shared with him as a matter of course by a man's children. Also, any special luxuries in food, or such things as betel-nut or tobacco, he will share with his children as well as with his wife. In all such small articles of indulgence, free distribution will also obtain between the chief or the headman and his vassals, though not in such a generous spirit, as within the family. In fact, everyone who possesses betel-nut or tobacco in excess of what he can actually consume on the spot, would be expected to give it away. This very special rule, which also happens to apply to such articles as are generally used by white men for trade, has largely contributed to the tenacity of the idea of the communistic native. In fact, many a man will carefully conceal any surplus so as to avoid the obligation of sharing it and yet escape the opprobrium attaching to meanness.

There is no comprehensive name for this class of free gifts in native terminology. The verb " to give " (*sayki*) would simply be used, and on inquiry as to whether there was repayment for such a gift, the natives would directly answer that this was a gift without repayment ; *mapula* being the general term for return gifts, and retributions, economic as well as otherwise. The natives undoubtedly would not think of free gifts as forming one class, as being all of the same nature. The acts of liberality on the part of the chief, the sharing of

* These natives have no idea of physiological fatherhood. See Chapter II, Division VI.

tobacco and betel-nut by anybody who has some to spare, would be taken as a matter of course. Gifts by a husband to a wife are considered also as rooted in the nature of this relationship. They have as a matter of fact a very coarse and direct way of formulating that such gifts are the *mapula* (payment) for matrimonial relations, a conception in harmony with the ideas underlying another type of gift, of which I shall speak presently, that given in return for sexual intercourse. Economically the two are entirely different, since those of husband to wife are casual gifts within a permanent relationship, whereas the others are definite payment for favours given on special occasions.

The most remarkable fact, however, is that the same explanation is given for the free gifts given by the father to his children ; that is to say, a gift given by a father to his son is said to be a repayment for the man's relationship to the son's mother. According to the matrilineal set of ideas about kinship, mother and son are one, but the father is a stranger (*tomakava*) to his son, an expression often used when these matters are discussed. There is no doubt, however, that the state of affairs is much more complex, for there is a very strong direct emotional attitude between father and child. The father wants always to give things to his child, as I have said, (compare Chapter II, Division VI), and this is very well realised by the natives themselves.

As a matter of fact, the psychology underlying these conditions is this : normally a man is emotionally attached to his wife, and has a very strong personal affection towards his children, and expresses these feelings by gifts, and more especially by trying to endow his children with as much of his wealth and position as he can. This, however, runs counter to the matrilineal principle as well as to the general rule that all gifts require repayment, and so these gifts are explained away by the natives in a manner that agrees with these rules. The above crude explanation of the natives by reference to sex payment is a document, which in a very illuminating manner shows up the conflict between the matrilineal theory and the actual sentiments of the natives, and also how necessary it is to check the explicit statements of natives, and the views contained in their terms and phraseology by direct observation of full-blooded life, in which we see man not only laying down rules and theories, but behaving under the impulse of instinct and emotion.

2. *Customary payments, re-paid irregularly, and without strict equivalence.*—The most important of these are the annual payments received at harvest time by a man from his wife's brothers (cf. Chapter II, Divisions IV and V). These regular and unfailing gifts are so substantial, that they form the bulk of a man's income in food. Sociologically, they are perhaps the strongest strand in the fabric of the Trobriands tribal constitution. They entail a life-long obligation of every man to work for his kinswomen and their families. When a boy begins to garden, he does it for his mother. When his sisters grow up and marry, he works for them. If he has neither mother nor sisters, his nearest female blood relation will claim the proceeds of his labour.*

The reciprocity in these gifts never amounts to their full value, but the recipient is supposed to give a valuable (*vaygu'a*) or a pig to his wife's brother from time to time. Again if he summons his wife's kinsmen to do communal work for him, according to the *kabutu* system, he pays them in food. In this case also the payments are not the full equivalent of the services rendered. Thus we see that the relationship between a man and his wife's kinsmen is full of mutual gifts and services, in which repayment, however, by the husband, is not equivalent and regular, but spasmodic and smaller in value than his own share ; and even if for some reason or other it ever fails, this does not relieve the others from their obligations. In the case of a chief, the duties of his numerous relatives-in-law have to be much more stringently observed ; that is, they have to give him much bigger harvest gifts, and they also have to keep pigs, and grow betel and coco-nut palms for him. For all this, they are rewarded by correspondingly large presents of valuables, which again, however, do not fully repay them for their contributions.

The tributes given by vassal village communities to a chief and usually repaid by small counter-gifts, also belong to this class. Besides these, there are the contributions given by one kinsman to another, when this latter has to carry out a mortuary distribution (*sagali*). Such contributions are some-

* Compare Plate XXXIII, where the yam houses of a headman are filled by his wife's brothers.

times, but irregularly and spasmodically, repaid by objects of small value.

The natives do not embrace this class under one term, but the word *urigubu*, which designates harvest gifts from the wife's brothers, stands for one of the most important conceptions of native sociology and economics. They have quite a clear idea about the many characteristics of the *urigubu* duties, which have have been described here, and about their far-reaching importance. The occasional counter gifts given by the husband to his wife's kinsmen are called *youlo*. The chief's tributes which we have put in this category are called *pokala*. The placing of these two types of payment in one category is justified both by the similar mechanism, and by the close resemblance between the *urigubu* gifts, when given to a chief, and the *pokala* received by him. There are even resemblances in the actual ceremonial, which however, would require too much of a detailed description to be more than mentioned here. The word *pokala* is a general term for the chief's tributes, and there are several other expressions which cover gifts of first fruit, gifts at the main harvest, and some other sub-divisions. There are also terms describing the various counter-gifts given by a chief to those who pay him tribute, according to whether they consist of pig's flesh or yams or fruit. I am not mentioning all these native words, in order not to overload the account with details, which would be irrelevant here.

3. *Payment for services rendered.* This class differs from the foregoing one in that here the payment is within limits defined by custom. It has to be given each time the service is performed, but we cannot speak here of direct economic equivalence, since one of the terms of the equation consists of a service, the value of which cannot be assessed, except by conventional estimates. All services done by specialists for individuals or for the community, belong here. The most important of these are undoubtedly the services of the magician. The garden magician, for instance, receives definite gifts from the community and from certain individuals. The sorcerer is paid by the man who asks him to kill or who desires to be healed. The presents given for magic of rain and fair weather are very considerable. I have already described the payments given to a canoe-builder. I shall have to speak later on of

those received by the specialists who make the various types of
vaygu'a.

Here also belong the payments, always associated with
love intrigues. Disinterested love is quite unknown among
these people of great sexual laxity. Every time a girl favours
her lover, some small gift has to be given immediately. This
is the case in the normal intrigues, going on every night in the
village between unmarried girls and boys, and also in more
ceremonial cases of indulgence, like the *katuyausi* custom, or
the mortuary consolations, mentioned in Chapter II, Division
II. A few areca-nuts, some betel pepper, a bit of tobacco,
some turtle-shell rings, or spondylus discs, such are the small
tokens of gratitude and appreciation never omitted by the
youth. An attractive girl need never go unprovided with the
small luxuries of life.

The big mortuary distributions of food, *sagali,* have already
been mentioned several times. On their economic side, these
distributions are payments for funerary services. The deceased
man's nearest maternal kinsman has to give food gifts to all the
villagers for their assuming mourning, that is to say, for
blackening their faces and cutting their hair. He pays some
other special people for wailing and grave digging ; a still
smaller group for cutting out the dead man's ulna and using it
as a lime spoon ; and the widow or widower for the prolonged and scrupulously to be observed period of strict
mourning.

All these details show how universal and strict is the idea
that every social obligation or duty, though it may not on any
account be evaded, has yet to be re-paid by a ceremonial gift.
The function of these ceremonial re-payments is, on the surface
of it, to thicken the social ties from which arise the obligations.

The similarity of the gifts and payments which we have put
into this category is expressed by the native use of the word
mapula (repayment, equivalent) in connection with all these
gifts. Thus in giving the reason why a certain present is made
to a magician, or why a share is allotted to a man at the
sagali (distribution), or why some valuable object is given to a
specialist, they would say : " This is the *mapula* for what he
has done." Another interesting identification contained in
linguistic usage is the calling of both magical payments and
payments to specialists : a ' restorative,' or, literally, a

'poultice.' Certain extra fees given to a magician are described as ' *katuwarina kaykela* ' or ' poultice for his leg ' ; as the magician, especially he of the garden or the sorcerer, has to take long walks in connection with his magic. The expression ' poultice of my back,' will be used by a canoe-builder who has been bending over his work, or ' poultice of my hand ' by a carver or stone-polisher. But the identity of these gifts is not in any way expressed in the detailed terminology. In fact, there is a list of words describing the various payments for magic, the gifts given to specialists, love payments, and the numerous types of gifts distinguished at the sagali. Thus a magical payment, of which a small part would be offered to ancestral spirits, is called *ula'ula ;* a substantial magical gift is called *sousula ;* a gift to a sorcerer is described by the verb *ibudipeta*, and there are many more special names. The gifts to the specialists are called *vewoulo*—the initial gift ; *yomelu*—a gift of food given after the object has been ceremonially handed over to the owner ; *karibudaboda*—a substantial gift of yams given at the next harvest. The gifts of food, made while the work is in progress are called *vakapula ;* but this latter term has much wider application, as it covers all the presents of cooked or raw food given to workers by the man, for whom they work. The sexual gifts are called *buwana* or *sebuwana*. I shall not enumerate the various terminological distinctions of *sagali* gifts, as this would be impossible to do, without entering upon the enormous subject of mortuary duties and distributions.

The classification of love gifts and *sagali* gifts in the same category with gifts to magicians and specialists, is a generalisation in which the natives would not be able to follow us. For them, the gifts given at *sagali* form a class in themselves and so do the love gifts. We may say that, from the economic point of view, we were correct in classing all these gifts together, because they all represent a definite type of equivalence ; also they correspond to the native idea that every service has to be paid for, an idea documented by the linguistic use of the word *mapula*. But within this class, the sub-divisions corresponding to native terminology represent important distinctions made by the natives between the three sub-classes ; love gifts, *sagali* gifts, and gifts for magical and professional services.

4. *Gifts returned in economically equivalent form* —We are enumerating the various types of exchange, as they gradually assume the appearance of trade. In this fourth class have been put such gifts as must be re-paid with almost strict equivalence. But it must be stressed that strict equivalence of two gifts does not assimilate them to trade altogether. There can be no more perfect equivalence between gift and counter-gift, than when A gives to B an object, and B on the same day returns the very same object to A. At a certain stage of the mortuary proceedings, such a gift is given and received back again by a deceased man's kinsmen and his widow's brothers. Yet it is obvious at once that no transaction could be further removed from trade. The above described gifts at the presentation of new canoes (*kabigidoya*) belong to this class. So do also numerous presents given to one community by another, on visits which are going to be returned soon. Payments for the lease of a garden plot are at least in certain districts of the Trobriands returned by a gift of equivalent value.

Sociologically, this class of gifts is characteristic of the relationship between friends (*luba'i*). Thus the *kabigidoya* takes place between friends, the Kula takes place between overseas partners and inland friends, but of course relations-in-law also belong *par excellence* to this category.

Other types of equivalent gifts which have to be mentioned here shortly, are the presents given by one household to another, at the *milamala*, the festive period associated with the return of the ancestral spirits to their villages. Offerings of cooked food are ceremonially exposed in houses for the use of the spirits, and after these have consumed the spiritual substance, the material one is given to a neighbouring household. These gifts are always reciprocal.

Again, a series of mutual gifts exchanged immediately after marriage between a man and his wife's father (not matrilineal kinsman in this case), have to be put into this category.

The economic similarity of these gifts is not expressed in terminology or even in linguistic use. All the gifts I have enumerated have their own special names, which I shall not adduce here, so as not to multiply irrelevant details of information. The natives have no comprehensive idea that such a class as I have spoken of exists. My generalisation is based upon the very interesting fact, that all through the tribal life we find scattered cases of direct exchange of equivalent gifts. Nothing perhaps could show up so clearly, how much the natives value the give and take of presents for its own sake.

5. *Exchange of Material Goods against Privileges, Titles and non-material Possessions.* Under this heading, I class transactions which approach trade, in so far as two owners, each possessing something they value highly, exchange it for something they value still more. The equivalence here is not so strict, at any rate not so measurable, as in the previous class, because in this one, one of the terms is usually a non-material possession, such as the knowledge of magic, the privilege to execute a dance, or the title to a garden plot, which latter very often is a mere title only. But in spite of this smaller measure of equivalence, their character of trade is more marked, just because of the element of mutual desire to carry out the transaction and of the mutual advantage.

Two important types of transaction belong to this class. One of them is the acquisition by a man of the goods or privileges which are due to him by inheritance from his maternal uncle or elder brother, but which he wishes to acquire before the elder's death. If a maternal uncle is to give up in his life time a garden, or to teach and hand over a system of magic, he has to be paid for that. As a rule several payments, and very substantial ones, have to be given to him, and he gradually relinquishes his rights, giving the garden land, bit by bit, teaching the magic in instalments. After the final payment, the title of ownership is definitely handed over to the younger man.

I have drawn attention already in the general description of the Trobriand Sociology (Chapter II, Division VI) to the remarkable contrast between matrilineal inheritance and that between father and son. It is noteworthy that what is considered by the natives rightful inheritance has yet to be paid for, and that a man who knows that in any case he would obtain a privilege sooner or later, if he wants it at once, must pay for it, and that heavily. None the less, this transaction takes place only when it appears desirable to both parties. There is no customary obligation on either of the two to enter on the exchange, and it has to be considered advantageous to both before it can be completed. The acquisition of magic is of course different, because that must naturally always be taught by the elder man to the younger in his life time.

The other type of transaction belonging to this class, is the payment for dances. Dances are "owned"; that is, the original inventor has the right of "producing" his dance and song in his village community. If another village takes a fancy to this song and dance, it has to purchase the right to perform it. This is done by handing ceremonially to the original village a substantial payment of food and valuables, after which the dance is taught to the new possessors.

In some rare cases, the title to garden-lands would pass from one community to another. For this again, the members and headman of the acquiring community would have to pay substantially to those who hand over their rights.

Another transaction which has to be mentioned here is the hire of a canoe, where a temporary transference of ownership takes place in return for a payment.

The generalisation by which this class has been formed, although it does not run counter to native terminology and ideas, is beyond their own grasp, and contains several of their sub-divisions, differentiated by distinct native terms. The name for the ceremonial purchase of a task or for the transfer of a garden plot is *laga*. This term denotes a very big and important transaction. For example, when a small pig is purchased by food or minor objects of value, they call this barter (*gimwali*) but when a more valuable pig is exchanged for *vaygu'a*, they call it *laga*.

The important conception of gradual acquisition in advance of matrilineal inheritance, is designated by the term *pokala*, a word which we have already met as signifying the tributes to the chief. It is a homonym, because its two meanings are distinct, and are clearly distinguished by the natives. There can be no doubt that these two meanings have developed out of a common one by gradual differentiation, but I have no data even to indicate this linguistic process. At present, it would be incorrect to strain after any connection between them, and indeed this is an example how necessary it is to be careful not to rely too much on native terminology for purposes of classification.

The term for the hire of a canoe is *toguna waga*.

6. *Ceremonial barter with deferred payment.*—In this class
we have to describe payments which are ceremonially offered,
and must be received and re-paid later on.   The exchange is
based on a permanent partnership, and the articles have to be
roughly equivalent in value.   Remembering the definition of
the Kula in Chapter III, it is easy to see that this big, ceremonial, circulating exchange belongs to this class.   It is ceremonial barter based on permanent partnership, where a gift
offered is always accepted, and after a time has to be re-paid
by an equivalent counter-gift.

There is also a ceremonial form of exchange of vegetable food
for fish, based on a standing partnership, and on the obligation
to accept and return an initial gift.   This is called *wasi*.   The
members of an inland village, where yams and taro are plentiful
have partners in a Lagoon village, where much fishing is done
but garden produce is scarce.   Each man has his partner, and
at times, when new food is harvested and also during the main
harvest, he and his fellow villagers will bring a big quantity of
vegetable food into the Lagoon village (see Plate XXXVI),
each man putting his share before his partner's house.   This is
an invitation, which never can be rejected, to return the gift
by its fixed equivalent in fish.

As soon as weather and previous engagements allow, the
fishermen go out to sea and notice is given to the inland village
of the fact.   The inlanders arrive on the beach, awaiting the
fishermen, who come back in a body, and their haul of fish is
taken directly from the canoes and carried to the inland village.
Such large quantities of fish are always acquired only in connection with big distributions of food (*sagali*).   It is remarkable
that in the inland villages these distributions must be carried
out in fish, whereas in the Lagoon villages, fish never can be
used for ceremonial purposes, vegetables being the only
article considered proper.   Thus the motive for exchange
here is not to get food in order to satisfy the primary
want of eating, but in order to satisfy the social need
of displaying large quantities of conventionally sanctioned
eatables.   Often when such a big fishing takes place,
great quantities of fish perish by becoming rotten before
they reach the man for whom they are finally destined.
But being rotten in no way detracts from the value of fish
in a *sagali*.

The equivalence of fish, given in return for vegetable food, is measured only roughly. A standard sized bunch of taro, or one of the ordinary baskets of *taytu* (small yams) will be repaid by a bundle of fish, some three to five kilograms in weight. The equivalence of the two payments, as well as the advantage obtained by one party at least, make this exchange approach barter.* But the element of trust enters into it largely, in the fact that the equivalence is left to the repayer ; and again, the initial gift which as a rule is always given by the inlanders, cannot be refused. And all these features distinguish this exchange from barter.

Similar to this ceremonial exchange are certain arrangements in which food is brought by individuals to the industrial villages of Kuboma, and the natives of that place return it by manufactured objects when these are made. In certain cases of production of *vaygu'a* (valuables) it is difficult to judge whether we have to do with the payment for services rendered (Class 3), or with the type of ceremonial barter belonging to this class. There is hardly any need to add that the two types of exchange contained in this class, the Kula and the *wasi* (fish barter) are kept very distinct in the minds of the natives. Indeed, the ceremonial exchange of valuables, the Kula, stands out as such a remarkable form of trade that in all respects, not only by the natives, but also by ourselves, it must be put into a class by itself. There is no doubt, however, that the technique of the *wasi* must have been influenced by the ideas and usages of the Kula, which is by far the more important and widespread of the two. The natives, when explaining one of these trades, often draw parallels to the other. And the existence of social partnership, of ceremonial sequence of gift, of the free yet unevadible equivalence, all these features appear in both forms. This shows that the natives have a definite mental attitude towards what they consider an honourable, ceremonial type of barter. The rigid exclusion of haggling, the formalities observed in handing over the gift, the obligation

* This advantage was probably in olden days a mutual one. Nowadays, when the fishermen can earn about ten or twenty times more by diving for pearls than by performing their share of the *wasi*, the exchange is as a rule a great burden on them. It is one of the most conspicuous examples of the tenacity of native custom that in spite of all the temptation which pearling offers them and in spite of the great pressure exercised upon them by the white traders, the fishermen never try to evade a *wasi*, and when they have received the inaugurating gift, the first calm day is always given to fishing, and not to pearling.

of accepting the initial gift and of returning it later on, all these express this attitude.

7. *Trade, Pure and Simple*.—The main characteristic of this form of exchange is found in the element of mutual advantage : each side acquires what is needed, and gives away a less useful article. Also we find here the equivalence between the articles adjusted during the transaction by haggling or bargaining.

This bartering, pure and simple, takes place mainly between the industrial communities of the interior, which manufacture on a large scale the wooden dishes, combs, lime pots, armlets and baskets and the agricultural districts of Kiriwina, the fishing communities of the West, and the sailing and trading communities of the South. The industrials, who are regarded as pariahs and treated with contumely, are nevertheless allowed to hawk their goods throughout the other districts. When they have plenty of articles on hand, they go to the other places, and ask for yams, coco-nuts, fish, and betel-nut, and for some ornaments, such as turtle shell, earrings and spondylus beads. They sit in groups and display their wares, saying "You have plenty of coco-nuts, and we have none. We have made fine wooden dishes. This one is worth forty nuts, and some betel-nut, and some betel pepper." The others then may answer, "Oh, no, I do not want it. You ask too much." "What will you give us ? " An offer may be made, and rejected by the pedlars, and so on, till a bargain is struck.

Again, at certain times, people from other villages may need some of the objects made in Kuboma, and will go there, and try to purchase some manufactured goods. People of rank as a rule will do it in the manner described in the previous paragraph, by giving an initial gift, and expecting a repayment. Others simply go and barter. As we saw in the description of the *kabigidoya*, the Sinaketans and Vakutans go there and purchase goods before each Kula expedition to serve for the subsidiary trade.

Thus the conception of pure barter (*gimwali*) stands out very clearly, and the natives make a definite distinction between this and other forms of exchange. Embodied in a word, this distinction is made more poignant still by the manner in which the word is used. When scornfully criticising bad conduct in Kula, or an improper manner of giving gifts, a native will say that " it was done like a *gimwali*." When asked, about a transaction, whether it belongs to one class or another, they will reply with an accent of depreciation " That was only a *gimwali*—(*gimwali wala !*) " In the course of ethnographic investigation, they give clear descriptions, almost definitions of *gimwali*, its lack of ceremony, the permissibility of haggling, the free manner in which it can be done between any two strangers. They state correctly and clearly its general conditions, and they tell readily which articles may be exchanged by *gimwali*.

Of course certain characteristics of pure barter, which we can perceive clearly as inherent in the facts, are quite beyond their theoretical grasp. Thus for instance, that the element of mutual advantage is prominent in *gimwali ;* that it refers exclusively to newly manufactured goods, because second-hand things are never *gimwali*, etc., etc. Such generalisations the ethnographer has to make for himself. Other properties of the *gimwali* embodied in custom are : absence of ceremonial, absence of magic, absence of special partnership—all these already mentioned above. In carrying out the transaction, the natives also behave quite differently here than in the other transactions. In all ceremonial forms of give and take, it is considered very undignified and against all etiquette, for the receiver to show any interest in the gift or any eagerness to take it. In ceremonial distributions as well as in the Kula, the present is thrown down by the giver, sometimes actually, sometimes only given in an abrupt manner, and often it is not even picked up by the receiver, but by some insignificant person in his following. In the *gimwali*, on the contrary, there is a pronounced interest shown in the exchange.

There is one instance of *gimwali* which deserves special attention. It is a barter of fish for vegetables, and stands out in sharp contrast therefore to the *wasi*, the ceremonial fish and yam exchange. It is called *vava*, and takes place between villages which have no standing *wasi* partnership and there-fore simply *gimwali* their produce when necessary (see Plate XXXVII).

This ends the short survey of the different types of exchange. It was necessary to give it, even though in a condensed form, in order to provide a background for the Kula. It gives us an idea of the great range and variety of the material give and take associated with the Trobriand tribal life. We see also that the rules of equivalence, as well as the formalities accompanying each transaction, are very well defined.

VII

It is easy to see that almost all the categories of gifts, which I have classified according to economic principles, are also based on some sociological relationship. Thus the first type of gifts, that is, the free gifts, take place in the relationship between husband and wife, and in that between parents and children. Again, the second class of gifts, that is, the obligatory ones, given without systematic repayment, are associated with relationship-in-law, mainly, though the chief's tributes also belong to this class.

If we drew up a scheme of sociological relations, each type of them would be defined by a special class of economic duties. There would be some parallelism between such a sociological classification of payments and presents, and the one given above. But such parallelism is only approximate. It will be therefore interesting to draw up a scheme of exchanges, classified according to the social relationship, to which they correspond. This will give us good insight into the economics of Trobriand sociology, as well as another view of the subject of payments and presents.

Going over the sociological outline in Chapter II, Divisions V and VI, we see that the family, the clan and sub-clan, the village community, the district and the tribe are the main social divisions of the Trobriands. To these groupings correspond definite bonds of social relationship. Thus, to the family, there correspond no less than three distinct types of relationship, according to native ideas. First of all there is the matrilineal kinship (*veyola*) which embraces people, who can trace common descent through their mothers. This is, to the natives, the blood relationship, the identity of flesh, and the real kinship. The marriage relation comprises that between husband and wife, and father and children. Finally, the relationship between the husband and the wife's matrilineal kinsmen forms the third class of personal ties corresponding to family. These three types of personal bonds are clearly distinguished in terminology, in the current linguistic usage, in custom, and in explicitly formulated ideas.

To the grouping into clans and sub-clans, there pertain the ties existing between clansmen and more especially between members of the same sub-clan, and on the other hand, the relationship between a man and members of different clans. Membership in the same sub-clan is a kind of extended kinship. The relationship to other clans is most important, where it assumes the form of special friendship called *luba'i*. The grouping into village communities results in the very important feature of fellow membership in the same village community. The distinction of rank associated with clanship, the division into village communities and districts, result, in the manner sketched out in Chapter II, in the subordination of commoners to chiefs. Finally, the general fact of membership in the tribe creates the bonds which unite every tribesman with another and which in olden days allowed of a free though not unlimited intercourse, and therefore of commercial relations. We have, therefore, eight types of personal relationship to distinguish. In the following table we see them enumerated with a short survey of their economic characteristics.

1. *Matrilineal kinship*.—The underlying idea that this means identity of blood and of substance is by no means forcibly expressed on its economic side. The right of inheritance, the common participation in certain titles of ownership, and a limited right to use one another's implements and objects of daily use are often restricted in practice by private jealousies and animosities. In economic gifts more especially, we find here the remarkable custom of purchasing during lifetime, by instalments, the titles to garden plots and trees and the knowledge of magic, which by right ought to pass at death from the older to the younger generation of matrilineal kinsmen. The economic identity of matrilineal kinsmen comes into prominence at the tribal distributions—*sagali*—where all of them have to share in the responsibilities of providing food.

2. *Marriage ties*.—(Husband and wife ; and derived from that, father and children). It is enough to tabulate this type of relationship here, and to remind the reader that it is characterised by free gifts, as has been minutely described in the foregoing classification of gifts, under (1).

3. *Relationship-in-law.*—These ties are in their economic aspect not reciprocal or symmetrical. That is, one side in it, the husband of the woman, is the economically favoured recipient, while the wife's brothers receive from him gifts of smaller value in the aggregate. As we know, this relationship is economically defined by the regular and substantial harvest gifts, by which the husband's storehouse is filled every year by his wife's brothers. They also have to perform certain services for him. For all this, they receive a gift of *vaygu'a* (valuables) from time to time, and some food in payment for services rendered.

4. *Clanship.*—The main economic identification of this group takes place during the *sagali*, although the responsibility for the food rests only with those actually related by blood with the deceased man. All the members of the sub-clan, and to a smaller extent members of the same clan within a village community, have to contribute by small presents given to the organisers of the *sagali*.

5. *The Relationship of Personal Friendship.*—Two men thus bound as a rule will carry on Kula between themselves, and, if they belong to an inland and Lagoon village respectively, they will be partners in the exchange of fish and vegetables (*wasi*).

6. *Fellow-citizenship in a Village Community.*—There are many types of presents given by one community to another. And, economically, the bonds of fellow-citizenship mean the obligation to contribute one's share to such a present. Again, at the mortuary divisions, *sagali*, the fellow-villagers of clans, differing from the deceased man's, receive a series of presents for the performance of mortuary duties.

7. *Relationship between Chiefs and Commoners.*—The tributes and services given to a chief by his vassals on the one hand, and the small but frequent gifts which he gives them, and the big and important contribution which he makes to all tribal enterprises are characteristic of this relationship.

8. *Relationship between any two tribesmen.*—This is character-ised by payments and presents, by occasional trade between two individuals, and by the sporadic free gifts of tobacco or betel-nut which no man would refuse to another unless they were on terms of hostility.

With this, the survey of gifts and presents is finished. The general importance of give and take to the social fabric of Boyowan society, the great amount of distinctions and subdivisions of the various gifts can leave no doubt as to the paramount rôle which economic acts and motives play in the life of these natives.

CHAPTER VII

THE DEPARTURE OF AN OVERSEAS EXPEDITION

We have brought the Kula narrative to the point where all the preparations have been made, the canoe is ready, its ceremonial launching and presentation have taken place, and the goods for the subsidiary trade have been collected. It remains only to load the canoes and to set sail. So far, in describing the construction, the *tasasoria* and *kabigidoya*, we spoke of the Trobrianders in general. Now we shall have to confine ourselves to one district, the southern part of the Island, and we shall follow a Kula expedition from Sinaketa to Dobu. For there are some differences between the various districts and each one must be treated separately. What is said of Sinaketa, however, will hold good so far as the other southern community, that of Vakuta, is concerned. The scene, therefore, of all that is described in the following two chapters will be set in one spot, that is, the group of some eight component villages lying on the flat, muddy shore of the Trobriand Lagoon, within about a stone's throw of one another. There is a short, sandy beach under a fringe of palm trees, and from there we can take a comprehensive view of the Lagoon, the wide semi-circle of its shore edged with the bright green of mangroves, backed by the high jungle on the raised coral ridge of the Raybwag. A few small, flat islands on the horizon just faintly thicken its line, and on a clear day the mountains of the d'Entrecasteaux are visible as blue shadows in the far distance.

From the beach, we step directly into one of the villages, a row of houses faced by another of yam-stores. Through this, leaving on our right a circular village, and passing through some empty spaces with groves of betel and coco-nut palms, we come to the main component village of Sinaketa, to Kasiyetana. There, overtopping the elegant native huts, stands an enormous corrugated iron shed, built on piles, but with the space between the floor and the ground filled up carefully with white coral stones. This monument testifies both to native vanity and to the strength of their superstitions—vanity in aping the white man's habit of raising the house, and native belief in the fear of the *bwaga'u* (sorcerer), whose most powerful sorcery is applied by burning magical herbs, and could not be warded off, were he able to creep under the house. It may be added that even the missionary teachers, natives of the Trobriands, always put a solid mass of stones to fill the space beneath their houses. To'udawada, the chief of Kasiyetana, is, by the way, the only man in Boyowa who has a corrugated iron house, and in fact in the whole of the island there are not more than a dozen houses which are not built exactly according to the traditional pattern. To'udawada is also the only native whom I ever saw wearing a sun-helmet ; otherwise he is a decent fellow (physically quite pleasant looking), tall, with a broad, intelligent face. Opposite his iron shanty are the fine native huts of his four wives.

Walking towards the North, over the black soil here and there pierced by coral, among tall trees and bits of jungle, fields and gardens, we come to Kanubayne, the village of Kouta'uya, the second most important chief in Sinaketa. Very likely we shall see him sitting on the platform of his hut or yam-house, a shrivelled up, toothless old man, wearing a big native wig. He, as well as To'udawada, belongs to the highest ranks of chieftainship, and they both consider themselves the equals of the chiefs of Kiriwina. But the power of each one is limited to his small, component village, and neither in ceremonial nor in wealth did they, at least in olden days, approach their kinsmen in the North. There is still another chief of the same rank in Sinaketa, who governs the small village of Oraywota. This is Sinakadi, a puffed up, unhealthy looking, bald and toothless old man, and a really contemptible and crooked character, despised by black and white alike. He has a well-established reputation of boarding white men's boats as soon as they arrive, with one or two of his young wives in the canoe, and of returning soon after, alone, but with plenty of tobacco and good merchandise. Lax as is the Trobriander's sense of honour and morality in such matters, this is too much even for them, and Sinakadi is accordingly not respected in his village.

The rest of the villages are ruled by headmen of inferior rank, but of not much less importance and power than the main chiefs. One of them, a queer old man, spare and lame but with an extremely dignified and deliberate manner, called Layseta, is renowned for his extensive knowledge of all sorts of magic, and for his long sojourns in foreign countries, such as the Amphletts and Dobu. We shall meet some of these chiefs later on in our wanderings. Having described the villages and headmen of Sinaketa let us return to our narrative.

A few days before the appointed date of the departure of the Kula expedition there is a great stir in the villages. Visiting parties arrive from the neighbourhood, bringing gifts mostly of food, to serve as provisions for the journey. They sit in front of the huts, talking and commenting, while the local people go about their business. In the evenings, long conferences are held over the fires, and late hours are kept. The preparation of food is mainly woman's work, whereas the men put the finishing touches to the canoes, and perform their magic.

Sociologically the group of the departing differentiates itself of course from those who remain. But even within that group a further differentiation takes place, brought about by their respective functions in the Kula. First of all there are the masters of the canoe, the *toliwaga*, who will play quite a definite part for the next few weeks. On each of them fall with greater stringency the taboos, whether those that have to be kept in Sinaketa or in Dobu. Each has to perform the magic and act in ceremonies. Each will also enjoy the main honours and privileges of the Kula. The members of the crew, the *usagelu*, some four to six men in each canoe, form another group. They sail the craft, perform certain magical rites, and as a rule do the Kula each on his own account. A couple of younger men in each canoe, who do not yet kula, but who help in the work of sailing, form another class, and are called *silasila*. Here and there a small boy will go with his father on a Kula expedition—such are called *dodo'u*—and makes himself useful by blowing the conch shell. Thus the whole fleet consists of four classes, that of the *toliwaga*, the *usagelu*, the helpers and the children. From Sinaketa, women, whether married or unmarried, never go on overseas expeditions, though a different custom prevails in the eastern part of the Trobriands.

Each *toliwaga* has to give a payment in food to his *usagelu*, and this is done in the form of a small ceremony of distribution of food called *mwalolo*, and held after the return from the expedition, in the central place of the village.

A few days before the sailing, the *toliwaga* starts his series of magical rites and begins to keep his taboos, the women busy themselves with the final preparation of the food, and the men trim the waga (*canoe*) for the imminent, long journey.

The taboo of the *toliwaga* refers to his sexual life. During the last two nights, he has in any case to be up late in connection with his magical performances, and with the visits of his friends and relatives from other villages, who bring provisions for the voyage, presents in trade goods, and who chat about the forthcoming expedition. But he has also to keep vigil far into the night as a customary injunction, and he has to sleep alone, though his wife may sleep in the same house.

The preparations of the canoe are begun by covering it with plaited mats called *yawarapu*. They are put on the platform, thus making it convenient for walking, sitting and spreading about of small objects. This, the first act of canoe trimming, is associated with a magical rite. The plaited leaves are chanted over by the *toliwaga* on the shore as they are put on the canoe. Or, in a different system of Kula magic the *toliwaga* medicates some ginger root and spits it on the mats in his hut. This is a specimen of the magical formula which would be used in such a rite :

Yawarapu Spell.

" Betel-nut, betel-nut, female betel-nut ; betel-nut, betel-nut, male betel-nut ; betel-nut of the ceremonial spitting ! "

" The chiefs' comrades ; the chiefs and their followers ; their sun, the afternoon sun ; their pig, a small pig. One only is my day "—here the reciter utters his own name—" their dawn, their morning."

This is the exordium of the spell. Then follows the main body. The two words *boraytupa* and *badederuma*, coupled together, are repeated with a string of other words. The first word of the couple means, freely translated, ' quick sailing,' and the second one, ' abundant haul.' The string of words which are in succession tacked on to this couple describe various forms of Kula necklaces.

The necklaces of different length and of different finish have each their own class names, of which there are about a dozen. After that, a list of words, referring to the human head, are recited :

" My head, my nose, my occiput, my tongue, my throat, my larynx, etc., etc." Finally, the various objects carried on a Kula expedition are mentioned. The goods to be given (*pari*) ; a ritually wrapped up bundle (*lilava*) ; the personal basket ; the sleeping mat ; big baskets ; the lime stick ; the lime pot and comb are uttered one after the other.

Finally the magician recites the end part of the spell ; " I shall kick the mountain, the mountain moves, the mountain tumbles down, the mountain starts on its ceremonial activities, the mountain acclaims, the mountain falls down, the mountain lies prostrate ! My spell shall go to the top of Dobu Mountain, my spell will penetrate the inside of my canoe. The body of my canoe will sink ; the float of my canoe will get under water. My fame is like thunder, my treading is like the roar of the flying witches."

The first part of this spell contains a reference to the betel-nut, this being one of the things which the natives expect to receive in the Kula. On the other hand, it is one of the substances which the natives charm over and give to the partner to induce him to *kula* with them. To which of these two acts the spell refers, it is impossible to decide, nor can the natives tell it. The part in which he extols his speed and success are typical of the magic formulæ, and can be found in many others.

The main part of the spell is as usual much easier to interpret. It implies, broadly speaking, the declaration : " I shall speed and be successful with regard to the various forms of *vaygu'a* ; I shall speed and be successful with my head, with my speech, with my appearance ; in all my trade goods and personal belongings." The final part of the spell describes the impression which is to be made by the man's magic upon ' the mountain,' which stands here for the district of Dobu and its inhabitants. In fact, the districts in the d'Entrecasteaux to which they are sailing are always called *koya* (mountain). The exaggerations, the metaphors, and the implicit insistence on the power of the spell are very characteristic of all magical spells.

The next day, or the day after, as there is often a delay in starting, a pig or two are given by the master of the expedition to all the participants. In the evening of that day, the owner of each canoe goes into the garden, and finds an aromatic mint plant (*sulumwoya*). Taking a sprig of it into his hand, he moves it to and fro, uttering a spell, and then he plucks it. This is the spell:

Sulumwoya Spell.*

" Who cuts the *sulumwoya* of Laba'i ? I, Kwoyregu, with my father, we cut the *sulumwoya* of Laba'i ! The roaring *sulumwoya*, it roars ; the quaking *sulumwoya*, it quakes ; the soughing *sulumwoya*, it soughs ; the boiling *sulumwoya*, it boils "

" My *sulumwoya*, it boils, my lime spoon, it boils, my lime pot, it boils, my comb . . . my basket . . . my small basket . . . my mat . . . my *lilava* bundle . . . my presentation goods (*pari*) . . ."
And with each of these terms, the word ' boils ' or ' foams up ' is repeated often several times. After that, the same verb ' it boils ' is repeated with all parts of the head, as in the previously quoted formula.

The last part runs thus : " Recently deceased spirit of my maternal uncle Mwoyalova, breathe thy spell over the head of Monikiniki. Breathe the spell upon the head of my light canoe. I shall kick the mountain ; the mountain tilts over ; the mountain subsides ; the mountain opens up ; the mountain jubilates ; it topples over. I shall *kula* so as to make my canoe sink. I shall *kula* so as to make my outrigger go under. My fame is like thunder, my treading is like the roar of the flying witches."

The exordium of this spell contains some mythical references, of which, however, my informants could give me only confused explanations. But it is clear in so far as it refers directly to the magical mint, and describes its magical efficiency. In the second part, there is again a list of words referring to objects used in the Kula, and to the personal appearance and persuasiveness of the magician. The verb with which they are repeated refers to the boiling of the mint and coco-nut oil which I shall presently have to mention,

* Compare the linguistic analysis of the original text of this spell, given in Chapter XVIII.

and it indicates that the magical properties of the mint are imparted to the *toliwaga* and his goods. In the last part, the magician invokes the spirit of his real maternal kinsman, from whom he obtained this spell, and asks him to impart magical virtue to his canoe. The mythological name, Monikiniki, with which there is no myth connected, except the tradition that he was the original owner of all these spells, stands here as synonym of the canoe. At the very end in the *dogina*, which contains several expressions identical with those in the end part of the *Yawarapu* spell, we have another example of the strongly exaggerated language so often used in magic.

After having thus ritually plucked the mint plant, the magician brings it home. There he finds one of his *usagelu* (members of crew) who helps him by boiling some coco-nut oil (*bulami*) in a small native clay pot. Into the boiling oil the mint plant is put, and, while it boils, a magical formula is uttered over it.

KAYMWALOYO SPELL.

" No betel-nut, no *doga* (ornament of circular boar's tusk), no betel-pod ! My power to change his mind ; my *mwasila* magic, my *mwase, mwasare, mwaserewai.*" This last sentence contains a play on words very characteristic of Kiriwinian magic. It is difficult to interpret the opening sentence. Probably it means something like this : " No betel-nut or pod, no gift of a *doga*, can be as strong as my *mwasila* and its power of changing my partner's mind in my favour ! "

Now comes the main part of the spell : " There is one *sulumwoya* (mint) of mine, a *sulumwoya* of Laba'i which I shall place on top of Gumasila."

" Thus shall I make a quick Kula on top of Gumasila ; thus shall I hide away my Kula on top of Gumasila ; thus shall I rob my Kula on top of Gumasila ; thus shall I forage my Kula on top of Gumasila ; thus shall I steal my Kula on top of Gumasila."

These last paragraphs are repeated several times, inserting instead of the name of the island of Gumasila the following ones : Kuyawaywo, Domdom, Tewara, Siyawawa, Sanaroa, Tu'utauna, Kamsareta, Gorebubu. All these are the successive names of places in which Kula is made. In this long spell, the magician follows the course of a Kula expedition, enumerating its most conspicuous landmarks. The last part in this formula is identical with the last part of the Yawarapu Spell, previously quoted : " I shall kick the mountain, etc."

After the recital of this spell over the oil and mint, the magician takes these substances, and places them in a receptacle made of banana leaf toughened by grilling. Nowadays a glass bottle is sometimes used instead. The receptacle is then attached to a stick thrust through the prow boards of the canoe and protruding slantwise over the nose. As we shall see later on, the aromatic oil will be used in anointing some objects on arrival at Dobu.

With this, however, the series of magical rites is not finished. The next day, early in the morning, the ritual bundle of representative trade goods, called *lilava*, is made up with the recital of a magical spell. A few objects of trade, a plaited armlet, a comb, a lime pot, a bundle of betel-nut are placed on a clean, new mat, and into the folded mat the spell is recited. Then the mat is rolled up, and over it another mat is placed, and one or two may be wrapped round ; thus it contains, hermetically sealed, the magical virtue of the spell. This bundle is placed afterwards in a special spot in the centre of the canoe, and is not opened till the expedition arrives in Dobu. There is a belief that a magical portent (*kariyala*) is associated with it. A gentle rain, accompanied by thunder and lightning, sets in whenever the *lilava* is opened. A sceptical European might add, that in the monsoon season it almost invariably rains on any afternoon, with the accompaniment of thunder, at the foot or on the slopes of such high hills as are found in the d'Entrecasteaux group. Of course when, in spite of that, a *kariyala* does not make its appearance, we all know something has been amiss in the performance of the magical rite over the *lilava* ! This is the spell recited over the tabooed *lilava* bundle.

Lilava Spell.

" I skirt the shore of the beach of Kaurakoma ; the beach of Kayli, the Kayli of Muyuwa." I cannot add any explanation which would make this phrase clearer. It obviously contains some mythological references to which I have no key. The spell runs on :

" I shall act magically on my mountain. . . Where shall I lie ? I shall lie in Legumatabu ; I shall dream, I shall have dream visions ; rain will come as my magical portent. . . his mind is on the alert ; he lies not, he sits not, he stands up and trembles, he stands up and is agitated ; the renown of Kewara is small, my own renown flares up. . ."

This whole period is repeated over and over again, each time the name of another place being inserted instead of that of Legumatabu. Legumatabu is a small coral island some two hundred yards long and a hundred yards wide, with a few pandanus trees growing on it, wild fowl and turtle laying their eggs in its sand. In this island, half way between Sinaketa and the Amphletts, the Sinaketan sailors often spend a night or two, if overtaken by bad weather or contrary winds.

This period contains first a direct allusion to the magical portent of the *lilava*. In its second half it describes the state of agitation of the Dobuan partner under the influence of this magic, a state of agitation which will prompt him to be generous in the Kula. I do not know whether the word Kewara is a proper name or what else it may mean, but the phrase contains a boast of the magician's own renown, very typical of magical formulæ.

The localities mentioned instead of Legumatabu in the successive repetitions of the period are : Yakum, another small coral island, Urasi, the Dobuan name for Gumasila, Tewara, Sanaro'a, and Tu'utauna, all localities known to us already from our description of Dobu.

This is a very long spell. After the recital, and a very lengthy one, of the last period with its variants, yet another change is introduced into it. Instead of the first phrase " where shall I lie ? etc." the new form runs "Where does the rainbow stand up ? It stands up on the top of Koyatabu," and after this the rest of the period is repeated : " I shall dream, I shall have dream visions, etc." This new form is again varied by uttering instead of Koyatabu, Kamsareta, Koyava'u, and Gorebubu.* This again carries us through the landscape ; but here, instead of the sleeping places we follow the beacons of the sailing expedition by mentioning the tops of the high mountains. The end part of this spell is again identical with that of the Yawarapu Spell.

* Koyatabu—the mountain on the North shore of Fergusson ; Kamsareta, —the highest hill on Domdom,—in the Amphletts ; Koyava'u—the mountain opposite Dobu island, on the North shore of Dawson Straits ; Gorebubu —the volcano on Dobu island.

This magical rite takes place on the morning of the last day. Immediately after the recital of the spell, and the rolling up of the *lilava*, it is carried to the canoe, and put into its place of honour. By that time the *usagelu* (members of the crew) have already made the canoe ready for sailing.

Each *masawa* canoe is divided into ten, eleven, or twelve compartments by the stout, horizontal poles called *riu*, which join the body of the canoe with the outrigger. Such a compartment is called *liku*, and each *liku* has its name and its function. Starting from the end of the canoe, the first *liku*, which, as is easily seen, is both narrow and shallow, is called *ogugwau*, ' in the mist,' and this is the proper place for the conch-shell. Small boys will sit there and blow the conch-shell on ceremonial occasions.

The next compartment is called *likumakava*, and there some of the food is stowed away. The third division is called *kayliku* and water-bottles made of coco-nut shells have their traditional place in it. The fourth *liku*, called *likuguya'u*, is, as its name indicates, the place for the *guya'u* or chief, which, it may be added, is unofficially used as a courtesy title for any headman, or man of importance. The baler, *yalumila*, always remains in this compartment. Then follow the central compartments, called *gebobo*, one, two or three, according to the size of the canoe. This is the place where the *lilava* is put on the platform, and where are placed the best food, not to be eaten till the arrival in Dobu, and all valuable trade articles. After that central division, the same divisions, as in the first part are met in inverse order (see Plate XXXIX).

When the canoe is going to carry much cargo, as is always the case on an expedition to Dobu, a square space is fenced round corresponding to the *gebobo* part of the canoe. A big sort of square hen-coop, or cage, is thus erected in the middle of the canoe, and this is full of bundles wrapped up in mats, and at times when the canoe is not travelling, it is usually covered over with a sail. In the bottom of the canoe a floor is made by a framework of sticks. On this, people can walk and things can rest, while the bilgewater flows underneath, and is baled out from time to time. On this framework, in the *gebobo*, four coco-nuts are placed, each in the corner of the square, while a spell is recited over them. It is after that, that the *lilava* and the choice food, and the rest of the trade are stowed away.

The following spell belongs to the class which is recited over the four coco-nuts.

Gebobo Spell.

"My father, my mother . . . Kula, *mwasila*." This short exordium, running in the compressed style proper to magical beginnings, is rather enigmatic, except for the mention of the Kula and *mwasila*, which explain themselves. The second part is less obscure :

"I shall fill my canoe with *bagido'u*, I shall fill my canoe with *bagiriku*, I shall fill my canoe with *bagidudu*, etc." All the specific names of the necklaces are enumerated. The last part runs as follows : "I shall anchor in the open sea, and my renown will go to the Lagoon, I shall anchor in the Lagoon, and my renown will go to the open sea. My companions will be on the open sea and on the Lagoon. My renown is like thunder, my treading is like earthquake."

This last part is similar to several of the other formulæ. This rite is obviously a Kula rite, judging from the spell, but the natives maintain that its special virtue is to make the food stuffs, loaded into the canoe, last longer. After this rite is over, the loading is done quickly, the *lilava* is put into its place of honour, and with it the best food to be eaten in Dobu. Some other choice food to serve as *pokala* (offerings) is also put in the gebobo, to be offered to overseas partners ; on it, the rest of the trade, called *pari*, is piled, and right on top of all are the personal belongings of the *usagelu* and the *toliwaga* in their respective baskets, shaped like travelling bags.

The people from the inland villages, *kulila'odila*, as they are called, are assembled on the beach. With them stand the women, the children, the old men, and the few people left to guard the village. The master of the fleet gets up and addresses the crowd on the shore, more or less in these words :

"Women, we others sail ; you remain in the village and look after the gardens and the houses ; you must keep chaste. When you get into the bush to get wood, may not one of you lag behind. When you go to the gardens to do work keep together. Return together with your younger sisters."

He also admonishes the people from the other villages to keep away, never to visit Sinaketa at night or in the evening, and never to come singly into the village. On hearing that,

the headman of an inland village will get up and speak in this
fashion :

> "Not thus, oh, our chief ; you go away, and your
> village will remain here as it is. Look, when you are here
> we come to see you. You sail away, we shall keep to our
> villages. When you return, we come again. Perhaps
> you will give us some betel-nut, some sago, some coco-nuts.
> Perhaps you will *kula* to us some necklace of shell beads."

After these harangues are over, the canoes sail away in a
body. Some of the women on the beach may weep at the
actual departure, but it is taboo to weep afterwards. The
woman are also supposed to keep the taboo, that is, not to
walk alone out of the village, not to receive male visitors, in
fact, to remain chaste and true to their husbands during their
absence. Should a woman commit misconduct, her husband's
canoe would be slow. As a rule there are recriminations
between husbands and wives and consequent bad feeling on the
return of the party ; whether the canoe should be blamed or
the wife it is difficult to say.

The women now look out for the rain and thunder, for the
sign that the men have opened the *lilava* (special magical
bundle). Then they know that the party has arrived on the
beach of Sarubwoyna, and performs now its final magic, and
prepares for its entrance into the villages of Tu'utauna, and
Bwayowa. The women are very anxious that the men should
succeed in arriving at Dobu, and that they should not be
compelled by bad weather to return from the Amphletts.
They have been preparing special grass skirts to put on, when
they meet the returning canoes on the beach ; they also hope
to receive the sago, which is considered a dainty, and some
of the ornaments, which their men bring them back from
Dobu. If for any reason the fleet returns prematurely, there
is great disappointment throughout the village, because this
means the expedition has been a failure, nothing has been
brought back to those left at home, and they have no opportunity of wearing their ceremonial dress.

Chapter VIII

THE FIRST HALT OF THE FLEET ON MUWA

I

After so many preparations and preliminaries, we might expect that, once embarked, the natives would make straight for the high mountains, which beckon them alluringly from the distant South. Quite on the contrary, they are satisfied with a very short stage the first day, and after sailing a few miles, they stop on a big sand bank called Muwa, lying to the south-west of the village of Sinaketa. Here, near the sandy shore, edged with old, gnarled trees, the canoes are moored by sticks, while the crews prepare for a ceremonial distribution of food, and arrange their camp for the night on the beach.

This somewhat puzzling delay is less incomprehensible, if we reflect that the natives, after having prepared for a distant expedition, now at last for the first time find themselves together, separated from the rest of the villagers. A sort of mustering and reviewing of forces, as a rule associated with a preliminary feast held by the party, is characteristic of all the expeditions or visits in the Trobriands.

I have spoken already about big and small expeditions, but I have not perhaps made quite clear that the natives themselves make a definite distinction between big, competitive Kula expeditions, called *uvalaku*, and sailings on a smaller scale, described as ' just Kula,' (" Kula wala "). The *uvalaku* are held every two or three years from each district, though nowadays, as in everything else, the natives are getting slack. One would be held, whenever there is a great agglomeration of *vaygu'a*, due to reasons which I shall describe later on. Some-times, a special event, such as the possession by one of the head men of an exceptionally fine pig, or of an object of high value, might give rise to an *uvalaku*. Thus, in 1918, a big competitive expedition (*uvalaku*) from Dobu was held ostensibly for the reason that Kauyaporu, one of the head men of Tu'utauna, owned a very large boar with tusks almost curling over into a circle. Again, plenty of food, or in olden days the completion of a successful war expedition, would form the *raison d'être* of an *uvalaku*. Of course these reasons, explicitly given by the natives, are, so to speak, accessory causes, for in reality an *uvalaku* would be held whenever its turn came, that is, barring great scarcity of food or the death of an important personage.

The *uvalaku* is a Kula expedition on an exceptionally big scale, carried on with a definite social organisation under scrupulous observance of all ceremonial and magical rites, and distinguished from the smaller expeditions by its size, by a competitive element, and by one or two additional features. On an *uvalaku*, all the canoes in the district will sail, and they will sail fully manned. Everybody will be very eager to take part in it. Side by side with this natural desire, however, there exists the idea that all the members of the crews are under an obligation to go on the expedition. This duty they owe to the chief, or master of the *uvalaku*. The *toli'uvalaku*, as he is called, is always one of the sectional chiefs or headmen. He plays the part of a master of ceremonies, on leaving the beach of Sinaketa, at the distributions of food, on arrival in the overseas villages, and on the ceremonial return home. A streamer of dried and bleached pandanus leaf, attached to the prows of his canoe on a stick, is the ostensible sign of the dignity. Such a streamer is called *tarabauba'u* in Kiriwinian, and *doya* in the Dobuan language. The headman, who is *toli'uvalaku* on an expedition, will as a rule receive more Kula gifts than the others. On him also will devolve the glory of this particular expedition. Thus the title of *toli*, in this case, is one of honorary and nominal ownership, resulting mainly in renown (*butura*) for its bearer, and as such highly valued by the natives.

From the economic and legal point of view, however, the obligation binding the members of the expedition to him is the most important sociological feature. He gives the distribution of food, in which the others participate, and this imposes on them the duty of carrying out the expedition, however hard this might be, however often they would have to stop or even return owing to bad weather, contrary winds, or, in olden, days, inter-ference by hostile natives. As the natives say,

PLATE XXXVIII

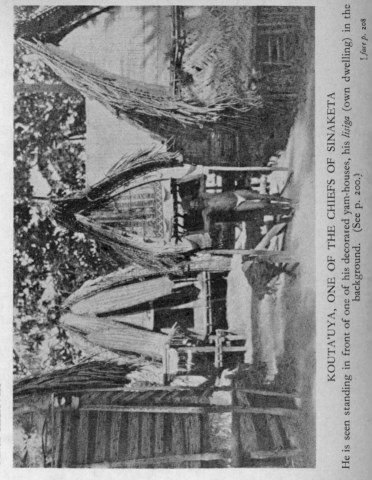

KOUTA'UYA, ONE OF THE CHIEFS OF SINAKETA

He is seen standing in front of one of his decorated yam-houses, his *liŝiga* (own dwelling) in the
background. (See p. 200.)

[*face p.* 208]

PLATE XXXIX

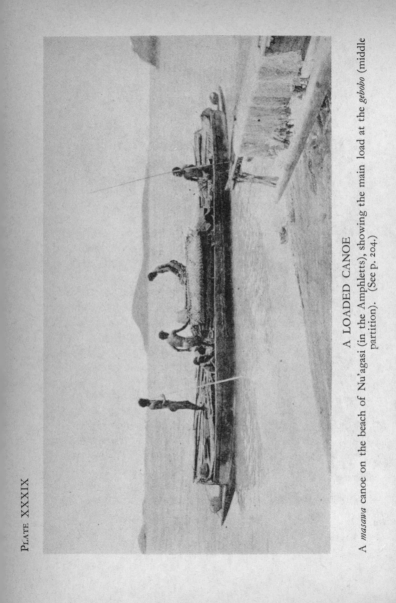

A LOADED CANOE

A *masawa* canoe on the beach of Nu'agasi (in the Amphletts), showing the main load at the *gebobo* (middle partition). (See p. 204.)

" We cannot return on *uvalaku*, for we have eaten of the pig, and we have chewed of the betel-nut given by the *toli'uvalaku*."

Only after the most distant community with whom the Sinaketans *kula* has been reached, and after due time has been allowed for the collection of any *vaygu'a* within reach, will the party start on the return journey. Concrete cases are quoted in which expeditions had to start several times from Sinaketa, always returning within a few days after all the provisions had been eaten on Muwa, from where a contrary wind would not allow the canoes to move south. Or again, a memorable expedition, some few decades ago, started once or twice, was becalmed in Vakuta, had to give a heavy payment to a wind magician in the village of Okinai, to provide them with a propitious northerly wind, and then, sailing South at last, met with a *vineylida*, one of the dreadful perils of the sea, a live stone which jumps from the bottom of the sea at a canoe. But in spite of all this, they persevered, reached Dobu in safety, and made a successful return.

Thus we see that, from a sociological point of view, the *uvalaku* is an enterprise partially financed by the *toli'uvalaku*, and therefore redounding to his credit, and bringing him honour ; while the obligation imposed on others by the food distributed to them, is to carry on the expedition to a successful end.

It is rather puzzling to find that, although everyone is eager for the expedition, although they all enjoy it equally and satisfy their ambition and increase their wealth by it, yet the element of compulsion and obligation is introduced into it ; for we are not accustomed to the idea of pleasure having to be forced on people. None the less, the *uvalaku* is not an isolated feature, for in almost all tribal enjoyments and festive entertainments on a big scale, the same principle obtains. The master of the festivities, by an initial distribution of food, imposes an obligation on the others, to carry through dancing, sports, or games of the season. And indeed, considering the ease with which native enthusiasms flag, with which jealousies, envies and quarrels creep in, and destroy the unanimity of social amusements, the need for compulsion from without to amuse oneself appears not so preposterous as at first sight.

I have said that an *uvalaku* expedition is distinguished

from an ordinary one, in so far also as the full ceremonial of the
Kula has to be observed.   Thus all the canoes must be either
new or relashed, and without exception they must be also re-
painted and redecorated.   The full ceremonial launching, *tasasoria*, and the presentation, *kabigodoya*, are carried out with
every detail only when the Kula takes the form of an *uvalaku*.
The pig or pigs killed in the village before departure are also
a special feature of the competitive Kula.   So is the *kayguya'u*
ceremonial distribution held on Muwa, just at the point of the
proceedings at which we have now arrived.   The *tanarere*, a
big display of *vaygu'a* and comparison of the individual
acquisitions at the end of an expedition, is another ceremonial
feature of the *uvalaku* and supplies some of the competitive
element.   There is also competition as to the speed, qualities
and beauties of the canoes at the beginning of such an expedition.   Some of the communities who present their *vaygu'a* to
an *uvalaku* expedition vie with one another, as to who will give
most, and in fact the element of emulation or competition runs
right through the proceedings.   In the following chapters, I
shall have, in several more points, occasion to distinguish an
uvalaku from an ordinary Kula sailing.

It must be added at once that, although all these ceremonial
features are compulsory only on an *uvalaku* sailing, and although
only then are they one and all of them unfailingly observed,
some and even all may also be kept during an ordinary Kula
expedition, especially if it happens to be a somewhat bigger one.
The same refers to the various magical rites—that is to say the
most important ones—which although performed on every
Kula expedition, are carried out with more punctilio on an
uvalaku.

Finally, a very important distinctive feature is the rule,
that no *vaygu'a* can be carried on the outbound sailing of an
uvalaku.   It must not be forgotten that a Kula overseas expedition sails, in order mainly to receive gifts and not to give them,
and on an *uvalaku* this rule is carried to its extreme, so that no
Kula valuables whatever may be given by the visiting party.
The natives sailing from Sinaketa to Dobu on ordinary Kula
may carry a few armshells with them, but when they sail on a
ceremonial competitive *uvalaku*, no armshell is ever taken.
For it must be remembered that Kula exchanges, as has been
explained in Chapter III, never take place simultaneously.

It is always a gift followed after a lapse of time by a counter-gift. Now on a *uvalaku* the natives would receive in Dobu a certain amount of gifts, which, within a year or so, would be returned to the Dobuans, when these pay a visit to Sinaketa. But there is always a considerable amount of valuables which the Dobuans owe to the Sinaketans, so that when now the Sinaketans go to Dobu, they will claim also these gifts due to them from previous occasions. All these technicalities of Kula exchange will become clearer in one of the subsequent chapters (Chapter XIV).

To sum up, the *uvalaku* is a ceremonial and competitive expedition. Ceremonial it is, in so far as it is connected with the special initial distribution of food, given by the master of the *uvalaku*. It is also ceremonial in that all the formalities of the Kula are kept rigorously and without exception, for in a sense every Kula sailing expedition is ceremonial. Competitive it is mainly in that at the end of it all the acquired articles are compared and counted. With this also the prohibition to carry *vaygu'a*, is connected, so as to give everyone an even start.

II

Returning now to the Sinaketan fleet assembled at Muwa, as soon as they have arrived there, that is, some time about noon, they proceed to the ceremonial distribution. Although the *toli'uvalaku* is master of ceremonies, in this case he as a rule sits and watches the initial proceedings from a distance. A group of his relatives or friends of lesser rank busy themselves with the work. It might be better perhaps here to give a more concrete account, since it is always difficult to visualise exactly how such things will proceed.

This was brought home to me when in March, 1918, I assisted at these initial stages of the Kula in the Amphlett Islands. The natives had been preparing for days for departure, and on the final date, I spent the whole morning observing and photographing the loading and trimming of the canoes, the farewells, and the setting out of the fleet. In the evening, after a busy day, as it was a full-moon night, I went for a long pull in a dinghey. Although in the Trobriands I had had accounts of the custom of the first halt, yet it gave me a surprise when on rounding a rocky point I came upon the whole crowd of Gumasila natives, who had departed on the Kula that morning, sitting in full-moon light on a beach, only a few miles from the village which they had left with so much to-do some ten hours before. With the fairly strong wind that day, I was thinking of them as camping at least half way to the Trobriands, on one of the small sand banks some twenty miles North. I went and sat for a moment among the morose and unfriendly Amphlett Islanders, who, unlike the Trobrianders, distinctly resented the inquisitive and blighting presence of an Ethnographer.

To return to our Sinaketan party, we can imagine the chiefs sitting high up on the shore under the gnarled, broad-leafed branches of the shady trees. They might perhaps be resting in one group, each with a few attendants, or else every headman and chief near his own canoe, To'udawada silently chewing betel-nut, with a heavy and bovine dignity, the excitable Koutauya chattering in a high pitched voice with some of his grown-up sons, among whom there are two or three of the finest men in Sinaketa. Further on, with a smaller group of attendants, sits the infamous Sinakadi, in conference with his successor to chieftainship, his sister's son, Gomaya, also a notorious scoundrel. On such occasions it is good form for chiefs not to busy themselves among the groups, nor to survey the proceedings, but to keep an aloof and detached attitude. In company with other notables, they discuss in the short, jerky sentences which make native languages so difficult to follow, the arrangements and prospects of the Kula, making now and then a mythological reference, forecasting the weather, and discussing the merits of the canoes.

In the meantime, the henchmen of the *toli'uvalaku*, his sons, his younger brothers, his relatives-in-law, prepare the distribution. As a rule, either To'udawada or Koutauya would be the *toli'uvalaku*. The one who at the given time has more wealth on hand and prospects of receiving more *vaygu'a*, would take over the dignity and the burdens. Sinakadi is much less wealthy, and probably it would be an exception for him and his predecessors and successors to play the part. The minor headmen of the other compound villages of Sinaketa would never fill the rôle.

Whoever is the master of the expedition for the time being will have brought over a couple of pigs, which will now be laid

on the beach and admired by the members of the expedition.
Soon some fires are lit, and the pigs, with a long pole thrust
through their tied feet, are hung upside down over the fires. A
dreadful squealing fills the air and delights the hearers. After
the pig has been singed to death, or rather, into insensibility,
it is taken off and cut open. Specialists cut it into appropriate
parts, ready for the distribution. Yams, taro, coco-nuts and
sugar cane have already been put into big heaps, as many as
there are canoes—that is, nowadays, eight. On these heaps,
some hands of ripe bananas and some betel-nut bunches are
placed. On the ground, beside them, on trays of plaited
coco-nut leaves, the lumps of meat are displayed. All this
food has been provided by the *toli'uvalaku*, who previously has
received as contributions towards it special presents, both from
his own and from his wife's kinsmen. In fact, if we try to draw
out all the strands of gifts and contributions connected with
such a distribution we would find that it is spun round into
such an intricate web, that even the lengthy account of the
foregoing chapter does not quite do it justice.

After the chief's helpers have arranged the heaps, they go
over them, seeing that the apportionment is correct, shifting
some of the food here and there, and memorising to whom each
heap will be given. Often in the final round, the *toli'uvalaku*
inspects the heaps himself, and then returns to his former seat.
Then comes the culminating act of the distribution. One of
the chief's henchmen, always a man of inferior rank, accompanied by the chief's helpers, walks down the row of heaps, and
at each of them screams out in a very loud voice :

" O, Siyagana, thy heap, there, O Siyagana, O ! " At
the next one he calls the name of another canoe : " O
Gumawora, thy heap, there ! O Gumawora O ! "

He goes thus over all the heaps, allotting each one to a
canoe. After that is finished, some of the younger boys of each
canoe go and fetch their heap. This is brought to their fire, the
meat is roasted, and the yams, the sugar cane and betel-nut
distributed among the crew, who presently sit down and eat,
each group by itself. We see that, although the *toli'uvalaku* is
responsible for the feast, and receives from the natives all the
credit for it, his active part in the proceedings is a small one,
and it is more nominal than real. On such occasions it would

perhaps be incorrect to call him 'master of ceremonies,' although
he assumes this rôle, as we shall see, on other occasions.
Nevertheless, for the natives, he is the centre of the proceedings.
His people do all the work there is to be done, and in certain
cases he would be referred to for a decision, on some question of
etiquette.

After the meal is over, the natives rest, chew betel-nut
and smoke, looking across the water towards the setting sun
—it is now probably late in the afternoon—towards where,
above the moored canoes, which rock and splash in the shallows,
there float the faint silhouettes of the mountains.   These are the
distant *Koya*, the high hills in the d'Entrecasteaux and
Amphletts, to which the elder natives have often already
sailed, and of which the younger have heard so many times in
myth, tales and magical spells.   Kula conversations will
predominate on such occasions, and names of distant partners,
and personal names of specially valuable *vaygu'a* will punctuate
the conversation and make it very obscure to those not initiated
into the technicalities and historical traditions of the Kula.
Recollections how a certain big spondylus necklace passed a
couple of years ago through Sinaketa, how So-and-so handed it
to So-and-so in Kiriwina, who again gave it to one of his
partners in Kitava (all the personal names of course being
mentioned) and how it went from there to Woodlark Island,
where its traces become lost—such reminiscences lead to
conjectures as to where the necklace might now be, and whether
there is a chance of meeting it in Dobu.   Famous exchanges are
cited, quarrels over Kula grievances, cases in which a man was
killed by magic for his too successful dealings in the Kula,
are told one after the other, and listened to with never failing
interest.   The younger men amuse themselves perhaps with
less serious discussions about the dangers awaiting them
on the sea, about the fierceness of the witches and dreadful beings in the *Koya*, while many a young Trobriander
would be warned at this stage of the unaccommodating
attitude of the women in Dobu, and of the fierceness of
their men folk.

After nightfall a number of small fires are lit on the beach.
The stiff pandanus mats, folded in the middle, are put over
each sleeper so as to form a small roof, and the whole crowd
settle down for the night.

III

Next morning, if there is a fair wind, or a hope of it, the natives are up very early, and all are feverishly active. Some fix up the masts and rigging of the canoes, doing it much more thoroughly and carefully than it was done on the previous morning, since there may be a whole day's sailing ahead of them perhaps with a strong wind, and under dangerous conditions. After all is done, the sails ready to be hoisted, the various ropes put into good trim, all the members of the crew sit at their posts, and each canoe waits some few yards from the beach for its *toliwaga* (master of the canoe). He remains on shore, in order to perform one of the several magical rites which, at this stage of sailing, break through the purely matter-of-fact events. All these rites of magic are directed towards the canoes, making them speedy, seaworthy and safe. In the first rite, some leaves are medicated by the *toliwaga* as he squats over them on the beach and recites a formula. The wording of this indicates that it is a speed magic, and this is also the explicit statement of the natives.

KADUMIYALA SPELL.

In this spell, the flying fish and the jumping gar fish are invoked at the beginning. Then the *toliwaga* urges his canoe to fly at its bows and at its stern. Then, in a long *tapwana*, he repeats a word signifying the magical imparting of speed, and with the names of the various parts of the canoe. The last part runs : " The canoe flies, the canoe flies in the morning, the canoe flies at sunrise, the canoe flies like a flying witch," ending up with the onomatopoetic words " *Saydidi, tatata, numsa*," which represent the flapping of pandanus streamers in the wind, or as others say, the noises made by the flying witches, as they move through the air on a stormy night.

After having uttered this spell into the leaves, the *toliwaga* gives them to one of the *usagelu* (members of the crew), who, wading round the *waga*, rubs with them first the *dobwana*, ' head ' of the canoe, then the middle of its body, and finally its *u'ula* (basis). Proceeding round on the side of the outrigger, he rubs the ' head ' again. It may be remembered here that, with the native canoes, fore and aft in the sailing sense are interchangeable, since the canoe must sail having always the wind on its outrigger side, and it often has to change stern to bows. But standing on a canoe so that the outrigger is on the left hand, and the body of the canoe on the right, a native will call the end of the canoe in front of him its head (*dabwana*), and that behind, its basis (*u'ula*).

After this is over, the *toliwaga* enters the canoe, the sail is hoisted, and the canoe rushes ahead. Now two or three pandanus streamers which had previously been medicated in the village by the *toliwaga* are tied to the rigging, and to the mast. The following is the spell which had been said over them :

Bisila Spell.

" Bora'i, Bora'i (a mythical name). Bora'i flies, it will fly ; Bora'i Bora'i, Bora'i stands up, it will stand up. In company with Bora'i—*sididi*. Break through your passage in Kadimwatu, pierce through thy Promontory of Salamwa. Go and attach your pandanus streamer in Salamwa, go and ascend the slope of Loma."

" Lift up the body of my canoe ; its body is like floating gossamer, its body is like dry banana leaf, its body is like fluff."

There is a definite association in the minds of the natives between the pandanus streamers, with which they usually decorate mast, rigging and sail, and the speed of the canoe. The decorative effect of the floating strips of pale, glittering, yellow is indeed wonderful, when the speed of the canoe makes them flutter in the wind. Like small banners of some stiff, golden fabric they envelope the sail and rigging with light, colour and movement.

The pandanus streamers, and especially their trembling, are a definite characteristic of Trobriand culture (see Plate XXIX). In some of their dances, the natives use long, bleached ribbons of pandanus, which the men hold in both hands, and set a-flutter while they dance. To do this well is one of the main achievements of a brilliant artist. On many festive occasions the *bisila* (pandanus streamers) are tied to houses on poles for decoration. They are thrust into armlets and belts as personal ornaments. The *vaygu'a* (valuables) when prepared for the Kula, are decorated with strips of *bisila*. In the Kula a chief will send to some distant partner a *bisila* streamer over which a special spell has been recited, and this will make the partner eager to bestow valuables on the sender. As we saw, a broad *bisila* streamer is attached to the canoe of a *toli'uvalaku* as his badge of honour. The flying witches (*mulukwausi*) are supposed to use pandanus streamers in order to acquire speed and levitation in their nightly flights through the air.

After the magical pandanus strips have been tied to the rigging, beside the non-magical, purely ornamental ones, the *toliwaga* sits at the *veva* rope, the sheet by which the sail is extended to the wind, and moving it to and fro he recites a spell.

KAYIKUNA VEVA SPELL.

Two verbs signifying magical influence are repeated with the prefix *bo*—which implies the conception of ' ritual ' or ' sacred ' or ' being tabooed.'* Then the *toliwaga* says : " I shall treat my canoe magically in its middle part, I shall treat it in its body. I shall take my *butia* (flower wreath), of the sweet-scented flowers. I shall put it on the head of my canoe."

Then a lengthy middle strophe is recited, in which all the parts of a canoe are named with two verbs one after the other. The verbs are : " To wreathe the canoe in a ritual manner," and " to paint it red in a ritual manner." The prefix *bo*-, added to the verbs, has been here translated, " in a ritual manner."*

The spell ends by a conclusion similar to that of many other canoe formulæ, " My canoe, thou art like a whirl-wind, like a vanishing shadow ! Disappear in the distance, become like mist, avaunt ! "

These are the three usual rites for the sake of speed at the beginning of the journey. If the canoe remains slow, however, an auxiliary rite is performed ; a piece of dried banana leaf is put between the gunwale and one of the inner frame sticks of the canoe, and a spell is recited over it. After that, they beat both ends of the canoe with this banana leaf. If the canoe is

* The prefix *bo*—has three different etymological derivations, each carrying its own shade of meaning. First, it may be the first part of the word *bomala*, in which case, its meaning will be " ritual" or " sacred." Secondly, it may be derived from the word *bu'a*, areca-nut, a substance very often used and mentioned in magic, both because it is a narcotic, and a beautiful, vermilion dye. Thirdly, the prefix may be a derivation from *butia*, the sweet scented flower made into wreaths, in which case it would usually be *bway*, but sometimes might become *bo*-, and would carry the meaning of " festive," " decorated." To a native, who does not look upon a spell as an ethnological document, but as an instrument of magical power, the prefix probably conveys all three meanings at once, and the word " ritual " covers best all these three meanings.

still heavy, and lags behind the others, a piece of *kuleya* (cooked and stale yam) is put on a mat, and the *toliwaga* medicates it with a spell which transfers the heaviness to the yam. The spell here recited is the same one which we met when the heavy log was being pulled into the village. The log was then beaten with a bunch of grass, accompanied by the recital of the spell, and then this bunch was thrown away.* In this case the piece of yam which has taken on the heaviness of the canoe is thrown overboard. Sometimes, however, even this is of no avail. The *toliwaga* then seats himself on the platform next to the steersman, and utters a spell over a piece of coco-nut husk, which is thrown into the water. This rite, called *Bisiboda patile* is a piece of evil-magic (*bulubwalata*), intended to keep all the other canoes back. If that does not help, the natives conclude that some taboos pertaining to the canoe might have been broken, and perhaps the *toliwaga* may feel some misgivings regarding the conduct of his wife or wives.

---

* See Division II of Chapter V.

CHAPTER IX

SAILING ON THE SEA-ARM OF PILOLU

I

Now at last the Kula expedition is properly set going. The canoes are started on a long stage, before them the sea-arm of Pilolu, stretching between the Trobriands and the d'Entre-casteaux. On the North, this portion of the sea is bounded by the Archipelago of the Trobriands, that is, by the islands of Vakuta, Boyowa and Kayleula, joining in the west on to the scattered belt of the Lousançay Islands. On the east, a long submerged reef runs from the southern end of Vakuta to the Amphletts, forming an extended barrier to sailing, but affording little protection from the eastern winds and seas. In the South, this barrier links on to the Amphletts, which together with the Northern coast of Fergusson and Goodenough, form the Southern shore of Pilolu. To the West, Pilolu opens up into the seas between the mainland of New Guinea and the Bismarck Archipelago. In fact, what the natives designate by the name of Pilolu is nothing else but the enormous basin of the Lousançay Lagoon, the largest coral atoll in the world. To the natives, the name of Pilolu is full of emotional associations, drawn from magic and myth ; it is connected with the experiences of past generations, told by the old men round the village fires and with adventure personally lived through.

As the Kula adventurers speed along with filled sails, the shallow Lagoon of the Trobriands soon falls away behind ; the dull green waters, sprinkled with patches of brown where seaweed grows high and rank, and lit up here and there with spots of bright emerald where a shallow bottom of clean sand shines through, give place to a deeper sea of strong green hue. The low strip of land, which surrounds the Trobriand Lagoon in a wide sweep, thins away and dissolves in the haze, and before them the southern mountains rise higher and higher. On a clear day, these are visible even from the Trobriands. The neat outlines of the Amphletts stand diminutive, yet firmer and more material, against the blue silhouettes of the higher mountains behind. These, like a far away cloud are draped in wreaths of cumuli, almost always clinging to their summits. The nearest of them, Koyatabu—the mountain of the taboo—* on the North end of Fergusson Island, a slim, somewhat tilted pyramid, forms a most alluring beacon, guiding the mariners due South. To the right of it, as we look towards the South-West, a broad, bulky mountain, the Koyabwaga'u—mountain of the sorcerers—marks the North-western corner of Fergusson Island. The mountains on Goodenough Island are visible only in very clear weather, and then very faintly.

Within a day or two, these disembodied, misty forms are to assume what for the Trobrianders seems marvellous shape and enormous bulk. They are to surround the Kula traders with their solid walls of precipitous rock and green jungle, furrowed with deep ravines and streaked with racing water-courses. The Trobrianders will sail deep, shaded bays, resounding with the, to them unknown, voice of waterfalls ; with the weird cries of strange birds which never visit the Trobriands, such as the laughing of the kookooburra (laughing jackass), and the melancholy call of the South Sea crow. The sea will change its colour once more, become pure blue, and beneath its transparent waters, a marvellous world of multi-coloured coral, fish and seaweed will unfold itself, a world which, through a strange geographical irony, the inhabitants of a coral island hardly ever can see at home, and must come to this volcanic region to discover.

In these surroundings, they will find also wonderful, heavy, compact stones of various colours and shapes, whereas at home the only stone is the insipid, white, dead coral. Here they can see, besides many types of granite and basalt and volcanic tuff, specimens of black obsidian, with its sharp edges and metallic ring, and sites full of red and yellow ochre. Besides big hills of volcanic ash, they will behold hot springs boiling up periodically. Of all these marvels the young Trobriander hears tales, and sees samples brought back to his country, and there is no

---

* The word *tabu*, in the meaning of taboo—prohibition—is used in its verbal form in the language of the Trobriands, but not very often. The noun "prohibition," "sacred thing," is always *bomala*, used with suffixed personal pronouns.

doubt that it is for him a wonderful experience to find himself amongst them for the first time, and that afterwards he eagerly seizes every opportunity that offers to sail again to the Koya. Thus the landscape now before them is a sort of promised land, a country spoken of in almost legendary tone.

And indeed the scenery here, on the borderland of the two different worlds, is singularly impressive. Sailing away from the Trobriands on my last expedition, I had to spend two days, weatherbound, on a small sandbank covered with a few pandanus trees, about midway between the Trobriands and the Amphletts. A darkened sea lay to the North, big thunderclouds hanging over where I knew there was the large flat island of Boyowa—the Trobriands. To the South, against a clearer sky, were the abrupt forms of the mountains, scattered over half of the horizon. The scenery seemed saturated with myth and legendary tales, with the strange adventures, hopes and fears of generations of native sailors. On this sandbank they had often camped, when becalmed or threatened with bad weather. On such an island, the great mythical hero, Kasabwaybwayreta stopped, and was marooned by his companions, only to escape through the sky Here again a mythical canoe once halted, in order to be re-caulked. As I sat there, looking towards the Southern mountains, so clearly visible, yet so inaccessible, I realised what must be the feelings of the Trobrianders, desirous to reach the Koya, to meet the strange people, and to *kula* with them, a desire made perhaps even more acute by a mixture of fear. For there, to the west of the Amphletts, they see the big bay of Gabu, where once the crews of a whole fleet of Trobriand canoes were killed and eaten by the inhabitants of unknown villages, in attempting to *kula* with them. And stories are also told of single canoes, drifted apart from the fleet and cast against the northern shore of Fergusson Island, of which all the crew perished at the hands of the cannibals. There are also legends of some inexperienced natives, who, visiting the neighbourhood of Deyde'i and arriving at the crystal water in the big stone basins there, plunged in, to meet a dreadful death in the almost boiling pool.

But though the legendary dangers on the distant shores may appall the native imagination, the perils of actual sailing are even more real. The sea over which they travel is seamed with reefs, studded with sandbanks and coral rocks awash.

And though in fair weather these are not so dangerous to a canoe as to a European boat, yet they are bad enough. The main dangers of native sailing, however, lie in the helplessness of a canoe. As we have said before, it cannot sail close to the wind, and therefore cannot beat. If the wind comes round, the canoe has to turn and retrace its course. This is very unpleasant, but not necessarily dangerous. If, however, the wind drops, and the canoe just happens to be in one of the strong tides, which run anything between three and five knots, or if it becomes disabled, and makes leeway at right angles to its course, the situation becomes dangerous. To the West, there lies the open sea, and once far out there, the canoe would have slender chances of ever returning. To the East, there runs the reef, on which in heavy weather a native canoe would surely be smashed. In May, 1918, a Dobuan canoe, returning home a few days after the rest of the fleet, was caught by a strong South-Easterly wind, so strong that it had to give up its course, and make North-West to one of the Lousançay Islands. It had been given up as lost, when in August it came back with a chance blow of the North-Westerly wind. It had had, however, a narrow escape in making the small island. Had it been blown further West, it would never have reached land at all.

There exist other tales of lost canoes, and it is a wonder that accidents are not more frequent, considering the conditions under which they have to sail. Sailing has to be done, so to speak, on straight lines across the sea. Once they deviate from this course, all sorts of dangers crop up. Not only that, but they must sail between fixed points on the land. For, and this of course refers to the olden days, if they had to go ashore, anywhere but in the district of a friendly tribe, the perils which met them were almost as bad as those of reefs and sharks. If the sailors missed the friendly villages of the Amphletts and of Dobu, everywhere else they would meet with extermination. Even nowadays, though the danger of being killed would be smaller—perhaps not absolutely non-existent—yet the natives would feel very uncomfortable at the idea of landing in a strange district, fearing not only death by violence, but even more by evil magic. Thus, as the natives sail across Pilolu, only very small sectors of their horizon present a safe goal for their journey.

On the East, indeed, beyond the dangerous barrier reef, there is a friendly horizon, marked for them by the Marshall Bennett Islands, and Woodlark, the country known under the term Omuyuwa. To the South, there is the Koya, also known as the land of the *kinana*, by which name the natives of the d'Entrecasteaux and the Amphletts are known generically. But to the South-West and West there is the deep open sea (*bebega*), and beyond that, lands inhabited by tailed people, and by people with wings, of whom very little more is known. To the North, beyond the reef of small coral islands, lying off the Trobriands, there are two countries, Kokopawa and Kaytalugi. Kokopawa is peopled with ordinary men and women, who walk about naked, and are great gardeners. Whether this country corresponds to the South coast of New Britain, where people really are without any clothing, it would be difficult to say.

The other country, Kaytalugi, is a land of women only, in which no man can survive. The women who live there are beautiful, big and strong, and they walk about naked, and with their bodily hair unshaven (which is contrary to the Trobriand custom). They are extremely dangerous to any man through the unbounded violence of their passion. The natives never tire of describing graphically how such women would satisfy their sensuous lust, if they got hold of some luckless, shipwrecked man. No one could survive, even for a short time, the amorous yet brutal attacks of these women. The natives compare this treatment to that customary at the *yousa*, the orgiastic mishandling of any man, caught at certain stages of female communal labour in Boyowa (cf. Chapter II, Division II). Not even the boys born on this island of Kaytalugi can survive a tender age. It must be remembered the natives see no need for male co-operation in continuing the race. Thus the women propagate the race, although every male needs must come to an untimely end before he can become a man.

None the less, there is a legend that some men from the village of Kaulagu, in eastern Boyowa, were blown in their canoe far North from the easterly course of a Kula expedition, and were stranded on the coast of Kaytalugi. There, having survived the first reception, they were apportioned individually and married. Having repaired their canoe, ostensibly for the

sake of bringing some fish to their wives, one night they put
food and water into it, and secretly sailed away. On their
return to their own village, they found their women married to
other men. However, such things never end tragically in the
Trobriands. As soon as their rightful lords reappeared their
women came back to them. Among other things these men
brought to Boyowa a variety of banana called *usikela*, not
known before.

II

Returning again to our Kula party, we see that, in journey-
ing across Pilolu, they move within the narrow confines of
familiar sailing ground, surrounded on all sides both by real
dangers and by lands of imaginary horrors. On their track,
however, the natives never go out of sight of land, and in the
event of mist or rain, they can always take sufficient bearings to
enable them to make for the nearest sand-bank or island.
This is never more than some six miles off, a distance which,
should the wind have dropped, may even be reached by
paddling.

Another thing that also makes their sailing not so dangerous
as one would imagine, is the regularity of the winds in this part
of the world. As a rule, in each of the two main seasons, there
is one prevailing direction of wind, which does not shift more
than within some ninety degrees. Thus, in the dry season,
from May to October, the trade wind blows almost incessantly
from the South-East or South, moving sometimes to the North-
East, but never beyond that As a matter of fact, however,
this season, just because of the constancy of the wind, does not
lend itself very well to native sailing. For although with this
wind it is easy to sail from South to North, or East to West,
it is impossible to retrace the course, and as the wind often
blows for months without veering, the natives prefer to do their
sailings between the seasons, or in the time when the monsoon
blows. Between the seasons—November, December or
March and April—the winds are not so constant, in fact they
shift from one position on the compass to another. On the
other hand, there is very seldom a strong blow at this time, and
so this is the ideal season for sailing In the hot summer
months, December till March, the monsoon blows from the
North-West or South-West, less regularly than a trade wind, but

PLATE XL

A WAGA SAILING ON A KULA EXPEDITION

A canoe fully loaded with a crew of twelve men, just about to furl sail, arriving in the Amphletts. Note the cargo at the *gebobo* and each man's personal buncle of folded mat on top of it. (See p. 228.)

PLATE XLI

THE RIGGING OF A CANOE

Each time before a canoe starts, its mast has to be put up and fixed by means of stays and a special arrangement of crescent-shaped cross-pieces and a rope, to be seen in the picture. (See p. 226.) Note the small *kewo'u* canoe to the left

[*face p.* 225

often culminating in violent storms which almost always come from the North-West. Thus the two strong winds to be met in these seas come from definite directions, and this minimises the danger. The natives also as a rule are able to foretell a day or two beforehand the approach of a squall. Rightly or wrongly, they associate the strength of the North-Westerly gales with the phases of the moon

There is, of course, a good deal of magic to make wind blow or to put it down. Like many other forms of magic, wind magic is localised in villages. The inhabitants of Simsim, the biggest village in the Lousançay Islands, and the furthest North-Westerly settlement of this district, are credited with the ability of controlling the North-Westerly wind, perhaps through association with their geographical position. Again, the control over the South-Easterly wind is granted to the inhabitants of Kitava, lying to the East of Boyowa. The Simsim people control all the winds which blow habitually during the rainy season, that is the winds on the western side of the compass, from North to South. The other half can be worked by the Kitavan spells.

Many men in Boyowa have learnt both spells and they practise the magic. The spells are chanted broadcast into the wind, without any other ritual. It is an impressive spectacle to walk through a village, during one of the devastating gales, which always arise at night and during which people leave their huts and assemble in cleared spaces. They are afraid the wind may lift their dwellings off the ground, or uproot a tree which might injure them in falling, an accident which actually did happen a year or two ago in Wawela, killing the chief's wife. Through the darkness from the doors of some of the huts, and from among the huddled groups, there resound loud voices, chanting, in a penetrating sing-song, the spells for abating the force of the wind. On such occasions, feeling myself somewhat nervous, I was deeply impressed by this persistent effort of frail, human voice, fraught with deep belief, pitting itself so feebly against the monotonous, overpowering force of the wind.

Taking the bearing by sight, and helped by the uniformity of winds, the natives have no need of even the most elementary knowledge of navigation. Barring accidents they never have to direct their course by the stars. Of these, they know certain outstanding constellations, sufficient to indicate for them the

direction, should they need it. They have names for the
Pleiades, for Orion, for the Southern Cross, and they also
recognise a few constellations of their own construction. Their
knowledge of the stars, as we have mentioned already in
Chapter II, Division V, is localised in the village of Wawela,
where it is handed over in the maternal line of the chiefs of the
village.

In order to understand better the customs and problems of
sailing, a few words must be said about the technique of
managing a canoe. As we have said before, the wind must
always strike the craft, on the outrigger side, so the sailing canoe
is always tilted with its float raised, and the platform slanting
towards the body of the canoe. This makes it necessary for
it to be able to change bows and stern at will ; for imagine
that a canoe going due South, has to sail with a North-Easterly
wind, then the *lamina* (outrigger) must be on the left hand, and
the canoe sails with what the natives call its " head " forward.
Now imagine that the wind turns to the North-West. Should
this happen in a violent squall, without warning, the canoe
would be at once submerged. But, as such a change would be
gradual, barring accidents, the natives could easily cope with it.
The mast, which is tied at the fourth cross-pole (*ri'u*) from
the temporary bows of the canoe, would be unbound, the canoe
would be turned 180 degrees around, so that its head would now
form the stern, its *u'ula* (foundation) would face South, and
become its bows, and the platform would be to our right,
facing West. The mast would be attached again to the fourth
cross-pole (*ri'u*), from the *u'ula* end, the sail hoisted, and the
canoe would glide along with the wind striking it again on its
outrigger side, but having changed bows to stern (see Plate XLI).

The natives have a set of nautical expressions to describe
the various operations of changing mast, of trimming the sail,
of paying out the sheet rope, of shifting the sail, so that it stands
up with its bottom end high, and its tip touching the canoe, or
else letting it lie with both boom and gaff almost horizontal.
And they have definite rules as to how the various manœuvres
should be carried out, according to the strength of the wind,
and to the quarter on which it strikes the canoe. They have
four expressions denoting a following wind, wind striking
the outrigger beam, wind striking the canoe from the *katala*
(built-out body), and wind striking the canoe on the

outrigger side close to the direction of sailing. There is no point, however, in adducing this native terminology here, as we shall not any further refer to it ; it is enough to know that they have got definite rules, and means of expressing them, with regard to the handling of a canoe.

It has been often remarked here, that the Trobriand canoes cannot sail close to the wind. They are very light, and shallow, and have very little water board, giving a small resistance against making lee-way. I think that this is also the reason, why they need two men to do the steering for the steering oars act as lee-boards. One of the men wields a big, elongated steering oar, called *kuriga*. He sits at the stern, of course, in the body of the canoe. The other man handles a smaller steering paddle, leaf-shaped, yet with a bigger blade than the paddling oars ; it is called *viyoyu*. He sits at the stern end of the platform, and does the steering through the sticks of the *pitapatile* (platform).

The other working members of the crew are the man at the sheet, the *tokwabila veva*, as he is called, who has to let out the *veva* or pull it in, according as the wind shifts and varies in strength.

Another man, as a rule, stands in the bows of the ship on the look-out, and if necessary, has to climb the mast in order to trim the rigging. Or again, he would have to bale the water from time to time, as this always leaks through, or splashes into the canoe. Thus four men are enough to man a canoe, though usually the functions of the baler and the man on the look-out and at the mast are divided.

When the wind drops, the men have to take to the small, leaf-shaped paddles, while one, as a rule, wields a pulling oar. But in order to give speed to a heavy *masawa* canoe, at least ten men would have to paddle and pull. As we shall see, on certain ceremonial occasions, the canoes have to be propelled by paddling, for instance when they approach their final destination, after having performed the great *mwasila* magic. When they arrive at a halting place, the canoes, if necessary, are beached. As a rule, however, the heavily loaded canoes on a Kula expedition, would be secured by both mooring and anchoring, according to the bottom. On muddy bottoms, such as that of the Trobriand Lagoon, a long stick would be thrust into the slime, and one end of the canoe lashed to it. From the other, a heavy stone, tied with a rope, would be thrown down as an anchor. Over a hard, rocky bottom, the anchor stone alone is used.

It can be easily understood that with such craft, and with such limitations in sailing, there are many real dangers which threaten the natives. If the wind is too strong, and the sea becomes too rough, a canoe may not be able to follow its course, and making lee-way, or even directly running before the wind, it may be driven into a quarter where there is no landfall to be made, or from where at best there is no returning at that season. This is what happened to the Dobuan boat mentioned before. Or else, a canoe becalmed and seized by the tide may not be able to make its way by means of paddling. Or in stormy weather, it may be smashed on rocks and sandbanks, or even unable to withstand the impact of waves. An open craft like a native canoe easily fills with sea water, and, in a heavy rain-storm, with rain water. In a calm sea this is not very dangerous, for the wooden canoe does not sink ; even if swamped, the water can be baled out and the canoe floats up. But in rough weather, a water-logged canoe loses its buoyancy and gets broken up. Last and not least, there is the danger of the canoe being pressed into the water, outrigger first, should the wind strike it on the opposite side. With so many real dangers around it, it is a marvellous thing, and to the credit of native seamanship, that accidents are comparatively rare.

We now know about the crew of the canoe and the different functions which every man has to fulfil. Remembering what has been said in Chapter IV, Division V, about the sociological division of functions in sailing, we can visualise concretely the craft with all its inmates, as it sails on the Pilolu ; the *toliwaga* usually sits near the mast in the compartment called *kayguya'u*. With him perhaps is one of his sons or young relatives, while another boy remains in the bows, near the conch-shell ready to sound it, whenever the occasion arises. Thus are employed the *toliwaga* and the *dodo'u* (small boys). The *usagelu* or members of the crew, some four or five strong, are each at his post, with perhaps one supernumerary to assist at any emergency, where the task would require it. On the platform are lounging some of the *silasila*, the youths not yet employed in any work, and not participating in the Kula, but there for their pleasure, and to learn how to manage a boat (see Plate XL).

III

All these people have not only special posts and modes of occupation assigned to them, but they have also to keep certain rules. The canoe on a Kula expedition, is surrounded by taboos, and many observances have to be strictly kept, else this or that might go wrong. Thus it is not allowed to ' point to objects with the hand ' (*yosala yamada*), or those who do it will become sick. A new canoe has many prohibitions connected with it, which are called *bomala wayugo* (the taboos of the lashing creeper). Eating and drinking are not allowed in a new canoe except after sunset. The breaking of this taboo would make the canoe very slow. On a very quick *waga* this rule might perhaps be disregarded, especially if one of the young boys were hungry or thirsty. The *toliwaga* would then bale in some sea-water, pour it over one of the lashings of the creeper with the words :

"I sprinkle thy eye, O *kudayuri* creeper, so that our crew might eat."

After that, he would give the boy something to eat and drink. Besides this eating and drinking taboo, on a new *waga* the other physiological needs must not be satisfied. In case of urgent necessity, a man jumps into the water, holding to one of the cross sticks of the outrigger, or if it were a small boy, he is lowered into the water by one of the elders. This taboo, if broken, would also make the canoe slow. These two taboos, however, as was said, are kept only on a new *waga*, that is on such a one which either sails for the first time, or else has been relashed and repainted before this trip. The taboos are in all cases not operative on the return journey. Women are not allowed to enter a new *waga* before it sails. Certain types of yams may not be carried on a canoe, which has been lashed with the rites of one of the *wayugo* magical systems. There are several systems of this magic (compare Chapter XVII, Division VII) and each has got its specific taboos. These last taboos are to be kept right through the sailing. On account of a magic to be described in the next chapter, the magic of safety as it might be called, a canoe has to be kept free from contact with earth, sand and stones. Hence the natives of Sinaketa do not beach their canoes if they can possibly avoid it.

Among the specific taboos of the Kula, called *bomala lilava* (taboos of the magical bundle) there is a strict rule referring to the entering of a canoe. This must not be entered from any other point but on the *vitovaria*, that is, the front side of the platform, facing the mast. A native has to scale the platform at this place, then, crouching low, pass to the back or front, and there descend into the body of the canoe, or sit down where he is. The compartment facing the *lilava* (magical bundle) is filled out with other trade goods. In front of it sits the chief, behind it the man who handles the sheets. The natives have special expressions which denote the various manners of illicitly entering a canoe, and, in some of the canoe exorcisms, these expressions are used to undo the evil effects of the breaking of these taboos. Other prohibitions, which the natives call the taboo of the *mwasila*, though not associated with the *lilava*, are those which do not allow of using flower wreaths, red ornaments, or red flowers in decorating the canoe or the bodies of the crew. The red colour of such ornaments is, according to native belief, magically incompatible with the aim of the expedition—the acquisition of the red spondylus necklaces. Also, yams may not be roasted on the outward journey, while later on, in Dobu, no local food may be eaten, and the natives have to subsist on their own provisions, until the first Kula gifts have been received.

There are, besides, definite rules, referring to the behaviour of one canoe towards another, but these vary considerably with the different villages. In Sinaketa, such rules are very few ; no fixed sequence is observed in the sailing order of the canoes, anyone of them can start first, and if one of them is swifter it may pass any of the others, even that of a chief. This, however, has to be done so that the slower canoe is not passed on the outrigger side. Should this happen, the transgressing canoe has to give the other one a peace offering (*lula*), because it has broken a *bomala lilava*, it has offended the magical bundle.

There is one interesting point with regard to priorities in Sinaketa, and to describe this we must hark back to the subject of canoe-building and launching. One of the sub-clans of the Lukwasisiga clan, the Tolabwaga sub-clan, have the right of priority in all the successive operations of piecing together, lashing, caulking, and painting of their canoes. All these stages of building and all the magic must first be done on the Tolabwaga canoe, and this canoe is also the first to be launched. Only afterwards, the chief's and the commoners' canoes may follow. A correct observance of this rule ' keeps the sea clean ' (*imilakatile bwarita*). If it were broken, and the chiefs had their canoes built or launched before the Tolabwaga, the Kula would not be successful.

> " We go to Dobu, no pig, no *soulava* necklace is given. We would tell the chiefs : ' Why have you first made your canoes ? The ancestor spirits have turned against us, for we have broken the old custom ! ' "

Once at sea, however, the chiefs are first again, in theory at least, for in practice the swiftest canoe may sail first.

In the sailing custom of Vakuta, the other South Boyowan community, who make the Kula with the Dobu, a sub-clan of the Lukwasisiga clan, called Tolawaga, have the privilege of priority in all the canoe-building operations. While at sea, they also retain one prerogative, denied to all the others : the man who steers with the smaller oar, the *tokabina viyoyu*, is allowed permanently to stand up on the platform. As the natives put it,

> " This is the sign of the Tolawaga (sub-clan) of Vakuta : wherever we see a man standing up at the *viyoyu*, we say : ' there sails the canoe of the Tolawaga ! ' "

The greatest privileges, however, granted to a sub-clan in sailing are those which are to be found in Kavataria. This fishing and sailing community from the North shore of the Lagoon makes distant and dangerous sailings to the North-Western end of Fergusson Island. These expeditions for sago, betel-nut, and pigs will be described in Chapter XXI. Their sea customs, however, have to be mentioned here.

The Kulutula sub-clan of the Lukwasisiga clan enjoy all the same privileges of priority in building, as the Tolabwaga and Tolawaga clans in the southern villages, only in a still higher degree. For their canoe has to pass each stage of construction on the first day, and only the day after can the others follow. This refers even to launching, the Kulutula canoe being launched one day, and on the next those of the chiefs and commoners. When the moment of starting arrives, the Kulutula canoe leaves the beach first, and during the sailing no one is allowed to pass ahead of it. When they arrive at the sandbanks or at an intermediate place in the Amphletts, the Kulutula have to anchor first, and first go ashore and make their camp ready. Only after that can the others follow. This priority expires at the final point of destination. When they arrive at the furthest Koya the Kulutula go ashore first, and they are the first to be presented with the welcoming gift of the ' foreigner ' (tokinana). He receives them with a bunch of betel-nut, which he beats against the head of the canoe, till the nuts scatter. On the return journey, the Kulutula clan sink again into their naturally inferior position.

It may be noted that all the three privileged sub-clans in the three villages belong to the Lukwasisiga clan, and that the names of two of them, Tolawaga, Tolabwaga have a striking resemblance to the word toliwaga, although these resemblances would have to be tested by some stricter methods of etymological comparison, than I have now at my disposal. The fact that these clans, under special circumstances of sailing, resume what may be a lost superiority points to an interesting historical survival. The name Kulutula is undoubtedly identical with Kulutalu, which is an independent totemic clan in the Eastern Marshall Bennetts and in Woodlark.*

IV

Let us return now to our Sinaketan fleet, moving southwards along the barrier reef and sighting one small island after the other. If they did not start very early from Muwa—and delay is one of the characteristics of native life—and if they were not favoured with a very good wind, they would probably have to put in at one of the small sand islands, Legumatabu, Gabuwana or Yakum. Here, on the western side, sheltered from the prevalent trade winds, there is a diminutive lagoon, bounded by two natural breakwaters of coral reef running from the Northern and Southern ends of the island. Fires are lit on the clean, white sand, under the scraggy pandanus trees, and the natives boil their yam food and the eggs of the wild sea fowl, collected on the spot. When darkness closes in and the fires draw them all into a circle, the Kula talk begins again.

* At a later date, I hope to work out certain historical hypotheses with regard to migrations and cultural strata in Eastern New Guinea. A considerable number of independent indices seem to corroborate certain simple hypotheses as to the stratification of the various cultural elements.

Let us listen to some such conversations, and try to steep ourselves in the atmosphere surrounding this handful of natives, cast for a while on to the narrow sandbank, far away from their homes, having to trust only to their frail canoes on the long journey which faces them.   Darkness, the roar of surf breaking on the reef, the dry rattle of the pandanus leaves in the wind, all produce a frame of mind in which it is easy to believe in the dangers of witches and all the beings usually hidden away, but ready to creep out at some special moment of horror.   The change of tone is unmistakable, when you get the natives to talk about these things on such an occasion, from the calm, often rationalistic way of treating them in broad daylight in an Ethnographer's tent.   Some of the most striking revelations I have received of this side of native belief and psychology were made to me on similar occasions.   Sitting on a lonely beach in Sanaroa, surrounded by a crew of Trobrianders, Dobuans, and a few local natives, I first heard the story of the jumping stones.   On a previous night, trying to anchor off Gumasila in the Amphletts, we had been caught by a violent squall, which tore one of our sails, and forced us to run before the wind. on a dark night, in the pouring rain.   Except for myself, all the members of the crew saw clearly the flying witches in the form of a flame at the mast head.   Whether this was St. Elmo's fire I could not judge, as I was in the cabin, seasick and indifferent to dangers, witches, and even ethnographic revelations.   Inspired by this incident, my crew told me how this is, as a rule, a sign of disaster, how such a light appeared a few years ago in a boat, which was sunk almost on the same spot where the squall had caught us ; but fortunately all were saved.   Starting from this, all sorts of dangers were spoken about, in a tone of deep conviction, rendered perfectly sincere by the experiences of the previous night, the surrounding darkness, and the difficulties of the situation—for we had to repair our sail and again attempt the difficult landing in the Amphletts.

I have always found that whenever natives are found under similar circumstances, surrounded by the darkness and the imminent possibility of danger, they naturally drift into a conversation about the various things and beings into which the fears and apprehensions of generations have traditionally crystallised.

Thus if we imagine that we listen to an account of the perils and horrors of the seas, sitting round the fire at Yakum or Legumatabu, we do not stray from reality. One of those who are specially versed in tradition, and who love to tell a story, might refer to one of his own experiences ; or to a well-known case from the past, while others would chime in, and comment, telling their own stories. General statements of belief would be given, while the younger men would listen to the tales so familiar, but always heard with renewed interest.

They would hear about an enormous octopus (*kwita*) which lies in wait for canoes, sailing over the open seas. It is not an ordinary *kwita* of exceptional size, but a special one, so gigantic that it would cover a whole village with its body ; its arms are thick as coco-nut palms, stretching right across the sea. With typical exaggeration, the natives will say : ' *ikanubwadi Pilolu*,' . . . ' he covers up all the Pilolu ' (the sea-arm between the Trobriands and the Amphletts). Its proper home is in the East, ' *o Muyuwa*,' as the natives describe that region of sea and islands, where also it is believed some magic is known against the dreadful creature. Only seldom does it come to the waters between the Trobriands and Amphletts, but there are people who have seen it there. One of the old men of Sinaketa tells how, coming from Dobu, when he was quite young, he sailed in a canoe ahead of the fleet, some canoes being to the right and some to the left behind him. Suddenly from his canoe, they saw the giant *kwita* right in front of them. Paralysed with fear, they fell silent, and the man himself, getting up on the platform, by signs warned the other canoes of the danger. At once they turned round, and the fleet divided into two, took big bends in their course, and thus gave the octopus a wide berth. For woe to the canoe caught by the giant *kwita* ! It would be held fast, unable to move for days, till the crew, dying of hunger and thirst, would decide to sacrifice one of the small boys of their number. Adorned with valuables, he would be thrown overboard, and then the *kwita*, satisfied, would let go its hold of the canoe, and set it free. Once a native, asked why a grown-up would not be sacrificed on such an occasion, gave me the answer :

> " A grown-up man would not like it ; a boy has got no mind. We take him by force and throw him to the *kwita*."

Another danger threatening a canoe on the high seas, is a big, special Rain, or Water falling from above, called *Sinamatanoginogi*. When in rain and bad weather a canoe, in spite of all the efforts to bale it out, fills with water, *Sinamatanoginogi* strikes it from above and breaks it up. Whether at the basis of this are the accidents with waterspouts, or cloud-bursts or simply extremely big waves breaking up the canoe, it is difficult to judge. On the whole, this belief is more easily accounted for than the previous one.

The most remarkable of these beliefs is that there are big, live stones, which lie in wait for sailing canoes, run after them, jump up and smash them to pieces. Whenever the natives have reasons to be afraid of them, all the members of the crew will keep silence, as laughter and loud talk attracts them. Sometimes they can be seen, at a distance, jumping out of the sea or moving on the water. In fact I have had them pointed to me, sailing off Koyatabu, and although I could see nothing, the natives, obviously, genuinely believed they saw them. Of one thing I am certain, however, that there was no reef awash there for miles around. The natives also know quite well that they are different from any reefs or shallows, for the live stones move, and when they perceive a canoe will pursue it, break it up on purpose and smash the men. Nor would these expert fishermen ever confuse a jumping fish with anything else, though in speaking of the stones they may compare them to a leaping dolphin or stingaree.

There are two names given to such stones. One of them, *nuwakekepaki*, applies to the stones met in the Dobuan seas. The other, *vineylida*, to those who live ' o Muyuwa.' Thus, in the open seas, the two spheres of culture meet, for the stones not only differ in name but also in nature. The *nuwakekepaki* are probably nothing but malevolent stones. The *vineylida* are inhabited by witches, or according to others, by evil male beings.* Sometimes a *vineylida* will spring to the surface, and hold fast the canoe, very much in the same manner as the giant octopus would do. And here again offerings would have to be given. A folded mat would first be thrown, in an attempt to deceive it ; if this were of no avail, a little boy would be anointed with coco-nut oil, adorned with arm-shells and *bagi* necklaces, and thrown over to the evil stones.

* The word vineylida suggests the former belief, as *vine*—female, *lida*-coral stone.

It is difficult to realise what natural phenomena or actual occurrences might be at the bottom of this belief, and the one of the giant octopus. We shall presently meet with a cycle of beliefs presenting the same striking features. We shall find a story told about human behaviour mixed up with supernatural elements, laying down the rules of what would happen, and how human beings would behave, in the same matter of fact way, as if ordinary events of tribal life were described. I shall have to comment on the psychology of these beliefs in the next chapter, where also the story is told. Of all the dangerous and frightful beings met with on a sailing expedition, the most unpleasant, the best known and most dreaded are the flying witches, the *yoyova* or *mulukwausi*. The former name means a woman endowed with such powers, whereas *mulukwausi* describes the second self of the woman, as it flies disembodied through the air. Thus, for instance, they would say that such and such a woman in Wawela is a *yoyova*. But sailing at night, one would have to be on the look out for *mulukwausi*, among whom might possibly be the double of that woman in Wawela. Very often, especially at moments when the speaker would be under the influence of fear of these beings, the deprecating euphemism—' *vivila* ' (women) would be used. And probably our Boyowan mariners would speak of them thus in their talk round the campfire, for fear of attracting them by sounding their real name. Dangerous as they always are, at sea they become infinitely more dreaded. For the belief is deep that in case of shipwreck or mishap at sea, no real evil can befall the crows except by the agency of the dreaded women.

As through their connection with shipwreck, they enter inevitably into our narrative, it will be better to leave our Kula expedition on the beach of Yakum in the midst of Pilolu, and to turn in the next chapter to Kiriwinian ethnography and give there an account of the natives' belief in the flying witches and their legend of shipwreck.

CHAPTER X

THE STORY OF SHIPWRECK

I

IN this chapter an account will be given of the ideas and beliefs associated with shipwreck, and of the various precautions which the natives take to insure their own safety. We shall find here a strange mixture of definite, matter of fact information, and of fantastic superstitions. Taking a critical, ethnographic side view, it may be said directly that the fanciful elements are intertwined with the realities in such a manner, that it is difficult to make a distinction between what is mere mytho-poetic fiction and what is a customary rule of behaviour, drawn from actual experience. The best way of presenting this material will be to give a consecutive account of a shipwreck, as it is told in Kiriwinian villages by the travelled old men to the younger generation. I shall adduce in it the several magical formulæ, the rules of behaviour, the part played by the miraculous fish, and the complex ritual of the saved party as they flee from the pursuing *mulukwausi*.

These—the flying witches—will play such an important part in the account, that I must begin with a detailed description of the various beliefs referring to them, though the subject has been touched upon once or twice before (Chapter II, Division VII, and other places). The sea and sailing upon it are intimately associated in the mind of a Boyowan with these women. They had to be mentioned in the description of canoe magic, and we shall see what an important part they play in the legends of canoe building. In his sailing, whether he goes to Kitava or further East, or whether he travels South to the Amphletts and Dobu, they form one of the main preoccupations of a Boyowan sailor. For they are not only dangerous to him, but to a certain extent, foreign. Boyowa, with the exception of Wawela and one or two other villages on the Eastern coast, and in the South of the island, is an ethnographic district, where the flying witches do not exist, although they visit it from time to time. Whereas all the surrounding tribes are full of women who practice this form of sorcery. Thus sailing South, the Boyowan is travelling straight into the heart of their domain.

These women have the power of making themselves invisible, and flying at night through the air. The orthodox belief is that a woman who is a *yoyova* can send forth a double which is invisible at will, but may appear in the form of a flying fox or of a night bird or a firefly. There is also a belief that a *yoyova* develops within her a something, shaped like an egg, or like a young, unripe coco-nut. This something is called as a matter of fact *kapuwana*, which is the word for a small coco-nut.* This idea remains in the native's mind in a vague, indefinite, undifferentiated form, and any attempt to elicit a more detailed definition by asking him such questions, as to whether the *kapuwana* is a material object or not, would be to smuggle our own categories into his belief, where they do not exist. The *kapuwana* is anyhow believed to be the something which in the nightly flights leaves the body of the *yoyova* and assumes the various forms in which the *mulukwausi* appears. Another variant of the belief about the *yoyova* is, that those who know their magic especially well, can fly themselves, bodily transporting themselves through the air.

But it can never be sufficiently emphasised that all these beliefs cannot be treated as consistent pieces of knowledge ; they flow into one another, and even the same native probably holds several views rationally inconsistent with one another. Even their terminology (compare the last Division of the foregoing chapter), cannot be taken as implying a strict distinction or definition. Thus, the word *yoyova* is applied to the woman as we meet her in the village, and the word *mulukwausi* will be used when we see something suspicious flying through the air. But it would be incorrect to systematise this use into a sort of doctrine and to say : " An individual woman is conceived as consisting of an actual living personality called *yoyova*, and of

---

* Professor Seligman has described the belief in similar beings on the North-East Coast of New Guinea. At Gelaria, inland of Bartle Bay, the flying witches can produce a double, or " sending," which they call *labuni*. " *Labuni* exists within women, and can be commanded by any woman who has had children. . . . It was said that the *labuni* existed in, or was derived from, an organ called *ipona*, situated in the flank, and literally meaning egg or eggs." *op. cit.*, p. 640. The equivalence of beliefs here is evident.

an immaterial, spiritual principle called *mulukwausi*, which in its potential form is the *kapuwana.''* In doing this we would do much what the Mediæval Scholastics did to the living faith of the early ages. The native feels and fears his belief rather than formulates it clearly to himself. He uses terms and expressions, and thus, as used by him, we must collect them as documents of belief, but abstain from working them out into a consistent theory ; for this represents neither the native's mind nor any other form of reality.

As we remember from Chapter II, the flying witches are a nefarious agency, second in importance to the *bwaga'u* (male sorcerer), but in efficiency far more deadly even than he himself. In contrast to the *bwaga'u*, who is simply a man in possession of a special form of magic, the *yoyova* have to be gradually initiated into their status. Only a small child, whose mother is a witch, can become a witch herself. When a witch gives birth to a female child, she medicates a piece of obsidian, and cuts off the navel string. The navel string is then buried, with the recital of a magical formula, in the house, and not, as is done in all ordinary cases, in the garden. Soon after, the witch will carry her daughter to the sea beach, utter a spell over some brine in a coco-nut cup, and give the child to drink. After that, the child is submerged in water and washed, a kind of witch's baptism ! Then she brings back the baby into the house, utters a spell over a mat, and folds her up in it. At night, she carries the baby through the air, and goes to a trysting place of other *yoyova*, where she presents her child ritually to them. In contrast to the usual custom of young mothers of sleeping over a small fire, a sorceress lies with her baby in the cold. As the child grows up, the mother will take it into her arms and carry it through the air on her nightly rounds. Entering girlhood at the age when the first grass skirt is put on a maiden, the little prospective witch will begin to fly herself.

Another system of training, running side by side with flying, consists in accustoming the child to participation in human flesh. Even before the growing witch will begin to fly on her own account, the mother will take her to the ghoulish repasts, where she and other witches sit over a corpse, eating its eyes, tongue, lungs, and entrails. There the little girl receives her first share of corpse flesh, and trains her taste to like this diet.

There are other forms of training ascribed to mothers solicitous that their daughters should grow up into efficient *yoyova* and *mulukwausi*. At night the mother will stand on one side of the hut, with the child in her hands, and throw the little one over the roof. Then quickly, with the speed only possible to a *yoyova*, she will move round, and catch the child on the other side. This happens before the child begins to fly, and is meant to accustom it to passing rapidly through the air. Or again, the child will be held by her feet, head down, and remain in this position while the mother utters a spell. Thus gradually, by all these means, the child acquires the powers and tastes of a *yoyova*.

It is easy to pick out such girls from other children. They will be recognisable by their crude tastes, and more especially by their habit of eating raw flesh of pigs or uncooked fish. And here we come to a point, where mythical superstition plays over into something more real, for I have been assured by reliable informants, and those not only natives, that there are cases of girls who will show a craving for raw meat, and when a pig is being quartered in the village will drink its blood and tear up its flesh. These statements I never could verify by direct observations, and they may be only the result of very strong belief projecting its own realities, as we see on every side in our own society in miraculous cures, spiritistic phenomena, etc., etc. If, however, the eating of raw flesh by girl children really occurs, this simply means that they play up to what they know is said and believed about them. This again is a phenomenon of social pyschology met with in many phases of Trobriand society and in our own.

This does not mean that the character of a *yoyova* is publicly donned. Indeed, though a man often owns up to the fact that he is a *bwaga'u*, and treats his speciality quite openly in conversation, a woman will never directly confess to being a *yoyova*, not even to her own husband. But she will certainly be marked by everyone as such a one, and she will often play up to the rôle, for it is always an advantage to be supposed to be endowed with supernatural powers. And moreover, being a sorceress is also a good source of income. A woman will often receive presents with the understanding that such and such a person has to be injured. She will openly take gifts, avowedly in payment for healing someone who has been hurt by another witch. Thus the character of a *yoyova* is, in a way, a public one and the most important and powerful witches will be enumerated by name. But no woman will ever openly speak about being one. Of course to have such a character would in no way spoil matrimonial chances, or do anything but enhance the social status of a woman.

So deep is the belief in the efficacy of magic, and in magic being the only means of acquiring extraordinary faculties, that all powers of a *yoyova* are attributed to magic. As we saw in the training of a young *yoyova*, magic has to be spoken at every stage in order to impart to her the character of a witch. A full blown *yoyova* has to utter special magic each time she wishes to be invisible, or when she wants to fly, or acquire higher speed, or penetrate darkness and distance in order to find out whether an accident is happening there. But like everything referring to this form of witchcraft, these formulæ never come to light. Although I was able to acquire a whole body of spells of the *bwaga'u* sorcery, I could not even lift the fringe of the impenetrable veil, surrounding the magic of the *yoyova*. As a matter of fact, there is not the slightest doubt for me that not one single rite, not one single word of this magic, have ever existed.

Once a *mulukwausi* is fully trained in her craft, she will often go at night to feed on corpses or to destroy shipwrecked mariners, for these are her two main pursuits. By a special sense, acquired through magic, she can ' hear,' as the natives say, that a man has died at such and such a place, or that a canoe is in danger. Even a young apprenticed *yoyova* will have her hearing so sharpened that she will tell her mother : " Mother, I hear, they cry ! " Which means that a man is dead or dying at some place. Or she will say : " Mother, a *waga* is sinking ! " And then they both will fly to the spot.

When she goes out on such an errand, the *yoyova* leaves her body behind. Then she climbs a tree, and reciting some magic, she ties a creeper to it. Then, she flies off, along this creeper, which snaps behind her. This is the moment when we see the fire flying through the sky. Whenever the natives see a falling star, they know it is a *mulukwausi* on her flight. Another version is that, when a *mulukwausi* recites a certain spell, a tree which stands somewhere near her destination bends down towards the other tree on which she is perched. She jumps from one top to the other, and it is then that we see the fire. According to some versions, the *mulukwausi*, that is, the witch in her flying state, moves about naked, leaving her skirt round the body, which remains asleep in the hut. Other versions depict her as tying her skirt tightly round her when flying, and beating her buttocks with a magical pandanus streamer. These latter versions are embodied in the magic quoted above in Chapter V.

Arrived at the place where lies the corpse, the *mulukwausi*, with others who have also flown to the spot, perches on some high object, the top of a tree or the gable of a hut. There they all wait till they can feast on the corpse, and such is their greed and appetite that they are also very dangerous to living men. People who collect round the dead body to mourn and wake over it often have a special spell against the *mulukwausi* recited over them, by the one who knows it. They are careful not to stray away from the others, and, during burial of the dead and afterwards, they believe the air to be infested with these dangerous witches, who spread the smell of carrion around them.

The *mulukwausi* will eat out the eyes, the tongue, and the 'insides' (*lopouia*) of the corpse; when they attack a living man they may simply hit him or kick him, and then he becomes more or less sick. But sometimes they get hold of an individual and treat him like a corpse and eat some of his organs, and then the man dies. It is possible to diagnose this, for such a person would quickly fail, losing his speech, his vision, sometimes suddenly being bereft of all power of movement. It is a less dangerous method to the living man when the *mulukwausi* instead of eating his 'insides' on the spot, simply remove them. They hide them in a place only known to themselves, in order to have provision for a future feast. In that case there is some hope for the victim. Another *yoyova*, summoned quickly by the relations of the dying and well paid by them, will, in the form of a *mulukwausi*, go forth, search for the missing organs, and, if she is fortunate enough to find and restore them, save the life of the victim.

Kenoriya, the favourite daughter of To'ulawa, the chief of Omarakana, while on a visit to another village, was deprived of her internal organs by the *mulukwausi*. When brought home, she could neither move nor speak, and lay down as if dead. Her mother and other relatives already began their mortuary wailing over her, the chief himself broke out into loud lamentations.

But nevertheless, as a forlorn hope, they sent for a woman from Wawela, a well-known *yoyova*, who after receiving valuables and food, flew out as a *mulukwausi*, and the very next night found Kenoriya's insides somewhere in the *raybwag*, near the beach of Kaulukuba, and restored her to health.

Another authentic story is that of the daughter of a Greek trader and a Kiriwinian woman from Oburaku. This story was told me by the lady herself, in perfectly correct English, learnt in one of the white settlements of New Guinea, where she had been brought up in the house of a leading missionary. But the story was not spoilt by any scepticism ; it was told with perfect simplicity and conviction.

When she was a little girl, a woman called Sewawela, from the Island of Kitava, but married to a man of Wawela, came to her parents' house and wanted to sell a mat. They did not buy it, and gave her only a little food, which, as she was a renowned *yoyova* and accustomed therefore to deferential treatment, made her angry. When night came, the little one was playing on the beach in front of the house, when the parents saw a big firefly hovering about the child. The insect then flew round the parents and went into the room. Seeing that there was something strange about the firefly, they called the girl and put her to bed at once. But she fell ill immediately, could not sleep all night, and the parents, with many native attendants, had to keep watch over her. Next morning, added the Kiriwinian mother, who was listening to her daughter telling me the tale, the girl " *boge ikarige ; kukula wala ipipisi*," " she was dead already, but her heart was still beating." All the women present broke out into the ceremonial lamentations. The father of the girl's mother, however, went to Wawela, and got hold of another *yoyova*, called Bomrimwari. She took some herbs and smeared her own body all over. Then she went out in the form of a *mulukwausi* in search of the girl's *lopoulo* (inside). She searched about and found it in the hut of Sewawela, where it lay on the shelf on which are kept the big clay-pots, in which the *mona* (taro pudding), is cooked ceremonially. There it lay " red as calico." Sewawela had left it there, while she went into the garden with her husband, meaning to eat it on her return. Had this happened, the girl could not have been saved. As soon as Bomrimwari found it, she made some magic over it then and there. Then she came back to the trader's compound, made some more magic over ginger-root, and water, and caused the *lopoulo* to return to its place. After that, the little girl soon got better. A substantial payment was given by the parents to the *yoyova* for saving their child.

Living in Oburaku, a village on the Southern half of Boyowa, I was on the boundary between the district where the *yoyova* do not exist, and the other one, to the East, where they are plentiful. On the other side of the Island, which is very narrow at this part, is the village of Wawela, where almost every woman is reputed to be a witch, and some are quite notorious. Going over the *raybwag* at night, the natives of Oburaku would point out certain fireflies which would suddenly disappear, not to relight again. These were the *mulukwausi*. Again, at night, swarms of flying foxes used to flap over the tall trees, making for the big, swampy Island of Boymapo'u which closes in the Lagoon opposite the village. These too were *mulukwausi*, travelling from the East, their real home. They also used to perch on the tops of the trees growing on the water's edge, and this was therefore an especially dangerous spot after sunset. I was often warned not to sit there on the platforms of the beached canoes, as I liked to do, watching the play of colours on the smooth, muddy waters, and on the bright mangroves. When I fell ill soon after, everybody decided that I had been ' kicked ' by the *mulukwausi*, and some magic was performed over me by my friend Molilakwa, the same who gave me some formulæ of *kayga'u*, the magic spoken at sea against witches. In this case his efforts were entirely successful, and my quick recovery was attributed by the natives solely to the spells.

II

What interests us most about *mulukwausi*, is their association with the sea and shipwreck. Very often they will roam over the sea, and meet at a trysting place on a reef. There they will partake of a special kind of coral, broken off from a reef, a kind called by the natives *nada*. This whets their appetite for human flesh, exactly as the drinking of salt water does with the *bwaga'u*. They have also some indirect power over the elements in the sea. Although the natives do not quite agree on the point, there is no doubt that a definite connection exists between the *mulukwausi* and all the other dangers which may be met in the sea, such as sharks, the ' gaping depth ' (*ikapwagega wiwitu*), many of the small sea animals, crabs, some of the shells and the other things to be mentioned presently, all of which are considered to be the cause of death of drowning men. Thus the belief is quite definite that, in being cast into the water by the shipwreck, men do not meet any real danger except by being eaten by the *mulukwausi*, the sharks, and the other animals. If by the proper magic these influences can be obviated, the drowning men will escape unscathed. The belief in the omnipotence of man, or rather, woman in this case, and of the equal power in antidoting by magic, governs all the ideas of these natives about shipwreck. The supreme remedy and insurance against any dangers lies in the magic of mist, called *kayga'u*, which, side by side with Kula magic, and the magic of the canoes, is the third of the indispensable magical equipments of a sailor.

A man who knows well the *kayga'u* is considered to be able to travel safely through the most dangerous seas. A renowned chief, Maniyuwa, who was reputed as one of the greatest masters in *kayga'u* as well as in other magic, died in Dobu on an expedition about two generations ago. His son, Maradiana, had learnt his father's *kayga'u*. Although the *mulukwausi* are extremely dangerous in the presence of a corpse, and though the natives would never dream of putting a dead body on a canoe, and thus multiplying the probabilities of an attack by the witches, still, Maradiana, trusting to his *kayga'u*, brought the corpse back to Boyowa without mishap. This act, a testimony to the daring sailor's great prowess, and to the efficiency of the *kayga'u* magic, is kept alive in the memory and tradition of the natives. One of my informants, boasting of his *kayga'u*, told me how once, on a return from Dobu, he performed his rites. Such a mist arose as a consequence of it that the rest of the canoes lost their way, and arrived in the island of Kayleula. Indeed, if we can speak of a belief being alive, that is, of having a strong hold over human imagination, the belief in the danger from *mulukwausi* at sea is emphatically such a one. In times of mental stress, in times of the slightest danger at sea, or when a dying or dead person is near, the natives at once respond emotionally in terms of this belief. No one could live among these natives, speaking their language, and following their tribal life, without constantly coming up against the belief in *mulukwausi*, and in the efficiency of the *kayga'u*.

As in all other magic, also here, there are various systems of *kayga'u*, that is, there are various formulæ, slightly differing in their expressions, though usually similar in their fundamental wordings and in certain ' key ' expressions. In each system, there are two main types of spells, the *giyotanawa*, or the *kayga'u* of the Underneath, and the *giyorokaywa*, or the *kayga'u* of the Above. The first one usually consists of a short formula or formulæ spoken over some stones and some lime in a lime pot and over some ginger root. This *giyotanawa*, as its name indicates, is magic directed against the evil agencies, awaiting the drowning men from below. Its spells close up ' the gaping depth ' and they screen off the shipwrecked men from the eyes of the sharks. They also protect them from the other evil things, which cause the death of a man in drowning. The several little sea worms found on the beach, the crabs, the poisonous fish, *soka*, and the spiky fish, *baiba'i*, as well as the jumping stones, whether *vineylida* or *nu'akekepaki*, are all warded off and blinded by the *giyotanawa*. Perhaps the most extraordinary belief in this connection is that the *tokwalu*, the carved human figures on the prow boards, the *guwaya*, the semi-human effigy on the mast top, as well as the canoe ribs would ' eat ' the drowning men if not magically ' treated.'

The *kayga'u* of the ' Above,' the *giyorokaywa*, consists of long spells, recited over some ginger root, on several occasions before sailing, and during bad weather or shipwreck. They are directed exclusively against the *mulukwausi*, and form therefore the more important class of the two. These spells must never be recited at night, as then the *mulukwausi* could see and hear the man, and make his magic inefficient. Again, the spell of the Above, when recited at sea, must be spoken so that the magician is not covered with spray, for if his mouth were wet with sea water, the smell would attract rather than disperse, the flying witches. The man who knows the *kayga'u* must also be very careful at meal times. Children may not speak, play about, or make any noise while he eats, nor should anyone go round him behind his back while he is thus engaged ; nor may they point out anything with the finger. Should the man be thus disturbed during his food, he would have to stop eating at once, and not resume it till the next meal time.

Now the leading idea of *kayga'u* is that it produces some sort of mist. The *mulukwausi* who follow the canoe, the sharks and live stones which lie in wait for it, the depth with all its horror, and the *débris* of the canoe ready to harm the owner, all these are blinded by the mist that arises in obedience to these spells. Thus the paralysing effect of these two main forms of magic and the specialised sphere of influence of each of them, are definite and clear dogmas of native belief.

But here again we must not try to press the interpretation of these dogmas too far. Some sort of mist covers the eyes of all the evil agencies or blinds them ; it makes the natives invisible from them. But to ask whether the *kayga'u* produces a real mist, visible also to man, or only a supernatural one, visible only to the *mulukwausi* ; or whether it simply blinds their eyes so that they see nothing, would be asking too much. The same native who will boast of having produced a real mist, so great that it led astray his companions, will next day perform the *kayga'u* in the village during a burial, and affirm that the *mulukwausi* are in a mist, though obviously a perfectly clear atmosphere surrounds the whole proceedings. The natives will tell how, sailing on a windy but clear day, after a *kayga'u* has been recited into the eye of the wind, they hear the shrieks of the *mulukwausi*, who, losing their companions and the scent of the trail, hail one another in the dark. Again, some expressions seem to represent the view that it is mainly an action on the eyes of the witches. ' *Idudubila matala mulukwausi*,'— ' It darkens the eyes of the mulukwausi,' or ' *Iguyugwayu* '— ' It blinds,' the natives will say. And when asked :

> "What do the *mulukwausi* see, then ? " they will answer : "They will see mist only. They do not see the places, they do not see the men, only mist."

Thus here, as in all cases of belief, there is a certain latitude, within which the opinions and views may vary, and only the broad outline, which surrounds them, is definitely fixed by tradition, embodied in ritual, and expressed by the phraseology of magical formulæ or by the statements of a myth.

I have thus defined the manner in which the natives face the dangers of the sea ; we have found, that the fundamental conceptions underlying this attitude are, that in shipwreck, men are entirely in the hands of the witches, and that from

this, only their own magical defence can save them. This
defence consists in the rites and formulæ of the *kayga'u*, of
which we have also learnt the leading principles. Now, a
consecutive description must be given of how this magic is
performed when a *toliwaga* sets out on an expedition. And
following up this expedition, it must be told how the natives
imagine a shipwreck, and what they believe the behaviour of
the shipwrecked party would be.

III

I shall give this narrative in a consecutive manner, as it was
told to me by some of the most experienced and renowned
Trobriand sailors in Sinaketa, Oburaku, and Omarakana. We
can imagine that exactly such a narrative would be told by a
veteran *toliwaga* to his *usagelu* on the beach of Yakum, as our
Kula party sit round the camp fires at night. One of the old
men, well-known for the excellence of his *kayga'u*, and boastful
of it, would tell his story, entering minutely into all the details,
however often the others might have heard about them before,
or even assisted at the performance of his magic. He would
then proceed to describe, with extreme realism, and dwelling
graphically on every point, the story of a shipwreck, very
much as if he had gone through one himself. As a matter of
fact, no one alive at present has had any personal experience
of such a catastrophe, though many have lived through frequent narrow escapes in stormy weather. Based on this, and
on what they have heard themselves of the tradition of ship-
wrecks, natives will tell the story with characteristic vividness.
Thus, the account given below is not only a summary of native
belief, it is an ethnographic document in itself, representing
the manner in which such type of narrative would be told
over camp fires, the same subject being over and over again
repeated by the same man, and listened to by the same
audience, exactly as we, when children, or the peasants of
Eastern Europe, will hearken to familiar fairy tales and
Märchen. The only deviation here from what would actually
take place in such a story-telling, is the insertion of magical
formulæ into the narrative. The speaker might indeed repeat
his magic, were he speaking in broad daylight, in his village, to a
group of close kinsmen and friends. But being on a small
island in the middle of the ocean, and at night, the recital of

spells would be a taboo of the *kayga'u* ; nor would a man ever recite his magic before a numerous audience, except on certain occasions at mortuary vigils, where people are expected to chant their magic aloud before hundreds of listeners.

Returning then again to our group of sailors, who sit under the stunted pandanus trees of Yakum, let us listen to one of the companions of the daring Maradiana, now dead, to one of the descendants of the great Maniyuwa. He will tell us how, early in the morning, on the day of departure from Sinaketa, or sometimes on the next morning, when they leave Muwa, he performs the first rite of *kayga'u*. Wrapping up a piece of *leyya* (wild ginger root) in a bit of dried banana leaf, he chants over it the long spell of the *giyorokaywa*, the *kayga'u* of the Above. He chants this spell into the leaf, holding it cup-shaped, with the morsel of ginger root at the bottom, so that the spell might enter into the substance to be medicated. After that, the leaf is immediately wrapped round, so as to imprison the magical virtue, and the magician ties the parcel round his left arm, with a piece of bast or string. Sometimes he will medicate two bits of ginger and make two parcels, of which the other will be placed in a string necklet, and carried on his breast. Our narrator, who is the master of one of the canoes, will probably not be the only one within the circle round the camp fire, who carries these bundles of medicated ginger ; for though a *toliwaga* must always perform this rite as well as know all the other magic of shipwreck, as a rule several of the older members of his crew also know it, and have also prepared their magical bundles.

This is one of the spells of the *giyorokaywa*, such as the old man said over the ginger root :

GIYOROKAYWA NO. 1 (LEYYA KAYGA'U).

" I will befog Muyuwa ! " (repeated). " I will befog Misima ! " (repeated). " The mist springs up ; the mist makes them tremble. I befog the front, I shut off the rear ; I befog the rear, I shut off the front. I fill with mist, mist springs up ; I fill with mist, the mist which makes them tremble."

This is the opening part of the formula, very clear, and easy to be translated. The mist is magically invoked, the word for mist being repeated with several verbal combinations, in a rhythmic and alliterative manner. The expression tremble, *maysisi*, refers to a peculiar belief, that when a sorcerer or sorceress approaches the victim, and this man paralyses them with a counter spell, they lose their bearings, and stand there trembling.

The main part of this spell opens up with the word *aga'u*,' ' I befog,' which, like all such leading words of a spell is first of all intoned in a long, drawn-out chant, and then quickly repeated with a series of words. Then the word ' *aga'u* ' is replaced by ' *aga'u sulu*,' ' I befog, lead astray,' which in its turn makes way for, ' *aga'u boda*,' ' I befog, shut off.' The list of words repeated in succession with each of these three expressions is a long one. It is headed by the words ' the eyes of the witches.' Then, ' the eyes of the sea-crab.' Then, always with the word ' eyes,' the animals, worms and insects which threaten drowning men in the sea, are enumerated. After they are exhausted, the various parts of the body are repeated ; then finally, a long list of villages is recited, preceded by the word *aga'u*, forming phrases such as : " I befog the eyes of the women of Wawela, etc."

Let us reconstruct a piece of this middle part in a consecutive manner. " I befog . . . . ! I befog, I befog, the eyes of the witches ! I befog the eyes of the little crabs ! I befog the eyes of the hermit crab ! I befog the eyes of the insects on the beach ! . . . etc."

" I befog the hand, I befog the foot, I befog the head, I befog the shoulders . . . . etc."

" I befog the eyes of the women of Wawela ; I befog the eyes of the women of Kaulasi ; I befog the eyes of the women of Kumilabwaga, I befog the eyes of the women of Vakuta. . . . etc., etc."

" I befog, lead astray, the eyes of the witches ; I befog, lead astray the eyes of the little crab ! . . . etc."

" I befog, shut off the eyes of the witches, I befog, shut off the eyes of the little crab . . . etc., etc."

It can easily be seen how long drawn such a spell is, especially as in this middle part, the magician will often come back to where he has started, and repeat the leading word over and over again with the others. Indeed, this can be taken as a typical *tapwana*, or middle part, of a long spell, where the leading words are, so to speak, well rubbed into the various other expressions. One feature of this middle part is remarkable, namely, that the beings from below, the crabs, the sea insects and worms are invoked, although the spell is one of the *giyorokaywa* type, the magic of the Above. This is an inconsistency frequently met with ; a contradiction between the ideas embodied in the spell, and the theory of the magic, as explicitly formulated by the informants. The parts of the body enumerated in the *tapwana* refer to the magician's own person, and to his companions in the canoe. By this part of the spell, he surrounds himself and all his companions with mist, which makes them invisible to all the evil influences.

After the long *tapwana* has been recited, there follows the last part, which, however, is not chanted in this case, but spoken in a low, persuasive, tender voice.

" I hit thy flanks ; I fold over thy mat, thy bleached mat of pandanus ; I shall make it into thy mantle. I take thy sleeping *doba* (grass skirt), I cover thy loins ; remain there, snore within thy house ! I alone myself" (here the reciter's name is uttered) " I shall remain in the sea, I shall swim ! "

This last part throws some interesting sidelights on native belief in *mulukwausi*. We see here the expression of the idea that the body of the witch remains in the house, whilst she herself goes out on her nefarious errand. Molilakwa, the magician of Oburaku who gave me this spell, said in commentary to this last part :

" The *yoyova* casts off her body (*inini wowola*—which really means ' peals off her skin ') ; she lies down and sleeps, we hear her snoring. Her covering (*kapwalela* that is, her outward body, her skin) remains in the house, and she herself flies (*titolela biyova*). Her skirt remains in the house, she flies naked. When she meets men, she eats us. In the morning, she puts on her body, and lies down in her hut. When we cover her loins with the *doba*, she cannot fly any more."

This last sentence refers to the magical act of covering, as expressed in the last part of the spell.

Here we find another variant of belief as to the nature of the *mulukwausi*, to be added to those mentioned before. Previously we met the belief of the disassociation of the woman into the part that remains, and the part that flies. But here the real personality is located in the flying part, whereas what remains is the ' covering.' To imagine the *mulukwausi*, the flying part, as a ' sending,' in the light of this belief, would not be correct. In general, such categories as ' agent,' and ' sending,' or as

' real self ' and ' emanation ' etc., etc., can be applied to native belief as rough approximations only, and the exact definition should be given in terms of native statement.

The final sentence of this spell, containing the wish to remain alone in the sea, to be allowed to swim and drift, is a testimony to the belief that without *mulukwausi*, there is no danger to a man adrift on a piece of wreckage among the foaming waves of a stormy sea.

After reciting this lengthy spell, the *toliwaga*, as he tells us in his narrative, has had to perform another rite, this time, over his lime-pot. Taking out the stopper of rolled palm leaf and plaited fibre from the baked and decorated gourd in which he keeps his lime, he utters another spell of the *giyorokaywa* cycle :

GIYOROKAYWA No. 2 (PWAKA KAYGA'U).

" There on Muruwa, I arise, I stand up ! Iwa, Sewatupa, at the head—I rumble, I disperse. Kasabwaybwayreta, Namedili, Toburitolu, Tobwebweso, Tauva'u, Bo'abwa'u, Rasarasa. They are lost, they disappear."

This beginning, full of archaic expressions, implicit meanings and allusions and personal names, is very obscure. The first words refer probably to the head-quarters of sorcery ; Muruwa (or Murua—Woodlark Island), Iwa, Sewatupa. The long list of personal names following afterwards contains some mythical ones, like Kasabwaybwayreta, and some others, which I cannot explain, though the words Tobwebweso, Tauva'u, and Bo'abwa'u suggest that this is a list in which some sorcerers' names figure. As a rule, in such spells, a list of names signifies that all those who have used and handed down this formula, are enumerated. In some cases the people mentioned are frankly mythical heroes. Sometimes a few mythical names are chanted, and then comes a string of actual people, forming a sort of pedigree of the spell. If these in this spell are ancestor names they all refer to mythical personalities, and not to real ancestors.* The last words contained an expression typical of the *kayga'u*. Then comes the middle part.

* Not all the spells which I have obtained have been equally well translated and commented upon. This one, although very valuable, for it is one of the spells of the old chief Maniyuwa, and one which had been recited when his corpse was brought over from Dobu by his son Maradiana, was obtained early in my ethnographic career, and Gomaya, Maradiana's son, from whom I got it, is a bad commentator. Nor could I find any other competent informant later on, who could completely elucidate it for me.

" I arise, I escape from *bara'u ;* I arise, I escape from *yoyova*. I arise, I escape from *mulukwausi*. I arise, I escape from *bowo'u*, etc.," repeating the leading words " I arise, I escape from— " with the words used to describe the flying witches in the various surrounding districts. Thus the word *bara'u* comes from Muyuwa (Woodlark Island), where it describes the sorceress, and not, as in other Massim districts, a male sorcerer. The words *yoyova, mulukwausi* need no explanation. *Bowo'u* is an Amphlettan word. Words from Dobu, Tubetube, etc., follow. Then the whole period is repeated, adding ' eyes of ' in the middle of each phrase, so that it runs :

" I arise, I escape from the eyes of the *bara'u*. I arise, I escape from the eyes of the *yoyova*, etc." The leading words, ' I arise, I escape from ' are then replaced by ' They wander astray,' which, again, make way to ' the sea is cleared off ' This whole middle part of the spell is clear, and needs no commentary. Then comes the concluding period (*dogina*) :

" I am a *manuderi* (small bird), I am a *kidikidi* (small sea bird), I am a floating log, I am a piece of sea-weed ; I shall produce mist till it encloses all, I shall befog, I shall shut off with fog. Mist, enveloped in mist, dissolving in mist am I. Clear is the sea, (the *mulukwausi* are) straying in mist." This part also needs no special commentary.

This is again a long spell of the *giyorokaywa* type, that is, directed against the *mulukwausi,* and in this the spell is consistent, for the *mulukwausi* alone are invoked in the middle period.

After the spell has been chanted into the lime pot, this is well stoppered, and not opened till the end of the journey. It must be noted that these two *giyorokaywa* spells have been spoken by our *toliwaga* in the village or on Muwa beach, and in day time. For, as said above, it is a taboo to utter them in the night or at sea. From the moment he has spoken these two spells, both medicated substances, the ginger root and the lime in the lime pot, remain near him. He has also in the canoe some stones of those brought from the Koya, and called *binabina*, in distinction to the dead coral, which is called *dakuna*. Over these stones, at the moment of the occurrence of danger, a spell of the Underneath, a *giyotanawa* will be recited. The following is a formula of this type, short as they always are.

Giyotanawa No. 1 (Dakuna Kayga'u).

" Man, bachelor, woman, young girl ; woman, young
girl, man, bachelor !   Traces, traces obliterated by cob-
webs ; traces, obliterated by turning up (the material in
which they were left) ; I press, I close down ! Sharks of
Dukutabuya, I press, I close down ; Sharks of Kaduwaga,
I press, I close down," etc., the sharks of Muwa, Galeya,
Bonari, and Kaulokoki being invoked in turn.   All these
words are names of marked parts of the sea, in and around
the Trobriand Lagoon.   The formula ends up with the
following peroration : " I press down thy neck, I open up
thy passage of Kiyawa, I kick thee down, O shark.   Duck
down under water, shark.   Die, shark, die away."

The commentary to the opening sentences given by my
informant, Molilakwa of Oburaku, was :

" This magic is taught to people when they are quite
young.   Hence the mention of young people."

The obliterating of traces will be made clearer by the account
which follows, in which we shall see that to obliterate traces,
to put off the scent the shark and *mulukwausi* are the main
concerns of the shipwrecked party.   The middle part refers to
sharks only, and so does the peroration.   The passage of
Kiyawa near Tuma is mentioned in several types of magical
exorcisms, when the evil influence is being banished.   This
passage lies between the main island and the island of Tuma,
and leads into the unknown regions of the North-Western seas.

It will be best to quote here another formula of the
giyotanawa type, and a very dramatic one.   For this is the
formula spoken at the critical moment of shipwreck.   At the
moment when the sailors decide to abandon the craft and to
plunge into the sea, the *toliwaga* stands up in the canoe, and
slowly turning round so as to throw his words towards all four
winds, intones in a loud voice this spell :

Giyotanawa No. 2.

" Foam, foam, breaking wave, wave ! I shall enter into
the breaking wave, I shall come out from behind it.   I
shall enter from behind into the wave, and I shall come
out in its breaking foam ! "
" Mist, gathering mist, encircling mist, surround,
surround me ! "

" Mist, gathering mist, encircling mist, surround, surround
    me, my mast !
Mist, gathering mist, etc.   . . .   surround me, the nose
    of my canoe.
Mist, etc.   . . .   surround me, my sail,
Mist, etc.   . . .   surround me, my steering oar,
Mist, etc.   . . .   surround me, my rigging,
Mist, etc.   . . .   surround me, my platform,"

.   .   .   .

And so on, enumerating one after the other all the parts
of the canoe and its accessories.   Then comes the final part
of the spell :
    " I shut off the skies with mist ; I make the sea tremble
with mist ; I close up your mouth, sharks, *bonubonu*
(small worms), *ginukwadewo* (other worms). Go underneath and we shall swim on top."

Little is needed as a commentary to this magic.   Its beginning is very clear, and singularly well depicts the situation in
which it is uttered.   The end refers directly to the primary
aim of the magic, to the warding off of the Underneath, of the
dangerous animals in the sea.   The only ambiguity refers to
the middle part, where the magical leading words of ' envelop-
ing by mist ' are associated with a list of names of the parts of
the canoe.   I am not certain whether this is to be interpreted,
in the sense that the *toliwaga* wants to surround his whole canoe
with mist so that it may not be seen by the sharks, etc., or
whether, on the contrary, just on the verge of abandoning his
canoe, and anxious to cut himself off from its various parts
which may turn on him and ' eat him,' he therefore wants to
surround each of them with mist so that it may be blinded.
The latter interpretation fits the above-quoted belief that
certain parts of the canoe, especially the carved human figures
on the prowboard and the mast, the ribs of the canoe, and
certain other parts of its construction, ' eat ' the shipwrecked
men.   But again, in this spell, there are enumerated not certain
parts, but every part, and that undoubtedly is not consistent
with this belief, so the question must remain open.

IV

I have anticipated some of the events of the consecutive
narrative of shipwreck, in order to give the two last mentioned
magical formulæ first, and not to have to interrupt the tale of

our *toliwaga*, to which we now return. We left it at the point
where, having said his first two *kayga'u* formulæ over the ginger
and into the lime pot, he embarks, keeping these two things
handy, and putting some *binabina* stones within his reach.
From here, his narrative becomes more dramatic. He describes the approaching storm :

NARRATIVE OF SHIPWRECK AND SALVAGE.

" The canoe sails fast ; the wind rises ; big waves come ;
the wind booms, du-du-du-du. . . The sails flutter ;
the *lamina* (outrigger) rises high ! All the *usagelu* crouch
on the *lamina*. I speak magic to calm the wind. The big
spell of the Sim-sim. They know all about *yavata* (North-
Westerley Monsoon wind). They live in the eye of the
yavata. The wind abates not, not a little bit. It booms,
it gains strength, it booms loud du-du-du-du-du. All the
usagelu are afraid. The *mulukwausi* scream, u-ú, u-ú,
u-ú, u ; their voices are heard in the wind. With the wind
they scream and come flying. The *veva* (sheet rope) is
torn from the hands of the *tokabinaveva*. The sail flutters
freely in the wind ; it is torn away. It flies far into the
sea ; it falls on the waters. The waves break over the
canoe. I stand up. I take the *binabina* stones ; I recite
the *kayga'u* over them, the *giyotanawa*, the spell of the
Underneath. The short spell, the very strong spell. I
throw the stones into the deep. They weigh down the
sharks, the *vineylida ;* they close the Gaping Depth. The
fish cannot see us. I stand up, I take my lime pot ; I
break it. The lime I throw into the wind. It wraps us up
in mist. Such a mist that no one can see us. The
mulukwausi lose sight of us. We hear them shout near by.
They shout u-û, u-û, u-ú, u. The sharks, the *bonubonu*,
the *soka* do not see us ; the water is turbid.. The canoe
is swamped, the water is in it. It drifts heavily, the
waves break over us. We break the *vatotuwa*, (the sticks
joining the float to the platform). The *lamina* (outrigger
float) is severed ; we jump from the *waga ;* we catch hold
of the *lamina*. On the *lamina* we drift. I utter the great
Kaytaria spell ; the big fish *iraviyaka* comes. It lifts us.
It takes the *lamina* on its back, and carries us. We drift,
we drift, we drift."

" We approach a shore ; the *iraviyaka* brings us there,
the *iraviyaka* puts us on the shallows. I take a stout pole,
I lift it off ; I speak a spell. The *iraviyaka* turns back
to the deep sea."

" We are all on the *dayaga* (fringing reef). We stand in
water. The water is cold, we all shiver with cold. We
do not go ashore. We are afraid of the *mulukwausi*. They
follow us ashore. They wait for us ashore. I take a
dakuna (piece of coral stone), I say a spell over it. I
throw the stone on the beach ; it makes a big thud ;
good ; the *mulukwausi* are not there. We go ashore.
Another time, I throw a stone, we hear nothing : *mulukwausi* are on the beach ; they catch it ; we hear nothing.
We remain on the *dayaga*. I take some *leyya* (ginger). I
spit it at the beach. I throw another stone. The
mulukwausi do not see it. It falls down ; we hear it. We
go ashore ; we sit on the sand in a row. We sit in one row,
one man near another, as on the *lamina* (in the same order
as they drifted on the *lamina*). I make a charm over the
comb ; all the *usagelu* comb their hair ; they tease their
hair a long time. They are very cold ; we do not make
the fire. First, I put order on the beach ; I take the piece
of *leyya*, I spit it over the beach. One time, when the
leyya is finished, I take some *kasita* leaves (the beach is
always full of these). I put them on the shore, I put a
stone on them, uttering a spell—afterwards, we make
fire. All sit round and warm themselves at the fire."

" At day time, we don't go to the village ; the *mulukwausi* would follow us. After dark, we go. Like on the
lamina, we march in the same order, one after the other.
I go last ; I chant a spell over a *libu* plant. I efface our
traces. I put the *libu* on our track ; I put the weeds
together. I make the path confused. I say a charm to
the spider, that he might make a cobweb. I say a charm
to the bush-hen, that she might turn up the soil."

" We go to the village. We enter the village, we pass
the main place. No one sees us ; we are in mist, we are
invisible. We enter the house of my *veyola* (maternal
kinsman), he medicates some *leyya ;* he spits (magically)
on all of us. The *mulukwausi* smell us ; they smell the
salt water on our skins. They come to the house, the house
trembles. A big wind shakes the house, we hear big thuds
against the house. The owner of the house medicates the
leyya and spits over us ; they cannot see us. A big fire
is made in the house ; plenty of smoke fills the house.
The *leyya* and the smoke blind their eyes. Five days we
sit in smoke, our skin smells of smoke ; our hair smells of
smoke ; the *mulukwausi* cannot smell us. Then I medicate
some water and coco-nut, the *usagelu* wash and annoint
themselves. They leave the house, they sit on the

kaukweda (spot before the house).   The owner of the house chases them away. ' Go, go to your wife ; ' we all go, we return to our houses.''

I have given here a reconstruction of a native account, as I have often heard it told with characteristic vividness : spoken in short, jerky sentences, with onamatopoetic representations of sound, the narrative exaggerates certain features, and omits others.   The excellency of the narrator's own magic, the violence of the elements at critical moments, he would always reiterate with monotonous insistence.   He would diverge into some correlated subject, jump ahead, missing out several stages, come back, and so on, so that the whole is quite incoherent and unintelligible to a white listener, though the native audience follows its trend perfectly well.   For it must be remembered that, when a native tells such a story, the events are already known to his listeners, who have grown up gradually becoming familiar with the narrow range of their tribal folklore.   Our *toliwaga*, telling this story over again on the sandbank of Yakum, would dwell on such points as allowed him to boast of his *kayga'u*, to describe the violence of the storm, to bear witness to the traditional effects of the magic.

It is necessary for an Ethnographer to listen several times to such a narrative, in order to have a fair chance of forming some coherent idea of its trend.   Afterwards, by means of direct examination, he can succeed in placing the facts in their proper sequence.   By questioning the informants about details of rite and magic, it is possible then to obtain interpretations and commentaries.   Thus the whole of a narrative can be constructed, the various fragments, with all their spontaneous freshness, can be put in their proper places, and this is what I have done in giving this account of shipwreck.*

A few words of comment must now be given on the text of the above narrative.   In it, a number of magical rites were mentioned, besides those which were described first with their spells.   Something must be said more in detail about the spells of the subsequent magical performances.   There are some eleven of them.   First comes the ritual invocation of the fish

---

* Such reconstructions are legitimate for an Ethnographer, as well as for a historian.   But it is a duty of the former as well as of the latter to show his sources as well as to explain how he has manipulated them.   In one of the next chapters, Chapter XVIII, Divisions XIV-XVII, a sample of this method-ological aspect of the work will be given, although the full elaboration of sources and methods must be postponed to another publication.

which helps the shipwrecked sailors. The spell corresponding to this, is called *kaytaria*, and it is an important formula, which every *toliwaga* is supposed to know. The question arises, has this rite ever been practised in reality ? Some of the actions taken by the shipwrecked natives, such as the cutting of the the outrigger float when the boat is abandoned, are quite rational. It would be dangerous to float on the big, unwieldy canoe which might be constantly turned round and round by the waves, and if smashed to pieces, might injure the sailors with its wreckage. In this fact, perhaps there is also the empirical basis for the belief that some fragments of the canoe ' eat ' the shipwrecked men. The round, symmetrical log of the *lamina*, on the other hand, will serve as an excellent lifebuoy. Perhaps a *toliwaga*, arrived at such a pass, would really utter the *kaytaria* spell. And if the party were saved, they would probably all declare, and, no doubt believe, that the fish had come to their summons, and somehow or other helped in the rescue.

It is less easy to imagine what elements in such an experience might have given rise to the myth that the natives, landed on the shore, magically lift the fish from the shallow waters by means of a charmed pole. This indeed seems a purely imaginary incident, and my main informant, Molilakwa of Oburaku, from whom I obtained the *kaytaria* spell, did not know the spell of the pole, and would have had to leave the *iraviaka* to its own fate in the shallows. Nor could I hear of anyone else professing to know this spell. The formula uttered over the stone to be thrown on the beach was equally unknown to the circle of my informants. Of course, in all such cases, when a man carrying on a system of magic would come to a gap in his knowledge, he would perform the rite without the spell, or utter the most suitable spell of the system. Thus here, as the stone is thrown in order to reconnoitre whether the *mulukwausi* are waiting for them, a spell of the *giyorokaywa*, the spell of the *mulukwausi*, might be uttered over the stone. Over the combs, as well as over the herbs on the beach, a *giyorokaywa* spell would be uttered, according to my informants, but probably, a different spell from the one spoken originally over the ginger root. Molilakwa, for instance, knows two spells of the *giyoro-kaywa*, both of which are suitable to be spoken over the ginger and over the beach respectively. Then there comes another spell, to be uttered over the *libu* plant, and in addressing the spider and the bush-hen. Molilakwa told me that the same spell would be said in the three cases, but neither he, nor anyone else, among my informants could give me this spell. The magic done in the village, while the shipwrecked men remained in the smoky hut, would be all accompanied by the *leyya* (ginger) spells.

One incident in the above narrative might have struck the reader as contradictory of the general theory of the *mulukwausi* belief, that, namely, where the narrator declares that the party on the beach have to wait till nightfall before they enter the village. The general belief expressed in all the *mulukwausi* legends, as well as in the taboos of the *kayga'u*, is that the witches are really dangerous only at night, when they can see and hear better. Such contradictions, as I have said, are often met in native belief, and in this, by the way, the savages do not differ from ourselves. My informant, from whom I had this version, simply said that such was the rule and the custom, and that they had to wait till night. In another account, on the other hand, I was told that the party must proceed to the village immediately after having performed the several rites on the beach, whether night or day.

There also arises the main question, regarding this narrative, to which allusion has been made already, namely, how far does it represent the normal behaviour in shipwreck, and how far is it a sort of standardised myth? There is no doubt that shipwreck in these seas, surrounded in many parts by islands, is not unlikely to end by the party's being saved. This again would result in some such explanation as that contained in our narrative. Naturally, I tried to record all the actual cases of shipwreck within the natives' memory. Some two generations ago, one of the chiefs of Omarakana, named Numakala, perished at sea, and with him all his crew. A canoe of another Eastern Trobriand village, Tilakaywa, was blown far North, and stranded in Kokopawa, from where it was sailed back by its crew, when the wind turned to the North-West. Although this canoe was not actually shipwrecked, its salvation is credited to *kayga'u* magic, and to the kind fish, *iraviyaka*. A very intelligent informant of mine explained this point of view in answer to some of my cavillings : " If this canoe had been wrecked, it would have been saved also."

A party from Muyuwa (Woodlark Island) were saved on the shore of Boyowa. In the South of the Island, several cases arc on record where canoes were wrecked and saved in the d'Entrecasteaux Islands or in the Amphletts. Once the whole crew were eaten by cannibals, getting ashore in a hostile district of Fergusson Island, and one man only escaped, and ran along the shore, south-eastwards towards Dobu. Thus there is a certain amount of historical evidence for the saving power of the magic, and the mixture of fanciful and real elements makes our story a good example of what could be called *standardised* or *universalised myth*—that is, a myth referring not to one historical event but to a type of occurrence, happening universally.

V

Let us now give the text of the remaining spells which belong to the above narrative, but have not been adduced there, so as not to spoil its flow. First of all there is the *kayluria* spell, that which the *toliwaga*, drifting alongside his crew on the detached canoe float, intones in a loud, slow voice, in order to attract the *iraviyaka*.

KAYTARIA SPELL.

" I lie, I shall lie down in my house, a big house. I shall sharpen my ear, I shall hear the roaring of the sea—it foams up, it makes a noise. At the bottom of Kausubiyai, come, lift me, take me, bring me to the top of Nabonabwana beach."

Then comes a sentence with mythological allusions which I could not succeed in translating. After that follows the main part of the spell :

" The *suyusayu* fish shall lift me up ; my child, the *suyusayu* shall lift me up ; my child's things, the *suyusayu* shall lift me up ; my basket, etc. ; my lime pot, etc. ; my lime spoon, etc. ; my house, etc. ; " repeating the words " the *suyusayu* fish shall lift me up " with various expressions describing the *toliwaga's* equipment as well as his child, presumably a member of the shipwrecked crew.

There is no end part to this spell, as it was given to me ; only the beginning is repeated after the main part. It is not impossible that Molilakwa himself, my informant, did not know the spell to the end. Such magic, once learnt by a native, never used, and recited perhaps once a year during a mortuary ceremony, or occasionally, in order to show off, is easily forgotten. There is a marked difference between the vacillating and uncertain way in which such spells are produced by informants, and the wonderful precision and the easy flow with which, for example, the spells, year after year performed in public, will trip off the tongue of the garden magician.

I cannot give a correct commentary to the mythological names Kausubiyai and Nabonabwana, in the first part of the spell. What this part means, whether the reclining individual who hears the noises of the sea is the magician, or whether it represents the sensations of the fish who hears the calling for help, I could not make out. The meaning of the middle part is plain, however. *Suyusayu* is another name for *iraviyaka*, indeed, its magical name used only in spells, and not when speaking of it in ordinary conversations.

The other formula to be given here is the other *giyorokaywa* spell, which would be used in spitting the ginger on the beach after rescue, and also in medicating the herbs, which will be put on the beach and beaten with a stone. This spell is associated with the myth of the origin of *kayga'u*, which must be related here, to make the formula clear.

Near the beginning of time, there lived in Kwayawata, one of the Marshall Bennetts, a family strange to our ideas of family life, but quite natural in the world of Kiriwinian mythology. It consisted of a man, Kalaytaytu, his sister, Isenadoga, and the youngest brother, a dog, Tokulubweydoga. Like other mythological personages, their names suggest that originally they must have conveyed some sort of description. *Doga* means the curved, almost circular, boar's tusk used as ornament. The name of the canine member of the family might mean something like Man-with-circular-tusks-in-his-head, and his sister's name, Woman-ornamented-with-*doga*. The eldest brother has in his name the word *taytu*, which signifies the staple food (small yams) of natives, and a verb, *kalay*, signifying ' to put on ornaments.' Not much profit, however, can be deduced from this etymology, as far as I can see, for the interpretation of this myth. I shall quote in a literal translation the short version of this myth, as I obtained it first, when the information was volunteered to me by Molilakwa in Oburaku.

Myth of Tokulubwaydoga.

" They live in Kwayawata ; one day Kalaytayta goes to fish, gets into a small canoe (*kewo'u*). Behind him swims the dog. He comes to Digumenu. They fish with the older brother. They catch fish ! The elder brother paddles ; that one again goes behind ; goes, returns to Kwayawata. They died ; came Modokei, he learned the *kayga'u*, the inside of Tokulubwaydoga. The name of their mother, the mother of Tokulubwaydoga, is Tobunaygu.''

This little fragment gives a good idea of what the first version is, even of so well fixed a piece of narrative as a myth. It has to be supplemented by inquiries as to the motives of the behaviour of the various personages, as to the relations of one event to the other. Thus, further questions revealed that the elder brother refused to take the dog with him on this fishing expedition. Tokulubwaydoga then determined to go all the same, and swam to Digumenu, following the canoe of his brother. This latter was astonished to see him, but none the less they went to work together. In fishing, the dog was more successful than his brother, and thus aroused his jealousy. The man then refused to take him back. Tokulubwaydoga then jumped into the water, and again swam and arrived safely in Kwayawata. The point of the story lies in the fact that the dog was able to do the swimming, because he knew the *kayga'u*, otherwise the sharks, *mulukwausi*, or other evil things would have eaten him. He got it from his mother, the lady Tobunaygu, who could teach him this magic because she was a *mulukwausi* herself. Another important point about this myth, also quite omitted from the first version volunteered to me, is its sociological aspect. First of all, there is the very interesting incident, unparalleled in Kiriwinian tradition : the mother of the three belonged to the Lukwasisiga clan. It was a most incongruous thing for a dog, who is the animal of the Lukuba clan, to be born into a Lukwasisiga family. However, there he was, and so he said :

" Good, I shall be a Lukuba, this is my clan.''

Now the incident of the quarrel receives its significance in so far as the dog, the only one to whom the mother gave the *kayga'u*, did not hand it over to his brother and sister who were of the Lukwasisiga clan, and so the magic went down only the dog's own clan, the Lukuba. It must be assumed (though this was not known to my informant) that Madokei, who learnt the magic from the dog, was also a Lukuba man.

Like all mythological mother-ancestresses, Tobunaygu had no husband, nor does this circumstance call forth any surprise or comment on the part of the natives, since the physiological aspect of fatherhood is not known among them, as I have repeatedly observed.

As can be seen, by comparing the original fragment, and the subsequent amplification by inquiries, the volunteered version misses out the most important points. The concatenation of events, the origin of the *kayga'u*, the important sociological details, have to be dragged out of the informant, or, to put it more correctly, he has to be made to enlarge on points, to roam over all the subjects covered by the myth, and from his statements then, one has to pick out and piece together the other bits of the puzzle. On the other hand, the names of the people, the unimportant statements of what they did and how they were occupied are unfailingly given.

Let us adduce now the *kayga'u*, which is said to be derived from the dog, and ultimately from his mother :

KAYGA'U OF TOKULUBWAYDOGA.

" Tobunaygu (repeated), Manemanaygu (repeated), my mother a snake, myself a snake ; myself a snake, my mother a snake. Tokulubwaydoga, Isenadoga, Matagagai, Kaĺaytaytu ; *bulumava'u tabugu* Madokei. I shall befog the front, I shall shut off the rear ; I shall befog the rear, I shall shut off the front."

This exordium contains at first the invocation of the name of the *mulukwausi*, who was the source of the spell. Its pendant Manemanaygu is, according to my informant, derived from an archaic word *nema*, equivalent to the present day *yama*, hand. " As the right hand is to the left one, so is Tobunaygu to Manemanaygu," which was expressed as a matter of fact in the less grammatically worded form ; " this right hand, this left " (clapped together) " so Tobunaygu, Manemanaygu."

Whether this analysis of my informant is correct must remain an open question. It must be remembered that magic is not taken by the natives as an ethnographic document, allowing of interpretations and developments, but as an instrument of power. The words are there to act, and not to teach. Questions as to the meaning of magic, as a rule, puzzled the informants, and therefore it is not easy to explain a formula or obtain a correct commentary upon it. All the same there are some natives who obviously have tried to get to the bottom of what the various words in magic represent.

To proceed with our commentary, the phrase " My mother a snake, etc.," was thus explained to me by Molilakwa : " Supposing we strike a snake, already it vanishes, it does not remain ; thus also we human beings, when *mulukwausi* catch us, we disappear." That is, we disappear after having spoken this magical formula, for in a formula the desired result is always expressed in anticipation. Molilakwa's description of a snake's behaviour is, according to my experience, not sound Natural History, but it probably expresses the underlying idea, namely the elusiveness of the snake, which would naturally be one of the metaphorical figures used in the spell.

The string of words following the invocation of the snake are all mythical names, four of which we found mentioned in the above myth, while the rest remain obscure. The last-named, that of Modokei, is preceded by the words *bulumavau tabugu*, which means, ' recent spirit of my ancestor,' which words are as a rule used in spells with reference to real grandfathers of the reciters.

The middle part of the spell proceeds :—

" I shall cover the eyes of the witches of Kitava ; I shall cover the eyes of the witches of Kumwageya ; I shall cover the eyes of the witches of Iwa ; I shall cover the eyes of the witches of Gawa, etc., etc.," enumerating all the villages and islands renowned for their witches. This list is again recited, substituting for the expression " I shall cover," in succession, " I shall befog," and " dew envelopes." This middle part needs no commentary.

The end of this formula runs as follows :

" I shall kick thy body, I shall take thy spirit skirt, I shall cover thy buttocks, I shall take thy mat, a pandanus mat, I shall take thy mantle. I shall strike thee with my foot, go, fly over Tuma, fly away. I myself in the sea (here the reciter's name is mentioned), I shall drift away, well." This last part of the spell is so much alike to the end of the spell first quoted in this chapter, that no commentary is needed.

The mythological and magical data presented in this chapter all bear upon the native belief in flying witches and dangers at sea, a belief in which elements of reality are strangely blended with traditionally fixed fancies, in a way, however, not uncommon to human belief in general. It is time now to return to our party on the beach at Yakum, who, after having spent the night there, next morning rig up their masts, and with a favourable wind, soon reach the waters of Gumasila and Domdom.

CHAPTER XI

IN THE AMPHLETTS—SOCIOLOGY OF THE KULA

I

OUR party, sailing from the North, reach first the main island of Gumasila, a tall, steep mountain with arched lines and great cliffs, suggesting vaguely some huge Gothic monument. To the left, a heavy pyramid, the island of Domdom, recedes behind the nearer mountain as the travellers approach. The fleet now sails along the westerly shore of Gumasila, on which side the jungle, interspersed with bald patches, ascends a steep slope, ribbed with rocky ridges, and creased by valleys which run at their foot into wide bays. Only here and there can be seen triangular clearings, signs of cultivation made by the natives from the other side of the island, where the two villages are situated. At the South-West end of Gumasila, a narrow promontory runs into a flat, low point with a sandy beach on both sides. On the North side of the point, hidden from the villages, the fleet comes to a halt, on the beach of Giyawana (called by the Trobrianders Giyasila). This is the place where all the fleets, arriving from the North, stop before approaching the villages. Here also the inhabitants of the Amphletts rest for a day, after the first false start they have made from the villages, and before they actually set off for the Trobriands. This beach, in short, is the Amphlettan counterpart of the sandbank Muwa. It was also here that I surprised the Gumasilan canoes on a full moon night, in March, 1918, after they had started to join the *uvalaku* expedition to Sinaketa.

On this beach, the Sinaketans perform the final stage of Kula magic, before approaching their partners in Gumasila. The same magic will be repeated before arriving in Dobu, and as a matter of fact, when the objective of the big *uvalaku* is Dobu, the full and ceremonial performance of the magic might usually be deferred till then. It will be better therefore to postpone the description of this magic till we have brought our fleet to the beach of Sarubwoyna. Here it will be enough to mention that on occasions when magic is performed, after an hour's or half hour's pause on the beach of Giyawana, all the men get into their canoes, take the paddles and oars, and the fleet sails round the point where, in a small, very picturesque bay, there lies the smaller village of Gumasila, called Nu'agasi (see Plate I). This village in olden days was perched on a narrow ledge some one hundred metres above the sea level, a fastness difficult of access, and overlooking all its approaches. Now, after the white man's influence has rendered unnecessary all precautions against raiding parties, the village has come down to the narrow strip of foreshore, a bridge between the sea and a small swamp formed at the foot of the hill. Some of the canoes will come to this beach, the others will sail further, under a precipitous black rock of some 150 metres high and 300 metres wide (see Plate XLII). Turning another corner, they arrive at the big village of Gumasila, built on artificial stone terraces, surrounded by dykes of small stones, forming square lagoons and diminutive harbours (compare the description given above in Chapter I, Division V). This is the old village which, practically inaccessible by sea, formed a fastness of a different kind from the other, high-perched villages typical of this district. Exposed to the full onslaught of the South-Easterly winds and seas, against which it was protected by its stone bulwarks and dykes, it was approachable only in all weathers by a small channel to the South, where a big rock and a reef shelter it from the rough waters.

Without any preliminary welcoming ceremony or formal reception, the Sinaketan guests now leave their canoes and disperse among the villagers, settle down in groups near the houses of their friends, and engage in betel chewing and conversations. They speak in Kiriwinian, a language which is universally known in the Amphletts. Almost as soon as they go ashore, they give to their partners presents of *pari* (opening gift), some small object, such as a comb, a lime pot, or a lime stick. After that, they await some Kula gifts to be given them. The most important headman will offer such a gift first to Kouta'uya, or To'udawada, whichever of them is the *toli'uvalaku* of the occasion. The soft, penetrating sound of a

conch-shell soon announces that the first gift has been given.
Other blasts of conch-shells follow, and the Kula is in full
swing. But here again, what happens in the Amphletts, is
only a minor interlude to the Sinaketan adventurers, bent on
the bigger goal in Dobu. And in order for us to remain in
harmony with the native perspective we shall also wait for the
detailed and circumstantial description of the Kula proceedings till we arrive on the beach of Tu'utauna, in Dobu.
The concrete account of how such a visiting fleet is received and
behaves on arrival will be given, when I describe a scene
I saw with my own eyes in the village of Nabwageta, another
Amphlett island, when sixty Dobuan canoes arrived there on
their *uvalaku, en route* for Boyowa.

To give a definite idea of the conversations which take
place between the visitors and the Amphlettans, I shall give a
sample noted down, during a visit of some Trobrianders to
Nu'agasi, the smaller village of Gumasila. A few canoes had
arrived a day or two before, in the neighbouring island,
Nabwageta, coming from the small Western islands of the
Trobriands on a Kula. One of them paddled across to Nu'agasi
with a crew of some six men, in order to offer *pari* gifts to their
partners and see what was to be done in the way of Kula. The
canoe was sighted from a distance, and its purpose was guessed
at once, as word had been brought before of the arrival in
Nabwageta of this small expedition. The headman of
Nu'agasi, Tovasana, hurried back to his house from my tent,
where I was taking great pains to obtain some ethnographic
information from him.

Tovasana is an outspoken character, and he is the most
important headman in the Amphletts. I am not using the
word ' chief,' for in the Amphletts, as I have said, the natives
do not observe either the court ceremonial with crouching and
bending, nor do the headmen have any power or economic
influence, at all comparable with those of the Trobriands.
Yet, although I came from the Trobriands, I was struck by the
authoritative tone used, and the amount of influence evidently
wielded by Tovasana. This is partly due undoubtedly to the
lack of white man's interference, which has so undermined
native authority and morality in the Trobriands, whereas the
Amphletts have so far escaped to a large extent Missionary
teaching and Government law and order. On the other hand,

however, the very narrow sphere of his powers, the authority
over a small village, consolidates the headman's influence. The
oldest and the most aristocratic by descent of all the headmen,
he is their acknowledged ' doyen.'

In order to receive his visitors he went to the beach in front
of his house and sat there on a log, looking impassively over
the sea. When the Trobrianders arrived each man took a
gift and went to his partner's house. The chief did not rise to
meet them, nor did they come in a body to greet him. The
toliwaga came towards the place where Tovasana was sitting ;
he carried a bundle of taro and a piece of *gugu'a* (objects of
small value, such as combs, lime pots, etc.) These he laid
down near the seated headman, who, however, took no notice
of it. A small boy, a grandchild of Tovasana, I think, took
up the gifts and put them into his house. Then, without
having yet exchanged a word, the *toliwaga* sat down on the
platform next to Tovasana. Under a shady tree, which
spread its branches like a canopy above the bleached canoe,
the men formed a picturesque group sitting cross-legged on the
platform. Beside the slim, youthful figure of the Kaduwaga
man, the old Tovasana, with his big, roughly carved features,
with his large aquiline nose sticking out from under an enormous
turban-like wig, looked like an old gnome. At first exchanging
merely a word or two, soon they dropped into more animated
conversation, and when other villagers and the rest of the
visitors joined them, the talk became general. As they spoke
in Kiriwinian, I was able to jot down the beginning of their
conversation.

Tovasana asked :
    " Where have you anchored ? "
    " In Nabwageta."
    " When did you come ? "
    " Yesterday."
    " From where did you start on the last day before
arriving ? "
    " From Gabuwana."
    " When ? "
    " The day before yesterday."
    " What wind ? "
    " Started from home with *yavata ;* wind changed.
Arrived on sandbank (Gabuwana) ; we slept ; so-and-so
made wind magic ; wind changed again ; good wind."

Then Tovasana asked the visitors about one of the chiefs from the island of Kayleula (to the West of Kiriwina), and when he was going to give him a big pair of *mwali*. The man answered they do not know ; to their knowledge that chief has no big *mwali* at present. Tovasana became very angry, and in a long harangue, lapsing here and there into the Gumasila language, he declared that he would never *kula* again with that chief, who is a *topiki* (mean man), who has owed him for a long time a pair of *mwali* as *yotile* (return gift), and who always is slow in making Kula. A string of other accusations about some clay pots given by Tovasana to the same chief, and some pigs promised and never given, were also made by the angry headman. The visitors listened to it with polite assent, uttering here and there some noncommital remark. They, in their turn, complained about some sago, which they had hoped to receive in Nabwageta, but which was churlishly refused for some reason or other to all the men of Kaduwaga, Kaysiga and Kuyawa.

Tovasana then asked them, " How long are you going to stay ? "

" Till Dobu men come."

" They will come," said Tovasana, " not in two days, not in three days, not in four days ; they will come tomorrow, or at the very last, the day after tomorrow."

" You go with them to Boyowa ? "

" I sail first to Vakuta, then to Sinaketa with the Dobu men. They sail to Susuwa beach to fish, I go to your villages, to Kaduwaga, to Kaysiga, to Kuyawa. Is there plenty of *mwali* in your villages ? "

" Yes, there are. So-and-so has . . ."

Here followed a long string of personal names of big armshells, the approximate number of smaller, nameless ones, and the names of the people in whose possession they were at the time.

The interest of both hearers and speakers was very obvious, and Tovasana gave the approximate dates of his movements to his visitors. Full moon was approaching, and the natives have got names for every day during the week before and after full moon, and the following and preceding days can therefore be reckoned. Also, every seven-day period within a moon is named after the quarter which falls in it. This allows the natives to fix dates with a fair exactitude. The present example shows the way in which, in olden times, the movements of the various expeditions were known over enormous areas ; nowadays, when white men's boats with native crews often move from one island to the other, the news spreads even more easily. In former times, small preliminary expeditions such as the one we have just been describing, would fix the dates and make arrangements often for as much as a year ahead.

The Kaduwaga men next inquired as to whether any strangers from the Trobriands were then staying in Gumasila. The answer was that there was in the village one man from Ba'u, and one from Sinaketa. Then inquiries were made as to how many Kula necklaces there were in Gumasila, and the conversation drifted again into Kula technicalities.

It is quite customary for men from the Trobriands to remain for a long time in the Amphletts, that is, from one expedition to another. For some weeks or even months, they live in the house of their partner, friend, or relative, careful to keep to the customs of the country. They will sit about with the men of the village and talk. They will help in the work and go out on fishing expeditions. These latter will be specially attractive to a Trobriander, a keen fisherman himself, who here finds an entirely new type of this pursuit. Whether an expedition would be made on one of the sandbanks, where the fishermen remain for a few days, casting their big nets for dugong and turtle ; or whether they would go out in a small canoe, trying to catch the jumping gar fish with a fishing kite ; or throwing a fish trap into the deep sea—all these would be a novelty to the Trobriander, accustomed only to the methods suitable to the shallow waters of the Lagoon, swarming with fish.

In one point the Trobriander would probably find his sojourn in the Amphletts uncongenial ; he would be entirely debarred from any intercourse with women. Accustomed in his country to easy intrigues, here he has completely to abstain, not only from sexual relations with women married or unmarried, but even from moving with them socially, in the free and happy manner characteristic of Boyowa. One of my main informants, Layseta, a Sinaketa man, who spent several years in the Amphletts, confessed to me, not without shame and regret, that he never succeeded in having any intrigues with the women there. To save his face, he claimed that he had had several Amphlett belles declaring their love to him, and offering their favours, but he always refused them :

" I feared ; I feared the *bowo'u* of Gumasila ; they are very bad."

The *bowo'u* are the local sorcerers of the Amphletts. Whatever we might think about Layseta's temptations—and his personal appearance and charm do not make his boastings very credible—and whether he was afraid of sorcery or of a sound thrashing, the fact remains that a Trobriander would have to change his usual mode of behaviour when in the Amphletts, and keep away from the women entirely. When big parties arrive in Gumasila, or Nabwageta, the women run away, and camp in the bush till the beach is clear.

The Amphlettans, on the contrary, were used to receive favours from unmarried women in Sinaketa. Nowadays, the male inhabitants of that village, always disapproving of the custom, though not to the extent of taking any action, tell the Amphlettans that the white man's Government has prohibited the men from Gumasila and Nabwageta to have sexual relations in Sinaketa. One of the very few occasions, when the men from the Amphletts showed any interest in talking to me was when they asked me whether this was true.

" The Sinaketa men tell us that we will go to jail if we sleep with girls in Sinaketa. Would the Government put us into jail, in truth ? "

As usually, I simply disclaimed all knowledge of the white man's arcana in such matters.

The small party of Kaduwaga men, whose visit to Tovasana I have just been describing, sat there for about two hours, smoked and chewed betel-nut, the conversation flagging now and then, and the men looking into the distance with the habitual self-important expression worn on such occasions. After the final words about mutual plans were exchanged, and a few pots had been brought by small boys to the canoe as *talo'i* (farewell gift to the visitors), they embarked, and paddled back three or four miles across to Nabwageta.

We must imagine the big Kula party from Sinaketa, whom we just watched landing in the two villages of Gumasila, behaving more or less in the same manner ; conducting similar conversations, offering the same type of *pari* gifts to their partners. Only everything happens of course on a much bigger scale. There is a big group seated before each house,

parties walk up and down the village, the sea in front of it
is covered with the gaudy, heavily laden canoes.   In the little
village, of which Tovasana is headman, the two chiefs, To'udawada and Kouta'uya, will be seated on the same platform, on
which we saw the old man receiving his other guests.   The
other headmen of the Sinaketans will have gone to the bigger
village round the corner, and will encamp there under the tall
palms, looking across the straits towards the pyramidal forms of
Domdom, and further South, to the main island fronting them
with the majestic form of Koyatabu.   Here, among the small
houses on piles, scattered picturesquely through the maze of
little harbours, lagoons and dykes, large groups of people will
be seated on mats of plaited coco-nut, each man as a rule under
the dwelling of his partner, chewing betel-nut stolidly, and
watching stealthily the pots being brought out to be presented
to them, and still more eagerly awaiting the giving of Kula
gifts, although he remains to a superficial glance quite
impassive.

II

In Chapter III I spoke about the sociology of Kula, and
gave a concise definition of partnership with its functions and
obligations.   I said there that people enter into this relationship in a definite manner, and remain in it for the rest of their
life.   I also said that the number of partners a man possesses,
depends upon his social position and rank.   The protective
character of an overseas partner becomes now clearer, after we
have realised the nervous tension with which each Kula party
in olden days would have approached a land full of *mulukwausi*,
bowo'u and other forms of sorcery, a land from which originate
the very *tauva'u* themselves.*   To have a friend there, one
who will not on the surface of it have bad intentions, is a great
boon.   What this really means to the natives can, however,
only be realised when we arrive at Dobu, learn the special
safety magic performed there and find how genuinely serious
these apprehensions are.

We must now make another short digression from our consecutive account, and discuss the several aspects of the sociology
of the Kula one after the other.

* See Chapter II, Division VII.

1. *Sociological Limitations to the Participation in the Kula.*—
Not everyone who lives within the cultural sphere of the Kula
does participate in it.   More especially in the Trobriand Islands,
there are whole districts which do not practise the Kula.   Thus
a series of villages in the North of the main Island, the villages
on the Island of Tuma, as well as the industrial villages of
Kuboma and the agricultural ones of Tilataula do not practise
Kula.   In villages like Sinaketa, Vakuta, Gumasila and
Nabwageta, every man carries on the Kula.   The same applies
to the small Islands which link up the big gaps of the Kula
chain, the Islands of Kitava, Iwa, Gawa and Kwayawata,
strewn on the seas between the Trobriands and Woodlark
Island, to Tubetube and Wari, etc., etc.   In the Dobuan
speaking district, on the other hand, I think that certain village
complexes either do not practice Kula at all, or else practice
it on a small scale, that is, their headmen have only a few
partners in the neighbouring villages.

In some of the big chiefs' villages in Kiriwina there
are certain people who never practice Kula.   Thus, in
a village where the headman has the rank of *guya'u*
(chief) or *gumguya'u* (minor chief) the commoners of the
lowest rank and unrelated to the headman are not supposed to carry on the Kula.   In olden days this rule would
be very strictly observed, and nowadays even, though somewhat relaxed, not many commoners of this description practice
the Kula.   Limitations as to entry into the Kula, therefore,
exist only in big Kula districts such as that of Dobu and of the
Trobriands, and they are partly local, excluding whole
villages, and partly social, excluding certain people of low
rank.

2. *The Relation of Partnership.*—The name for an overseas
partner is in the Trobriand language *karayta'u ;* ' my partner '
is styled *ulo karayta'u, ulo* being the possessive pronoun of
remote relation.   In Gumasila he is called *ulo ta'u*, which means
simply ' my man ' ; in Dobuan, *yegu gumagi*.   The inland
partners are known in Kiriwinian by the term denoting a friend,
' *lubaygu*,' the suffixed possessive pronoun *gu* being that of
nearest possession.

Only after this relationship has been established between
two men, can the two make Kula with one another.   An
overseas visitor would as a rule go to his partner's house and

offer him a small present as *pari*. This again would be returned by the local man by means of a *talo'i* present. There would not be any great intimacy between two overseas partners. But, in sharp contrast to the essential hostility between two strange tribesmen, such a relationship of friendship would stand out as the most remarkable deviation from the general rule. In inland relations between two partners of neighbouring villages, the closeness and intimacy would be relatively small as compared to other ties. This relation was defined to me in these words :

" My partner same as my clansman (*kakaveyogu*)—he might fight me. My real kinsman (*veyogu*), same navel-string, would always side with us."

The best way of obtaining detailed information, and of eliminating any errors which might have crept into ethnographic generalisations, is to collect concrete data. I have drawn up a complete list of the partners of Kouta'uya, who is one of the biggest Kula men in the whole Ring ; another list of a smaller Sinaketa headman, Toybayoba ; and of course I know several complements of partners of smaller men, who, as as rule, have about four to six partners each.

The full list of Kouta'uya includes fifty-five men in the Northern Half of Boyowa, that is, in Luba, Kulumata and Kiriwina. From these the chief receives armshells. To the South, his partners in the Southern districts of Boyowa and Vakuta are twenty-three by number ; in the Amphletts eleven, and twenty-seven in Dobu. Thus we see that the numbers to the South and North almost balance, the Southern exceeding the Northern by six. These numbers include his partners in Sinaketa, where he makes Kula with all his fellow chiefs, and with all the headmen of the divisional villages, and in his own little village he *kulas* with his sons. But even there, everyone of his partners is either South or North to him, that is, either gives him the necklaces or armshells.

All the clans are represented in the list. Often when asked with regard to the name of some man, why he is in partnership with him, the answer would be—" Because he is my kinsman," which means, in this case, clansman of equal rank. Men of other clans are included, as ' friends,' or relatives-in-law, or for some other reason more or less imaginary. I shall speak presently of the mechanism through which the man enters on this relation.

The list of Toybayoba's partners includes twelve men to the North, four in Southern Boyowa, three in the Amphletts and eleven in Dobu, the balance here also being on the Southern side. As said above, minor men might have anything between four to ten partners all told, whereas there are men in northern Boyowa who have only two partners, one on each side of the ring, so to speak, with whom they make Kula.

In drawing up these lists, which I shall not reproduce here in extenso, another striking feature comes to light : on both sides, there is a definite geographical limit, beyond which a man cannot have any partners. For all men in the village of Sinaketa, for instance, this limit, as regards the armshells, coincides with the furthest boundary of Kiriwina ; that is, no man from Sinaketa has any partners in Kitava, which is the next Kula district beyond Kiriwina. South, in the direction from which the *soulava* are received, the villages at the South-East end of Fergusson Island are the last places where partners of Sinaketan men are still to be found. The small Island of Dobu itself lies just beyond this boundary, and no man in this Island or in any of the villages on Normanby Island makes Kula with the Sinaketans (compare the circles, indicating Kula Communities on Map V).

Beyond these districts, the men still know the names of what could be called their partners-once-removed, that is, the partners of their partners. In the case of a man who has only a couple of partners on each side, who, again being modest men, have also only one or two, this relationship is not devoid of importance. If I, in Sinaketa, have one partner, say in Kiriwina, who again has one partner in Kitava, it is no small matter for me to learn that this Kitava man just obtained a splendid pair of armshells. For this means that there is about a quarter of a chance of my receiving these armshells, on the supposition that the Kitavan and Kiriwinian have two partners each between whom they can choose in bestowing them. In the case of a big chief like Kouta'uya, however, the number of once-removed partners becomes so great that they lose any personal significance for him. Kouta'uya has some twenty-five partners in Kiriwina ; among them To'uluwa, the big chief, makes Kula with more than half of all the men in Kitava.

Some other of Kouta'uya's partners in Kiriwina, of lesser rank, yet quite important, also make Kula with a great number, so that probably practically everybody in Kitava is Kouta'uya's partner-once-removed.

If we were to imagine that on the Kula Ring there are many people who have only one partner on each side, then the Ring would consist of a large number of closed circuits, on each of which the same articles would constantly pass. Thus if A in Kiriwina always *kulas* with B in Sinaketa who *kulas* with C in Tubetube, who *kulas* with D in Murua, who *kulas* with E in Kitava, who *kulas* with A in Kiriwina, then A B C D E F would form such one strand in the big Kula circuit. If an armshell got into the hands of one of them, it could never leave this strand. But the Kula Ring is nothing approaching this, because every small Kula partner has, as a rule, on one side or the other, a big one, that is a chief. And every chief plays the part of a shunting-station for Kula objects. Having so many partners on each side, he constantly transfers an object from one strand to another. Thus, any article which on its rounds has travelled through the hands of certain men, may on its second round come through an entirely different channel. This, of course, supplies a large part of the zest and excitement of the Kula exchange.

The designation of such a partner-once-removed in the language of Kiriwina is *muri-muri*. A man will say that such and such a one is ' my partner-once-removed,' ' *ulo murimuri.*' Another expression connected with this relationship is to inquire ' whose hand ' has passed on such and such a *vaygu'a*. When To'uluwa gives a pair of armshells to Kouta'uya, this latter will ask : ' *availe yamala* (whose hand) ' ? The answer is ' *yamala Pwata'i,*' (' the hand of Pwatai '). And, as a rule, more or less the following conversation will ensue : " who gave this pair of armshells to Pwata'i ? " " how long were they kept by a man in the Island of Yeguma, and then distributed on the occasion of a *so'i* (feast) ? " " when they had been the last time in Boyowa ? " etc., etc.

3. *Entering the Kula Relationship.*—In order to become a practising member of the Kula, a man must have passed the stage of adolescence; he must have the status and rank required, that is in such villages where this condition is demanded ; he must know the magic of the Kula ; and last, not least, he

must be in possession of a piece of *vaygu'a*. The membership, with all its concomitant implications, may be received from the father, who teaches his son the magic, gives him a piece of *vaygu'a*, and provides him with a partner, very often in his own person.

Supposing one of the sons of Kouta'uya has reached the stage where a lad may begin to *kula*. The chief will have been teaching him the spells for some time already. Moreover the lad, who from childhood has taken part in overseas expeditions, has many a time seen the rites performed and heard the spells uttered. When the time is ripe, Kouta'uya, having the conch-shell blown, and with all due formalities, presents a *soulava* to his son. This latter, soon afterwards, goes somewhere North. Perhaps he goes only to one of the neighbouring villages within Sinaketa, perhaps he accompanies his father on a visit as far North as Omarakana, and in any case he makes Kula, either with one of his father's friends and partners, or with a special friend of his own. Thus, at one stroke, the lad is equipped with magic, *vaygu'a*, and two partners, one of whom is his father. His northern partner will give him in due course an armshell, and this he will probably offer to his father. The transactions once started continue. His father soon gives him another *vaygu'a*, which he may *kula* with the same northern partner, or he may try to establish another partnership. The next *mwali* (armshells) he receives from the North, he will probably give to another partner in the South, and thus establish a new relationship. A chief's son, who is always a commoner himself (since the chief cannot marry within his own sub-clan and the son has the status of his mother), would not multiply his partners beyond the limit numerically given by the above mentioned partners of Toybayoba.

Not everyone, however, is as fortunate as to be the son of a chief, which in the Trobriands is, on the whole, one of the most enviable positions, since it confers many privileges, and entails no special responsibilities. A young chief himself would have to pay substantially for establishing his position in the Kula, for a chief is always the son of a woman of high rank, and the nephew of a chief, though his father may be a commoner of small influence only. In any case, his maternal uncle will expect from him some *pokala* (offerings by instalment), in payment for magic, *vaygu'a*, and finally for a leading position in

the Kula. The young chief would marry, and thus acquire
wealth within limits, and with this he would have to give
presents to his maternal uncle, who in turn would introduce
him into the Kula, exactly as a chief does his son, only not dis-
interestedly.

A commoner enters into the Kula like a chief, with the only
exception that everything is on a smaller scale, the amount of
the *pokala* which he gives to his maternal uncle, the *vaygu'a*
which he receives, and the number of partners with whom he
kulas. When a man gives to another a piece of *vaygu'a*, of the
Kula kind, but not as a Kula exchange but as a gift, let us say as
youlo (gift in repayment for the harvest supply offerings, see
above, Chapter VI, Division VI), this *vaygu'a* does not leave
the Kula Ring. The receiver, if he had not been in the Kula
yet, enters into it by acquiring the *vaygu'a*, and can then choose
his partner, and go on with the exchange.

There is one important qualification of the statement
made at the beginning of this section. I said there that a man
entering the Kula Ring, must learn the *mwasila* magic. This
refers only to those who practise overseas Kula. For people
who do only the inland exchange, magic is not necessary, and in
fact it is never learned by them.

4. *Participation of Women in the Kula.*—As I have said in
the general descriptive chapter on the Kula tribes, the position
of women among them is by no means characterised by oppres-
sion or social insignificance. They have their own sphere of
influence, which, in certain cases and in certain tribes, is of great
importance. The Kula, however, is essentially a man's type of
activity. As mentioned above, in the section between
Sinaketa and Dobu, women do not sail on the big expeditions.
From Kiriwina young, unmarried girls would sail East to
Kitava, Iwa, and Gawa, and from these Islands even old,
married women, indeed whole families, come to Kiriwina.
But they do not carry on overseas Kula exchange, neither
among themselves, nor with men.

In Kiriwina, some women, notably the chief's wives, are
admitted to the honour and privilege of exchanging *vaygu'a*,
though in such cases the transactions are done *en famille*. To
take a concrete case, in October or November, 1915, To'uluwa,
the chief of Omarakana, brought a fine haul of *mwali* from
Kitava. The best pair of these he presented to his veteran wife,

Bokuyoba, a wife whom he had inherited from his elder brother Numakala. Bokuyoba in turn gave the pair, without much delay, to Kadamwasila, the favourite wife of the chief, the mother of five sons and one daughter. She again gave it to her son, Namwana Guyau, who *kula'd* it on to some of his southern partners. Next time he receives a *soulava* necklace, he will give it, not to his father directly, but to his mother, who will hand it over to her senior colleague, and this venerable lady will give it to To'uluwa. The whole transaction is evidently a complimentary interpolation of the two *giyovila* (chief's wives) in between the simple transaction of the chief giving the *vaygu'a* to his son. This interpolation gives the women much pleasure, and is highly valued by them. In fact, at that time I heard more about that than about all the rest of the exchanges associated with this overseas trip.

In Southern Boyowa, that is in Sinaketa and Vakuta, the rôle of women is similar, but they play besides another part. A man would sometimes send his wife with a Kula gift to his partner in the neighbouring village. On some occasions, when he needs *vaygu'a* very badly, as for instance when he is expecting some *uvalaku* visitors, his wife may help him to obtain the *vaygu'a* from that partner. For, though this latter might refuse to give it to his Sinaketan partner, he would not do so to his wife. It must be added that no sexual motives are associated with it, and that it is only a sort of customary compliment paid to the fair sex.

In Dobu, the wife, or the sister of a man, is always credited with a great influence over his Kula decisions. Therefore, there is a special form of magic, used by the Sinaketans, in order to act on the minds of the Dobuan women. Although, in matters of sex, a Trobriander would have absolutely to keep aloof from Dobuan women, married or unmarried, he would approach them with nice speeches and gifts in matters of Kula. He would reproach an unmarried girl with her brother's conduct towards him. She would then ask for a piece of betel nut. This would be given with some magic spoken over it, and the girl, it is believed, would then influence her brother to *kula* with his partner.*

---

* I cannot tell what sort of influence this would be, exercised by a sister over her brother in Dobu. I do not even know whether, in that district, there obtains the same taboo between brother and sister as in the Trobriands.

III

In the short outline of the Amphlett tribe which was given in Chapter II, Division IV, I called them 'typical monopolists,' both with reference to their economic position and to their character. Monopolists they are in two respects, namely as manufacturers of the wonderful clay pots which form the only supply for the surrounding districts ; and in the second place, as a commercial community, situated half-way between the populous country of Dobu, with its rich gardens and coco-nut plantations, on the one hand, and the Trobriands, the main industrial community in Eastern New Guinea on the other.

The expression ' monopolists ' must, however, be correctly understood. The Amphletts are not a centre of commercial middle-men, constantly busy importing and exporting desirable utilities. Only about once or twice a year, a big expedition comes to their Islands, and every few months they themselves will sail South-East or North and again receive visits from smaller expeditions from one of the neighbours or the other. It is through just such small expeditions that they collect a relatively considerable amount of utilities from all surrounding districts, and these they can give to such visitors as need and desire them. Nor would they impose high prices on any such exchange, but they are certainly considered less liberal, less ready to give or to trade and always on the look out for higher return gifts and extras. In their bartering away of the clay pots, they also cannot ask extortionate prices, such as, according to the laws of supply and demand, they could impose on their neighbours. For, no more than any other natives, can they run counter to customary rules, which regulate this exchange as much as all others. Indeed, considering the great amount of trouble which they have in obtaining the clay, and the high degree of skill necessary to produce the pots, the prices for which they sell them are very low. But here again, their manners over this transaction are distinctly haughty, and they are well aware of their value as potters and distributors of pots to the other natives.

A few more words must be said about their pot making industry as well as about the trade in these islands.

The natives of the Amphletts are exclusive manufacturers of pottery, within a wide radius. They are the only purveyors to the Trobrianders, to the inhabitants of the Marshall Bennett Islands, and also, I believe, all the claypots in Woodlark come from the Amphletts.* To the South, they export their pots to Dobu, Du'a'u, and further South as far as Milne Bay. This is not all, however, for although in some of these farther districts the Amphlett pots are used side by side with other ones, they are infinitely superior to any earthenware found in the whole of British New Guinea. Of a large size, yet extremely thin, they possess great durability, and in form they are extremely well shaped and finished (see Plate XLVI).

The best Amphlett pots owe their high quality to the excellence of their material as well as their workmanship. The clay for them has to be imported into the Islands from Yayawana, a quarry on the Northern shore of Fergusson Island, about a day's journey from the Amphletts. Only a very inferior clay can be found in the islands of Gumasila and Nabwageta, good enough to make small pots, but quite useless for the big ones.

There is a legend, explaining why the good clay cannot be obtained nowadays in the Amphletts. In olden days, two brothers, Torosipupu and Tolikilaki, lived on one of the summits of Gumasila called Tomonumonu. There was plenty of fine clay there at that time. One day Torosipupu went to fish with a trap. He caught a very fine giant clam-shell. When he came back, Tolikilaki said : " O my shell ! I shall eat it ! " Torosipupu refused it and answered with a very obscene allusion to the bivalvular mollusc and to the uses he was going to make of it. Tolikilaki asked again ; Torosipupu refused. They quarrelled. Tolikilaki then took part of the clay with him, and went to Yayawana on the main island. Torosipupu afterwards took the rest and followed him. What were their further destinies, the legend does not say. But on Gumasila there remained only very poor clay, which is all that can be found there ever since.

Since then, the men have to go about twice yearly to Yayawana in order to bring the clay from which the women afterwards will manufacture the pots. It takes them about a day to reach Yayawana, to which, as it lies to the South West,

* This is the information which I obtained during my short visit to Murua (Woodlark Island), and which was confirmed by the Trobriand Islanders. Professor Seligmann states, also, that the sepulchral pots, found in this island come from the Amphletts. *Op. cit.*, p. 731. Compare also pp. 15 and 535.

they can travel with any of the prevailing winds and return equally well. They remain for a couple of days there, digging the clay, drying it and filling a few *vataga* baskets with it. I estimate that each canoe carries about two ton weight on its return journey. This will last the women for half a year's production. The pale, straw-coloured clay is kept under the houses in big troughs made of sides of discarded canoes.

In olden days, before the white man's advent, the conditions were a little more complicated. Only one island, Kwatouto, being on friendly terms with the natives had the freedom of the Northern shore. Whether the other islands used also to fetch the clay from there, doing so armed and ready for attack ; or whether they used to acquire the clay by barter from Kwatouto, I could not definitely establish. The information one receives in the Amphletts is exceedingly unsatisfactory, and my several informants gave contradictory accounts on this point. The fact seems clear in my case, that Kwatouto, then as now, was the source of the best pottery, but that both Gumasila and Nabwageta also always manufactured pots, though perhaps inferior ones. The fourth island, Domdom, never participated in this trade, and up to the present there is not a single woman in Domdom who can shape a pot.

The manufucturing of this article, as said, is exclusively the work of women. They sit in groups of two or three under the houses, surrounded by big clumps of clay and the implements of their craft, and produce in these very shabby and mean conditions, veritable masterpieces of their art. Personally I had only the opportunity of seeing groups of very old women at work, although I spent about a month in the Amphletts.

With regard to the technology of pot-making, the method is that of first roughly moulding the clay into its form and then beating with a spatula and subsequently scraping the walls to the required thinness with a mussel-shell. To give the description in detail, a woman starts first by kneading a certain amount of clay for a long time. Of this material she makes two semi-circular clumps, or several clumps, if a big pot is to be made. These clumps are then placed in a ring, touching one another upon a flat stone or board, so that they form a thick, circular roll (Plate XLIV, top). The woman now begins to work this roll with both hands, gradually pressing it together, and at the same time bringing it up all round into a slanting wall (see Plate XLIV, bottom). Her left hand works as a rule on the inside, and her right on the outside of this wall ; gradually it begins to shape into a semi-spherical dome. On the top of the dome there is a hole, through which the woman thrusts her left hand, working with it on the inside, of the dome (see Plate XLV, top). At first the main movements of her hands were from downward up, flattening out the rolls into thin walls. The traces of her fingers going up and down on the outside leave longitudinal furrows (see details on Plate XLV, top). Towards the end of this stage her hands move round and round, leaving concentric, horizontal marks on the dome. This is continued until the pot has assumed a good curvature all round.

It seems almost a miracle to see how, in a relatively short time, out of this after all brittle material, and with no implements whatever, a woman will shape a practically faultless hemisphere, often up to a metre in diameter.

After the required shape has been obtained the woman takes a small spatula of light-wood into her right hand and she proceeds to tap the clay gently (see Plate XLV, bottom). This stage lasts a fairly long time, for big pots about an hour. After the dome has been sufficiently worked in this way small pieces of clay are gradually fitted in at the top, closing the orifice, and the top of the dome is beaten again. In the case of small pots the beating is done only after the orifice has been closed. The pot is put with the mat into the sun, where it remains for a day or two to harden. It is then turned round, so that its mouth is now uppermost, and its bottom is carefully placed into a basket. Then, round the rim of the mouth, a flat strip of clay is placed horizontally, turned towards the inside, forming a graceful lip. Three small lumps of clay are put 120° distance from each other near the lip as ornaments, and, with a pointed stick, a design is scratched in round the lip and sometimes down the outside of the body. In this state the pot is again left in the sun for some length of time.

After it has sufficiently hardened to be handled with safety, though it must be done with the utmost care, it is placed on some dried sticks, mouth downwards, supported by stones put between the sticks. It is surrounded with twigs and pieces of wood on its outside, fire is kindled, the sticks below bake it from the inside, and those from above on the outside. The final result is a beautiful pot, of a brick red colour when new, though after several uses it becomes completely black. Its shape is not quite semi-spherical ; it is rather half an elipsoid, like the broader half of an egg, cut off in the middle. The whole gives the feeling of perfection in form and of elegance, unparalleled in any South Sea pottery, I know (see Plate XLVI).

These pots in Kiriwinian language *kuria*, are called by the Amphlett natives *kuyana* or *va'ega*. The biggest specimens are about a metre across their mouth, and some sixty centimetres deep ; they are used exclusively for the ceremonial cooking of *mona* (see Plate XXXV), and are called *kwoylamona* (in the Amphletts : *nokunu*). The second size *kwoylakalagila* (in the Amphletts, *nopa'eva*) are used for ordinary boiling of yams or taro. *Kwoylugwawaga* (Amphletts, *nobadala*), are used for the same purposes but are much smaller. An especial size, *kwoylamegwa* (Amphletts, *nosipoma*) are used in sorcery. The smallest ones, which I do not remember ever having seen in the Trobriands though there is a Trobriand word for them, *kwoylakekita*, are used for everyday cooking in the Amphletts where they are called *va'ega*, in the narrower sense of the word.

I have expatiated on this singular and artistic achievement of the natives of the Amphletts, because from all points of view it is important to know the details of a craft so far in advance of any similar achievement within the Melanesian region.

A few words must now be said about trade in the Amphletts. The central position of this little archipelago situated between, on one side, the big, flat, extremely fertile coral islands, which, however, are deprived of many indispensable, natural resources ; and on the other, the rich jungle and varied mineral supplies of the volcanic regions in the d'Entrecasteaux archipelago, indicates on which lines this trade would be likely to develop. To this natural inequality between them and their neighbours are added social elements. The Trobrianders are skilful, industrious, and economically highly organised. In this respect, even the Dobuans stand on a lower level, and the other inhabitants of the d'Entrecasteaux much more so.

If we imagine a commercial diagram drawn on the map, we would first of all notice the export in pottery, radiating from the Amphletts as its source. In the inverse direction, flowing towards them, would be imports in food such as sago, pigs, coco-nut, betel-nut, taro and yams. An article very important in olden days, which had to be imported into the Amphletts, was the stone for implements coming *via* the Trobriands from Woodlark Island. These indeed would be traded on by the Amphlettans, as all the d'Entrecasteaux relied, for the most part at least, on the imports from Woodlark, according to information I obtained in the Amphletts. The Amphlett islands further depended on the Trobriands for the following articles : wooden dishes, manufactured in Bwoytalu ; lime-pots manufactured in several villages of Kuboma ; three-tiered baskets and folding baskets, made in Luya ; ebony lime pots and mussel shells, these latter fished mainly by the village of Kavataria in the lagoon. These articles were paid for, or matched as presents by the following ones : first of all, of course the pots ; secondly, turtle-shell earrings, special nose sticks, red ochre, pummice stone and obsidian, all of these obtainable locally. Further, the natives of the Amphletts procured on Fergusson Island, for the Trobrianders, wild banana seeds used for necklaces, strips of rattan used as belts and for lashing, feathers of the cassowary and red parrot, used for dancing decorations, plaited fibre-belts, bamboo and barbed spears.

It may be added that in olden days, the natives in the Amphletts would not sail freely to all the places on the main island. Each Amphlett village community had a district on the mainland, with which they were on friendly terms and with which they could trade without incurring any danger. Thus, as said above, only the village of Kwatouto, in the southern-most inhabited Amphlett island, was free to go unmolested to the district round Yayawana, from whence they obtained the pale yellow clay, so excellent for pottery. The natives of Nabwageta had a few villages eastwards from Yayawana to deal with, and those of Gumasila went further East still. Domdom natives were never great traders or sailors. The trading conditions in the islands were further complicated by the constant internal quarrels and warfare between the districts. Kwatouto and Domdom on the one side, Gumasila and Nabwageta on the other were allies, and between these two factions there was a constant, smouldering hostility, preventing any development of friendly commercial intercourse, and breaking out now and then into open warfare. This was the reason why the villages were all perched on high, inaccessible ledges, or like Gumasila, were built so as to be protected by the sea and reefs from attack.

The influence of the surrounding great districts, that is, of the Trobriands and of Dobu upon the Amphletts neither was nor is merely commercial. From the limited linguistic material collected in the Amphletts, I can only say that their language is related both to that of the Trobriands and of Dobu. Their social organisation resembles closely that of the Trobrianders with the exception of chieftainship, which is lacking in the Amphletts. In their beliefs as to sorcery, spirits, etc., they seem to be more akin to the Dobuans than to the Trobrianders. Their canoe magic has come form the Trobriands, but the art of building their canoes is that of Dobu, which as we have seen before is also the one adopted by the Trobrianders. The magic of the Kula, known in the Amphletts, is partly adopted from the Trobriands, and partly from Dobu. There is only one indigenous system of magic which originated in the islands. Long ago there lived a man of the Malasi clan, who had his abode in the rock of Selawaya, which stands out of the jungle, above the big village of Gumasila. This man knew the magic of *ayowa*, which is the name given to *mwasila* (Kula magic) in the language of the Amphletts and of Dobu. Some people passed near the stone while it was being recited within it ; they learned it, and handed it over to their descendants.

IV

One more point of importance must be mentioned here, a point bearing upon the intertribal relations in this district. As we saw, some Trobriand people remain sometimes on prolonged visits in the Amphletts. This custom, however, is never reciprocated, and people from the Amphletts never visit for any length of time their Northern neighbours. The same refers to the relations between the Trobriands and the district of Dobu. In discussing the lists of Kula partners of Kouta'uya and Toybayoba, I was told about some of their Southern partners, that they were *veyola* (maternal kinsmen) of my informant. On further inquiry it appeared that these people were emigrants from the Trobriands, who settled down in Tewara, Sanaroa or the big Dobuan settlements on the North-West shores of Dawson Straits.

PLATE XLII

[face p. 288

SCENERY IN THE AMPHLETTS. (See p. 268.)

PLATE XLIII

LANDING IN THE MAIN VILLAGE OF GUMASILA. (See p. 272.)

Plate XLIV

TECHNOLOGY OF POT MAKING (I)

Top picture : the clumps of clay have been put in a circle and joined up, forming a thick, circular roll.   Bottom picture : the roll is being worked upwards, caving in all round.   (See p. 284.)

Plate XLV

TECHNOLOGY OF POT MAKING (II)

Top picture : the dome-shaped mass of clay is worked near the hole in the top ; presently the latter will be closed, and, as this is a small pot, only after that is the pot beaten, as shown in the picture below. (See p. 285.)

When I asked whether, on the contrary, there were any cases of Dobuans settling in Boyowa, it was emphatically denied that such a thing could happen. And indeed, in the numerous genealogical data which I have collected from all over the district, there is no trace of migration from the South, although frequent migrations occur within the district and some from the Marshall Bennett Islands. In general, all these migrations within the Trobriands show also a marked tendency to move form North to South. Thus, the most aristocratic sub-clan, the Tabalu, originated in the Northernmost village of Laba'i. But now their stronghold is further South in Omarakana, and the members of the same sub-clan are ruling in Olivilevi, and Tukwa'ukwa, that is in the middle of the island. Some of them even migrated as far South as Vakuta, where they established a feeble imitation of chieftainship, never being able to subdue the other natives to any extent. Several sub-clans, now firmly established in the Middle and Southern portions of the island, trace their descent from the North, and in the Amphletts there are also a couple of cases of sub-clans immigrated from Boyowa.

In contrast to this migration of people from North to South, we have noted the spread of one of the main cultural elements, of the canoe, from South to North. We saw how the *nagega*, the big, sea-worthy, but heavy and slow canoe has been superseded by the *masawa* or *tadobu*, which spread a few generations ago, till it arrived at the island of Kitava. It is more difficult to follow the movements of beliefs. But I have reason to assume that beliefs in sorcery, more especially in the *mulukwausi* and *tauva'u*, move from South to North.

In the next Chapter, we shall return to our Sinaketan expedition, in order to move them for a short distance along their route into the first settlements of the Dobu speaking people These places will suggest a new theme for a lengthy digression, this time into the mythological subjects and legends connected with the Kula.

CHAPTER XII

IN TEWARA AND SANAROA—MYTHOLOGY OF THE KULA

I

AT daybreak the party leave the Amphletts. This is the stage when the parting gifts, the *talo'i* are given. The clay pots, the several kinds of produce of the islands and of the Koya, which had been laid aside the previous day, are now brought to the canoes (see Plate XLVII). Neither the giver nor the main receiver, the *toliwaga*, take much notice of the proceedings, great nonchalance about give and take being the correct attitude prescribed by good manners. Children bring the objects, and the junior members of the crew stow them away. The general behaviour of the crowds, ashore and in the canoes, is as unostentatious at this moment of parting as it was at the arrival. No more farewells than greetings are spoken or shouted, nor are there any visible or formal signs of grief, or of hope of meeting again, or of any other emotions. The busy, self-absorbed crews push off stolidly, step the mast, set sail, and glide away.

They now approach the broad front of Koyatabu, which with a favourable wind, they might reach within two hours or so. They probably sail near enough to get a clear view of the big trees standing on the edge of the jungle, and of the long waterfall dividing the mountain's flank right down the middle ; of the triangular patches under cultivation, covered with the vine of yams and big leaves of taro. They could also perceive here and there smoke curling out of the jungle where, hidden under the trees, there lies a village, composed of a few miserable huts. Nowadays these villages have come down to the water's edge, in order to supplement their garden yield with fish. In olden days they were all high up on the slope, and their huts hardly ever visible from the sea.

The inhabitants of these small and ramshackle villages are shy and timid, though in olden days they would have been dangerous to the Trobrianders. They speak a language which differs from that of Dobu and is usually called by the natives ' the Basima talk.' There seem to be about four or five various languages on the island of Fergusson, besides that of Dobu. My acquaintance with the Basima natives is very small, due only to two forced landings in their district. They struck me as being physically of a different type from the Dobuans, though this is only an impression. They have got no boats, and do the little sailing they require on small rafts of three or five logs tied together. Their houses are smaller and less well-made than those in Dobu. Further investigation of these natives would be very interesting, and probably also very difficult, as is always the case when studying very small communities, living at the same time right out of touch with any white man.

This land must remain, for the present anyhow, veiled for ourselves, as it also is for the Trobriand natives. For these, indeed, the few attempts which they occasionally made to come into contact with these natives, and the few mishaps which brought them to their shores, were all far from encouraging in results, and only strengthened the traditional superstitious fear of them. Several generations ago, a canoe or two from Burakwa, in the island of Kayeula, made an exploring trip to the district of Gabu, lying in a wide bay under the North-West flank of Koyatabu. The natives of Gabu, receiving them at first with a show of interest, and pretending to enter into commercial relations, afterwards fell on them treacherously and slew the chief Toraya and all his companions. This story has become famous, and indeed one of the outstanding historical events of the Trobriands, because Tomakam, the slain chief's younger brother, went to the Koya of Gabu, and killed the head man of one of the villages, avenging thus his brother's death. He then composed a song and a dance which is performed to this day in Kiriwina, and has indeed one of the finest melodies in the islands.

This is the verbatim account of the story as it was told to me by To'uluwa himself, the chief of Omarakana, who at present ' owns ' this Gumagabu dance, his ancestors having acquired it from the descendants of Tomakam by a *laga*

payment.* It is a commentary to the song, and begins only with
the avenging expedition of Tomakam, which is also the theme
of the song.

THE STORY OF GUMAGABU

" Tomakam got a new *waga*. He blew the conch shell
and went to the Koya. He spoke to his mother " (that
is, before leaving), " ' My mother, you remain, I shall
sail. One conch shell you hear, it will be a conch shell of a
necklace.' " (That is, it will be a sign that he has been
successful in getting a good Kula necklace). " ' The
second conch shell will be the conch shell of the dead man;
the sign that I have already carried out my revenge. I
shall sail, I shall anchor, I shall sleep. The second day I
shall sail, I shall anchor, I shall sleep. The third day I
shall anchor in a village, having already arrived in the
Mountain. The fourth day I shall give *pari*, the *Kinana*
(the Southern foreigner) will come, I shall hit him. The
fifth day I shall return. I shall sail fast, till night grows
on the sea. The next day I shall anchor at Burakwa.
You hear the conch shell, you sleep in the house, arise.
One blow you hear of the shell—the blow of the *bagi*
(necklace). Two blows you hear, the blow of the dead
man ! Then the men of Burakwa will say : ' Two conch
shells, two necklaces,' then, you come out of the house,
you speak : ' Men of Burakwa, from one side of the village
and from the other ; indeed you mocked my son,
Tomakam. Your speech was—go, carry out thy
vendetta in Gabu. The first conch shell is that of the
necklace, the second conch shell is that of the dead man.
I have spoken!'" (Here ends the speech of Tomakam to
his mother.)

" He anchored in the village in the Koya. He told
his younger brother : ' Go, tell the *Kinana* men these
words : Your friend has a sore leg, well, if we together go
to the canoe he will give the *pari !* ' The younger brother
went and spoke those words to the head-man of the
Kinana : ' Some green coco-nuts, some betel-nut, some
pig, bring this to us and we shall give you *pari*. Your
arm-shells, your big stone blade, your boar's tusk, your
whale-bone spatula await you in the canoe. The message
for you is that your friend has a sore leg and cannot walk.'
Says the *Kinana* man : ' Well, let us go ! ' "

" He caught a pig, he collected betel-nut, sugar cane,
bananas, necklaces, betel-pod, he said : ' Well, let us go

* See Chapter VI, Division VI.

together to the canoe.' *Pu'u* he gives the necklace ; *pu'u*, the pig ; then he gave the coco-nut, the betel-nut, the sugar cane, the bananas. Tomakam lay on one side ; his leg he wrapped up in a white, soft pandanus mat. Before he had spoken to his younger brother '' : (i.e., he gave him this instruction also, when he sent him to meet the people of Gabu) : " ' You all come with the *Kinana* man. Do not remain in the village.' Then '' (after the first gifts were exchanged) " the *Kinana* man stood up in the canoe. His betel-pod fell down. Spoke Tomakam, addressing the *Kinana* man : ' My friend, pick up the betel-pod. It fell and went down into the canoe.' ' The *Kinana* man bent down, he took the betel-pod. Tomakam saw that the *Kinana* bent down, he took an axe, and sitting he made a stroke at him. He cut off his neck. Then Tomakam took the head, threw the body into the sea. The head he stuck on a stick of his canoe. They sailed, they arrived in their village. He caught a pig, prepared a taro pudding, cut sugar cane, they had a big feast, he invented this song.''

Such was the story told me by the chief of Omarakana about the song and dance of Gumagabu, which at that time they were singing and performing in his village. I have adduced it in full, in an almost literal translation from the native text, in order to show it side by side with the song. The narrative thus reproduced shows characteristic gaps, and it does not cover even the incidents of the song.

The following is a free translation of the song, which, in its original native text, is very condensed and impressionistic. A word or two indicates rather than describes whole scenes and incidents, and the traditional commentary, handed on in a native community side by side with the song, is necessary for a full understanding.

The Gumagabu Song

I

> The stranger of Gumagabu sits on the top of the mountain.
> ' Go on top of the mountain, the towering mountain. . . .'
> ——They cry for Toraya. . . . .——
>
> The stranger of Gumagabu sits on the slope of the mountain.
> ——The fringe of small clouds lifts above Boyowa ;
> The mother cries for Toraya——

' I shall take my revenge.'
The mother cries for Toraya.

II

Our mother, Dibwaruna, dreams on the mat.
She dreams about the killing.
' Revenge the wailing ;
Anchor ; hit the Gabu strangers ! '
——The stranger comes out ;
The chief gives him the *pari ;*
' I shall give you the *doga ;*
Bring me things from the mountain to the canoe ! '

III

We exchange our *vaygu'a ;*
The rumour of my arrival spreads through the Koya
We talk and talk.
He bends and is killed.
His companions run away ;
His body is thrown into the sea ;
The companions of the *Kinana* run away,
We sail home.

IV

Next day, the sea foams up,
The chief's canoe stops on the reef ;
The storm approaches ;
The chief is afraid of drowning.
The conch shell is blown :
It sounds in the mountain.
They all weep on the reef.

V

They paddle in the chief's canoe ;
They circle round the point of Bewara.
' I have hung my basket.
I have met him.'
So cries the chief,
So cries repeatedly the chief.

VI

Women in festive decoration
Walk on the beach.
Nawaruva puts on her turtle rings ;
She puts on her *luluga'u* skirt.
In the village of my fathers, in Burakwa.
There is plenty of food ;
Plenty is brought in for distribution.

The character of this song is extremely elliptic, one might even say futuristic, since several scenes are crowded simultaneously into the picture. In the first strophe we see the *Kinana*, by which word all the tribesmen from the d'Entrecasteaux Archipelago are designated in Boyowa, on the top of his Mountain in Gabu. Immediately afterwards, we are informed of the intentions of Tomakam to ascend the mountain, while the women cry for Toraya, for the slain chief—probably his kinswomen and widows. The next picture again spans over the wide seas, and on the one shore we see the Gabuan sitting on the slopes of his hill and far away on the other, under the fringe of small clouds lifting above Boyowa, the mother cries for her son, the murdered chief. Tomakam takes a resolve, ' I shall take my revenge,' hearing her cry.

In the second strophe, the mother dreams about the expedition ; the words about revenge to be taken on the Gabu men and the directions to anchor and hit him are probably taken from her dream. Then suddenly we are transported right across to the mountain, the expedition having arrived there already. The strangers, the *Kinana* are coming down to the canoe, and we assist at the words spoken between them and the people of Buakwa.

Then in the third strophe, we arrive at the culminating scene of the drama ; even here, however, the hero, who is also his own bard, could not help introducing a few boastful words about his renown resounding in the Koya. In a few words the tragedy is described : the *Kinana* bends down, is killed, and his body is thrown into the water. About his head we hear nothing in this verse.

In the next one, a storm overtakes the returning party. Signals of distress are re-echoed by the mountain, and like Homeric heroes, our party are not ashamed to weep in fear and anguish. Somehow they escape, however, and in the next verse, they are already near their village and Tomakam, their leader, bursts into a pæan of triumph. It is not quite clear what the allusion to the basket means, whether he keeps there his Kula trophies or the slain enemy's head ; this latter, in contradiction to what we heard in the prose story of its being impaled. The song ends with a description of a feast. The woman mentioned there is Tomakam's daughter, who puts on festive attire in order to welcome her father.

Comparing now the song with the story, we see that they do not quite tally. In the story, there is the dramatic interest of the mother's intervention. We gather from it that Tomakam, goaded by the aspersions of his fellow-villagers, wishes to make his return as effective as possible. He arranges the signals of the two conch shell blasts with his mother, and asks her to harangue the people at the moment of his return. All this finds no expression in the song. The ruse of the chief's sore leg is also omitted from there, which, however, does not mean that the hero was ashamed of it. On the other hand, the storm described in the song is omitted from the story, and there is a discrepancy about the head of the Gabu man, and we do not know whether it really is conveyed in a basket as the song has it or impaled, as the story relates !

I have adduced in detail the story and the song, because they are a good illustration of the native's attitude towards the dangers, and towards the heroic romance of the Koya. They are also interesting as documents, showing which salient points would strike the natives' imagination in such a dramatic occurrence. Both in the story and in the song, we find emphasised the motives of social duty, of satisfied self-regard and ambition ; again, the dangers on the reef, the subterfuge in killing, finally the festivities on return home. Much that would interest us in the whole story is omitted, as anyone can see for himself.

Other stories, though not made illustrious through being set into a song, are told about the Koya. I met myself an old man in the island of Vakuta, who, as a boy, had been captured with a whole party by a village community of Dobu-speaking people on Normanby Island. The men and another small boy of the party were killed and eaten, but some women took pity on him, and he was spared, to be brought up amongst them. There is another man, either alive or recently dead in Kavataria, who had a similar experience in Fergusson Island. Another man called Kaypoyla, from the small island of Kuyawa in the Western Trobriands, was stranded with his crew somewhere in the West of Fergusson Island, but not in the district where they used to trade. His companions were killed and eaten. He was taken alive and kept to fatten for a proximate feast. His host, or rather the host of the feast in which he was going to furnish the *pièce de résistence*, was away inland, to invite the guests, while the host's wife went for a moment behind the house, sweeping the ground. Kaypoyla jumped up and ran to the shore. Being chased by some other men from the settlement, he concealed himself in the branches of a big tree standing on the beach, and was not found by his pursuers. At night he came down, took a canoe or a raft, and paddled along the coast. He used to sleep on shore during the night, and paddle on in day time. One night he slept among some sago-palms, and, awakening in the morning, found himself, to his terror, surrounded by *Kinana* men. What was his joyful surprise after all, when he recognised among them his friend and Kula partner, with whom he always used to trade ! After some time, he was sent back home in his partner's canoe.

Many such stories have a wide currency, and they supply one of the heroic elements in tribal life, an element which now, with the establishment of white man's influence, has vanished. Yet even now the gloomy shores which our party are leaving to the right, the tall jungle, the deep valleys, the hill-tops darkened with trailing clouds, all this is a dim mysterious background, adding to the awe and solemnity of the Kula, though not entering into it. The sphere of activities of our traders lies at the foot of the high mountains, there, where a chain of rocks and islands lies scattered along the coast. Some of them are passed immediately after leaving Gumasila. Then, after a good distance, a small rock, called Gurewaya, is met, remarkable for the taboos associated with it. Close behind it, two islands, Tewara and Uwama, are separated by a narrow passage, the mythical straits of Kadimwatu. There is a village on the first-mentioned, and the natives of this make gardens on both islands. The village is not very big ; it may have some sixty to eighty inhabitants, as it can man three canoes for the Kula. It has no commercial or industrial importance, but is notable because of its mythological associations. This island is the home of the mythological hero, Kasabwaybwayreta, whose story is one of the most important legends of the Kula. Here indeed, in Tewara, we are right within the mythological heart of the Kula. In fact, we entered its legendary area with the moment the Sinaketan fleet sailed out of the Lagoon into the deep waters of Pilolu.

II

Once more we must pause, this time in an attempt to grasp the natives' mental attitude towards the mythological aspect of the Kula. Right through this account it has been our constant endeavour to realise the vision of the world, as it is reflected in the minds of the natives. The frequent references to the scenery have not been given only to enliven the narrative, or even to enable the reader to visualise the setting of the native customs. I have attempted to show how the scene of his actions appears actually to the native, to describe his impressions and feelings with regard to it, as I was able to read them in his folk-lore, in his conversations at home, and in his behaviour when passing through this scenery itself.

Here we must try to reconstruct the influence of myth upon this vast landscape, as it colours it, gives it meaning, and transforms it into something live and familiar. What was a mere rock, now becomes a personality ; what was a speck on the horizon becomes a beacon, hallowed by romantic associations with heroes ; a meaningless configuration of landscape acquires a significance, obscure no doubt, but full of intense emotion. Sailing with natives, especially with novices to the Kula, I often observed how deep was their interest in sections of landscape impregnated with legendary meaning, how the elder ones would point and explain, the younger would gaze and wonder, while the talk was full of mythological names. It is the addition of the human interest to the natural features, possessing in themselves less power of appealing to a native man than to us, which makes the difference for him in looking at the scenery. A stone hurled by one of the heroes into the sea after an escaping canoe ; a sea passage broken between two islands by a magical canoe ; here two people turned into rock ; there a petrified *waga*—all this makes the landscape represent a continuous story or else the culminating dramatic incident of a familiar legend. This power of transforming the landscape, the visible environment, is one only of the many influences which myth exercises upon the general outlook of the natives. Although here we are studying myth only in its connection with the Kula, even within these narrow limits some of its broader connections will be apparent, notably its influence upon sociology, magic and ceremonial.

The question which presents itself first, in trying to grasp the native outlook on the subject is : what is myth to the natives ? How do they conceive and define it ? Have they any line of demarcation between the mythical and the actual reality, and if so, how do they draw this line ?

Their folk-lore, that is, the verbal tradition, the store of tales, legends, and texts handed on by previous generations, is composed of the following classes : first of all, there is what the natives call *libogwo*, ' old talk,' but which we would call tradition ; secondly, *kukwanebu*, fairy tales, recited for amusement, at definite seasons, and relating avowedly untrue events ; thirdly, *wosi*, the various songs, and *vinavina*, ditties, chanted at play or under other special circumstances ; and last, not least, *megwa* or *yopa*, the magical spells. All these classes are strictly distinguished from one another by name, function, social setting, and by certain formal characteristics. This brief outline of the Boyowan folk-lore in general must suffice here, as we cannot enter into more details, and the only class which interests us in the present connection is the first one, that called *libogwo*.

This, the ' old talk,' the body of ancient tradition, believed to be true, consists on the one hand of historical tales, such as the deeds of past chiefs, exploits in the Koya, stories of shipwreck, etc. On the other hand, the *libogwo* class also contains what the natives call *lili'u*—myths, narratives, deeply believed by them, held by them in reverence, and exercising an active influence on their conduct and tribal life. Now the natives distinguish definitely between myth and historic account, but this distinction is difficult to formulate, and cannot be stated but in a somewhat deliberate manner.

First of all, it must be borne in mind, that a native would not trouble spontaneously to analyse such distinctions and to put them into words. If an Ethnographer succeeded in making the problem clear to an intelligent informant (and I have tried and succeeded in doing this) the native would simply state :

" We all know that the stories about Tudava, about Kudayuri, about Tokosikuna, are *lili'u ;* our fathers, our *kadada* (our maternal uncles) told us so ; and we always hear these tales ; we know them well ; we know that there are no other tales besides them, which are *lili'u.* Thus, whenever we hear a story, we know whether it is a *lili'u* or not."

Indeed, whenever a story is told, any native, even a boy, would be able to say whether this is one of his tribal *lili'u* or not. For the other tales, that is the historical ones, they have no special word, but they would describe the events as happening among ' humans like ourselves.' Thus tradition, from which the store of tales is received, hands them on labelled as *lili'u*, and the definition of a *lili'u*, is that it is a story transmitted with such a label. And even this definition is contained by the facts themselves, and not explicitly stated by the natives in their current stock of expressions.

For us, however, even this is not sufficient, and we have to search further, in order to see whether we cannot find other indices, other characteristic features which differentiate the world of mythical events from that of real ones. A reflection which would naturally present itself would be this : " Surely the natives place their myths in ancient, pre-historic times, while they put historical events into recent ages ? " There is some truth in this, in so far as most of the historical events related by the natives are quite recent, have occurred within the community where they are told and can be directly connected with people and conditions existing at present, by memory of living man, by genealogies or other records. On the other hand, when historical events are told from other districts, and cannot be directly linked with the present, it would be erroneous to imagine that the natives place them into ..definite compartment of time different from that of the myth. For it must be realised that these natives do not conceive of a past as of a lengthy duration, unrolling itself in successive stages of time. They have no idea of a long vista of historical occurrences, narrowing down and dimming as they recede towards a distant background of legend and myth, which stands out as something entirely different from the nearer planes. This view, so characteristic of the naive, historical thinking among ourselves, is entirely foreign to the natives. Whenever they speak of some event of the past, they distinguish whether it happened within their own memory or that of their fathers' or not. But, once beyond this line of demarcation, all the past events are placed by them on one plane, and there are no gradations of ' long ago ' and ' very long ago.' Any idea of epochs in time is absent from their mind ; the past is one vast storehouse of events, and the line of demarcation between myth and history does not coincide with any division into definite and distinct periods of time. Indeed, I have found very often that when they told me some story of the past, for me obviously mythological, they would deem it necessary to emphasise that this did not happen in their fathers' time or in their grand-fathers' time, but long ago, and that it is a *lili'u*.

Again, they have no idea of what could be called the evolution of the world or the evolution of society ; that is, they do not look back towards a series of successive changes, which happened in nature or in humanity, as we do. We, in our religious and scientific outlook alike, know that earth ages and that humanity ages, and we think of both in these terms ; for them, both are eternally the same, eternally youthful. Thus, in judging the remoteness of traditional events, they cannot use the co-ordinates of a social setting constantly in change and divided into epochs. To give a concrete example, in the myths of Torosipupu and Tolikalaki, we saw them having the same interest and concerns, engaged in the same type of fishing, using the same means of locomotion as the present natives do. The mythical personages of the natives' legends, as we shall presently see, live in the same houses, eat the same food, handle the same weapons and implements as those in use at present. Whereas in any of our historical stories, legends or myths, we have a whole set of changed cultural conditions, which allow us to co-ordinate any event with a certain epoch, and which make us feel that a distant historical event, and still more, a mythological one, is happening in a setting of cultural conditions entirely different from those in which we are living now. In the very telling of the stories of, let us say, Joan of Arc, Solomon, Achilles, King Arthur, we have to mention all sorts of things and conditions long since disappeared from among us, which make even a superficial and an uneducated listener realise that it is a story of a remote and different past.

I have said just now that the mythical personages in the Trobriand tradition are living the same type of life, under the same social and cultural conditions as the present natives. This needs one qualification, and in this we shall find a very remarkable criterion for a distinction between what is legendary and what is historical : in the mythical world, although surrounding conditions were similar, all sorts of events happened which do not happen nowadays, and people were endowed with powers such as present men and their historical ancestors do not possess. In mythical times, human beings come out of the ground, they change into animals, and these become people again ; men and women rejuvenate and slough their skins ; flying canoes speed through the air, and things are transformed into stone.

Now this line of demarcation between the world of myth and that of actual reality—the simple difference that in the former things happen which never occur nowadays—is undoubtedly felt and realised by the natives, though they themselves could not put it into words. They know quite well that to-day no one emerges from underground ; that people do not change into animals, and *vice versa ;* nor do they give birth to them ; that present-day canoes do not fly. I had the opportunity of grasping their mental attitude towards such things by the following occurrence. The Fijian missionary teacher in Omarakana was telling them about white man's flying machines. They inquired from me, whether this was true, and when I corroborated the Fijian's report and showed them pictures of aeroplanes in an illustrated paper, they asked me whether this happened nowadays or whether it were a *lili'u.* This circumstance made it clear to me then, that the natives would have a tendency, when meeting with an extraordinary and to them supernatural event, either to discard it as untrue, or relegate it into the regions of the *lili'u.* This does not mean, however, that the untrue and the mythical are the same or even similar to them. Certain stories told to them, they insist on treating as *sasopa* (lies), and maintain that they are not *lili'u.* For instance, those opposed to missionary teaching will not accept the view that Biblical stories told to them are a *lili'u,* but they reject them as *sasopa.* Many a time did I hear such a conservative native arguing thus :—

> " Our stories about Tudava are true ; this is a *lili'u.* If you go to Laba'i you can see the cave in which Tudava was born, you can see the beach where he played as a boy. You can see his footmark in a stone at a place in the Raybwag. But where are the traces of Yesu Keriso ? Who ever saw any signs of the tales told by the misinari ? Indeed they are not *lili'u.*"

To sum up, the distinction between the *lili'u* and actual or historical reality is drawn firmly, and there is a definite cleavage between the two. *Prima facie*, this distinction is based on the fact that all myth is labelled as such and known to be such to all natives. A further distinctive mark of the world of *lili'u* lies in the super-normal, supernatural character of certain events which happen in it. The supernatural is believed to be true, and this truth is sanctioned by tradition, and by the various signs and traces left behind by mythical events, more especially by the magical powers handed on by the ancestors who lived in times of *lili'u*. This magical inheritance is no doubt the most palpable link between the present and the mythical past. But this past must not be imagined to form a pre-historic, very distant background, something which preceded a long evolution of mankind. It is rather the past, but extremely near reality, very much alive and true to the natives.

As I have just said, there is one point on which the cleavage between myth and present reality, however deep, is bridged over in native ideas. The extraordinary powers which men possess in myths are mostly due to their knowledge of magic. This knowledge is, in many cases, lost, and therefore the powers of doing these marvellous things are either completely gone, or else considerably reduced. If the magic could be recovered, men would fly again in their canoes, they could rejuvenate, defy ogres, and perform the many heroic deeds which they did in ancient times. Thus, magic, and the powers conferred by it, are really the link between mythical tradition and the present day. Myth has crystallised into magical formulæ, and magic in its turn bears testimony to the authenticity of myth. Often the main function of myth is to serve as a foundation for a system of magic, and, wherever magic forms the backbone of an institution, a myth is also to be found at the base of it. In this perhaps, lies the greatest sociological importance of myth, that is, in its action upon institutions through the associated magic. The sociological point of view and the idea of the natives coincide here in a remarkable manner. In this book we see this exemplified in one concrete case, in that of the relation between the mythology, the magic, and the social institution of the Kula.

Thus we can define myth as a narrative of events which are to the native supernatural, in this sense, that he knows well

that to-day they do not happen.   At the same time he believes
deeply that they did happen then.   The socially sanctioned
narratives of these events ; the traces which they left on the
surface of the earth ; the magic in which they left behind part
of their supernatural powers, the social institutions which are
associated with the practice of this magic—all this brings about
the fact that a myth is for the native a living actuality, though
it has happened long ago and in an order of things when people
were endowed with supernatural powers.

I have said before that the natives do not possess any
historical perspective, that they do not range events—except
of course, those of the most recent decades—into any successive
stages.   They also do not classify their myths into any divisions
with regard to their antiquity.   But in looking at their myths,
it becomes at once obvious that they represent events, some of
which must have happened prior to others.   For there is a
group of stories describing the origin of humanity, the emerging
of the various social units from underground.   Another group
of mythical tales gives accounts of how certain important
institutions were introduced and how certain customs crystallised.   Again, there are myths referring to small changes in
culture, or to the introduction of new details and minor customs.
Broadly speaking, the mythical folk-lore of the Trobrianders
can be divided into three groups referring to three different
strata of events.   In order to give a general idea of Trobriand
mythology, it will be good to give a short characterisation of
each of these groups.

1. *The Oldest Myths*, referring to the origin of human
beings ; to the sociology of the sub-clans and villages ; to the
establishment of permanent relations between this world and
the next.   These myths describe events which took place just
at the moment when the earth began to be peopled from
underneath.   Humanity existed, somewhere underground, since
people emerged from there on the surface of Boyowa, in full
decoration, equipped with magic, belonging to social divisions,
and obeying definite laws and customs.   But beyond this we
know nothing about what they did underground.   There is,
however, a series of myths, of which one is attached to every one
of the more important sub-clans, about various ancestors
coming out of the ground, and almost at once, doing some
important deed, which gives a definite character to the sub-clan.

PLATE XLVI

FINE SPECIMENS OF AMPHLETT POTS

The largest type of cooking pots, used only for the preparation of taro pudding, are an article of high value and often handled and displayed in connection with ceremonial distributions (*sagali*) and communal cooking.

(See p. 283.)

PLATE XLVII

A CANOE IN GUMASILA LOADING POTS

The main article of export from the Amphletts has to be stowed away very carefully. (See p. 290.)

Plate XLVIII

A KULA FLEET HALTING TO PERFORM THE FINAL RITES OF MWASILA

This photograph was taken in the Trobriands, and it shows the Dobuan fleet just arriving and its final halt (cf. Chapter XVI, Division II). The scene on the beach of Sarubwoyna would present an identical picture. Note the two men in the forefront, wading ashore to procure the leaves for the Kaykakaya. (See p. 335.)

PLATE XLIX

THE BEAUTY MAGIC OF THE MWASILA

The whole fleet are preparing for the final approach; in each canoe magic is spoken over cosmetics and every
man combs his hair, anoints his body, and paints his face.   (See p. 335.)

[face p. 305

Certain mythological versions about the nether world belong also to this series.

2. *Kultur myths.*—Here belong stories about ogres and their conquerors; about human beings who established definite customs and cultural features; about the origin of certain institutions. These myths are different from the foregoing ones, in so far as they refer to a time when humanity was already established on the surface of the earth, and when all the social divisions had already assumed a definite character. The main cycle of myths which belong here, are those of a culture hero, Tudava, who slays an ogre and thus allows people to live in Boyowa again, whence they all had fled in fear of being eaten A story about the origins of cannibalism belongs here also, and about the origin of garden making.

3. *Myths in which figure only ordinary human beings*, though endowed with extraordinary magical powers. These myths are distinguished from the foregoing ones, by the fact that no ogres or non-human persons figure in them, and that they refer to the origin, not of whole aspects of culture, such as cannibalism or garden-making, but to definite institutions or definite forms of magic. Here comes the myth about the origins of sorcery, the myth about the origins of love magic, the myth of the flying canoe, and finally the several Kula myths. The line of division between these three categories is, of course, not a rigid one, and many a myth could be placed in two or even three of these classes, according to its several features or episodes. But each myth contains as a rule one main subject, and if we take only this, there is hardly ever the slightest doubt as to where it should be placed.

A point which might appear contradictory in superficial reading is that before, we stressed the fact that the natives had no idea of change, yet here we spoke of myths about ' origins ' of institutions. It is important to realise that, though natives do speak about times when humanity was not upon the earth, of times when there were no gardens, etc., yet all these things arrive ready-made ; they do not change or evolve. The first people, who came from underground, came up adorned with the same trinkets, carrying their lime-pot and chewing their betel-nut. The event, the emergence from the earth was mythical, that is, such as does not happen now ; but the human beings and the country which received them were such as exist to-day.

III

The myths of the Kula are scattered along a section of the present Kula circuit. Beginning with a place in Eastern Woodlark Island, the village of Wamwara, the mythological centres are spread round almost in a semi-circle, right down to the island of Tewara, where we have left for the present our party from Sinaketa.

In Wamwara there lived an individual called Gere'u, who, according to one myth, was the originator of the Kula. In the island of Digumenu, West of Woodlark Island, Tokosikuna, another hero of the Kula, had his early home, though he finished his career in Gumasila, in the Amphletts. Kitava, the westernmost of the Marshall Bennetts, is the centre of canoe magic associated with the Kula. It is also the home of Monikiniki, whose name figures in many formulæ of the Kula magic, though there is no explicit myth about him, except that he was the first man to practice an important system of *mwasila* (Kula magic), probably the most widespread system of the present day. Further West, in Wawela, we are at the other end of the Kasabwaybwayreta myth, which starts in Tewara, and goes over to Wawela in its narrative of events, to return to Tewara again. This mythological narrative touches the island of Boyowa at its southernmost point, the passage Giribwa, which divides it from Vakuta. Almost all myths have one of their incidents laid in a small island between Vakuta and the Amphletts, called Gabuwana. One of the myths leads us to the Amphletts, that of Tokosikuna ; another has its beginning and end in Tewara. Such is the geography of the Kula myths on the big sector between Murua and Dobu.

Although I do not know the other half through investigations made on the spot, I have spoken with natives from those districts, and I think that there are no myths localised anywhere on the sector Murua (Woodlark Island), Tubetube, and Dobu. What I am quite certain of, however, is that the whole of the Trobriands, except the two points mentioned before, lie outside the mythological area of the Kula. No Kula stories, associated with any village in the Northern half of Boyowa exist, nor does any of the mythical heroes of the other stories ever come to the Northern or Western provinces of the Trobriands. Such extremely important centres as Sinaketa and Omarakana are never mentioned. This would point, on the surface of it, to the fact that in olden days, the island of Boyowa, except its Southern end and the Eastern settlement of Wawela, either did not enter at all or did not play an important part in the Kula.

I shall give a somewhat abbreviated account of the various stories, and then adduce in extenso the one last mentioned, perhaps the most noteworthy of all the Kula myths, that of Kasabwaybwayreta, as well as the very important canoe myth, that of the flying *waga* of Kudayuri.

The Muruan myth, which I obtained only in a very bald outline, is localised in the village of Wamwara, at the Eastern end of the island. A man called Gere'u, of the Lukuba clan, knew very well the *mwasila* magic, and wherever he went, all the valuables were given to him, so that all the others returned empty-handed. He went to Gawa and Iwa, and as soon as he appeared, *pu-pu* went the conch shells, and everybody gave him the *bagi* necklaces. He returned to his village, full of glory and of Kula spoils. Then he went to Du'a'u, and obtained again an enormous amount of arm-shells. He settled the direction in which the Kula valuables have to move. *Bagi* necklaces have ' to go,' and the arm-shells ' to come.' As this was spoken on Boyowa, ' go ' meant to travel from Boyowa to Woodlark, ' come ' to travel from Gere'u's village to Sinaketa. The culture hero Gere'u was finally killed, through envy of his success in the Kula.

I obtained two versions about the mythological hero, Tokosikuna of Digumenu. In the first of them, he is represented as a complete cripple, without hands and feet, who has to be carried by his two daughters into the canoe. They sail on a Kula expedition through Iwa, Gawa, through the Straits of Giribwa to Gumasila. Then they put him on a platform, where he takes a meal and goes to sleep. They leave him there and go into a garden which they see on a hill above, in order to gather some food. On coming back, they find him dead. On hearing their wailing, an ogre comes out, marries one of them and adopts the other. As he was very ugly, however, the girls killed him in an obscene manner, and then settled in the island. This obviously mutilated and superficial version does not give us many clues to the native ideas about the Kula.

The other version is much more interesting. Tokosikuna, according to it, is also slightly crippled, lame, very ugly, and with a pitted skin ; so ugly indeed that he could not marry. Far North, in the mythical land of Kokopawa, they play a flute so beautifully that the chief of Digumenu, the village of Tokosikuna, hears it. He wishes to obtain the flute. Many men set out, but all fail, and they have to return half way, because it is so far. Tokosikuna goes, and, through a mixture of cunning and daring, he succeeds in getting possession of the flute, and in returning safely to Digumenu. There, through magic which one is led to infer he has acquired on his journey, he changes his appearance, becomes young, smooth-skinned and beautiful. The *guya'u* (chief) who is away in his garden, hears the flute played in his village, and returning there, he sees Tokosikuna sitting on a high platform, playing the flute and looking beautiful. " Well," he says, " all my daughters, all my granddaughters, my nieces and my sisters, you all marry Tokosikuna ! Your husbands, you leave behind ! You marry Tokosikuna, for he has brought the flute from the distant land ! " So Tokosikuna married all the women.

The other men did not take it very well, of course. They decided to get rid of Tokosikuna by stratagem. They said : " The chief would like to eat giant clam-shell, let us go and fish it." " And how shall I catch it ? " asks Tokosikuna. " You put your head, where the clam-shell gapes open." (This of course would mean death, as the clam-shell would close, and, if a really big one, would easily cut off his head). Tokosikuna, however, dived and with his two hands, broke a clam-shell open, a deed of super-human strength. The others were angry, and planned another form of revenge. They arranged a shark-fishing, advising Tokosikuna to catch the fish with his hands. But he simply strangled the big shark, and put it into the canoe. Then, he tears asunder a boar's mouth, bringing them thus to despair. Finally they decide to get rid of him at sea. They try to kill him first by letting the heavy tree, felled for the *waga*, fall on him. But he supports it with his outstretched arms, and does no harm to himself. At the time of lashing, his companions wrap some *wayaugo* (lashing creeper) into a soft pandanus leaf ; then they persuade him to use pandanus only for the lashing of his canoe, which he does indeed, deceived by seeing them use what apparently is the same. Then they sail, the other men in good, sea-worthy canoes, he in an entirely unseaworthy one, lashed only with the soft, brittle pandanus leaf.

And here begins the real Kula part of the myth The expedition arrives at Gawa, where Tokosikuna remains with his canoe on the beach, while the other men go to the village to *kula*. They collect all the smaller armshells of the *soulava* type, but the big ones, the *bagi*, remain in the village, for the local men are unwilling to give them.   Then Tokosikuna starts for the village after all the others have returned.   After a short while, he arrives from the village, carrying all the *bagido'u bagidudu*, and *bagiriku*—that is, all the most valuable types of spondylus necklaces.   The same happens in Iwa and Kitava. His companions from the other canoes go first and succeed only in collecting the inferior kinds of valuables.   He afterwards enters the village, and easily obtains the high grades of necklace, which had been refused to the others.   These become very angry ; in Kitava, they inspect the lashings of his canoe, and see that they are rotten.   " Oh well, to-morrow, Vakuta ! The day after, Gumasila,—he will drown in Pilolu."   In Vakuta the same happens as before, and the wrath of his unsuccessful companions increases.

They sail and passing the sandbank of Gabula (this is the Trobriand name for Gabuwana, as the Amphlettans pronounce it) Tokosikuna eases his helm ; then, as he tries to bring the canoe up to the wind again, his lashings snap, and the canoe sinks.   He swims in the waves, carrying the basket-full of valuables in one arm.   He calls out to the other canoes : " Come and take your *bagi !* I shall get into your *waga !* " " You married all our women," they answer, " now, sharks will eat you !   We shall go to make Kula in Dobu ! "   Tokosikuna, however, swims safely to the point called Kamsareta, in the island of Domdom.   From there he beholds the rock of Selawaya standing out of the jungle on the eastern slope of Gumasila.   " This is a big rock, I shall go and live there," and turning towards the Digumenu canoes, he utters a curse :

" You will get nothing in Dobu but poor necklaces, *soulava* of the type of *tutumuyuwa* and *tutuyanabwa*.   The big *bagido'u* will stop with me."   He remains in the Amphletts and does not return to Digumenu.   And here ends the myth.

I have given an extensive summary of this myth, including its first part, which has nothing to do with the Kula, because it gives a full character sketch of the hero as a daring sailor and adventurer. It shows, how Tokosikuna, after his Northern trip, acquired magic which allowed him to change his ugly and weak frame into a powerful body with a beautiful appearance. The first part also contains the reference to his great success with women, an association between Kula magic and love magic, which as we shall see, is not without importance. In this first part, that is, up to the moment when they start on the Kula, Tokosikuna appears as a hero, endowed with extraordinary powers, due to his knowledge of magic.

In this myth, as we see, no events are related through which the natural appearance of the landscape is changed. Therefore this myth is typical of what I have called the most recent stratum of mythology. This is further confirmed by the circumstance that no allusion is made in it to any origins, not even to the origins of the *mwasila* magic. For, as the myth is at present told and commented upon, all the men who go on the Kula expedition with our hero, know a system of Kula magic, the *mwasila* of Monikiniki. Tokosikuna's superiority rests with his special beauty magic ; with his capacity to display enormous strength, and to face with impunity great dangers ; with his ability to escape from drowning, finally, with his knowledge of the evil magic, *bulubwalata*, with which he prevents his companions from doing successful Kula. This last point was contained in a commentary upon this myth, given to me by the man who narrated it. When I speak about the Kula magic more explicitly further on, the reader will see that the four points of superiority just mentioned correspond to the categories into which we have to group the Kula magic, when it is classified according to its leading ideas, according to the goal towards which it aims.

One magic Tokosikuna does not know. We see from the myth that he is ignorant of the nature of the *wayugo*, the lashing creeper. He is therefore obviously not a canoe-builder, nor acquainted with canoe-building magic. This is the point on which his companions are able to catch him.

Geographically, this myth links Digumenu with the Amphletts, as also did the previous version of the Tokosikuna story. The hero, here as there, settles finally in Gumasila, and the element of migration is contained in both versions. Again, in the last story, Tokosikuna decides to settle in the Amphletts, on seeing the Selawaya rock. If we remember the Gumasilan legend about the origin of Kula magic, it also refers to the same rock. I did not obtain the name of the individual who is believed to have lived on the Selawaya rock, but it obviously is the same myth, only very mutilated in the Gumasilan version.

IV

Moving Westwards from Digumenu, to which the Tokosi-kuna myth belongs, the next important centre of Kula magic is the island of Kitava. With this place, the magical system of Monikiniki is associated by tradition, though no special story is told about this individual. A very important myth, on the other hand, localised in Kitava, is the one which serves as foundation for canoe magic. I have obtained three independent versions of this myth, and they agree substantially. I shall adduce at length the story as it was told to me by the best informant, and written down in Kiriwinian, and after that, I shall show on what points the other versions vary. I shall not omit from the full account certain tedious repetitions and obviously inessential details, for they are indispensable for imparting to the narrative the characteristic flavour of native folk-lore.

To understand the following account, it is necessary to realise that Kitava is a raised coral island. Its inland part is elevated to a height of about three hundred feet. Behind the flat beach, a steep coral wall rises, and from its summit the land gently falls towards the central declivity. It is in this central part that the villages are situated, and it would be quite impossible to transport a canoe from any village to the beach. Thus, in Kitava, unlike what happens with some of the Lagoon villages of Boyowa, the canoes have to be always dug out and lashed on the beach.

THE MYTH OF THE FLYING CANOE OF KUDAYURI.

" Mokatuboda of the Lukuba clan and his younger brother Toweyre'i lived in the village of Kudayuri. With them lived their three sisters Kayguremwo, Na'ukuwakula and Murumweyri'a. They had all come out from underground in the spot called Labikewo, in Kitava. These people were the *u'ula* (foundation, basis, here : first possessors) of the *ligogu* and *wayugo* magic."

" All the men of Kitava decided on a great Kula expedition to the Koya. The men of Kumwageya, Kaybutu,
Kabululo and Lalela made their canoes. They scooped out
the inside of the *waga*, they carved the *tabuyo* and *lagim*
(decorated prow boards), they made the *budaka* (lateral
gunwale planks). They brought the component parts to
the beach, in order to make the *yowaga* (to put and lash
them together)."

" The Kudayuri people made their canoe in the village.
Mokatuboda, the head man of the Kudayuri village, ordered
them to do so. They were angry : ' Very heavy canoe.
Who will carry it to the beach ? ' He said : ' No, not so ;
it will be well. I shall just lash my *waga* in the village.'
He refused to move the canoe ; it remained in the village.
The other people pieced their canoe on the beach ; he
pieced it together in the village. They lashed it with the
wayugo creeper on the beach ; he lashed his in the village.
They caulked their canoes on the sea-shore ; he caulked
his in the village. They painted their canoes on the beach
with black ; he blackened his in the village. They made
the *youlala* (painted red and white) on the beach ; he
made the *youlala* in the village. They sewed their sail on
the beach ; he did it in the village. They rigged up the
mast and rigging on the beach ; he in the village. After
that, the men of Kitava made *tasasoria* (trial run) and *kabigidoya* (visit of ceremonial presentation), but the Kudayuri
canoe did not make either."

" By and by, all the men of Kitava ordered their women
to prepare the food. The women one day put all the
food, the *gugu'a* (personal belongings), the *pari* (presents
and trade goods) into the canoe. The people of Kudayuri
had all these things put into their canoe in the village.
The headman of the Kudayuri, Mokatuboda, asked all his
younger brothers, all the members of his crew, to bring
some of their *pari*, and he performed magic over it, and
made a *lilava* (magical bundle) of it."

" The people of other villages went to the beach ; each
canoe was manned by its *usagelu* (members of the crew).
The man of Kudayuri ordered his crew to man his canoe
in the village. They of the other villages stepped the mast
on the shore ; he stepped the mast in the village. They
prepared the rigging on the shore ; he prepared the
rigging in the village. They hoisted the sail on the sea ;
he spoke ' May our sail be hoisted,' and his companions
hoisted the sail. He spoke : ' Sit in your places, every
man ! ' He went into the house, he took his *ligogu* (adze),

he took some coco-nut oil, he took a staff. He spoke magic over the adze, over the coco-nut oil. He came out of the house, he approached the canoe. A small dog of his called Tokulubweydoga jumped into the canoe.* He spoke to his crew : ' Pull up the sail higher.' They pulled at the halyard. He rubbed the staff with the coco-nut oil. He knocked the canoe's skids with the staff. Then he struck with his ligogu the *u'ula* of his canoe and the *dobwana* (that is, both ends of the canoe). He jumped into the canoe, sat down, and the canoe flew ! "

" A rock stood before it. It pierced the rock in two, and flew through it. He bent down, he looked ; his companions (that is, the other canoes of Kitava) sailed on the sea. He spoke to his younger brothers, (that is to his relatives in the canoe) : ' Bail out the water, pour it out ! ' Those who sailed on the earth thought it was rain, this water which they poured out from above."

" They (the other canoes) sailed to Giribwa, they saw a canoe anchored there. They said : ' Is that the canoe from Dobu ? ' They thought so, they wanted to *lebu* (take by force, but not necessarily as a hostile act) the *buna* (big cowrie) shells of the Dobu people. Then they saw the dog walking on the beach. They said : ' Wi-i-i ! This is Tokulubweydoga, the dog of the Lukuba ! This canoe they lashed in the village, in the village of Kudayuri. Which way did it come ? It was anchored in the jungle ! ' They approached the people of Kudayuri, they spoke : ' Which way did you come ? ' ' Oh, I came together with you (the same way).' ' It rained. Did it rain over you ? ' ' Oh yes, it has rained over me.' "

" Next day, they (the men of the other villages of Kitava), sailed to Vakuta and went ashore. They made their Kula. The next day they sailed, and he (Mokatuboda) remained in Vakuta. When they disappeared on the sea, his canoe flew. He flew from Vakuta. When they (the other crews) arrived in Gumasila, he was there on the promontory of Lububuyama. They said : ' This canoe is like the canoe of our companions,' and the dog came out. ' This is the dog of the Lukuba clan of Kudayuri.' They asked him again which way he came ; he said he came the same way as they. They made the Kula in Gumasila. He said : ' You sail first, I shall sail later on.' They were astonished · ' Which way does he sail ? ' They slept in Gumasila."

* The reader will note that this is the same name, which another mythical dog bore, also of the Lukuba clan as all dogs are, the one namely from whom the *kayga'u* magic is traced. Cf. Chapter X, Division V.

" Next day they sailed to Tewara, they arrived at the beach of Kadimwatu. They saw his canoe anchored there, the dog came out and ran along the beach. They spoke to the Kudayuri men, ' How did you come here ? ' ' We came with you, the same way we came.' They made Kula in Tewara. Next day, they sailed to Bwayowa (village in Dobu district). He flew, and anchored at the beach Sarubwoyna. They arrived there, they saw : ' Oh, look at the canoe, are these fishermen from Dobu ? ' The dog came out. They recognised the dog. They asked him (Mokatuboda) which way he came : ' I came with you, I anchored here.' They went to the village of Bwayowa, they made Kula in the village, they loaded their canoes. They received presents from the Dobu people at parting, and the Kitava men sailed on the return journey. They sailed first, and he flew through the air.' "

On the return journey, at every stage, they see him first, they ask him which way he went, and he gives them some sort of answer as the above ones.

" From Giribwa they sailed to Kitava ; he remained in Giribwa ; he flew from Giribwa ; he went to Kitava, to the beach. His *gugu'a* (personal belongings) were being carried to the village when his companions came paddling along, and saw his canoe anchored and the dog running on the beach. All the other men were very angry, because his canoe flew."

" They remained in Kitava. Next year, they made their gardens, all the men of Kitava. The sun was very strong, there was no rain at all. The sun burned their gardens. This man (the head man of Kudayuri, Mokatuboda) went into the garden. He remained there, he made a *bulubwalata* (evil magic) of the rain. A small cloud came and rained on his garden only, and their gardens the sun burned. They (the other men of Kitava) went and saw their gardens. They arrived there, they saw all was dead, already the sun had burned them. They went to his garden and it was all wet : yams, *taitu*, taro, all was fine. They spoke : ' Let us kill him so that he might die. We shall then speak magic over the clouds, and it will rain over our gardens.' "

" The real, keen magic, the Kudayuri man (i.e. Mokatuboda) did not give to them ; he gave them not the magic of the *ligogu* (adze) ; he gave them not the magic of *kunisalili* (rain magic) ; he gave them not the magic of the *wayugo* (lashing creeper), of the coco-nut oil and staff. Toweyre'i, his younger brother, thought that he had already received the magic, but he was mistaken. His elder brother gave him only part of the magic, the real one he kept back."

" They came (to Mokatuboda, the head man of Kudayuri), he sat in his village. His brothers and maternal nephews sharpened the spear, they hit him, he died."

" Next year, they decided to make a big Kula expedition, to Dobu. The old *waga*, cut and lashed by Mokatuboda, was no more good, the lashings had perished. Then Toweyre'i, the younger brother, cut a new one to replace the old. The people of Kumwageya and Lalela (the other villages in Kitava) heard that Toweyre'i cuts his *waga*, and they also cut theirs. They pieced and lashed their canoes on the beach. Toweyre'i did it in the village."

Here the native narrative enumerates every detail of canoe making, drawing the contrast between the proceedings on the beach of the other Kitavans, and of Toweyre'i building the canoe in the village of Kudayuri. It is an exact repetition of what was said at the beginning, when Mokatuboda was building his canoe, and I shall not adduce it here. The narrative arrives at the critical moment when all the members of the crew are seated in the canoe ready for the flight.

" Toweyre'i went into the house and made magic over the adze and the coco-nut oil. He came out, smeared a staff with the oil, knocked the skids of the canoe. He then did as his elder brother did. He struck both ends of the canoe with the adze. He jumped into the canoe and sat down ; but the *waga* did not fly. Toweyre'i went into the house and cried for his elder brother, whom he had slain ; he had killed him without knowing his magic. The people of Kumwageya and Lalela went to Dobu and made their Kula. The people of Kudayuri remained in the village."

" The three sisters were very angry with Toweyre'i, for he killed the elder brother and did not learn his magic. They themselves had learnt the *ligogu*, the *wayugo* magic ; they had it already in their *lopoula* (belly). They could fly through the air, they were *yoyova*. In Kitava they lived on the top of Botigale'a hill. They said : ' Let us leave Kitava and fly away.' They flew through the air. One of them, Na'ukuwakula, flew to the West, pierced through the sea-passage Dikuwa'i (somewhere in the Western Trobriands) ; she arrived at Simsim (one of the Lousançay). There she turned into a stone, she stands in the sea."

" The two others flew first (due West) to the beach of Yalumugwa (on the Eastern shore of Boyowa). There they tried to pierce the coral rock named Yakayba—it was too hard. They went (further South on the Eastern shore) through the sea-passage of Vilasasa and tried to pierce the rock Kuyaluya—they couldn't. They went (further South) and tried to pierce the rock of Kawakari— it was too hard. They went (further South). They tried to pierce the rocks at Giribwa. They succeeded. That is why there is now a sea passage at Giribwa (the straits dividing the main island of Boyowa from the island of Vakuta)."

" They flew (further South) towards Dobu. They came to the island of Tewara. They came to the beach of Kadimwatu and pierced it. This is where the straits of Kadimwatu are now between the islands of Tewara and Uwama. They went to Dobu ; they travelled further South, to the promontory of Saramwa (near Dobu island). They spoke : ' Shall we go round the point or pierce right through ? ' They went round the point. They met another obstacle and pierced it through, making the Straits of Loma (at the Western end of Dawson Straits). They came back, they returned and settled near Tewara. They turned into stones ; they stand in the sea. One of them cast her eyes on Dobu, this is Murumweyri'a ; she eats men, and the Dobuans are cannibals. The other one, Kayguremwo, does not eat men, and her face is turned towards Boyowa. The people of Boyowa do not eat man."

This story is extremely clear in its general outline, and very dramatic, and all its incidents and developments have a high degree of consistency and psychological motivation. It is perhaps the most telling of all myths from this part of the world which came under my notice. It is also a good example of what has been said before in Division II. Namely that the identical conditions, sociological and cultural, which obtain at the present time, are also reflected in mythical narratives. The only exception to this is the much higher efficiency of magic found in the world of myth. The tale of Kudayuri, on the one hand, describes minutely the sociological conditions of the heroes, their occupations and concerns, and all these do not differ at all from the present ones. On the other hand, it shows the hero endowed with a truly super-normal power through his magic of canoe building and of rain making. Nor could it be more convincingly stated than is done in this narrative that the full knowledge of the right magic was solely responsible for these supernatural powers.

In its enumeration of the various details of tribal life, this myth is truly a fount of ethnographic information. Its statements, when made complete and explicit by native comment, contain a good deal of what is to be known about the sociology, technology and organisation of canoe-making, sailing, and of the Kula. If followed up into detail, the incidents of this narrative make us acquainted for instance, with the division into clans ; with the origin and local character of these latter ; with ownership of magic and its association with the totemic group. In almost all mythological narratives of the Trobriands, the clan, the sub-clan and the locality of the heroes are stated. In the above version, we see that the heroes have emerged at a certain spot, and that they themselves came from underground ; that is, that they are the first representatives of their totemic sub-clan on the surface of the earth. In the two other versions, this last point was not explicitly stated, though I think it is implied in the incidents of this myth, for obviously the flying canoe is built for the first time, as it is for the last. In other versions, I was told that the hole from which this sub-clan emerged is also called Kudayuri, and that the name of their magical system is Viluvayaba.

Passing to the following part of the tale, we find in it a description of canoe-building, and this was given to me in the same detailed manner in all three versions. Here again, if we would substitute for the short sentences a fuller account of what happens, such as could be elicited from any intelligent native informant ; if for each word describing the stages of canoe-building we insert a full description of the processes for which these words stand—we would have in this myth an almost complete, ethnographic account of canoe-building. We would see the canoe pieced together, lashed, caulked, painted, rigged out, provided with a sail till it lies ready to be launched. Besides the successive enumeration of technical stages, we have in this myth a clear picture of the rôle played by the headman, who is the nominal owner of the canoe, and who speaks of it as his canoe and at the same time directs its building ; overrides the wishes of others, and is responsible for the magic. We have even the mention of the *tasasoria* and *kabigidoya*, and several allusions to the Kula expedition of which the canoe-building in this myth is represented as a preliminary stage. The frequent, tedious repetitions and enumerations of customary sequences of events, interesting as data of folk-lore, are not less valuable as ethnographic documents, and as illustrations of the natives' attitude towards custom. Incidentally, this feature of native mythology shows that the task of serving as ethnographic informant is not so foreign and difficult to a native as might at first appear. He is quite used to recite one after the other the various stages of customary proceedings in his own narratives, and he does it with an almost pedantic accuracy and completeness, and it is an easy task for him to transfer these qualities to the accounts, which he is called upon to make in the service of ethnography.

The dramatic effect of the climax of the story, of the unexpected flight of the canoe is clearly brought out in the narrative, and it was given to me in all its three versions. In all three, the members of the crew are made to pass through the numerous preparatory stages of sailing. And the parallel drawn between the reasonable proceedings of their fellows on the beach, and the absurd manner in which they are made to get ready in the middle of the village, some few hundred feet above the sea, makes the tension more palpable and the sudden *denouement* more effective. In all accounts of this myth, the magic is also performed just before the flight, and its performance is explicitly mentioned and included as an important episode in the story.

The incident of bailing some water out of a canoe which never touched the sea, seems to show some inconsistency. If we remember, however, that water is poured into a canoe, while it is built, in order to prevent its drying and consequently its shrinking, cracking and warping, the inconsistency and flaw in the narrative disappear. I may add that the bailing and rain incident is contained in one of my three versions only.

The episode of the dog is more significant and more important to the natives, and is mentioned in all three versions. The dog is the animal associated with the Lukuba clan ; that is, the natives will say that the dog is a Lukuba, as the pig is a Malasi, and the igwana a Lukulabuta. In several stories about the origin and relative rank of the clans, each of them is represented by its totemic animal. Thus the igwana is the first to emerge from underground. Hence the Lukulabuta are the oldest clan. The dog and the pig dispute with one another the priority of rank, the dog basing his claims on his earlier appearance on the earth, for he followed immediately the igwana ; the pig, asserting himself in virtue of not eating unclean things. The pig won the day, and therefore the Malasi clan are considered to be the clan of the highest rank, though this is really reached only in one of its sub-clans, that of the Tabalu of Omarakana. The incident of the *lebu* (taking by force) of some ornaments from the Dobuans refers to the custom of using friendly violence in certain Kula transactions (see chapter XIV, Division II).

In the second part of the story, we find the hero endowed again with magical powers far superior to those of the present-day wizards. They can make rain, or stay the clouds, it is true, but he is able to create a small cloud which pours copious rain over his own gardens, and leaves the others to be shrivelled up by the sun. This part of the narrative does not touch the canoe problem, and it is of interest to us only in so far as it again shows what appears to the natives the real source of their hero's supernatural powers.

The motives which lead to the killing of Mokatuboda are not stated explicitly in the narrative. No myth as a rule enters very much into the subjective side of its events. But, from the lengthy, indeed wearisome repetition of how the other Kitava men constantly find the Kudayuri canoe outrunning them, how they are astonished and angry, it is clear that his success must have made many enemies to Mokatuboda. What is not so easily explained, is the fact that he is killed, not by the other Kitava men, but by his own kinsmen. One of the versions mentions his brothers and his sister's sons as the slayers. One of them states that the people of Kitava ask Toweyre'i, the younger brother, whether he has already acquired the flying magic and the rain magic, and only after an affirmative is received, is Mokatuboda killed by his younger brother, in connivance with the other people. An interesting variant is added to this version, according to which Toweyre'i kills his elder brother in the garden. He then comes back to the village and instructs and admonishes Mokatuboda's children to take the body, to give it the mortuary attentions, to prepare for the burial. Then he himself arranges the *sagali*, the big mortuary distribution of food. In this we find an interesting document of native custom and ideas. Toweyre'i, in spite of having killed his brother, is still the man who has to arrange the mortuary proceedings, act as master of ceremonies, and pay for the functions performed in them by others. He personally may neither touch the corpse, nor do any act of mourning or burial ; nevertheless he, as the nearest of kin of the dead man, is the bereaved one, is the one from whom a limb has been severed, so to speak. A man whose brother has died cannot mourn any more than he could mourn for himself.* To return to the motives of killing, as this was done according to all accounts by Mokatuboda's own kinsmen, with the approval of the other men, envy, ambition, the desire to succeed the head-man in his dignity, must have been mixed with spite against him. In fact, we see that Toweyre'i proceeds confidently to perform the magic, and bursts out into wailing only after he has discovered he has been duped.

Now we come to one of the most remarkable incidents of the whole myth, that namely which brings into connection the *yoyova*, or the flying witches, with the flying canoe, and with such speed of a canoe, as is imparted to it by magic. In the spells of swiftness there are frequent allusions to the *yoyova* or *mulukwausi*. This can be clearly seen in the spell of the *wayugo*, already adduced (Chapter V, Division III), and which is still to be analysed linguistically (Chapter XVIII, Divisions II to IV). The *kariyala* (magical portent, cf. Chapter XVII, Division VII) of the *wayugo* spell consists in shooting stars, that is, when a *wayugo* rite is performed at night over the creeper coils, there will be stars falling in the sky. And again, when a magician, knowing this system of magic, dies, shooting stars will be seen. Now, as we have seen (Chapter X, Division I), falling stars are *mulukwausi* in their flight.

In this story of the Kudayuri we see the mythological ground for this association. The same magic which allowed the canoe to sail through the air gives the three sisters of Kudayuri their power of being *mulukwausi*, and of flying. In this myth they are also endowed with the power of cleaving the rocks, a power which they share with the canoe, which

---

* Cf. Professor C. G. Seligman, " The Melanesians," Chapter LIV, " Burial and Mourning Ceremonies " (among the natives of the Trobriand Islands, of Woodlark and the Marshall Bennetts).

cleft a rock immediately after leaving the village. The three sisters cleave rocks and pierce the land in several places. My native commentators assured me that when the canoe first visited Giribwa and Kadimwatu at the beginning of this myth, the land was still joined at these places and there was a beach at each of them. The *mulukwausi* tried to pierce Boyowa at several spots along the Eastern coast, but succeeded only at Giribwa. The myth thus has the archaic stamp of referring to deep changes in natural features. The two sisters, who fly to the South return from the furthest point and settle near Tewara, in which there is some analogy to several other myths in which heroes from the Marshall Bennett Islands settle down somewhere between the Amphletts and Dobu. One of them turns her eyes northwards towards the non-cannibal people of Boyowa and she is said to be averse to cannibalism. Probably this is a sort of mythological explanation of why the Boyowan people do not eat men and the Dobuans do, an explanation to which there is an analogy in another myth shortly to be adduced, that of Atu'a'ine and Aturamo'a, and a better one still in a myth about the origins of cannibalism, which I cannot quote here.

In all these traditions, so far, the heroes belonged to the clan of Lukuba. To it belong Gere'u, Tokosikuna, the Kudayuri family and their dog, and also the dog, Tokulubway-doga of the myth told in Chapter X, Division V. I may add that, in some legends told about the origin of humanity, this clan emerges first from underground and in some it emerges second in time, but as the clan of highest rank, though in this it has to yield afterwards to the Malasi. The main Kultur-hero of Kiriwina, the ogre-slayer Tudava, belongs, also to the clan of Lukuba. There is even a historic fact, which agrees with this mythological primacy, and subsequent eclipse. The Lukuba were, some six or seven generations ago, the leading clan in Vakuta, and then they had to surrender the chieftainship of this place to the Malasi clan, when the sub-clan of the Tabalu, the Malasi chiefs of the highest rank in Kiriwina, migrated South, and settled down in Vakuta. In the myths quoted here, the Lukuba are leading canoe-builders, sailors, and adventurers, that is with one exception, that of Tokosikuna, who, though excelling in all other respects, knows nothing of canoe construction.

V

Let us now proceed to the last named mythological centre, and taking a very big step from the Marshall Bennetts, return to Tewara, and to its myth of the origin of the Kula. I shall tell this myth in a translation, closely following the original account, obtained in Kiriwinian from an informant at Oburaku. I had an opportunity of checking and amending his narrative, by the information obtained from a native of Sanaro'a in pidgin English.

The Story of Kasabwaybwayreta and Gumakarakedakeda

" Kasabwaybwayreta lived in Tewara. He heard the renown of a *soulava* (spondylus necklace) which was lying (kept) in Wawela. Its name was Gumakarakedakeda. He said to his children : ' Let us go to Wawela, make Kula to get this *soulava*.' He put into his canoe unripe coco-nut, undeveloped betel-nut, green bananas."

" They went to Wawela ; they anchored in Wawela. His sons went ashore, they went to obtain Gumakara-kedakeda. He remained in the canoe. His son made offering of food, they (the Wawela people) refused. Kasabwaybwayreta spoke a charm over the betel-nut : it yellowed (became ripe) ; he spoke the charm over the coco-nut : its soft kernel swelled ; he charmed the bananas : they ripened. He took off his hair, his gray hair ; his wrinkled skin, it remained in the canoe. He rose, he went, he gave a *pokala* offering of food, he received the valuable necklace as Kula gift, for he was already a beautiful man. He went, he put it down, he thrust it into his hair. He came to the canoe, he took his covering (the sloughed skin) ; he donned the wrinkles, the gray hairs, he remained."

" His sons arrived, they took their places in the canoe, they sailed to Giribwa. They cooked their food. He called his grandson ; ' Oh, my grandson, come here, look for my lice.' The grandson came there, stepped near him. Kasabwaybwayreta spoke, telling him : ' My grandson, catch my lice in the middle (of my hair).' His grandson parted his hair ; he saw the valuable necklace, Gumakarakedakeda remaining there in the hair of Kasabwaybwayreta. ' Ee. . .' he spoke to his father, telling him, ' My father, Kasabwaybwayreta already obtained Gumakarakedakeda.' ' O, no, he did not obtain it ! I am a chief, I am beautiful, I have not obtained that valuable. Indeed, would this wrinkled old man have obtained the necklace ? No, indeed ! ' ' Truly, my father, he has obtained it already. I have seen it ; already it remains in his hair ! ' ' "

" All the water-vessels are empty already ; the son went into the canoe, spilled the water so that it ran out, and only the empty vessels (made of coco-nut shell) remained. Later on they sailed, they went to an island, Gabula (Gabuwana in Amphlettan and in Dobuan). This man, Kasabwaybwayreta wanted water, and spoke to his son. This man picked up the water vessels—no, they were all empty. They went on the beach of Gabula, the *usagelu* (members of the crew) dug out their water-holes (in the beach). This man remained in the canoe and called out : ' O my grandson, bring me here my water, go there and dip out my water ! ' The grandson said : ' No, come here and dip out (yourself) ! ' Later on, they dipped out water, they finished, and Kasabwaybwayreta came. They muddied the water, it was muddy. He sat down, he waited."

" They went, they sailed in the canoe. Kasabwaybway-reta called out, ' O, my son, why do you cast me off ? ' Spoke the son : ' I think you have obtained Gumakara-kedakeda ! ' ' O, by and by, my son, when we arrive in the village, I shall give it to you ! ' ' O, no ! Well, you remain, I shall go ! ' " He takes a stone, a *binabina* one, this man Kasabwaybwayreta, he throws so that he might make a hole in the canoe, and the men might go into the sea. No ! they sped away, they went, this stone stands up, it has made an island in the sea. They went, they anchored in Tewara. They (the villagers) asked : ' And where is Kasabwaybwayreta ? ' ' O, his son got angry with him, already he had obtained Gumakarakedakeda ! ' "

' 'Well, then, this man Kasabwaybwayreta remained in the island Gabula. He saw Tokom'mwawa (evening star) approach. He spoke : ' My friend, come here, let me just enter into your canoe ! ' ' O no, I shall go to another place.' There came Kaylateku (Sirius). He asked him : ' Let me go with you.' He refused. There came Kayyousi (Southern Cross). Kasabwaybwayreta wanted to go with him. He refused. There came Umnakayva'u, (Alpha and Beta Centauri). He wanted a place in his canoe. He refused. There came Kibi (three stars widely distant, forming no constellation in our sky-chart). He also refused to take Kasabwaybwayreta.

There came Uluwa (the Pleiades). Kasabwaybwayreta asked him to take him. Uluwa said : ' You wait, you look out, there will come Kaykiyadiga, he will take you.' There came Kaykiyadiga (the three central stars in Orion's belt). Kasabwaybwayreta asked him : ' My friend, which way will you go ? ' ' I shall come down on top of Taryebutu mountain. I shall go down, I shall go away.' ' Oh, my friend, come here, let me just sit down (on you).' ' Oh come,—see on one side there is a va'i (stingaree) on the other side, there is the lo'u (a fish with poisonous spikes) ; you sit in the middle, it will be well ! Where is your village ? ' ' My village is Tewara.' ' What stands in the site of your village ? ' ' In the site of my village, there stands a busa tree ! ''

" They went there. Already the village of Kasabwaybwayreta is straight below them. He charmed this busa tree, it arose, it went straight up into the skies. Kasabwaybwayreta changed place (from Orion's belt on to the tree), he sat on the busa tree. He spoke : ' Oh, my friend, break asunder this necklace. Part of it, I shall give you ; part of it, I shall carry to Tewara.' He gave part of it to his companion. This busa tree came down to the ground. He was angry because his son left him behind. He went underground inside. He there remained for a long time. The dogs came there, and they dug and dug. They dug him out. He came out on top, he became a tauva'u (evil spirit, see Chapter II, Division VII.) He hits human beings. That is why in Tewara the village is that of sorcerers and witches, because of Kasabwaybwayreta.''

To make this somewhat obscure narrative clearer, a short commentary is necessary. The first part tells of a Kula expedition in which the hero, his son, his grandson, and some other members of the crew take part. His son takes with him good, fresh food, to give as solicitory offering and thus tempt his partners to present him with the famous necklace. The son is a young man and also a chief of renown. The later stages are clearer ; by means of magic, the hero changes himself into a young, attractive man, and makes his own unripe, bad fruit into splendid gifts to be offered to his partner. He obtains the prize without difficulty, and hides it in his hair. Then, in a moment of weakness, and for motives which it is impossible to find out from native commentators, he on purpose reveals the necklace to his grandson. Most likely, the motive was vanity. His son, and probably also the other companions, become very angry and set a trap for him. They arrange things so that he has to go for his own water on the beach of Gabula. When they have already got theirs and while he is dipping it out, they sail away, leaving him marooned on the sand-bank. Like Polyphemus after the escaping party of Odysseus, he throws a stone at the treacherous canoe, but it misses its mark, and becomes an outstanding rock in the sea.

The episode of his release by the stars is quite clear. Arrived at the village, he makes a tree rise by his magic, and after he has given the bigger part of his necklace to his rescuer, he descends, with the smaller part. His going underground and subsequent turning into a *tauva'u* shows how bitter he feels towards humanity. As usual, the presence of such a powerful, evil personality in the village, gives its stamp to the whole community, and this latter produces sorcerers and witches. All these additions and comments I obtained in cross-questioning my original informant.

The Dobuan informant from Sanaro'a introduced one or two variants into the second part of the narrative. According to him, Kasabwaybwayreta marries while in the sky, and remains there long enough to beget three male and two female children. After he has made up his mind to descend to earth again, he makes a hole in the heavens, looks down and sees a betel-nut tree in his village. Then he speaks to his child, ' When I go down, you pull at one end of the necklace.' He climbs down by means of the necklace on to the betel palm and pulls at one end of Gumakarakedakeda. It breaks, a big piece remains in the skies, the small one goes with him below. Arrived in the village, he arranges a feast, and invites all the villagers to it. He speaks some magic over the food and after they have eaten it, the villagers are turned into birds. This last act is quite in harmony with his profession of *tauva'u*, which he assumed in the previous version of the myth. My Dobuan informant also added, by way of commentary, that the companions of Kasabwaybwayreta were angry with him, because he obtained the necklace in Boyowa, which was not the right direction for a necklace to travel in the Kula. This, however, is obviously a rationalisation of the events of the myth.

Comparing the previously related story of Tokosikuna with this one, we see at once a clear resemblance between them in several features. In both, the heroes start as old, decrepit, and very ugly men. By their magical powers, they rejuvenate in the course of the story, the one permanently, the other just sloughing off his skin for the purpose of a Kula transaction. In both cases, the hero is definitely superior in the Kula, and by this arouses the envy and hatred of his companions. Again, in both stories, the companions decide to punish the hero, and the island or sandbank of Gabuwana is the scene of the punishment. In both, the hero finally settles in the South, only in one case it is his original home, while in the other he has migrated there from one of the Marshall Bennett Islands. An anomaly in the Kasabwaybwayreta myth, namely, that he fetches his necklace from the North, whereas the normal direction for necklaces to travel is from South to North in this region, makes us suspect that perhaps this story is a transformation of a legend about a man who made the Kula from the North. Ill-treated by his companions, he settled in Tewara, and becoming a local Kultur-hero, was afterwards described as belonging to the place. However this might be, and the hypothetical interpretation is mine, and not obtained from the natives, the two stories are so similar that they must be regarded obviously as variants of the same myth, and not as independent traditions.

VI

So much about the ethnographic analysis of these myths. Let us now return to the general, sociological considerations with which we opened this digression into mythology. We are now better able to realise to what extent and in what manner Kula myths influence the native outlook.

The main social force governing all tribal life could be described as the inertia of custom, the love of uniformity of behaviour. The great moral philosopher was wrong when he formulated his *categorical imperative*, which was to serve human beings as a fundamental guiding principle of behaviour. In advising us to act so that our behaviour might be taken as a norm of universal law, he reversed the natural state of things. The real rule guiding human behaviour is this : " what everyone else does, what appears as norm of general conduct, this is right, moral and proper. Let me look over the fence and see what my neighbour does, and take it as a rule for my behaviour." So acts every 'man-in-the-street' in our own society, so has acted the average member of any society through the past ages, and so acts the present-day savage; and the lower his level of cultural development, the greater stickler he will be for good manners, propriety and form, and the more incomprehensive and odious to him will be the non-conforming point of view. Systems of social philosophy have been built to explain and interpret or misinterpret this general principle. Tarde's 'Imitation,' Giddings' 'Consciousness of Kind,' Durkheim's 'Collective Ideas,' and many such conceptions as 'social consciousness,' 'the soul of a nation,' 'group mind' or nowa-days prevalent and highly fashionable ideas about 'suggestibility of the crowd,' 'the instinct of herd,' etc., etc., try to cover this simple empirical truth. Most of these systems, especially those evoking the Phantom of Collective Soul are futile, to my mind, in so far as they try to explain in the terms of a hypothesis that which is most fundamental in sociology, and can therefore be reduced to nothing else, but must be simply recognised and accepted as the basis of our science. To frame verbal definitions and quibble over terms does not seem to bring us much more forward in a new branch of learning, where a knowledge of facts is above all needed.

Whatever might be the case with any theoretical interpretations of this principle, in this place, we must simply emphasise that a strict adherence to custom, to that which is done by everyone else, is the main rule of conduct among our natives in the Trobriands. An important corollary to this rule declares that the past is more important than the present. What has been done by the father—or, as the Trobriander would say, by the maternal uncle—is even more important as norm of behaviour than what is done by the brother. It is to the behaviour of the past generations that the Trobriander instinctively looks for his guidance. Thus the mythical events which relate what has been done, not by the immediate ancestors but by mythical, illustrious forbears, must evidently carry an enormous social weight. The stories of important past events are hallowed because they belong to the great mythical generations and because they are generally accepted as truth, for everybody knows and tells them. They bear the sanction of righteousness and propriety in virtue of these two qualities of preterity and universality.

Thus, through the operation of what might be called the elementary law of sociology, myth possesses the normative power of fixing custom, of sanctioning modes of behaviour, of giving dignity and importance to an institution. The Kula receives from these ancient stories its stamp of extreme importance and value. The rules of commercial honour, of generosity and punctiliousness in all its operations, acquire through this their binding force. This is what we could call the normative influence of myth on custom.

The Kula myth, however, exercises another kind of appeal. In the Kula, we have a type of enterprise where the vast possibilities of success are very much influenced by chance. A man, whether he be rich or poor in partners, may, according to his luck, return with a relatively big or a small haul from an expedition. Thus the imagination of the adventurers, as in all forms of gambling, must be bent towards lucky hits and turns of extraordinarily good chance. The Kula myths feed this imagination on stories of extreme good luck, and at the same time show that it lies in the hands of man to bring this luck on himself, provided he acquires the necessary magical lore.

I have said before that the mythological events are distinct from those happening nowadays, in so far as they are extraordinary and super-normal. This adds both to their authoritative character and to their desirability. It sets them before the native as a specially valuable standard of conduct, and as an ideal towards which their desires must go out.

VII

But I also said before that, distinct as it is, the mythical world is not separated by an unbridgable gulf from the present order of events. Indeed, though an ideal must be always beyond what actually exists, yet it must appear just within reach of realisation if it is to be effective at all. Now, after we have become acquainted with their stories, we can see clearly what was meant when it was said, that magic acts as a link between the mythical and the actual realities. In the canoe myth, for instance, the flying, the super-normal achievement of the Kudayuri canoe, is conceived only as the highest degree of the virtue of speed, which is still being imparted nowadays to canoes by magic. The magical heritage of the Kudayuri clan is still there, making the canoes sail fast. Had it been transmitted in its complete form, any present canoe, like the mythical one, could be seen flying. In the Kula myths also, magic is found to give super-normal powers of beauty, strength and immunity from danger. The mythological events demonstrate the truth of the claims of magic. Their validity is established by a sort of retrospective, mythical empiry. But magic, as it is practised nowadays, accomplishes the same effects, only in a smaller degree. Natives believe deeply that the formulæ and rites of *mwasila* magic make those who carry them out attractive, irresistible and safe from dangers (compare next chapter).

Another feature which brings the mythical events into direct connection with the present state of affairs, is the sociology of mythical personages. They all are associated with certain localities, as are the present local groups. They belong to the same system of totemic division into clans and sub-clans as obtains nowadays. Thus, members of a sub-clan, or a local unit, can claim a mythical hero as their direct ancestor, and members of a clan can boast of him as of a clansman. Indeed, myths, like songs and fairy stories, are ' owned ' by certain sub-clans This does not mean that other people would abstain from telling them, but members of the sub-clan are supposed to possess the most intimate knowledge of the mythical events, and to be an authority in interpreting them. And indeed, it is a rule that a myth will be best known in its own locality, that is, known with all the details and free from any adulterations or not quite genuine additions and fusions.

This better knowledge can be easily understood, if we remember that myth is very often connected with magic in the Trobriands, and that this latter is a possession, kept by some members of the local group. Now, to know the magic, and to understand it properly, it is necessary to be well acquainted with the myth. This is the reason why the myth must be better known in the local group with which it is connected. In some cases, the local group has not only to practise the magic associated with the myth, but it has to look after the observ- ance of certain rites, ceremonies and taboos connected with it. In this case, the sociology of the mythical events is intimately bound up with the social divisions as they exist now. But even in such myths as those of the Kula, which have become the property of all clans and local groups within the district, the explicit statement of the hero's clan, sub-clan and of his village gives the whole myth a stamp of actuality and reality. Side by side with magic, the sociological continuity bridges over the gap between the mythical and the actual. And indeed the magical and the sociological bridges run side by side.

I spoke above (beginning of Division II) of the enlivening influence of myth upon landscape. Here it must be noted also that the mythically changed features of the landscape bear testimony in the native's mind to the truth of the myth. The mythical word receives its substance in rock and hill, in the changes in land and sea. The pierced sea-passages, the cleft boulders, the petrified human beings, all these bring the mythological world close to the natives, make it tangible and permanent. On the other hand, the story thus powerfully illustrated, re-acts on the landscape, fills it with dramatic happenings, which, fixed there for ever, give it a definite meaning. With this I shall close these general remarks on mythology though with myth and mythical events we shall constantly meet in further inquiries.

VIII

As we return to our party, who, sailing past the mythical centre of Tewara, make for the island of Sanaro'a, the first thing to be related about them, brings us straight to another mythological story. As the natives enter the district of Siayawawa, they pass a stone or rock, called Sinatemubadiye'i. I have not seen it, but the natives tell me it lies among the mangroves in a tidal creek. Like the stone Gurewaya, mentioned before, this one also enjoys certain privileges, and offerings are given to it.

The natives do not tarry in this unimportant district. Their final goal is now in sight. Beyond the sea, which is here land-locked like a lake, the hills of Dobu, topped by Koyava'u loom before them. In the distance to their right as they sail South, the broad Easterly flank of Koyatabu runs down to the water, forming a deep valley ; behind them spreads the wide plain of Sanaro'a, with a few volcanic cones at its Northern end, and far to the left the mountains of Normanby unfold in a long chain. They sail straight South, making for the beach of Sarubwoyna, where they will have to pause for a ritual halt in

order to carry out the final preparations and magic. They
steer towards two black rocks, which mark the Northern end of
Sarubwoyna beach as they stand, one at the base, the other
at the end of a narrow, sandy spit. These are the two rocks
Atu'a'ine and Aturamo'a, the most important of the tabooed
places, at which natives lay offerings when starting or arriving
on Kula expeditions. The rock among the mangroves of
Siyawawa is connected with these two by a mythical story.
The three—two men whom we see now before us in petrified
form, and one woman—came to this district from somewhere
'Omuyuwa,' that is, from Woodlark Island or the Marshall
Bennetts. This is the story :

MYTH OF ATU'A'INE, ATURAMO'A AND SINATEMUBADIYE'I.

"They were two brothers and a sister. They came
first to the creek called Kadawaga in Siyawawa. The
woman lost her comb. She spoke to her brethren : ' My
brothers, my comb fell down.' They answered her :
' Good, return, take your comb.' She found it and took
it, and next day she said : ' Well, I shall remain here
already, as Sinatemubadiye'i.' "

"The brothers went on. When they arrived at the
shore of the main island, Atu'a'ine said : ' Aturamo'a,
how shall we go ? Shall we look towards the sea ? ' Said
Aturamo'a ; ' O, no, let us look towards the jungle.'
Aturamo'a went ahead, deceiving his brother, for he was a
cannibal. He wanted to look towards the jungle, so that
he might eat men. Thus Aturamo'a went ahead, and his
eyes turned towards the jungle. Atu'a'ine turned his eyes,
looked over the sea, he spoke : ' Why did you deceive me,
Aturamo'a ? Whilst I am looking towards the sea, you
look towards the jungle.' Aturamo'a later on returned
and came towards the sea. He spoke, ' Good, you
Atu'a'ine, look towards the sea, I shall look to the jungle ! '
This man, who sits near the jungle, is a cannibal, the one
who sits near the sea is good."

This short version of the myth I obtained in Sinaketa.
The story shows us three people migrating for unknown reasons
from the North-East to this district. The sister, after having
lost her comb, decides to remain in Siyawawa, and turns into
the rock Sinatemubadiye'i. The brothers go only a few miles
further, to undergo the same transformation at the Northern end
of Sarubwoyna beach. There is the characteristic distinction

between the cannibal and the non-cannibal. As the story was told to me in Boyowa, that is, in the district where they were not man-eaters, the qualification of ' good ' was given to the non-cannibal hero, who became the rock further out to sea. The same distinction is to be found in the previously quoted myth of the Kudayuri sisters who flew to Dobu, and it is to be found also in a myth, told about the origins of cannibalism, which I shall not quote here. The association between the jungle and cannibalism on the one hand, and between the sea and abstention from human flesh on the other, is the same as the one in the Kudayuri myth. In that myth, the rock which looks towards the South is cannibal, while the Northern one is not, and for the natives this is the reason why the Dobuans do eat human flesh and the Boyowans do not. The designation of one of these rocks as a man-eater (*tokamlata'u*) has no further meaning, more especially it is not associated with the belief that any special dangers surround the rock.

The importance of these two rocks, Atu'a'ine and Aturamo'a lies, however, not so much in the truncated myth as in the ritual surrounding them. Thus, all three stones receive an offering—*pokala*—consisting of a bit of coco-nut, a stale yam, a piece of sugar cane and banana. As the canoes go past, the offerings are placed on the stone, or thrown towards it, with the words :

> " Old man (or in the case of Sinatemubadiyei, ' old woman ') " here comes your coco-nut, your sugar cane, your bananas, bring me good luck so that I may go and make my Kula quickly in Tu'utauna."

This offering is given by the Boyowan canoes on their way to Dobu, and by the Dobuans as they start on the Kula Northwards, to Boyowa. Besides the offerings, certain taboos and observances are kept at these rocks. Thus, any people passing close to the rock would have to bathe in the sea out of their canoes, and the children in the canoes would be sprinkled with sea-water. This is done to prevent disease. A man who would go for the first time to *kula* in Dobu would not be allowed to eat food in the vicinity of these rocks. A pig, or a green coco-nut would not be placed on the soil in this neighbourhood, but would have to be put on a mat. A novice in the Kula would have to make a point of going and bathing at the foot of Atu'a'ine and Aturamo'a.

The Dobuans *pokala* some other stones, to which the Boyowans do not give any offerings. The previously mentioned Gureweya rock receives its share from the Dobuans, who believe that if they passed it close by without making a *pokala*, they would become covered with sores and die. Passing Gureweya, they would not stand up in their canoes, nor would they eat any food when camping on a beach within sight of Gureweya. If they did so, they would become seasick, fall asleep, and their canoe would drift away into the unknown. I do not know whether there is any myth in Dobu about the Gureweya stone. There is a belief that a big snake is coiled on the top of this rock, which looks after the observance of the taboos, and in case of breach of any of them would send down sickness on them. Some of the taboos of Gureweya are also kept by the Boyowans, but I do not exactly know which.

I obtained from a Dobuan informant a series of names of other, similar stones, lying to the East of Dobu, on the route between there and Tubtube. Thus, somewhere in the district of Du'a'u, there is a rock called Kokorakakedakeda. Besides this, near a place called Makaydokodoko there is a stone, Tabudaya. Further East, near Bunama, a small stone called Sinada enjoys some Kula prestige. In a spot Sina'ena, which I cannot place on the map, there is a stone called Taryadabwoyro, with eye, nose, legs and hind-quarters shaped like those of a pig. This stone is called ' the mother of all the pigs,' and the district of Sina'ena is renowned for the abundance of these animals there.

The only mythical fragment about any of these stones which I obtained is the one quoted above. Like the two Kula myths previously adduced, it is a story of a migration from North to South. There is no allusion to the Kula in the narrative, but as the stones are *pokala'd* in the Kula, there is evidently some association between it and them. To understand this association better, it must be realised that similar offerings are given in certain forms of magic to ancestral spirits and to spirits of Kultur-heroes, who have founded the institution in which the magic is practised. This suggests the conclusion that Atu'a'ine and Aturamo'a are heroes of the Kula like Tokosikuna and Kasabwaybwayreta ; and that their story is another variant of the fundamental Kula myth.

Chapter XIII

ON THE BEACH OF SARUBWOYNA

I

When the Sinaketan fleet passes the two mythical rocks of Atu'a'ine and Aturamoa, the final goal of the expedition has been already reached. For before them, there stretch in a wide expanse the N.W. shores of Dawson Straits, where on the wide beach, there are scattered the villages of Bwayowa, Tu'utauna and Deyde'i, at the foot of Koyava'u. This latter, the Boyowans call Koyaviguna—the final mountain. Immediately behind the two rocks, there stretches the beach of Sarubwoyna, its clean, white sand edging the shallow curve of a small bay. This is the place where the crews, nearing their final destination, have to make a halt, to prepare themselves magically for approaching their partners in Dobu. As, on their start from Sinaketa, they stopped for some time on Muwa and there performed the last act of their inaugurating rites and ceremonies, so in the same manner this beach is the place where they once more muster their forces after the journey has been accomplished.

This is the place which was already mentioned in Chapter II when, in giving a description of the district, we imagined ourselves passing near this beach and meeting there a large fleet of canoes, whose crews were engaged in some mysterious activities. I said there that up to a hundred canoes might have been seen anchored near the beach, and indeed, on a big *uvalaku* expedition in olden days such a figure could easily have been reached. For, on a rough estimate, Sinaketa could have produced some twenty canoes ; the Vakutans could have joined them with about forty ; the Amphlettans with another twenty ; and twenty more would have followed from Tewara, Siyawawa, and Sanaroa. Some of them would indeed not have taken part in the Kula, but have followed only out of sheer curiosity, just as in the big *uvalaku* expedition, which I accompanied in 1918 from Dobu to Sinaketa, the sixty Dobuan canoes were joined by some twelve canoes from the Amphletts and about as many again from Vakuta.

The Sinaketans having arrived at this beach, now stop, moor the canoes near the shore, adorn their persons, and perform a whole series of magical rites. Within a short space of time they crowd in a great number of short rites, accompanied by formulæ as a rule not very long. In fact, from the moment they have arrived at Sarubwoyna up to their entry into the village, they do not cease doing one magical act or another, and the *toliwaga* never stop incessantly muttering their spells. To the observer, a spectacle of feverish activity unfolds itself, a spectacle which I witnessed in 1918 when I assisted at an analogous performance of the Dobuan Kula fleet approaching Sinaketa.

The fleet halts ; the sails are furled, the masts dismounted, the canoes moored (see Plate XLVIII). In each canoe, the elder men begin to undo their baskets and take out their personal belongings. The younger ones run ashore and gather copious supplies of leaves which they bring back into the canoes. Then the older men again murmur magical formulæ over the leaves and over other substances. In this, the *toliwaga* is assisted by others. Then, they all wash in sea-water, and rub themselves with the medicated leaves. Coco-nuts are broken, scraped, medicated, and the skin is rubbed with the mess, which greases it and gives it a shining surface. A comb is chanted over, and the hair teased out with it (see Plate XLIX). Then, with crushed betel-nut mixed with lime, they draw red ornamental designs on their faces, while others use the *sayyaku*, an aromatic resinous stuff, and draw similar lines in black. The fine-smelling mint plant, which has been chanted over at home before starting, is taken out of its little receptacle where it was preserved in coco-nut oil. The herb is inserted into the armlets, while the few drops of oil are smeared over the body, and over the *lilava*, the magical bundle of *pari* (trade goods).

All the magic which is spoken over the native cosmetics is the *mwasila* (Kula magic) of beauty. The main aim of these spells is the same one which we found so clearly expressed in myth ; to make the man beautiful, attractive, and irresistible

to his Kula partner.   In the myths we saw how an old, ugly and
ungainly man becomes transformed by his magic into a radiant
and charming youth.   Now this mythical episode is nothing
else but an exaggerated version of what happens every time,
when the *mwasila* of beauty is spoken on Sarubwoyna beach or
on other similar points of approach.   As my informants over
and over again told me, when explaining the meaning of these
rites :

> " Here we are ugly ; we eat bad fish, bad food ; our
> faces remain ugly.   We want to sail to Dobu ; we keep
> taboos, we don't eat bad food.   We go to Sarubwoyna ;
> we wash ; we charm the leaves of *silasila ;* we charm the
> coco-nut ; we *putuma* (anoint ourselves) ; we make our red
> paint and black paint ; we put in our fine-smelling *vana*
> (herb ornament in armlets) ; we arrive in Dobu beautiful
> looking.   Our partner looks at us, sees our faces are
> beautiful ; he throws the *vaygu'a* at us."

The bad fish and bad food here mentioned are the articles
which are tabooed to those who know the *mwasila*, and a man
may often unwittingly break such a taboo.

There is no doubt that a deep belief in the efficacy of such
magic might almost make it effective.   Although actual beauty
cannot be imparted by spells, yet the feeling of being beautiful
through magic may give assurance, and influence people in
their behaviour and deportment, and as in the transaction it
is the manner of the soliciting party which matters, this magic,
no doubt, achieves its aim by pyschological means.

This branch of Kula magic has two counter-parts in the
other magical lore of the Trobrianders.   One of them is the love
magic, through which people are rendered attractive and
irresistible.   Their belief in these spells is such that a man
would always attribute all his success in love to their efficiency.
Another type closely analogous to the beauty magic of the
Kula is the specific beauty magic practised before big dances
and festivities.

Let us now give one or two samples of the magic which is
performed on Sarubwoyna beach.   The ritual in all of it is
exceedingly simple.   In each case the formula is spoken over
a certain substance, and then this substance is applied to the
body.   The first rite to be performed is that of ceremonial
washing.   The *toliwaga* brings his mouth close to the big

bundles of herbs, brought from the shore and utters the
formula called *kaykakaya* (the ablution formula) over them.
After an ablution, these leaves are rubbed over the skins of
all those in the canoe who practise Kula. Then, in the
same succession as I mention them, the coco-nut, the comb, the
ordinary or the aromatic black paint or the betel-nut are
charmed over.* Only one, as a rule, of the paints is used. In
some cases the *toliwaga* does the spell for everybody. In other
cases, a man who knows, say, the betel-nut or the comb spell,
will do it for himself or even for all others. In some cases
again, out of all these rites, only the *kaykakaya* (ablution)
and one of the others will be performed.

KAYKAKAYA SPELL

" O *katatuna* fish, O *marabwaga* fish, *yabwau* fish,
reregu fish ! "

" Their red paint, with which they are painted ; their
red paint, with which they are adorned."

" Alone they visit, together we visit ; alone they visit,
together we visit a chief."

" They take me to their bosom ; they hug me."

" The great woman befriends me, where the pots are
boiling ; the good woman befriends me, on the sitting
platform."

" Two pigeons stand and turn round ; two parrots fly
about."

"No more it is my mother, my mother art thou, O woman
of Dobu ! No more it is my father, my father art thou, O
man of Dobu ! No more it is the high platform, the high
platform are his arms ; no more it is the sitting platform,
the sitting platform are his legs ; no more it is my lime
spoon, my lime spoon is his tongue ; no more it is my
lime pot, my lime pot is his gullet."

This formula then passes into the same ending as the
sulumwoya spell, quoted previously, Chapter VII, which
runs : " Recently deceased spirit of my maternal uncle,
etc."

At the beginning of this spell, we find enumerated a series of
fish names. These fishes all have red markings on their bodies,
and they are tabooed to the people, who recite the *mwasila* magic
and do the Kula. If eaten, they would give a man an ugly
appearance. The above quoted saying of one of my informants :

---

* Compare also No. VI (A), in the Synoptic Table of Kula magic, in
Chapter XVII, p. 418.

" we eat bad fish, we are ugly," refers to these fishes amongst others. In this formula, the invocation is partly an appeal for assistance, and partly a sort of exorcism, which is meant to undo the evil effects of breaking the taboo of eating these fish. As this formula is associated with the ritual washing, the whole proceding possesses a sort of magical consistency, which obtains within an exceedingly obscure and confused concatenation of ideas : the redness of the fish, the red painting on the human bodies for beauty, the invocation of the fishing magic, the taboo on this fish. These ideas hang together somehow, but it would be unwise and incorrect to attempt to put them into any logical order or sequence.* The sentence about ‘ visiting,’ in this spell could not be made clear by any of my native informants. I venture to suggest that the fish are invited to assist the adventurer on his Kula visit, and to help him with their beauty.

The next few sentences refer to the reception he anticipates at Dobu, in the forcible and exaggerated language of magic. The words which have been here translated by ‘ take to his bosom,’ ‘ hug,’ ‘ befriend,’ are the terms used to describe the fondling and rocking and hugging of small children. According to native custom, it would not be considered effeminate or ridiculous for men to put their arms round each other and walk or sit about thus. And it must be added, this is done without any homo-sexual intention, at least of the grosser type. None the less, no such fondling would really take place between the Dobuans and their Kula partners. The mention of the ‘ great woman,’ the ‘ great good woman ’ refers to the wife and sister of the partner, who, as we have said before, are considered to wield great influence in the transactions.

The two pigeons and the two parrots express metaphorically the friendship between the reciter of this magic and his partner. The long list that follows expresses the exchange of his ordinary relations for his Dobuan friends. An exaggerated description follows of the intimacy between him and his partner, on whose arms and legs he will sit, and from whose mouth he will partake of the betel chewing materials.

I shall give a sample of another of these spells, associated with adornment and personal beauty. This is the spell spoken

* There can be no better expression to denote the mutual relation of all these ideas than that used by Frazer to describe one of the typical forms of magic thought, the ‘ contagion of ideas.’ The subjective, psychological process leads the natives to the belief in magical contagion of things.

over the betel-nut with which the *tol:waga* and the members of
his canoe draw lines of vermilion red on their faces.   Young
betel-nut, when crushed with lime in a small mortar, produces
pigment of wonderful brightness and intensity.   Travellers in
the countries of the Indian Ocean and parts of the Pacific know
it well, as the paint that colours the lips and tongues of the
natives.

Talo Spell

" Red paint, red paint of the *udawada* fish !   Red paint,
red paint, of the *mwaylili* fish !   At the one end of the
aromatic pandanus flower-petal ;   at the other end of the
Duwaku flower.   There are two red paints of mine, they
flare up, they flash."

" My head, it flares up, it flashes ;   my red paint, it
flares up, it flashes,

    My facial blacking, it flares up, it flashes ;
    My aromatic paint, it flares up, it flashes ;
    My little basket, it flares up, it flashes ;
    My lime spoon, it flares up, it flashes ;
    My lime pot, it flares up, it flashes ;
    My comb, it flares up, it flashes."

And so on, enumerating the various personal appurtenances, such as the mat, the stock-in-trade, the big basket,
the charmed bundle (*lilava*) and then again the various
parts of his head, that is his nose, his occiput, his tongue,
his throat, his larynx, his eyes, and his mouth.   The whole
series of words is again repeated with another leading
word instead of " it flares up, it flashes."   The new
word, ' *mitapwaypwa'i* ' is a compound, expressing a desire,
a coveting, nascent in the eyes.   The eyes are, according
to native psycho-physical theories, the seat of admiration,
wish and appetite in matters of sex, of greed for food, and
for material possessions.   Here, this expression conveys
that the Dobuan partner, will, on beholding his visitor,
desire to make Kula with him.

The spell ends :   " My head is made bright, my face
flashes.   I have acquired a beautiful shape, like that of a
chief ;   I have acquired a shape that is good.   I am the only
one ;   my renown stands alone."

At the beginning we have again the mention of two
fishes ;   evidently the redness of the fish is the right redness for
the Kula !   I am unable to explain the meaning of the second
sentence, except that the petals of the pandanus flower are
slightly coloured at one end, and that they are considered as

one of the finest and most attractive ornaments. The middle part and the end of this spell need no commentary.

These two spells will be sufficient to indicate the general character of the beauty magic of the Kula. One more spell must be adduced here, that of the conch shell. This shell is as a rule medicated at this stage of the Kula proceedings. Sometimes, however, the *toliwaga* would, before departure from home, utter the formula into the opening of the conch shell, and close this up carefully, so that the virtue might not evaporate. The conch shell is made of a big specimen of the *Cassis cornuta* shell, at the broad end of which the apex of the spiral windings is knocked out, so as to form a mouth-piece. The spell is not uttered into the mouthpiece, but into the broad opening between the lips, both orifices being afterwards closed with coco-nut husk fibre until the shell has actually to be blown.

The Spell of the Ta'uya (Conch Shell)

" *Mwanita, Mwanita*! Come there together ; I will make you come there together ! Come here together ; I will make you come here together ! The rainbow appears there ; I will make the rainbow appear there ! The rainbow appears here ; I will make the rainbow here."

" Who comes ahead with the Kula ? I " (here the name of the reciter is uttered), " come ahead with the Kula, I shall be the only chief ; I shall be the only old man ; I shall be the only one to meet my partner on the road. My renown stands alone ; my name is the only one. Beautiful valuables are exchanged here with my partner ; Beautiful valuables are exchanged there with my partner ; The contents of my partner's basket are mustered."

After this exordium there comes a middle part, constructed on the general principle of one word's being repeated with a series of others. The keyword here is an expression denoting the state of excitement which seizes a partner, and makes him give generous Kula offerings. This word here is repeated first with a series of words, describing the various personal belongings of the partner, his dog, his belt; his tabooed coco-nut and betel-nut ; and then, with a new series of terms denoting the different classes of Kula valuables which are expected to be given. This part could therefore be translated thus :—

" A state of excitement seizes his dog, his belt, his *gwara* " (taboo on coco-nuts and betel-nuts) " his *bagido'u* necklace, his *bagiriku* necklace, his *bagidudu* necklace, etc." The spell ends in a typical manner : " I shall *kula*, I shall rob my Kula ; I shall steal my Kula ; I shall pilfer my Kula. I shall *kula* so as to make my canoe sink ; I shall *kula* so as to make my outrigger go under. My fame is like thunder, my steps are like earthquake ! "

The first word of this spell, *mwanita*, is the native name for a long worm covered with rings of black armour. I was told that it is mentioned here because of its similarity to the spondylus shell necklaces, which also consist of many rings. I obtained this formula in Sinaketa, hence this interpretation heeds only the necklaces, though the simile might also obviously be extended to armshells, for a number of armshells threaded on a string, as they can be seen on Plate LX, presents also a likeness to the *mwanita* worm. It may be added here that Sinaketa is one of these Kula communities in which the overseas expeditions are done only in one direction, to the South, from where only the spondylus necklaces are fetched. Its counterpart, Kiriwina, to the North, carries on again only one-sided overseas Kula. The formulæ which I obtained in Kiriwina differ from those of Sinaketa in their main parts : whenever there is a list of spondylus necklaces in a Sinaketan *tapwana* (main part) a list of the several varieties of armshells would be used in a Kiriwinian *tapwana*. In Kitava, where, as in several other Kula communities, the overseas expeditions are carried out in both directions, the same formula would be used by the same man with two different main parts, according as to whether he was sailing East to fetch *mwali*, or West to fetch *soulava*. No changes, however, would be made in the beginning of a spell.

The sentence ' come here together ' refers to the collected valuables. The play on ' there ' and ' here,' represented in the native language by the sounds ' m ' and ' w,' which are used as interchangeable formatives, is very frequent in magic ; (see Chapter XVIII, Division XII). The rainbow here invoked is a *kariyala* (magical portent) of this formula. When the conch shell is blown, and the fleet approaches the shore, a rainbow will appear in the skies.

The rest of the exordium is taken up by the usual boasts and exaggerations typical of magic. The middle part needs no commentary. It is clear that the sound of the conch shell is meant to arouse the partner to do his duty eagerly. The magic spoken into the conch shell heightens and strengthens this effect.

II

After the beauty magic and the spell over the conch shell are finished—and the whole performance does not take more than half an hour or so—every man, in full festive array, takes his place in his canoe. The sails have been folded and the masts removed, and the final stage is done by paddling. The canoes close in, not in any very regular formation, but keeping near to one another, the canoe of the *toli'uvalaku* as a rule moving in the van. In each canoe, the *toliwaga* sits at his proper place in the middle of the canoe near the *gebobo* (special erection made for cargo). One man sits in the front, right against the prow-board, and another at the stern on the platform. All the remaining members of the canoe wield the paddles, while the small boy or the junior member of the crew, sits near the front, ready to blow the conch shell. The oarsmen swing their leaf-shaped paddles with long, energetic and swift strokes, letting the water spray off them and the glistening blades flash in the sunlight—a ceremonial stroke which they call *kavikavila* (lightening).

As the canoes begin to move, the three men, so far idle, intone a chant, reciting a special magical formula, each a different one. The man in the front, holding his hand on the *tabuyo* (oval prow-board), recites a spell, called *kayikuna tabuyo* (the swaying of the prow-board). The *toliwaga* in the middle recites the powerful formula called *kavalikuliku* (the earthquake spell), a formula which makes " the mountain tremble and subside." The man at the stern recites what is called *kaytavilena moynawaga*, a name which I cannot very well explain, which literally means, " the changing of the canoe entrance." Thus, laden with magical force, which is poured forth irresistibly on to the mountain, the canoes advance towards the goal of their enterprise. With the voices of the reciters mingle the soft, penetrating sounds of the conch shell, blending their various pitches into a weird, disturbing harmony. Samples of the three spells must be given here.

Kayikuna Tabuyo

" Moruborogu, Mosilava'u ! "

" Fish-hawk, fall on thy prey, catch it.

My prow-board, O fish-hawk, fall on thy prey, catch it."
This key expression, the invocation of the fish-hawk, is
repeated with a string of words, denoting, first, the ornamental parts of the canoe ; afterwards, certain of its
constructive parts ; and finally, the lime-pot, the lime stick
the comb, the paddles, the mats, the *lilava* (magical
bundle), and the *usagelu* (members of the crew).   The spell
ends with the words :—

" I shall *kula*, I shall rob my Kula, etc.," as in the
previously given formula of the conch shell.

The first two words of this spell are personal names of men,
as the initial syllable Mo- indicates, but no information about
them was available.   The allusion to the fish-hawk in the main
part suggests a connection between the action of the rite, that
is, the moving of the *tabuyo*, with this part of the spell, for the
ornamental prow-boards are called synonymously *buribwari*
(fish-hawk).   On the other hand, the expression : " Fish-hawk,
fall on thy prey," is no doubt also a magical simile, expressing
the idea : " As a fish-hawk falls on his prey and carries it off,
so let this canoe fall on the Kula valuables and carry them off."
The association of this simile with the act of shaking the prow-
boards is very suggestive.   It may be an attempt to assimilate
the whole canoe and all its parts to a fish-hawk falling on its
prey, through the special mediation of the ornamental prow-
board.

The spell recited by the *toliwaga* in the middle of the canoe
runs thus :—

Kavalikuliku

" I anchor at the open sea beach, my renown reaches
the Lagoon ; I anchor at the Lagoon, my renown reaches
the open sea beach."

" I hit the mountain ; the mountain shivers ; the
mountain subsides ; the mountain trembles ; the mountain
falls down ; the mountain falls asunder.   I kick the ground
on which the mountain stands.   I bring together, I
gather."

" The mountain is encountered in the Kula ; we encounter the mountain in the Kula."

The expression, *kubara, takuba, kubara*, which we have
here translated by " the mountain is met in the Kula, etc."

is then repeated with a long string of words denoting the various classes of valuables to be received in the Kula. It ends with the conclusion already quoted : " My renown is like thunder, my steps are like earthquake."

The opening two sentences are clear ; they contain a typical magical exaggeration, and equally typical permutation of words. Then comes the terrible verbal onslaught on " the mountain," in which the dreadful upheaval is carried on in words. " The mountain " (*koya*) stands here for the community of partners, for the partner, for his mind. It was very difficult to translate the expression *kubara, takuba kubara.* It is evidently an archaic word, and I have found it in several formulæ of the *mwasila.* It seems to mean something like an encounter between the approaching fleet and the *koya.* The word for sea battle is *kubilia* in the Trobriand language, and *kubara* in that of the Amphletts and Dobu, and as often the words of the partner's language are mixed up into these formulæ, this etymology and translation seem to be the correct ones.

The third formula, that of the man in the stern, is as follows :—

Kaytavilena Mwoynawaga

" Crocodile, fall down, take thy man ! push him down under the *gebobo !* (part of the canoe where the cargo is stowed away)."

" Crocodile, bring me the necklace, bring me the *bagido'u,* etc."

The formula is ended by the usual phrase : " I shall *kula*, I shall rob my Kula, etc.," as in the two previously quoted spells (Ta'uyo and Kayikuna tabuyo).

This formula is obviously a pendant to the first of these three spells, and the crocodile is here invoked instead of the fish hawk, with the same significance. The rest of the spell is clear, the crocodile being appealed to, to bring all the different classes of the spondylus shell valuables.

It is interesting to reflect upon the psychological importance of this magic. There is a deep belief in its efficiency, a belief cherished not only by those who advance chanting it, but shared also by the men awaiting the visitors on the shore. The Dobuans know that powerful forces are at work upon them.

They must feel the wave of magical influence slowly advancing, spreading over their villages. They hear the appeal of the conch-shell, wafting the magic to them in its irresistible note. They can guess the murmur of the many voices accompanying it. They know what is expected from them, and they rise to the occasion. On the part of the approaching party, this magic, the chant of the many voices blended with the *ta'uyo* (conch shell), expresses their hopes and desires and their rising excitement ; their attempt to " shake the mountain," to stir it to its very foundations.

At the same time, a new emotion arises in their minds, that of awe and apprehension ; and another form of magic has to come to their assistance at this juncture, to give expression to this fear and to assuage it—the magic of safety. Spells of this magic have been spoken previously, perhaps on the beach of Sarubwoyna alongside with the rest, perhaps even earlier, at one of the intermediate stages of the journey. But the rite will be performed at the moment of setting foot ashore, and as this is also the psychological moment to which the magic corresponds, it must be described here.

It seems absurd, from the rational point of view, that the natives, who know that they are expected, indeed, who have been invited to come, should yet feel uncertain about the good will of their partners, with whom they have so often traded, whom they have received in visit, and themselves visited and re-visited again and again. Coming on a customary and peaceful errand, why should they have any apprehensions of danger, and develop a special magical apparatus to meet the natives of Dobu ? This is a logical way of reasoning, but custom is not logical, and the emotional attitude of man has a greater sway over custom than has reason. The main attitude of a native to other, alien groups is that of hostility and mistrust. The fact that to a native every stranger is an enemy, is an ethnographic feature reported from all parts of the world. The Trobriander is not an exception in this respect, and beyond his own, narrow social horizon, a wall of suspicion, misunderstanding and latent enmity divides him from even near neighbours. The Kula breaks it through at definite geographical points, and by means of special customary transactions. But, like everything extraordinary and exceptional, this waiving of the general taboo on strangers must be justified and bridged over by magic.

Indeed, the customary behaviour of the Dobuans and of the visitors expresses this state of affairs with singular accuracy. It is the customary rule that the Trobrianders should be received first with a show of hostility and fierceness ; treated almost as intruders. But this attitude entirely subsides after the visitors have ritually spat over the village on their arrival. The natives express their ideas on this subject very characteristically :

> " The Dobu man is not good as we are. He is fierce, he is a man-eater ! When we come to Dobu, we fear him, he might kill us. But see ! I spit the charmed ginger root, and their mind turns. They lay down their spears, they receive us well."

III

This show of hostility is fixed into a definite ceremonial attitude when the Dobuan village, which consists of a collection of hamlets, has been laid under a taboo. On the death of a man of importance in any of the hamlets, the whole community undergoes the so called *gwara* taboo. The coco-nut and betel-nut palms around and within the village are not allowed to be scaled, and the fruit must not be touched by the Dobuans themselves, and still less by strangers. This state of affairs lasts a varying length of time, according to the importance of the dead man, and to other circumstances. Only after the *gwara* has run out its course, and is ripe for expiring, do the Kiriwinians dare to come on a visit to Dobu, having been advised beforehand of the circumstance. But then, when they arrive, the Dobuans put up a show of real hostility, for the visitors will have to break the taboo, they will have to scale the palms, and take the forbidden fruit. This is in accordance with a wide-spread Papuo-Melanesian type of custom of finishing tabooed periods : in all cases, someone else, who is not under the taboo, has to put an end to it, or to force the imposer of the taboo to break it. And in all cases, there is some show of violence and struggle on the part of the one who has to allow it to be broken. In this case, as the Kiriwinian natives put it :

> " Supposing we do not perform the *ka'ubana'i* (safety magic), we are afraid, when there is a *gwara* in Dobu, The Dobuans put on war paint, take spear in hand, and a

puluta (sword club) ; they sit and look at us. We run into the village ; we climb the tree. He runs at us ' Don't climb,' he cries. Then we spit *leyya* (ginger root) at him. He throws down his spear, he goes back and smiles. The women take the spears away. We spit all around the village. Then he is pleased. He speaks : ' You climb your coco-nut, your betel-nut ; cut your bananas.' "

Thus the taboo is broken, the *gwara* is finished, and the customary and histrionic moment of tension is over, which must have been none the less a strain on the nerves of both parties.

This is the lengthy formula which a *toliwaga* utters over several bits of ginger root, which are afterwards distributed among his crew, each of whom carries a piece when getting ashore.

Ka'ubana'i

" Floating spirit of Nikiniki !
Duduba, Kirakira." (These words are untranslatable).
" It ebbs, it ebbs away !
Thy fury ebbs, it ebbs away, O man of Dobu !
Thy war paint ebbs, it ebbs away, O man of Dobu !
Thy sting ebbs, it ebbs away, O man of Dobu !
Thy anger ebbs, it ebbs away, O man of Dobu !
Thy chasing away ebbs, it ebbs away, O man of Dobu ! "
A long string of various expressings denoting hostile passions, disinclination to make Kula, and all the paraphernalia of war are here enumerated. Thus, such words as " Kula refusal," " growling," " sulking," " dislike " ; further : " weapon," " bamboo knife," " club-sword," " large-barbed spear," " small-barbed spear," " round club," " war blackening," " red war paint," are uttered one after the other. Moreover, all of them are repeated in their Dobuan equivalents after the list has been exhausted in Kiriwinian. When this series has been exhausted with reference to the man of Dobu, part of it is repeated with the addition " Woman of Dobu," the mention of weapons, however, being omitted. But this does not end this extremely long formula. After the protracted litany has been finished, the reciter chants :

" Who emerges at the top of Kinana ? I " (here the name of the reciter is mentioned) " emerge on the top of Kinana."
Then the whole litany is again repeated, the key word, instead of, " it ebbs, it ebbs away " being " the dog sniffs."

In connection with all the other words, this would run, more or less, in a free translation :—

" Thy fury, O man of Dobu, is as when the dog sniffs," or, more explicitly :—

" Thy fury, O man of Dobu, should abate as the fury of a dog abates when it comes and sniffs at a new-comer."

The simile of the dog must be very strongly ingrained in the magical tradition, for in two more versions of this formula, obtained from different informants, I received as key-words the expressions : " The dog plays about," and " The dog is docile." The final part of this formula is identical with that of the Kaykakaya spell previously given in this chapter :—

" No more it is my mother, my mother art thou, O woman of Dobu, etc.," running into the ending " Recently deceased, etc."

In comment on this formula, there is first of all the name mentioned in the first line, that of Nikiniki, or Monikiniki, as it is usually pronounced, with the prefix of masculinity, *mo-*. He is described as " A man, an ancient man ; no myth about him ; he spoke the magic." Indeed, the main system of *mwasila* magic is named after him, but none of my informants knew any legend about him.

The first key word of the middle part is quite clear. It describes the ebbing away of the Dobuans' passions and of their outward trappings. It is noteworthy that the word for ' ebbing ' here used, is in the Dobuan, and not in the Kiriwinian language. The reference to the dog already explained may be still made clearer in terms of native comment. One explanation is simple :—

" They invoke the dog in the *mwasila*, because when master of dog comes, the dog stands up and licks ; in the same way, the inclinations of the Dobu people." Another explanation is more sophisticated : " The reason is that dogs play about nose to nose. Supposing we mentioned the word, as it was of old arranged, the valuables do the same. Supposing we had given away armshells, the necklace will come, they will meet."

This means, by invoking the dog in this magic, according to old magical tradition, we also influence the Kula gifts. This explanation is undoubtedly far-fetched, and probably does not express the real meaning of the spell. It would have no meaning in association with the list of passions and weapons, but I have adduced it as an example of native scholasticism.

The dog is also a taboo associated with this magic.   When a man, who practices the *ka'ubana'i* eats and a dog howls within his hearing, he has to leave his food, else his magic would ' blunt.'

Safe under the auspices of this magic, the Trobriand sailors land on the beach of Tu'utauna, where we shall follow them in the next chapter.

Chapter XIV

THE KULA IN DOBU—TECHNICALITIES OF THE EXCHANGE

I

In the last chapter, we spoke about the institution of *gwara* (mortuary taboo) and of the threatening reception accorded to the visiting party, at the time when it is laid upon the village, and when it has to be lifted. When there is no *gwara*, and the arriving fleet are on an *uvalaku* expedition, there will be a big and ceremonial welcome. The canoes, as they approach, will range themselves in a long row facing the shore. The point selected will be the beach, corresponding to a hamlet where the main partner of the *toli'uvalaku* lives. The canoe of the *toli'uvalaku*, of the master of the *uvalaku* expedition, will range itself at the end of the row. The *toli'uvalaku* will get up on to the platform and harangue the natives assembled on the beach. He will try to appeal to their ambition, so that they might give the visitors a large amount of valuables and surpass all other occasions. After that, his partner on the shore will blow a conch-shell, and, wading through the water, advance towards the canoe, and offer the first gift of valuables to the master of the expedition. This may be followed by another gift, again given to the *toli'uvalaku*. Other blasts then follow, and men disengage themselves from the throng on the shore, approaching the canoes with necklaces for their partners. A certain order of seniority will be observed in this. The necklaces are always carried ceremonially ; as a rule they will be tied by both ends to a stick, and carried hanging down, with the pendant at the bottom (see Plate LXI). Sometimes, when a *vaygu'a* (valuable) is carried to the canoes by a woman (a headman's wife or sister) it will be put into a basket and carried on her head.

II

After this ceremonial reception, the fleet disperses. As we remember from Chapter II, the villages in Dobu are not built in compact blocks of houses, but scattered in hamlets, each of about a dozen huts. The fleet now sails along the shore, every canoe anchoring in front of the hamlet in which its *toliwaga* has his main partner.

We have at last arrived at the point when the real Kula has begun. So far, it was all preparations, and sailing with its concomitant adventure, and a little bit of preliminary Kula in the Amphletts. It was all full of excitement and emotion, pointing always towards the final goal, the big Kula in Dobu. Now we have at last reached the climax. The net result will be the acquisition of a few dirty, greasy, and insignificant looking native trinkets, each of them a string of flat, partly discoloured, partly raspberry-pink or brick-red discs, threaded one behind the other into a long, cylindrical roll. In the eyes of the natives, however, this result receives its meaning from the social forces of tradition and custom, which give the imprint of value to these objects, and surround them with a halo of romance. It seems fit here to make these few reflections upon the native psychology on this point, and to attempt to grasp its real significance.

It may help us towards this understanding to reflect, that not far from the scenes of the Kula, large numbers of white adventurers have toiled and suffered, and many of them given their lives, in order to acquire what to the natives would appear as insignificant and filthy as their *bagi* are to us—a few nuggets of gold. Nearer, even, in the very Trobriand Lagoon, there are found valuable pearls. In olden days, when the natives on opening a shell to eat it, found a *waytuna*, as they called it, a ' seed ' of the pearl shell, they would throw it to their children to play with. Now they see a number of white men straining all their forces in competition to acquire as many of these worthless things as they can. The parallel is very close. In both cases, the conventionalised value attached to an object carries with it power, renown, and the pleasure of increasing them both. In the case of the white man, this is infinitely more complex and indirect, but not essentially different from that of the natives. If we would imagine that a great number of celebrated gems are let loose among us, and travel from hand to hand—that Koh-i-noor and Orloff and other celebrated diamonds, emeralds and rubies—were on a continuous round tour, and to be obtained through luck, daring and enterprise, we would have a still closer analogy. Even though the possession of them would be a short and temporary one, the renown of having possessed them and the mania of ' collectioneering ' would add its spur to the lust for wealth.

This general, human, psychological foundation of the Kula must be kept constantly in mind. If we want, however, to understand its specific forms, we have to look for the details and technicalities of the transaction. A short outline of these has been given before in Chapter III. Here, after we have acquired a better knowledge of preliminaries, and a more thorough grasp of native psychology and custom, we shall be more ready to enter into a detailed description.

The main principle of the Kula exchange has been laid down in the before-mentioned chapter ; the Kula exchange has always to be a *gift*, followed by a *counter-gift ;* it can never be a barter, a direct exchange with assessment of equivalents and with haggling. There must be always in the Kula two transactions, distinct in name, in nature and in time. The exchange is opened by an initial or opening gift called *vaga*, and closed by a final or return present called *yotile*. They are both ceremonial gifts, they have to be accompanied by the blow of a conch shell, and the present is given ostentatiously and in public. The native term " to throw " a valuable describes well the nature of the act. For, though the valuable has to be handed over by the giver, the receiver hardly takes any notice of it, and seldom receives it actually into his hands. The etiquette of the transaction requires that the gift should be given in an off-hand, abrupt, almost angry manner, and received with equivalent nochalance and disdain. A slight modification in this is introduced when, as it happens sometimes, in the Trobriands, and in the Trobriands only, the *vaygu'a* is given by a chief to a commoner, in which case the commoner would take it into his hand, and show some appreciation of it. In all other cases, the valuable would be placed within the reach of the receiver, and an insignificant member of his following would pick it up.

It is not very easy to unravel the various motives which combine to make up this customary behaviour on receiving and

giving a gift. The part played by the receiver is perhaps not
so difficult to interpret. Right through their ceremonial and
commercial give and take, there runs the crude and fundamental human dissatisfaction with the value received. A native
will always, when speaking about a transaction, insist on the
magnitude and value of the gift he gave, and minimise those of
the equivalent accepted. Side by side with this, there is the
essential native reluctance to appear in want of anything, a
reluctance which is most pronounced in the case of food, as we
have said before (Chapter VI, Division IV). Both these
motives combine to produce the, after all, very human and
understandable attitude of disdain at the reception of a gift.
In the case of the donor, the histrionic anger with which he
gives an object might be, in the first place, a direct expression
of the natural human dislike of parting with a possession.
Added to this, there is the attempt to enhance the apparent
value of the gift by showing what a wrench it is to give it away.
This is the interpretation of the etiquette in giving and taking
at which I have arrived after many observations of native
behaviour, and through many conversations and casual remarks
of the natives.

The two gifts of the Kula are also distinct in time. It is
quite obvious this must be so in the case of an overseas expedition of an *uvalaku* type, on which no valuables whatever are
taken with them by the visiting party, and so, any valuable
received on such an occasion, whether as *vaga* or *yotile*, cannot
therefore be exchanged at the same time. But even when the
exchange takes place in the same village during an inland
Kula, there must be an interval between the two gifts, of a few
minutes at least.

There are also deep differences in the nature of the two
gifts. The *vaga*, as the opening gift of the exchange, has to
be given spontaneously, that is, there is no enforcement of any
duty in giving it. There are means of soliciting it, (*wawoyla*),
but no pressure can be employed. The *yotile*, however, that is,
the valuable which is given in return for the valuable previously
received, is given under pressure of a certain obligation. If I
have given a *vaga* (opening gift of valuable) to a partner of
mine, let us say a year ago, and now, when on a visit, I find
that he has an equivalent *vaygu'a*, I shall consider it his duty
to give it to me. If he does not do so, I am angry with him,

and justified in being so. Not only that, if I can by any chance lay my hand on his *vaygu'a* and carry if off by force (*lebu*), I am entitled by custom to do this, although my partner in that case may become very irate. The quarrel over that would again be half histrionic, half real.

Another difference between a *vaga* and a *yotile* occurs in overseas expeditions which are not *uvalaku*. On such expeditions, valuables sometimes are carried, but only such as are due already for a past *vaga*, and are to be given as *yotile*. Opening gifts, *vaga*, are never taken overseas.

As mentioned above, the *vaga*, entails more wooing or soliciting than the *yotile*. This process, called by the natives *wawoyla*, consists, among others of a series of solicitary gifts. One type of such gifts is called *pokala*, and consists of food.* In the myth of Kasabwaybwayreta, narrated in Chapter XII, this type of gift was mentioned. As a rule, a considerable amount of food is taken on an expedition, and when a good valuable is known to be in the possession of a man, some of this food will be presented to him, with the words : " I *pokala* your valuable ; give it to me." If the owner is not inclined to part with his valuable, he will not accept the *pokala*. If accepted, it is an intimation that the *vaygu'a* will sooner or later be given to the man who offers the *pokala*. The owner, however, may not be prepared to part with it at once, and may wish to receive more solicitary gifts.

Another type of such a gift is called *kaributu*, and consists of a valuable which, as a rule, is not one of those which are regularly *kulaed*. Thus, a small polished axe blade, or a valuable belt is given with the words : " I *kaributu* your necklace (or armshells) ; I shall take it and carry it off " This gift again may only be accepted if there is an intention to satisfy the giver with the desired *vaygu'a*. A very famous and great valuable will often be solicited by gift of *pokala* and of *kaributu*, one following the other. If, after one or two of such solicitory gifts, the big *vaygu'a* is finally given, the satisfied receiver will often give some more food to his partner, which gift is called *kwaypolu*.

The food gifts would be returned on a similar occasion if it arises. But there would be no strict equivalence in the

---

* It will be noted, that this is the third meaning in which the term *pokala* is used by the natives. (Cf. Chapter VI, Division VI.)

matter of food. The *kaributu* gift of a valuable, however, would always have to be returned later on, in an equivalent form. It may be added that the *pokala* offerings of food would be most often given from a district, where food is more abundant than in the district to which it is carried. Thus, the Sinaketans would bring *pokala* to the Amphletts, but they would seldom or never *pokala* the Dobuans, who are very rich in food. Again, within the Trobriands, a *pokala* would be offered from the Northern agricultural district of Kiriwina to men of Sinaketa, but not inversely.

Another peculiar type of gift connected with the Kula is called *korotomna*. After a Sinaketan has given a necklace to a man of Kiriwina, and this latter receives a minor valuable from his partner further East, this minor valuable will be given to the Sinaketan as the *korotomna* of his necklace. This gift usually consists of a lime spatula of whalebone ornamented with spondylus discs, and it has to be repaid.

It must be noted that all these expressions are given in the language of the Trobriands, and they refer to the gifts exchanged between the Northern and Southern Trobriands on the one hand, and these latter and the Amphletts on the other. In an overseas expedition from Sinaketa to Dobu, the solicitary gifts would be rather given wholesale, as the visitors' gifts of *pari*, and the subtle distinctions in name and in technicality would not be observed. That this must be so becomes clear, if we realise that, whereas, between the Northern and Southern Trobriands the news about an exceptionally good valuable spreads easily and quickly, this is not the case between Dobu and Boyowa. Going over to Dobu, therefore, a man has to make up his mind, whether he will give any solicitory presents to his partner, what and how much he will give him, without knowing whether he has any specially fine valuables to expect from him or not. If, however, there was any exceptionally valuable gift in the visitors' *pari*, it will have to be returned later on by the Dobuans.

Another important type of gift essential to the Kula is that of the intermediary gifts, called *basi*. Let us imagine that a Sinaketan man has given a very fine pair of armshells to his Dobuan partner at their last meeting in Sinaketa. Now, arriving in Dobu, he finds that his partner has not got any necklace equivalent in value to the armshells given. He none the less will expect his partner to give him meanwhile a neck-lace, even though it be of inferior value. Such a gift is a *basi*, that is, not a return of the highly valuable *vaga*, but a gift given to fill in the gap. This *basi* will have to be repaid by a small equivalent pair of armshells at a later date. And the Dobuan on his side has still to repay the big armshells he received, and for which he has as yet got no equivalent in his possession. As soon as this is obtained, it will be given, and will close the trans-action as a clinching gift, or *kudu*. Both these names imply figures of speech. *Kudu* means ' tooth,' and is a good name for a gift which clinches or bites. *Basi* means to pierce, or to stab, and this is the literal translation of a native comment on this name :

> " We say *basi*, for it does not truly bite, like a *kudu* (tooth) ; it just *basi* (pierces) the surface ; makes it lighter."

The equivalence of the two gifts, *vaga* and *yotile*, is expressed by the word *kudu* (tooth) and *bigeda* (it will bite). Another figure of speech describing the equivalence is contained in the word *va'i*, to marry. When two of the opposite valuables meet in the Kula and are exchanged, it is said that these two have married. The armshells are conceived as a female prin-ciple, and the necklaces as the male. An interesting comment on these ideas was given to me by one of the informants. As mentioned above, a gift of food is never given from Sinaketa to Kiriwina, obviously because it would be a case of bringing coals to Newcastle. When I asked why this is so, I received the answer :

> " We do not now *kwaypolu* or *pokala* the *mwali*, for they are women, and there is no reason to *kwaypolu* or *pokala* them."

There is little logic in this comment, but it evidently includes some idea about the smaller value of the female principle. Or else perhaps it refers to the fundamental idea of the married status, namely that it is for the woman's family to provide the man with food.

The idea of equivalence in the Kula transaction is very strong and definite, and when the receiver is not satisfied with the *yotile* (return gift) he will violently complain that it is not a proper ‘ tooth ’ (*kudu*) for his opening gift, that it is not a real ‘ marriage,’ that it is not properly ‘ bitten.’

These terms, given in the Kiriwinian language, cover about half of the Kula ring from Woodlark Island and even further East, from Nada (Loughlan Islands) as far as the Southern Trobriands. In the language of Dobu, the same word is used for *vaga* and *basi*, while *yotile* is pronounced *yotura*, and *kudu* is *udu*. The same terms are used in the Amphletts.

So much about the actual regulations of the Kula transactions. With regard to the further general rules, the definition of Kula partnership and sociology has been discussed in detail in Chapter XI. As to the rule that the valuables have always to travel and never to stop, nothing has to be added to what has been said about this in Chapter III, for there are no exceptions to this rule. A few more words must be said on the subject of the valuables used in the Kula. I said in Chapter III, stating the case briefly, that in one direction travel the armshells, whilst in the opposite, following the hands of the clock, travel the necklaces. It must now be added that the *mwali*—armshells—are accompanied by another article, the *doga*, or circular boar’s tusks. In olden days, the *doga* were almost as important as the *mwali* in the stream of the Kula. Nowadays, hardly any at all are to be met as Kula articles. It is not easy to explain the reason for this change. In an institution having the importance and traditional tenacity which we find in the Kula, there can be no question of the interference of fashion to bring about changes. The only reason which I can suggest is that nowadays, with immensely increased intertribal intercourse, there is a great drainage on all Kula valuables by other districts lying outside the Kula. Now, on the one hand the *doga* are extremely valued on the main-land of New Guinea, much more, I assume, than they are within the Kula district. The drainage therefore would affect the *doga* much more strongly than any other articles, one of which, the spondylus necklaces, are actually imported into the Kula region from without, and even manufactured by white men in considerable quantities for native consumption. The armshells are produced within the district in sufficient numbers to replace any leakage, but *doga* are extremely difficult to reproduce as they are connected with a rare freak of nature—a boar with a circular tusk.

One more article which travels in the same direction as the *mwali*, consists of the *bosu*, the big lime spatulæ made of whale-bone and decorated with spondylus shells. They are not strictly speaking Kula articles, but play a part as the *korotomna* gifts mentioned above and nowadays are hardly to be met with. With the necklaces, there travel only as an unimportant subsidiary Kula article, belts made of the same red spondylus shell. They would be given as return presents for small armshells, as *basi*, etc.

There is one important exception in the respective movements of necklace and armshell. A certain type of spondylus shell strings, much bigger and coarser than the strings which are used in the Kula, are produced in Sinaketa, as we saw in the last Chapter. These strings, called *katudababile* in Kiriwinian, or *sama'upa* in Dobuan, are sometimes exported from Sinaketa to Dobu as Kula gifts, and function therefore as armshells. These *katudababile*, however, never complete the Kula ring, in the wrong direction, as they never return to the Trobriands from the East. Part of them are absorbed into the districts outside the Kula, part of them come back again to Sinaketa, and join the other necklaces in their circular movement.

Another class of articles, which often take a subsidiary part in the Kula exchange, consists of the large and thin polished axe blades, called in the Kiriwinian language *beku*. They are never used for any practical purposes, and fulfil only the function of tokens of wealth and objects of parade. In the Kula they would be given as *kaributu* (solicitary gifts), and would go both ways. As they are quarried in Woodlark Island and polished in Kiriwina, they would, however, move in the direction from the Trobriands to Dobu more frequently than in the opposite one.

To summarise this subject, it may be said that the proper Kula articles are on the one hand, the armshells (*mwali*), and the curved tusks (*doga*) ; and, on the other hand, the fine, long necklaces (*soulava* or *bagi*), of which there are many sub-classes. An index of the special position of these three articles is that they are the only ones, or at least, by far the most important ones, mentioned in the spells. Later on, I shall enumerate all the sub-classes and varieties of these articles.

Although, as we have seen, there is both a good deal of ceremony attached to the transaction and a good deal of decorum, one might even say commercial honour, implied in the technicalities of the exchange, there is much room left as well for quarrelling and friction. If a man obtains a very fine valuable, which he is not already under an obligation to offer as *yotile* (return payment), there will be a number of his partners, who will compete to receive it. As only one can be successful, all the others will be thwarted and more or less offended and full of malice. Still more room for bad blood is left in the matter of equivalence. As the valuables exchanged cannot be measured or even compared with one another by an exact standard ; as there are no definite correspondences or indices of correlation between the various kinds of the valuables, it is not easy to satisfy a man who has given a *vaygu'a* of high value. On receiving a repayment (*yotile*), which he does not consider equivalent, he will not actually make a scene about it, or even show his displeasure openly in the act. But he will feel a deep resentment, which will express itself in frequent recriminations and abuse. These, though not made to his partner's face, will reach his ears sooner or later. Eventually, the universal method of settling differences may be resorted to—that of black magic, and a sorcerer will be paid to cast some evil spell over the offending party.

When speaking about some celebrated *vaygu'a*, a native will praise its value in the words : " Many men died because of it "—which does not mean that they died in battle or fight, but were killed by black magic. Again, there is a system of signs by which one can recognise, on inspecting the corpse the day after death, for what reasons it has been bewitched. Among these signs there are one or two which mean that the man has been done away with, because of his success in Kula, or because he has offended somebody in connection with it. The mixture of punctilio and decorum, on the one hand, with passionate resentment and greed on the other, must be realised as underlying all the transactions, and giving the leading psychological tone to the natives' interest. The obligation of fairness and decency is based on the general rule, that it is highly improper and dishonourable to be mean. Thus, though a man will generally strive to belittle the thing received, it must not be forgotten that the man who gave it was genuinely eager to do his best. And after all, in some cases when a man receives a really fine valuable, he will boast of it and be frankly satisfied.

Such a success is attributed of course not to his partner's generosity, but to his own magic.

A feature which is universally recognised as reprehensible and discreditable, is a tendency to retain a number of valuables and be slow in passing them on. A man who did this would be called " hard in the Kula." The following is a native description of this feature as exhibited by the natives of the Amphletts.

" The Gumasila, their Kula is very hard ; they are mean, they are retentive. They would like to take hold of one *soulava*, of two, of three big ones, of four perhaps. A man would *pokala* them, he would *pokapokala ;* if he is a kinsman he will get a *soulava*. The Kayleula only, and the Gumasila are mean. The Dobu, the Du'a'u, the Kitava are good. Coming to Muyuwa—they are like Gumasila."

This means that a man in Gumasila would let a number of necklaces accumulate in his possession ; would require plenty of food as *pokala*—a characteristic reduplication describes the insistance and perseverance in *pokala*—and even then he would give a necklace to a kinsman only. When I inquired from the same informant whether such a mean man would also run a risk of being killed by sorcery, he answered :

" A man, who is very much ahead in the Kula—he will die—the mean man not ; he will sit in peace.

III

Returning now to the concrete proceedings of the Kula, let us follow the movements of a Sinaketan *toliwaga*. He has presumably received a necklace or two on his arrival ; but he has more partners and he expects more valuables. Before he receives his fill, he has to keep a taboo. He may not partake of any local food, neither yams, nor coco-nuts, nor betel pepper or nut. According to their belief, if he transgressed this taboo he would not receive any more valuables. He tries also to soften the heart of his partner by feigning disease. He will remain in his canoe and send word that he is ill. The Dobu man will know what such a conventional disease means. None the less, he may yield to this mode of persuasion. If this ruse does not succeed, the man may have recourse to magic. There is a formula called *kwoygapani* or ' enmeshing magic,' which seduces the mind of a man on whom it is practised, makes him silly, and thus amenable to persuasion. The formula is recited over a betel-nut or two, and these are given to the partner and to his wife or sister.

KWOYGAPANI SPELL

" O *kwega* leaf ; O friendly *kwega* leaf ; O *kwega* leaf hither ; O *kwega* leaf thither ! "

" I shall enter through the mouth of the woman of Dobu ; I shall come out through the mouth of the man of Dobu. I shall enter through the mouth of the man of Dobu ; I shall come out through the mouth of the woman of Dobu."

" Seducing *kwega* leaf ; enmeshing *kwega* leaf ; the mind of the woman of Dobu is seduced by the *kwega* leaf, is enmeshed by the *kwega* leaf."

The expression " is seduced," " is enmeshed " by the *kwega* leaf, is repeated with a string of words such as : " Thy mind, O man of Dobu," " thy refusal, O woman of Dobu," " Thy disinclination, O woman of Dobu," " Thy bowels, thy tongue, thy liver," going thus over all the organs of understanding and feeling, and over the words which describe these faculties. The last part is identical with that of one or two formulæ previously quoted :

" No more it is my mother ; my mother art thou, O woman of Dobu, etc." (Compare the Kaykakaya and Ka'ubana'i spells of the previous chapter.)

Kwega is a plant, probably belonging to the same family as betel pepper, and its leaves are chewed with areca-nut and lime, when real betel-pods (*mwayye*) are not available. The *kwega* is, remarkably enough, invoked in more than one magical formula, instead of the real betel-pod. The middle part is quite clear. In it, the seducing and enmeshing power of the *kwega* is cast over all the mental faculties of the Dobuan, and on the anatomical seats of these faculties. After the application of this magic, all the resources of the soliciting man are exhausted. He has to give up hope, and take to eating the fruit of Dobu, as his taboo lapses.

Side by side with the Kula, the subsidiary exchange of ordinary goods takes place. In Chapter VI, Division VI, we have classified the various types of *give and take*, as they are to be found in the Trobriand Islands. The inter-tribal transactions which now take place in Dobu also fit into that scheme

The Kula itself belongs to class (6), ' Ceremonial Barter with deferred payment.' The offering of the *pari*, of landing gifts by the visitors, returned by the *talo'i* or farewell gifts from the hosts fall into the class (4) of presents more or less equivalent. Finally, between the visitors and the local people there takes place, also, barter pure and simple (*gimwali*). Between partners, however, there is never a direct exchange of the *gimwali* type. The local man will as a rule contribute a bigger present, for the *talo'i* always exceeds the *pari* in quantity and value, and small presents are also given to the visitors during their stay. Of course, if in the *pari* there were included gifts of high value, like a stone blade or a good lime spoon, such solicitary gifts would always be returned in strictly equivalent form. The rest would be liberally exceeded in value.

The trade takes place between the visitors and local natives, who are not their partners, but who must belong to the community with whom the Kula is made. Thus, Numanuma, Tu'utauna and Bwayowa are the three communities which form what we have called the ' Kula community' or ' Kula unit,' with whom the Sinaketans stand in the relation of partnership. And a Sinaketa man will *gimwali* (trade) only with a man from one of these villages who is not his personal partner. To use a native statement :

> " Some of our goods we give in *pari ;* some we keep back ; later on, we *gimwali* it. They bring their areca-nut, their sago, they put it down. They want some article of ours, they say : ' I want this stone blade.' We give it, we put the betel-nut, the sago into our canoe. If they give us, however, a not sufficient quantity, we rate them. Then they bring more."

This is a clear definition of the *gimwali*, with haggling and adjustment of equivalence in the act.

When the visiting party from Sinaketa arrive, the natives from the neighbouring districts, that is, from the small island of Dobu proper, from the other side of Dawson Straits, from Deyde'i, the village to the South, will assemble in the three Kula villages. These natives from other districts bring with them a certain amount of goods. But they must not trade directly with the visitors from Boyowa. They must exchange their goods with the local natives, and these again will trade them with the Sinaketans. Thus the hosts from the Kula community act as intermediaries in any trading relations between the Sinaketans and the inhabitants of more remote districts.

To sum up the sociology of these transactions, we may say that the visitor enters into a threefold relation with the Dobuan natives. First, there is his partner, with whom he exchanges general gifts on the basis of free give and take, a type of transaction, running side by side with the Kula proper. Then there is the local resident, not his personal Kula partner, with whom he carries on *gimwali*. Finally there is the stranger with whom an indirect exchange is carried on through the intermediation of the local men. With all this, it must not be imagined that the commercial aspect of the gathering is at all conspicuous. The concourse of the natives is great, mainly owing to their curiosity, to see the ceremonial reception of the *uvalaku* party. But if I say that every visitor from Boyowa, brings and carries away about half-a-dozen articles, I do not under-state the case. Some of these articles the Sinaketan has acquired in the industrial districts of Boyowa during his preliminary trading expedition (see Chapter VI, Division III). On these he scores a definite gain. A few samples of the prices paid in Boyowa and those received in Dobu will indicate the amount of this gain.

Kuboma to Sinaketa.		Dobu to Sinaketa.
1 *tanepopo* basket =	12 coco-nuts	=12 coco-nuts + sago + 1 belt
1 comb =	4 coco-nuts	4 coco-nuts + 1 bunch of betel
1 armlet =	8 coco-nuts	8 coco-nuts + 2 bundles of betel
1 lime pot =	12 coco-nuts	=12 coco-nuts + 2 pieces of sago

This table shows in its second column the prices paid by the Sinaketans to the industrial villages of Kuboma, a district in the Northern Trobriands. In the third column what they receive in Dobu is recorded. The table has been obtained from a Sinaketan informant, and it probably is far from accurate, and the transactions are sure to vary greatly in the gain which they afford. There is no doubt, however, that for each article, the Sinaketan would ask the price which he paid for them as well as some extra article.

Thus we see that there is in this transaction a definite gain obtained by the middlemen. The natives of Sinaketa act as intermediaries between the industrial centres of the Trobriands and Dobu, whereas their hosts play the same rôle between the Sinaketans and the men from the outlying districts.

Besides trading and obtaining of Kula valuables, the natives of Sinaketa visit their friends and their distant relatives, who, as we saw before, are to be found in this district owing to migrations. The visitors walk across the flat, fertile plain from one hamlet to the other, enjoying some of the marvellous and unknown sights of this district. They are shown the hot springs of Numanuma and of Deyde'i, which are in constant eruption. Every few minutes, the water boils up in one spring after another of each group, throwing up jets of spray a few metres high. The plain around these springs is barren, with nothing but here and there a stunted kind of eucalyptus tree. This is the only place in the whole of Eastern New Guinea where as far as I know, eucalyptus trees are to be found. This was at least the information of some intelligent natives, in whose company I visited the springs, and who had travelled all over the Eastern islands and the East end of the mainland.

The land-locked bays and lagoons, the Northern end of Dawson Strait, enclosed like a lake by mountains and volcanic cones, all this must also appear strange and beautiful to the Trobrianders. In the villages, they are entertained by their male friends, the language spoken by both parties being that of Dobu, which differs completely from Kiriwinian, but which the Sinaketans learn in early youth. It is remarkable that no one in Dobu speaks Kiriwinian.

As said above, no sexual relations of any description take place between the visitors and the women of Dobu. As one of the informants told me :

> " We do not sleep with women of Dobu, for Dobu is the final mountain (Koyaviguna Dobu); it is a taboo of the *mwasila* magic."

But when I enquired, whether the results of breaking this taboo would be baneful to their success in Kula only, the reply was that they were afraid of breaking it, and that it was

ordained of old (*tokunabogwo ayguri*) that no man should interfere with the women of Dobu. As a matter of fact, the
Sinaketans are altogether afraid of the Dobuans, and they
would take good care not to offend them in any way.

After some three or four days' sojourn in Dobu, the
Sinaketan fleet starts on its return journey. There is no
special ceremony of farewell. In the early morning, they
receive their *talo'i* (farewell gifts) of food, betel-nut, objects of
use and sometimes also a Kula valuable is enclosed amongst the
the *talo'i*.   Heavily laden as they are, they lighten their canoes
by means of a magic called *kaylupa*, and sail away northwards
once more.

Chapter XV

THE JOURNEY HOME—THE FISHING AND WORKING OF THE KALOMA SHELL

I

THE return journey of the Sinaketan fleet is made by following exactly the same route as the one by which they came to Dobu. In each inhabited island, in every village, where a halt had previously been made, they stop again, for a day or a few hours. In the hamlets of Sanaroa, in Tewara and in the Amphletts, the partners are revisited. Some Kula valuables are received on the way back, and all the *talo'i* gifts from those intermediate partners are also collected on the return journey. In each of these villages people are eager to hear about the reception which the *uvalaku* party have received in Dobu ; the yield in valuables is discussed, and comparisons are drawn between the present occasion and previous records.

No magic is performed now, no ceremonial takes place, and there would be very little indeed to say about the return journey but for two important incidents ; the fishing for spondylus shell (*kaloma*) in Sanaroa Lagoon, and the display and comparison of the yield of Kula valuables on Muwa beach.

The natives of Sinaketa, as we have seen in the last chapter, acquire a certain amount of the Koya produce by means of trade. There are, however, certain articles, useful yet unobtainable in the Trobriands, and freely accessible in the Koya, and to these the Trobrianders help themselves. The glassy forms of lava, known as obsidian, can be found in great quantities over the slopes of the hills in Sanaroa and Dobu. This article, in olden days, served the Trobrianders as material for razors, scrapers, and sharp, delicate, cutting instruments. Pummice-stone abounding in this district is collected and carried to the Trobriands, where it is used for polishing. Red ochre is also procured there by the visitors, and so are the hard, basaltic stones (*binabina*) used for hammering and pounding and for magical purposes.   Finally, very fine silica sand, called *maya*, is collected on some of the beaches, and imported into the Trobriands, where it is used for polishing stone blades, of the kind which serve as tokens of value and which are manufactured up to the present day.

II

But by far the most important of the articles which the Trobrianders collect for themselves are the spondylus shells. These are freely, though by no means easily, accessible in the coral outcrops of Sanaroa Lagoon.   It is from this shell that the small circular perforated discs (*kaloma*) are made, out of which the necklaces of the Kula are composed, and which also serve for ornamenting almost all the articles of value or of artistic finish which are used within the Kula district.   But, only in two localities within the district are these discs manufactured, in Sinaketa and in Vakuta, both villages in Southern Boyowa. The shell can be found also in the Trobriand Lagoon, facing these two villages.   But the specimens found in Sanaroa are much better in colour, and I think more easily procured. The fishing in this latter locality, however, is done by the Sinaketans only.

Whether the fishing is done in their own Lagoon, near an uninhabited island called Nanoula, or in Sanaroa, it is always a big, ceremonial affair, in which the whole community takes part in a body.   The magic, or at least part of it, is done for the whole community by the magician of the *kaloma* (*towosina kaloma*), who also fixes the dates, and conducts the ceremonial part of the proceedings.   As the spondylus shell furnishes one of the essential episodes of a Kula expedition, a detailed account both of fishing and of manufacturing must be here given.   The native name, *kaloma* (in the Southern Massim districts the word *sapi-sapi* is used) describes both the shell and the manufactured discs.   The shell is the large spondylus shell, containing a crystalline layer of a red colour, varying from dirty brick-red to a soft, raspberry pink, the latter being by far the most prized.   It lives in the cavities of coral outcrop, scattered among shallow mud-bottomed lagoons.

This shell is, according to tradition, associated with the village of Sinaketa.   According to a Sinaketan legend, once upon a time, three *guya'u* (chief) women, belonging to the

Tabalu sub-clan of the Malasi clan, wandered along, each choosing her place to settle in. The eldest selected the village of Omarakana ; the second went to Gumilababa ; the youngest settled in Sinaketa. She had *kaloma* discs in her basket, and they were threaded on a long, thin stick, called *viduna*, such as is used in the final stage of manufacture. She remained first in a place called Kaybwa'u, but a dog howled, and she moved further on. She heard again a dog howling, and she took a *kaboma* (wooden plate) and went on to the fringing reef to collect shells. She found there the *momoka* (white spondylus), and she exclaimed: " Oh, this is the *kaloma !* " She looked closer, and said : " Oh no, you are not red. Your name is *momoka*." She took then the stick with the *kaloma* discs and thrust it into a hole of the reef. It stood there, but when she looked at it, she said : " Oh, the people from inland would come and see you and pluck you off." She went, she pulled out the stick ; she went into a canoe, and she paddled. She paddled out into the sea. She anchored there, pulled the discs off the stick, and she threw them into the sea so that they might come into the coral outcrop. She said : " It is forbidden that the inland natives should take the valuables. The people of Sinaketa only must dive." Thus only the Sinaketa people know the magic, and how to dive.

This myth presents certain remarkable characteristics. I shall not enter into its sociology, though it differs in that respect from the Kiriwinian myths, in which the equality of the Sinaketan and the Gumilababan chiefs with those of Omarakana is not acknowledged. It is characteristic that the Malasi woman in this myth shows an aversion to the dog, the totem animal of the Lukuba clan, a clan which according to mythical and historical data had to recede before and yield its priority to the Malasi (compare Chapter XII, Division IV). Another detail of interest is that she brings the *kaloma* on their sticks, as they appear in the final stage of manufacturing. In this form, also, she tries to plant them on the reef. The finished *kaloma*, however, to use the words of one of my informants, " looked at her, the water swinging it to and fro ; flashing its red eyes." And the woman, seeing it, pulls out the too accessible and too inviting *kaloma* and scatters them over the deep sea. Thus she makes them inaccessible to the uninitiated inland villagers, and monopolises them for Sinaketa. There can be no doubt that the villages of Vakuta have learnt this industry from the Sinaketans. The myth is hardly known in Vakuta, only a few are experts in diving and manufacturing ; there is a tradition about a late transference of this industry there ; finally the Vakutans have never fished for *kaloma* in the Sanaroa Lagoon.

Now let us describe the technicalities and the ceremonial connected with the fishing for *kaloma*. It will be better to give an account of how this is done in the Lagoon of Sinaketa, round the sandbank of Nanoula, as this is the normal and typical form of *kaloma* fishing. Moreover, when the Sinaketans do it in Sanaroa, the proceedings are very much the same, with just one or two phases missed out.

The office of magician of the *kaloma* (*towosina kaloma*) is hereditary in two sub-clans, belonging to the Malasi clan, and one of them is that of the main chief of Kasi'etana. After the Monsoon season is over, that is, some time in March or April, *ogibukuvi* (i.e., in the season of the new yams) the magician gives the order for preparations. The community give him a gift called *sousula*, one or two bringing a *vaygu'a*, the rest supplying *gugu'a* (ordinary chattels), and some food. Then they prepare the canoes, and get ready the *binabina* stones, with which the spondylus shell will be knocked off the reef.

Next day, in the morning, the magician performs a rite called ' *kaykwa'una la'i*,' ' the attracting of the reef,' for, as in the case of several other marine beings, the main seat of the *kaloma* is far away. Its dwelling place is the reef Ketabu, somewhere between Sanaroa and Dobu. In order to make it move and come towards Nanoula, it is necessary to recite the above-named spell. This is done by the magician as he walks up and down on the Sinaketa beach and casts his words into the open, over the sea, towards the distant seat of the *kaloma*. The *kaloma* then ' stand up ' (*itolise*) that is start from their original coral outcrop (*vatu*) and come into the Lagoon of Sinaketa. This spell, I obtained from To'udavada, the present chief of Kasi'etana, and descendant of the original giver of this shell, the woman of the myth. It begins with a long list of ancestral names ; then follows a boastful picture of how the whole fleet admires the magical success of the magician's spell. The key-word in the main part is the word ' *itolo* ' : ' it stands up,' i.e., ' it starts,' and with this, there are enumerated all the various classes of the *kaloma* shell, differentiated according to size, colour and quality. It ends up with another boast ; " My canoe is overladed with shell so that it sinks," which is repeated with varying phraseology.

This spell the magician may utter once only, or he may repeat it several times on successive days. He fixes then the final date for the fishing expedition. On the evening before that date, the men perform some private magic, every one in his own house. The hammering stone, the *gabila*, which is always a *binabina* (it is a stone imported from the Koya), is charmed over. As a rule it is put on a piece of dried banana leaf with some red hibiscus blossoms and leaves or flowers of red colour. A formula is uttered over it, and the whole is then wrapped up in the banana leaf and kept there until it is used. This will make the stone a lucky one in hitting off many shells, and it will make the shells very red.

Another rite of private magic consists in charming a large mussel shell, with which, on the next morning, the body of the canoe will be scraped. This makes the sea clear, so that the diver may easily see and frequently find his spondylus shells.

Next morning the whole fleets starts on the expedition. Some food has been taken into the canoes, as the fishing usually lasts for a few days, the nights being spent on the beach of Nanoula. When the canoes arrive at a certain point, about half-way between Sinaketa and Nanoula, they all range themselves in a row. The canoe of the magician is at the right flank, and he medicates a bunch of red hibiscus flowers, some red croton leaves, and the leaves of the red-blossomed mangrove — red coloured substances being used to make the shell red, magically. Then, passing in front of all the other canoes, he rubs their prows with the bundle of leaves. After that, the canoes at both ends of the row begin to punt along, the row evolving into a circle, through which presently the canoe of the magician passes, punting along its diameter. At this place in the Lagoon, there is a small *vatu* (coral outcrop) called Vitukwayla'i. This is called the *vatu* of the *baloma* (spirits). At this *vatu* the magician's canoe stops, and he orders some of its crew to dive down and here to begin the gathering of shells.

Some more private magic is performed later on by each canoe on its own account. The anchor stone is charmed with some red hibiscus flowers, in order to make the spondylus shell red.   There is another private magic called ' sweeping of the sea,' which, like the magic of the mussel shell, mentioned above, makes the sea clear and transparent.   Finally, there is an evil magic called ' besprinkling with salt water.'   If a man does it over the others, he will annul the effects of their magic, and frustrate their efforts, while he himself would arouse astonishment and suspicion by the amount of shell collected. Such a man would dive down into the water, take some brine into his mouth, and emerging, spray it towards the other canoes, while he utters the evil charm.

So much for the magic and the ceremonial associated with the spondylus fishing in the Trobriand Lagoon.   In Sanaroa, exactly the same proceedings take place, except that there is no attracting of the reef, probably because they are already at the original seat of the *kaloma*.   Again I was told that some of the private magic would be performed in Sinaketa before the fleet sailed on the Kula expedition   The objects medicated would be then kept, well wrapped in dried leaves.

It may be added that neither in the one Lagoon nor in the other are there any private, proprietory rights to coral outcrops. The whole community of Sinaketa have their fishing grounds in the Lagoon, within which every man may hunt for his spondylus shell, and catch his fish at times.   If the other spondylus fishing community, the Vakutans, encroached upon their grounds, there would be trouble, and in olden days, fighting. Private ownership in coral outcrops exists in the Northern villages of the Lagoon, that is in Kavataria, and the villages on the island of Kayleula.

III

We must now follow the later stages of the *kaloma* industry. The technology of the proceedings is so mixed up with remarkable sociological and economic arrangements that it will be better to indicate it first in its main outlines.   The spondylus consists of a shell, the size and shape of a hollowed out half of a pear, and of a flat, small lid.   It is only the first part which is worked.   First it has to be broken into pieces with a *binabina* or an *utukema* (green stone imported from Woodlark Island) as shown on Plate L (A).   On each piece, then, can be seen the stratification of the shell : the outside layer of soft, chalky substance ; under this, the layer of red, hard, calcareous material, and then the inmost, white, crystalline stratum. Both the outside and inside have to be rubbed off, but first each piece has to be roughly rounded up, so as to form a thick circular lump. Such a lump (see foregrounds of Plates L (A), L (B)) is then put in the hole of a cylindrical piece of wood. This latter serves as a handle with which the lumps are rubbed on a piece of flat sandstone (see Plate L (B)). The rubbing is carried on so far till the outside and inside layers are gone, and there remains only a red, flat tablet, polished on both sides. In the middle of it, a hole is drilled through by means of a pump drill—*gigi'u*—(see Plate LI), and a number of such perforated discs are then threaded on a thin, but tough stick (see Plate LII), with which we have already met in the myth. Then the cylindrical roll is rubbed round and round on the flat sandstone, until its form becomes perfectly symmetrical (see Plate LII). Thus a number of flat, circular discs, polished all round and perforated in the middle, are produced. The breaking and the drilling, like the diving are done exclusively by men. The polishing is as a rule woman's work.

This technology is associated with an interesting sociological relation between the maker and the man for whom the article is made. As has been stated in Chapter II, one of the main features of the Trobriand organisation consists of the mutual duties between a man and his wife's maternal kinsmen. They have to supply him regularly with yams at harvest time, while he gives them the present of a valuable now and then. The manufacture of *kaloma* valuables in Sinaketa is very often associated with this relationship. The Sinaketan manufacturer makes his *kutadababile* (necklace of large beads) for one of his relatives-in-law, while this latter pays him in food. In accordance with this custom, it happens very frequently that a Sinaketan man marries a woman from one of the agricultural inland villages, or even a woman of Kiriwina. Of course, if he has no relatives-in-law in one of these villages, he will have friends or distant relatives, and he will make the string for one or the other of them. Or else he will produce one for himself, and launch it into the Kula. But the most typical and interesting case is, when the necklace is produced to order for a man who repays it according to a remarkable economic system, a system similar to the payments in instalments, which I have mentioned with regard to canoe making. I shall give here, following closely the native text, a translation of an account of the payments for *kaloma* making.

ACCOUNT OF THE KALOMA MAKING

Supposing some man from inland lives in Kiriwina or in Luba or in one of the villages nearby ; he wants a *katuda-babile*. He would request an expert fisherman who knows how to dive for *kaloma*. This man agrees ; he dives, he dives . . . till it is sufficient ; his *vataga* (large folding basket) is already full, this man (the inlander) hears the rumour ; he, the master of the *kaloma* (that is, the man for whom the necklace will be made) says : " Good ! I shall just have a look ! " He would come, he would see, he would not give any *vakapula* payment. He (here the Sinaketan diver is meant) would say : " Go, tomorrow, I shall break the shell, come here, give me *vakapula*." Next day, he (the inlander) would cook food, he would bring, he would give *vakapula ;* he (the diver) would break the shell. Next day, the same. He (the inlander) would give the *vakapula*, he (the diver) would break the shell. Supposing the breaking is already finished, he (the diver) would say : " Good ! already the breaking is finished, I shall polish." Next day, he (the inlander) would cook food, would bring bananas, coco-nut, betel-nut, sugar cane, would give it as *vakapula ;* this man (the diver) polishes. The polishing already finished, he would speak : " Good ! To-morrow I shall drill." This man (the inlander) would bring food, bananas, coco-nuts, sugar cane, he would give it as *vakapula :* it would be abundant, for soon already the necklace will be finished. The same, he would give a big *vakapula* on the occasion of the rounding up of the cylinder, for soon everything will be finished. When finished, we thread it on a string, we wash it. (Note the change from the third singular into the first plural). We give it to our wife, we blow the conch shell ; she would go, she would carry his valuable to this man, our relative-in-law. Next day, he would *yomelu ;* he would catch a pig, he would break off a bunch of betel-nut, he would cut sugar cane, bananas, he would fill the baskets with food, and spike the coco-nut on a multi-forked piece of wood. By-and-by he would bring it. Our house would be filled up. Later on we would make a distribution of the bananas, of the sugar cane, of the betel-nut. We give it to our helpers. We sit, we sit (i.e., we wait) ; at harvest time he brings yams, he *karibudaboda* (he gives the payment of that name), the necklace. He would bring the food and fill out our yam house.

This narrative, like many pieces of native information, needs certain corrections of perspective. In the first place, events here succeed one another with a rapidity quite foreign to the extremely leisurely way in which natives usually accomplish such a lengthy process as the making of a *katudababile*. The amount of food which, in the usual manner, is enumerated over and over again in this narrative would probably not be exaggerated, for—such is native economy—a man who makes a necklace to order would get about twice as much or even more for it than it would fetch in any other transaction. On the other hand, it must be remembered that what is represented here as the final payment, the *karibudaboda*, is nothing else but the normal filling up of the yam house, always done by a man's relations-in-law. None the less, in a year in which a *katudababile* would be made, the ordinary yearly harvest gift would be styled the ' *karibudaboda* payment for the necklace.' The giving of the necklace to the wife, who afterwards carries it to her brother or kinsman, is also characteristic of the relation between relatives-in-law.

In Sinaketa and Vakuta only the necklaces made of bigger shell and tapering towards the end are made. The real Kula article, in which the discs are much thinner, smaller in diameter and even in size from one end of the necklace to the other, these were introduced into the Kula at other points, and I shall speak about this subject in one of the following chapters (Chapter XXI), where the other branches of the Kula are described.

IV

Now, having come to an end of this digression on *kaloma*, let us return for another short while to our Sinaketan party, whom we have left on the Lagoon of Sanaroa. Having obtained a sufficient amount of the shells, they set sail, and re-visiting Tewara and Gumasila, stopping perhaps for a night on one of the sandbanks of Pilolu, they arrive at last in their home Lagoon. But before rejoining their people in their villages, they stop for the last halt on Muwa. Here they make what is called *tanarere*, a comparison and display of the valuables obtained on this trip. From each canoe, a mat or two are spread on the sand beach, and the men put their necklaces on the mat. Thus a long row of valuables lies on the beach, and the members of the expedition walk up and down, admire, and count them. The chiefs would, of course, have always the greatest haul, more especially the one who has been the *toli'uvalaku* on that expedition.

After this is over, they return to the village. Each canoe blows its conch shell, a blast for each valuable that it contains. When a canoe has obtained no *vaygu'a* at all, this means great shame and distress for its members, and especially for the *toliwaga*. Such a canoe is said to *bisikureya*, which means literally ' to keep a fast.'

On the beach all the villagers are astir. The women, who have put on their new grass petticoats (*sevata'i*) specially made for this occasion, enter the water and approach the canoes to unload them. No special greetings pass between them and their husbands. They are interested in the food brought from Dobu, more especially in the sago.

People from other villages assemble also in great numbers to greet the incoming party. Those who have supplied their friends or relatives with provisions for their journey, receive now sago, betel-nuts and coco-nuts in repayment. Some of the welcoming crowd have come in order to make Kula. Even from the distant districts of Luba and Kiriwina natives will travel to Sinaketa, having a fair idea of the date of the arrival of the Kula party from Dobu. The expedition will be talked over, the yield counted, the recent history of the important valuables described. But this stage leads us already into the subject of inland Kula, which will form the subject of one of the following chapters.

Chapter XVI

THE RETURN VISIT OF THE DOBUANS TO SINAKETA

I

In the twelve preceding chapters, we have followed an expedition from Sinaketa to Dobu. But branching off at almost every step from its straight track, we studied the various associated institutions and underlying beliefs; we quoted magical formulæ, and told mythical stories, and thus we broke up the continuous thread of the narrative. In this chapter, as we are already acquainted with the customs, beliefs and institutions implied in the Kula, we are ready to follow a straight and consecutive tale of an expedition in the inverse direction, from Dobu to Sinaketa.

As I have seen, indeed followed, a big *uvalaku* expedition from the South to the Trobriands, I shall be able to give some of the scenes from direct impression, and not from reconstruction. Such a reconstruction for one who has seen much of the natives' tribal life and has a good grip over intelligent informants is neither very difficult nor need it be fanciful at all. Indeed, towards the end of my second visit, I had several times opportunities to check such a reconstruction by witnessing the actual occurrence, for after my first year's stay in the Trobriands I had written out already some of my material. As a rule, even in minute details, my reconstructions hardly differed from reality, as the tests have shown. None the less, it is possible for an Ethnographer to enter into concrete details with more conviction when he describes things actually seen.

In September, 1917, an *uvalaku* expedition was led by Kouta'uya from Sinaketa to Dobu. The Vakutans joining them on the way, and the canoes of the Amphletts following them also, some forty canoes finally arrived at the western shore of Dawson Straits. It was arranged then and there that a return expedition from that district should visit Sinaketa in

about six months' time. Kauyaporu, the *esa'esa* (headman)
of Kesora'i hamlet in the village of Bwayowa, had a pig with
circular tusks. He decided therefore to arrange an *uvalaku*
expedition, at the beginning of which the pig was to be killed
and feasted upon and its tusks turned into ornaments.

When, in November, 1917, I passed through the district,
the preparing of the canoes was already afoot. All of those,
which still could be repaired, had been taken to pieces and were
being relashed, recaulked and repainted. In some hamlets,
new dugouts were being scooped. After a few months stay in
the Trobriands, I went South again in March, 1918, intending
to spend some time in the Amphletts. Landing there is always
difficult, as there are no anchorages near the shore, and it is
quite impossible to disembark in rough weather at night. I
arrived late in a small cutter, and had to cruise between
Gumasila and Domdom, intending to wait till daybreak and
then effect a landing. In the middle of the night, however,
a violent north-westerly squall came down, and making a
split in the main-sail, forced us to run before the wind, southwards towards Dobu. It was on this night that the native
boys employed in the boat, saw the *mulukwausi* flaming up at
the head of the mast. The wind dropped before daybreak,
and we entered the Lagoon of Sanaroa, in order to repair the
sail. During the three days we stopped there, I roamed over
the country, climbing its volcanic cones, paddling up the
creeks and visiting the villages scattered on the coral plain.
Everywhere I saw signs of the approaching departure for
Boyowa ; the natives preparing their canoes on the beach to
be loaded, collecting food in the gardens and making sago in
the jungle. At the head of one of the creeks, in the midst of a
sago swamp, there was a long, low shelter which serves as a
dwelling to Dobuan natives from the main Island when they
come to gather sago. This swamp was said to be reserved to
a certain community of Tu'utauna.

Another day I came upon a party of local natives from
Sanaroa, who were pounding sago pulp out of a palm, and
sluicing it with water. A big tree had been felled, its bark
stripped in the middle of the trunk in a large square, and the
soft, fleshy interior laid open. There were three men standing
in a row before it and pounding away at it. A few more men
waited to relieve the tired ones. The pounding instruments,

half club, half adzes, had thick but not very broad blades of green stone, of the same type as I have seen among the Mailu natives of the South Coast.*

The pulp was then carried in baskets to a neighbouring stream. At this spot there was a natural trough, one of the big, convex scales, which form the basis of the sago leaf. In the middle of it, a sieve was made of a piece of coco-nut spathing, a fibre which covers the root of a coco-nut leaf, and looks at first sight exactly like a piece of roughly woven material. Water was directed so that it flowed into the trough at its broad end, coming out at the narrow one. The sago pulp was put at the top, the water carried away with it the powdered sago starch, while the wooden, husky fibres were retained by the sieve. The starch was then carried with the water into a big wooden canoe-shaped trough ; there the heavier starch settled down, while the water welled over the brim. When there is plenty of starch, the water is drained off carefully and the starch is placed into another of the trough-shaped, sago leaf bases, where it is allowed to dry. In such receptacles it is then carried on a trading expedition, and is thus counted as one unit of sago.

I watched the proceedings for a long time with great interest. There is something fascinating about the big, anti-deluvian-looking sago palm, so malignant and unapproachable in its unhealthy, prickly swamp, being turned by man into food by such simple and direct methods. The sago produced and eaten by the natives is a tough, starchy stuff, of dirty white colour, very unpalatable. It has the consistency of rubber, and the taste of very poor, unleavened bread. It is not clear, like the article which is sold under the name of sago in our groceries but is mealy, tough, and almost elastic. The natives consider it a great delicacy, and bake it into little cakes, or boil it into dumplings.

The main fleet of the Dobuans started some time in the second half of March from their villages, and went first to the beach of Sarubwoyna, where they held a ceremonial distribution of food, *eguya'i*, as it is called in Dobu. Then, offering the *pokala* to Aturamo'a and Atu'a'ine, they sailed by way of Sanaroa and Tewara, passing the tabooed rock of Gurewaya to

---

* See the Author's Memoir, "The Natives of Mailu" in Transactions of the R. Society of S. Australia for 1915, p. 598.

the Amphletts. The wind was light and changeable, weak S.W. breezes prevailing. The progress of this stage of the journey must have been very slow. The natives must have spent a few nights on the intermediate islands and sandbanks, a few canoes' crews camping at one spot.

At that time I had already succeeded in reaching the Amphletts, and had been busy for two or three weeks doing ethnographic work, though not very successfully ; for, as I have already once or twice remarked, the natives here are very bad informants. I knew of course that the Dobuan fleet was soon to come, but as my experience had taught me to mistrust native time-tables and fixtures of date, I did not expect them to be punctual. In this, however, I was mistaken. On a Kula expedition, when the dates are once fixed, the natives make real and strenuous efforts to keep to them. In the Amphletts the people were busy preparing for the expedition, because they had the intention of joining the Dobuans and proceeding with them to the Trobriands. A few canoes went to the mainland to fetch sago, pots were being mustered and made ready for stowing away, canoes were overhauled. When the small expedition returned from the mainland with sago, after a week or so, a *sagali* (in Amphlettan ; *madare*), that is, a ceremonial distribution of food was held on the neighbouring island, Nabwageta.

My arrival was a very untoward event to the natives, and complicated matters, causing great annoyance to Tovasana, the main headman. I had landed in his own little village, Nu'agasi, on the island of Gumasila, for it was impossible to anchor near the big village, nor would there have been room for pitching a tent. Now, in the Amphletts, a white man is an exceedingly rare occurrence, and to my knowledge, only once before, a white trader remained there for a few weeks. To leave me alone with the women and one or two old men was impossible, according to their ideas and fears, and none of the younger men wanted to forgo the privilege and pleasure of taking part in the expedition. At last, I promised them to move to the neighbouring island of Nabwageta, as soon as the men were gone, and with this they were satisfied.

As the date fixed for the arrival of the Dobuans approached, the excitement grew. Little by little the news arrived, and was eagerly received and conveyed to me : " Some sixty canoes

of the Dobuans are coming," " the fleet is anchored off Tewara,"
" each canoe is heavily laden with food and gifts," " Kauyaporu
sails in his canoe, he is *toli'uvalaku*, and has a big pandanus
streamer attached to the prow." A string of other names
followed which had very little meaning for me, since I was
not acquainted with the Dobuan natives. From another part
of the world, from the Trobriands, the goal of the whole expedition, news reached us again : " To'uluwa, the chief of Kiriwina has gone to Kitava—he will soon come back, bringing
plenty of *mwali*." " The Sinaketans are going there to fetch
some of the *mwali*." " The Vakutans have been in Kitava and
brought back great numbers of *mwali*." It was astonishing to
hear all this news, arriving at a small island, apparently completely isolated with its tiny population, within these savage
and little navigated seas ; news only a few days old, yet
reporting events which had occurred at a travelling distance of
some hundred miles.

It was interesting to follow up the way it had come. The
earlier news about the Dobuans had been brought by the
canoes, which had fetched the sago to Gumasila from the main
island. A few days later, a canoe from one of the main island
villages had arrived here, and on its way had passed the
Dobuans in Tewara. The news from the Trobriands in the
North had been brought by the Kuyawa canoe which had
arrived a couple of days before in Nabwageta (and whose
visit to Nu'agasi I have described in Chapter XI). All these
movements were not accidental, but connected with the
uvalaku expedition. To show the complexity, as well as the
precise timing of the various movements and events, so perfectly synchronised over a vast area, in connection with the
uvalaku, I have tabulated them in the Chart, facing this page,
in which almost all the dates are quite exact, being based
on my own observations. This Chart also gives a clear,
synoptic picture of an *uvalaku*, and it will be useful to refer to
it, in reading this Chapter.

In olden days, not less than now, there must have been an
ebulition in the inter-tribal relations, and a great stirring
from one place to another, whenever an *uvalaku* Kula was
afoot. Thus, news would be carried rapidly over great distances, the movements of the vast numbers of natives would be
co-ordinated, and dates fixed. As has been said already, a

TIME-TABLE OF THE UVALAKU EXPEDITION, DOBU TO SINAKETA, 1918

THE PREVIOUS UVALAKU

DATE

September, 1917 .. The expedition, led by Kouta'uya from Sinaketa to Dobu.

PREPARATORY STAGE

Oct., 1917—Feb., 1918 Building of new canoes and repairing of old ones, in the district of N.W. Dobu.

Feb.—March, 1918 .. Sago making, collecting of trade and food.

Middle of March   Launching, fitting and loading of the canoes ; preliminary magic.

THE SAILING

About 25th March .. The Dobuan canoes start on their overseas trip.

About same time .. [In Boyowa : the Vakutans return from Kitava with a good haul of *mwali*].

Same time   .. [In the Amphletts : preparations to sail ; collecting food ; repairing canoes.]

About 28th March .. [In Boyowa : To'uluwa returns from Kitava bringing *mwali*.]

Same time   .. [In the Amphletts : news reach of the approaching fleet from Dobu ; of the doings in Boyowa.]

29th March   .. [In the Amphletts : part of the canoes sail ahead to Vakuta.]

31st March   .. The Dobuan fleet arrives in the Amphletts.

1st April   .. They proceed on their journey to Boyowa.

2nd April   .. [In the Amphletts : rest of local canoes sail to Boyowa.]

Same day   .. [In Boyowa : the Sinaketans go to Kiriwina.]

3rd April   .. [In Boyowa : they return with the armshells.]

THE ARRIVAL OF THE DOBUANS IN BOYOWA

3rd April   .. The Dobuan fleet appears in Vakuta.

3rd-5th April .·. They receive Kula gifts, exchange presents and trade in Vakuta.

6th April   .. Arrival of the Dobuan fleet in Sinaketa, magic at the beach of Kaykuyawa, ceremonial reception.

6th-10th April .. The Dobuans (as well as the Amphlettans) remain in Sinaketa, receiving Kula presents, giving *pari* gifts and trading.

10th April   .. They all leave Sinaketa, receiving *talo'i* (farewell) gifts. The Dobuans sail south (and the Amphlettans to Kayleula and the smaller Western Trobriand Islands).

10th-14th April .. The Dobuans are engaged in fishing in the S. Lagoon.

RETURN JOURNEY

14th April   .. They reappear in Vakuta, and receive their *talo'i* (farewell) gifts.

15th April   .. They leave Vakuta.

About 20th or 21st .. *Tanarere* (competitive display and comparison) on the beach of Sarubwoyna, and return to Dobu.

culminating event of an expedition, in this case the arrival
of the Dobuan fleet in Sinaketa, would be always so timed as to
happen on, or just before, a full moon, and this would serve
as a general orientation for the preliminary movements, such
as in this case, the visits of the single canoes.

Indeed, from that moment, the events on and about the
Amphlett Islands moved rapidly. The day after the visit
from the Kuyawan canoes, the canoes of the main village of
Gumasila sailed off to the Trobriands, starting therefore a few
days ahead of the Dobuan *uvalaku* fleet. I rowed over in a
dinghy to the big village, and watched the loading and departing
of the canoes. There was a bustle in the village, and even a
few old women could be seen helping the men in their tasks.
The large canoes were being pushed into the water from their
supports, on which they were beached. They had been already
prepared for the journey there, their platforms covered with
plaited palm leaves, frames put in their bottoms to support the
cargo, boards placed crossways within the canoe to serve as
seats for the crew, the mast, rigging and sail laid handy. The
loading, however, begins only after the canoe is in water.
The large, trough-shaped chunks of sago were put at the bottom,
while men and women carefully brought out the big clay pots,
stowing them away with many precautions in special places in
the middle (see Plate XLVII). Then, one after the other,
the canoes went off, paddling round the southern end of the
island towards the West. At about ten o'clock in the morning,
the last canoe disappeared round the promontory, and the
village remained practically empty. There was no saying of
farewells, not a trace of any emotion on the part of those
leaving or those remaining. But it must be remembered that,
owing to my presence, no women except one or two old hags,
were visible on the shore. All my best informants gone, I
intended to move to Nabwageta next morning. At sunset, I
made a long excursion in my dinghy round the western shores
of Gumasila, and it was on that occasion that I discovered all
those who had left that morning on the Kula sitting on Giyasila
beach, in accordance with the Kula custom of a preliminary halt,
such as the one on Muwa described in Chapter VII.

Next morning, I left for the neighbouring island and village
of Nabwageta, and only after he saw me safely off, Tovasana
and his party left in his canoe, following the others to Vakuta.

In Nabwageta, the whole community were in the midst of their final preparations for departure, for they intended to wait for the Dobuans and sail with them to Kiriwina. All their canoes were being painted and renovated, a sail was being repaired on the beach (see Plate LIII). There were some minor distributions of food taking place in the village, the stuff being over and over again allotted and re-allotted, smaller pieces carved out of the big chunks and put into special wrappings. This constant handling of food is one of the most prominent features of tribal life in that part of the world. As I arrived, a sail for one of the canoes was just being finished by a group of men. In another canoe, I saw them mending the outrigger by attaching the small log of light, dry wood to make the old, water-logged float more buoyant. I could also watch in detail the final trimming of the canoes, the putting up of the additional frames, of the coco-nut mats, the making of the little cage in the central part for the pots and for the *lilava* (the sacred bundle), I was, nevertheless, not on sufficiently intimate terms with these Nabwageta natives to be allowed to witness any of the magic. Their system of *mwasila* is identical with that of Boyowa, in fact, it is borrowed from there.

Next day—in this village again I had difficulty in finding any good informants, a difficulty increased by the feverish occupation of all the men—I went for a long row in the afternoon with my two 'boys,' hoping to reach the island of Domdom. A strong current, which in this part is at places so pronounced that it breaks out into steep, tidal waves, made it impossible to reach our goal. Returning in the dark, my boys suddenly grew alert and excited, like hounds picking up a scent. I could perceive nothing in the dark, but they had discerned two canoes moving westwards. Within about half-an-hour, a fire became visible twinkling on the beach of a small, deserted island South of Domdom ; evidently some Dobuans were camping there. The excitement and intense interest shown by my boys, one a Dobuan, the other from Sariba (Southern Massim), gave me an inkling of the magnitude of this event —the vanguard of a big Kula fleet slowly creeping up towards one of its intermediate halting places. It also brought home to me vividly the inter-tribal character of this institution, which unites in one common and strongly emotional interest so many scattered communities. That night, as we learnt afterwards, a good number of canoes had anchored on the outlying deserted islands of the Amphletts, waiting for the rest of the fleet to arrive.   When we came that evening to Nabwageta, the news had already been received of the important event, and the whole village was astir.

Next day, the weather was particularly fine and clear, with the distant mountains wreathed only in light cumuli, their alluring outlines designed in transparent blue.   Early in the afternoon, with a blast of conch shell, a Dobuan waga, in full paint and decoration, and with the rich pandanus mat of the sail glowing like gold against the blue sea, came sailing round the promontory.   One after the other, at intervals of a few minutes each, other canoes came along, all sailing up to some hundred yards from the beach, and then, after furling the sail, paddling towards the shore (see Plate XL).   This was not a ceremonial approach, as the aim of the expedition this time did not embrace the Amphletts, but was directed towards the Trobriands only, Vakuta, and Sinaketa ; these canoes had put in only for an intermediate halt.   Nevertheless, it was a great event, especially as the canoes of Nabwageta were going to join with the fleet later on.   Out of the sixty or so Dobuan canoes, only about twenty-five with some 250 men in them had come to Nabwageta, the others having gone to the big village of Gumasila.   In any case, there were about five times as many men gathered in the village as one usually sees.   There was no Kula done at all, no conch-shells were blown on the shore, nor do I think were any presents given or received by either party. The men sat in groups round their friends' houses, the most distinguished visitors collected about the dwelling of Tobwa'ina, the main headman of Nabwageta.

Many canoes were anchored along the coast beyond the village beach, some tucked away into small coves, others moored in sheltered shallows.   The men sat on the shore round fires, preparing their food, which they took out of the provisions carried on the canoes.   Only the water did they obtain from the island, filling their coco-nut-made water vessels from the springs.   About a dozen canoes were actually moored at the village beach.   Late at night, I walked along the shore to observe their sleeping arrangements.   In the clear, moonlit night, the small fires burnt with a red, subdued glow ; there was always one of them between each two sleepers, consisting of

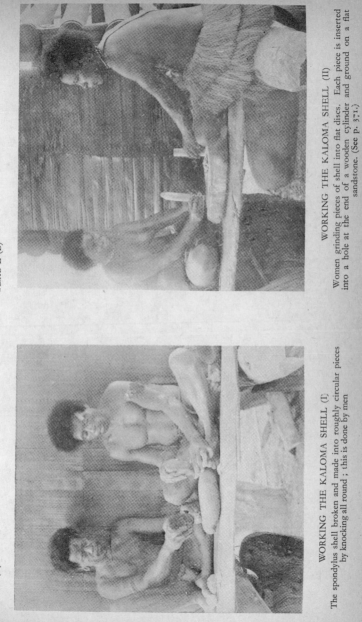

PLATE L (A)

PLATE L (B)

WORKING THE KALOMA SHELL (I)

The spondylus shell broken and made into roughly circular pieces by knocking all round ; this is done by men

WORKING THE KALOMA SHELL (II)

Women grinding pieces of shell into flat discs. Each piece is inserted into a hole at the end of a wooden cylinder and ground on a flat sandstone. (See p. 371.)

[face p. 384

PLATE LI

WORKING THE KALOMA SHELL (III)
By means of a pump drill, a hole is bored in each disc.   (See p. 372.)

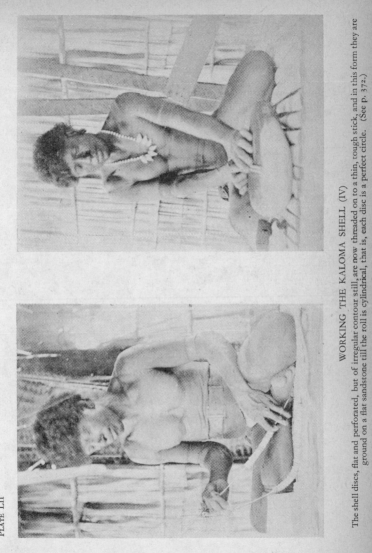

PLATE LII

WORKING THE KALOMA SHELL (IV)

The shell discs, flat and perforated, but of irregular contour still, are now threaded on to a thin, rough stick, and in this form they are ground on a flat sandstone till the roll is cylindrical, that is, each disc is a perfect circle. (See p. 372.)

Plate LIII

ON THE BEACH OF NABWAGETA

In the middle of the picture a sail is seen, hung on a scaffolding of sticks ; natives are pausing in their work of overhauling it and patching it up. (See p. 383.)

three burning sticks, gradually pushed in as they were consumed. The men slept with the big, stiff pandanus mats over
them ; each mat is folded in the middle, and when put on the
ground, forms a kind of miniature prismatic tent. All along
the beach, it was almost a continuous row of man alternating
with fire, the dun-coloured mats being nearly invisible against
the sand in the full moonlight. It must have been a very light
sleep for every now and then, a man stirred, peeping up from
under his shell, re-adjusting the fire, and casting a searching
glance over the surroundings. It would be difficult to say
whether mosquitoes or cold wind or fear of sorcery disturbed
their sleep most, but I should say the last.

The next morning, early, and without any warning, the
whole fleet sailed away. At about 8 o'clock the last canoe
punted towards the offing, where they stepped their mast and
hoisted their sail. There were no farewell gifts, no conch
shell blowing, and the Dobuans this time left their resting place
as they had come, without ceremony or display. The morning
after, the Nabwagetans followed them. I was left in the village
with a few cripples, the women and one or two men who had
remained perhaps to look after the village, perhaps specially to
keep watch over me and see that I did no mischief. Not one
of them was a good informant. Through a mistake of mine,
I had missed the cutter which had come two days before to the
island of Gumasila and left without me. With bad luck and
bad weather, I might have had to wait a few weeks, if not
months in Nabwageta. I could perhaps have sailed in a native
canoe, but this could only be done without bedding, tent, or
even writing outfit and photographic apparatus, and so my
travelling would have been quite useless. It was a piece of
great good luck that a day or two afterwards, a motor launch,
whose owner had heard about my staying in the Amphletts,
anchored in front of Nabwageta village, and within an hour I
was speeding towards the Trobriands again, following the
tracks of the Kula fleet.

II

On the next morning, as we slowly made our way along the
channels in the opalescent, green lagoon, and as I watched
a fleet of small, local canoes fishing in their muddy waters,
and could recognise on the surrounding flat shores a dozen

well-known villages, my spirits rose, and I felt well pleased
to have left the picturesque, but ethnographically barren
Amphletts for the Trobriands, with their scores of excellent
informants.

Moreover, the Amphletts, in the persons of their male
inhabitants were soon to join me here. I went ashore in
Sinaketa, where everybody was full of the great moment which
was soon to arrive. For the Dobuan fleet was known to be
coming, though on that morning, so far, no news had reached
them of its whereabouts. As a matter of fact, the Dobuans,
who had left Nabwageta forty-eight hours ahead of me, had
made a slow journey with light winds, and sailing a course to
the East of mine, had arrived that morning only in Vakuta.

All the rumours which had been reported to me in the
Amphletts about the previous movements of the Trobriand
natives had been correct. Thus the natives of Vakuta had
really been to the East, to Kitava, and had brought with them
a big haul of armshells. To'uluwa, the chief of Kiriwina, had
visited Kitava later, and about five or six days before had
returned from there, bringing with him 213 pairs of armshells.
The Sinaketans then had gone to Kiriwina, and out of the
213 pairs had succeeded in securing 154. As there had been
previously 150 pairs in Sinaketa, a total of 304 was awaiting
the Dobuans. On the morning of my arrival, the Sinaketan
party had just returned from Kiriwina, hurrying home so as to
have everything ready for the reception of the Dobuans. Of
these, we got the news that very afternoon—news which
travelled overland from one village to another, and reached us
from Vakuta with great rapidity. We were also told that the
uvalaku fleet would be at Sinaketa within two or three days.

This period I utilised in refurbishing my information about
that phase of the Kula, which I was going to witness, and
trying to get a clear outline of every detail of all that was going
soon to happen. It is extremely important in sociological
work to know well beforehand the underlying rules and the
fundamental ideas of an occurrence, especially if big masses of
natives are concerned in it. Otherwise, the really important
events may be obliterated by quite irrelevant and accidental
movements of the crowd, and thus the significance of what he
sees may be lost to the observer. No doubt if one could repeat
one's observations on the same phenomenon over and over

again, the essential and relevant features would stand out by their regularity and permanence. If, however, as it often happens in ethnographic field-work, one gets the opportunity only once of witnessing a public ceremony, it is necessary to have its anatomy well dissected beforehand, and then concentrate upon observing how these outlines are followed up concretely, gauge the tone of the general behaviour, the touches of emotion or passion, many small yet significant details which nothing but actual observation can reveal, and which throw much light upon the real, inner relation of the native to his institution. So I was busy going over my old entries and checking them and putting my material into shape in a detailed and concrete manner.

On the third day, as I was sitting and taking notes in the afternoon, word ran all round the villages that the Dobuan canoes had been sighted. And indeed, as I hastened towards the shore, there could be seen, far away, like small petals floating on the horizon, the sails of the advancing fleet. I jumped at once into a canoe, and was punted along towards the promontory of Kaykuyawa, about a mile to the South of Sinaketa. There, one after the other, the Dobuan canoes were arriving, dropping their sails and undoing the mast as they moored, until the whole fleet, numbering now over eighty canoes, were assembled before me (see Plate XLVIII). From each a few men waded ashore, returning with big bunches of leaves. I saw them wash and smear themselves and perform the successive stages of native, festive adornment (see Plate XLIX). Each article was medicated by some man or another in the canoe before it was used or put on. The most carefully handled articles of ornamentation were the ineffective looking, dried up herbs, taken out of their little receptacles, where they had remained since they had been becharmed in Dobu, and now stuck into the armlets. The whole thing went on quickly, almost feverishly, making more the impression of a piece of technical business being expeditiously performed, than of a solemn and elaborate ceremony taking place. But the ceremonial element was soon to show itself.

After the preparations were finished, the whole fleet formed itself into a compact body, not quite regular, but with a certain order, about four or five canoes being in a row, and one row behind the other. In this formation they punted along over the Lagoon, too shallow for paddling, towards the beach of Sinaketa. When they were within about ten minutes of the shore, all the conch shells began to be sounded, and the murmur of recited magic rose from the canoes. I could not come sufficiently near the canoes, for reason of etiquette, to be able to see the exact arrangement of the reciters, but I was told that it was the same as that observed by the Trobrianders on their approach to Dobu, described in Chapter XIII. The general effect was powerful, when this wonderfully painted and fully decorated fleet was gliding swiftly over the green waters of the Lagoon towards the palm grove above the sand beach, at that moment thick with expectant natives. But I imagine that the arrival of a Trobriand fleet in Dobu must be considerably more effective even than that. The much more picturesque landscape, the ceremonial paddling with the leaf-shaped oars over the deep water, the higher sense of danger and tension, than that which the Dobuans feel, when coming to visit the meek Trobrianders, all this must make it even more dramatic and impressive than the scene I have just described.

Within some twenty metres from the shore, the canoes formed themselves into a double row, the canoe of the *toli'uvalaku* on the left flank of the first row. Kauyaporu, as soon as all the craft were in position, rose in his canoe, and in a loud voice, addressed in Dobuan those standing on the shore. His words, preserved in the memory of his hearers, were transmitted to me that same evening in their Kiriwinian equivalent. He spoke :

> " Who will be first in the Kula ? The people of Vakuta or yourselves ? I deem you will have the lead ! Bring armshells, one basketful, two baskets ; catch pigs ; pluck coco-nuts ; pluck betel-nut ! For this is my *uvalaku*. By and by, thou, Kouta'uya, wilt make an *uvalaku*, and we shall give thee then plenty of *vaygu'a* ! "

So spoke Kauyaporu, addressing his main partner, Kouta'uya, the second chief of Sinaketa. He did not address To'udawada, the most important chief, because he was not his main partner.

As soon as the speech was finished, Kouta'uya waded through the water from the beach, carrying a pair of armshells in each hand. Behind him came a small boy, the youngest son, blowing a conch shell. He was followed again by two men, who between them had a stick resting on their shoulders, on which several pairs of *mwali* (armshells) were displayed. This procession waded towards the canoe of Kauyaporu, whom Kouta'uya addressed in these words, throwing the armshells on the platform of the canoe :

"This is a *vaga* (opening gift) ! In due time, I shall make a *uvalaku* to Dobu ; thou shalt return to me a big *soulava* (necklace) as *kudu* (equivalent gift) for this. Plenty more armshells thou wilt receive now. There are plenty of armshells in Sinaketa. We know there were plenty of armshells in Vakuta. By and by thou and thy *usagelu* come ashore, I shall catch a pig. I shall give you plenty of food, coco-nuts, betel-nut, sugar cane, bananas ! "

As soon as he was back on the shore, his wife, the eldest one, with a *peta* basket on her head, containing a pair of armshells, went into the water and carried it to Kauyaporu's canoe, the boy with the conch shell following her also. After that, conch shells were blown on all sides on the shore, and single men or groups detached themselves from the rest, and waded towards the canoes. The *mwali* were carried with ceremony on sticks or in outstretched arm. But the grossly exaggerated way of putting one pair of armshells into a basket which was big enough to hold some four score, was only done by the chief's wife. All this lasted for perhaps half-an-hour, while the setting sun poured down its glowing light on the painted canoes, the yellow beach, and the lively bronze forms moving upon it. Then, in a few moments the Dobuan canoes were partly beached, partly moored, whilst their crews spread over the seven villages of Sinaketa. Large groups could be seen sitting on platforms chewing betel nut and conversing in Dobuan with their hosts (see Plate LVI).

For three days, the Dobuans remained in Sinaketa. Every now and then, blasts of conch shell announced that a Kula transaction had taken place, that is, that a pair of armshells had been handed over to one of the visitors. Swarms of people from the other districts had assembled in Sinaketa ; every day, natives from the inland villages of Southern Boyowa crowded into their capital, whilst people from Kuboma, Luba, and Kiriwina, that is, the Central and Northern districts, were camping in their relatives' houses, in yam stores and under provisional shelters. Reckoning that the number of the visitors, that is, the Dobuans, the Amphlettans and the Vakutans, who had joined them on their way, amounted to some eight hundred ; that the Sinaketans numbered about five hundred people, and that some twelve hundred had come from the other villages, it will be seen that the crowd in and about Sinaketa was considerable, numbering over two thousand.

The Trobriand natives, of course, looked after their own provisions. The Dobuans had also brought a considerable amount of food with them, and would receive some additional vegetables and pigs' flesh from their hosts, while they acquired fish from some of the other villages of Boyowa. As a matter of fact, stingaree, shark and some other fish are the only articles for which the Dobuans barter on their own account. The rest of the trade, in the same way as is done in Dobu by the Sinaketans, must be done with the community who receive visitors, that is, with Sinaketa. The Sinaketans buy from the manufacturing districts of Boyowa the same industrial products that they take with them to Dobu, that is baskets, lime pots, lime spatulæ, etc. Then they sell these to the Dobuans in just the same manner and with the same profit as was described in Chapter XV. As has been said there also, a man of Sinaketa would never trade with his partner, but with some other Dobuan. Between the partners, only presents are exchanged. The gift offered by the Dobuans to the Sinaketans is called *vata'i*, and it differs only in name and not in its economic or sociological nature from the *pari* gift offered by the Boyowans to their overseas partners. The *talo'i*, or farewell gift offered to them is as a rule more substantial than the *vata'i*.

The Dobuans, during their stay in Sinaketa, lived on the beach or in their canoes (see Plates LIV and XX). Skilfully rigged up with canopies of golden mats covering parts of the craft, their painted hulls glowing in the sun against the green water, some of the canoes presented the spectacle of some gorgeously fantastic pleasure boat (see Plate LV). The natives waded about amongst them, making the Lagoon lively with movement, talk and laughter. Groups camped on the sea shore, boiling food in the large clay pots, smoking and chewing betel-nut. Big parties of Trobrianders walked among them, discreetly but curiously watching them. Women were not very conspicuous in the whole proceedings, nor did I hear any scandal about intrigues, although such may have taken place.

III

On the fourth day, conch shells were blown again in the morning, though on the last of the three days their sounds had almost died out. These were the signs of the departure. Food and small presents were brought to the canoes as *talo'i*, and a few *mwali* were given at the last, for which the conch shells were blown. Without any ceremony or farewell speeches, the Dobuan canoes sailed away, one after the other.

Their journey home was also interrupted by a customary halt for fishing, but this time for fish, not shell. Some of them stop on the beach of Muwa, but the bulk camp on a beach called Susuwa, half way between Sinaketa and Vakuta, where they catch the fish by means of a poisonous root, which they have brought for this purpose from home. This time, they remained three days in Susuwa and Muwa, and then sailed to Vakuta to receive there *talo'i*. Their further journey I could not trace step by step, but afterwards I heard that quickly, and without any accident, they had reached their homes.

Their *tanarere* on Sarubwoyna beach—that is, the competitive display of the yield—gave more or less the following results :

From Sinaketa they received 304 armshells.

From Vakuta they received 344 armshells.

The total therefore was 648. As there were about sixty canoes making the proper *uvalaku* from Dobu, that is, not counting those from the Amphletts and Vakuta which joined on the way and appeared before Sinaketa, there were at the outside some five hundred Dobuan natives on that expedition. Out of these, however, not more than half were grown-up, Kula making men. So that, on the average, there were nearly thirteen armshells for every five men. Some would not get more than one pair, some perhaps even none, whilst the headmen received large quantities.

We shall follow in a later chapter the movements of some at least of those who had collected in Sinaketa from the other districts, in connection with the Kula. It did not take them more than a few days to disperse completely, and for the village to resume its ordinary aspect and routine.

Chapter XVII

MAGIC AND THE KULA

I

In treating of the various customs and practices of the Kula, I had at every step to enter into the description of magical rites and into the analysis of spells. This had to be done, first of all, because magic looms paramount in the natives' view of the Kula. Again, all magical formulæ disclose essentials of belief and illustrate typical ideas in a manner so thorough and telling that no other road could lead us as straight into the inner mind of the native. Finally, there is a direct, ethnographic interest in knowing the details of magical performance, which has such an overweening influence over tribal life, and enters so deeply into the make-up of the natives mentality.

It is now necessary to complete our knowledge of magic and to focus all the dispersed data into one coherent picture. So far, the many scattered references and numerous concrete details have not furnished a general idea, of what magic means to the natives ; how they imagine the working of the magical forces ; what are their implied and expressed views on the nature of magical power. Collecting all the material which has already been presented in the previous chapters, and supplementing it with native and ethnographic comments, we shall be able to arrive at a certain synthesis, respecting the Kiriwinian theory of magic.

All the data which have been so far mustered disclose the extreme importance of magic in the Kula. But if it were a question of treating of any other aspect of the tribal life of these natives, it would also be found that, whenever they approach any concern of vital importance, they summon magic to their aid. It can be said without exaggeration that magic, according to their ideas, governs human destinies ; that it supplies man with the power of mastering the forces of nature ; and that it

is his weapon and armour against the many dangers which
crowd in upon him on every side. Thus, in what is most essential to man, that is in his health and bodily welfare, he is but
a plaything of the powers of sorcery, of evil spirits and of
certain beings, controlled by black magic. Death in almost all
its forms is the result of one of these agencies. Permanent ill-
health and all kinds of acute sickness, in fact everything,
except such easily explainable ailments as physical overstrain
or slight colds, are attributed to magic. I have spoken
(Chapter II) of the several ways in which the evil powers bring
disease and death. The *tauva'u*, who bring epidemics and the
tokway, who inflict shooting pains and minor ailments, are the
only examples of non-human beings' exerting any direct
influence on human destinies, and even the members of this
restricted pantheon of demonology only occasionally descend
among the mortals to put into action their potential powers.
By far the deepest dread and most constant concern of the
natives are with the *bwaga'u*, the entirely human sorcerers,
who carry out their work exclusively by means of magic.
Second to them in the quantity of magical output and in the
frequency of their exploits, are the *mulukwausi*, the flying
witches, which have been described in detail in Chapter XI.
They are a good example of how every belief in a superior power
is at the bottom a belief in magic. Magic gives to these beings
the capacity to destroy human life and to command other agents
of destruction. Magic also gives man the power and the means
to defend himself, and if properly applied, to frustrate all the
nefarious attempts of the *mulukwausi*. Comparing the two
agencies, it may be said that in every-day life, the sorcerer is
by far the most feared and is most frequently believed to be at
work ; while the *mulukwausi* enter upon the scene at certain
dramatic moments, such as the presence of death, a catastrophe
on land, and more especially at sea ; but then, they enter with
even deadlier weapons than the *bwaga'u*. Health, the normal
state of human beings can, if once lost, be regained by magic
and by magic only. There is no such thing as natural recovery,
return to health being always due to the removal of the evil
magic by means of magical counter-action.

All those crises of life, which are associated with fear of
danger, with the awakening of passions or of strong emotions,
have also their magical accompaniment. The birth of a child

is always ushered in by magic, in order to make the child prosper, and to neutralise the dangers and evil influences. There is no rite or magic at puberty; but then, with this people, puberty does not present any very definite crisis in the life of the individual, as their sexual life starts long before puberty arrives, and gradually shapes and develops as the organism matures. The passion of love, however, has a very elaborate magical counterpart, embodied in many rites and formulæ, to which a great importance is attached, and all success in sexual life is ascribed to it. The evil results of illicit love—that is love within the clan, which, by the way, is considered by these natives as the main class of sexual immorality—can also be counteracted by a special type of magic.

The main social interests, ambition in gardening, ambition in successful Kula, vanity and display of personal charms in dancing—all find their expression in magic. There is a form of beauty magic, performed ceremonially over the dancers, and there is also a kind of safety magic at dances, whose object is to prevent the evil magic of envious sorcerers. Particular garden magic, performed by an individual over his crops and seeds, as well as the evil magic which he casts on the gardens of his rivals, express the private ambitions in gardening, as contrasted with the interests of the whole village, which are catered for by communal garden magic.

Natural forces of great importance to man, such as rain and sunshine, the appropriate alternative operation of which makes his crops thrive; or wind, which must be controlled for purposes of sailing and fishing, are also governed by magic. The magic of rain and sunshine can be used for good, as well as for nefarious purposes, and in this they have a special interest in the Trobriands, because the most powerful system of this magic is in the hands of the paramount chiefs of Kiriwina. By bringing about a prolonged drought, the chiefs of Omarakana have always been able to express their general displeasure with their subjects, and thus enhance their wholesale power, independently of any other mechanism, which they might have used for forcing their will on private individuals or on whole communities.

The basic, food-providing economic activities, which in the Trobriands are mainly gardening and fishing, are also completely magic-ridden. The success of these pursuits is of course largely due to luck, chance or accident, and to the natives they require supernatural assistance. We had examples of economic magic in describing the construction of a canoe, and the fishing for *kaloma* shell. The communal garden-magic and the fishing magic of certain village communities show to a higher degree even than the cases described, the feature which we found so distinct in canoe magic, namely : that the rites and formulæ are not a mere appendage, running side by side with economic efforts, without exercising any influence over these. On the contrary, it may be said that a belief in magic is one of the main, psychological forces which allow for organisation and systemisation of economic effort in the Trobriands.* The capacity for art, as well as the inspiration in it, is also ascribed to the influence of magic.

The passions of hatred, envy, and jealousy, besides finding their expression in the all powerful sorcery of the *bwaga'u* and *mulukwausi*, are also responsible for many forms of witchery, known by the generic term of *bulubwalata*. The classical forms of this magic have as their object the estrangement of the affections of a wife or a sweetheart, or the destruction of the domestic attachment of a pig. The pig is sent away into the bush, having been made to take a dislike to its master and to its domestic habits ; the wife, though the spells used to estrange her are slightly different, can be made also to take a dislike to her domestic life, abandon her husband and return to her parents. There is a *bulubwalata* of gardens, of canoes, of Kula, of *kaloma*, in fact of everything, and a good deal of beneficial magic is taken up with exorcising the results of *bulubwalata*.

The list of magic is not quite exhausted yet. There is the magic of conditional curses, performed in order to guard property from possible harm, inflicted by others ; there is war-magic ; there is magic associated with taboos put on coco-nuts and betel-nuts, in order to make them grow and multiply ; there is magic to avert thunder and resuscitate people who are struck by lightning ; there is the magic of tooth-ache, and a magic to make food last a long time.

All this shows the wide diffusion of magic, its extreme importance and also the fact that it is always strongest there,

* These views have been elaborated in the previously quoted article on " Primitive Economics " in the *Economic Journal*, March, 1921.

where vital interests are concerned ; where violent passions or emotions are awakened ; when mysterious forces are opposed to man's endeavours ; and when he has to recognise that there is something which eludes his most careful calculations, his most conscientious preparations and efforts.

II

Let us now proceed to formulate some short statement of the essential conception of magic, as it is entertained by the natives. All statement of belief, found among human beings so widely different from us, is full of difficulties and pitfalls, which perhaps beset us most there, where we try to arrive at the very foundation of the belief—that is, at the most general ideas which underlie a series of practices and a body of traditions. In dealing with a native community at the stage of development which we find in the Trobriands, we cannot expect to obtain a definite, precise and abstract statement from a philosopher, belonging to the community itself. The native takes his fundamental assumptions for granted, and if he reasons or inquires into matters of belief, it would be always only as regards details and concrete applications. Any attempts on the part of the Ethnographer to induce his informant to formulate such a general statement would have to be in the form of leading questions of the worst type because in these leading questions he would have to introduce words and concepts essentially foreign to the native. Once the informant grasped their meaning, his outlook would be warped by our own ideas having been poured into it. Thus the Ethnographer must draw the generalisation for himself, must formulate the abstract statement without the direct help of a native informant.

I am saying *direct help* because the generalisation must be entirely based on indirect data supplied by the natives. In the course of collecting information, of discussing formulæ and translating their text, a considerable number of opinions on matters of detail will be set forth by the natives. Such spontaneous opinions, if placed in a correctly constructed mosaic, might almost of themselves give us a true picture, might almost cover the whole field of native belief. And then our task would only be to summarise this picture in an abstract formula.

The Ethnographer, however, possesses an even better supply of evidence from which to draw his conclusions. The objective items of culture, into which belief has crystallised in the form of tradition, myth, spell and rite are the most important source of knowledge. In them, we can face the same realities of belief as the native faces in his intimate intercourse with the magical, the same realities which he not only professes with his tongue, but lives through partly in imagination and partly in actual experience. An analysis of the contents of the spells, the study of the manner in which they are uttered; in which the concomitant rites are performed ; the study of the natives' behaviour, of the actors as well as of the spectators; the knowledge of the social position and social functions, of the magical expert—all this reveals to us, not only the bare structure of their ideas on magic, but also the associated sentiments and emotions, and the nature of magic as a social force.

An Ethnographer who, from the study of such objective data, has been able to penetrate into the natives' attitude, to formulate a general theory of magic, can *then* test his conclusions by direct questionings. For he will be already in a position to use native terminology and to move along the lines of native thought, and in his questionings he will be able to accept the lead of his informant instead of misleading the latter and himself by leading questions. More especially in obtaining opinions of actual occurrences from the natives, he will not have to move in abstract generalities, but will be able to translate them into concrete applications and into the native modes of thought.

In arriving at such general conclusions about vast aspects of primitive human thought and custom, the Ethnographer's is a creative work, in so far as he brings to light phenomena of human nature which, in their entirety, had remained hidden even from those in whom they happened. It is creative in the same sense as is the construction of general principles of natural science, where objective laws of very wide application lie hidden till brought forth by the investigating human mind. In the same sense, however, as the principles of natural science are empirical, so are also the final generalisations of ethnographic sociology because, though expressly stated for the first time by the investigator, they are none the less objective realities of human thinking, feeling and behaviour.

III

We can start from the question of how the natives imagine their magic to have originated. If we would ask even the most intelligent informant some such concretely framed questions as : " Where has your magic been made ? How do you imagine its invention ? "—they would necessarily remain unanswered. Not even a warped and half-suggested reply would be forthcoming. Yet there is an answer to this question, or rather to its generalised equivalent. Examining the mythology of one form of magic after the other, we find that there are in every one either explicitly stated or implied views about how magic has become known to man. As we register these views, compare them, and arrive at a generalisation, we easily see, why our imaginary question, put to the natives, would have to remain unanswered. For, according to native belief, embedded in all traditions and all institutions, magic is never conceived as having been made or invented. Magic has been handed on as a thing which has always been there. It is conceived as an intrinsic ingredient of everything that vitally affects man. The words, by which a magician exercises his power over a thing or a process, are believed to be co-existent with them. The magical formula and its subject matter were born together.

In some cases, tradition represents them literally as being ' born ' by the same woman. Thus, rain was brought forth by a woman of Kasana'i, and the magic came with it, and has been handed on ever since in this woman's sub-clan. Again, the mythical mother of the Kultur-hero Tudava gave birth, among other plants and animals, also to the *kalala* fish. The magic of this fish is also due to her. In the short myth about the origin of *kayga'u* magic—the one to protect drowning sailors from witches and other dangers—we saw that the mother, who gave birth to the Tokulubweydoga dog, also handed the magic over to him. In all these cases, however, the myth does not point to these women's inventing or composing the magic ; indeed, it is explicitly stated by some natives that the women had learned the magic from their matrilineal ancestors. In the last case, the woman is said in the myth to have known the magic by tradition.

Other myths are more rudimentary, yet, though less circumstantial about the origin of the magic, show us just as unmistakably that magic is a primeval thing, indeed, in the literal sense of the word, autochthonous. Thus, the Kula magic in Gumasila came out of the rock of Selawaya ; the canoe magic out of the hole in the ground, brought by the men, who originally emerged with it ; garden magic is always conceived as being carried from underground by the first ancestors, who emerged out of the original hole of that locality. Several minor forms of magic of local currency, such as fish magic, practised in one village only, wind magic, etc., are also imagined to have been carried out of the ground. All the forms of sorcery have been handed over to people by non-human beings, who passed them on but did not create them. The *bwaga'u* sorcery is due to a crab, who gave it to a mythical personage, in whose *dala* (sub-clan) the magic was carried on and from it distributed all over the islands. The *tokway* (wood-sprites) have taught man certain forms of evil magic. There are no myths in Kiriwina about the origin of flying witch magic. From other districts, however, I have obtained rudimentary information pointing to the fact that they were instructed in this magic by a mythical, malevolent being called Taukuri-pokapoka, with whom even now some sort of relations are kept up, culminating in nocturnal meetings and sexual orgies which remind one very strongly of the Walpurgisnacht.

Love magic, the magic of thunder and lightning, are accounted for by definite events. But in neither of them are we led to imagine that the formula is invented, in fact, there is a sort of *petitio principii* in all these myths, for on the one hand they set out to account for how magic came, and on the other, in all of them magic is represented as being there, ready made. But the *petitio principii* is due only to a false attitude of mind with which we approach these tales. Because, to the native mind, they set out to tell, not how magic originated, but how magic was brought within the reach of one or other of the Boyowan local groups or sub-clans.

Thus it may be said, in formulating a generalisation from all these data, that magic is never invented. In olden days, when mythical things happened, magic came from underground, or was given to a man by some non-human being, or was handed on to descendants by the original ancestress, who also brought forth the phenomenon governed by the magic. In actual cases of the present times and of the near-past generations whom the natives of to-day knew personally, the magic is given by one man to another, as a rule by the father to his son or by the maternal kinsman. But its very essence is the impossibility of its being manufactured or invented by man, its complete resistance to any change or modification by him. It has existed ever since the beginning of things ; it creates, but is never created ; it modifies, but must never be modified.

It is now easy to see that no questions about the origins of magic, such as we formulated before, could have been asked of a native informant without distorting the evidence in the very act of questioning, while more general and quite abstract and colourless inquiries cannot be made intelligible to him. He has grown up into a world where certain processes, certain activities have their magic, which is as much an attribute of theirs' as anything else. Some people have been traditionally instructed how this magic runs, and they know it; how men came by magic is told in numerous mythical narratives. That is the correct statement of the native point of view. Once arrived at this conclusion inductively, we can of course, test our conclusions by direct questions, or by a leading question, for the matter of that. To the question : " where human beings found magic ? " I obtained the following answer :—

> " All magic, they found long ago in the nether world. We do not find ever a spell in a dream ; should we say so, this would be a lie. The spirits never give us a spell. Songs and dances they do give us, that is true, but no magic."

This statement, expressing the belief in a very clear and direct manner, I had confirmed, reiterated with variations and amplifications, by ever so many informants. They all emphasise the fact that magic has its roots in tradition, that it is the most immutable and most valuable traditional item, that it cannot leak into human knowledge by any present human intercourse with spirits or with any non-human beings such as the *tokway* or *tauva'u*. The property of having been received from previous generations is so marked that any breach of continuity in this succession cannot be imagined, and any addition by an actual human being would make the magic spurious.

At the same time, magic is conceived as something essentially human. It is not a force of nature, captured by man

Plate LIV

THE DOBUAN CANOES PULLED UP ON SINAKETA BEACH . (See p. 390.)

Plate LV

SOME CANOES MOORED ON THE SHALLOW LAGOON NEAR THE SHORE.
(See p. 390.)

Plate LVI

DOBUAN VISITORS IN SINAKETA

Top picture : the Kula visitors and hosts sitting side by side on a house platform in Sinaketa. Bottom picture : to the right Tovasana, wearing a wig of pandanus fibre, holding his lime pot and spatula and ornamented with *buna* shell on his leg, sits with Kauyaporu (on the left), the chief of the Dobuans, on the platform of one of the Sinaketan chiefs. Note the aromatic herbs in Kauyaporu's armlets. (See p. 389.)

PLATE LVII

A MAGICAL SPELL ASSOCIATED WITH PREGNANCY

The women are bent over a special garment to be worn by the pregnant woman. They almost touch it with their mouths so that it may be well pervaded with their breath which conveys the virtues of the spell. (See p. 405)

PLATE LVIII

A RITE OF WAR MAGIC

Kanukubusi, the last war wizard of Kiriwina (see Div. V), showing, in reconstruction, the manner in which he used to charm the shields in olden days. (See p. 406.)

Plate LIX

A RITE OF GARDEN MAGIC

An offering of cooked food is exposed to the spirits for some time in the garden. The magician, with the ceremonial axe on his arm, is seen squatting to the right. In the forefront, a big bundle of leaves which he will presently charm over. (See p. 407.)

[face p. 401

through some means and put to his service ; it is essentially the assertion of man's intrinsic power over nature. In saying that, I, of course translate native belief into abstract terms, which they would not use themselves for its expression. None the less it is embodied in all their items of folk-lore and ways of using magic and thinking about it. In all the traditions, we find that magic is always in possession of man, or at least of anthropomorphic beings. It is carried out from underground by man. It is not conceived as having been there somewhere outside his knowledge and then captured. On the contrary, as we saw, often the very things which are governed by magic have been brought forth by man, as for instance rain, the *kalala* fish ; or disease, created by the anthropmorphic crab.

The close sociological association of magic with a given sub-clan emphasises this anthropocentric conception of magic. In the majority of cases indeed, magic refers to human activities or to the response of nature to human activities, rather than to natural forces alone. Thus, in gardening and in fishing, it is the behaviour of plants and animals tended or pursued by man ; in the canoe magic, in the carver's magic, the object is a human-made thing ; in the Kula, in love magic, in many forms of food magic, it is human nature on to which the force is directed. Disease is not conceived as an extraneous force, coming from outside and settling on the man, it is directly a man-made, sorcerer-made something. We may, therefore, amplify the above given definition, and say that magic is a traditionally handed on power of man over his own creations, over things once brought forth by man, or over responses of nature to his activities.

There is one more important aspect of the question of which I have spoken already—the relation of magic to myth. It has been stated in Chapter XII, that myth moves in the realm of the supernatural, or better, super-normal, and that magic bridges over the gap between that and present-day reality. Now this statement acquires a new importance ; magic appears to us as the essence of traditional continuity with ancestral times. Not only, as I have emphasised in this chapter, is it never conceived as a new invention, but it is identical in its nature with the supernatural power which forms the atmosphere of mythical events. Some of this power may have been lost on its way down to our times—mythical stories relate how it has been lost ; but never has anything been added to it. There is nothing in it now which has not been in it in the ancient, hoary times of myth. In this the natives have a definitely regressive view of the relation between now and before ; in this they have their counterpart to a Golden Age, and to a Garden of Eden of sorts. Thus we fall back upon the recognition of the same truth, whether we approach the matter by looking for beginnings of magic, or by studying the relations between the present and the mythical reality. Magic is a thing never invented and never tampered with, by man or any other agency.

This, of course, means that it is so in native belief. It hardly needs explicitly stating that in reality magic must constantly change. The memory of men is not such, that it could hand over verbally exactly what it had received, and, like any other item of traditional lore, a magical formula is in reality constantly being re-shaped as it passes from one generation to another, and even within the mind of the same man. As a matter of fact, even from the material collected by me in the Trobriands, it can be unmistakably recognised that certain formulæ are much older than others, and indeed, that some parts of spells, and even some whole spells, are of recent invention. Here I cannot do more than refer to this interesting subject, which, for its full development, needs a good deal of linguistic analysis, as well as of other forms of " higher criticism."

All these considerations have brought us very near to the essential problem : what does magic really mean to the natives ? So far, we have seen that it is an inherent power of man over those things which vitally affect him, a power always handed over through tradition.* About the beginnings of magic they know as little, and are occupied as little as about the beginnings of the world. Their myths describe the origin of

* The association of magic with any vital interest is demonstrated by the case of pearling. Here, through the advent of white men, a new and very lucrative and absorbing pursuit has opened up for the natives. A form of magic is now in existence, associated with this fishing. This of course apparently contradicts the native dogma that magic cannot be invented. The natives, if faced with this contradiction, explain that it is really an old magic of shell fishing which refers to all the shells found at the bottom of the Lagoon, but which so far had only been used with regard to fishing for the Conus. In fact, this magic is nothing but the adaptation of the *mwali* (armshell) magic to the pearls. I doubt, none the less, whether even such a transference or adaptation would have taken place before the foundations of native belief and custom had been shaken by the well-intentioned but not always wise and beneficent teachings and rulings of the white man and by the introduction of trade.

social institutions and the peopling of the world by men.   But the world is taken for granted, and so is the magic.   They ask no questions about *magiogony* any more than they do about *cosmogony*.

IV

So far we have not gone beyond the examination of myths and of what we can learn from them about the nature of magic. To gain a deeper insight into this subject, we must study more closely the concrete data about magical performance.   Even in the foregoing chapters a sufficient material has been collected to allow of correct inferences, and I shall only here and there have to allude to other forms of magic, besides that of canoe, Kula and sailing.

I have spoken so far about " magic " in a wholesale manner, as if it were all of one piece.   As a matter of fact, magic all the world over, however rudimentary or developed it might be, presents three essential aspects.   In its performance there enter always some words spoken or chanted, some actions carried out, and there are always the minister or ministers of the ceremony.   In analysing the concrete details of magical performances, therefore, we have to distinguish the *formula*, *the rite*, and *the condition of the performer*.

These three factors stand out quite clearly and definitely in the Trobriand magic, whether we examine the facts themselves or the natives' way of looking at them.   It may be said at once that in this society the relative importance of the three factors is not quite the same.   The spell is by far the most important constituent of magic.   In their linguistic use, although these natives have a special word, *yopa*, they very often use the word magic, *megwa*, to describe a spell.   The spell is the part of the magic which is kept secret and known only to the esoteric circle of practitioners.   When a magic is handed over, whether by purchase, gift, or inheritance, only the spell has to be taught to the new recipient, and as already once said before, it is usually taught in instalments, while the payment is received in that manner.   When one speaks about magical knowledge, or in inquiries whether an individual knows some magic this invari-ably refers to the formula, for the nature of the rite is always quite public property.   Even from the examples given in this book, it can be seen how simple are the rites and how elaborate often the formulæ. To direct questions on the subject, the natives always reply that the spell is the more important part. The question : " where is the real strength of magic ? " would receive the reply : " in the spell." The condition of the magician is, like the rite, essential to the performance of the magic, but it also is considered by the natives as subservient to the spell.

All this must be made clearer by the examination of actual facts. First of all, let us examine the relation between spell and rite ; and to this purpose it will be best to group the various magical performances into several classes according to the complexity of the concomitant rite. We shall begin with the simplest rites.

Spells uttered directly without concomitant rite.—We had one or two examples of such magic where the performer simply utters a formula directly into space. For example, the communal magician of the *kaloma* (spondylus shell) fishing performs the first act by walking on the beach and reciting his spell towards the sea. In the moment of actual shipwreck, before abandoning the canoe, the *toliwaga* launches his last *kayga'u* directly into the elements. Again, he lets his voice float over the waters, when invoking the marvellous fish, who will bring the drowning party to some friendly shore. The final spell of the Kula, by which the approaching canoe ' shakes the mountain,' chanted by a trio of magical reciters, is thrown directly towards the Koya. The clearing of the sea in the *kaloma* fishing is also done this way, and many more examples could be adduced from garden magic, wind magic, and other classes not described in this book.

The natives have a special expression for such acts ; they say that the formula is recited ' by the mouth only,' ' *o wadola wala.*' This form of magic with such a rudimentary rite is, however, relatively uncommon. Although one could say that there is no rite at all in such cases, for the magician does not manipulate anything or perform any action beyond speaking, yet from another point of view, the whole performance is ritual in so far as he has always to cast his voice towards the element, or being, which he addresses. Indeed here, as in all other cases, the voice of the reciter has to be somehow or other conveyed to the object which he wishes to becharm. We see, moreover, that in all these instances, the nature of this object is such that it can be directly reached by the voice, whilst on the other hand, there would be some difficulty in applying any substance or performing any action over, let us say, wind, or a shell growing on a distant reef or the Koya (mountain).

Spells accompanied by simple rites of impregnation.—A large number of the cases described in this book falls under this heading. We saw quite at the beginning (Chapter V, Division II and III) how the magician charms the blade of his adze, the ropes by which the canoe had been pulled, the lashing creeper, the caulking, and the paint of the canoe. Among the Kula rites, the initial magic over the aromatic mint, over the *lilava* (magical bundle) over the *gebobo* (central part of canoe) ; all the beauty magic on Sarubwoyna beach, over coco-nuts, over the facial paints as well as the conch shell magic, belong here. In all these performances an object is put well within reach of the voice, and in an appropriate position. Often, the object is placed within a receptacle or covering so that the voice enters an enclosed space and is concentrated upon the substance to be charmed. Thus, when the *lilava* is chanted over, the voice is cast into the mats, which are afterwards carefully wrapped up. The aromatic mint is charmed, lying at the bottom of a bag made of baked and thus toughened banana leaf, which afterwards is carefully folded together and bound with string. Again, the adze blade is first of all half wrapped up in a banana leaf, and the voice enters the blade and the inside of the leaf, which subsequently is folded over and tied over the blade. In the magic of the conch shell, I drew attention to the fact that immediately after the charm has been spoken, both holes of the instrument are carefully stuffed up. In all cases where an object is going to be used immediately, not so many precautions are taken, but always, without any exception, the mouth is put quite close to the object medicated (see Plate LVII) and wherever possible, this latter is placed in some sort of cavity, such as a folded piece of leaf, or even the two palms of the hand put together. All this shows that it is essential to a correct performance of magic, that the voice should be conveyed directly to the substance, if possible enclosed and condensed round it, and then, imprisoned permanently there by means of some wrapping. Thus, in this type of rite, the action serves mainly to convey carefully and to retain the spell round the object.

It may be noted that in almost all cases described, the substance harmed in the rite is not the final aim of the magic, but forms only a constituent part of the object in view or is an accessory of it, or an instrument used in its making. Thus the *wayugo* creeper, the *kaybasi* (caulking), the paint, the prow-boards, all these are constituent parts of the canoe, and the magic performed over them does not aim at giving them any qualities, but aims at imparting swiftness and lightness to the canoe of which they are parts only. Again, the herbs and the colours of the coco-nut ointment medicated in the Kula are accessories of the final end of this magic, that is, of the personal beauty and attractiveness of the performer. The adze, the breaking stone in *kaloma* magic are implements used in obtaining the object, towards which the magic is directed. There are only a few instances in which the simple rite of impregnation is directly performed on the object in view. If we compare this type of rite with the one of the previous category, we see that the difference lies mainly in the size of the object. If you want to cast a charm over a mountain, over a reef, or over the wind, you cannot put your object into a little bag made of banana leaf. Nor can you put there the human mind. And as a rule, the final objects of magical rites are not small things, which could be easily handled. In the magic described in this book, there is, I think, not one single instance, in which the substance handled in the rite and impregnated by condensing the charm upon it artificially, is the final object of the spell. In war magic the points of the spears are made effective and the shields are made spear-proof (see Plate LVIII) by magic uttered over them. In private garden magic, the planted yams are made fruitful by a spell, and a few more examples could be adduced from other types of magic.

Spells accompanied by a rite of transference.—When we compare the rite of medicating the adze blade with the rite of medicating some dried grass, with which the canoe is afterwards beaten, we see that, in the second case, the magic is uttered over a something, which has no intrinsic connection with the final object of the magic, that is, with the canoe. It is neither to become a part of it, nor to be used as an implement in its manufacture. We have here the introduction for purposes of the rite, of a special medium, used to absorb the magical force, and to transfer it to the final object. We can therefore call rites where such mediums are used *rites of transference*. When a stick is charmed to be used afterwards for the magical knocking out of a canoe ; or a mussel-shell, with which the canoe will be scraped; or a piece of coco-nut husk, which will be thrown into the water to remove the heaviness of the canoe ; or a pandanus streamer, which will give it swiftness, there is introduced into every one of these rites a substance which has to play a magical rôle only. The rite, therefore, is not the simple charming of a part or of a constructive implement, which will enter into the composition or be used in the making of an object. The rite here is more autonomous, possesses more of its own significance. The beating of a canoe with two bunches of grass, one after the other, in order first to extract its heaviness and then impart to it lightness, has a meaning parallel to the spell but independent of it. So has also the throwing down of the coco-nut husk. The flutter of the pandanus streamers has direct association with speed, as the natives explicitly state. As the *bisila* streamers flutter in the wind, so should the canoe and the sail shake with the swiftness of their going. In the case of the ginger, which is spat over the Dobuans feigning hostility, the inherent quality of the substance, which our pharmacopæas describe as a *stimulant*, makes the meaning of the rite plain. We can easily see that some of the rites are rather more creative than others. That is, the very act performed produces, according to native ideas, a more definite effect than in others. So it is with the spitting of the ginger, and still more directly the spilling of the lime, in order to produce a mist, and shut the eyes of the *mulukwausi*. These two, for instance, are more creative than the hanging up of the pandanus streamer.

Spells accompanied by offerings and invocations.—In the very first rite described in this book, we saw an offering being laid before, and an invocation being addressed to the wood sprite, *tokway*. There are a number of rites, accompanied by offerings given to ancestral spirits, whose participation in the offering is solicited. Such rites are performed in garden magic (see Plate LIX) in fishing magic, and in weather magic. It must, however, be said at once that there is no worship and no sacrificial offering involved in these rites, that is, not of the usual description, because the spirits are not imagined to serve as agents of the magician, in carrying out the bidding of his magic. We shall return to the subject presently. Here it will be enough to notice that the only instance of such a spell we have come across—that is, the invocation of the *tokway*—has its concomitant offering made only as a sort of compensation for having chased him out, or as a means of persuading him to go. Probably it is the first rather than the second, because the *tokway* has no free choice left, after he has been exorcised. He must obey the bidding of the magician.

This survey shows clearly that the virtue, the force, the effective principle of magic lies in the spell. We saw that in many cases, the spell is quite sufficient, if directly breathed upon the object. Again, in what may be called the prevalent type of ritual, the action which accompanies the utterance of the formula serves only to direct and condense the spell upon the object. In all such cases the rite lacks all independent significance, all autonomous function. In some cases, the rite introduces a substance which is used for magical purposes only. As a rule, the substance then intensifies, through a parallel action, the meaning of the spell. On the whole, it may be said that the main creative power of magic resides in the formula ; that the rite serves to convey, or transfer it to the object, in certain cases emphasising the meaning of the spell through the nature of the transferring medium, as well as through the manner in which it is finally applied. It is hardly necessary to state that in the Trobriand magic, there are no rites performed without the spell.

V

It is also evident in studying the manner in which the force of the spell is conveyed to the object, that the voice of the reciter transfers the virtue. Indeed, as has been repeatedly pointed out, in quoting the formulæ, and as we shall have to discuss later still, the magical words are, so to speak, rubbed in by constant repetition to the substance. To understand this better we must inquire into the natives' conceptions of psychophysiology. The mind, *nanola*, by which term intelligence, power of discrimination, capacity for learning magical formulæ, and all forms of non-manual skill are described, as well as moral qualities, resides somewhere in the larynx. The natives will always point to the organs of speech, where the *nanola* resides. The man who cannot speak through any defect of his organs, is identified in name (*tonagowa*) and in treatment with all those mentally deficient. The memory, however, the store of formulæ and traditions learned by heart, resides deeper, in the belly. A man will be said to have a good *nanola*, when he can acquire many formulæ, but though they enter through the larynx, naturally, as he learns them, repeating word for word, he has to stow them away in a bigger and more commodious receptacle ; they sink down right to the bottom of his abdomen. I made the discovery of this anatomical truth, while collecting war magic, from Kanukubusi, the last office holder of the long succession of war magicians to the chiefs of Omarakana. Kanukubusi is an old man, with a big head, a broad, high forehead, a stumpy nose, and no chin, the meekest and most docile of my informants, with a permanently puzzled and frightened expression on his honest countenance (see Plate LVIII). I found this mild old man very trustworthy and accurate, an excellent informant indeed, within the narrow sphere of his speciality, which he and his predecessors had used to make ' anger flare up in the *nanola* ' of Omarakana men, to make the enemy fly in terror, pursued and slaughtered by the victorious warriors. I paid him well for the few formulæ he gave me, and inquired at the end of our first session, whether he had any more magic to produce. With pride, he struck his belly several times, and answered : " Plenty more lies there ! " I at once checked his statement by an independent informant, and learned that everybody carries his magic in his abdomen.

There exist also certain ideas about stratification of magic, namely, that certain forms of magic have to be learnt first, so that they sink down, while others come on top. But these ideas are vague and contradictory, whereas the main idea, that magic rests in the belly, is clear and definite. This fact gives us a new insight into native ideas about magic. The force of magic, crystallised in the magical formulæ, is carried by men of the present generation in their bodies. They are the depositories of this most valuable legacy of the past. The force of magic does not reside in the things ; it resides within man and can escape only through his voice.

VI

So far, we only spoke of the relation between spell and rite. The last point, however, brings us to the problem of the condition of the performer. His belly is a tabernacle of magical force. Such a privilege carries its dangers and obligations. It is clear that you cannot stuff foreign matter indiscriminately into a place, where extremely valuable possessions are kept. Food restrictions, therefore, become imperative. Many of them are directly determined by the contents of the spell. We saw some examples of this, as when red fish, invoked in magic, is tabooed to the performer; or the dog, spoken about in the Ka'ubanai spell, may not be heard howling while the man eats. In other cases, the object which is the aim of the magic, cannot be partaken by the magician. This is the rule in the case of shark fishing, *kalala* fishing, and other forms of fishing magic. The garden magician is also debarred from partaking of new crops, up to a certain period. There is hardly any clear doctrine, as to why things mentioned in magical formulæ, whether they are the aims of the magic or only co-operating factors, should not be eaten. There is just the general apprehension that the formula would be damaged by it. There are other taboos, binding the magician, some of them permanent, some of them temporary, during the season of his magical performance. We saw some permanent ones, as in the case of the man who knows Kayga'u magic, and is not allowed to eat while children make noises. The temporary ones, such as the sexual abstinence during the first rites of the Kula, could be supplemented by numerous examples from other forms of magic. Thus, in order to bring about rain, the magician paints himself black and has to remain unwashed and unkempt for some time. The shark magician has to keep his house open, to remove his pubic leaf and to sit with his legs apart, while the fishing and the magic last, " so that the shark's mouth might remain gaping." But we cannot enter too much into enumeration of these taboos and observances, and have only to make it clear that the proper behaviour of the magician is one of the essentials of magic, and that in many cases this behaviour is dictated by the contents of the spell.

The taboos and observances are not the only conditions which a man must fulfil in order to carry out certain forms of magic. In many cases the most important condition is his membership in a social group, for many forms of magic are strictly local, and must be performed by one, who is the descendant of the mythical, original owner of the magic. Thus in every case of garden magic, a magic which to the natives ranks first among all the other types of beneficent magic, the performer must be genealogically related to the first ancestor, who locally emerged from the hole. Certain exceptions to this rule are to be found only in cases where a family of high rank has come and usurped the headmanship of the group, but these exceptions are rare. In the case of the several systems of local fishing magic, the office of magician is hereditary, and associated with the locality. The important rain and sun magic which have been ' born ' in Kasana'i, can only be performed by the chiefs of that spot, who have ursurped this important privilege from the original local headman. The succession, is of course, always matrilineal. A man may make a gift of such a magic to his son, but this latter may be obliged to relinquish the privilege at his father's death, and he never will be allowed to hand it over to his son, unless this latter belongs again to the local group, through cross-cousin marriage. Even in trans-actions where magic is sold or given away from one clan to another, the prestige of certain local groups as main specialists and experts in a branch of magic still remain. For instance, the black magic, though practised all over the place and no more localised, is still believed to be best known in the villages of Ba'u and Bwoytalu, where the original crab fell down from the skies, and brought with him the magic. The Kula magic is also spread over the whole district, yet it is still associated with definite localities.

To summarise these sociological observations, we may say that, where the local character of magic is still maintained, the magician has to belong to the *dala* (sub-clan or local group) of the mythical ancestor. In all other cases, the local character of magic is still recognised, even though it does not influence the sociology of the magician.

The traditional character of magic and the magical filiation of the performer find their expression in another important feature of the spells. In some of them, as we have seen, references to mythical events are made, or names of mythical ancestors are uttered. Even more often, we find a whole list of names, beginning with the mythical founder of the magic, and ending with the name of the immediate predecessor, that is, of the man from whom the magic was obtained by the actual performer. Such a list links up the present magician by a sort

of magical pedigree with all those, who had previously been
using this formula. In other formulæ again, the magician
identifies himself with some mythical individual, and utters the
latter's name in the first person. Thus, in the spell uttered
whilst plucking the mint plant, we found the phrase : " I,
Kwoyregu, with my father, we cut the *sulumwoya* of Laba'i."
Both the actual genealogical descent of the magician from the
mythical ancestors, and the magical filiation expressed in the
formulæ show again the paramount importance of tradition, in
this case acting on the sociological determination of the performer. He is placed in a definite social group of those, who
by birth, or what could be called ' magical adoption', have had
the right of performing this magic. In the very act of uttering
the spell, the magician bears testimony to his indebtedness to
the past by the enumeration of magical names, and by references to myth and mythical events. Both the sociological
restrictions, wherever they still exist, and the magical filiation
confirm once more the dependence of magic on tradition. On
the other hand, both show, as also do the taboos, that the
obligations imposed on the magician and the conditions he has to
fulfil, are largely derived from the spell.

VII

Closely connected with the questions discussed in the
preceding division, is the subject of the *systems of magic* and
the distinction between ' systematic ' and ' independent '
magical rites and formulæ. As we saw in the beginning of this
chapter, the whole body of magic naturally falls into several
big divisions, each of them corresponding to a department of
nature, such as wind or weather ; to some activity of man,
such as gardening, fishing, hunting or warfare ; or to some real
or imaginary force, such as artistic inspiration, witchcraft,
personal charm or prowess.

There is, however, an important distinction to be made
within each such division of magic ; some of the rites and spells
are isolated and independent, they can be used by themselves,
whenever the need arises. Such are almost all the incantations
of wind magic ; some spells of individual garden magic ;
formulæ against toothache, and minor ailments ; some spells
of hunting and food collecting ; a few rites of love magic and

of the magic of carving. When a man, for instance, paddles along the Lagoon in his canoe and an unfavourable wind sets in, he will utter a spell to make it abate and change. The same spell would be recited in the village, when there arises a wind so strong as to be dangerous. The incantation is a free, individual act, which may be performed and is performed in any of the circumstances which require it.

It is quite another matter with the spells belonging to what I have called here *systematic magic*. Such magic consists of a connected and consecutive body of incantations and concomitant rites, no one of which can be torn out of its sequence and performed by itself. They have to be carried out one after the other in a determined order, and the more important of them, at least, can never be omitted, once the series has been started. Such a series is always closely connected with some activity, such as the building of a canoe or an overseas Kula voyage, a fishing expedition or the making and harvesting of a garden. It will not be difficult for us to realise the nature of systematic magic, for in this book almost all the rites and spells described belong to this class. In general, in the Trobriands, the independent uncorollated rites and formulæ are quite an insignificant minority, both in number and in importance.

Let us consider one of the forms of systematic magic previously described, whether canoe magic or that of the Kula, whether the *kayga'u* formulæ, or the magical ritual of *kaloma* fishing. The first general fact to be noted here is, that we are in the presence of a type of enterprise or activity, which is never embarked upon without magic. No canoe will be built, no *uvalaku* started, no *kaloma* fished, without its magic ceremonial. This ceremonial will be scrupulously observed in its main features, that is, some of the most important formulæ will never be omitted, as some minor ones might be, a fact which has been previously noted. The association between the practical activity and its magical concomitant is very intimate. The stages and acts of the first, and the rites and spells of the latter, correspond to each other one by one. Certain rites have to be done in order to inaugurate certain activities ; others have to be performed at the end of the practical work ; others again are part and parcel of the activity. But each of the rites and spells is to the native mind, quite as indispensable for the success of the enterprise, as is the practical activity. Thus, the *tokway* has to be expelled, or the tree would be entirely unsuitable for a canoe ; the adze, the lashing creeper, the caulking and the paint have to be charmed, or else the canoe would be heavy and unwieldy, and such an omission might even prove dangerous to life. Going mentally over the various cases quoted in the previous chapters, it can be easily seen, how this intimate association between enterprise and magic imparts to systematic magic its specific character. The consecutive progress of work and of magic are inseparable, just because, according to native ideas, work needs magic, and magic has only meaning as an indispensable ingredient of work.

Both work and magic are directed towards the same aim ; to construct a swift and a stable canoe ; to obtain a good Kula yield ; to insure safety from drowning and so on. Thus we see that systematic magic consists in a body of rites and spells associated with one enterprise, directed towards one aim, and progressing in a consecutive series of performances which have to be carried out in their proper place. The point—the proper understanding of what is meant by systematic magic—is of the greatest theoretical importance because it reveals the nature of the relation between magical and practical activities, and shows how deeply the two are connected with one another. It is one of these points, also, which cannot be properly explained and grasped without the help of a Chart. In the appended " Table of Kula Magic and of the Corresponding Activities," I have prepared such a Chart, in which has been summarised the substance of several of the foregoing Chapters. The Table allows of a rapid survey of the consecutive activities of the Kula in their relation to magic, beginning with the first act of canoe-building and finishing with the return home. It shows the salient features of systematic magic in general, and of the *mwasila* and canoe magic in particular. It shows the relation between magical, ritual and practical activities, the correlated sequence of the two, their rolling off, stage after stage, and side by side, towards one central aim—a successful Kula. The Table thus serves to illustrate the meaning of the expression ' systematic magic,' and it provides a firm outline of the essentials, magical, ceremonial and practical, of the Kula.

TABLE OF KULA MAGIC AND OF THE CORRESPONDING ACTIVITIES.

I—FIRST STAGE OF CANOE-BUILDING (CHAPTER V, DIVISION II)

Season and approximate duration	Place	Activity		Magic
Beginning: June—August.	*Raybwag.*	Felling of tree, (done by the builder and helpers);	inaugurated by	the *Vabusi Tokway* (offering and spell) aiming at the expulsion of the wood sprite from the tree (performed by owner or builder).
Immediately afterwards.	Same place.	Trimming of the log-canoe (done by builder with helpers).		No magic.
A few days later.	Road.	Pulling the log (done by all villagers);	helped out by	double rite of lightness (*Kaymomwa'u* and *Kaygagabile*).
On morning after arrival at village.	Main place in the village.	The log is left as it is;	until	the magical act (*Kapitunena Duku*) ceremonially inaugurating the work over the canoe.
Evening of the same day.	Main place in the village.	Working out of the outside of the log.		No magic accompanying it.
Several days or weeks following.	Main place.	Scooping out of the inside of the canoe;	inaugurated by	*Ligogu* spell, over the *havilali*, the adze with the movable handle.
Towards the end of the foregoing period.	In the village before builder's house.	Other parts of canoe made ready by builder and helpers.		No magic.
After all work is over.				Concluding rite: *Kapitunena Nanola Waga*.

All the magic of this stage is canoe magic. It is performed only when a new canoe is built and not when an old one is renovated. The spells are uttered by the builder and not by the owner, except the first one. Work at this stage is done by one man mainly, the builder and carver, with the help of a few men; except for the pulling of the log, in which many men assist.

II—THE SECOND STAGE OF CANOE BUILDING (CHAPTER V, DIVISION III)

Time	Place	Activity		Magic
First day of work.	On the sea-front of a Lagoon village, or on a beach of one of the Eastern villages.	Fixing the prow-boards;	inaugurated by	*Katuliliva Tabuyo* rite, performed over the ornamental prow-boards by the *toliwaga*. It belongs to the *mwasila* (Kula magic).
		The following activities are	inaugurated by	*Vakakaya* rite. A magical, ceremonial cleansing of the canoe, performed by the owner or builder to remove all evil influence and thus to make the canoe fast.
(At times, the lashing cannot be done in one day and has to be continued into another session.)		Lashing of the canoe;	associated with	the *Wayugo* spell (lashing creeper) rite; the most important of the magical performances in the second stage. Done by builder or owner to make canoe swifter and stronger.
Second sitting : during this the caulking is done and the three exorcisms performed afterwards.	On the sea-front of a Lagoon village or on a beach of one of the Eastern villages.	Caulking of the canoe;	associated with	*Kaybasi* (caulking) magic; spell uttered over caulking by builder or owner to make canoe safe. *Vakasulu*, an exorcism. *Vaguri*, an exorcism. *Kayyapena waga* an exorcism.
		Painting of the canoe;	associated with	Magic of ; *Kaykoulo* (black paint) *Malakava* (red paint). *Pwaka* (white paint).

III—The Ceremonial Launching of a Canoe (Chapter VI, Division I)

Activity		Magic
The launching and trial run	inaugurated by	*Kaytalula wadola waga* rite, belonging to the *mwasila* cycle of magic.

After this, there comes the interval, filled out by the *Kabigidoya* (ceremonial visiting,) by the preliminary trade and other preparations for the expedition overseas.

IV—The Magic during, and Preparations before the Departure (Chapter VII)

Time : some three to seven days before setting sail.

Activity		Magic
Preparing the canoe for sailing (placing of the mats on the platform, and of the frames in the body) ;	inaugurated by	*Yawarapu* rite over the coco-palm leaves, done by the *toliwaga* to ensure success in the Kula.
		Kayikuna sulumwoya rite over the aromatic mint.
		Kaymwaloyo rite over the mint boiled in coco-nut oil, performed by the *toliwaga*.
Packing of the trade goods ;	associated with	*Gebobo* rite (called also : *Kipwo'i sikwabu*), made over four coco-nuts by a friend or relative in law of the *toliwaga*, to make all the food last (the spell expresses only the desire for a good Kula.)

All this magic belongs to the *mwasila*, and it has to be performed by the *toliwaga*, with the exception of the last spell.

V—Canoe Magic, performed at the Final Start on Overseas Voyage (Chapter VIII, Division III)

The series of rites starts at the moment when the canoes are ready to set sail on the long voyage on Pilolu. They are not associated with a progressive series of acts ; they all refer to one aim : canoe speed and reliability. They are all performed by the *toliwaga*.

Activity : overseas sailing, inaugurated by a Series of Magical Rites.

	Kadumiyala, ritual rubbing or cleansing of the canoe with leaves charmed over.
Time : morning of the second day of the expedition.	*Bisila* magic ; pandanus streamers, previously chanted over are tied to the mast and rigging.
Place : the beach of Muwa.	*Kayikuna veva* ; swaying the sheet rope uttering an incantation.
Aim of Magic : imparting of speed to canoe.	
Performer of the Rites : the *toliwaga*	*Vabusi momwa'u* ; "expelling the heaviness" out of a canoe by means of a stale potato.
	Bisiboda patile ; a rite of evil magic to make other canoes slow and thus achieve relative speed.

VI—The Mwasila, performed on Arrival at the Final Destination

(A) BEAUTY MAGIC (Chapter XIII, Division I)

Activity : washing, anointing and painting.

Place : the beach, on or near which the party rest before starting on the last stage (on the way to Dobu ; Sarubwoyna beach. On the way to Sinaketa : Kaykuyawa).

Performers : the spells are uttered usually by the *toliwaga*, sometimes by an elder member of the crew.

Kaykakaya—ritual washing and rubbing with charmed leaves.

Luya (coco-nut) spell—over the scraped coco-nut used for anointing.

Sinata (comb) spell—over the comb.

Sayyaku—aromatic black paint.

Bowa—ordinary charcoal blacking.

Talo—red paint of crushed arecanut.

(B) MAGIC OF THE FINAL APPROACH (Chapter XIII, Division II)

Activity : the fleet are paddling (on the approach to Dobu) or punting (to Sinaketa) in a body.

Performers : in each canoe, simultaneously, the *toliwaga* and two members of the crew.

Aim : to "shake the mountain," to produce an impression on the partners awaiting on the beach.

Ta'uya—the ritual blowing of the conch shell, which has been charmed over before.

Kayikuna-tabuyo—the swaying of the front prow-board while the spell is being uttered.

Kavalikuliku—the spell by the *toliwaga*.

Kaytavilena mwoynawaga—the incantation uttered at the stern towards the *Koya*.

(C) MAGIC OF SAFETY (Chapter XIII, Division III)

Activity	Magic
Entering the Dobuan village (this magic is performed only when Boyowans come to the *Koya*).	*Ka'ubana'i*, charm uttered over ginger, which is then ritually spat over the Dobuan village and the partners, and makes their hearts soft.

(D) MAGIC OF PERSUASION (Chapter XIV, Division III)

Activity	Magic
The wooing in Kula (*wawoyla*) of the of the overseas partner by the visitor.	*Kwoygapani*—a spell uttered over a piece of areca-nut, given subsequently to the partner.

VII—A Canoe Spell, uttered on the Departure Home (Chapter XIV, Division III)

Activity	Magic
Loading of the canoe with the gifts received from overseas partners, with the trade gain, and with the provisions for the home journey.	*Kaylupa*—a spell to make the canoe lighter, to "lift" it out of the water.

Within each department of systematic magic, there are again various *systems of magic*. Thus we saw that, although the type of rite and formula is the same in all villages, the actual details, let us say, of the *wayugo* magic, are not identical, but vary according to the system with which a given reciter is acquainted. The differences are, as a rule, less pronounced in the rites, which are generally very simple in the Trobriand magic, and are identical in all the systems, but the formulæ differ completely in their wording. Thus, in the *wayugo* magic (Chapter V, Division III) we found only a slight difference in the rite, but one or two *wayugo* spells, which I have also recorded, differ essentially from the one given in the text.

Each system of magic has a more or less developed mythological pedigree, and in connection with it a local character, a point which has been elaborated in the previous Division. The *wayugo* spell given in Chapter V, and all the spells of canoe-building quoted in this book belong to the Kaykudayuri system of canoe magic. This system is believed to have been known and recited by the mythical builder of the flying canoe, and to have been handed down to his descendants, that is, as we know, in an incomplete form. As has been said in the previous Division, the knowledge and the use of this magic and of other systems does not abide strictly within the original clan, but it spreads outside of it, and it becomes known to many people who are connected with the original owner by a sort of magical filiation.

According to native belief, all these people know identical formulæ. In fact, in the course of years and of repeated transmission, considerable differences have been introduced, and nowadays many of the ' real Kudayuri ' spells differ from one another completely.

A system of magic is therefore a number of magical formulæ, forming one consecutive series. The main system of canoe magic is that of the Kaykudayuri, which is associated with the place of the same name in Kitava. This system comprises the whole series of canoe-building spells, from the expelling of the *tokway* to the final exorcisms. Another comprehensive system is called Kaykapayouko, and is localised in the island of Kayleula. An important system called Ilumte'ulo is nowadays claimed by Sinaketa, but probably hails from Dobu. The mythological data of some of these systems are not known to me, and some of them seem to be exceedingly rudimentary, not going beyond the assertion that such and such a system originated at such and such a place, and was originally the property of such and such a clan. Of the systems of *mwasila*, the best known in South Boyowa is that called Monikiniki, to which belong the majority of the formulæ here quoted. This system is sometimes loosely associated with the myth of Tokosikuna, who is sometimes said to have been the original owner of the system. According to another version, Monikiniki is the name of the original owner. The Dobuan *mwasila* is called Kasabwaybwayreta, and is ascribed to that hero. From Muyuwa, hails the Momroveta system of Kula magic, while in Kiriwina the system of Monikiniki is usually recited, and only a few formulæ are inserted into it, belonging to a local magic, called Kwoygapani (a name not to be confused with the name in a formula quoted in Chapter XIV). In the light of these remarks, the many references to ' magical systems ' given in the text, will become clear, so there is no need to add more here.

VIII

We saw before in the chapter on mythology that magic bridges over the cleavage between the super-normal world of myth and the normal, ordinary happenings of to-day. But then, this bridge itself must necessarily touch the super-normal, it must lead into that domain. Magic surely, therefore, must partake of the supernatural character ? There is no doubt that it is so. The effects of magic, although constantly witnessed, and although considered as a fundamental fact, are regarded as something distinctly different from the effects of other human activities. The natives realise quite well that the speed and buoyancy of a canoe are due to the knowledge and work of the constructor ; they are well acquainted with the properties of good material and of good craftsmanship. Yet the magic of swiftness adds something more to even the best constructed canoe. This superadded quality is regarded very much like the properties of the mythical canoe which made it fly through the air, though in the present day canoes these properties have dwindled down to mere surpassing speed.

The language of spells expresses this belief through the constant allusions to myth, similes in which the present canoe is invited to imitate the mythical one. In the explicit comments on the Kudayuri myth, the natives also state definitely that the prodigious speed which well-charmed canoes develop is the legacy and counterpart of the old flying speed. Thus the effects of magic are something superadded to all the other effects produced by human effort and by natural qualities. The same is to be found in love magic. The importance of a fine face and figure, of ornaments, decorations and nice scents, is well recognised as being of attractive value, yet almost every man ascribes his success to the perfection of his love magic. The force of magic is considered as something independent of, and surpassing even, the power of all other personal charms. A statement very often met with expresses this quite well :

" Look, I am not good looking, yet so many girls want me. The reason of that is that I have good magic."

In garden magic, soil, rain, proper work, are given their full due. None the less, no one would dream of making a garden without the full magical performance being done over it. Garden magic is thought to make just this difference, which a man hopes for from ' chance,' or ' good luck,' when he sees everybody round him working as hard as he can, and in all other respects under similar conditions to himself. So we see that, in all these cases, magical influence runs parallel to and independently of the effects of human work and natural conditions. It produces these differences and those unexpected results, which cannot be explained by any of the other factors.

So far, we see that magic represents, so to speak, a different sort of reality. When I call this different sort ' super-natural ' or ' super-normal,' one of the criteria which I use here lies in the emotional reaction of the natives. This, of course, is most pronounced in the case of evil magic. The sorcerer is not only feared because of his bad intentions. He is also feared as ghosts are feared by us, as an uncanny manifestation. One is afraid of meeting him in the dark, not so much because he might do any harm, but because his appearance is dreadful and because he has at his bidding all sorts of powers and faculties which are denied to those not versed in black magic. His sweat glows, night birds run with him to give him warning ; he can become invisible at will and produce paralysing fear in those he meets. In short, the same hysterical dread, associated amongst ourselves with the idea of haunted places, is produced by the sorcerers in the minds of the natives. And it must be added that the natives have no such emotion of dread at all with regard to the spirits of the departed. The horror which they have of the *bwaga'u* is even stronger in the case of the *mulukwausi*, to whom all sorts of most uncanny properties are attributed. Their ghoulish feasting on corpses, their capacity of flying, of making themselves invisible, of changing into night birds, all this inspires the natives with extreme terror.

The other magicians and their art do not inspire such strong emotions in the natives, and of course in any case the emotion would not be that of dread. There is a very great value and attachment to systems of local magic, and their effects are distinctly considered as an asset for a community.

Each form of magic also has its associated magical portent, *kariyala*. When a magic formula is spoken, a violent natural upheaval will take place. For example, when garden magic is performed, there will be thunder and lightning ; with certain forms of Kula magic, a rainbow will appear in the skies. Others will produce shower clouds. The portent of a mild storm, accompanying the opening of the magical bundle (*lilava*) has already been quoted. The *kayga'u* may produce a tidal wave, whereas an earthquake will be the result of other forms of magic. War magic, in an unexpectedly bucolic way, affects only some plants and birds. In certain forms of magic, a portent would take place whenever the formula is uttered, in others, this will not be so regular, but a *kariyala* will invariably occur when a magician dies. When asked, what is the real cause of any of these natural phenomena enumerated, they will say :

"Magic is the real cause (*u'ula*) ; they are a *kariyala* of magic."

Another point, where magic touches the super-normal or supernatural, is in the association of spirits with certain magical performances. A special type of magical payment, the *ula'ula*, is at the same time an offering to the *baloma* (spirits). The magician will detach a small bit of the large quantity of food brought to him, and put it down on some special place, with the words :

"Partake, O spirits, of your *ula'ula*, and make my magic thrive."

At certain ceremonies, the spirits are supposed to be present (see Plate LIX). When something goes wrong with magic, or it is badly performed, ' the spirits will become angry,' as it is often expressed by the natives. In some cases the *baloma* will appear in dreams and advise the magician what to do. As this is the most active interference of the spirits in human affairs, as far as magic is concerned, I shall quote in free translation some statements obtained on the matter.

" The owners of fish magic will often dream that there is plentiful fish. The cause of it is the magician's ancestor spirit. Such a magician would then say : ' The ancestral spirit has instructed me in the night, that we should go to catch fish ! And indeed, when we get there, we find plenty of fish, and we cast the nets.' "

" Mokudeya, the maternal uncle of Narugo," who is, the main fishing magician of Oburaku " comes to his nephew in a dream and instructs him : ' Tomorrow, cast the nets for fish in Kwabwawa ! ' Narugo then says : ' Let us come, the old man instructed me last night.' "

" The *kaloma* (spondylus shell) magician of Sinaketa dreams about a plentiful patch of *kaloma* shell. Next morning, he would dive and knock it off on the reef. Or he dreams of a canoe, and he then paddles and casts the anchor at that place. To'udawada, Luvayam, Sinakadi dream that they knock it off in plenty. When next morning we go there, it is plentiful."

In all these examples (except the last) we see that the spirits act as advisors and helpers. They fill the rôle of guardian of the traditions when they get angry because of a bad performance, or as associates and sympathisers when they share the magician's *ula'ula*. But they are not agencies which get to work directly. In the Trobriand demonology, the magician does not command the spirits to go and set to work. The work is done by the agency of the spell, assisted by the accompanying ritual, and performed by the proper magician. The spirits stand in the same relation, as the performer does, to the magical force, which alone is active. They can help him to wield it properly, but they can never become his instruments.

To summarise the results of what we have learned about the super-normal nature of magic, it may be said that it has a definite character of its own, which differentiates it from the non-magical actions of man. The manner in which the magical force is conceived to act, parallel to the ordinary efforts but independent of them ; the emotional reaction to certain types of magic and magician ; the *kariyala ;* the intercourse with spirits during the performances, all these properties differentiate magic from the ordinary activities of man.

In native terminology, the realm of the magical is called by the word *megwa*, which describes the ' magical performance,' the ' spell,' the ' force ' or ' virtue ' of magic, and can be used as adjective to describe in general everything which presents a magical character. Used as a verb, the words *megwa, miga-megwa, miga,* all of which are variations of the same root, mean : ' to perform magic,' ' to utter a spell,' ' to carry out a rite.' If the natives want to express that certain actions are done in connection with magic, and not with work, and that certain effects are due to magical forces, and not to other efforts, they used the word *megwa* as a substantive or adjective. It is never used to describe any virtue residing in a man or a thing, nor for any action which is independent of a spell.

The associated concept of taboo is covered by the Kiriwinian word *bomala* (with suffixed possessive pronouns). It means a ' prohibition,' something which a man is not allowed to do under any circumstances. It is used for magical taboos, for prohibitions associated with rank, for restrictions in regard to food generally considered as unclean, as, for example, the flesh of lizards, snakes, dogs and man. There is hardly any trace of the meaning of ' sacred ' attached to the word *bomala*. If anywhere, it can be found in the use of the word *boma*, for a tabooed grove where men usually are not allowed to enter, and where traditional spots, often original holes where men came out and whence magic issued, are to be found. The expression *toboma* (*to-*, prefix denoting personal noun) means a man of high rank, but hardly a sacred man.

IX

Finally, a few words must be said about the sociological or ceremonial setting of magic. Reference has often been made to the simplicity of rites, and to their matter-of-fact character. This has been mentioned with reference to canoe-building, and in garden magic we would have found equally simple and purely businesslike performances. In calling a

magical action ' ceremonial ' we imply that it was done with a
big public attendance ; under the observance of definite rules
of behaviour by the spectators as well as by the performer,
such as general silence, reverent attention to what is being
done, with at least a show of some interest.   Now if, in the
middle of some work, a man quickly performs an action whilst
others talk and laugh and leave him entirely on one side, this
gives a definite sociological stamp to the magical actions, and
does not allow us to use the term ' ceremonial,' as the distinguishing mark of the magical acts.   Some of them, it is
true, do have this character.   For instance, the initial rite with
which the *kaloma* fishing begins, requires the assistance of the
whole fleet, and a definite type of behaviour on the part of the
crews, while the magician officiates for all of them, but with
their assistance, in the complex evolutions of the fleet.   Similar
rites are to be found in two or three systems of fishing magic,
and in several rites of the garden magic of certain villages.   In
fact, the initial rite of garden magic is everywhere connected
with a ceremonial performance.   The garden rite, associated
with the ceremonial offering of food to spirits, and attended by
a body of villagers, a scene of which is shown on Plate LIX,
has been elsewhere described.*   One or two rites in war magic
imply the active assistance of large numbers of men, and take
the form of big ceremonies.   Thus we see that magical rites
may or may not be ceremonial, but that the *ceremonial* is by
no means an outstanding or universal feature of Trobriand
magic.

X

We found that taboos are associated with magic, in so far
as it is the magician who has to observe them.   There are,
however, certain forms of restrictions or prohibitions, set up for
special purposes, and associated with magic in a somewhat
different form.   Thus, in an institution called *kaytubutabu* we
find a ban made on the consumption of coco-nuts and betel-nuts,
associated with a specific magic to make them grow.   There is
also a protective taboo, used to prevent the theft of ripening
fruits or nuts, too far away from the village to be watched.   In
these cases a small parcel of medicated substance is placed on

* See article by the Author on the " Baloma, spirits of the dead in the
Trobriand Islands."   J. A. I., 1917.

the tree or near it, on a small stick. The magic spoken over such a substance is a ' conditional curse,' to use the excellent term introduced by Professsor Westermarck. The conditional curse would fall upon anyone who would touch the fruits of that tree, and would bring upon him one form of disease or another. This is the only form of magic, in which the personal agency is invoked, for in some of these spells, the *tokway* (wood sprite) is invited to take up his abode on the *kaytapaku*, that is the stick, with the substance on it, and to guard the fruit. Some such small divergencies from the general trend of native belief are always to be found. Sometimes they contain important clues, and a deeper insight into the facts, sometimes they mean nothing, and only emphasise the fact, that it is not possible to find absolute consistency in human belief. Only a deeper analysis, and a comparative study of similar phenomena can decide which is the case.

XI

In order to complete the survey of all the characteristics of magic, I shall rapidly mention here the economic aspect of the position of magician, although the data referring to it have already been given, scattered through the previous chapters. I have spoken of the matrilineal inheritance of magic, and of the deviations from it which consist in inheritance from father to son, and in the transmission of magic by purchase (Chapter II, Divison VI, and Chapter VI, Division VI under (5)). This latter transaction may take place under two names, which really cover two essentially different operations ; the *pokala* or payment to a maternal kinsman from whom one is going to obtain the magic, and the *laga*, which is the purchase of magic from a stranger. Only certain forms of magic can freely pass from one clan or sub-clan to another, and are purchasable by the *laga* system. The majority of magical systems are local, and can descend only in the same sub-clan with an occasional deviation to the son of a member, from whom, however, the magic must return to the sub-clan again. A further economic feature of magic is the payment, which the magician receives for his services. There are many types of payment ; some given occasionally by an individual for a definite act of magic, as in the case of sorcery or healing magic ; others, paid at regular intervals by the whole community, as in the case of garden and fishing magic. In some cases the payments are considerable, as in sorcery, in rain and fine weather magic, and in garden magic. In others, they amount to little more than a mere formal offering.

XII

In all this, we have been dealing with general characteristics of Boyowan (Trobriand) magic. This has been done mainly on the basis of the material presented in this volume, with only a few examples from other branches of magic. The result so far can be set down thus : magic to the natives represents a special department ; it is a specific power, essentially human, autonomous and independent in its action. This power is an inherent property of certain words, uttered with the performance of certain actions by the man entitled to do it through his social traditions and through certain observances which he has to keep. The words and acts have this power in their own right, and their action is direct and not mediated by any other agency. Their power is not derived from the authority of spirits or demons or supernatural beings. It is not conceived as having been wrested from nature. The belief in the power of words and rites as a fundamental and irreducible force is the ultimate, basic dogma of their magical creed. Hence we find established the ideas that one never can tamper with, change or improve spells ; that tradition is the only source from which they can be derived ; that it has brought them down from times lying beyond the speculation of man, that there can be no spontaneous generation of magic.

We are naturally led now to inquire one stage further into the manner in which the magical words and rites act. Obviously the only way to obtain correct information on this point is to analyse and compare a great number of well authenticated formulæ, and minutely recorded rites. Even the collection of Kula magic here partially given in free translation, would allow us to arrive at certain interesting conclusions. But we can go deeper still with the help of linguistic analysis, and we shall proceed to this inquiry in the next chapter.

Chapter XVIII

THE POWER OF WORDS IN MAGIC—SOME LINGUISTIC DATA

I

THE aim of this Chapter is to show by a linguistic analysis of two magical texts, and by a general survey of a greater number, what sort of words are believed to exercise magical power. This, of course, does not mean that we are under the delusion that the composers or inventers of magic had a theory about the efficiency of words, and carried this theory into practice by inventing the formula. But, as the moral ideas and rules prevalent in society, though not codified, can be found out by analysing human behaviour ; as we reach the underlying principles of law and social propriety by examining customs and manners ; as in the study of rites, we see some definite tenets of belief and dogmas—so, in analysing the direct verbal expressions of certain modes of thinking in the magical formulæ, we are justified in assuming that these modes of thinking must have somehow guided those who shaped them. The exact manner in which we must imagine the relation between a typical way of thinking in a society on the one hand, and the fixed, crystallised results of this thinking on the other, is a problem of Social Psychology. For this branch of science we are, in ethnography, under the obligation of gathering material, but we need not encroach upon its field of study.

Thus much may, however, be put down, that, in whatever manner we might imagine a spell to have come into existence, it cannot be considered as the creation of one man ; for as has been said before, if we examine any one of them, not with the eyes of the natives, but as outside critics, each spell shows unmistakable signs of being a collection of linguistic additions from different epochs. There is in practically every one of them a good deal of archaic material, but not a single one bears the stamp of having come down to us in the same form in which it must have presented itself a few generations ago. So that it may be said that a spell is constantly being remoulded as it passes through the chain of magicians, each probably leaving his mark, however small, upon it. It is the general attitude in matters of magical belief common to all of the successive holders which will be at the bottom of all the regularities, all the typical features found in the spells.

I shall adduce a formula of canoe magic and one of the spells belonging to the *mwasila*, choosing two texts of which a translation and a commentary of average quality have been obtained, and which show clearly the several characteristic features of verbal magic. Those who are not interested in linguistic technicalities and details of method, may omit the following division, and take up the trend of our argument at division XII.

II

The following text is the *wayugo* spell, obtained from Layseta, the headman of Kopila, one of the sub-villages of Sinaketa. The commentary was obtained from himself, and from another informant, Motago'i, a man of exceptional intelligence, and a very straightforward and a reliable informant. This spell has been given in free translation before in Chapter VI, and, as has been said there, the rite consists simply in chanting the words over five coils of the *wayugo* creeeper put on a wooden platter between two mats.

WAYUGO SPELL

A. U'ULA (INITIAL PART)

1 *Kala*   *bosisi'ula*,   *kala*   *bomwalela*.
1 His   ritual eating of fish,   his   tabooed inside.

2 *Papapa*,   *silubida*,   *monagakalava*.
2 Flutter,   betel plant,   leaving behind.

3   *Tubugu Kalabotawosi*,   *Tubugu Kwaysa'i*,
3 Grandfather Kalabotawosi,   grandfather Kwaysa'i,

   Tubugu Pulupolu,   *Tubugu Semkuku*,
   grandfather Pulupolu,   grandfather Semkuku,

3   *Tubugu Kabatuwayaga,*   *Tubugu Ugwaboda,*
    grandfather Kabatuwayaga,   grandfather Ugwaboda,

    Tubugu Kitava,   *Bulumava'u Nawabudoga,*
    grandfather Kitava,   new spirit Nawabudoga,

        kaykapwapu   *Mogilawota.*
    immediate predecessor   Mogilawota.

4   *Kusilase*   *onikota,*   *bukwa'u'i kambu'a.*
4   You sit   on canoe slips, you chew your areca-nut.

5   *Kwawoyse*   *bisalena*   *Kaykudayuri*
5   You take   his pandanus streamer (of) Kaykudayuri

    Kusaylase   *odabana*   *Teula*
    you place (it)   on top   (of) Teula.

6   *Basivila,*   *basivilake'i*   *Kitava miTo'uru,*
6   I might turn,   I might turn on   Kitava your Touru,

        mimilaveta   *Pilolu.*
    your sea-arm   Pilolu.

7   *Nagayne*   *isipukayse*   *girina*   *Kaykudayuri.*
7   To-day   they kindle   festive fire (of) Kaykudayuri.

8   *Kumwam*   *dabem*   *Siyaygana,*
8   Thou bind together   thy skirt   Siyaygana,

    bukuyova.
    thou fly.

9   *Bakabima*   *kaykabila,*   *bakipatuma*
9   I might clutch   the adze handle,   I might grip

        yogwayogula
    the component sticks.

10 *Baterera*   *odabana*   *Kuyawa.*
10 I might fly   on top (of)   Kuyawa.

B. Tapwana (Main Part)

11 *Odabana Kuyawa,*   *odabana Kuyawa* . . . ;
11 On top (of) Kuyawa,   on top (of) Kuyawa . . . ;
                                   (repeated several times)

        bayokokoba   *odabana Kuyawa ;*
    I might become like smoke   on top (of) Kuyawa ;
        bayowaysulu   *odabana Kuyawa ;*
    I might become invisible   on top (of) Kuyawa ;
        bayovivilu'a, etc. ;
    I might become as a wind eddy, etc. ;

11   *bayomwaleta, etc. ;*   *bayokarige, etc. ;*
I might become alone, etc. ;   I might become as dead, etc. ;

    bayotamwa'u, etc ;   *bayogugwa'u, etc. ;*
I might disappear, etc. ;   I might become like mist, etc. ;

12 The verses 9, 10 and 11 are repeated, substituting Dikutuva for Kuyawa.

13 The verses 9, 10 and 11 are repeated, substituting La'u for Kuyawa. After this, the *u'ula* is repeated, and then a secondary *tapwana* follows.

14   *Bakalatatava,*   *bakalatatava*   . . . . ;
14 I might heel over,   I might heel over . . . . ;
                                (repeated several times)

ula sibu   *bakalatatava ;*   *ulo koumwali*
my keel   I might heel over ;   my canoe gunwale

   bakalatatava ;   *uli sirota, etc. ;*
I might heel over ;   my canoe bottom, etc. ;

ulo katukulu, etc. ;   *ulo gelu, etc. ;*   *ulo kaysuya, etc. ;*
my prow, etc. ;   my rib, etc. ;   my threading stick, etc. ;

  uli tabuyo, etc. ;   *uli lagim, etc. ;*
my prowboard, etc. ;   my transverse board, etc. ;

 ulo kawaydala, etc.
my canoe side, etc.

The *u'ula* is repeated again and the spell is closed by the *dogina* (concluding part).

C. Dogina (Conclusion)

15   *Kalubasisi*   *kalubayo'u ;*   *kuvaylise mayena,*
15 (Untranslatable)   flying(?) ;   you hit his tongue,

 kuvaylise bubuwala,   *kulakwoyse*   *kala*   *sibu*   *waga.*
 you hit   his chest,   you untie   his   keel   canoe.

16 *Wagam,*   *kousi,*   *wagam,*   *vivilu'a,*
16 Canoe (thou art) ghost,   canoe, (thou art) wind eddy,

  kuyokarige   *Siyaygana,*   *bukuyova.*
  thou vanish   Siyaygana,   thou fly.

17 *Kwarisasa*   *kamkarikeda*   *Kadimwatu ;*
17 Thou pierce   thy sea-passage   Kadimwatu ;

    kwaripwo   *kabaluna*   *Saramwa ;*
  thou break through   nose his   Saramwa ;

kwabadibadi   *Loma.*
thou meet   Loma.

18	*Kuyokarige,*		*kuyotamwa'u,*	
18	Thou become as dead,		thou disappear,	

	kuyovivilu'a		*kuyogugwa'u.*	
	thou become as a wind eddy,		thou become like mist.	

19	*Kusola*	*kammayamaya,*	*kwotutine*	*kamgulupeya;*
19	Thou mould	the fine sand,	thou cut	thy seaweed;

	kuna,	*kugoguna*	*kambwoymatala.*	
	thou go,	thou put on	thy butia wreath.	

We have here the native text, translated word for word, each expression and formative affix being rendered by its English equivalent. In obtaining such a verbatim translation and subsequently putting it into a free, intelligible English rendering, there are two main difficulties to be overcome. A considerable proportion of the words found in magic do not belong to ordinary speech, but are archaisms, mythical names and strange compounds, formed according to unusual linguistic rules. Thus the first task is to elucidate the obsolete expressions, the mythical references, and to find the present day equivalents of any archaic words. Even if we obtain a series of meanings corresponding to each term of the original text, there is often considerable difficulty in linking these meanings together. Magic is not built up in the narrative style; it does not serve to communicate ideas from one person to another; it does not purport to contain a consecutive, consistent meaning. It is an instrument serving special purposes, intended for the exercise of man's specific power over things, and *its meaning*, giving this word a wider sense, can be understood only in correlation to this aim. It will not be therefore a meaning of logically or topically concatenated ideas, but of expressions fitting into one another and into the whole, according to what could be called a magical order of thinking, or perhaps more correctly, a magical order of expressing, of launching words towards their aim. It is clear that this magical order of verbal concatenations—I am purposely avoiding the expression 'magical logic' for there is no logic in the case—must be known and familiar to anyone who wishes really to understand the spells. There is therefore a great initial difficulty in 'reading' such documents, and only an acquaintance with a great number makes one more confident and more competent.

III

In the ordinary routine of working out such texts, I tried to obtain from the magician the equivalents, word for word, of the more cryptic expressions. As a rule the magician himself knows a good deal more than anyone else about the mythical references, and about certain esoteric expressions contained in the spell. There are some unintelligent old men, unfortunately, who rattle off a formula, and who evidently never were interested about its significance or else forgot all about it, and are no good as commentators. Often a fairly good informant, quite capable of reciting a spell slowly and intelligibly, without losing his thread, will be of no use as linguistic informant, that is in helping to obtain a definition of a word, in assisting to break it up into its formative parts; in explaining which words belong to ordinary speech, which are dialectic, which are archaic, and which are purely magical compounds. I had only a few informants who could help me in this way, and among them the previously mentioned Motago'i was one of the best.

The analysis to which I now proceed can be given only in an approximate manner, for in a full one, a long disquisition on grammar would have to be given first. It will be enough, however, to show in broad outline the main linguistic features of a spell, as well as the methods which have been used in constructing the free translation given in the previous chapters.

The formula here quoted, shows the typical tripartition of the longer spells. The first part is called *u'ula*. This word means the 'bottom part' of a tree or post, the 'foundation' of any structure, and in more figurative uses, it means 'reason' 'cause,' or, again, 'beginning.' It is in this last sense that the natives apply it to the first strophe of a song, and to the exordium of a magical formula. The second part of the spell is called *tapwana*, literally: 'surface,' 'skin,' 'body,' 'trunk,' 'middle part' of a tree, 'main part' of a road, and thus 'main part' of a spell or song. The word *dogina*, literally the 'tip' or 'end,' used for the 'tip' of a tree or the 'end' of a tail, is used to designate the 'final part' or the 'conclusion' of a spell. Sometimes the word *dabwana*, 'top,' or 'head,' (not human head) is substituted for *dogina*. Thus the spell must be imagined turned upside down, its beginning put at the basis, the *u'ula*, its main part where the middle trunk would be, and its end at the tip, the *dogina*.

The opening words of the *u'ula* in this spell are short, cutting, pithy expressions, each standing for its own cycle of ideas, for a sentence or even a whole story. In this they are typical of the beginnings of Kiriwinian spells. They are also typical, in the great difficulty which they present to the interpreter. Out of the seven words contained in phrases 1 and 2, four do not belong to ordinary speech, and are obscure compounds. Thus the words *bosisi'ula* and *bomwalela* are made up first of the prefix *bo-*, which carries with it the meaning of ' tabooed,' ' belonging to magic,' and of the two roots *sisiula* and *mwalela*, neither of which is a complete word. The first is the root part of the word *visisi'ula*, which designates a custom associated with this magic. At certain times, in connection with the performance of the *wayugo* rite, the magician has fits of trembling and then he has to be given some baked fish, and after partaking of it his trembling fit passes. The natives say that he trembles like a *bisila* (pandanus streamer) and that this shows that his magic is good, since the trembling of the pandanus is a symbol of speed. *Mwalela* is derived from *olumwalela* which means ' inside.' With the prefix *bo-* the word can be translated ' the tabooed inside.'

It is even more difficult to interpret the general meaning of these two expressions, than to find out their literal equivalents. We have an allusion to a ritual eating of fish, associated with a trembling which symbolises speed, and we have an expression ' tabooed inside.' The custom of eating fish after trembling has a magical importance. It adds to the efficiency of magic, as all such observances do. The force or merit of this observance, which, dissociated from the spell and the rite can have no direct effect, is made available by being mentioned in the formula ; it is so to speak, magically discounted. This is the best way in which I can interpret the two words of ritual eating and of tabooed interior of the magician.

The three words of sentence 2 have each to tell its own story. The word *papapa*, ' flutter,' stands for a phrase : " let the canoe speed so that the pandanus leaves flutter." Of course the word expresses much more than this sentence, because it is intelligible only to those who are acquainted with the part played by the pandanus leaves in the decoration of canoes, with the native ideas about magical association between flutter and speed, and with the ritual use of pandanus streamers. Therefore the word has a meaning only if taken with the context of this formula, in connection with its aim, with the various associated ideas and customs. To the native, who knows all this and in whose mind the whole context rises, when he hears or repeats 'papapa,' the word quivers with magical force. The word *silubida*, an especial magical transformation of *lilobida*, stands for a certain variety of the betel pepper plant. The word *monagakalava* is again an elaborate compound carrying the meaning 'to leave behind.' The betel plant is a common magical ingredient, and in this spell, the ancestral spirits will presently be invited to chew betel-nut. 'Leaving behind' undoubtedly refers to the other canoes which will be outrun by that of the reciter. Both these words, therefore, can be placed without much difficulty into the context of this spell. It is quite clear, as has been said , that each of these expressions stands alone and represents a self-contained cycle of ideas. The two expressions of sentence 1 probably do belong to one another, but even they represent each one-half of a complex story.

Then, in 3, there comes a long list of names of ancestors, all of whom are said to be real men who had lived in Kitava, the home of this magic. The words *kwaysa'i*, 'stormy sea,' and *pulupolu*, 'boiling up,' 'foaming up,' suggest that the names are significant and therefore mythical. Nawabudoga, a Kitavan man, was father of the last-mentioned one, Mogilawota, a maternal relative of the present owner, We see here, therefore, a good case of 'magical filiation,' by which the present owner, a man of Sinaketa, is connected with the mythical district of Kitava.

The following two sentences, 4 and 5, are linguistically much clearer and simpler, and they present connected sequences of words. They are an invocation to ancestral spirits, asking them to join the magician at the canoe, which is called here Kaykudayuri, 'the craft of the Kudayuri,'' and to place the pandanus streamers on the top of Teulo. This, in an exaggerated and figurative speech, expresses an invitation to the spirits to follow the man on his trip. It must be noted that, according to the present belief at least, the spirits are not conceived as agents or forces which carry the canoe at the behest of the magician, but as passive companions only. Sentence 6 contains a scornful address to his companions ; the magician in prospect sees himself sailing ahead towards the mountains; as he turns round, the Kitava men, that is his companions, are far behind on the beach of To'uru, and the whole sea-arm of Pilolu still lies before them.

In 7, the same trend of ideas is followed ; the custom of kindling the fire by the first canoe is alluded to, and the magician sees himself carrying out this privilege. It is to be noted that he speaks always of his canoe under the name of Kudayuri, that is of the mythical flying canoe of ancient times. In 8, the canoe is addressed as a flying witch, who is asked to bind her skirt together and to fly. In 9, the magician verbally retraces an incident from the original myth of Kudayuri. He takes the adze handle, gets hold of the canoe, and strikes it, whereupon the canoe flies.

Thus the *u'ula* begins with archaic, condensed compounds each carrying a self-contained cycle of magical meaning. Then follows a list of forbears ; then more explicit and, at the same time more dramatic sentences ; an invocation to ancestral spirits, the anticipated victory in speed, the reconstructed mythical incident.

IV

Let us pass now to the *tapwana*. This is always the longest part of a spell, since we have a whole list of words which have to be repeated with several key expressions, of which in the present case there are three. Moreover, the magician can *ad libitum* repeat the same words over and over again with a key word. He will not go in any fixed order over all the words of the list, but is allowed, in this part of the formula, to return and repeat with one key-word the various items of the list.

It will be best to say here a few words about the manner in which the magical formulæ are actually recited. The opening words are always intoned with a strong, melodious cadence which is not permanently fixed, but varies with the magician. The first words are repeated some several times. Thus here, *kala bosisi'ula* would be reiterated three or four times, and so would be the following two words (*kala bomwalela*). The words of No. 2 are recited slowly and ponderously but not repeated.

The list of ancestors is run over quickly and perfunctorily. The rest of the *u'ula*, its dramatic part so to speak, is spoken with less melody, more with the ordinary speaking voice and more rapidly.

Then comes the last sentence of the *u'ula*, which in almost all spells links it up with the main part. This is always intoned slowly, solemnly and distinctly ; the voice drops at the end by the interval of a tone. In the *tapwana*, the key word, or key expression, which forms always the concluding part of the *u'ula*, is taken up again. It is repeated several times, as if to fix or rub it well in. Then, dropping into a quick, continuous stream of utterance, the magician runs over one word of the list after the other. The key-word is inserted between each of them, said sometimes once, sometimes two or three times. It gives an effect as if the key-word were being rubbed in into every one of the other expressions. They as a rule spoken more slowly, mark the rhythm of this part. The reciting of the last part of a spell, the *dogina* or *dabwana*, is more perfunctory, usually it is rather spoken than chanted.

After this digression, let us return to the analysis of our spell. It is a rule that the *tapwana*, the main part of a formula, is easier to translate, expressed in less archaic and less condensed terms, than the *u'ula*. The *tapwana* of this spell has quite easy key-words, both in its first and in its second part. In the first one (phrase 11) the key-words are of mythical nature, referring to localities associated with the flying of one of the Kudayuri sisters. In the second *tapwana*, the key-word means : ' I might heel over ' or ' I shall heel over,' that is with speed. And this expression stands here for : ' I shall overtake,' and the list of words pronounced with this verb denotes the various parts of a canoe. The second part of the *tapwana* (phrase 14) is much more typical than the first, because the key word is a verb, whilst the list words are nouns. It is typical also, in that the verb expresses, in a simple and direct manner, the magical effect of the spell (the overtaking of the other canoes) whereas the sum of the words of the list gives the object of the spell, that is, the canoe. Such *tapwana*, in which the magical action is expressed as a verb, while in the list of words we have mentioned the various parts of a garden or of fishing nets, or weapons or parts of the human body, are to be found in all classes of magic.

The first part of the *tapwana* (phrases 11, 12, and 13) is less typical, in so far that the verbs depicting various magical actions are relegated into the list, while the key-words are adverbial expressions of locality. The verbal links of the long chain express all and one in a metaphoric manner the speed of the canoe. ' I shall fly, I shall become like smoke, I shall become invisible, I shall become as a wind eddy, etc," are all rather picturesque, concrete descriptions of surpassing speed. They present also a linguistic symmetry and singularity. The prefix *ba-* is the form of the future or potential tense, which I have literally translated 'might,' but which stands here for ' shall ' The formative prefix *yo-* is a causative, and stands for ' become as ' or ' become like.' Then follows the root : *kokoba-* ' smoke which trails in clouds above a burning garden.' Hence the expression *bayokokoba*, in its full concrete meaning, could be translated : ' I shall become like clouds of trailing smoke.' Again, *boyowaysula* in its full meaning could be translated : ' I shall become invisible as distant spray.' The only abstract word in this list is *tamwa'u*, which literally means, ' to disappear.' So, in this *tapwana*, the list consists of a number of formally similar words, each expressing the same general meaning in a concrete metaphorical manner. The length of the whole *tapwana* (main body) of the spell can be imagined, since in the middle between its two sections the *u'ula* is recited once more.

The last part of this spell, the *dogina*, contains an explicit allusion to the Kudayuri myth and to several geographic localities, which are mentioned in that myth. It also shows the usual *crescendo*, characteristic of the conclusions of a spell. The final results are anticipated in exaggerated, forceful language.

V

So much about the *wayugo* spell. I shall adduce now another spell of a somewhat different type, belonging to the *mwasila* (Kula magic). It is distinctly a more modern formula ; there are hardly any archaic expressions ; words are not used, as independent sentences each ; on the whole it is easily understandable and has a consecutive meaning.

KAYIKUNA SULUMWOYA (also called SUMGEYYATA)

A. U'ula (Initial Part)

1 *Avayta'u*   *netata'i*   *sulumwoyala*   *Laba'i ?*
1 Who   cuts   the mint plant of   Laba'i ?

   Yaygu,   *Kwoyregu,*   *sogu*   *tamagu,*
   I,   Kwoyregu,   together with   my father,

   katata'i   *sulumwoyala*   *Laba'i.*
   we cut   the mint plant of   Laba'i.

2   *Silimwaynunuva,*   *inunuva ;*   *silimwayniku,*
2 The roaring sulumwoya, it roars ; the quaking sulumwoya

   iniku ;   *silimwayyega,*   *iyega ;*
   it quakes ;   the soughing sulumwoya,   it soughs ;

    silimwaypolu,   *ipolu.*
   the boiling sulumwoya,   it boils.

B.—Tapwana (Main Part)

3   *Ipolu,*   *ipolu*   *ipolu* . .   *agu sulumwoya*
3 It boils,   it boils,   it boils . .   my mint plant

   ipolu ;   *agu*   *vana,*   *ipolu ;*   *agu*
   it boils ;   my   herb ornaments,   it boils ;   my

    kena   *ipolu ;*   *agu*   *yaguma*   *ipolu ;*
   lime spatula   it boils ;   my   lime pot   it boils ;

   agu   *sinata*   *ipolu ;*   *agu*   *mo'i*   *ipolu ;*
   my   comb   it boils ;   my   mat   it boils ;

   agu   *pari*   *ipolu ;*   *agu*   *vataga*
   my   presentation goods   it boils ;   my   big basket

   ipolu ;   *agu*   *kauyo*   *ipolu ;*   *agu*
   it boils ;   my   personal basket   it boils ;   my

    lilava   *ipolu.*
   magical bundle   it boils.

   Dabagu   *ipolu ;*   *kabulugu*   *ipolu ;*   *kaygadugu*
   my head   it boils ;   my nose   it boils ; my occiput

   ipolu ;   *mayyegu*   *ipolu ;*   *tabagu*   *ipolu ;*
   it boils ;   my tongue   it boils ;   my larynx   it boils ;

    kawagu   *ipolu ;*   *wadogu*   *ipolu ;*
   my speaking organ   it boils ;   my mouth   it boils ;

   ula   *woyla*   *ipolu.*
   my   Kula courting   it boils.

C.—Dogina (Conclusion)

4 *Bulumava'u*   *kadagu*   *Mwoyalova*
4 New spirit   my maternal uncle   Mwoyalova

  kuvapwo   *dabana*   *Monikiniki,*
  thou breathe   (the spell over) the head (of) Monikiniki,

  kuvapokayma   *dabana*   *agu*
  thou breathe   (the spell over) the head (of)   my

  touto'u.
  light wood.

5 *Avaliwo*   *koya—*   *isikila*   *koya* ;
5 I kick   the mountain—   it tilts over,   the mountain ;

  imwaliku   *koya* ;   *ikaywa'u*   *koya* ;
  it subsides,   the mountain ;   it opens up, the mountain ;

   isabwani   *koya* ;   *itakubile*
  it jubilates,   the mountain ;   it topples over,

    koya ;   *itakubilatala*   *koya.*
  the mountain ;   it topples down,   the mountain.

6 *Avapwoyma*   *dabana*   *Koyava'u ;*
6 I breathe   (a spell over)   the head (of)   Koyava'u ;

  avapokayma   *lopoum*   *Siyaygana*;
  I charm   thy inside   (of)   Siyaygana (canoe) ;

  akulubeku   *wagana*   *akulisonu*   *lumanena.*
  I drown   the waga   I submerge   the lamina.

7 *Gala*   *butugu,*   *butugu*   *pilapala* ;   *gala*
7 Not   my renown   my renown   thunder ;   not

   valigu,   *valigu*   *tumwadudu*
  my treading,   my treading   noise made by flying witches (?)

  tudududu.
  tudududu.

The opening sentences of the formula are so clear that the translation word for word explains itself without any closer commentary, except of course as far as the names are concerned. Laba'i is a village in the North of Kiriwina, and it plays a considerable part in the mythology of the origin of man, since several of the principal sub-clans emerged there from underground. Laba'i is also the home of the mythical culture-hero Tudava. The mythology of the Kula, however, does not include Laba'i amongst the places, on which it touches. Perhaps this somewhat anomalous features of the formula may be connected with its obvious linguistic modernity ? The other personal name mentioned in this spell is Kwoyregu, on which Layseta, who gave me this magic, commented in the following manner :

> " A man, he lived in Laba'i, the master of the magic. It was not this man who first knew the magic of Moni-kiniki. That magic was partly found by Tokosikuna, partly in olden days in Sinaketa."

In explaining this commentary it must be noted that the informant was a Sinaketan man, hence his local patriotism, for there is no definite, mythological version connecting the early practice of the *mwasila* with the village of Sinaketa. As we saw, Tokosikuna is indeed one of the mythical heroes with whose story the magic of *mwasila* is associated. Monikiniki is the name of one of the systems of the *mwasila* magic, which usually is said to come from a man of that name.

Phrase 2 of this spell contains four couples, each consisting of a compound and a verb. The substantival compounds have all, according to the alliterative symmetry so dear to Kiriwinian magic, the prefix *silimway-*, derived from *sulumwoya*, the mint plant. Such play on words, especially on what is the leading word in a spell, as *sulumwoya* is here, shows that the purely phonetic handling of words must be associated with the idea or feeling of their inherent power. The keyword of the *tapwana* (phrase 3), has been translated, literally ' it boils.' Perhaps it might have been translated in its other slightly different meaning ' it foams.' Probably it has both meanings to the mind of the native reciter. I think that the use of a word fraught with two meanings at the same time is one of the characteristics of native language. In this spell, for instance, the word *polu* appears as one in a series of such verbs as ' to roar,' ' to quake,' ' to sough,' all carrying the meaning of ' noise,' ' commotion,' ' stir,' a meaning which is in harmony with the magical effects to be produced by the *mwasila* magic. In this context the obvious translation of the word would be : ' to foam.' On the other hand, this spell is said over a piece of mint, which will be preserved in boiled coco-nut oil, and the double meaning here contained might be paraphrased in this manner : " as the oil of the *sulumwoya* boils, so may my renown (or the eagerness of my partner?) foam up." Thus the word *polu* would link up the meaning of the rite of boiling with the context of this spell. This explanation, however, has not been obtained from a native informant, though it is undoubtedly in keeping with the general type of current explanations. What I have called before the magical concatenation of magical ideas consists in just such connections of words and their meanings.

The *dogina* (final part) contains one or two typical features. For instance, in phrase 4, the maternal uncle of the present reciter is asked to breathe the spell over the head of Monikiniki. In this, the present owner of the spell identifies his canoe with that of the mythical hero. In 5, 6 and 7, we have several grandiloquent expressions such as that refering to the commotion on the mountain ; that comparing his renown to thunder, and his treading to the noise made by *mulukwausi ;* and that describing how the *waga* will sink, through being overfilled with valuables. The last part would, as usual, be recited in a much more perfunctory and quick manner, giving it the effect of piling up words, one forceful phrase following another It ends with the onomatopoetic sound *tudududu* . . . which stands for the roll of the thunder.

VI

The two specimens of magic here given in the original with a verbal translation, show how the linguistic analysis allows us a much deeper insight into the magical value of words, as it is felt by the natives. On the one hand, the various phonetic characteristics show the handling of words when these have to convey magical force. On the other hand, only an analysis word for word of the spells could give us a good insight into the frequently mentioned magical concatenation of ideas and verbal expressions. It is, however, impossible to adduce here all the spells in their full original version with linguistic comments, as this would lead us into a treatise on the language of magic. We may, however, quickly pass over some of the other spells and point out in them the salient features of magical expression, and thus amplify the results so far obtained by the detailed analysis of these two spells.

Of course these two examples belong to the longer type consisting of three parts. Many of the spells previously quoted in free translation contain no main part, though it is possible to

distinguish their *u'ula* (exordium) from their *dogina* (finale).
The very first spell quoted in Chapter VI, the formula of the
Vabusi Tokway (the expulsion of the wood sprite) is an
anomalous one. It is an invocation, and it is not even chanted
but has to be spoken in a low persuasive voice. It consists of
two parts : in the first one the word *kubusi* (' thou comest
down ') used as an imperative, ' come down ! ' is repeated with
all sorts of descriptions and circumscriptions of the wood-
sprites. In the second part, several sentences are repeated to
make the wood-sprite feel that he has been chased away. Both
the keyword of the first part, *kubusi*, and the sentences of the
second part have a direct force of their own. It must be
realised that, for the natives, it is a great insult to be told to go
away. *Yoba*, the ' expulsion,' the ' command to go,' stands in
a category of its own. People are *yoba'd*, expelled from communities in certain circumstances, and a man would never
dream of remaining, when thus treated. Therefore the words
in this spell possess a force due to social sanctions of native
custom. The next spell, given in Chapter VI, the *Kaymomwa'u*,
is also anomalous for it consists of one part only. The word
kubusi, ' come down ' is also repeated here, with various words
designating defilements and broken taboos. These qualities
are, however, not thought of as personified beings. The force
of the word is probably also derived from the ideas about the
yoba.

The second spell, which is a pendant to the *Kaymomwa'u*,
the *Kaygagabile*, or spell of lightness, begins with a typical
u'ula :—

> *Susuwayliguwa (repeated) ;*   *Titavaguwa (repeated)*
> He fails to outrun me ;   the canoe trembles with speed ;
>
> *mabuguwa (repeated) ;*   *mabugu,*   *mabugamugwa ;*
> magical word ;   mabugu,   mabugu-ancient ;
>
> *mabugu, mabuguva'u.*
> mabugu, mabugu-new.

The first two words are compounds with prefixes and suffixes
added for magical purposes, as a sort of magical trimming.
The untranslatable word, said by the natives to be *megwa
wala* (' just magic ') is repeated several times in symmetry with
the previous two words and then with the two suffixes ;
ancient and new. Such repetitions with prefixes or suffixes of

antithetic meaning are a frequent feature of magical trimming of words. This exordium affords a clear example of the magical play on words, of transformations for the sake of rhythm and symmetry; of repetitions of the same words with antithetic affixes. In the following part of the spell, the word *ka'i* (tree) is repeated with verbs :—' the tree flies ' etc., and it functions as a key-word. It is difficult to decide whether this part is a true *tapwana* or only one of the not infrequent examples of an *u'ula* with a keyword.

Let us survey a few more of the *u'ula* (first parts) of the canoe spells, and then proceed to the examination of the middle parts and ends. In the next spell of Chapter VI, the Kapitunena Duku spell, the word *bavisivisi*, ' I shall wave them back,' (that is; the other canoes), is repeated ponderously several times. The opening of a spell with one word, which summarises in a metaphorical manner the aim of the spell is often found in Kiriwinian magic. In this spell there follow the words :—

Sîyá		*dábanâ*	*Tókunâ*	*inenâ*.
Siya hill	(on)	top of	Takuna	the women

Sinegu	*bwaga'u*,	*tatogu*	*bwaga'u*.
My mother	sorcerer,	myself	sorcerer.

These words are pronounced with a heavy, thumping rhythm, as indicated by the sharp and circumflex accents. The second line shows a rhythmic and symmetrical arrangement of words. The remainder of the *u'ula* of this spell is similar to the same part in the *wayugo* spell, which has been given here in full native text (compare the free translations of both spells in previous Chapters).

In the *ligogu* spell of the same Chapter, the *u'ula* opens with another juggling of words :—

virayra'i (repeated) ;		*morayra'i (repeated)* ;	
female rayra'i ;		male rayra'i ;	

basilabusi		*Wayayla*,	*basilalaguwa*	
I shall penetrate	(at)	Wayayla,	I shall emerge	(at)

Oyanaki ;	*basilalaguwa*		*Wayayla*,
Oyanaki ;	I shall emerge	(at)	Wayayla,

basilabusi	*Oyanaki* ;
I shall penetrate	Oyanaki ;

This part of the *u'ula* has not been translated in the text, as its meaning is ' magical ' and can be better grasped in connection with the native text. The word *rayra'i* is a magical word only. It is first given with the antithetic opposition of the male and female prefixes *vi-* and *mo-*. The following phrase is a typical example of a geographical antithesis. The two names refer to the promontories facing one other across the sea passage Kaulokoki, between Boyowa and Kayleula. Why those two points are mentioned I could not find out.

In the *kadumiyala* spell, given in Chapter IX, we have the following opening :—

> *Vinapega, pega ; vinamwana, mwana ;*
> *nam mayouyai, makariyouya'i, odabwana ;*
> *nam mayouya'i, makariyouya'i, o'u'ula.*

In the first line, we have the symmetrically uttered and prefixed names of the two flying or jumping fishes, *pega* and *mwana*. The prefix *vina-* is probably the female prefix and may convey the meaning of flying's being associated with women, that is with the flying witches. The second and third verse contain a play on the root *yova* or *yo'u* ' to fly,' reduplicated and with several affixes added. These two verses are brought into a sort of antithesis by the last two words, *odabwana* and *o'u'ula*, or ' at the top,' and ' at the bottom,' or here, probably, at the one end of the canoe and at the other.

In the *Bisila* spell, given in the same chapter, we have the beginning :—

> *Bora'i, bora'i, borayyova, biyova ;*
> *Bora'i, bora'i, borayteta, biteta.*

The word *bora'i* seems to be again a purely magical one. The prefix *bo-* carries the meaning of tabooed, or ritual ; the root *ra'i* suggests similarity with the above quoted magical word *rayra'i*, which is obviously merely a reduplicated form of *ra'i*. This is therefore a rhythmically constructed play on the magical root *ra'i*, and the words *yova*, ' to fly,' and *teta*, ' to be poised ' ' to soar.'

The *Kayikuna veva* spell presents the following rhythmic and symmetrical exordium :—

> *Bosuyasuya (repeated) ; boraguragu (repeated).*
> *Bosuya olumwalela ; boyragu okatalena.*

The   su*asila* (Kula magic) spells, quoted or mentioned
except t   ginning with the *u'ula*.
ment and   *rwpu* spell (Chapter VII) we have the begin-
and *kata*he
features y ex   *vinaygau, vinaygu ;*
          ting   *mwanaygu, mwanaygu* . . .
          er can
          d simila   (areca-nut) is repeated and used as a prefix
The   *buriwada*   etic roots -*vinay*- (female), and -*mwanay*-
much lo   the reef-   uffix -*gu* (first possessive pronoun).
Many sp   e aim of   o (Chapter VII) begins :—
regular   ght.   *la doga, gala mwayye* . . .
Duku.
list of c   a solemn manner, and then follows the play on
spoken   described above in the free translation of this

ma   s of th
          c feature   rthmic beginning, spoken with regular, strongly
These v   nomat   is to be found in the *Kaykakaya* spell (Chapter
which r   the thre
althoug   *la* spel   *iyanâ, márabwága iyanâ* . . .
languag   e of th   ul arrangements of words, with alliterative pre-
flavour   n as th   rticle and with antithetic uses of word couples
Some o   ere th   d in several other spells.
meanin   panior
manner   ng s   The *Talo* formula (Chapter XIII) :
the key   ons   *lawada, udawada*
of the c   spel   *aylili, mwaylili* . . .
archaic   ry   The *Ta'uya* spell (Chapter XIII) :
terms a   ng   *onimwanita ;*
          o   *derideriwa ;*
Ano   *deriderima* . . .
spell in   The *Ka'ubana'i* spell (Chapter XIII) :
been t   *Nikiniki,*
na- is   *Nikiniki* . . .
unabl   The *Kwoygapani* spell (Chapter XIV) :
beat   *weganubwa'i, nubwa'i ;*
In th   *kweganuwa'i, nuwa'i ;*
ing   *kweganuma'i, numa'i* . . .
ma   *written them down here without full comment, to
pr   sho*   ormal phonetic characteristics, which are indeed in
          all   *s* quite similar to the samples previously quoted
t   and   ed.

X

The main parts of the spells in the magic of the Kula do not essentially differ in their characteristics from the *tapwana* of the canoe magic. In their form, some key-words are simply verbs used without any transformation in their narrative tense. Thus in the *Talo* (red paint) formula, the pair of verbs *ikata* (' it flares up '), *inamila* (' it flashes ') is used with various nouns describing parts of the human head. The key-words of the *Kayikuna Tabuyo* (Chapter XIII) are also grammatically simple : *buribwari, kuvakaku kuvakipusa* (' fish-hawk, fall on thy prey, catch it ')—the verbs being in the second person of the narrative tense.

In other cases we find the key-word transformed by reduplication, composition or by affixes. In the Yawarapu spell (Chapter VII) the pair *horaytupa, badederuma* repeated as key expressions is a compound which I did not succeed in analysing completely, though the consensus of my informants makes me satisfied with the approximate translation :—' Quick sailing, abundant haul.' In the *Gebobo* spell (Chapter VII) the expression *tutube tubeyama* is a play on the root *tubwo* used as a rule verbally and meaning ' to be full in the face,' ' to be fine looking.' In the *Ta'uya* spell (Chapter XIII) there is the reduplication *munumweynise* of the root *mwana* or *mwayna* expressing the ' itching ' or ' state of excitement.' In the *ka'ubanai* the first key-expression *ida dabara* is an archaic or dialectical couple (the root is *dabara*, and *ida* is only a phonetic addition), which signifies ' to ebb.' The other key-expressions ' *ka'ukwa yaruyaru*,' ' *ka'ukwa mwasara*,' ' *ka'ukwa mwasara baremwasemwasara* ' have all the verbal part irregularly reduplicated and in the last expression repeated and transformed. The last formula of the *mwasila* (Kula magic) given in Chapter XIV, has a pair of expressions used as key-phrase : ' *kwoygapani, pani ; kwoyga'ulu, ulu.*' The word *kwega*, a variety of betel plant, is used in a modified form as a prefix and compounded with the verbal roots *pani* (seduce) and *ulu* (enmesh).

As to the final parts of this class of spell, I have said before that it is much less variable than the initial and main parts of a formula. Within the same cycle or system, the *dogina* often varies little and a man will often use the same one with all his

spells. The sample given with the *sulumwoya* text will therefore be sufficient to show the various characteristics of this part
of the *mwasila* spell, and there is no need to say anything more
about it.

XI

A very rapid survey of the phonetic characters of the
kayga'u spells (Chapter XI) must be sufficient and we shall
confine ourselves to their *tapwana*. The word *gwa'u* or *ga'u*
means 'mist' or 'fog'; verbally used with the meaning
'to make mist' ' to befog,' it has always the form *ga'u*. In the
main parts of some of the formulæ of this class, this phonetically
very expressive word is used with very great sound effect. For
example in the *giyorokaywa* spell No. 1, the key-words are
aga'u (' I befog '), *aga'usulu* (' I befog, lead astray ') ; *aga'uboda*
(' I befog, shut off '). Spoken, at the beginning of the *tapwana*
slowly and sonorously, and then quickly and insistently these
words produce a really 'magical' effect—that is as far as the
hearers' subjective impressions are concerned. Even more
impressive and onomatopoetic is the phrase used as key-
expression in the *Giyotanawa* No. 2 :

> *Ga'u, yaga'u, yagaga'u, yaga'u, bode, bodegu !*

This sentence, giving the vowels a full Italian value, such as
they receive in the Melanesian pronunciation, does certainly
have an impressive ring ; fittingly enough, because this is the
dramatic spell, uttered into the wind in the sinking *waga*, the
final effort of magic to blind and mislead the *mulukwausi*. The
causative prefix *ya* is used here with a nominal expression
yaga'u which has been translated 'gathering mist ' ; the
reduplicated one *yagaga'u* I have rendered by ' encircling mist.'
It can be seen from this example how feebly the equivalents
can be given of the magical phrases in which so much is
expressed by phonetic or onomatopoetic means.

The other spells have much less inspired key-words.
Giyotanawa No. 1 uses the word *atumboda*, translated ' I press,'
' I close down,' which literally renders the meanings of the
verbs *tum*, ' to press,' and *boda*, ' to close.' The *Giyorokaywa*
No. 2 has the somewhat archaic key-words spoken in a couple :
' *apeyra yauredi*,' ' I arise,' ' I escape ' and the grammatically
irregular expression *suluya*, ' to lead astray.'

The main part of the Kaytaria spell, by which the benevolent fish is summoned to the rescue of the drowning party has
the key-phrase ' *bigabaygu suyusayu :* the *suyusayu* fish shall
lift me up.' This expression is noteworthy : even in this spell,
which might be regarded as an invocation of the helpful animal,
it is not addressed in the second person. The result is verbally
anticipated, proving that the spell is to act through the direct
force of the words and not as an appeal to the animal.

XII

With this, the survey of linguistic samples from various
spells is closed, and we can briefly summarise our results. The
belief in the efficiency of a formula results in various peculiarities of the language in which it is couched, both as regards
meaning and sound. The native is deeply convinced of this
mysterious, intrinsic power of certain words ; words which are
believed to have their virtue in their own right, so to speak ;
having come into existence from primeval times and exercising
their influence directly.

To start first with the meaning of the magical expressions,
we have seen that in this respect they are plain and direct
enough. Most of the key-words simply state the magical
action, for example when in one of the spells the key-word
napuwoye, ' I impart magical virtue (of speed '), or in another
the key-words ' to paint red in a festive manner, to wreathe in a
festive manner,' simply describe what the magician is doing.
Much more often the principal expressions, that is the initial
words and the key-words, of a spell refer to its aim, as for
instance, when we find words and phrases denoting ' speed ' in
canoe magic ; or, in Kula magic, designations for ' success '
' abundant haul,' ' excitement,' ' beauty.' Still more often the
aim of magic is stated in a metaphorical manner, by similes
and double meanings. In other parts of the spell, where the
magical meaning is imprisoned not so much in single words
and expressions, as in explicit phraseology and long periods,
we found that the predominant features are : lists of ancestral
names ; invocations of ancestral spirits ; mythological
allusions ; similes and exaggerations ; depreciating contrasts
between the companions and the reciter—most of them expressing an anticipation of the favourable results aimed at in the
spell. Again, certain parts of the spell contain systematic,

meticulous enumerations, the reciter going over the parts of a canoe one by one; the successive stages of a journey; the various Kula goods and valuables; the parts of the human head; the numerous places from which the flying witches are believed to come. Such enumerations as a rule strive at an almost pedantic completeness.

Passing to the phonetic characteristics, we saw that a word will often be used in a shape quite different from those in which it is used in ordinary speech; that it will show notable changes in form and sound. Such phonetic peculiarities are most conspicuous in the main words, that is in the key-words and initial words. They are sometimes truncated, more often provided with additions, such as symmetrical or antithetic affixes; formatives added for the sake of sound. By these means there are produced effects of rhythm, alliteration and rhyme, often heightened and accentuated by actual vocal accent. We found play on words by symmetrical couples of sounds, with antithetic meaning like *mo-* and *vi-*, or *mwana-* and *vina-*, both couples signifying 'male' and 'female' respectively; or *-mugwa* (ancient) and *-va'u* (new); or *ma-* (hither) and *wa-* (thither), etc., etc. Especially we found the prefix *bo-*, carrying the meaning of ritual or tabooed, with derivation from *bomala ;* or with the meaning 'red,' 'festive' in its derivation from *bu'a* (areca-nut); onomatopoetic sounds such as *sididi* or *saydidi, tatata, numsa,* in imitation of speed noises, of the wailing of wind, rustling of sail, swish of pandanus leaves; *tududu,* in imitation of the thunder claps; and the rhythmical, expressive, though perhaps not directly onomatopoetic, sentence :

Ga'u, yaga'u, yagaga'u, yaga'u, bode, bodegu.

XIII

If we now turn to the substances used in the magical rites, as means of ritual transference of the spell, we find in canoe magic, dried lalang grass, dried banana leaf, dried pandanus leaf, all used in the magic of lightness. A stale potato is employed to carry away the heaviness of the canoe; although on another occasion heaviness is thrown away with a bunch of lalang grass. The leaves of two or three shrubs and weeds, which as a rule the natives take to dry their skin after bathing, are used for magical cleansing of a canoe body, and a stick and a torch serve in other rites of exorcism. In the rite associated with the blackening of a canoe, charred remains of several light substances such as lalang grass, the nest of a small, swift bird, the wings of a bat, coco-nut husk and the twigs of an extremely light mimosa tree are employed.

It is easy to see that, not less than the words, the substances here used are associated with the aim of the magic, that is, with lightness, with swiftness and with flying.

In the magic of the Kula we find betel-nut, crushed with lime in a mortar, used to redden the tip of the canoe. Betel-nut is also given to a partner, after it has been charmed over with a seducing spell. Aromatic mint, boiled in coco-nut oil and ginger root are also used in the *mwasila*. The conch-shell, and the cosmetic ingredients, charmed over on Sarubwoyna beach are really part of the outfit, and so is the *lilava* bundle. All the substances used in this magic are associated either with beauty and attractiveness (betel-nut, cosmetics, the mint plant) or with excitement (conch-shell, chewed betel-nut). Here therefore, it is not with the final aim—which is the obtaining of valuables —that the magic is concerned, but with the intermediate one, that is that of being agreeable to one's partner, of putting him into a state of excitement about the Kula.

XIV

I wish to close this chapter by adducing a few texts of native information. In the previous chapters, several statements and narratives have been put into the natives' mouths and given in quotations. I wish now to show some of the actual linguistic data from which such quotations have been derived. Numerous utterances of the natives were taken down by me as they were spoken. Whenever there was a native expression covering a point of crucial importance, or a characteristic thought, or one neatly formulated, or else one especially hazy and opalescent in meaning—I noted them down in quick handwriting as they were spoken. A number of such texts, apart from their linguistic importance, will serve as documents embodying the native ideas without any foreign admixture, and it will also show the long way which lies between the crude native statement and its explicit, ethnographic presentation. For what strikes us at first sight most forcibly in these texts is their extreme bareness, the scantiness of information which they appear to contain. Couched in a condensed, disjointed, one might say telegraphic style, they seem to lack almost everything which could throw light on the subject of our study. For they lack concatenation of ideas, and they contain few concrete details, and few really apt generalisations. It must be remembered, however, that, whatever might be the importance of such texts, they are not the only source of ethnographic information, not even the most important one. The observer has to read them in the context of tribal life. Many of the customs of behaviour, of the sociological data, which are barely mentioned in the texts, have become familiar to the Ethnographer through personal observation and the direct study of the objective manifestations and of data referring to their social constitution (compare the observations on Method in the Introduction). On the other hand, a better knowledge of and acquaintance with the means of linguistic expression makes the language itself much more significant to one who not only knows how it is used but uses it himself. After all, if natives could furnish us with correct, explicit and consistent accounts of their tribal organisation, customs and ideas, there would be no difficulty in ethnographic work. Unfortunately, the native can neither get outside his tribal atmospheres and see it objectively, nor if he could, would he have intellectual and linguistic means sufficient to express it. And so the Ethnographer has to collect objective data, such as maps, plans, genealogies, lists of possessions, accounts of inheritance, censuses of village communities. He has to study the behaviour of the native, to talk with him under all sorts of conditions, and to write down his words. And then, from all these diverse data, to construct his synthesis, the picture of a community and of the individuals in it. But I have dwelt on these aspects of method already in the Introduction and here I want only to exemplify them with regard to the linguistic material directly representing some of the natives' thoughts on ethnographic subjects.

XV

I shall give here first a text on the subject of the priority in sailing, which as described in Chapter IX, is the privilege of a certain sub-clan in Sinaketa. I was discussing with a very good informant, Toybayoba of Sinaketa, the customs of launching the canoes, and I tried, as usually, to keep my interlocutor as much as possible to concrete details and to the stating of the full sequence of events. In his account he uttered this sentence :

" The Tolabwaga launch their canoe first ; by this the face of the sea is cleared."

I thereupon perceived that a new subject had been brought within my notice, and I headed my informant on to it, and obtained the following text, sentence after sentence :—

THE TOLABWAGA SUB-CLAN AND THEIR SEA-FARING PRIVILEGES

1 *Bikugwo,*   *ikapusi*   *siwaga*
1 He might be first   he fall down   their canoe
         (it is launched)

   Tolabwaga,   *boge*   *bimilakatile*   *bwarita.*
   Tolabwaga,   already   he might be clear   sea.

2 *Igau*   *kumaydona*   *gweguya,*   *tokay*
2 Later on   all   chiefs,   commoner

   siwaga   *ikapusisi*   *oluvyeki.*
   their canoe   they fall down   behind.
         (are launched)

3 *Kidama*   *takapusi*   *takugwo*
3 Supposing   we fall down,   we are first

    bitavilidasi   *baloma ;*   *bitana*
    they might turn (on) us   spirits ;   we might go

   Dobu,   *gala*   *tabani*   *bunukwa*   *soulava.*
   Dobu,   no   we find   pig   necklace.

4 *Makawala*   *yuwayoulo :*   *bikugwo*   *isipusi*
4 Alike   (lashing creeper)   he (it) might be first   they bind

   siwayugo,   *iga'u*   *yakidasi.*
   their wayugo lashing,   later on   ourselves.

5 *Takeulo*   *Dobu,*   *gala*   *bikugwasi*
5 We sail   Dobu,   no   they might be first

   Tolabwaga ;   *okovalawa*   *boge*   *aywokwo.*
   Tolabwaga ;   on sea front   already   he was over.

6 *Obwarita*　　　*tananamse*　　　　*kayne*　　　*isakauli*
6 In sea　　　we consider　　　whether　　　he run

　　taytala　　　　　*lawaga*,　　　　*ikugwo*.
　one (masculine)　　　his canoe,　　　he is first.

7 *Gala*　　　*bikaraywagasi*　　　　　*patile*.
7 No　　　they might command　　　canoe fleet.

8 *Dobu*,　　*gweguya*　　　　　*bikugwasi*,
8 Dobu,　　　chiefs　　　they might be first,

　　biwayse　　　　　*kaypatile*　　　*gweguya*.
　they might come there　　　canoe fleet　　　chiefs.

9 *M'tage*　　　*Tolabwaga*　　　*boge*　　　*aywokwo*
9 Indeed　　　Tolabwaga　　　already　　　he (it) was over

　sikaraywaga　　　　　*ovalu*.
　their command　　　in village.

The Tolabwaga sub-clan belong to the Lukwasisiga clan,
and live at present in Kasi'etana.　Only one man and two
women are surviving.

10 *Simwasila*　　　　　*siwaga*　　　*migavala*,　　　*vivila*
10 Their Kula magic　　　their canoe　　　magic his,　　　woman

　boge　　　*iyousayse*.
　already　　　they grasp.

11　　" *Datukwasi*　　　　　*boge*　　　*kasakaymi*
11 " Our magical property　　　already　　　we give you

megwa　　　*kwaraywagasi*　　　*lagayle* ! "
magic　　　you command　　　to-day ! "

Thus would they say on handing their magic to their
male descendants.

Informant's Commentary.

Commenting on verse 3, the expression, ' *bitalividasi
baloma*,' my informant said :—

　　' *Bitavilida* ' :　　　　　*bilivalasi*　　　*baloma*
' They might turn (on) us ' :　　　they might say　　　spirit
" *Avaka*　　*pela*　　*gala*　　　*ikugwo*　　　*Tolabwaga*,
" What　　　for　　　no　　　he is first　　　Tolabwaga,

kukugwasi　　　*gumgweguya* ;　　　*kayuviyuvisa*
you are first　　　sub-chiefs ;　　　sweepers of the sea
Tolabwaga ! "
Tolabwaga ! "

13 *Tavagi*   *gaga*   *igiburuwasi,*   *ninasi*   *igaga,*
13 We do   bad   they angry   mind theirs'   he bad

    pela   *magisi*   *batayamata*   *tokunabogwo*
    for   desire theirs   we might watch   long ago

    aygura.
    he has decreed.

The verbal translation renders word for word the individual meaning of every particle and root, according to a definite grammatical and lexcographical scheme which has been adopted for this text in common with a few hundred more. In this place, I cannot give the commentary and justification of the linguistic details, which will be fairly obvious to a Melanesian scholar, who might, however, find some new and even controversial features in my translation. To other readers, these details are of small interest. I have not included in this translation any distinction between the inclusive and exclusive first person, dual and plural. Of the two tenses which are to be found in this text, the narrative one is translated by the English verb in infinitive, the potential, by the addition of the word 'might.' In brackets underneath, the special meaning of a word in its context is indicated, or some comments are added.

The free translation of the text must now be given :—

FREE TRANSLATION.

1 The Tolabwaga canoe would be launched first ; by this the face of the sea is cleared.

2 Afterwards, all the chiefs', the commoners' canoes are launched.

3 If we would launch our canoes first, the spirits (of ancestors) would be angry with us ; we would go to Dobu and we would receive no pigs, no necklaces.

4 It is likewise with the lashing of the canoe : first, the Tolabwaga would bind the lashing creeper and afterwards ourselves.

5 On our journey to Dobu, the Tolabwaga would not sail ahead, for their priority ends on the beach of Sinaketa.

6 On the sea it is according to our wish, and if one man's canoe runs fast, he would be first.

7 They (the Tolabwaga) do not wield the command of the canoe fleet.

8 In Dobu, the chiefs would be first ; the chiefs would arrive there at the head of the fleet.

9 But the supremacy of the Tolabwaga ends here already, in the village.

10 The Kula magic, the magic of the canoe, belonging to the Tolabwaga clan has passed already into the hands of their womenfolk.

11 (These would say speaking to their male children) :— " We shall give you the magic, the magical inheritance, you rule henceforward."

12 When the spirits become angry, they would tell us :— " Why are the Tolabwaga not first and you minor chiefs are ahead ?   Are not the Tolabwaga cleaners of the sea ? "

13 When we do wrong, they (the spirits) are angry, their minds are malevolent, for they desire that we should keep to the old customs.

XVI

Comparing the free translation with the literal one, it is easy to see that certain additions have been made, sentences have been subordinated and co-ordinated by various English conjunctions which are either completely absent from the native text, or else represented by such very vague particles as *boge* (already), and *m'tage* (indeed). On these linguistic questions I cannot enlarge here, but it will be good to go over each sentence in succession, and to show how much it was necessary to add from the general store of sociological and ethnographic knowledge, in order to make it intelligible.

1. The meaning of the word ' fall down ' is specialised here by the context, and I translated it by ' launch.'   The particle *boge* had to be translated here by ' by this.'   The words about the ' clearing of the sea ' suggested at once to me that there was a special ancient custom in question.   Then there is the name of the sub-clan Tolabwaga.   In order to understand the full meaning of this phrase, it is necessary to realise that this name stands for a sub-clan ; and then one has to be well acquainted with native sociology, in order to grasp what such a privilege, vested in a sub-clan, might mean.   Thus, a word like this can in the first place be understood only in the context of its phrase, and on the basis of a certain linguistic knowledge.   But its fuller meaning becomes intelligible only in the context of the

native life and of native sociology. Again the expression referring to the clearing of the sea required a further comment, for which I asked my informant, and was answered by Phrase 3.

2. In this phrase the expressions ' chiefs,' ' commoners ' etc., are fully intelligible only to one, who has a definition of these words in terms of native sociology. Indeed, only the knowledge of the usual supremacy of the chiefs allows one to gauge their importance and the survival character of this custom, by which this importance is diminished for a time.

3. Here, we have the explanation of the obscure clause in phrase 1, ' A clear sea ' means the good temper of the spirits which again means good luck. The question as to whether the spirits are to be imagined as actively interfering or helping still remained open. I asked for a further elucidation, which was given to me in the text of Phrases 12 and 13.

4. This contains a condensed reference to the stages of ship-building, previous to launching. This, of course, to be understood, pre-supposes a knowledge of these various activities.

5 to 9. The limitations of the powers of the Tolabwaga sub-clan are outlined, giving interesting side-lights on the rôle played by females as repositories of family (sub-clan) traditions. Needless to say, this statement would be entirely meaningless without the knowledge of the natives' matrilineal institutions, of their customs of inheritance and of property in magic. The correct knowledge of these facts can only be gathered by a collection of objective, ethnographic documents, such as concrete data about cases of actual inheritance, etc.

12 and 13. Here it is explained how far the *baloma* would become angry and how they would act if a custom were broken. It can be distinctly seen from it that the anger of the spirits is only a phrase, covering all these forces which keep the natives to the observance of old customs. The *baloma* would go no further than to reproach them for breaking the old rules, and there are no definite ideas among these natives about actual punishment being meted out by offended spirits.

These considerations show convincingly that no linguistic analysis can disclose the full meaning of a text without the help of an adequate knowledge of the sociology, of the customs and of the beliefs, current in a given society.

XVII

Another sample of a native text may be given here, as it is of especial interest, in that it throws light upon the previously given magical formula of the *wayugo*. It is the text I obtained trying to find the meaning of the word *bosisi'ula*, which figures at the beginning of the above-mentioned spell. According to two informants of Sinaketa, the word *visisi'una* refers to the belief already described, that the owner of a *wayugo* charm is liable to fits of trembling, during which he trembles as a *bisila* (pandanus) streamer trembles in the wind. He then should ritually eat some baked fish, and this is called *visisi'una*. Such a man would then ask somebody of his household :—

" *Kugabu, kumaye, avisisi'una.*"
" Thou bake, thou bring, I ritually eat."

Or someone else would urge his wife or daughter :—

" *Kugabu, kumaye, ivisisi'una.*"
" Thou bake, thou bring, he eats ritually."

Again, asked for a direct equation, my informant said :—

" *Ivisisi'una — bigabu,   tomwaya   ikam.*"
" Ivisisi'una — he bake,   old man   he eat."

The following text contains a more explicit definition of the term, which I was trying at that time to make clear and to translate by an appropriate English expression.

EXPLANATION OF WORD VISISI'UNA

A.—First Informant.

1 *Pela   isewo   wayugo,   itatatuva   wowola*
1 For   he learn   wayugo,   he (it) tremble   body his
         (the creeper magic)

   matauna,   isa'u (or *isewo*)   *wayugo.*
   this (man),   (who)   he learn   wayugo.

2 " *Nanakwa,   kugabu   kusayki,   tomwaya*
2 " Quick,   thou bake   thou give   old man
                       (magician)

   ivisisi'una   boge   itatatuva   kana
   he ritually eats,   already   he tremble   his

     bisila,   kana   wayugo"
   pandanus streamer,   his   wayugo creeper."

B.—Second Informant.

3	*Tayta*		*isewo*	*bisila,*	*gala*	*bikam*
3	(If) one (man)		he learn	bisila,	not	he might eat

yena,	*boge*	*itatuva*	*wowola.*
fish,	already	he tremble	body his.

FREE TRANSLATION.

(A.) 1. The body of a man who has learned the *wayugo* spell, trembles, because he learned the spell. (Someone seeing him tremble, would tell someone of his household :)

2 " Quick, bake fish, give to the old man that he might ritually eat, his pandanus streamer trembles, his *wayugo*."

(B.) 3 A man who learns the *bisila* magic and does not eat fish will tremble.

This text, with its foregoing short comments and with its two versions will give an inkling of how I was able to obtain from my native informants the definition of unknown and sometimes very involved expressions and how, in the act of doing it, I was given additional enlightenment on obscure details of belief and custom.

It will also be interesting to give another text referring to the *gwara* custom. I have given in Chapter XIV a native definition of this custom, and of the reception accorded to the Trobrianders in Dobu when there is a taboo on palms there. The statement was based on the following text, and on certain other additional notes.

GWARA IN DOBU AND THE KA'UBANA'I MAGIC

1	*Tama*	*Dobu*	*ikarigava'u—*	*gwara :*	*bu'a*
1	We come (to) Dobu,		he die anew—	gwara :	areca

bilalava	*usi*	*bimwanogu,*	*nuya*
he might ripen	banana	he might ripen,	coco-nut

bibabayse	*ka'i*	*kayketoki.*
they might spike	stick	small stick.

2	*Gala*	*ka'ubana'i,*	*takokola :*	*ikawoyse*
2	No	ka'ubana'i,	we fright :	they take (put on)

bowa	*kayyala,*	*kema ;*	*isisuse*
war paints	spear,	axe ;	they sit

biginayda
they might look at us.

3 *Batana   ovalu   tasakaulo,   gala   tanouno*
3 We go   in village   we run,   no   we walk.

   batawa   tamwoyne   bu'a.
   we might arrive   we (i.d.) climb   areca.

4 *Idou :   " E !   Gala   bukumwoyne   bu'a."*
4 He cries   " E !   No   thou mightst climb   areca."

5 *Bogwe   ika'u   kayyala,   mwada*
5 Already   he take   spear,   mayhap

   biwoyda.
   he might hit us.

6   *Tapula   nayya   ka'ubana'i :*
6 We ritually spit   wild ginger root   ka'ubana'i :

   ika'ita   ima,   igigila   iluwaymo
   he return   he come   he laugh,   he throw

   kayyala,   kema.
   spear,   axe.

7   *Tapula   valu   kumaydona,   boge   itamwa'u*
7 We ritually spit   village   all,   already   he vanish

   ninasi   ilukwaydasi :
   mind theirs',   they tell us :

8 " *Bweyna,   kumwoynasi   kami   bu'a,   nuya,*
8 " Good,   you climb   your   areca,   coco-nut (palms)

   kami   usi   kuta'isi."
   your   banana   you cut."

In comment added :

9 *Gala   ikarige   veyola   ninasi   bweyna.*
9 No   he die   kinsman his,   mind their   well.

10 *Vivila   kayyala   ikawo,   pela   tokamsita'u.*
10 Woman   spear her   she take   for   cannibals.

FREE TRANSLATION

1 We come to Dobu, (there) someone has recently died—
  there is a gwala : the areca nut will ripen, the bananas will
  ripen, they will stick up coco-nuts on small spikes.

2 If there is no ka'ubana'i charm made—we are afraid : they
  (sc. the Dobuans) put on war paint, take up spear and axe,
  they sit (waiting) and look at us.

3 We go into the village running, not walking ; we arrive
  and climb the areca palm.

4 He (the Dobuan) shouts : " Don't climb the areca palm ! "

5 Already he takes the spear, so as to hit us.

6 We ritually spit about wild ginger root charmed with the ka'ubana'i spell—he returns, comes to us, laughs, he throws away spear and axe.

7 We ritually bespit the whole village, already their intention vanishes, they tell us :

8 " Well, climb your areca palm and your coco-nut, cut your banana."

9 If no kinsman had died, their intentions are good.

10 A woman would also take up a spear, as they (the Dobuans) are cannibals.

These three texts will be quite sufficient to give an idea of the method of dealing with linguistic evidence, and of the documentary value of immediately recorded native opinions. They will also make clear what I have said before, that only a good, working knowledge of a native language on the one hand, and a familiarity with their social organisation and tribal life on the other, would make it possible to read all the full significance into these texts.

Chapter XIX

THE INLAND KULA

I

AFTER the somewhat long digression on magic, we can now return once more to the description of the Kula. So far, we have been treating only one incident in it, the overseas expedition between Sinaketa and Dobu, and the return visit. But in dealing with this one typical stage we have received a picture of the whole Kula, and we have incidentally learnt all about the fundamentals of the exchange, the magic, the mythology, and the other associated aspects. Now it remains to put the finishing touches to the general picture, that is, to say a few words, first about the manner in which it is conducted within a district, and then to follow the exchange on the remaining part of the ring. The exchange within each Kula community has been called the ' inland Kula.' This part of the subject I know from personal experience in the Trobriands only. All that will be said therefore in this chapter will apply primarily to that part of the ring. As Boyowa, however, is by far the biggest and most densely populated piece of land within the Kula, it is clear that in treating the inland exchange in that island, we treat it in its most developed and typical form.

It has been mentioned before, in Chapter XVI that in April, 1918, To'uluwa had come to Sinaketa in connection with the *uvalaku* visit of the Dobuans. To'uluwa is the present chief of Omarakana, indeed, the last chief of Kiriwina, for after his death no one will succeed him. His power has been broken by the interference of Government officials and the influence of Mission work. The power of the Trobriand chief lay mainly in his wealth, and this he was able to keep constantly at a high level through the institution of polygamy. Now that he is forbidden to acquire more wives, though he may keep his old ones ; and now that his successor will not be allowed to follow this immemorial custom of polygamy practised by their dynasty, the power of the chief has no basis, and has to a great extent collapsed.

I may add that this interference, inflicted for no comprehensible purposes, except if it be an exceedingly parochial and narrow-minded application of our sense of morality and propriety, has no legal basis whatever in the regulations of that Colony, and could not be justified either formally or on account of any results it may produce. Indeed, the undermining of old-established authority, of tribal morals and customs tends on the one hand completely to demoralise the natives and to make them unamenable to any law or rule, while on the other hand, by destroying the whole fabric of tribal life, it deprives them of many of their most cherished diversions, ways of enjoying life, and social pleasures. Now once you make life unattractive for a man, whether savage or civilised, you cut the taproot of his vitality. The rapid dying out of native races is, I am deeply convinced, due more to wanton interference with their pleasures and normal occupations, to the marring of their joy of life as they conceive it, than to any other cause. In the Trobriands, for instance, the chief has always been the organiser of all the big, tribal festivities. He received large contributions from the commoners under various legal obligations (see Chap. VI, Division VI) but he gave away all his wealth again in the form of big, ceremonial distributions, of presents at festivities, of food gifts to the partakers in dances, tribal sports and diversions. These were the pleasures in which the natives found real zest, which largely gave meaning to their lives. Nowadays all these pursuits have greatly slackened, because of the lack of concentration of wealth and power in the chief's hands. He can neither afford to finance the big pastimes of yore, nor has he influence enough to give the same energetic initiative to start them going. After his death, things will be worse still. There are reasons to fear, and even natives express their misgivings, that in a generation or two the Kula will become entirely disorganised.

It is a well-known fact that the resistance and health of a native depend on auto-suggestion more even than is the case with ourselves, though new developments in psychotherapy seem to indicate that medicine has up till now largely under-rated the general influence of this factor. Even the old ethnographic observers, more in Polynesia perhaps than anywhere else, have reported clear, unmistakable instances in which the loss of interest in life and the determination to die brought about death without any other cause. My own experience, though I have no one very striking case to cite, bears this out fully from all sorts of corroborating types of evidence. It is therefore not going beyond what is fully granted by facts, to maintain that a general loss of interest in life, of the *joie de vivre*, the cutting of all the bonds of intense interest, which bind members of a human community to existence, will result in their giving up the desire to live altogether, and that there-fore they will fall an easy prey to any disease, as well as fail to multiply.

A wise administration of natives would, on the one hand, try to govern *through* the chief, using his authority along the lines of old law, usage, and custom ; on the other hand it would try to maintain all which really makes life worth living for the natives, for it is the most precious inheritance, which they have from the past ages, and it is no good to try to substitute other interests for those lost. It is easy to hand over one's vices to a man racially and culturally different ; but nothing is as difficult to impart as a keen interest in the sports and amuse-ments of other people. Even from one European nation to another, the last stronghold of national peculiarity can be found in its traditional diversions, and without diversion and amuse-ment a culture and a race cannot survive. The application of a heavy, indeed, crushing machinery of European law and moral regulations, with their various sanctions, simply destroys the whole delicate fabric of tribal authority, eradicating good and bad alike, and leaves nothing but anarchy, bewilderment and ill will.*

* An example of this ill-judged attitude of interference is to be found even in a book written by an exceptionally well informed and enlightened missionary, " In Far New Guinea," by Henry Newton. In describing the feasts and dancing of the natives, he admits these to be a necessity of tribal life : " On the whole the feasting and dancing are good ; they give excitement and relaxation to the young men, and tone the drab colours of life." He himself tells us that, " the time comes when the old men stop the dancing. They begin to growl because the gardens are neglected, and they want to know if dancing will give the people food, so the order is given that the drums are to be hung up, and the people settle down to work." But in spite of Mr. Newton's recognition of this natural, tribal authority, in spite of the fact that he really admits the views given in our

With a mere show of his former authority, therefore, poor old To'uluwa arrived with a handful of followers at Sinaketa. He still keeps to all the strict observances and onerous duties with which his exalted position was weighted in olden days. Thus, he may not partake of ever so many kinds of food, considered to be unclean for the members of the sub-clan of Tabalu. He may not even touch any defiled objects, that have been in contact with unclean food ; he may not eat from dishes or drink out of vessels which have been used previously by other people. When he goes to Sinaketa, for instance, where even the highest chiefs do not keep the taboos, he remains almost on starvation diet ; he can only eat the food which has been brought from his own village, or drink and eat green coco-nut. Of the honours attaching to his position, not many are observed. In olden days, on his approach to a village, a runner would enter first,

---

text, he cannot refrain from saying : " Seriously, however, for the benefit of the people themselves, it would be a good thing if there could be some regulations —if dancing were not allowed after midnight, for while it lasts nothing else is done.—The gardens suffer and it would help the people to learn self-restraint and so strengthen their characters if the dancing could be regulated." He goes on to admit quite candidly that it would be difficult to enforce such a regulation because " to the native mind, it would seem that it was the comfort of the white man, not the benefit of the native which was the reason for the regulation." And to my mind also, I am afraid !

The following quotations from a recent scientific work published by the Oxford Press—" The Northern d'Entrecasteaux," by D. Jenness, and the Rev. A. Ballantyne, 1920—are also examples of the dangerous and heedless tampering with the one authority that now binds the natives, the one discipline they can be relied upon to observe—that of their own tribal tradition. The relations of a church member who died, were " counselled to drop the harsher elements in their mourning," and instead of the people being bidden " to observe each jot and tittle of their old, time-honoured rites," they were advised from that day forth to leave off " those which had no meaning." It is strange to find a trained ethnologist, confessing that old, time-honoured rites have no meaning ! And one might feel tempted to ask : for *whom* it is that these customs have no meaning, for the natives or for the writers of the passage quoted ?

The following incident is even more telling. A native headman of an inland village was supposed to keep concealed in his hut a magic pot, the " greatest ruler of winds, rain, and sunshine," a pot which had " come down from times immemorial," which according to some of the natives " in the beginning simply was." According to the Authors, the owner of the pot used to descend on the coastal natives and " levy tribute," threatening them with the magical powers of the pot if they refused. Some of the coastal natives went to the Missionary and asked him to interfere or get the magistrate to do so. It was arranged they should all go with the Missionary and seize the pot. But on the day " only one man turned up." When the Missionary went, however, the natives blocked his path, and only through threats of punishments by the magistrate, were they induced to temporarily leave the village and thus to allow him to seize the pot ! A few days later the Missionary accordingly took possession of the pot, which he broke. The Authors go on to say that after this incident " everyone was contented and happy ; " except, one might add, the natives and those who would see in such occurrences the speedy destruction of native culture, and the final disintegration of the race.

and in a loud voice cry out "*O Guya'u*," whereupon all the people would stand in readiness, and at the chief's approach the commoners would throw themselves on the ground, the headman would squat down, and men of rank would bend their heads. Even now, no commoner in the Trobriands would stand erect in the presence of To'uluwa. But he no more announces his arrival in such a loud and proud manner, and he takes his dues as they are given, not demanding them with any show of authority.

II

On that occasion in Sinaketa, I met him again after about two years interval since the time when I lived as his neighbour in Omarakana for some eight months, my tent pitched side by side with his *lisiga* (chief's man's abode). I found him changed and aged, his tall figure more bent, his large face, with its expression half of benevolence and half of cunning, wrinkled and clouded over. He had some grievances to tell about the offhand treatment which had been given to him in Sinaketa, where he had received no necklaces at all, although a few days before the Sinaketans had carried from Kiriwina over 150 pairs of arm-shells. Indeed, the relative change of position between the chiefs of Sinaketa and himself is a permanent sore point with the old chief. All coastal natives, and especially the headman of Sinaketa, have become very rich owing to the introduced industry of pearling, where their services are paid for by the white men in tobacco, betel-nut, and *vaygu'a*. But To'uluwa, ruined through white man's influence, receives nothing from pearling, and compared to his Sinaketan inferiors, is a pauper. So after a day or two in Sinaketa, highly displeased, and vowing never to return again, he went back to Omarakana, his residence, and thither we shall follow him.

For Omarakana is still the centre of the Trobriand inland Kula, and, in certain respects, still one of the most important places on the ring. It is probably the only locality where the Kula is or ever was to some extent concentrated in the hands of one man, and it is also the capital of the important district of Kiriwina, which dominates all the inland Kula of the Northern Trobriands, and links up the island of Kitava with the western islands of Kuyleula and Kuyawa. It is also an important link between Kitava and Sinaketa, though between these two last mentioned places there are some minor means of communication, as we shall presently see.

Previously, in Chapter III, in the definition of the fundamentals of the Kula, we saw that the population of the Ring can be divided into what we called *Kula communities*. These divisions, as we remember, were distinguished by the fact that each one makes overseas expeditions of its own. For example, the Sinaketans, as we saw, make their trips to Dobu in a body, and although the Vakutans may go with them at the same time, the two fleets sail and act as independent units. Again, the whole district of Kiriwina sails to the East, to Kitava, as one fleet. But no Sinaketan canoe could ever form part of it. Another distinguishing characteristic of a Kula community is that the furthest limits of partnership are the same for all its members. Thus for instance, a man from any village in Kiriwina, provided he is in the Kula, may have a partner anywhere up to the furthest limits of the Sinaketa district in the South, and in any of the villages of the island of Kitava to the East. But beyond that, no Kiriwinian, not even To'uluwa himself, can enter into Kula partnership. There are again certain differences between the manner of conducting transactions within a Kula community on the one hand, and between members of two communities on the other.

Kiriwina is one of such Kula communities, and Sinaketa is another. Yet the two are not divided by sea, and the style of exchange, when this is carried on between two Kula communities which lie in the same district, differs also from that of overseas Kula. Our first task here will be therefore to mark out clearly the lines of distinction between :

1. The transactions of Kula carried on overseas, from one district to another.

2. Kula between two distinct but contiguous ' Kula communities.'

3. Transactions within a ' Kula community.'

The facts belonging to the first heading have been described at length, and it will be enough to point out in what the second type differs from the first. Obviously, when two districts on the same island, such as Kiriwina and Sinaketa, make the exchange there is no overseas sailing, no preparation of canoes, no launching, no *kabigidoya*. Sometimes big joint expeditions are made by the one community to the other and a great haul of *vaygu'a* is carried home. As an example of that, we may mention the visit made by the Sinaketans to Kiriwina in the last days of March, 1918, when a great number of *mwali* were brought, in readiness for the Dobuan *uvalaku* visit. When such an important visit is made from one Trobriand district to another, some of the Kula magic will be performed, but obviously not all, for there is no *lilava* bundle to be medicated, since no trade is carried ; no dangerous cannibals have to be tamed by the *ka'ubana'i* rite, for the hosts are, and always have been, friendly neighbours. But some of the beauty magic, and the enticing formula over betel nut would be recited to obtain as many valuables as possible. There is nothing corresponding to *uvalaku* in such big visits between neighbouring districts, though I think that they would be held only in connection with some *uvalaku* visit from another part of the ring to one of the two districts, as was the case in the example quoted, that is the Sinaketan visit to Kiriwina (Chapter XVI). Of course there is no associated trade on such expeditions, for there is very little to exchange between Sinaketa and Kiriwina, and what there is, is done independently, in a regular manner all the year round. Partnership between people of such two Kula communities is very much the same as within one of them. It obtains between people speaking the same language, having the same customs and institutions, many of whom are united by bonds of actual kinship or relationship-in-law. For, as has been mentioned already, marriages between Sinaketa and Kiriwina take place frequently, especially between natives of high rank. The rule is, in such cases, that a man of Sinaketa marries a woman of Kiriwina.

III

Let us pass now to the relation between categories 2 and 3, that is between Kula of two contiguous ' Kula communities,' and the Kula within one of them. First of all, in the inland Kula within the same community, there never take place big, wholesale transactions. The circulation of *vaygu'a* consists of individual exchanges, sometimes more frequent, that is, whenever an overseas expedition has come home laden with many valuables, sometimes done at long intervals. No magic is

performed in this type of Kula, and though there is a certain
amount of ceremony accompanying each gift, there are no big,
public gatherings. A concrete description of an actual case
may serve best to illustrate these general statements.

During the eight months I stayed in Omarakana in 1915-
1916, I had the opportunity of watching many cases of inland
Kula, as there was a constant come and go between Kiriwina
and Kitava, and subsequent to each influx of armshells from
the East, a series of exchanges took place. In the month
of November, To'uluwa went with his canoe on a small expedition across the sea to Kitava, and brought back a good haul of
mwali (armshells). He arrived on an evening on the beach of
Kaulukuba, and word was sent over to the village that next day
he would come up with his trophies. In the morning, blows of
conch-shell, heard from the distance, announced the approach
of the returning party, and soon, preceded by one of his
small sons carrying the conch-shell, To'uluwa made his
appearance followed by his companions. Each man carried
a few pairs which he had obtained, whilst the chief's share
was brought in on a stick, hanging down in a chaplet (see
Plate LX).

The people in the village sat before their huts, and according
to native custom, there was no special concourse to meet the
chief, nor any outward signs of excitement. The chief went
straight to one of his *bulaviyaka*, that is, one of his wives' houses,
and sat on the platform before it, waiting for some food to come.
That would be the place where he would seat himself, if he
wanted just to have a domestic chat with some of his wives and
children. Had any strangers been there, he would have
received them at his place of official reception, in front of
his *lisiga*, the extremely large and high chief's house, standing
in the inner row of yam houses, and facing the main place, the
baku (see Plate II). On that occasion he went to the hut of
Kadamwasila, his favourite wife, the mother of four sons
and one daughter. She is quite old now, but she was the
first wife married by To'uluwa himself, that is, not inherited,
and there is an unmistakable attachment and affection between
the two, even now. Though the chief has several much younger
and one or two really fine looking wives, he is usually to be found
talking and taking his food with Kadamwasila. He has also
a few older wives, whom, according to the custom, he inherited

from his predecessor, in that case, his elder brother. The eldest of them, Bokuyoba, the Dean of the Body of the chief's wives, has been twice inherited; she is now a source of income——for her male kinsmen have to supply yams to the chief—and an object of veneration, and is now even relieved of the duty of cooking the chief's food.

To'uluwa sat, ate, and talked about his journey to myself and some of the village elders assembled there. He spoke of the amount of *mwali* at present in Kitava, told us from whom and how he obtained those at which we were then looking, naming the most important ones, and giving bits of their histories. He commented on the state of gardens in Kitava, which in one respect, in the production of the big yams (*kuvi*) are the admiration of all the surrounding districts. He spoke also about future Kula arrangements, expeditions to arrive from the East in Kiriwina, and of his own planned movements.

On the afternoon of the same day, people from other villages began to assemble, partly to hear the news of the chief's expedition, partly in order to find out what they could obtain themselves from him. Headmen from all the dependent villages sat in one group round the chief, who now had moved to the official reception ground, in front of his *lisiga*. Their followers, in company with the chief's henchmen, and other inhabitants of Omarakana, squatted all over the *baku* (central place), engaged in conversation. The talk in each group was of the same subjects, and did not differ much from the conversation, I had heard from the chief on his arrival. The newly acquired armshells were handed round, admired, named, and the manner of their acquisition described.

Next day, several *soulava* (spondylus shell necklaces) were brought to Omarakana by the various men from neighbouring villages to the West, and ceremonially offered to To'uluwa (see Plates LXI, LXII, and Frontispiece). This was, in each case a *vaga* (opening gift), for which the giver expected to receive his *yotile* (clinching gift) at once from the store of *mwali*. In this case we see the influence of chieftainship in the relation between Kula partners. In the inland Kula of Kiriwina, all gifts would be brought to To'uluwa, and he would never have to fetch or carry his presents. Moreover, he would always be given and never give the opening gift (*vaga*) ; while his gift would invariably be a *yotile*. So that the chief sometimes owes a Kula gift to a commoner, but a commoner never owes a gift to a chief. The difference between the rules of procedure here and those of an *uvalaku* overseas expedition is clear : in a competitive overseas expedition, valuables for exchange are never carried by the visiting party, who only receive gifts and bring them back home ; in the inland Kula, the determining factor is the relative social position of the two partners. Gifts are brought to the man of superior by the man of inferior rank, and the latter has also to initiate the exchange.

The following entry is quoted literally from my notes, made in Omarakana, on November the 13th, 1915. " This morning, the headman of Wagaluma brought a *bagido'u* (fine necklace). At the entrance to the village (it is Omarakana), they (the party) halted, blew the conch shell, put themselves in order. Then, the conch shell blower went ahead, the men of highest rank took the stick with the *bagido'u*, a boy carrying the heavy wooden bell pendant on a *kaboma* (wooden dish)." This requires a commentary. The ceremonial way of carrying the spondylus shell necklaces is by attaching each end to a stick, so that the necklace hangs down with the pendant at its lowest point (see Frontispiece and Pl. LXI and LXII). In the case of very long and fine necklaces, in which the pendant is accordingly big and heavy, while the actual necklace is thin and fragile, the pendant has to be taken off and carried apart. Resuming the narrative :—" The headman approached To'uluwa and said : ' *Agukuleya, ikanawo ; lagayla lamaye ; yoku kayne gala mwali.*' This he said in thrusting the stick into the thatch of the chief's house." The words literally mean : ' My *kuleya* (food left over), take it ; I brought it to-day ; have you perhaps no armshells ? ' The expression ' food left over,' applied to the gift was a depreciating term, meaning something which is an overflow or unwanted scrap. Thus he was ironically depreciating his gift, and at the same time implying that much wealth still remained in his possession. By this, in an oblique manner, he bragged about his own riches, and with the last phrase, expressing doubt as to whether To'uluwa had any armshells, he threw a taunt at the chief. This time the gift was returned immediately by a fine pair of armshells.

It was in connection with the same expedition that the little exchange between two of the chief's wives took place, mentioned before (in Chapter XI, Division II, under 4) and one or two more domestic Kula acts were performed, a son of To'uluwa offering him a necklace (see Plates LXI and LXII) and receiving a pair of armshells afterwards. Many more transactions took place in those two days or so ; sounds of conch shells were heard on all sides as they were blown first in the village from which the men started, then on the way, then at the entrance to Omarakana, and finally at the moment of giving. Again, after some time another blast announced the return gift by To'uluwa, and the receding sounds of the conch marked the stages of the going home of the party. To'uluwa himself never receives a gift with his own hands; it is always hung up in his house or platform, and then somebody of his household takes charge of it ; but the commoner receives the armshell himself from the hands of the chief. There was much life and movement in the village during this time of concentrated exchange ; parties came and went with *vaygu'a*, others arrived as mere spectators, and the place was always full of a gazing crowd. The soft sounds of the conch shell, so characteristic of all South Sea experiences, gave a special flavour to the festive and ceremonial atmosphere of those days.

Not all the armshells brought from Kitava were thus at once given away. Some of them were kept for the purposes of more distant Kula ; or to be given on some future, special occasion when a present had to be handed over in association with some ceremony. In the inland Kula, there is always an outbreak of transactions whenever a big quantity of valuables is imported into the district. And afterwards, sporadic transactions happen now and then. For the minor partners who had received armshells from To'uluwa would not all of them keep them for any length of time, but part of them would be sooner or later passed on in inland transactions. But, however these valuables might spread over the district, they would be always available when an expedition from another Kula community would come and claim them. When the party from Sinaketa came in March, 1918, to Omarakana, all those who owned armshells would either come to the capital or else be visited in their villages by their Sinaketan partners. Of the 154 or so armshells obtained in Kiriwina on that occasion, only thirty came from To'uluwa himself, and fifty from Omarakana altogether, while the rest were given from other villages, in the following proportions :

Liluta	..	..	..	14
Osapola	..	..	..	14
Mtawa	..	..	..	6
Kurokaywa		..	..	15
Omarakana (To'uluwa)			..	30
Omarakana (other men)			..	20
Yalumugwa		..	..	14
Kasana'i	..	..	..	16
Other villages		..	..	25
				154

Thus the inner Kula does not affect the flow of the main stream, and, however, the valuables might change hands within the ' Kula community,' it matters little for the outside flow.

IV

It will be necessary to give a more detailed account of the actual conditions obtaining in Boyowa wth regard to the limits of the various Kula communities in that district. Looking at Map IV, p. 50, we see there the boundaries of Kiriwina, which is the easternmost Kula community in the Northern part of the islands. To the west of it the provinces of Tilataula, Kuboma, and Kulumata form another Kula community, or, it would be more correct to say, some of the men in these districts make the inland Kula with members of neighbouring communities. But these three provinces do not form as a whole a Kula community. In the first place, many villages are quite outside the Kula, that is, not even their headmen belong to the inter-tribal exchange. Remarkably enough, all the big industrial centres, such as Bwoytalu, Luya, Yalaka, Kadukway-kela, Buduwaylaka, do not take part in the Kula. An interesting myth localised in Yalaka tells how the inhabitants of that village, prevented by custom from seeing the world on Kula expeditions, attempted to erect a high pillar reaching to heaven, so as to find a field for their adventures in the skies. Unfortunately, it fell down, and only one man remained above, who is now responsible for thunder and lightning.

Another important omission in the Kula is that of the Northern villages of Laba'i, Kaybola, Lu'ebila, Idaleaka, Kapwani and Yuwada. If we remember that Laba'i is the very centre of Kiriwinian mythology, that there lies the very hole out of which the original ancestors of the four clans emerged from underground, that the highest chiefs of Kiriwina trace their descent from Laba'i, this omission appears all the more remarkable and mysterious.

Thus the whole Western half of the Northern Trobriands forms a unit of sorts in the chain of Kula communities, but it cannot be considered as a fully fledged one, for only sporadic individuals belong to it, and again, that district as a whole, or even individual canoes from it, never take part in any overseas Kula expedition. The village of Kavataria makes big overseas sailings to the Western d'Entrecasteaux Islands. Though these expeditions really have nothing to do with the Kula we shall say a few words about this in the next chapter but one.

Passing now to the West, we find the island of Kayleula, which, together with two or three smaller islands, to its South, Kuyawa, Manuwata, and Nubiyam, form a ' Kula community' of its own. This community is again slightly anomalous, for they make Kula only on a small scale, on the one hand with the chiefs and headmen of Kiriwina, and of the North-Western district of Boyowa, and on the other hand with the Amphletts, but never with Dobu. They also used to make long and perilous trips to the Western d'Entrecasteaux, sailing further West and for longer distances than the natives of Kavataria.

The main Kula communities in the South of Boyowa, Sinaketa and Vakuta, have been described already, and sufficiently defined in the previous chapters. Sinaketa is the centre for inland Kula of the South, which, though on a smaller scale than the inland Kula of the North, still unites half-a-dozen villages round Sinaketa. That village also carries on Kula with three coastal villages in the East, Okayaulo, Bwaga, and Kumilabwaga, who link it up with Kitava, to where they make journeys from time to time. These villages form again the sort of imperfect ' Kula community,' or perhaps one on a very small scale, for they would never have an *uvalaku* of their own, and the amount of transactions which pass through them is very small. Another such small community, independent as regards

Kula, is the village of Wawela. The district of Luba, which sometimes joins with Kiriwina in carrying on a big expedition, also sometimes joins with Wawela on small expeditions. Such nondescript or intermediate phenomena of transition are always to be found in studying the life of native races, where most social rules have not got the same precision as with us. There is among them neither any strong, psychological tendency to consistent thinking, nor are the local peculiarities and exceptions rubbed off by the influence of example or competition.

I cannot say very much about the inland Kula in other regions besides the Trobriands. I have seen it done in Woodlark Island, at the very beginning of my work among the Northern Massim, and that was the first time that I came across any of the symptoms of the Kula. Early in 1915, in the village of Dikoyas, I heard conch shells blown, there was a general commotion in the village, and I saw the presentation of a large *bagido'u*. I, of course, inquired about the meaning of the custom, and was told that this is one of the exchanges of presents made when visiting friends. At that time I had no inkling that I had been a witness of a detailed manifestation, of what I subsequently found out was Kula. On the whole, however, I have been told by natives from Kitava and Gawa, later on whilst working in the Trobriands, that the customs of Kula exchange there are identical with those obtaining in Kiriwina. And the same I was told is the case in Dobu. It must be realised, however, that the inland Kula must be somewhat different in a community where, as in Kitava, for instance, the strands of the Kula all come together in a small space, and the stream of valuables, which has been flowing through the broad area of the Trobriands, there concentrates into three small villages. If we estimate the inhabitants of the Trobriands with Vakuta at up to ten thousand, while those of Kitava at no more than five hundred, there will be about twenty times as many valuables per head of inhabitants in Kitava as compared to the Trobriands.

Another such place of concentration is the island of Tubetube, and I think one or two places in Woodlark Island, where the village of Yanabwa is said to be an independent link in the chain, through which every article has to pass. But this brings us already to the Eastern Kula, which will form the subject of the next chapter.

Chapter XX

EXPEDITIONS BETWEEN KIRIWINA AND KITAVA

I

THE subject of which this book treats and the material at our disposal are nearly exhausted. In describing the Southern branch of the Kula (between Sinaketa and Dobu) I entered into the details of its rules and associated aspects, and almost all that was said there refers to the Kula as a whole. In speaking of the N.E. branch of the Kula, which I am now about to describe, there will not therefore be very much new to tell. All the general rules of exchange and types of behaviour are the same as those previously defined. Here we have also big *uvalaku* expeditions and small, non-ceremonial sailings. The type of partnership between Kiriwinians and Kitavans is the same here, as the one obtaining within the Trobriands, and described in the last chapter. For the natives of the Eastern islands, from Kitava to Woodlark, have the same social organisation and the same culture as the Trobrianders, and speak the same language with dialectical differences only. Never any but friendly relations have obtained between them and many people are united by bonds of real kinship across the seas, for there have been migrations between the districts, and marriages are also not infrequent. Thus the general relations between overseas partners are different here from those between Sinaketa and Dobu. The visiting is not associated with any deep apprehensions, there is no *ka'ubana'i* (danger magic), and the relations between the visitors and hosts are much more free and easy and intimate. The rest of the Kula magic (except the *ka'ubana'i*) is identical with that in the South, and indeed much of it, as used all over Boyowa, has been received from the Kitavans. Many of the preliminary customs and arrangements of the Kula, the preparation of the canoes, ceremonial launching and *kabigidoya* are the same here. In fact, the launching described in Chapter VI was the one I saw on the beach of Omarakana.

On the actual expeditions, much of the ceremonial and all the rules of the Kula gifts, as well as of the *pari* and *talo'i*, the initial and farewell presents, are the same as in the South-Western branch of the Kula. The best plan will be to tell the story of a typical *uvalaku* expedition from Kiriwina to Kitava, noting the similarities and emphasising the differences, while one or two points of divergence will claim our special attention. There is a small, but interesting incident called *youlawada*, a custom which allows a visiting party to attack and damage the house ornaments of a man, to whom they bring a gift. Another important speciality of this Eastern Kula is the association of a mortuary feast called *so'i* with particularly abundant distributions of *vaygu'a*.

I had opportunities of collecting notes about the North-Eastern Kula and of making observations during my residence in Omarakana, in 1915-1916. I saw several expeditions from Kitava arrive on the beach, and camp for a few days. To'uluwa went twice to Kitava, and his return from one of these visits has been described in the last chapter. He also once started for an expedition there, of which I was a member. There was a change of wind, some time in September, and with the North wind which we hoped would last for a few hours, it would have been possible to cross to Kitava and to return at our pleasure with the prevailing South-Easterly. Half-way to our goal, the wind changed and we had to return, to my great disappointment, though this gave me a good example of the entire dependence of the natives on the weather. Unfortunately, To'uluwa got it into his head that I had brought him bad luck, and so when he planned his next trip, I was not taken into his confidence or allowed to form one of the party. Two years later, when I lived in Oburaka, about half-way between the Northern and Southernmost end of Boyowa, several expeditions from Kitava visited Wawela, a village lying across on the other side of the island, which here is no more than a mile and a half-wide ; and one or two expeditions left from Wawela for Kitava. The only big expedition which came under my notice was the *uvalaku* which was to leave some time in April or May, 1916, from Kiriwina to the East. I saw only the preparatory stages, of which the launching was described in Chapter VII.

Let us imagine that we follow the course of this Kiriwinian *uvalaku*. The first general intimation that it would take place, came after one of the visits which To'ulawa made to Kitava. He had heard there that a considerable quantity of armshells was soon to come to the island, for, as we shall see by the end of this Chapter, such big, concerted movements of valuables along the ring take place from time to time. To'ulawa then and there made arrangements with his chief partner, Kwaywaya, to make an *uvalaku*, which was to be the means of carrying on the big movement of the *mwali*. On his return to Omarakana, when the headmen of the other Kiriwinian villages assembled, the plans of the *uvalaku* were talked over and details arranged. Even in olden days, before the chief's power was undermined, though he used to take the initiative, and give decisions in important matters, he had to put the case before the other headmen, and listen to what they had to say. Their opinions on the occasion of which we are speaking, would hardly ever be in contradiction to his wishes, and it was decided without much discussion to make the *uvalaku* in about six months' time. Soon after, the rebuilding or refitting of the canoes began, in the manner previously described. The only slight difference in the preparations between Kiriwina and Sinaketa lies in the preliminary trade. The Kiriwinians have to go inland to the industrial districts of Kuboma, and they go there every man on his own account, to acquire the articles needed.

It will be best to say here at once all that is necessary about the trade between Kiriwina and Kitava. As these two districts are geologically and in other respects much more similar to one another than Sinaketa and Dobu are, the trade is not of such vital importance, with one notable exception, as we shall see. The articles of subsidiary trade, which a Kiriwinian expedition would carry with them to Kitava, are the following :—wooden combs ; various classes of lime pots ; armlets, plaited of fern fibre ; turtle-shell earrings ; mussel shell ; coils of lashing creeper (*wayugo*) ; plaited fern belts, made originally in the d'Entrecasteaux. Of these articles, the most important are probably the mussel shells, used for scraping and as knives, the various kinds of lime pots, which are a speciality of Kuboma, and last, but not least, the *wayugo*. I am not quite certain as to whether this creeper is not to be

PLATE LX

ARMSHELLS BROUGHT FROM KITAVA

The personal share of To'uluwa from the haul of armshells brought to Omarakana in October, 1915. (See p. 471.)

[face p. 480

PLATE LXI

BRINGING IN A SOULAVA

The party, the second man blowing the conch shell and the leader carrying the necklace on a stick, approach the chief's house. (See p. 472.)

PLATE LXII

OFFERING THE SOULAVA

The necklace is thrust on its stick into the chief's house. Both this plate and the foregoing one represent an act of purely domestic Kula, one of the sons of To'uluwa offering his father a necklace. Hence the scanty attendance of the general public. (See p. 472.)

found in Kitava, but as it grows only on marshy soil, it is hardly probable that it would thrive on a high, raised, coral island. In that case, the creeper is certainly the most indispensable of all the trade articles imported into Kitava from the Trobriands.

The Trobrianders import from the smaller islands a class of grass skirt made of coco-nut leaves ; exceptionally well finished urn-shaped baskets ; small hand-baskets ; specially bleached pandanus mats ; ornaments made of fragments of conus shell ; certain classes of cowrie shell, used for ornamenting belts ; ebony lime spatulæ ; ebony walking staves ; sword-clubs carved in ebony ; and an aromatic black paint, made of charred sandal wood. None of these articles is of vital importance, as all of them, though perhaps in slightly different or even inferior quality, are manufactured or found in the Trobriands.

There was one article, however, which, in the olden days, was of surpassing utility to the Trobriand natives, and which they could obtain only from Kitava, though it came originally from further East, from Murua (Woodlark Island). These were the *kukumuli*, or roughly shaped pieces of green-stone, which were then polished in the Trobriands, and in this state used as stone implements, while the biggest of them, very large and thin and well polished all over, became a specially important class of *vaygu'a* (articles of high value). Although the practical use of stone implements has naturally been done away with by the introduction of steel and iron, the *beku* (valuable axe blades) have still an undiminished, indeed, an increased value, as the white traders have to use them for purchasing pearls from the natives. It is important to note that although all the raw material for these stone implements and valuables had to be imported from Kitava, the finished valuables were and are re-exported again, as Kiriwina is still the main polishing district.

As to the manner in which the trade was done between the Kiriwinians and Kitavans, all that has been said previously on the subject of inter-tribal trade holds good ; part of the goods carried were given as presents, part of them were exchanged with non-partners, some were gifts received from the partners on leaving.

II

Returning to To'ulawa and his companions, as time went on there was more and more stir in the villages. As usually, all sorts of ambitious plans were framed, and the youthful members of the party hoped that they would reach Muyuwa (or Murua, Woodlark Island) where Kula was not done, but where Kiriwinian parties sometimes went in order to witness certain festivities. On the subject of Muyuwa, Bagido'u, the elderly heir apparent of Omarakana, who however, as said in the previous chapter, will never succeed his uncle, had to tell his own experiences. As a small boy, he sailed there with one of the big chiefs of Omarakana, his maternal grandfather. They went to Suloga, the place where the green stone was quarried.

" There," spoke Bagido'u, " there was a big *dubwadebula* (grotto or rock shelf). The members of the Lukulabuta clan (this clan is called Kulutalu in Muyuwa) of Suloga, were the *toli* (masters, owners) of this *dubwadebula*, and could quarry the stone. They knew some *megwa* (magic) ; they charmed their axeblades, and hit the walls of the *dubwadebula*. The *kukumali* (pieces of stone) fell down. When the men of Boyowa came to Suloga, they gave *pari* (presents) to the Lukulabuta men of Suloga. They gave them *paya* (turtle shell), *kwasi* (armlets), *sinata* (combs). Then, the Suloga men would show us the *kukumali*, and tell us : ' Take them with you, take plenty.' Good *kukumali*, which could be made into a *beku* (big wealth-blades) we would pay for ; we would give our *vaygu'a* (valuables) in exchange. At parting, they would give us more *kukumali* as *talo'i* (farewell gift)."

It must be remembered, in comment on this narrative, that when Bagido'u went to Suloga, some thirty or forty years ago, the iron and steel had already long before rendered the small *kukumali* quite useless and worthless to the natives, while the big *kukumali* had still their full value, as material for the large blades which serve as tokens of wealth. Hence, the big ones had still to be paid for, and hence also the generous invitation to take as many of the small ones, as they liked, an invitation of which the visitors, with corresponding delicacy, refused to avail themselves.*

---

* I have not seen the site of Suloga myself. Interesting details are to be found in " The Melanesians " of Professor Seligman, who visited the spot himself, and who has collected a number of specimens in the locality, as well as many data about the production of the blades. *Op. cit.*, pp. 530-533.

Another hero of the occasion was old Ibena, one of the Tabalu (members of the highest rank) of Kasana'i, the sister village of Omarakana. He has spent a long time on the island of Iwa, and knew the myths and magic of the Eastern archipelago very well. He would sit down and tell for hours various stories of famous Kula expeditions, of mythological incidents, and of the peculiar customs of the Eastern islands. It was from him that I first obtained my information about the *mulukwausi* and their customs, about shipwreck and the means of saving the party, about the love magic of Iwa, and many other facts, which only a man of cosmopolitan experience and culture, like Ibena, would know and understand thoroughly. He was a good informant, eager to instruct and to display his wisdom and knowledge, and not devoid of imagination ; of the licentious and libidinous women of Kaytalugi (see Chapter X) and of what a man has to suffer there, he would speak as if he had been there himself. At this time, he was specially loquacious about the Kula, and associated customs, inspired as he was by the hope of re-visiting his old haunts, and by the admiration and reverence shown to him by his listeners, myself included.

The other members of the audience were most interested in his accounts of how they make gardens in Kitava, Iwa and Gawa ; of the special dances performed there, of the technicalities of Kula, and of the great efficiency of the Iwan love magic.

At that time, I was able to obtain more information about the Kula, and that more easily and in a shorter while, than I had, with strenuous efforts, for months before. It is by taking advantage of such epochs, when the interest of the natives is centred round a certain subject, that ethnographic evidence can be collected in the easiest and most reliable manner. Natives will willingly state customs and rules, and they will also accurately and with interest follow up concrete cases. Here, for instance, they would trace the way in which a given pair of armshells had passed through the hands of several individuals, and was now supposed to have come round again to Kitava—and in such a way one receives from the natives definite ethnographic documents, realities of thought, and details of belief, instead of forced artificial verbiage.

I saw the proceedings as far as the ceremonial launching of the chiefs' canoes in Kasana'i and Omarakana (cf. Chapter VI), when the natives assembled in big numbers, and various festivities took place. Afterwards when everything was ready for sailing, a similar crowd gathered on the beach, though less numerous than the previous one, for only the neighbouring villages were there instead of the whole district. The chief addressed the crowd, enjoining strict taboos on strangers entering the village while the men were away. Such taboos, on the surface at least, are very carefully kept, as I had opportunities to observe during the two previous absences of To'uluwa. Early in the evening, everybody retired into his or her house, the outside fires were extinguished and when I walked through the village, it was quite deserted and except for a few old men specially keeping watch, no one was to be seen. Strangers would be careful not to pass even through the outskirts of the village after sunset, and would take another road to avoid the grove of Omarakana.

Even men from the sister-village of Kasana'i were excluded from entering the capital, and on one occasion when two or three of them wanted to visit their friends, they were stopped from doing it by some of the old men, with a considerable display of indignation and authority. As it happened, a day or two afterwards, but still while the Kula party were away, one of the favourite sons of To'uluwa, called Nabwasu'a who had not gone on the expedition, was caught *in flagrante delicto* of adultery with the youngest wife of the very old chief of Kasana'i. The people of the latter village were highly incensed, not without an admixture of malicious amusement. One of these who had been expelled two nights before from Omarakana took a conch shell and with its blast announced to the wide world the shame and scandal of Omarakana. As a conch shell is blown only on very important and ceremonial occasion, this was a slap in the face of the supposedly virtuous community, and a reproach of its hypocrisy. A man of Kasana'i, speaking in a loud vocie, addressed the people of Omarakana :—

> " You don't allow us to enter your village ; you call us adulterous (*tokaylasi*) ; but we wanted only to go and visit our friends. And look here, Nabwasu'a committed adultery in our village ! "

The *uvalaku* party, to whom we now return, would cross the sea in a few hours and arrive in Kitava. Their manner of sailing, the arrangement of men in the canoe, the taboos of sailing are the same as in Sinaketa. My knowledge of their canoe magic is much smaller than of that in Southern Boyowa, but I think they have got far fewer rites. The sailing on these seas is on the whole easier, for there are fewer reefs, and the two prevailing winds would either bring them towards the Eastern islands, or push them back towards the long coast of Boyowa. The natives of Kiriwina are on the other hand far less expert sailors than the Sinaketans.

They have the same beliefs about the dangers at sea, especially about the participation of the flying witches in shipwreck. The history of such a calamity and the means of escape from it, given in one of the foregoing chapters (Chapter X), refers to these seas, as well as to the sea-arm of Pilolu.

These natives, as well as the Southern Boyowans, feel and appreciate the romance of sailing ; they are visibly excited at the idea of an expedition, they enjoy even the sight of the open sea on the Eastern coast beyond the *raybwag* (coral ridge), and often walk there on mere pleasure parties. The Eastern coast is much finer than the beach of the Lagoon ; steep, dark rocks alternate there with fine, sandy beaches, the tall jungle spreading over the higher and lower parts of the shore. The sailing to Kitava does not present, however, the same contrasts as an expedition to the d'Entrecasteaux Islands from Southern Boyowa. The natives remain still in the world of raised coral islands, which they know from their own home. Even the island of Muyuwa (or Murua, Woodlark Island) where I spent a short time, does not present such a definite contrast in landscape as that between the Trobriands and the Koya. I do not know from personal experience the Marshall Bennett Islands, but from an excellent description given by Professor Seligman, they seem to be good specimens of small raised atolls.[*]

With regard to magic, the most important initial rites over the *lilava* and *sulumwoya* are done in the village by the *toliwaga* (compare above, Chapter VII). The magic over the four coco-nuts in the canoe is not performed in Kiriwina. On arrival at the beach in Kitava, all the rites of beauty magic, as

* Cf. *Op. cit.*, pp. 670-672.

well as the magic over the conch shell are recited in a manner identical to that in Sarubwoyna (Chapter XIII). Here, however, the natives have to make the last stage of the journey on foot.

The party, headed by a small boy, probably a youngest son of the *toliwaga*, after whom the chief and the others follow, would march towards the village which is situated beyond the elevated ridge. When *soulava* (necklaces) are brought by the party—which, it must be remembered is never the case on an *uvalaku*—they would be carried ceremonially on sticks by some men following the chief. In that case, that is when the party are bringing Kula gifts—the *youlawada* ceremony is performed. On entering the village, the party march on briskly without looking to right or left, and, whilst the boy blows frantically the conch shell, and all the men in the party emit the intermittent ceremonial scream called *tilaykiki*, others throw stones and spears at the *kavalapu*, the ornamental carved and painted boards running in a Gothic arch round the eaves of a chief's house or yam house. Almost all the *kavalapu* in the Eastern villages are slightly injured, that of To uluwa having one of its ends knocked off. The damage is not repaired, as it is a mark of distinction.

This custom is not known in the Kula between Sinaketa and Dobu or Sinaketa and Kiriwina. It begins on the Eastern shore of the Trobriands, and is carried on as far as Tubetube where it stops again, for it is not practised in Wari (Teste Island) or on the portion of the Kula between Tubetube and Dobu. I myself never saw it practised in the Trobriands, but I saw a similar custom among the Massim of the South Coast of New Guinea. At a *so'i* feast which I witnessed in three different villages as it progressed from one to the other, the party who brought in gifts of pigs to a man attempted to do some damage to his trees or his house. A pig is always slung by its legs on a long, stout pole, dangling head downwards (see Plates V and LXIII) : with this pole the natives would ram a young coco-nut or betel-nut palm or a fruit tree and if not stopped by the owners would break or uproot it, the pig squealing and the women of the damaged party screaming in unison. Again, a party entering a village with gifts to one of the inhabitants, would throw miniature spears at his house. A distinct show of fierceness and hostility is displayed on both sides by the natives on such occasions. Although the somewhat histrionic attack, and the slight but real damage to property were sanctioned by tribal usage, not infrequently among the Southern Massim serious quarrels and scrimmages were started by it. This custom has been observed by Professor Seligman among the natives of Bartle Bay. " As a man passed the house, they speared the wall with the branches they had been waving, and left them stuck in the walls." And again : ". . . the people bringing them (the pigs) in, carried branches of trees or pieces of stick with a wisp of grass tied to the end, and with these speared the house of the man to whom the pigs were given."*

When we remember what has been said about the style in which all gifts are given ; that is, so to speak, thrown down fiercely and almost contemptuously by the giver ; when we remember the taunts with which gifts are often accompanied, as well as the manner in which they are received, the *youlawada* custom appears only as an exaggerated form of this manner of giving, fixed into a definite ceremonial. It is interesting from this point of view to note that the *youlawada* is only done in association with *vaga* (initial gifts) and not with the *yotile* (return gifts).

The Kiriwinian party, after having paid their preliminary ceremonial visit in the village, given their gifts, both of the Kula and of the *pari* type, and had a long chat with their partners and friends, return in the evening to the beach, where they camp near their canoes. Sometimes temporary huts are erected, sometimes in fine weather the natives sleep under mats on the sand beach. Food is brought to them from the village by young, unmarried girls, who very often on that occasion arrange their intrigues with the visitors. The party will remain for a few days paying calls to the other villages of the island, talking, inspecting the gardens and hoping for more Kula presents. The food of Kitava is not tabooed to the chiefs, as the Kitavans abstain from the worst abominations. At parting the visitors receive their *talo'i* gifts which are brought down to their canoes.

The visits are returned by the Kitavans in very much the same manner. They camp on the sand beaches of the Eastern Coast. When weather-bound they erect temporary habitations,

* Op. cit., description of the Walaga feast, pp. 594-603.

and I have seen whole families, men, women, and children living for days on some of the Eastern shores. For it is the custom of the men of Kitava to carry their women and small children on their trips. The Kiriwinians take sometimes unmarried girls, but they would never take their wives and small children, whilst in the South no Sinaketan women at all go on a Kula voyage however small and unimportant a one it may be. From big *uvalaku* expeditions, women are excluded in all the districts.

It has been mentioned in the last chapter that Kitava enjoys a privileged position in the Ring, for every single piece of valuables has to pass through it. The island of Kitava is a ' Kula community ' in itself. All its neighbours to the West, the Kula communities of Kiriwina, Luba, Wawela, Southern Boyowa (that is, the villages of Okayyaulo, Bwaga and Kumilabwaga) cannot skip Kitava when they are exchanging, and the same refers to the Kitavan neighbours in the East. In other words, a man from the Eastern islands beyond Kitava, if he wants to pass an armshell westwards, has to give it to a Kitava man, and may not give it directly to some one beyond. The islands East of Kitava, Iwa, Gawa, and Kwayawata form one community. This is shown on Map V, where each ' Kula community ' is represented by one circle. The Kula stream, after having concentrated in Kitava, spreads out again, but by no means as broadly as when it runs to the Westward, and overflows over the broad area of the Trobriands. Another point, in which the Kula of Kitava differs from that of Sinaketa or Kiriwina, a point on which I have touched already once before (in Chapter XIII, Division I) is that the small island has to make overseas exchanges on both sides. As we saw, the Sinaketans carry on big expeditions and make *uvalaku* only to their Southern partners, so that they receive only the one Kula article, the necklaces in this manner, while their armshells come to them by inland Kula, from their Northern and Eastern neighbours. The same *mutatis mutandis* refers to the Kiriwinians, who receive all their necklaces overland and make overseas Kula for their armshells only. The two islands of Kitava and Vakuta, as well as the other Marshall Bennetts are, so to speak, ambidextrous in the Kula and have to fetch and carry both articles overseas. This, of course, results primarily from the geographical position in a district and a glance at Map V will easily show which Kula communities have to carry all their transactions overseas and which of them have to do one half of them overland. These latter are only the Trobriand districts mentioned in the previous Chapter and the districts in Dobu.

III

This exhausts all the peculiarities of the Kula in Kitava except one, and that a very important one. It has been mentioned before, in fact it is obvious from the account of the *uvalaku* custom that the Kula does not run with an even flow, but in violent gushes. Thus the *uvalaku* expedition from Dobu described in Chapter XVI carried about 800 pairs of armshells from Boyowa. Such sudden rushes of the Kula articles are associated with an important institution, which is not known in the Trobriands or in Dobu, but which we find in Kitava and further along the Ring, as far as Tubetube (see Map V). When a man dies, custom imposes a taboo upon the inhabitants of that village. This means that no one on a visit is received in the village, and no Kula articles are given away from there. The community lying under the taboo, however, expect to receive as many Kula gifts as possible, and busy themselves in that matter. After a certain time, a big ceremony and distribution of goods, called *so'i* is held, and invitations are sent out to all the Kula partners, and, in the case of a big affair, even to people from districts beyond the boundary of partnership. A big distribution of food takes place in which all the guests receive their share, and then the Kula valuables are given in great quantities to the partners of that community.

The association of taboo on economic goods with mourning is a wide-spread feature of the Melanesian customs in New Guinea. I found it among the Mailu on the South Coast of New Guinea, where a taboo, called *gora*, is put on coco-nuts as one of the features of mourning.* The same institution, as we saw, obtains in Dobu. Similar taboos are to be found among the Southern Massim.†

The importance of such economic taboos at times of mourning is due to another wide-spread association, that

---

* See the Author's Memoir in the Transactions of the Royal Society of S. Australia. "The Natives of Mailu," pp. 580-588.

† Cf. Professor C. G. Seligman. Op. cit., Chapter XLIV.

namely which obtains between mourning and feasts, or, more correctly, distributions of food, which are made at intervals during a more or less prolonged period after a person's death. An especially big feast, or rather distribution, is made at the end of the period, and on this occasion the accumulated goods, usually coco-nut, betel-nut and pigs, are distributed. Death among all the coastal natives of Eastern New Guinea causes a great and permanent disturbance in the equilibrium of tribal life. On the one hand, there is the stemming of the normal flow of economic consumption. On the other hand, an innumerable series of rites, ceremonies and festive distributions, which one and all create all sorts of reciprocal obligations, take up the best part of the energy, attention and time of the natives for a period of a few months, or a couple of years according to the importance of the dead. The immense social and economic upheaval which occurs after each death is one of the most salient features of the culture of these natives, and one also which on its surface strikes us as enigmatic and which entices into all sorts of speculations and reflections. What makes the problem still more obscure and complex is the fact that all these taboos, feasts, and rites have nothing whatever to do, in the belief of the natives, with the spirit of the deceased. This latter has gone at once and settled definitely in another world, entirely oblivious of what happens in the villages and especially of what is done in memory of his former existence.

The *so'i* (distribution of food) as found in Kitava is the final act in a long series of minor distributions. What distinguishes it from its Boyowan counterparts and the similar ceremonies among the other Massim, is the accumulation of Kula goods. In this case, as we have said, the taboo extends also to the valuables. Immediately after death has occurred in a village, a large stick is placed on the reef in front of its landing beach, and a conch shell is tied to it. This is a sign that no visitors will be received who come to ask for Kula goods. Besides this, a taboo is also imposed on coco-nut, betel-nut and pigs.

These details, as well as the following ones, I received from an intelligent and reliable Kitavan informant, who has settled in Sinaketa. He told me that according to the importance of the death, and the speed with which the goods were accumulating after a year or so, word would be sent round to all the partners and *muri-muri* (partners once removed).

" When all are assembled," my informant told me, " the *sagali* (distribution) begins. They *sagali* first *kaulo* (yam food), then *bulukwa* (pig). When pig is plentiful it would be given in halves ; when not, it will be quartered. A big heap of yam food, of coco-nut, betel-nut, and banana would be placed for each canoe. Side by side with this row, a row of pig meat would be placed. One man calls out for the yam heaps, another for the pig-meat ; the name of each canoe is called out. If it were a whole pig, they would say, *To'uluwa kam visibala !* (To'uluwa, your whole pig) ! Otherwise they would call out, ' *Mililuta, kami bulukwa !* ' (Men of Liluta, your pig). And again, ' *Mililuta, kami gogula !* ' (Men of Liluta, your heap). They take it, take their heap to their canoe. There, the *toliwaga* (master of the canoe) would make another small *sagali*. Those, who live near by, singe their meat, and carry it home in their canoes. Those who live far away, roast the pig, and eat it on the beach."

It will be noted that the supreme chief's name would be uttered when his and his companion's share is allotted. With the shares of men of less importance, the name of the village is called out. As on all such occasions, the strangers do not eat their food in public, and even its re-distribution is done in the privacy of their camping place near the canoe.

After the distribution of the food, and of course before this is taken away by the parties, the master of the *so'i* goes into his house and takes out a specially good piece of valuable. With a blast of the conch shell, he gives it to the most distinguished of his partners present. Others follow his example, and soon the village is filled with conch shell blasts, and all the members of the community are busy presenting gifts to their partners. First, the initial gifts (*vaga*) are given, and only after this is over, such valuables as have been due of old to their partners, and which have to be given as clinching gifts (*yotile*) are handed over.

After the whole public distribution is finished and the guests have gone, the members of the sub-clan who organised it, at sunset make a small distribution of their own, called *kaymelu*. With that the *so'i* and the whole period of mourning and of consecutive distributions, is over. I have said before that this account of the *so'i* has been obtained only through the statements of several informants, one especially very clear and reliable. But it has not been checked by personal observation, and as is always the case with such material, there is no guarantee of its being complete.

From the point of view in which it interests us, however, that is, in connection with the Kula, the outstanding fact is well established ; a mortuary taboo temporarily holds up the flow of Kula goods, and a big quantity of valuables thus dammed up, is suddenly let loose by the *so'i* and spreads in a big wave along the circuit. The big wave of armshells, for instance, which travelled along and was taken up by the *uvalaku* expedition of the Dobuans, was the ripple of a *so'i* feast, held one or two months previously at full moon in Yanabwa, a village of Woodlark Island. When I was leaving Boyowa, in September, 1918, a mortuary taboo was in force in the Island of Yeguma, or Egum, as it is pronounced in the Eastern district (the Alcester Islands of the map). Kwaywaya, the chief of Kitava whom I met on his visit in Sinaketa, told me that the people of Yeguma had sent him a sprouting coco-nut, with the message : " When its leaves develop, we shall *sagali* (make the distribution)." They had kept a coco-nut at the same stage of development in their village, and sent others to to all the neighbouring communities. This would give a first approach in fixing the date, which would be appointed more precisely when the feast was close at hand.

The custom of associating the *so'i* with Kula is practised as far as Tubetube. In Dobu, there is no distribution of valuables at the mortuary feast. They have there another custom, however ; at the final mortuary distribution, they like to adorn themselves with armshells and necklaces of the Kula—a custom entirely foreign to the Trobrianders. In Dobu therefore, an approaching mortuary feast also tends to dam up the valuables which after its performance, will ebb away in two waves of *mwali* and *so'ulava* along both branches of the Kula. But they have no custom of distributing these valuables during the final mortuary feast, and therefore the release of the *vaygu'a* would not be as sudden as in a *so'i*.

The same word—*so'i*—is used to denote the mortuary festivities over a wide area in the country of the Massim. Thus, the natives of Bonabona and Su'a'u, on the South Coast of New Guinea celebrate annually in November to January festivities, associated with dancing, gifts of pigs, the building of new houses, the erection of a platform and several other features. These feasts, which are held in an inter-connected series each year in several different localities, I had opportunities, as mentioned before, to see in three places, but not to study. Whether they are associated with some form of exchange of valuables I do not know. Mortuary feasts in other districts of the Massim are also called *so'i*.* What is the relation between these feasts and those of the Northern Massim I am unable to say.†

These considerations bring us more and more to the point, where the two branches of the Kula which we have been following up from the Trobriands Southwards and Eastwards bend back again and meet. On this remaining part of the Kula, on which my information, however, is scanty, a few words will be said in the next Chapter.

---

* Cf. Professor C. G. Seligman. *Op. cit.*, p. 584.

† The ethnographic researches at present carried on in Su'a'u by Mr. W. E. Armstrong, of Cambridge, will no doubt throw light on this subject.

Chapter XXI

THE REMAINING BRANCHES AND OFFSHOOTS OF THE KULA

I

In this chapter the ring of the Kula has to be closed by a description of its remaining portions. It will also be found indispensable to speak about its offshoots, that is, the trade and the expeditions, regularly carried on from certain points of the ring to outlying places. We have come across such off-shoots already, when we realised that the Western Trobriands, especially the village of Kavataria, and the settlements on the island of Kayleula make non-Kula trading expeditions to the islands of Fergusson and Goodenough. Such expeditions would naturally belong to a full picture of the Kula, with its various associations. This is even more the case, as this lateral trade is associated with the import and export of some of the Kula valuables in and out of the ring.

We have brought the description of our Southern expedition as far as Dawson Straits, and on the Eastern route, we reached Woodlark Island in the last chapter. We have to link up these two points. The saying, that a chain is not stronger than its weakest link does not, let us hope, apply to Ethnology. For indeed my knowledge of the remaining links of the Kula chain is far less complete than that contained in the previous chapters. Fortunately, what has been said there, remains true and valid, whatever might happen in the South-Eastern portion of the Kula. And again, there is no doubt that the fundamentals of the transaction are identical all over the ring, though some variations in detail probably occur. I had the opportunity of questioning informants from almost every place in the Kula, and the similarity of the main outlines is established beyond a doubt. Moreover, the information about some aspect of trade in the Southern Massim district contained in Professor

Seligman's book, entirely, though indirectly, corroborates my results.   But it is necessary to state emphatically and explicitly that the data given in this chapter are not in the same category as the rest of the information contained in this book.   The latter was obtained from natives among whom I lived, and the bulk of it has been controlled and verified by personal experiences and observations (compare Table I in the Introduction). The material referring to the South Eastern branch was obtained by cursory examination of natives from that district, whom I met abroad, not in their own country, whilst I have not been in any of the places between Woodlark Island and Dobu.

Starting at Woodlark Island, and keeping Map V before our eyes—we come at once on to an interesting ramification of the Kula.   To the East of Woodlark, lies the coral group of the Loughlans, inhabited by natives speaking the same language as in Woodlark.   They are in the ring, but it seems to be a *cul-de-sac* Kula, for as I was told, the valuables, which go there return again to Woodlark.   This is quite an unusual complication, a kind of eddy in the otherwise progressive current.   I could not ascertain whether the difficulty is solved by the districts being sub-divided, a small ring being formed within it, and each class of articles moving on it in an opposite direction ; or whether some other arrangement has been adopted.   Again, one of my informants told me that some of the *vaygu'a* went directly from the Loughlans South to Misima, but I was unable to verify this statement and this whole part of the Kula must remain with a sketchy outline.

Whatever might be the routes on which the Kula articles travel South from Woodlark Island, there is no doubt whatever that they all, or almost all, converge in the important commercial centre of Tubetube.   This small island, according to Professor Seligman, is not even self-supporting as far as food goes ; nor are they a greatly industrial community.   They are to a great extent engaged in trade, and probably gain part of their support from this activity.   " Tubetube has become a trading community, whose inhabitants are recognised as traders and middlemen over a very considerable area, extending westwards . . .   to Rogea and eastward to Murua."* Tubetube is known even in the Trobriands as one of the crucial points of the Kula, and it is well known that, whatever happens in

* Seligman. *Op. cit.*, p. 524.

the small island in the way of mortuary taboos and big feasts will affect the flow of valuables in Boyowa.

There is no doubt whatever that Tubetube had direct relations with Murua (to use the Tubetube pronunciation of the native name for Woodlark Island) to the North-East, and with Dobu to the North-West. I saw a canoe from the small island beached at Dobu, and in Woodlark I was told that men from Tubetube used to come there from time to time. Professor Seligman also describes in detail the manner and the stages of their sailings to Woodlark Island :

" Their trade route to Murua . . . was, as they made it, about 120-135 miles. They would usually go during the monsoon, and come back on the trade, as those winds served their itinerary best. Presuming that wind and weather served them throughout the passage, they slept the first night on an island called Ore, a couple of miles or so from Dawson Island. The next night they made Panamoti, the third night they slept at Tokunu (the Alcesters), and by the fourth night, they might reach Murua."* This description reminds us very much of the route on which we previously had followed the Sinaketans to Dobu—the same short stages with intermediate camping on sandbanks or islands, the same taking advantage of favourable following winds.

From Kitava Eastward as far as Tubetube, a different type of canoe was used, the *nagega*, mentioned already in Chapter V, Division IV. As we saw there, it was very much the same in principles of construction as the Trobriand canoe, but it was bigger, of a greater carrying capacity, and more seaworthy. It was at the same time slower, but had one great advantage over the swifter counterpart ; having more waterboard, it made less leeway in its sailing, and could be sailed against the wind. It would thus allow the natives to cross distances and to face changes in the weather, either of which would compel the frailer and swifter canoe of Dobu and Kiriwina to turn back.

To the Northern shores of Normanby Island (Du'a'u) and to Dobu, the men of Tubetube would sail with the S.E. trade wind and return with the blow of the monsoon. According to Professor Seligman, such a trip to Dobu would take them also about four days, under the most favourable conditions.†

* *Op. cit.*, p. 538.
† *Ibid.*

PLATE LXIII

CEREMONIAL DESTRUCTION DURING A SO'I FEAST

This picture was taken on the South coast of New Guinea. (cf. p. 486 and Div. III of Ch. II.)

PLATE LXIV

NAGEGA CANOE

This type of canoe is manufactured by the North Eastern Massim and it is used in the South Eastern branch of the Kula.
(See p. 496, and Ch. V, Div. IV.)

[face p. 497

Thus, one fundamental fact can be regarded as definitely established ; the main centre of the Kula in its South-Eastern branch, was the small island of Tubetube. And this island was in direct communication with two points to which we have followed the Kula in two directions, starting from the Trobriands ; that is, with Dobu and with Woodlark Island.

On points of detail, some queries must be left unsolved. Were the visits returned by the Dobuans and Muruans? According to all probability, yes, but I possess no definite certainty on this point.

Another question is whether the natives of Tubetube were direct partners of Murua or Dobu. We have seen that natives of Kiriwina sail not infrequently to Iwa, Gawa, Kwayawata and even to Woodlark ; yet they are not partners (*karayta'u*) of these natives, but partners once removed (*murimuri*). I have definite information that the natives of Dobu Island proper and of Du'a'u, who, as we remember are not partners of the Southern Boyowans, stood in direct relation of partnership to the Tubetube. I believe also that the natives of Woodlark made direct Kula exchange with those of Tubetube.

The fact, however, that there is a direct line of communication between Murua-Tubetube-Dobu does not preclude the possibility of other and more complex routes running parallel with the direct one. Indeed, I know that the island of Wari, (Teste Island) lying almost due South of Tubetube is also in the Kula. The big island of Misima (St. Aignan Island) about a hundred miles East of Tubetube forms also part of the ring. Thus a much wider circle runs from Woodlark Island, perhaps from the Loughlans through Misima, the neighbouring small island of Panayati, Wari, and further West, through the group of islands quite close to the East end of New Guinea, that is, the islands of Sariba, Roge'a, and Basilaki, and then northwards again towards Normanby Island. This duplicated circuit in the South-East has its North-Western counterpart in the double ramification which unites Kitava with Dobu. The short route runs direct from Kitava to Vakuta and from Vakuta to Dobu. Besides this, however, there are several longer ones. In one of them the stages are as follows : Kitava, Okayaulo, or Kitava, Wawela, thence Sinaketa, then Dobu direct ; or *via* the Amphletts. Another and still wider ramification would run thus : Kitava, to Kiriwina, Kiriwina to Sinaketa, etc. ; or, the widest, Kiriwina to western Boyowa, then Kayleula, thence Amphletts, and from there to Dobu.   This last route was not only longest in distance, but owing to the notorious ' hardness ' of both the natives of Kayleula and of the Amphletts, would take up much more time.   A glance at Map V, and also at the more detailed map of the Trobriands (Map IV) will make all this clear.

A more detailed knowledge of the North-Western routes allowed us to see the complications and irregularities obtaining there ; that the district of Western Boyowa carried on exclusively the inland Kula, and that merely in the person of a few headmen of a few villages ; that Kayleula made Kula on a small scale with the communities in the Amphletts, and that all these, as well as the villages on the Eastern shore of Southern Boyowa, were what we described as semi-independent Kula communities.   Such details and peculiarities no doubt also exist with regard to the South-Eastern ramifications of the Kula, but must be taken here for granted.

Following the various threads further on, I have no doubt that the islands lying near the East end of New Guinea— Roge'a, Sariba, Basilaki—are and were in olden days in the Kula ring, communicating in the East with Tubetube and Wari, while to the North they were in contact with the natives of Normanby Island.   Whether the large village complex lying at East Cape was also in the Kula I cannot definitely say.   In any case all the strands led to the Eastern shores of Dawson Straits, by way of the North-Eastern shores of Normanby Island.   From here, from the district of Dobu, we have traced the further lines with complete exactness and detail.

Of the various details of these expeditions and technicalities of the Kula observed in them, I have not much material available.   The rules of actual exchange, the ceremonial of conch blowing, the code of honour or morality or vanity, perhaps, compelling people to give equivalent articles for what they have received, all these are the same all along the ring.   So is also the Kula magic, with variations in details.

II

One subject on which more must be said is that of the associated trade.   A new and important article of exchange accompanies the transaction in the South-Eastern branch of the Kula : the big, sea-going canoes. The main centres of manufacture, and to a great extent manufacture for export, were the islands of Gawa and Panayati. In these places, canoes were constructed for export to the southern districts where the natives did not know how to build such canoes (compare Chapter I, Division III). In olden days the natives of Woodlark Island, before its present depopulation, also probably made some canoes for exchange in external trade. I have seen these canoes owned by natives in the Southern Massim district as far as Orangerie Bay, over two hundred miles from the place where they were manufactured. The trading of this article ran along with the Kula lines of communication as there is no doubt that the natives of Tubetube and Wari were the main distributors and middlemen in this trade.

How far canoe exchange was associated directly with Kula transactions, I cannot say definitely. Judging from the data given by Professor Seligman,* armshells were paid by natives of Tubetube for canoes purchased from Panamoti in the North. Thus, the *mwali* in this commercial transaction, travelled in a direction opposite to that in which they must move in the Kula ring. This, again, suggests complete independence of the two transactions. Besides the canoes, another important article of trade in the southern portion are the clay pots manufactured both in Tubetube and Wari. Besides this, the two islands of " merchant venturers," as they are called by Professor Seligman, carry on their Kula expeditions, and most likely independent of them also, they trade almost all the various articles of industry manufactured in the neighbouring districts and distributed by the two communities. This subject has been treated so fully by Professor Seligman in Chapter XL of his " Melanesians " that a reference here will suffice.†

Having now before us the whole ring of the Kula, we may inquire how far is this ring in contact commercially with other outlying districts, and, more especially, how far are certain

---

* Cf. *Op. cit.*, pp. 536-537.

† I cannot follow Professor Seligman in his use of the word *currency*, which is not very clearly defined by him. This word can be correctly applied to the armshells, spondylus discs, big polished blades of green stones, etc., only if we give it simply the meaning of "objects" or "tokens of wealth." *Currency* as a rule means a medium of exchange and standard of value, and none of the Massim valuables fulfil these functions.

articles of trade imported into it and others drawn out of it ?
What will interest us most in this connection is the entry into
the ring and the exit out of it of the articles of Kula proper,
the *mwali* (armshells) and the *soulava* (necklaces).

III

One such offshoot of the Kula ring we met in the Trobriands,
to wit, the expeditions from the Western village of Kavataria,
and from the island of Kayleula, to the Koya of Fergusson and
Goodenough.   We shall begin with a brief account of these
expeditions.*   The preparations are very much the same, as in
Sinaketa.   The canoes are built with more or less the same
magic (cf. Chapter V), they are launched ceremonially and the
trial run, the *tasasoria*, also takes place (Chapter VI).   The
island of Kayleula is by far the more important centre of canoe
building.   Whether some of the Kavataria canoes were not
actually made in Kayleula and purchased by the Kavatarians
in olden days, I do not definitely know, though I think this was
the case.   Nowadays, the community of Kavataria are completely absorbed by the pearling industry, and since about a
generation ago have given up the expeditions, and even do not
own any canoes.   The collecting of trade articles, the magic
performed over the *lilava*, the *yawarapu*, and the *sulumwoya*
are the same as those described before (Chapter VII) except,
that is, that there exists a different system of *mwasila* in the
island of Kayleula, a system which was used also by the
Kavatarians.   It must be remembered in this connection that

---

* A short article on this subject has been published by the Rev. M. Gilmour,
now head of the Methodist Mission in New Guinea. (Annual Report of British
New Guinea, 1904-5, p. 71.)   I used this article in the field, going over it with
several natives of Kavataria, and I found it substantially correct, and on the
whole formulated with precision.   The need for extreme compression of
statement has, however, led the Author into one or two ambiguities.   Thus,
the constant mention of " feasting " might give a wrong impression, for it is
always the matter of a public distribution of food, which is then eaten apart,
or in small groups, while the word " feast " suggests eating in common.   Again,
the data about the " sea-chief," as Mr. Gilmour calls the leader of the privileged
clan in Kavataria (cf. Chapter IX, Division III), seemed to me over-stated,
when he is said to be "supreme," to have " the right of determining an
expedition," and especially when it is said that he " had the right of first choice
of a canoe."   This latter phrase must involve a misunderstanding ; as we
saw, each sub-clan (that is, each sub-division of the village) build their own
canoe, and a subsequent swapping and free choice are out of the question.
Mr. Gilmour was fully acquainted with the facts of the Kula, as I learnt from
personal conversation.   In this article, he mentions it only in one phrase, saying
that some of the expeditions " were principally concerned in the exchange of
the circulated articles of native wealth. . . . in which trade was only a
secondary consideration."

the natives of Kayleula did make Kula on a small scale with
the Amphlettans, and that their *mwasila* was connected with
the Kula.* But the main object of the Kavatarian and
Kayleulan *mwasila* was their non-Kula trade with the natives
of Fergusson and Goodenough. This is quite clear from Mr.
Gilmour's account, and it was also corroborated by my informants. They told me that the *mwasila* is done because of the
kavaylu'a (fine food) that is, of the sago and betel-nut and pigs,
the main objects of their expedition :

> " If they (the Western Boyowans) would not make
> *mwasila*, they (the Western d'Entrecasteaux natives)
> would fight them. They are foolish men, the people of the
> Koya, not like people of Dobu, who are human beings.
> Those in the Koya are wild, eaters of man. If they
> (Kavataria and Kayleula) would make no *mwasila*, they
> would refuse them betel-nut, refuse them sago."

The sailing is characterised by the priority enjoyed by the
Kulutula clan, who, as we have seen in a previous chapter
(Chapter IX, Division III) sail ahead and have the privilege of
landing first on any beach, on which they stop. On arrival,
they perform the beauty magic, and sailing towards the beach,
the magic of " shaking the mountain " is also recited. In the
Koya, the transactions resemble to a certain extent those of
the Kula. As my informant said :

> " When they anchor, first of all they give the *pari ;* they
> give combs, lime pots, wooden dishes, lime spatulæ,
> plenty of *gugu'a* (objects of use). At the *talo'i* (farewell
> gifts) this will be repaid."

The following transaction, the main trade, is carried on as
gimwali. The natives of the Koya would bring the sago or the
betel-nut, put it on the beach near the canoes and say :

> " I want a *beku* (ceremonial axe blade)." And here my
> informants were positive that real bargaining would take
> place. " If they give us an insufficient quantity, we

---

* Mr. Gilmour's statement to the contrary namely that " the trips from
the West—Kavataria and Kaileuna—were pure trading expeditions " (*loc.
cit.*)—is incorrect. First, I am inclined to think that some of the Kavataria
men did make the Kula in the Amphletts, where they always stopped on their
way South, but this might have been only on a very small scale, and entirely
overshadowed by the main object of the expedition, which was the trade with
the Southern Koya. Secondly, as to the natives of Kayleula, I am certain that
they made the Kula, from conclusive data collected both in the Trobriands and
in the Amphletts.

expostulate, then they bring another portion. They would go to the village, fetch some more goods, return and give it to us,   If it is enough, we give him the *beku*."

Thus the barter would be carried on till the visitors had exhausted their stock in trade and received as much from the local natives as they could.

These expeditions are interesting in that we see the same type of magic and a number of similar customs, as in the Kula, associated with ordinary trading expeditions.   I am not certain about the nature of partnership obtaining in these trading relations, except that Kavataria and Kayleula have their own districts each with whom they trade.

As said already, the main objects for which they make these distant trips are sago, betel-nut, pig ; also the various feathers, especially those of the cassowary and the red parrot ; rattan-cane belts ; plaited fibre belts ; obsidian ; fine sand for polishing axe blades ; red ochre ; pummice stone ; and other products of the jungle and of the volcanic mountains.   For that, they exported to the Koya, to mention the most valuable first, armshells, the valuable axe blades, boars' tusks and imitations ; and, of lesser value, wooden dishes, combs, lime pots, armlets, baskets, *wayugo* creeper, mussel shells and lime spatulæ of ebony.   Spondylus shell necklaces were not exported to the Koya.

IV

Another important activity of the two districts of Kavataria and Kayleula is their production of armshells.   As Sinaketa and Vakuta are the only two places in the Trobriands where spondylus discs are made, so Kavataria and Kayleula are the only localities where the natives fished for the large *Conus millepunctatus* shell, and made out of it the ornaments so highly valued yet so seldom used.   The main reason for the exclusive monopoly, held by these two places in the manufacture of *mwali*, is the inertia of custom and usage which traditionally assigns to them this sort of fishing and manufacture.   For the shells are scattered all over the Lagoon, nor is the fishing and diving for them more difficult than any of the pursuits practised by all the Lagoon villages.   Only the communities mentioned, however, carry it on, and they only are in possession of a system of elaborate magic, at least as complex as that of the *kaloma*.

The actual manufacturing of the armshells presents also no difficulties. The ornament is made out of a belt of the shell cut out nearest to its base. With a stone, the natives knock out the circular base along the rim, and they also knock a circle at some distance from the base and parallel to it, by which the broad band of shell is severed, from which the ornament is to be made. It has then to be polished, and this is done on the outside by rubbing off the soft calcareous surface on a flat sandstone. The interior is polished off with a long, cylindrical stone.*

It was the custom in Kavataria that when a man found a fine Conus shell, he would give it to his wife's brother as a *youlo* present, who in turn would send the finder a return present of food, such as specially fine yams, bananas, betel-nut, and also a pig if it were an especially fine shell. He then would work out the shell for himself. This arrangement is a pendant to the one described with reference to Sinaketa, where a man would fish as well as work out a necklace for one of his wife's kinsmen.

An even more interesting custom obtains in Kayleula. A pair of shells would be fished and broken in one of the villages of that island, or in one of its small sister islands, Kuyawa and Manuwata. In this unfinished state, as a band of coarse shell, called as such *makavayna*, it is then brought to the Amphletts, and there given as a Kula gift. The Gumasila man, who receives the shells, will then polish them up, and in that state again *kula* them to Dobu. The Dobuan who receives them then bores holes in the side, where one rim overlaps the other (clearly to be seen on Plate XVI) and attaches there the ornaments of black, wild banana seeds, and spondylus discs. Thus, only after it has travelled some one hundred miles and passed through two stages of the Kula, has the *mwali* received its proper shape and final outfit.

In this manner does a new-born Kula article enter into the ring, taking shape as it goes through its first few stages, and at the same time, if it is a specially fine specimen, it is christened

* I have given a more detailed description of this process which I had often opportunities to observe among the Mailu on the South coast. I never saw the making of an armshell in the Trobriands, but the two processes are identical according to detailed information which I obtained. (Compare the monograph on " The Natives of Mailu " by the Author, in the Transactions of the Royal Society of S. Australia, 1915, pp. 643-644.

by its maker. Some of the names express simply local associations. Thus, a celebrated pair of *mwali*, of which the shell was found not long ago by a Kavataria man near the island of Nanoula, is named after that place. It may be added that, in each pair there is always a ' right ' and a ' left ' one, the first the bigger and more important of the two, and it is after that the name is given. Of course, they never are found at the same time, but if a man has succeeded in obtaining a specially fine specimen, he will be busy trying to find its slightly inferior companion, or some of his relatives-in-law, friends or kinsmen will give him one. ' Nanoula ' is one of the most celebrated pairs, and it was known all over the Trobriands, at that moment, that it was soon to come to Kitava, and the general interest hung round the question who was going to get it in Boyowa. A pair called ' Sopimanuwata,' which means, ' water of Manuwata ' was found in olden days by a man of that island close to its shores. Another famous pair, made in Kayleula, was called ' Bulivada,' after a fish of this name. The larger shell of this pair was found, according to tradition, broken, with a hole near its apex. When they brought it to the surface they found a small *bulivada* fish which had taken up its abode in the shell. Another pair was called ' Gomane ikola,' which means ' it is entangled in a net,' as, according to the story, it was brought up in a net. There are many other celebrated *mwali*, the names of which are so familiar that boys and girls are named after them. But the majority of the names cannot be traced as to their origins.

Another point at which the armshells enter into the ring is Woodlark Island. I do not know for certain, but I believe that the industry is quite or almost extinct now in that island. In the olden days, Murua probably was quite as productive a centre of this manufacture as the Trobriands, and in these latter though Kayleula and the Western islands fish and work the *mwali* as much as ever, the natives of Kavataria are almost entirely out of it, busy all the time diving for pearls. Both the main places of origin of the armshells, therefore, are within the Kula ring. After they are made, or, as we saw in Kayleula, in the process of making, they enter the circulation. Their entry into the ring is not accompanied by any special rite or custom, and indeed it does not differ from an ordinary act of exchange. If the man who found the shell and made the *mwali* were not in the Kula himself, as might happen in Kavataria or Kayleula, he would have a relative, a brother-in-law, or a head man to whom he would give it in the form of one or other of the many gifts and payments obligatory in this society.

V

Let us follow the ring of the Kula, noticing its commercial side tracks, of which so far we only described the trading routes of Kavataria and Kayleula. To the Eastward, the section from Kitava to Woodlark Island is the one big portion of the Kula from which no lateral offshoots issue, and on which all the trade follows the same routes as the Kula. The other branch, of which I have got a good knowledge, that from the Trobriands to Dobu, has the commercial relations of which I have just spoken. The Amphletts, as described in Chapter XI trade with the natives of Fergusson Island. The Dobuan-speaking natives from Tewara, Sanaroa, and the Dawson Straits make exchange, though perhaps not on a very big scale, with the inland natives of Fergusson. The Dobuan-speaking communities on Normanby Island, and the natives of Du'a'u, on the Northern coast of Normanby, all of whom are in the Kula, trade with the other natives of Normanby Island who are not in the ring, and with the natives of the mainland of New Guinea from East Cape Westwards. But, all this trade affects little the main current of the Kula. From its main stream, possibly some of the less valuable articles ebb away into the jungle, which, in its turn, gives its produce to the coast.

The most important leakage out and into the main stream takes place on the Southern section, mainly at Tubetube and Wari, and at some points of lesser importance around these two main centres. The North coast of New Guinea was connected with this district through the seafaring community at East Cape. But this side branch is of very small importance as regards the main articles of the Kula. It is the two connections to East and West, at the extreme southern point of the Kula ring, which matter most. One of them links up the South Coast of New Guinea with the Kula ring, the other joins the ring to the big islands of Sud-Est (Tagula) and Rossel with several adjacent small islands.

The South Coast, going from East to West, is at first inhabited by natives of the Massim stock, speaking the Su'a'u and Bonabona dialects. These are in constant intercourse with the Southern section of the Kula district, that is with the natives of Rogea, Sariba, Basilaki, Tubetube and Wari. The Massim of the Southern coast are again in commercial relations with the Mailu, and from this point, a chain of trading relations unites the Eastern districts with the Central ones, inhabited by the Motu. The Motu again as we know from Captain Barton's contribution to Professor Seligman's work, are in annual trading relations with the Gulf of Papua, so that an article could travel from the delta of any of the Papuan rivers to Woodlark in the Trobriands, and many things were in fact traded over all this distance.

There is, however, one movement which specially interests us from the Kula point of view, namely that of the two types of Kula valuables. One of these articles, the armshells, travels on the South Coast from East to West. There is no doubt that this article leaks out from the Kula current at its Southernmost point, and is carried away towards Port Moresby, where the value of armshells is, and was, in olden days much higher than in the Eastern district. I found in Mailu that the local native traders purchased, for pigs, armshells in the Su'a'u district, and carried them West towards Aroma, Hula, and Kerepunu. Professor Seligman, from his notes taken at Port Moresby, informs us that Hula, Aroma, and Kerepunu import armshells into Port Moresby. Some of these armshells, according to the same authority, travel further West as far as the Gulf of Papua.*

It was much more difficult to ascertain what was the direction in which the spondylus shell necklaces moved on the Southern Coast. Nowadays, the industry of making these articles, which was once very highly developed among the Port Moresby natives is partially, though not completely in decay. I have myself still had the opportunity of watching the natives of Bo'era at work on the *ageva*, the very small and fine shell discs, such as the very finest *bagi* would consist of. They were using in their manufacture a native pump-drill with a quartz point, in a place within a few miles of a large white settlement, in a district where white man's influence on a big scale has been exercised for the last fifty years. Yet, this is only a vestige of the once extremely developed industry. My inquiries into this subject could not be exhaustive, for when I worked on the South Coast, I did not have the problem before me, and on my second and third expeditions to New Guinea I only passed through Port Moresby. But I think it may be considered certain that in olden days the shell strings moved from Port Moresby Eastwards and were introduced into the Kula ring, at the East end of New Guinea.

However this might be, unquestionable sources of this Kula article are the islands of Sud-Est, Rossel, and the surrounding small islands. The best spondylus shell, with the reddest colours is fished in these seas, and the natives are expert workers of the discs, and export the finished article to the island of Wari, and, I believe, to the islands of Misima and Panayati. The most important articles for which the necklaces are traded are the canoes, and the large polished axe blades.

Casting now a glance at the Kula ring we see that one class of Kula article, the *mwali* or armshells, are produced within the ring at two points, that is, in Woodlark Island and in Western Boyowa. The other article, that is the *soulava* or *bagi* (necklaces) are poured into the ring at its southernmost point. One of these sources (Rossel Island) is still active, the other (Port Moresby) most probably furnished a good supply in olden days, but is now disconnected with the Kula ring. The necklaces produced in Sinaketa are not the real Kula article, and though they are sometimes exchanged they sooner or later disappear from the ring according to a sort of Gresham's Law, which operates here on an article which is not money, and therefore acts in the opposite sense ! The third type of valuable which sometimes flows in the Kula stream but is not really of it, the large green stone axe blades, finely polished all over, are, as we know, or more correctly were, quarried in Woodlark Island, and polished in the district of Kiriwina in the Trobriands. Another polishing centre is, or was, I believe, the island of Misima.

We see that the two sources of the *mwali* and *soulava* are at the Northern and Southern ends of the ring ; the arm-shells being manufactured in the extreme North, the necklaces entering at the Southern end. It is noteworthy that on the Eastern portion of the ring, on the section Woodlark-Boyowa-Dobu-Tubetube, the two articles travel in the natural direction, that is, each is exported from the districts of its origin towards one, where it is not made or procured. On the other branch, Woodlark-Yeguma-Tubetube, the current of the Kula is inverse to a natural, commercial movement of the articles, for here, the Tubetube people import armshells into Murua, thus bringing coals to Newcastle, while the Muruans bring necklaces to Tubetube and Wari, that is, to the points at which the necklaces flow into the ring from the outside. These considerations are important for anyone who would like to reflect on the origins, or history of the Kula, since the natural movement of valuables was no doubt the original one, and the Western half of the Kula from this point of view appears to be the older.

But here we have come to an end of all the descriptive data referring to the Kula, and some general remarks which I have to make upon it, will be reserved for the next and last chapter.

CHAPTER XXII

THE MEANING OF THE KULA

WE have been following the various routes and ramifications of
the Kula, entering minutely and meticulously into its rules
and customs, its beliefs and practices, and the mythological
tradition spun round it, till, arriving at the end of our information, we have made its two ends meet. We shall now put
aside the magnifying glass of detailed examination and look
from a distance at the subject of our inquiry, take in the
whole institution with one glance, let it assume a definite shape
before us. This shape will perhaps strike us as being something unusual, something not met before in ethnological studies.
It will be well to make an attempt at finding its place among
the other subjects of systematic ethnology, at gauging its
significance, at assessing how much we have learned by
becoming acquainted with it.

After all there is no value in isolated facts for science,
however striking and novel they might seem in themselves.
Genuine scientific research differs from mere curio-hunting
in that the latter runs after the quaint, singular and freakish—
the craving for the sensational and the mania of collecting
providing its twofold stimulus. Science on the other hand has
to analyse and classify facts in order to place them in an
organic whole, to incorporate them in one of the systems in
which it tries to group the various aspects of reality.

I shall not, of course enter upon any speculations or add
any hypothetical assumptions to the empirical data contained
in the foregoing chapters. I shall confine myself to some
reflections on the most general aspect of the institution, and try
to express somewhat more clearly what to me appears the
mental attitude at the bottom of the various Kula customs.
These general points of view ought, I think, to be considered and
tested in further field-work done on subjects akin to the Kula

as well as in theoretical research, and might thus prove fertile for future scientific work. In this form it may be granted that it is the privilege of the chronicler of a novel phenomenon to pass it over to the consideration of fellow-workers ; but it is his duty as well as his privilege. For, apart from his first-hand acquaintance with the facts—and indeed, if his account is good, he ought to have succeeded in transferring the best part of his knowledge to the reader—the fundamental aspects and characteristics of an ethnographic phenomenon for being general are none the less empirical. It is therefore the chronicler's task to finish his account by a comprehensive, synthetic *coup d'oeil* upon the institution described.

As said the Kula seems to be, to a certain extent, a novel type of ethnological fact. Its novelty lies partly in the size of its sociological and geographical extent. A big, inter-tribal relationship, uniting with definite social bonds a vast area and great numbers of people, binding them with definite ties of reciprocal obligations, making them follow minute rules and observations in a concerted manner—the Kula is a sociological mechanism of surpassing size and complexity, considering the level of culture on which we find it. Nor can this wide network of social co-relations and cultural influences be considered for a moment as ephemeral, new or precarious. For its highly developed mythology and its magical ritual show how deeply it has taken root in the tradition of these natives and of what ancient growth it must be.

Another unusual feature is the character of the transaction itself, which is the proper substance of the Kula. A half commercial, half ceremonial exchange, it is carried out for its own sake, in fulfilment of a deep desire to possess. But here again, it is not ordinary possession, but a special type, in which a man owns for a short time, and in an alternating manner, individual specimens of two classes of objects. Though the ownership is incomplete in point of permanency, it is in turn enhanced in point of numbers successively possessed, and may be called a cumulative possession.

Another aspect of great, perhaps the greatest, importance and which perhaps reveals best the unusual character of the Kula is the natives' mental attitude towards the tokens of wealth. These latter are neither used nor regarded as money or currency, and they resemble these economic instruments very little, if indeed there is any resemblance at all, except that both money and *vaygu'a* represent condensed wealth. *Vaygu'a* is never used as medium of exchange or as measure of value, which are the two most important functions of currency or money. Each piece of *vaygu'a* of the Kula type has one main object throughout its existence—to be possessed and exchanged; has one main function and serves one main purpose—to circulate round the Kula ring, to be owned and displayed in a certain manner, of which we shall speak presently. And the exchange which each piece of *vaygu'a* constantly undergoes is of a very special kind ; limited in the geographical direction in which it can take place, narrowly circumscribed in the social circle of men between whom it may be done, it is subject to all sorts of strict rules and regulations ; it can neither be described as barter, nor as simply giving and receiving of presents, nor in any sense is it a play at exchange. In fact it is *Kula*, an exchange of an entirely novel type. And it is just through this exchange, through their being constantly within reach and the object of competitive desire, through being the means of arousing envy and conferring social distinction and renown, that these objects attain their high value. Indeed, they form one of the leading interests in native life, and are one of the main items in the inventory of their culture. Thus, one of the most important and unusual features of the Kula is the existence of the Kula *vaygu'a*, the incessantly circulating and ever exchangeable valuables, owing their value to this very circulation and its character.

The acts of exchange of the valuables have to conform to a definite code. The main tenet of this declares that the transaction is not a bargain. The equivalence of the values exchanged is essential, but it must be the result of the repayer's own sense of what is due to custom and to his own dignity. The ceremonial attached to the act of giving, the manner of carrying and handling the *vaygu'a* shows distinctly that this is regarded as something else than mere merchandise. Indeed it is to the native something that confers dignity, that exalts him, and which he therefore treats with veneration and affection. Their behaviour at the transaction, makes it clear that the *vaygu'a* is regarded, not only as possessing high value, but that it is treated also in a ritual manner, and arouses emotional reaction. This recognition is confirmed and deepened by the consideration of some other uses of *vaygu'a*, in which uses other valuables, such as *kaloma* belts and large stone blades also function, besides the Kula articles.

Thus, when a malignant spirit, *tauva'u* (see Chapter II, Division VII) is found in or near the village in the shape of a snake or a land crab, some *vaygu'a* is put before it ceremonially and this is not done so much in order to bribe the spirit sacrificially by a gift as rather to exercise a direct action on his mind, and to make it benevolent. In the annual festive and dancing period, the *milamala*, the spirits return to their villages. The Kula valuables at that time in the hands of the community, as well as the permanent *vaygu'a*, such as stone blades, *kaloma* belts, and *doga* pendants, are exhibited sacrifically to the spirits on a platform, an arrangement and custom called *yolova* (compare Chapter II, Division VII). Thus the *vaygu'a* represent the most effective offering to be given to the spirits, through which they can be put into a pleasant state of mind; " to make their minds good," as the stereotyped phrase of the natives runs. In the *yolova* an offering is made to the spirits of what is most valued by the living. The shadowy visitors are supposed to take the spirit or shadow part of the *vaygu'a* home, and make a *tanarere* of it on the beach of Tuma, just as a Kula party make a *tanarere* of the acquired valuables on their home beach (cf. Chapter XV, Division IV). In all this there is a clear expression of the mental attitude of the natives, who regard the *vaygu'a* as supremely good in themselves, and not as convertible wealth, or as potential ornaments, or even as instruments of power. To possess *vaygu'a* is exhilarating, comforting, soothing in itself. They will look at *vaygu'a* and handle it for hours; even a touch of it imparts under circumstances its virtue.

This is most clearly expressed by a custom observed at death. A dying man is surrounded and overlaid with valuables which all his relatives and relatives-in-law bring in loan for the occasion, to take it back when all is over while the man's own *vaygu'a* are left on the corpse for some time after death (see Plate LXV). Various rationalised versions and justifications of this custom are given. Thus it is said to be a gift to Topileta, the keeper of the nether world ; or, again, that it has to be taken in its spiritual form to procure a high social standing in Tuma, or simply, that it is laid to adorn and make happier the

PLATE LXV

A CORPSE COVERED WITH VALUABLES

A great number of valuables, including large axe blades, with which this man was covered at dying, have been already withdrawn. Only personal possessions are left on the corpse, and they will be removed immediately before the interment.   (See p. 512.)

last moments of the dying. All these beliefs no doubt exist side by side, and they are all compatible with, and indeed express, the underlying emotional attitude ; the comforting action of the valuables. It is applied to the dying as something full of good, as something exercising a pleasant action, soothing and fortifying at the same time. They put it on his forehead, they put it on his chest, they rub his belly and his ribs with it, they dangle some of the *vaygu'a* before his nose. I have often seen them do that, in fact, observed them do it for hours, and I believe there is a complex, emotional and intellectual attitude at the bottom of it ; the desire to inspire with life ; and at the same time to prepare for death ; to hold him fast to this one, and to equip for the other world ; but above all, the deep feeling that the *vaygu'a* are the supreme comfort, that to surround a man with them, even in his most evil moment, makes this moment less evil. The same mental attitude is probably at the bottom of the custom which prescribes that the widow's brothers should give a *vaygu'a* to the brothers of the dead man, the same *vaygu'a* being given back on the same day. But it is kept just long enough to be of comfort to those, who, according to native kinship ideas, are most directly hit by the death.

In all this we find the expression of the same mental attitude, the extreme value attached to condensed wealth, the serious, respectful way of treating it, the idea and the feeling that it is the reservoir of highest good. The *vaygu'a* are valued in quite a different manner from that in which we value our wealth. The Biblical symbol of the golden calf might even be better applied to their attitude than to ours, although it would be not quite correct to say that they ' worship ' the *vaygu'a*, for they worship nothing. The *vaygu'a* might perhaps be called " objects of cult " in the sense expressed by the facts of the Kula, and the data just adduced ; that is, in so far as they are handled ritually in some of the most important acts of native life.

Thus, in several aspects, the Kula presents to us a new type of phenomenon, lying on the borderland between the commercial and the ceremonial and expressing a complex and interesting attitude of mind. But though it is novel, it can hardly be unique. For we can scarcely imagine that a social phenomenon on such a scale, and obviously so deeply connected with funda-mental layers of human nature, should only be a sport and a freak, found in one spot of the earth alone. Once we have found this new type of ethnographic fact, we may hope that similar or kindred ones will be found elsewhere. For the history of our science shows many cases in which a new type of phenomena having been discovered, taken up by theory, discussed and analysed, was found subsequently all the world over. The *tabu*, the Polynesian word and the Polynesian custom, has served as prototype and eponym to similar regulations found among all the savage and barbarous as well as civilised races. Totemism, found first among one tribe of North American Indians and brought to light by the work of Frazer, has later on been documented so widely and fully from everywhere, that in re-writing his early small book, its historian could fill out four volumes. The conception of *mana*, discovered in a small Melanesian community has, by the work of Hubert and Mauss, Marett and others, been proved of fundamental importance, and there is no doubt that *mana*, whether named or unnamed, figures and figures largely in the magical beliefs and practices of all natives. These are the most classical and best known examples, and they could be multiplied by others were it necessary. Phenomena of the ' totemic type ' or of the ' mana type ' or of the ' tabu type ' are to be found in all ethnographic provinces, since each of these concepts stands for a fundamental attitude of the savage towards reality.

So with the Kula, if it represents a novel, but not freakish, indeed, a fundamental type of human activity and of the mental attitude of man, we may expect to find allied and kindred phenomena in various other ethnographic provinces. And we may be on the lookout for economic transactions, expressing a reverential, almost worshipping attitude towards the valuables exchanged or handled ; implying a novel type of ownership, temporary, intermittent, and cumulative ; involving a vast and complex social mechanism and systems of economic enterprises, by means of which it is carried out. Such is the Kula type of semi-economic, semi-ceremonial activities. It would be futile, no doubt, to expect that exact replicas of this institution should be found anywhere and with the same details, such as the circular path on which the valuables move, the fixed direction in which each class has to travel, and existence of solicitory and intermediate gifts. All these technicalities are important and interesting, but they are probably connected in one way or another with the special local conditions of the Kula. What we can expect to find in other parts of the world are the fundamental ideas of the Kula, and its social arrangements in their main outline, and for these the field-worker might be on the look-out.

For the theoretical student, mainly interested in problems of evolution, the Kula might supply some reflections about the origins of wealth and value, of trade and economic relations in general. It might also shed some light upon the development of ceremonial life, and upon the influence of economic aims and and ambitions upon the evolution of intertribal intercourse and of primitive international law. For the student mainly viewing the problems of Ethnology from the point of view of the contact of cultures, and interested in the spread of institutions, beliefs and objects by transmission, the Kula is no less important. Here is a new type of inter-tribal contact, of relations between several communities slightly but definitely differing in culture, and a relation not spasmodic or accidental but regulated and permanent. Quite apart from the fact that in trying to explain how the Kula relationship between the various tribes originated, we are confronted with a definite problem of culture contact.

These few remarks must suffice, as I cannot enter into any theoretical speculations myself. There is one aspect of the Kula, however, to which attention must be drawn from the point of view of its theoretical importance. We have seen that this institution presents several aspects closely intertwined and influencing one another. To take only two, economic enterprise and magical ritual form one inseparable whole, the forces of the magical belief and the efforts of man moulding and influencing one another. How this is happening has been described before in detail in the previous chapters.*

But it seems to me that a deeper analysis and comparison of the manner in which two aspects of culture functionally depend on one another might afford some interesting material for theoretical reflection. Indeed, it seems to me that there is room for a new type of theory. The succession in time, and the influence of the previous stage upon the subsequent, is the main subject of evolutionary studies, such as are practised by the classical school of British Anthropology (Tylor, Frazer,

* Also in the before quoted article in the *Economic Journal*, March, 1921.

Westermarck, Sydney Hartland, Crawley). The ethnological school (Ratzel, Foy, Gräbner, W. Schmidt, Rivers, and Eliott-Smith) studies the influence of cultures by contact, infiltration and transmission. The influence of environment on cultural institutions and race is studied by anthropo-geography (Ratzel and others). The influence on one another of the various aspects of an institution, the study of the social and psychological mechanism on which the institution is based, are a type of theoretical studies which has been practised up till now in a tentative way only, but I venture to foretell will come into their own sooner or later. This kind of research will pave the way and provide the material for the others.

At one or two places in the previous chapters, a somewhat detailed digression was made in order to criticise the view about the economic nature of primitive man, as it survives in our mental habits as well as in some text books—the conception of a rational being who wants nothing but to satisfy his simplest needs and does it according to the economic principle of least effort. This economic man always knows exactly where his material interests lie, and makes for them in a straight line. At the bottom of the so-called materialistic conception of history lies a somewhat analogous idea of a human being, who, in everything he devises and pursues, has nothing but his material advantage of a purely utilitarian type at heart. Now I hope that whatever the meaning of the Kula might be for Ethnology, for the general science of culture, the meaning of the Kula will consist in being instrumental to dispell such crude, rationalistic conceptions of primitive mankind, and to induce both the speculator and the observer to deepen the analysis of economic facts. Indeed, the Kula shows us that the whole conception of primitive value ; the very incorrect habit of calling all objects of value ' money ' or ' currency ' ; the current ideas of primitive trade and primitive ownership—all these have to be revised in the light of our institution.

At the beginning of this book, in the Introduction, I, in a way, promised the reader that he should receive a vivid impression of the events enabling him to see them in their native perspective, at the same time without for one moment losing sight of the method by which I have obtained my data. I have tried to present everything as far as possible in terms of concrete fact, letting the natives speak for themselves, perform their transactions, pursue their activities before the reader's mental vision. I have tried to pave my account with fact and details, equip it with documents, with figures, with instances of actual occurrence. But at the same time, my conviction, as expressed over and over again, is that what matters really is not the detail, not the fact, but the scientific use we make of it. Thus the details and technicalities of the Kula acquire their meaning in so far only as they express some central attitude of mind of the natives, and thus broaden our knowledge, widen our outlook and deepen our grasp of human nature.

What interests me really in the study of the native is his outlook on things, his *Weltanschauung*, the breath of life and reality which he breathes and by which he lives. Every human culture gives its members a definite vision of the world, a definite zest of life. In the roamings over human history, and over the surface of the earth, it is the possibility of seeing life and the world from the various angles, peculiar to each culture, that has always charmed me most, and inspired me with real desire to penetrate other cultures, to understand other types of life.

To pause for a moment before a quaint and singular fact ; to be amused at it, and see its outward strangeness ; to look at it as a curio and collect it into the museum of one's memory or into one's store of anecdotes—this attitude of mind has always been foreign and repugnant to me. Some people are unable to grasp the inner meaning and the psychological reality of all that is outwardly strange, at first sight incomprehensible, in a different culture. These people are not born to be ethnologists. It is in the love of the final synthesis, achieved by the assimilation and comprehension of all the items of a culture and still more in the love of the variety and independence of the various cultures that lies the test of the real worker in the true Science of Man.

There is, however, one point of view deeper yet and more important than the love of tasting of the variety of human modes of life, and that is the desire to turn such knowledge into wisdom. Though it may be given to us for a moment to enter into the soul of a savage and through his eyes to look at the outer world and feel ourselves what it must feel to *him* to be himself—yet our final goal is to enrich and deepen our own world's vision, to understand our own nature and to make it finer, intellectually and artistically. In grasping the essential outlook of others, with the reverence and real understanding, due even to savages, we cannot but help widening our own. We cannot possibly reach the final Socratic wisdom of knowing ourselves if we never leave the narrow confinement of the customs, beliefs and prejudices into which every man is born. Nothing can teach us a better lesson in this matter of ultimate importance than the habit of mind which allows us to treat the beliefs and values of another man from his point of view. Nor has civilised humanity ever needed such tolerance more than now, when prejudice, ill will and vindictiveness are dividing each European nation from another, when all the ideals, cherished and proclaimed as the highest achievements of civilisation, science and religion, have been thrown to the winds. The Science of Man, in its most refined and deepest version should lead us to such knowledge and to tolerance and generosity, based on the understanding of other men's point of view.

The study of Ethnology—so often mistaken by its very votaries for an idle hunting after curios, for a ramble among the savage and fantastic shapes of " barbarous customs and crude superstitions "—might become one of the most deeply philosophic, enlightening and elevating disciplines of scientific research. Alas ! the time is short for Ethnology, and will this truth of its real meaning and importance dawn before it is too late ?

INDEX

INDEX